Law and Practice *of* the United Nations

D1496229

Law and Practice *of* the United Nations

....

Documents and Commentary

Simon Chesterman

New York University School of Law Singapore Programme,
NUS Faculty of Law

Thomas M. Franck

New York University School of Law

David M. Malone

Canadian High Commission

New York   Oxford
OXFORD UNIVERSITY PRESS
2008

Oxford University Press, Inc., publishes works that further Oxford University's
objective of excellence in research, scholarship, and education.

Oxford   New York
Auckland   Cape Town   Dar es Salaam   Hong Kong   Karachi
Kuala Lumpur   Madrid   Melbourne   Mexico City   Nairobi
New Delhi   Shanghai   Taipei   Toronto

With offices in
Argentina   Austria   Brazil   Chile   Czech Republic   France   Greece
Guatemala   Hungary   Italy   Japan   Poland   Portugal   Singapore
South Korea   Switzerland   Thailand   Turkey   Ukraine   Vietnam

Published by Oxford University Press, Inc.
198 Madison Avenue, New York, New York 10016
http://www.oup.com

Oxford is a registered trademark of Oxford University Press

Library of Congress Cataloging-in-Publication Data

Chesterman, Simon.
  Law and practice of the United Nations : documents and commentary / Simon Chesterman,
Thomas M. Franck, David M. Malone.
    p. cm.
ISBN 978-0-19-530842-6 (hardback)—ISBN 978-0-19-530843-3 (pbk.)   1. United Nations.
2. International agencies.   3. International organization.   I. Franck, Thomas M.
II. Malone, David, 1954–   III. Title.
KZ4986.C54 2008
341.23—dc22   2007020232

Printed in the United States of America
on acid-free paper.

For Lilly Sucharipa-Behrmann,
with admiration

Summary Contents

Contents

Acknowledgments

The authors would like to thank the many students who participated in the seminar that formed the basis for this volume, Constitutional Law of the United Nations, offered at New York University School of Law by Professor Franck since 1957. Professors Malone and Chesterman taught the course with Professor Franck in the years 1999–2003 and 2004–2006 respectively. Others who have helped lead the seminar over the years include Mohamed ElBaradei, Herbert Reis, and Lilly Sucharipa-Behrmann. Particular thanks are also due to Shelley Fenchel, the effective anchor of course administration and sympathetic channel for so many of our students throughout the period in which these materials were assembled and used, on an experimental basis, at NYU. We are all deeply grateful to her. Invaluable research assistance in preparing the volume was provided by Surabhi Ranganathan, Ralf Kanitz, and Anna Pollock. The text benefited from close reading by, among others, Christopher Bradley, Hasan M. Ibrahim, Jerry Kramer, and several anonymous reviewers.

About the Authors

Simon Chesterman is Global Professor and Director of the New York University School of Law Singapore Programme and an Associate Professor at the National University of Singapore. His books include *Shared Secrets: Intelligence and Collective Security, You, the People: The United Nations, Transitional Administration, and State-Building*, and *Just War or Just Peace? Humanitarian Intervention and International Law*, which was awarded the American Society of International Law Certificate of Merit. Edited works include *Secretary or General? The UN Secretary-General in World Politics* and *Making States Work: State Failure and the Crisis of Governance* (edited with Michael Ignatieff and Ramesh Thakur).

Thomas M. Franck is Murry and Ida Becker Professor of Law Emeritus at New York University School of Law. The author of more than 20 books (most recently, *Recourse to Force: State Action Against Threats and Armed Attacks*) and a two-time Guggenheim Fellowship winner, Franck received the Christopher Medal for Resignation in Protest. The American Society of International Law has awarded him a Certificate of Merit for four of his books: *United States Foreign Relations Law: Documents and Sources; Nation Against Nation: What Happened to the UN Dream and What the US Can Do About It; Political Questions/Judicial Answers: Does the Rule of Law Apply to Foreign Affairs?*; and *Fairness in International Law and Institutions*. Franck has acted as legal advisor or counsel to many foreign governments, including Tanganyika, Kenya, Zanzibar, Mauritius, Solomon Islands, El Salvador, Bosnia and Herzegovina, and Chad.

David M. Malone is Canada's High Commissioner for India and Ambassador to Bhutan and Nepal. From 2004 to 2006, he oversaw economic and multilateral diplomacy within Canada's Foreign Ministry. He is a former Canadian Ambassador to the United Nations. From 1998 to 2004, he was President of the International Peace Academy, an independent research institution on security issues working closely along side the United Nations, particularly its Security Council, and a variety of regional organizations. During these years, he also taught at the NYU School of Law and at Sciences Po in Paris. His books include *The UN Security Council: From the Cold War to the 21st Century* (edited with Lynne Rienner, 2004); and *Greed & Grievance: Economic Agendas in Civil Wars* (edited with Mats Berdal, Lynne Rienner, 2000). In 2006 he published *The International Struggle over Iraq: Politics in the UN Security Council, 1980–2005*. David Malone's views reflected in this volume are his own, and not those of the Canadian government.

Law and Practice *of* the United Nations

Introduction

This book is designed for students of international law and international relations studying the United Nations. By examining primary materials focused on the normative context within which the United Nations functions, students will develop an understanding of the interaction between law and practice. This is essential to a proper understanding of the UN Organization, but also to the possibilities and limitations of multilateral institutions more generally.

The book is organized in four parts. Part I, "Relevance," raises some preliminary questions about the role, legitimacy, and effectiveness of the United Nations, particularly in the area of peace and security. Part II, "Capacity," brings together materials on the nature and status of the United Nations. Part III, "Practice," examines how the United Nations has exercised its various powers. Part IV, "Accountability," concludes with materials on responsibility and accountability of the United Nations and its agents.

Each chapter begins with a short introductory essay by the authors. This describes how the documents that follow illustrate a set of legal, institutional, and political issues relevant to the practice of diplomacy and the development of public international law through the United Nations. Each chapter includes questions that may guide discussion of the primary materials and suggested further reading for additional secondary sources.

The emphasis on primary materials serves two purposes. First, such materials enable a realistic presentation of the work of international diplomacy; the negotiation and interpretation of such texts is an important part of what actually takes place at the United Nations and other international organizations. Secondly, it is hoped that students of these texts will develop the ability to read them critically, parsing not only the meaning but the politics behind such documents. Importantly, this second aim includes understanding the different types of material presented in this volume, each of which must be read differently: treaties and resolutions based on political compromises, judicial opinions that are based on legal reasoning, policy documents intended to justify specific actions, advocacy intended to pursue a national or other interest, and so on.

The book is not intended to be a comprehensive reference work, which would require far more material. A volume such as this is can hardly aim to be unputdownable. But its authors must guard against it becoming unpickupable. Accordingly, the present work draws selectively from six decades of practice to examine underlying themes and principles concerning the normative context within which the United Nations operates. For teaching purposes, it will be helpful to supplement the materials provided here with items currently on the agenda of the United Nations.

Given the normative focus of the book, the most important questions examined here tend to be what a body like the United Nations *may* or *must* do, rather than what it *might* or *should* do. The former are properly topics of legal analysis; the latter are more suggestive of policy questions in which law is a relevant but rarely conclusive factor. Whether the issue is sending peacekeepers to Darfur, establishing the Oil-for-Food Programme in Iraq, or coordinating relief in the wake of the 2004 Indian Ocean tsunami, the question of choosing the best policy will typically be a political one—the role of law is in defining the universe from which that choice is made or, more rarely, clarifying the extent of legal compulsion.

The focus on legal and normative considerations means it is only possible to get a snapshot of what actually happens on the ground. For example, the volume addresses the role of the United Nations in debates over economic development and the elaboration of new concepts and norms (such as the Millennium Development Goals and the Right to Development), but it does not examine UN development programming as such. Similarly, we consider the legal and political context of humanitarian assistance but do not directly focus on the programming and implementation quandaries that UN humanitarian staff face on a daily basis.

Within a domestic legal setting, the means of determining the limits of centralized power and the legal obligations of that authority are usually set out in a constitution or basic law. Though such analogies must be pursued with caution, the rest of this introduction raises basic questions about the nature of the United Nations and its Charter, framed around the question of whether that document might itself be considered a constitution. In our own teaching this question has been a recurrent theme and it may be helpful to revisit this question as one progresses through the text that follows. The complete text of the Charter is included in the appendix at the end of the book.

Is the UN Charter a Constitution?[1]

The Charter of the United Nations is, of course, a treaty. That it also happens to be one of the most-widely ratified treaties in the history of international

---

[1] This text draws upon passages first published in Thomas M. Franck, "Is the UN Charter a Constitution?" in Jochen Abr Frowein, *et al.* (eds.), *Verhandeln für den Frieden— Negotiating for Peace: Liber Amicorum Tono Eitel* (Berlin: Springer, 2003), pp. 95–106.

relations does signal the concomitant fact that it is not an ordinary treaty. But, a constitution? That, surely, would be a claim requiring very persuasive evidence.

Implicit in the claim is the even more controversial proposition that the members of the United Nations, by the fact of their membership, have not merely become parties to a treaty but members of a *community*.It is demonstrably possible to have a community without a formal constitution, but it is difficult to imagine a constitution without a community.

In traditional Lockeian jurisprudential parlance, a community is constituted by a contract (that is, a treaty, in the system of states) in which the parties agree to be bound together for certain specified purposes. Such a *social contract*by which persons (or, in our instance, states) agree to enter a continuing relationship differs from an ordinary contract (or ordinary treaty) in that it *constitutes* an ongoing *process* of interaction and not simply a substantive set of rules. In that sense, the chosen instrument—by which the rights and obligations of an ongoing relationship are determined and agreed—becomes not merely normative but *constitutive*.

Such a constitutive instrument is distinguished in several ways. First is its tendency toward pervasive *perpetuity*. Real constitutions are usually hard to escape. The great US civil war (1861–1865) was fought to establish that states of the Union, once enlisted, had no right of exit. The theory behind this aspect of a constitutive instrument is that, unlike many (although not all) simple contracts or treaties, an agreement that establishes an on-going community creates a web of criss-crossing mutual expectations, duties, and entitlements that, being a carefully knotted skein, are not readily disentangled. To permit one to exit can be seen as a derogation from the legitimate expectations of all the remaining members and as an act that may be construed as damaging the community as a whole.

Does the UN Charter have this perpetuity-characteristic of a constitution? Notably, it has no provision for states' withdrawal from the Organization created by it. In this, the Charter constitutes a deliberate departure from the Covenant of the League of Nations, in which provision was made in Article 1(3) for exit upon giving two years' notice. At San Francisco, the issue was considered and it was decided to pass it over in silence in recognition of the Organization's aspiration to universality and what was designated as "the highest duty of the nations . . . to continue their cooperation within the Organization for the preservation of international peace and security."

In practice, the United Nations has studiously avoided validating a right of exit. In 1965, the Government of Indonesia, irked by failure to get support for its claim to North Borneo and Sarawak, announced its withdrawal from the Organization; but, when it changed its mind later, its delegation was seated in the General Assembly as if the withdrawal had been null and void. When the union between Egypt and Syria was dissolved in 1961, Syria automatically regained its seat, which had been in abeyance during its submergence as a partner in the United Arab Republic. Clearly, the institution has applied the

Charter in such a way as to reinforce the tendency towards perpetuity of membership.

This tendency of the constitutive instrument to effect such pervasive perpetuity is underscored by a remarkable universalizing provision of the Charter that is not only absent from other treaties, but which may, indeed, be said to contradict the very essence of the ordinary contractual relationship. Article 2(6) provides that the "Organization shall ensure that states which are not Members of the United Nations act in accordance with the [Charter's] Principles so far as may be necessary for the maintenance of international peace and security." This provision not only seeks to ensure that states cannot escape the basic obligations established by the instrument—not even by purporting to refuse, or quitting, membership—but also purports to revoke the basic international legal principle that a sovereign state cannot be bound in law except by a free act of its own volition. The principles of the Charter claim the adherence not only of those states that have ratified that instrument, but also of those that have not. This is not a sustainable claim when advanced by parties to an ordinary treaty, but it is one enforced by the UN system. The Charter establishes a process by which one of its principal organs, the Security Council, may make a determination that the conduct of a state—member or non-member—constitutes a "threat to the peace, breach of the peace, or act of aggression" (Article 39) and may decide to bring collective measures to bear—ranging from diplomatic sanctions (Article 41) to military force (Article 42)—to ensure the compliance of the wrongdoer with community standards. None of this comports with the normal expectations of treaty law but does bear resemblance to a social compact or constitution.

A second characteristic is its *indelibleness*. Real constitutions are not easily nipped and tucked or reconfigured to meet the needs of contemporary fashion. The Charter, like a constitutive instrument, is extraordinarily hard to amend. Except for a series of amendments in 1963–1973, which increased the size of the Security Council and the Economic and Social Council, there has been a notable absence of revision in its main terms, most evident in the important but frustrating recent assays to legitimate the Security Council by making it more inclusive and representative of the shifts in power that have occurred during the first six decades of the Organization's existence. As with many national constitutions, the Charter (Article 109) creates a contract intended obdurately to withstand the vicissitudes of shifting political values and fortunes. To that end, proposed amendments must be put to a conference of all the members, be adopted by a two-thirds vote, and be ratified by two-thirds of the member governments, including those of all the permanent members of the Security Council. It is deliberate that this should be such a daunting hurdle to reform, and it is more characteristic of a constitution, rather than of an ordinary treaty.

Another aspect of indelibleness is that the Charter does not permit the sort of pick-and-choose approach that traditionally has made many multilateral treaties exemplars of unequal obligations among the parties. No reservations may be entered by any parties. All members are bound, identically, to all of the same provisions of the constitutive instrument.

A third characteristic of a constitutive instrument is its *primacy*. A constitutive instrument is usually accorded pre-eminence among legal instruments available to the community it serves. That there are normative constructs with priority over all others, implicitly, is what distinguishes "constitutional governance" from "parliamentary supremacy." Not every community has such a principle of priority. In the British system, entrenchment of constitutive norms cannot be achieved without encountering the general rule that all acts of parliament are of equal effect and that the last in time repeals any inconsistent prior enactment. While it is thus demonstrably possible for a community to develop around a principle of normative equality, where normative priority is fundamental to a community's system of law, it will always be found lodged in a constitutional instrument. In such states, organized around the principle of constitutional supremacy, the constitutive instrument trumps all inconsistent acts of governance, whether earlier or later in origin, save only amendments to the constitution itself. It is significant, in this respect, that the Charter (Article 103) makes the following claim:

> In the event of a conflict between the obligations of the Members of the United Nations under the present Charter and their obligations under any other international agreement, their obligations under the present Charter shall prevail.

Such an assertion of instrumental supremacy over both prior and subsequent commitments of states in the exercise of their sovereign rights strongly suggests an intent to create the constitutive foundations of a functioning community. This trumping of subsequent treaties by operation of the Charter (and by operation of decisions of the Security Council when exercising its Charter-bestowed powers) was tacitly acknowledged by the International Court of Justice (ICJ) at the interim measures phase of the *Lockerbie* case.[2]

A fourth characteristic of a constitutive instrument is its aspiration to *institutional autochthony*. Perhaps the most important characteristic of a constitution is that it creates a machine that runs by itself. This unique legal quality of constitutions has two components. First, the autochthonous instrument establishes the basic *loci* of governmental power and designates the appropriate parameters of power allotted to each. The legislative power may be defined and vested in a parliamentary assembly, the executive power in a presidency, and the judicial function in various courts. There may also be a sharing-out of powers between the center and the constituent provinces. Second, there is usually provision for the umpiring and implementing of these allocations of function and jurisdiction. In some constitutional systems—such as those of Germany, Canada, Australia, the United States,

---

[2] See chapter 3 in this volume.

and, increasingly, France—this "umpiring function" is assigned to courts. In others, it is shared by courts and political, administrative, or even religious bodies.

A constituent instrument may discharge these two requisites efficiently or inefficiently, but discharge them it must. The autochthony of a constitutional instrument is demonstrated by the capacity of institutions created by it to function through a decision-making and rule-applying process that does not require, in each instance, a negotiation to secure the consent of all the participating parties. Such return to instrumental renegotiation will be obviated by lodging the power to create new obligations in a judiciary, an administrative-executive secretariat and/or a political-parliamentary institution. The UN Charter has established forms of all three.

The Charter thus markedly simulates the requisites of a constitutive instrument. In Article 7(1) it sets out the jurisdictional parameters, and delimits the functions, of the principal organs through which the Organization is to operate: the General Assembly, the Security Council, the Economic and Social Council, the Trusteeship Council (now defunct), the International Court of Justice, and the Secretariat. At the founders' conference in 1945 at San Francisco, there were vigorous debates about the "umpiring function," with a narrow majority favoring the Court as sole final arbiter; but the Big Powers resisted such judicial supremacy. In the event, it was decided, fractiously, that the *kompetenz-kompetenz* should be exercised, first, by each principal organ in its own assigned bailiwick and, secondarily, by the Court when an issue arose in litigation between two member states or when the judges were requested by the Council or Assembly to render an advisory opinion (Article 96). Efficient or not, the result was that the Charter designed an instrument that could run by itself.

To ensure this, it provided a Secretariat, which was to operate free of instruction by the states of the civil servants' nationality. The international public servants were to constitute the intendancy of the machine, headed by an impartial Secretary-General vested with sufficient power and resources to ensure the integrity of the process (Articles 97–101).

The independence of the Secretariat is an important part of the Charter's constitutionalism, for it was established to ensure that the United Nations would not be merely a continuing conference of states (in the sense, for example, of the Congress of Vienna) but that, to paraphrase Mark Twain in another context, there would demonstrably be "a *there* there." In instituting this independence, the Charter does not merely state that the Secretary-General and his or her staff "shall not seek or receive instructions from any government or any other authority external to the Organization," but further requires member states "to respect the exclusively international character of the responsibilities of the Secretary-General and the staff and not to seek to influence them in the discharge of their responsibilities" (Article 100). One can reasonably conclude that the Charter may be, in form, a treaty among state-parties, but it is one which intentionally created a legal entity with rights and responsibilities separate from those of the members. For example, Article 99 bestows on the Secretary-General broad authority to "bring to the attention of the Security Council any matter which in his opinion may threaten the maintenance of international peace and security." This power has been used creatively by successive Secretaries-General to establish an important and independent jurisdiction to investigate looming crises and to propose initiatives for pre-empting them.

The General Assembly, the system's parliamentary institution, has also been endowed with autochthonous jurisdiction. An example is Article 17 of the Charter, which imposes on all members the duty to bear expenses approved and apportioned by the requisite majority. That this obligation is binding even on states that opposed and voted against a particular activity of the Organization has been made clear by the ICJ in the *Certain Expenses* case. It is thus apparent that when a voting majority of members decides to undertake a task, it is not legally open to opponents of that project to continue their opposition to it by withholding their share of contributions necessary to cover the cost of carrying it out.[3] This illustrates that membership by a sovereign state in the Organization necessarily involves adherence to a system of governance that, to some degree, is capable of generating new obligations not specified in the Charter itself, and to do so without the consent of all the parties to the compact.

The same autochthony is illustrated by the action of the Security Council in creating courts to bring to trial persons accused of war crimes and crimes against humanity in the Former Yugoslavia and Rwanda. Acting under its mandatory Chapter VII powers, the Council created entirely new obligations on all member states—including any opposed to this action—that oblige them to surrender for trial any persons (including their own citizens) indicted by the new courts. The Council also defined the law that the new tribunals were to apply. None of this could be said to have been expressed in the original treaty establishing the United Nations. Instead, the Charter established the institutional jurisdiction and powers that enabled the Security Council to create a new set of courts, define the law these tribunals were to apply, and endow them with jurisdiction over persons, wherever found, accused of violating those laws by an international prosecutor whose office and jurisdiction were also created by decision of the Council.

Perpetuity, indelibleness, primacy, and institutional autochthony: these four characteristics of the UN Charter relate that unique treaty more proximately to a constitution than to an ordinary contractual normative arrangement. But does it make any difference? Indeed it does. Whether or not the Charter is a constitution affects the way in which the norms of systemic interaction are to be interpreted by the judiciary, by the political organs, and by the Secretary-General.

Contracts between private parties, and bilateral treaties, should be construed narrowly to reflect precisely the literal text and the intent of the

---

[3] See chapter 6 in this volume.

negotiators at the time of their negotiation. A constitution, however, calls for another interpretative mode altogether. As the Judicial Committee of the Imperial Privy Council observed, when speaking of the Canadian constitution, such an instrument, meant to last for the ages, should be seen as "a living tree."[4] The same expansive view of constitutional interpretation has been taken by the US Supreme Court, not least by Chief Justice John Marshall in *McCulloch v. Maryland*, in which he construed the constitution's "necessary and proper" clause to permit Congress to exercise powers not specifically assigned to it but which, nevertheless, are "appropriate" to carrying out the "letter and spirit of the Constitution."[5] As Justice Holmes said in *Missouri v. Holland*, "when we are dealing with words that are also a constituent act . . . we must realize that they have called into life a being the development of which could not have been foreseen completely by the most gifted of its begetters. It was enough for them to realize or to hope that they had created an organism."[6] Applied to the interpretation of the UN Charter, this means, at the least, that the constitutive instrument establishing the United Nations should be read broadly so as to advance, rather than encumber, its institutional ability to accomplish the purposes for which it was created.

Gratifyingly, this is what has been happening. In the seminal *Reparations* case, the ICJ was called upon to pronounce whether the United Nations has the legal capacity to bring a claim for damages in its own right against a state on behalf of one of its officials, killed while on active duty in that state. The Charter, as the Court observed, is silent as to the matter. Its view is worth quoting *in extenso*:

> In the opinion of the Court, the Organization was intended to exercise and enjoy, and is in fact exercising and enjoying, functions and rights which can only be explained on the basis of the possession of a large measure of international personality and the capacity to operate upon an international plane. It is at present the supreme type of international organization, and it could not carry out the intentions of its founders if it was devoid of international personality. It must be acknowledged that its Members, by entrusting certain functions to it, with the attendant duties and responsibilities, have clothed it with the competence required to enable those functions to be effectively discharged. Accordingly, the Court has come to the conclusion that the Organization is an international person.[7]

This was taken to mean that the United Nations "is a subject of international law and capable of possessing international rights and duties, and

---

[4] *Edwards v. Attorney-General for Canada*, [1930] AC 124 (PC), at p. 136 (Lord Sankey).
[5] *McCulloch v. Maryland*, 17 US 316, 421 (1819).
[6] *Missouri v. Holland*, 252 US 416, 433 (1920) (Holmes, J.).
[7] *Reparation for Injuries Suffered in the Service of the United Nations (Advisory Opinion)* (1949) ICJ Rep. 174, pp. 179-180.

that it has capacity to maintain its rights by bringing international claims."[8]

This was not, however, a necessary inference from the *text* of the Charter, nor was it one that could have been derived from reading the Charter as if it were an ordinary contract between nations. In such a more traditional mode of treaty interpretation, the Court would have said that if the parties had wished to invest the United Nations with legal personality and its prerogatives, they could have said so explicitly. That they did *not* would be taken to imply that no such constitutive endowment was intended. Fortunately, the Court has had the wisdom to eschew such extrapolations from contract law and to construe the Charter as a living tree.

Another example is afforded by the way in which the Security Council (and then the Court) has construed Article 27(3) of the Charter. This provision states:

> Decisions of the Security Council on all [non-procedural] matters shall be made by an affirmative vote of nine members including the concurring votes of the permanent members.

In practice, however, the members have for many years, and in hundreds of votes, interpreted an abstention by a permanent member as not constituting a veto. This is a sensible embroidery of the text that has the great advantage of allowing a permanent member to abstain—thereby expressing reservations—without killing an otherwise widely accepted initiative of the majority. In a 1971 advisory opinion, the ICJ gave its approval to this auto-interpretation by the Council of the legal consequences of a permanent member's abstention, even though a literal reading of the text in a narrow contractual mode would have compelled the opposite conclusion.[9]

Whether the Charter continues to be regarded as a "living tree" will be further tested by the system's current response to *les petites crises* of law engendered by *les grandes crises* of politics: the 1999 war in Kosovo, the invasion and occupation of Iraq from 2003, ongoing efforts to counter the threats of terrorism and proliferation of weapons of mass destruction.[10]

NATO's action in Kosovo was not authorized in advance by the Security Council. Neither, earlier in the same decade, was the decision by the West African Community (ECOWAS) to despatch a military force (ECOMOG) to end the fighting and enforce a truce in Liberia and Sierra Leone. The Security Council, however, did turn down by twelve votes to three a resolution offered by Russia to condemn the NATO intervention and, thereafter, the Council

---

[8] Ibid.
[9] *Legal Consequences for States of the Continued Presence of South Africa in Namibia (South-West Africa) Notwithstanding Security Council Resolution 276 (1970) (Advisory Opinion)* (1971) ICJ Rep 16.
[10] See further chapter 2 in this volume.

agreed to participate in the "rapid implementation" of the settlement that had been imposed on Yugoslavia by the interveners. This might be construed as a form of *nunc pro tunc* authorization. In the West African case, the Council did not authorize the ECOMOG interventions until many months after they had begun, and, even then, did so only tacitly.

While these precedents cannot yet be said to have confirmed an accepted rule for construing Article 53 in a more flexible, less literal, manner, it is possible that future practice will confirm a normative expectation not precisely configured by that of the states gathered in San Francisco in 1945. It is entirely conceivable, for example, that the requirement for Security Council consent to military action by a regional organization could become—through practice of the Council and/or decision of the ICJ—a less rigid requirement that could be satisfied by *subsequent* approval or acquiescence. Such transformation-in-practice of the text of a written contractual instrument would be inadmissible, except in instances where the instrument is also a constitution of an organic community.

This does not argue, of course, that every departure from strict textuality by the Security Council, General Assembly, or Secretariat should be construed as Charter reform. In any legal system based at least in part on customary practice it is always both necessary, and necessarily difficult, to draw a line between the violation of law and its adaptation through practice. While it is necessary to acknowledge that the Charter, as treaty law, is not as evidently amenable to the reconstructive effects of practice as is "mere" custom, it is also true that, in construing a constitution, the practice of the organs created by it tend to have an important place in determining what that instrument means at any particular juncture of its history. Without reference to the historically evolved practices of the US President and Congress, for example, any effort to understand the constitutional law pertaining to the making of both war and international commitments solely by reliance on the text would be horrendously misleading. A constitution develops its own customary law of interpretation in part through the dynamic interaction of the parts of the system it has set in motion and that penumbra is formed through practice.

A simple forward-looking example will suffice. Suppose the Security Council, determined to oversee the disarmament of an aggressor state defeated in a conflict that had been authorized in accordance with Charter Chapter VII, were to create an international inspectorate with authority to investigate compliance. Suppose, further, that in authorizing this process of inspection, the Council stipulated that violations reported by the inspectors would give rise to a right of any state or "coalition of the willing" to use sufficient force to compel compliance *if the report were approved by any ten members of the Council* in a procedural vote to accept it. Is there any reason why the permanent members of the Security Council, utilizing such a resolution, could not make this arrangement—a commitment *in futuro* not to cast a veto that would prevent enforcement of the agreed disarmament inspection rules? Such an arrangement would have the practical advantage of ensuring that no one state could bar the use of force if the inspectors found a serious violation of their mandate, but that, equally, it would not relegate enforcement to the sole judgment of the inspectors or any one member state. It could be argued that the effect of such a resolution would be to devalue the power of the veto stipulated by Article 27 of the Charter. But, if the Charter is indeed a constitution, then the agreement of the members, including the permanent members, to restrain use of the veto in a particular circumstance would surely carry legal as well as political significance.

Thus, it appears, the question—is the UN Charter a constitution?—is not one of purely theoretical interest, nor one of import only to academics. Indeed, how it is answered may well determine the ability of the Organization to continue to reinvent itself in the face of new challenges, thereby assuring its enduring relevance to the needs of states and the emergence of an international community.

A Note on Sources

Many of the documents used in this volume are available in full on the Internet. The UN Document system, indicated by the UN document symbol "UN Doc. xxx," enables retrieval of a document, normally in all six UN languages, from the website http://documents.un.org. Another useful site from which to obtain the most current materials on matters currently on the agenda of the various UN bodies is http://www.un.org/documents.

The United Nations System

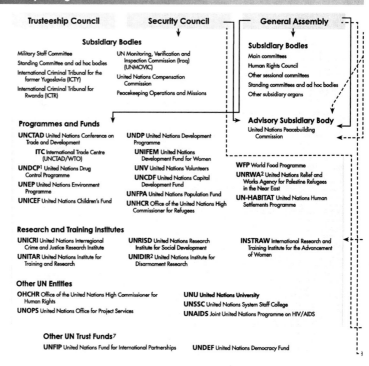

Trusteeship Council **Security Council** **General Assembly**

Subsidiary Bodies

Military Staff Committee

Standing Committee and ad hoc bodies

International Criminal Tribunal for the former Yugoslavia (ICTY)

International Criminal Tribunal for Rwanda (ICTR)

UN Monitoring, Verification and Inspection Commission (Iraq) (UNMOVIC)

United Nations Compensation Commission

Peacekeeping Operations and Missions

Subsidiary Bodies

Main committees

Human Rights Council

Other sessional committees

Standing committees and ad hoc bodies

Other subsidiary organs

Programmes and Funds

UNCTAD United Nations Conference on Trade and Development

    ITC International Trade Centre (UNCTAD/WTO)

UNDCP[1] United Nations Drug Control Programme

UNEP United Nations Environment Programme

UNICEF United Nations Children's Fund

UNDP United Nations Development Programme

    UNIFEM United Nations Development Fund for Women

    UNV United Nations Volunteers

UNCDF United Nations Capital Development Fund

UNFPA United Nations Population Fund

UNHCR Office of the United Nations High Commissioner for Refugees

Advisory Subsidiary Body

United Nations Peacebuilding Commission

WFP World Food Programme

UNRWA[2] United Nations Relief and Works Agency for Palestine Refugees in the Near East

UN-HABITAT United Nations Human Settlements Programme

Research and Training Institutes

UNICRI United Nations Interregional Crime and Justice Research Institute

UNITAR United Nations Institute for Training and Research

UNRISD United Nations Research Institute for Social Development

UNIDIR[2] United Nations Institute for Disarmament Research

INSTRAW International Research and Training Institute for the Advancement of Women

Other UN Entities

OHCHR Office of the United Nations High Commissioner for Human Rights

UNOPS United Nations Office for Project Services

UNU United Nations University

UNSSC United Nations System Staff College

UNAIDS Joint United Nations Programme on HIV/AIDS

Other UN Trust Funds[7]

UNFIP United Nations Fund for International Partnerships

UNDEF United Nations Democracy Fund

NOTES: Solid lines from a Principal Organ indicate a direct reporting relationship; dashes indicate a non-subsidiary relationship.

[1] The UN Drug Control Programme is part of the UN Office on Drugs and Crime

[2] UNRWA and UNIDIR report only to the GA

[3] The United Nations Ethics Office and the United Nations Ombudsman's Office report directly to the Secretary-General

[4] IAEA reports to the Security Council and the General Assembly (GA)

[5] The CTBTO Prep.Com and OPCW report to the GA

[6] Specialized agencies are autonomous organizations working with the UN and each other through the coordinating machinery of the ECOSOC at the intergovernmental level, and through the Chief Executives Board for coordination (CEB) at the inter-secretariat level

[7] UNFIP is an autonomous trust fund operating under the leadership of the United Nations Deputy Secretary-General. UNDEF's advisory board recommends funding proposals for approval by the Secretary-General.

Economic and Social Council

Functional Commissions

Commissions on:
- Narcotic Drugs
- Crime Prevention and Criminal Justice
- Science and Technology for Development
- Sustainable Development
- Status of Women
- Population and Development
- Commission for Social Development
- Statistical Commission

Regional Commissions

Economic Commission for Africa (ECA)

Economic Commission for Europe (ECE)

Economic Commission for Latin America and the Caribbean (ECLAC)

Economic and Social Commission for Asia and the Pacific (ESCAP)

Economic and Social Commission for Western Asia (ESCWA)

Other Bodies

Permanent Forum on Indigenous Issues (PFII)

United Nations Forum on Forests

Sessional and standing committees

Expert, ad hoc and related bodies

Related Organizations

WTO World Trade Organization

IAEA[4] International Atomic Energy Agency

CTBTO Prep.Com[5] PrepCom for the Nuclear-Test-Ban-Treaty Organization

OPCW[5] Organization for the Prohibition of Chemical Weapons

International Court of Justice

Specialized Agencies[6]

ILO International Labour Organization

FAO Food and Agriculture Organization of the United Nations

UNESCO United Nations Educational, Scientific and Cultural Organization

WHO World Health Organization

World Bank Group

IBRD International Bank for Reconstruction and Development

IDA International Development Association

IFC International Finance Corporation

MIGA Multilateral Investment Guarantee Agency

ICSID International Centre for Settlement of Investment Disputes

IMF International Monetary Fund

ICAO International Civil Aviation Organization

IMO International Maritime Organization

ITU International Telecommunication Union

UPU Universal Postal Union

WMO World Meteorological Organization

WIPO World Intellectual Property Organization

IFAD International Fund for Agricultural Development

UNIDO United Nations Industrial Development Organization

UNWTO World Tourism Organization

Secretariat

Departments and Offices

OSG[3] Office of the Secretary-General

OIOS Office of Internal Oversight Services

OLA Office of Legal Affairs

DPA Department of Political Affairs

DDA Department for Disarmament Affairs

DPKO Department of Peacekeeping Operations

OCHA Office for the Coordination of Humanitarian Affairs

DESA Department of Economic and Social Affairs

DGACM Department for General Assembly and Conference Management

DPI Department of Public Information

DM Department of Management

OHRLLS Office of the High Representative for the Least Developed Countries, Landlocked Developing Countries and Small Island Developing States

DSS Department of Safety and Security

UNODC United Nations Office on Drugs and Crime

☙❧

UNOG UN Office at Geneva

UNOV UN Office at Vienna

UNON UN Office at Nairobi

Published by the United Nations
Department of Public Information
06-39572—August 2006—10,000—DPI/2431

Part One **Relevance**

chapter one
. . . .

The UN Charter

The role of international law in international relations and in the nature of relations between states after 1945 remains heavily influenced by the two World Wars (1914–1918 and 1939–1945) that wracked Europe and, in the case of World War II, the Pacific Basin and much in between. The human, economic, and material costs of these wars were so devastating that the design of an international system to prevent their recurrence proved of the highest priority both in 1919 and in 1945. The failures of design and implementation of the League of Nations contributed to the march to war of the 1930s, but the League's collapse did not discourage US presidents Franklin D. Roosevelt and Harry S. Truman from their belief that only a strengthened collective security system could prevent, in the language of the UN Charter, "the scourge of war." The provisions of the Charter, drawing on manifold sources, were much debated prior to and during the San Francisco Conference of 1945, at the conclusion of which its terms were adopted by participating states. These debates still provide useful insights for those seeking to ascertain the intentions of the founders of the UN.

While the League's Covenant emphasized a legal approach to the prevention of war, by placing specific obligations on all its members, the UN Charter anticipated more proactive, pragmatic, and political strategies. Unlike the Covenant, the Charter recognized that the United Nations would not be effective in keeping the peace if it were challenged by a great power, and thus that collective action by the great powers to protect the peace was critical to the success of the UN.

Key differences between the League Covenant and the UN Charter can be summed up as follows: (a) the United States was to be at the core of the Organization and its key organ, the Security Council, from the outset (the US Senate had prevented the United States from joining the League); (b) the United States and four other powerful states were given special privileges, including permanent seats on the Security Council and veto powers to induce their active involvement in the Organization; and (c) the Security Council was empowered to impose, indeed enforce, its decisions when adopted under the terms of Chapter VII of the UN Charter. While the veto power was a topic of controversy at the San Francisco Conference (as were criteria for future membership, the extent to which regional organizations and alliances were to be subordinated to the Security Council's oversight, and the status of non-self governing territories and more broadly the future of the colonial and trusteeship system), realism won out over concern for the equality of states, an important principle formally enshrined in the Charter, discussed below.

Remarkably, the UN Charter, to a much greater extent than is generally recognized in superficial examinations of international relations, continues to guide the practice of states and broader debate on critical issues such as the use of force. Much has occurred since 1945 to complement, enrich, and qualify the terms of the Charter, but the text itself has stood up remarkably well to the test of time. It has lent itself to evolving interpretations of several of its key provisions as the circumstances of international relations evolved also, but its key principles remain intact. The notion of respect for the rule of law internationally is at the heart of the Charter, and at the heart of the foreign policy of most countries.

Not surprisingly, its central features address threats to the peace and how to manage them. While the Charter's stated central purpose is to prevent war, its key security provisions are couched in more reactive terms, dealing primarily with how to deal with threats to the peace. A broader vision, enshrined in the sweeping opening lines of the Charter, lays out how war itself is to be averted—through efforts to achieve interlocking security, economic, and social goals (including the attainment of human rights for all equally) that, it was hoped, would make the recourse to violent conflict redundant.

UN CHARTER, PREAMBLE

WE THE PEOPLES OF THE UNITED NATIONS DETERMINED

to save succeeding generations from the scourge of war, which twice in our lifetime has brought untold sorrow to mankind, and

to reaffirm faith in fundamental human rights, in the dignity and worth of the human person, in the equal rights of men and women and of nations large and small, and

to establish conditions under which justice and respect for the obligations arising from treaties and other sources of international law can be maintained, and

to promote social progress and better standards of life in larger freedom, AND FOR THESE ENDS

to practice tolerance and live together in peace with one another as good neighbours, and

to unite our strength to maintain international peace and security, and

to ensure by the acceptance of principles and the institution of methods, that armed force shall not be used, save in the common interest, and

to employ international machinery for the promotion of the economic and social advancement of all peoples,
HAVE RESOLVED TO COMBINE OUR EFFORTS TO ACCOMPLISH THESE AIMS

Accordingly, our respective Governments, through representatives assembled in the city of San Francisco, who have exhibited their full powers found to be in good and due form, have agreed to the present Charter of the United Nations and do hereby establish an international organization to be known as the United Nations.

Soon after the adoption of the Charter, the Cold War divided most members of the United Nations into rival blocs centered on Washington and Moscow. Avoiding nuclear war became the central challenge of the Cold War years, one in which the United Nations sometimes served as a meeting ground for ideological sparring. The Security Council Chamber was the cockpit for public confrontation between Moscow and Washington during the Cuban Missile Crisis of 1961, without doubt the most dangerous moment in international relations since 1945.

The Cold War seriously impeded implementation of many of the Charter's aims. It gave rise to many "regional" conflicts in Central America, Southern and Eastern Africa, South-East Asia, and elsewhere, pitting proxies of the superpowers against each other. It also acted as a brake on achievement of the Charter's ambitious economic and social goals. But, in retrospect, surprisingly, it did not slow (and may have accelerated) the remarkable development of norms through myriad treaties and through practice, initiated by the Universal Declaration of Human Rights in 1948. The Security Council, while marginal to many of the conflicts of the Cold War period, remained intact to assume much greater responsibilities in the post–Cold War era.

The Charter's focus on security, while eminently sensible for those countries that had experienced the two World Wars first hand, came to be challenged in the 1960s and 1970s by the many newly decolonized developing countries for which economic development was the over-riding objective. Since those years, serious tensions have existed within the Organization over its central goals, reflected, for example, in preparatory discussions of the UN Summit of 2005. But the related claims and counter-claims of states continue to draw upon the Charter and many of the texts developed under its authority by UN member states since 1945.

This chapter explores the question of why states still ground so many of their aspirations and arguments in the provisions of the Charter. As in domestic law, the discipline imposed by international law aims to protect all from all—an attractive proposition in theory, though sometimes inconvenient in practice for those with the power to disregard international criticism. Though explanations for compliance with or deviation from international norms are many, it is at least noteworthy that even when the most powerful member states violate the terms of the Charter, in particular since the end of the Cold War, they generally articulate justifications that draw upon UN decisions and practices—even if only after the fact.

Such extreme cases will be considered in chapter 2. The present chapter first examines the provisions of the Charter before tackling three recent turning points in its interpretation and implementation: the reinvigoration of the UN Security Council as a means of ensuring international peace and security after the Cold War; attempts to put development back at the heart of the UN agenda in 2000; and efforts to respond to the challenges to the effectiveness and legitimacy of the UN following the US-led invasion of Iraq in 2003.

1.1 Select Provisions of the Charter

What were the concerns of delegates at the San Francisco conference and how were the design flaws of the League of Nations remedied? Chapter I of the Charter outlines the new Organization's purposes and principles.

UN CHARTER, CHAPTER I—PURPOSES AND PRINCIPLES

Article 1

The Purposes of the United Nations are:

1. To maintain international peace and security, and to that end: to take effective collective measures for the prevention and removal of threats to the peace, and for the suppression of acts of aggression or other breaches of the peace, and to bring about by peaceful means, and in conformity with the principles of justice and international law, adjustment or settlement of international disputes or situations which might lead to a breach of the peace;
2. To develop friendly relations among nations based on respect for the principle of equal rights and self-determination of peoples, and to take other appropriate measures to strengthen universal peace;
3. To achieve international cooperation in solving international problems of an economic, social, cultural, or humanitarian character, and in promoting and encouraging respect for human rights and for fundamental freedoms for all without distinction as to race, sex, language, or religion; and
4. To be a centre for harmonizing the actions of nations in the attainment of these common ends.

Article 2

The Organization and its Members, in pursuit of the Purposes stated in Article 1, shall act in accordance with the following Principles.

1. The Organization is based on the principle of the sovereign equality of all its Members.
2. All Members, in order to ensure to all of them the rights and benefits resulting from membership, shall fulfil in good faith the obligations assumed by them in accordance with the present Charter.
3. All Members shall settle their international disputes by peaceful means in such a manner that international peace and security, and justice, are not endangered.
4. All Members shall refrain in their international relations from the threat or use of force against the territorial integrity or political independence of any state, or in any other manner inconsistent with the Purposes of the United Nations.
5. All Members shall give the United Nations every assistance in any action it takes in accordance with the present Charter, and shall refrain from giving assistance to any state against which the United Nations is taking preventive or enforcement action.
6. The Organization shall ensure that states which are not Members of the United Nations act in accordance with these Principles so far as may be necessary for the maintenance of international peace and security.
7. Nothing contained in the present Charter shall authorize the United Nations to intervene in matters which are essentially within the domestic jurisdiction of any state or shall require the Members to submit such matters to settlement under the present Charter; but this principle shall not prejudice the application of enforcement measures under Chapter VII.

"Sovereign equality" is, some argue, the constitutive fiction of the international order. We have already seen how the accordance of special privileges to major powers was an important departure from the League of Nations intended to ensure the participation of major states in its successor body. Article 2 nevertheless puts this at the heart of the Organization. At the San Francisco conference, aspects of sovereign equality addressed by delegates included: (a) the legal equality of states, (b) the enjoyment by each state of the rights inherent in full sovereignty, (c) respect for the personality of the state, as well as its territorial integrity and political independence, and (d) the compliance by the state with its international duties and obligations.[1]

---

[1] In fact, the UN was founded on the basis of a compromise between the reality of power politics and the legal principle of sovereign equality, a compromise highly relevant to efforts at achieving UN reform ever since. On security matters, the UN founders sought to avoid the equalization of state power through a consensus system. In 1963, the UN Special Committee on Principles of International Law Concerning Friendly Relations and Cooperation Among States, established under GA Res. 1966

Other principles relate to state behavior in the event of threats to the peace. However, the very last provision of Article 2 is the one cited most often in UN debates. This paragraph was initially interpreted as highly restrictive of the capacity of the United Nations to involve itself in the internal affairs of states, except at the invitation of the governments of those states or under treaty terms freely entered into by them. The UN was not to be an intrusive organization. There was not much reason to revisit this interpretation of the text as long as the provisions of Chapter VII of the Charter remained largely a dead letter, as they were for the most part from 1945 until 1990.

Before the action against Iraq in 1990–1991, the Council had authorized what might be considered enforcement actions only twice: in 1950 the Council "recommended" action in Korea under the unified command of the United States;[2] in 1966 it *"called upon"* the United Kingdom to use force to prevent the violation of sanctions against Southern Rhodesia.[3] In addition, the Council authorized the use of force by the United Nations and the Secretary-General in the course of the peacekeeping operation in the Congo.[4] The Council also imposed mandatory sanctions on two occasions in this period: the economic blockade of Southern Rhodesia (1966–1979)[5] and the arms embargo on South Africa (1977–1994).[6]

In its first forty-four years, twenty-four Security Council resolutions cited or used the terms of Chapter VII; by 1993 it was adopting that many such resolutions every year. This repeated recourse to the terms of Chapter VII was seen by some as a challenge to traditional conceptions of sovereignty, but more worrying to some member states was the manner in which this reflected a larger erosion of the protections of Article 2(7).

Chapter II of the Charter deals with membership. As in any club, the threshold for membership is set by requirements, in this case it being "open to . . . peace-loving states which accept the obligations contained in the . . . Charter and, in the judgment of the Organization, are able and willing to carry out these obligations" (Article 4). As a means of regulating membership, provision is made for the suspension of membership of countries against which the Security Council has taken action on a case-by-case basis. This was, arguably, the basis upon which South Africa and the Serb splinter state

---

(XVII), considered various proposals to expand or explain the meaning of sovereign equality, eventually adopting some not terribly illuminating consensus conclusions to be found in 20 UN GAOR, agenda items 90 and 94, p. 134, UN Doc. A/5746 (1965).
[2] See chapter 8 in this volume.
[3] See chapter 10 in this volume.
[4] See chapter 6 in this volume.
[5] SC Res. 232 (1966); SC Res. 253 (1968); SC Res. 277 (1970).
[6] SC Res. 418 (1977).

emerging from the Former Yugoslavia lost access to their seats in the General Assembly for some years (Article 5).[7]

Chapter III of the Charter establishes the Organization's "principal organs," defined as a General Assembly, a Security Council, an Economic and Social Council, a Trusteeship Council, an International Court of Justice, and a Secretariat. Importantly, the Charter does not set a hierarchy as between these organs and, while providing for particular responsibilities and powers of each, does not regulate how they should relate to each other.[8] Further, it does not narrowly delineate the competence of each organ. Thus, the principal organs largely set their own competence. This is particularly true of the Security Council, provided with the most extensive powers of all. While the General Assembly in Article 10 is empowered to "make recommendations" to the membership and to the Security Council, the Security Council can take decisions which, if adopted under the provisions of Chapter VII of the Charter, are binding on all states. The scope of the Council's discretion remaining undefined in the Charter text, this has left open a fairly vast field for improvisation under the general heading of peace and security, of which the Council has been exploring the full extent since 1990, for example addressing the spread of AIDS in Africa as a security threat.

The core of the Charter lies in Chapters V–VII relating to the Security Council's powers and functions, the Charter's directives for the pacific settlement of disputes, and the responses it envisages to breaches of the peace.

The Council's membership has, for some years, been quite controversial. In order to secure the continuing engagement of the great powers in the work of the Organization, five of them—China (initially the Nationalist Kuomintang regime, confined from 1949 to the island of Taiwan, but from 1971 the Communist mainland government with its capital in Beijing), France, the Soviet Union (later succeeded by the Russian Federation), the United Kingdom, and the United States—were granted permanent seats and the right to veto any "substantive" resolution advanced for decision. While this provision has, by and large, kept all five countries engaged in the Organization, other member states have been less satisfied. For one thing, during the Cold War years vetoes proliferated, contributing to the marginalization at that time of the Council. On the other, several of these countries have waned as major powers, while others such as Japan, Germany, India, and Brazil have since emerged or re-emerged as major players. Efforts aimed at addressing imbalances among member states have failed to date, although it was possible in

---

[7] Article 19 stipulates that member states can also lose their right to vote in the General Assembly when in arrear of dues to the UN by more than two years. See further chapter 5 in this volume.

[8] An exception is the provision in Article 12 concerning the General Assembly's competences with respect to matters being dealt with by the Security Council. This is discussed further in the *Certain Expenses* case in chapter 6.

the period 1963–1965 to add four non-permanent seats (for a total of ten, and a Council membership of fifteen) to grant greater representation to newly decolonized countries.

Each of Chapter VI and Chapter VII, with their carefully constructed and implicitly incremental approaches, are worth considering in their entirety. Chapter VII provides the Council with by far the most sweeping powers of any multilateral institution to date. They continue to serve as the foundation of virtually all action the Council undertakes, while their terms, more broadly, also affect actions of individual governments and of regional organizations.

UN CHARTER, CHAPTER VI—PACIFIC SETTLEMENT OF DISPUTES

Article 33

1. The parties to any dispute, the continuance of which is likely to endanger the maintenance of international peace and security, shall, first of all, seek a solution by negotiation, enquiry, mediation, conciliation, arbitration, judicial settlement, resort to regional agencies or arrangements, or other peaceful means of their own choice.

2. The Security Council shall, when it deems necessary, call upon the parties to settle their dispute by such means.

Article 34

The Security Council may investigate any dispute, or any situation which might lead to international friction or give rise to a dispute, in order to determine whether the continuance of the dispute or situation is likely to endanger the maintenance of international peace and security.

Article 35

1. Any Member of the United Nations may bring any dispute, or any situation of the nature referred to in Article 34, to the attention of the Security Council or of the General Assembly.

2. A state which is not a Member of the United Nations may bring to the attention of the Security Council or of the General Assembly any dispute to which it is a party if it accepts in advance, for the purposes of the dispute, the obligations of pacific settlement provided in the present Charter.

3. The proceedings of the General Assembly in respect of matters brought to its attention under this Article will be subject to the provisions of Articles 11 and 12.

Article 36

1. The Security Council may, at any stage of a dispute of the nature referred to in Article 33 or of a situation of like nature, recommend appropriate procedures or methods of adjustment.

2. The Security Council should take into consideration any procedures for the settlement of the dispute which have already been adopted by the parties.

3. In making recommendations under this Article the Security Council should also take into consideration that legal disputes should as a general rule be referred by the parties to the International Court of Justice in accordance with the provisions of the Statute of the Court.

Article 37

1. Should the parties to a dispute of the nature referred to in Article 33 fail to settle it by the means indicated in that Article, they shall refer it to the Security Council.

2. If the Security Council deems that the continuance of the dispute is in fact likely to endanger the maintenance of international peace and security, it shall decide whether to take action under Article 36 or to recommend such terms of settlement as it may consider appropriate.

Article 38

Without prejudice to the provisions of Articles 33 to 37, the Security Council may, if all the parties to any dispute so request, make recommendations to the parties with a view to a pacific settlement of the dispute.

UN CHARTER, CHAPTER VII—ACTION WITH RESPECT TO THREATS TO THE PEACE, BREACHES OF THE PEACE, AND ACTS OF AGGRESSION

Article 39

The Security Council shall determine the existence of any threat to the peace, breach of the peace, or act of aggression and shall make recommendations, or decide what measures shall be taken in accordance with Articles 41 and 42, to maintain or restore international peace and security.

Article 40

In order to prevent an aggravation of the situation, the Security Council may, before making the recommendations or deciding upon the measures provided for in Article 39, call upon the parties concerned to comply with such provisional measures as it deems necessary or desirable. Such provisional measures shall be without prejudice to the rights, claims, or position of the parties concerned. The Security Council shall duly take account of failure to comply with such provisional measures.

Article 41

The Security Council may decide what measures not involving the use of armed force are to be employed to give effect to its decisions, and it may call upon the Members of the United Nations to apply such measures. These may include complete or partial interruption of economic relations and of rail, sea, air, postal, telegraphic, radio, and other means of communication, and the severance of diplomatic relations.

Article 42

Should the Security Council consider that measures provided for in Article 41 would be inadequate or have proved to be inadequate, it may take such action by air, sea, or land forces as may be necessary to maintain or restore international peace and security. Such action may include demonstrations, blockade, and other operations by air, sea, or land forces of Members of the United Nations.

Article 43

1. All Members of the United Nations, in order to contribute to the maintenance of international peace and security, undertake to make available to the Security Council, on its call and in accordance with a special agreement or agreements, armed forces, assistance, and facilities, including rights of passage, necessary for the purpose of maintaining international peace and security.

2. Such agreement or agreements shall govern the numbers and types of forces, their degree of readiness and general location, and the nature of the facilities and assistance to be provided.

3. The agreement or agreements shall be negotiated as soon as possible on the initiative of the Security Council. They shall be concluded between the Security Council and Members or between the Security Council and groups of Members and shall be subject to ratification by the signatory states in accordance with their respective constitutional processes.

Article 44

When the Security Council has decided to use force it shall, before calling upon a Member not represented on it to provide armed forces in fulfilment of the obligations assumed under Article 43, invite that Member, if the Member so desires, to participate in the decisions of the Security Council concerning the employment of contingents of that Member's armed forces.

Article 45

In order to enable the United Nations to take urgent military measures, Members shall hold immediately available national air-force contingents for combined international enforcement action. The strength and degree of readiness of these contingents and plans for their combined action shall be determined within the limits laid down in the special agreement or agreements referred to in Article 43, by the Security Council with the assistance of the Military Staff Committee.

Article 42

Plans for the application of armed force shall be made by the Security Council with the assistance of the Military Staff Committee.

Article 47

1. There shall be established a Military Staff Committee to advise and assist the Security Council on all questions relating to the Security Council's military requirements for the maintenance of international peace and security, the employment and command of forces placed at its disposal, the regulation of armaments, and possible disarmament.

2. The Military Staff Committee shall consist of the Chiefs of Staff of the permanent members of the Security Council or their representatives. Any Member of the United Nations not permanently represented on the Committee shall be invited by the Committee to be associated with it when the efficient discharge of the Committee's responsibilities requires the participation of that Member in its work.

3. The Military Staff Committee shall be responsible under the Security Council for the strategic direction of any armed forces placed at the disposal of the Security Council. Questions relating to the command of such forces shall be worked out subsequently.

4. The Military Staff Committee, with the authorization of the Security Council and after consultation with appropriate regional agencies, may establish regional sub-committees.

Article 48

1. The action required to carry out the decisions of the Security Council for the maintenance of international peace and security shall be taken by all the Members of the United Nations or by some of them, as the Security Council may determine.

2. Such decisions shall be carried out by the Members of the United Nations directly and through their action in the appropriate international agencies of which they are members.

Article 49

The Members of the United Nations shall join in affording mutual assistance in carrying out the measures decided upon by the Security Council.

Article 50

If preventive or enforcement measures against any state are taken by the Security Council, any other state, whether a Member of the United Nations or not, which finds itself confronted with special economic problems arising from the carrying out of those measures shall have the right to consult the Security Council with regard to a solution of those problems.

Article 51

Nothing in the present Charter shall impair the inherent right of individual or collective self-defence if an armed attack occurs against a Member of the United Nations, until the Security Council has taken measures necessary to maintain international peace and security. Measures taken by Members in the exercise of this right of self-defence shall be immediately reported to the Security Council and shall not in any way affect the authority and responsibility of the Security Council under the present Charter to take at any time such action as it deems necessary in order to maintain or restore international peace and security.

The Charter covers much other ground. For example, Chapter VIII discusses Regional Arrangements (mostly seen nowadays as applying to Regional Organizations such as the Organization of American States, the European Union, and the African Union), which it casts as subsidiary to (but not in competition with) the Security Council in the "pacific settlement of local disputes," reserving for the Council the mandating of any coercive action required.[9] In practice, with the Security Council heavily burdened by a very ambitious agenda combined with limited means since 1990, partnerships between the United Nations and a number of regional organizations, arrangements and military alliances (such as NATO) have proliferated in recent years, providing regional organizations with a much greater role in the Council's strategies than was the case during the Cold War years.

While both the League Covenant and the UN Charter emphasized the maintenance of peace as a primary objective, the Charter recognizes the importance of international cooperation in dealing with economic and social problems, as well as the need to safeguard basic human rights in order to prevent another war. This is not surprising, given the role of economics and social dislocation in the lead up to World War II, and the extent to which denial of human rights had been associated with aggressive regimes. In Chapters IX and X, the Charter discusses the UN's role and action in the economic and social spheres, in Article 55 citing its central aims as being the promotion of "(a) higher standards of living, full employment, and conditions of economic and social progress and development; (b) solutions of international economic, social, health, and related problems; and international cultural and educational co-operation; and (c) universal respect for, and observance of, human rights and fundamental freedoms for all without distinction as to race, sex, language, or religion."

In fact, extraordinary progress has been achieved on basic living standards, life expectancy, the struggle against disease and the attainment of literacy since 1945, much of it due to the efforts of various agencies that had not yet fully taken shape in 1945. Some of this activity occurs within the UN umbrella, in its Development Programme (UNDP). Other activities are vaguely associated with the Organization. The International Bank for Reconstruction and Development (the World Bank) and the International Monetary Fund, created as part of the UN system, since 1945 have become independent of UN oversight and cooperate with the United Nations only loosely. The General Agreement on Trade and Tariffs (GATT) of 1948, and its successor institution, the World Trade Organization (WTO) were never organically linked to the United Nations. Meaningful economic development activity and its related institutional architecture thus developed outside the United Nations. Its normative role, however, remains significant, for example through the Millennium Development commitments of the year 2000 and the related Millennium Development Goals. These topics are revisited in chapter 11.

On human rights and fundamental freedoms, major progress has also been made, but on these issues the United Nations has been front and center, and continues to serve as the anchor of the international human rights system,

---

[9] Article 53 provides that "No enforcement action shall be taken under regional arrangements or by regional agencies without the authorization of the Security Council."

discussed in chapter 13. Here, too, parallel and complementary developments occur in a dense "confederal" relation to the United Nations. The human rights activities pursued by the Human Rights Committee under the International Covenant on Civil and Political Rights (ICCPR) are but one example.

Chapters XI–XIII of the Charter address non-self governing territories and the practice of trusteeship, applied by the League of Nations (as mandates) and subsequently the United Nations to a number of entities of uncertain status, the administration of which was typically entrusted to a colonial power. While trusteeship narrowly defined was irrelevant to most colonial territories, the process of widespread decolonization, initiated with the independence of India and Pakistan in 1947 and accelerating through the 1950s and 1960s, was a defining feature of the international agenda. With the independence of the last Trust Territory, Palau, in 1994, the Trusteeship Council became dormant, but the needs of several territories, particularly war-torn ones, for governance has led to the revival of a notion of "virtual trusteeship" in instances where the United Nations has taken on oversight and administration for several years of such places as East Timor and Kosovo. We will return to this in chapter 9.

The International Court of Justice, whose Statute is annexed to the Charter, is discussed in Chapter XIV. While the Court has played an important role in adjudicating disputes between states, and could play an even more active such role in the future, it is the dramatic development of other specialized courts and tribunals for trade, criminal law, and law of the sea that has largely monopolized the limelight. See further chapter 3.

The other "principal organ" of the United Nations, the Secretariat, is addressed rather summarily in Chapter XV of the Charter. The Secretary-General is cast very much as the chief administrative officer of the institution rather than as its global leader. That said, in Article 99, the Secretary-General is provided with an important opening into the procedures and proceedings of the UN's most powerful body. He or she "may bring to the attention of the Security Council any matter which in his opinion may threaten the maintenance of international peace and security." Successive Secretaries-General have built on this provision to enhance the position's international leadership functions in the prevention and management of violent conflict.

Several important miscellaneous provisions round out the Charter. Article 103 gives precedence to obligations under the UN Charter over any other commitments by member states. Article 104 provides an early indication of the need for the United Nations to enjoy legal standing to carry out its many functions: "The Organization shall enjoy in the territory of each of its Members such legal capacity as may be necessary for the exercise of its functions and the fulfilment of its purposes," to which Article 105 adds provision for legal immunities and privileges for the Organization. Subsequent articles deal with procedures for amending the Charter, its signature and ratification.

The entire text of the Charter is reproduced in the appendix to this volume.

QUESTIONS ....

1. The UN Charter lists four purposes in Article 1. What institutions and powers does it include to advance these purposes? Can they be ranked in order of importance?
2. Former Secretary-General of the UN Dag Hammarskjöld said in 1954 that the United Nations was created not to bring humanity to heaven but to save it from hell. Against what standards should the success or failure of the United Nations be judged?
3. Is the UN Charter like a national constitution? In what aspects is it like one; in what aspects is it not? How does this affect: (a) international relations; (b) member states of the UN; and (c) other entities?

1.2 The New Interventionism: The UN Charter After the Cold War

The first major crisis of the post–Cold War era emerged soon after the fall of the Berlin Wall, with Iraq's 1990 invasion and then annexation of Kuwait. This was a potentially explosive development given the economic and geo-strategic sensitivity of the Gulf area, where so much of the world's oil production is concentrated. US President George H. W. Bush responded through a strategy centered on the Security Council's capacity to authorize progressively more severe coercive measures. On 11 September 1990, six weeks after Iraq's invasion, President Bush spoke to a Joint Session of Congress.

GEORGE H. W. BUSH, ADDRESS BEFORE A JOINT SESSION OF CONGRESS, 11 SEPTEMBER 1990

Our objectives in the Persian Gulf are clear, our goals defined and familiar: Iraq must withdraw from Kuwait completely, immediately, and without condition. Kuwait's legitimate government must be restored. The security and stability of the Persian Gulf must be assured. And American citizens abroad must be protected. These goals are not ours alone. They've been endorsed by the United Nations Security Council five times in as many weeks. Most countries share our concern for principle. And many have a stake in the stability of the Persian Gulf. This is not, as Saddam Hussein would have it, the United States against Iraq. It is Iraq against the world.

As you know, I've just returned from a very productive meeting with Soviet President Gorbachev. And I am pleased that we are working together to build a new relationship. In Helsinki, our joint statement affirmed to the world our shared resolve to counter Iraq's threat to peace. Let me quote: "We are united in the belief that Iraq's aggression must not be tolerated. No peaceful international order is possible if larger states can devour their smaller neighbors." Clearly, no longer can a dictator count on East-West confrontation to stymie concerted United Nations action against aggression. A new partnership of nations has begun.

We stand today at a unique and extraordinary moment. The crisis in the Persian Gulf, as grave as it is, also offers a rare opportunity to move toward an historic period of cooperation. Out of these troubled times, our fifth objective—a new world order—can emerge: a new era—freer from the threat of terror, stronger in the pursuit of justice, and more secure in the quest for peace. An era in which the nations of the world, East and West, North and South, can prosper and live in harmony. A hundred generations have searched for this elusive path to peace, while a thousand wars raged across the span of human endeavor. Today that new world is struggling to be born, a world quite different from the one we've known. A world where the rule of law supplants the rule of the jungle. A world in which nations recognize the shared responsibility for freedom and justice. A world where the strong respect the rights of the weak. This is the vision that I shared with President Gorbachev in Helsinki. He and other leaders from Europe, the Gulf, and around the world understand that how we manage this crisis today could shape the future for generations to come.

The test we face is great, and so are the stakes. This is the first assault on the new world that we seek, the first test of our mettle. Had we not responded to this first provocation with clarity of purpose, if we do not continue to demonstrate our determination, it would be a signal to actual and potential despots around the world. America and the world must defend common vital interests—and we will. America and the world must support the rule of law—and we will. America and the world must stand up to aggression—and we will. And one thing more: In the pursuit of these goals America will not be intimidated.

Vital issues of principle are at stake. Saddam Hussein is literally trying to wipe a country off the face of the Earth. We do not exaggerate. Nor do we exaggerate when we say Saddam Hussein will fail. Vital economic interests are at risk as well. Iraq itself controls some 10 percent of the world's proven oil reserves. Iraq plus Kuwait controls twice that. An Iraq permitted to swallow Kuwait would have the economic and military power, as well as the arrogance, to intimidate and coerce its neighbors—neighbors who control the lion's share of the world's remaining oil reserves. We cannot permit a resource so vital to be dominated by one so ruthless. And we won't.

We can now point to five United Nations Security Council resolutions that condemn Iraq's aggression. They call for Iraq's immediate and unconditional withdrawal, the restoration of Kuwait's legitimate government, and categorically reject Iraq's cynical and self-serving attempt to annex Kuwait. Finally, the United Nations has demanded the release of all foreign nationals held hostage against their will and in contravention of international law. It is a mockery of human decency to call these people "guests." They are hostages, and the whole world knows it. . . .

Prime Minister Margaret Thatcher, a dependable ally, said it all: "We do not bargain over hostages. We will not stoop to the level of using human beings as bargaining chips ever." Of course, of course, our hearts go out to the hostages and to their families. But our policy cannot change, and it will not change. America and the world will not be blackmailed by this ruthless policy.

We're now in sight of a United Nations that performs as envisioned by its founders. We owe much to the outstanding leadership of Secretary-General Javier Perez de Cuellar. The United Nations is backing up its words with action. The Security Council has imposed mandatory economic sanctions on Iraq, designed to force Iraq to relinquish the spoils of its illegal conquest. The Security Council has also taken the decisive step of authorizing the use of all means necessary to ensure compliance with these sanctions. Together with our friends and allies, ships of the United States Navy are today patrolling Mideast waters. They've already intercepted more than 700 ships to enforce the sanctions. Three regional leaders I spoke with just yesterday told me that these sanctions are working. Iraq is feeling the heat. We continue to hope that Iraq's leaders will recalculate just what their aggression has cost them. They are cut off from world trade, unable to sell their oil. And only a tiny fraction of goods gets through. . . .

I cannot predict just how long it will take to convince Iraq to withdraw from Kuwait. Sanctions will take time to have their full intended effect. We will continue to review all options with our allies, but let it be clear: we will not let this aggression stand.[10]

As we now know, sanctions were not enough to persuade Saddam Hussein to abandon Kuwait. After several months of gradually increasing pressure, the Security Council, acting explicitly under Chapter VII of the Charter, adopted Security Council resolution 678 on 29 November 1990, authorizing member states to use "all necessary means" to evict Iraq from Kuwait and thus to restore international peace and security in the area. Military action by a broad US-led coalition of countries acted on this mandate in January 1991. (This action—and the contrast with the US-led invasion of Iraq in 2003—is discussed in chapter 2.)

One year later, on 31 January 1992, largely in response to these momentous developments that made clear a new willingness of the Security Council to unify on key threats, the first ever Security Council Summit convened. The President of the Council was authorized to discuss the conclusions of Council leaders in the following terms. This statement represents a high water mark in the belief among world leaders that the Security Council could and would play the central role multilaterally on security issues in the post–Cold War era:

---

[10] Full text available from http://millercenter.virginia.edu/scripps/diglibrary/prez speeches/ghbush/ghb_1990_0911.html.

SECURITY COUNCIL SUMMIT STATEMENT CONCERNING THE COUNCIL'S RESPONSIBILITY IN THE MAINTENANCE OF INTERNATIONAL PEACE AND SECURITY, 31 JANUARY 1992[11]

This meeting takes place at a time of momentous change. The ending of the Cold War has raised hopes for a safer, more equitable and more humane world. Rapid progress has been made, in many regions of the world, towards democracy and responsive forms of government, as well as towards achieving the Purposes set out in the Charter. The completion of the dismantling of apartheid in South Africa would constitute a major contribution to these Purposes and positive trends, including to the encouragement of respect for human rights and fundamental freedoms.

Last year, under the authority of the United Nations, the international community succeeded in enabling Kuwait to regain its sovereignty and territorial integrity, which it had lost as a result of Iraqi aggression. The resolutions adopted by the Security Council remain essential to the restoration of peace and stability in the region and must be fully implemented. At the same time the members of the Council are concerned by the humanitarian situation of the innocent civilian population of Iraq.

The members of the Council . . . welcome the role the United Nations has been able to play under the Charter in progress towards settling long-standing regional disputes, and will work for further progress towards their resolution. They applaud the valuable contribution being made by United Nations peacekeeping forces now operating in Asia, Africa, Latin America and Europe.

The members of the Council note that United Nations peacekeeping tasks have increased and broadened considerably in recent years. Election monitoring, human rights verification and the repatriation of refugees have in the settlement of some regional conflicts, at the request or with the agreement of the parties concerned, been integral parts of the Security Council's effort to maintain international peace and security. They welcome these developments.

The members of the Council also recognize that change, however welcome, has brought new risks for stability and security. Some of the most acute problems result from changes to State structures. . . .

The international community therefore faces new challenges in the search for peace. All Member States expect the United Nations to play a central role at this crucial stage. The members of the Council stress the importance of strengthening and improving the United Nations to increase its effectiveness. They are determined to assume fully their responsibilities within the United Nations Organization in the framework of the Charter.

---

[11]UN Doc. S/23500 (1992).

The absence of war and military conflicts amongst States does not in itself ensure international peace and security. The non-military sources of instability in the economic, social, humanitarian and ecological fields have become threats to peace and security. The United Nations membership as a whole, working through the appropriate bodies, needs to give the highest priority to the solution of these matters.

The members of the Council pledge their commitment to international law and to the United Nations Charter. All disputes between States should be peacefully resolved in accordance with the provisions of the Charter.

The members of the Council reaffirm their commitment to the collective security system of the Charter to deal with threats to peace and to reverse acts of aggression.

The members of the Council express their deep concern over acts of international terrorism and emphasize the need for the international community to deal effectively with all such acts.

To strengthen the effectiveness of these commitments, and in order that the Security Council should have the means to discharge its primary responsibility under the Charter for the maintenance of international peace and security, the members of the Council have decided on the following approach.

They invite the Secretary-General to prepare, for circulation to the Members of the United Nations by 1 July 1992, his analysis and recommendations on ways of strengthening and making more efficient within the framework and provisions of the Charter the capacity of the United Nations for preventive diplomacy, for peacemaking and for peacekeeping. . . .

The members of the Council, while fully conscious of the responsibilities of other organs of the United Nations in the fields of disarmament, arms control and non-proliferation, reaffirm the crucial contribution which progress in these areas can make to the maintenance of international peace and security. They express their commitment to take concrete steps to enhance the effectiveness of the United Nations in these areas.

The members of the Council underline the need for all Member States to fulfil their obligations in relation to arms control and disarmament; to prevent the proliferation in all its aspects of all weapons of mass destruction; to avoid excessive and destabilizing accumulations and transfers of arms; and to resolve peacefully in accordance with the Charter any problems concerning these matters threatening or disrupting the maintenance of regional and global stability. . . .

In conclusion, the members of the Security Council affirm their determination to build on the initiative of their meeting in order to secure positive advances in promoting International peace and security. They agree that the United Nations Secretary-General has a crucial role to play. . . .

The members of the Council agree that the world now has the best chance of achieving international peace and security since the foundation of the United Nations. They undertake to work in close cooperation with other United Nations Member States in their own efforts to achieve this, as well as to address urgently all the other problems, in particular those of economic and social development, requiring the collective response of the international community. They recognize that peace and prosperity are indivisible and that lasting peace and stability require effective international cooperation for the eradication of poverty and the promotion of a better life for all in larger freedom.[12]

QUESTIONS

4. How important is international law, such as that reflected in the UN Charter, in the conduct of international relations? President Bush referred to the rule of law supplanting the rule of the jungle in international affairs. What might this mean?
5. The United Nations in the 1990s experienced crises of legitimacy but also crises of expectations. Were statements such as that adopted by the Security Council in January 1992 overly ambitious?

1.3 Putting Development Back on the Agenda

By 2000, a sense had developed among member states that the UN's economic development objectives were being neglected. This led to a Millennium Summit focused mostly on development challenges facing the globe, although a number of salient security issues, for example relating to weapons of mass destruction and the trade in small arms, received prominent attention.

MILLENNIUM DECLARATION, 8 SEPTEMBER 2000[13]

2. We recognize that, in addition to our separate responsibilities to our individual societies, we have a collective responsibility to uphold the principles of human dignity, equality and equity at the global level. As leaders we have a duty therefore to all the world's people, especially the most vulnerable and, in particular, the children of the world, to whom the future belongs.
 3. We reaffirm our commitment to the purposes and principles of the Charter of the United Nations, which have proved timeless and universal.

---

[12] UN Doc. S/23500, 31 January 1992.
[13] GA Res. 55/2 (2000).

Indeed, their relevance and capacity to inspire have increased, as nations and peoples have become increasingly interconnected and interdependent.

4. We are determined to establish a just and lasting peace all over the world in accordance with the purposes and principles of the Charter. We rededicate ourselves to support all efforts to uphold the sovereign equality of all States, respect for their territorial integrity and political independence, resolution of disputes by peaceful means and in conformity with the principles of justice and international law, the right to self-determination of peoples which remain under colonial domination and foreign occupation, non-interference in the internal affairs of States, respect for human rights and fundamental freedoms, respect for the equal rights of all without distinction as to race, sex, language or religion and international cooperation in solving international problems of an economic, social, cultural or humanitarian character.

5. We believe that the central challenge we face today is to ensure that globalization becomes a positive force for all the world's people. For while globalization offers great opportunities, at present its benefits are very unevenly shared, while its costs are unevenly distributed. We recognize that developing countries and countries with economies in transition face special difficulties in responding to this central challenge. Thus, only through broad and sustained efforts to create a shared future, based upon our common humanity in all its diversity, can globalization be made fully inclusive and equitable. These efforts must include policies and measures, at the global level, which correspond to the needs of developing countries and economies in transition and are formulated and implemented with their effective participation.

6. We consider certain fundamental values to be essential to international relations in the twenty-first century. These include:

- **Freedom.** Men and women have the right to live their lives and raise their children in dignity, free from hunger and from the fear of violence, oppression or injustice. Democratic and participatory governance based on the will of the people best assures these rights.
- **Equality.** No individual and no nation must be denied the opportunity to benefit from development. The equal rights and opportunities of women and men must be assured.
- **Solidarity.** Global challenges must be managed in a way that distributes the costs and burdens fairly in accordance with basic principles of equity and social justice. Those who suffer or who benefit least deserve help from those who benefit most.
- **Tolerance.** Human beings must respect one other, in all their diversity of belief, culture and language. Differences within and between societies should be neither feared nor repressed, but cherished as a precious asset of humanity. A culture of peace and dialogue among all civilizations should be actively promoted.
- **Respect for nature.** Prudence must be shown in the management of all living species and natural resources, in accordance with the precepts of

sustainable development. Only in this way can the immeasurable riches provided to us by nature be preserved and passed on to our descendants. The current unsustainable patterns of production and consumption must be changed in the interest of our future welfare and that of our descendants.

• **Shared responsibility.** Responsibility for managing worldwide economic and social development, as well as threats to international peace and security, must be shared among the nations of the world and should be exercised multilaterally. As the most universal and most representative organization in the world, the United Nations must play the central role.

7. In order to translate these shared values into actions, we have identified key objectives to which we assign special significance. . . .

11. We will spare no effort to free our fellow men, women and children from the abject and dehumanizing conditions of extreme poverty, to which more than a billion of them are currently subjected. We are committed to making the right to development a reality for everyone and to freeing the entire human race from want.

12. We resolve therefore to create an environment—at the national and global levels alike—which is conducive to development and to the elimination of poverty.

13. Success in meeting these objectives depends, inter alia, on good governance within each country. It also depends on good governance at the international level and on transparency in the financial, monetary and trading systems. We are committed to an open, equitable, rule-based, predictable and non-discriminatory multilateral trading and financial system.

14. We are concerned about the obstacles developing countries face in mobilizing the resources needed to finance their sustained development. . . .

15. We call on the industrialized countries:

• To adopt . . . a policy of duty- and quota-free access for essentially all exports from the least developed countries;

• To implement the enhanced programme of debt relief for the heavily indebted poor countries without further delay and to agree to cancel all official bilateral debts of those countries in return for their making demonstrable commitments to poverty reduction; and

• To grant more generous development assistance, especially to countries that are genuinely making an effort to apply their resources to poverty reduction.

16. We are also determined to deal comprehensively and effectively with the debt problems of low- and middle-income developing countries, through various national and international measures designed to make their debt sustainable in the long term. . . .

19. We resolve further:

• To halve, by the year 2015, the proportion of the world's people whose income is less than one dollar a day and the proportion of people who suffer from hunger and, by the same date, to halve the proportion of people who are unable to reach or to afford safe drinking water.

- To ensure that, by the same date, children everywhere, boys and girls alike, will be able to complete a full course of primary schooling and that girls and boys will have equal access to all levels of education.
- By the same date, to have reduced maternal mortality by three quarters, and under-five child mortality by two thirds, of their current rates.
- To have, by then, halted, and begun to reverse, the spread of HIV/AIDS, the scourge of malaria and other major diseases that afflict humanity.
- To provide special assistance to children orphaned by HIV/AIDS.
- By 2020, to have achieved a significant improvement in the lives of at least 100 million slum dwellers as proposed in the "Cities Without Slums" initiative.

   20. We also resolve:

- To promote gender equality and the empowerment of women as effective ways to combat poverty, hunger and disease and to stimulate development that is truly sustainable.
- To develop and implement strategies that give young people everywhere a real chance to find decent and productive work.
- To encourage the pharmaceutical industry to make essential drugs more widely available and affordable by all who need them in developing countries.
- To develop strong partnerships with the private sector and with civil society organizations in pursuit of development and poverty eradication.
- To ensure that the benefits of new technologies, especially information and communication technologies, in conformity with recommendations contained in the ECOSOC 2000 Ministerial Declaration, are available to all. . . .
- To make every effort to ensure the entry into force of the Kyoto Protocol, preferably by the tenth anniversary of the United Nations Conference on Environment and Development in 2002, and to embark on the required reduction in emissions of greenhouse gases.
- To intensify our collective efforts for the management, conservation and sustainable development of all types of forests.
- To press for the full implementation of the Convention on Biological Diversity and the Convention to Combat Desertification in those Countries Experiencing Serious Drought and/or Desertification, particularly in Africa.
- To stop the unsustainable exploitation of water resources by developing water management strategies at the regional, national and local levels, which promote both equitable access and adequate supplies.
- To intensify cooperation to reduce the number and effects of natural and man-made disasters.

- To ensure free access to information on the human genome sequence. . . .
- To respect fully and uphold the Universal Declaration of Human Rights.
- To strive for the full protection and promotion in all our countries of civil, political, economic, social and cultural rights for all.
- To strengthen the capacity of all our countries to implement the principles and practices of democracy and respect for human rights, including minority rights.
- To combat all forms of violence against women and to implement the Convention on the Elimination of All Forms of Discrimination against Women.
- To take measures to ensure respect for and protection of the human rights of migrants, migrant workers and their families, to eliminate the increasing acts of racism and xenophobia in many societies and to promote greater harmony and tolerance in all societies.
- To work collectively for more inclusive political processes, allowing genuine participation by all citizens in all our countries.
- To ensure the freedom of the media to perform their essential role and the right of the public to have access to information. . . .
- To expand and strengthen the protection of civilians in complex emergencies, in conformity with international humanitarian law.
- To strengthen international cooperation, including burden sharing in, and the coordination of humanitarian assistance to, countries hosting refugees and to help all refugees and displaced persons to return voluntarily to their homes, in safety and dignity and to be smoothly reintegrated into their societies.
- To encourage the ratification and full implementation of the Convention on the Rights of the Child and its optional protocols on the involvement of children in armed conflict and on the sale of children, child prostitution and child pornography. . . .
- To give full support to the political and institutional structures of emerging democracies in Africa.
- To encourage and sustain regional and subregional mechanisms for preventing conflict and promoting political stability, and to ensure a reliable flow of resources for peacekeeping operations on the continent.
- To take special measures to address the challenges of poverty eradication and sustainable development in Africa, including debt cancellation, improved market access, enhanced Official Development Assistance and increased flows of Foreign Direct Investment, as well as transfers of technology.
- To help Africa build up its capacity to tackle the spread of the HIV/AIDS pandemic and other infectious diseases.

Further commitments in other fields were also identified. In sum, it was a vast project but one of critical importance to the majority of humanity. As member states settled down to work on implementing this program of action, two developments shook the United Nations: the first, the terrorist attacks against New York and Washington on 11 September 2001, the second, a damaging deadlock in the UN Security Council over Iraq in March 2003. These events, which Secretary-General Kofi Annan saw as potentially undermining the role of the UN in managing international security, led to a flurry of activity culminating in his report "In Larger Freedom." This was intended to chart a course for the UN Summit of 2005 (initially conceived in 2000 to follow on the Millennium Summit's development objectives).

IN LARGER FREEDOM: TOWARDS DEVELOPMENT, SECURITY, AND HUMAN RIGHTS FOR ALL (REPORT OF THE SECRETARY-GENERAL), 21 MARCH 2005[14]

6. In the Millennium Declaration, world leaders were confident that humanity could, in the years ahead, make measurable progress towards peace, security, disarmament, human rights, democracy and good governance. They called for a global partnership for development to achieve agreed goals by 2015. They vowed to protect the vulnerable and meet the special needs of Africa. And they agreed that the United Nations needed to become more, not less, actively engaged in shaping our common future. . . .

8. Much has happened since the adoption of the Millennium Declaration to compel such an approach. Small networks of non-State actors—terrorists—have, since the horrendous attacks of 11 September 2001, made even the most powerful States feel vulnerable. At the same time, many States have begun to feel that the sheer imbalance of power in the world is a source of instability. Divisions between major powers on key issues have revealed a lack of consensus about goals and methods. Meanwhile, over 40 countries have been scarred by violent conflict. Today, the number of internally displaced people stands at roughly 25 million, nearly one third of whom are beyond the reach of United Nations assistance, in addition to the global refugee population of 11 to 12 million, and some of them have been the victims of war crimes and crimes against humanity.

9. Many countries have been torn apart and hollowed out by violence of a different sort. HIV/AIDS, the plague of the modern world, has killed over 20 million men, women and children and the number of people infected has surged to over 40 million. The promise of the Millennium Development Goals

---

[14] UN Doc. A/59/2005 (2005).

still remains distant for many. More than one billion people still live below the extreme poverty line of one dollar per day, and 20,000 die from poverty each day. Overall global wealth has grown but is less and less evenly distributed within countries, within regions and in the world as a whole. While there has been real progress towards some of the Goals in some countries, too few Governments—from both the developed and developing world—have taken sufficient action to reach the targets by 2015. And while important work has been done on issues as diverse as migration and climate change, the scale of such long-term challenges is far greater than our collective action to date to meet them.

10. Events in recent years have also led to declining public confidence in the United Nations itself, often for opposite reasons. For instance, both sides of the debate on the Iraq war feel let down by the Organization—for failing, as one side saw it, to enforce its own resolutions, or as the other side saw it, for not being able to prevent a premature or unnecessary war. Yet most people who criticize the United Nations do so precisely because they think the Organization is vitally important to our world. Declining confidence in the institution is matched by a growing belief in the importance of effective multilateralism.

11. I do not suggest that there has been no good news in the last five years. On the contrary, there is plenty we can point to which demonstrates that collective action can produce real results, from the impressive unity of the world after 11 September 2001 to the resolution of a number of civil conflicts, and from the appreciable increase of resources for development to the steady progress achieved in building peace and democracy in some war-torn lands. We should never despair. Our problems are not beyond our power to meet them. But we cannot be content with incomplete successes and we cannot make do with incremental responses to the shortcomings that have been revealed. Instead, we must come together to bring about far-reaching change. . . .

16. Not only are development, security and human rights all imperative; they also reinforce each other. This relationship has only been strengthened in our era of rapid technological advances, increasing economic interdependence, globalization and dramatic geopolitical change. While poverty and denial of human rights may not be said to "cause" civil war, terrorism or organized crime, they all greatly increase the risk of instability and violence. Similarly, war and atrocities are far from the only reasons that countries are trapped in poverty, but they undoubtedly set back development. Again, catastrophic terrorism on one side of the globe, for example an attack against a major financial centre in a rich country, could affect the development prospects of millions on the other by causing a major economic downturn and plunging millions into poverty. And countries which are well governed and respect the human rights of their citizens are better placed to avoid the horrors of conflict and to overcome obstacles to development. . . .

19. . . . Sovereign States are the basic and indispensable building blocks of the international system. It is their job to guarantee the rights of their citizens, to protect them from crime, violence and aggression, and to provide the framework of freedom under law in which individuals can prosper and society develop. If States are fragile, the peoples of the world will not enjoy the security, development and justice that are their right. Therefore, one of the great challenges of the new millennium is to ensure that all States are strong enough to meet the many challenges they face.

20. States, however, cannot do the job alone. We need an active civil society and a dynamic private sector. Both occupy an increasingly large and important share of the space formerly reserved for States alone, and it is plain that the goals outlined here will not be achieved without their full engagement.

21. . . . As globalization shrinks distances around the globe and these issues become increasingly interconnected, the comparative advantages of the United Nations become ever more evident. So too, however, do some of its real weaknesses. From overhauling basic management practices and building a more transparent, efficient and effective United Nations system to revamping our major intergovernmental institutions so that they reflect today's world and advance the priorities set forth in the present report, we must reshape the Organization in ways not previously imagined and with a boldness and speed not previously shown. . . .

24. In today's world, no State, however powerful, can protect itself on its own. Likewise, no country, weak or strong, can realize prosperity in a vacuum. We can and must act together. We owe it to each other to do so, and we owe each other an account of how we do so. If we live up to those mutual commitments, we can make the new millennium worthy of its name.

Two other key issues had been identified by the Secretary-General's High-Level Panel on Threats, Challenges and Change. Among other things, its report contemplated the nature of sovereignty in a changing world and endorsed the notion of "sovereignty as responsibility," adopting the concept of a "responsibility to protect." It also addressed the related issue of the need for the Security Council to consider criteria governing its approach to the use of force.[15]

---

[15] The Report of the High-Level Panel is also discussed in chapters 4, 9, 13, and 17.

. . . .

REPORT OF THE HIGH-LEVEL PANEL ON THREATS, CHALLENGES, AND CHANGE: A MORE SECURE WORLD: OUR SHARED RESPONSIBILITY, 1 DECEMBER 2004[16]

29. In signing the Charter of the United Nations, States not only benefit from the privileges of sovereignty but also accept its responsibilities. Whatever perceptions may have prevailed when the Westphalian system first gave rise to the notion of State sovereignty, today it clearly carries with it the obligation of a State to protect the welfare of its own peoples and meet its obligations to the wider international community. But history teaches us all too clearly that it cannot be assumed that every State will always be able, or willing, to meet its responsibilities to protect its own people and avoid harming its neighbours. And in those circumstances, the principles of collective security mean that some portion of those responsibilities should be taken up by the international community, acting in accordance with the Charter of the United Nations and the Universal Declaration of Human Rights, to help build the necessary capacity or supply the necessary protection, as the case may be. . . .

183. The framers of the Charter of the United Nations recognized that force may be necessary for the "prevention and removal of threats to the peace, and for the suppression of acts of aggression or other breaches of the peace." Military force, legally and properly applied, is a vital component of any workable system of collective security, whether defined in the traditional narrow sense or more broadly as we would prefer. But few contemporary policy issues cause more difficulty, or involve higher stakes, than the principles concerning its use and application to individual cases. . . .

185. The Charter of the United Nations, in Article 2.4, expressly prohibits Member States from using or threatening force against each other, allowing only two exceptions: self-defence under Article 51, and military measures authorized by the Security Council under Chapter VII (and by extension for regional organizations under Chapter VIII) in response to "any threat to the peace, breach of the peace or act of aggression."

186. For the first 44 years of the United Nations, Member States often violated these rules and used military force literally hundreds of times, with a paralysed Security Council passing very few Chapter VII resolutions and Article 51 only rarely providing credible cover. Since the end of the cold war, however, the yearning for an international system governed by the rule of law has grown. There is little evident international acceptance of the idea of security being best preserved by a balance of power, or by any single—even benignly motivated—superpower.

---

[16]UN Doc. A/59/565 (2004).

187. But in seeking to apply the express language of the Charter, three particularly difficult questions arise in practice: first, when a State claims the right to strike preventively, in self-defence, in response to a threat which is not imminent; secondly, when a State appears to be posing an external threat, actual or potential, to other States or people outside its borders, but there is disagreement in the Security Council as to what to do about it; and thirdly, where the threat is primarily internal, to a State's own people.

188. The language of [Article 51 of the Charter] is restrictive: "Nothing in the present Charter shall impair the inherent right of individual or collective self-defence if an armed attack occurs against a member of the United Nations, until the Security Council has taken measures to maintain international peace and security." However, a threatened State, according to long established international law, can take military action as long as the threatened attack is imminent, no other means would deflect it and the action is proportionate. The problem arises where the threat in question is not imminent but still claimed to be real: for example the acquisition, with allegedly hostile intent, of nuclear weapons-making capability.

189. Can a State, without going to the Security Council, claim in these circumstances the right to act, in anticipatory self-defence, not just pre-emptively (against an imminent or proximate threat) but preventively (against a non-imminent or non-proximate one)? Those who say "yes" argue that the potential harm from some threats (e.g., terrorists armed with a nuclear weapon) is so great that one simply cannot risk waiting until they become imminent, and that less harm may be done (e.g., avoiding a nuclear exchange or radioactive fallout from a reactor destruction) by acting earlier.

190. The short answer is that if there are good arguments for preventive military action, with good evidence to support them, they should be put to the Security Council, which can authorize such action if it chooses to. If it does not so choose, there will be, by definition, time to pursue other strategies, including persuasion, negotiation, deterrence and containment—and to visit again the military option.

191. For those impatient with such a response, the answer must be that, in a world full of perceived potential threats, the risk to the global order and the norm of non—intervention on which it continues to be based is simply too great for the legality of unilateral preventive action, as distinct from collectively endorsed action, to be accepted. Allowing one to so act is to allow all.

192. We do not favour the rewriting or reinterpretation of Article 51.

193. In the case of a State posing a threat to other States, people outside its borders or to international order more generally, the language of Chapter VII is inherently broad enough, and has been interpreted broadly enough, to allow the Security Council to approve any coercive action at all, including military action, against a State when it deems this "necessary to maintain or restore international peace and security." That is the case whether the threat is occurring now, in the imminent future or more distant future; whether it involves the State's own actions or those of non-State actors it harbours or

supports; or whether it takes the form of an act or omission, an actual or potential act of violence or simply a challenge to the Council's authority.

194. We emphasize that the concerns we expressed about the legality of the preventive use of military force in the case of self-defence under Article 51 are not applicable in the case of collective action authorized under Chapter VII. . . .

195. Questions of legality apart, there will be issues of prudence, or legitimacy, about whether such preventive action should be taken: crucial among them is whether there is credible evidence of the reality of the threat in question (taking into account both capability and specific intent) and whether the military response is the only reasonable one in the circumstances. We address these issues further below.

196. It may be that some States will always feel that they have the obligation to their own citizens, and the capacity, to do whatever they feel they need to do, unburdened by the constraints of collective Security Council process. But however understandable that approach may have been in the cold war years, when the United Nations was manifestly not operating as an effective collective security system, the world has now changed and expectations about legal compliance are very much higher.

197. One of the reasons why States may want to bypass the Security Council is a lack of confidence in the quality and objectivity of its decision-making. The Council's decisions have often been less than consistent, less than persuasive and less than fully responsive to very real State and human security needs. But the solution is not to reduce the Council to impotence and irrelevance: it is to work from within to reform it, including in the ways we pro pose in the present report. . . .

199. The Charter of the United Nations is not as clear as it could be when it comes to saving lives within countries in situations of mass atrocity. It "re-affirm(s) faith in fundamental human rights" but does not do much to protect them, and Article 2.7 prohibits intervention "in matters which are essentially within the jurisdiction of any State." There has been, as a result, a long-standing argument in the international community between those who insist on a "right to intervene" in man-made catastrophes and those who argue that the Security Council, for all its powers under Chapter VII to "maintain or restore international security," is prohibited from authorizing any coercive action against sovereign States for whatever happens within their borders.

200. Under the Convention on the Prevention and Punishment of the Crime of Genocide (Genocide Convention), States have agreed that genocide, whether committed in time of peace or in time of war, is a crime under international law which they undertake to prevent and punish. Since then it has been understood that genocide anywhere is a threat to the security of all and should never be tolerated.

The principle of non-intervention in internal affairs cannot be used to protect genocidal acts or other atrocities, such as large-scale violations of international humanitarian law or large-scale ethnic cleansing, which can properly be considered a threat to international security and as such provoke action by the Security Council.

201. The successive humanitarian disasters in Somalia, Bosnia and Herzegovina, Rwanda, Kosovo and now Darfur, Sudan, have concentrated attention not on the immunities of sovereign Governments but their responsibilities, both to their own people and to the wider international community. There is a growing recognition that the issue is not the "right to intervene" of any State, but the "responsibility to protect" of every State when it comes to people suffering from avoidable catastrophe—mass murder and rape, ethnic cleansing by forcible expulsion and terror, and deliberate starvation and exposure to disease. And there is a growing acceptance that while sovereign Governments have the primary responsibility to protect their own citizens from such catastrophes, when they are unable or unwilling to do so that responsibility should be taken up by the wider international community—with it spanning a continuum involving prevention, response to violence, if necessary, and rebuilding shattered societies. The primary focus should be on assisting the cessation of violence through mediation and other tools and the protection of people through such measures as the dispatch of humanitarian, human rights and police missions. Force, if it needs to be used, should be deployed as a last resort.

202. The Security Council so far has been neither very consistent nor very effective in dealing with these cases, very often acting too late, too hesitantly or not at all. But step by step, the Council and the wider international community have come to accept that, under Chapter VII and in pursuit of the emerging norm of a collective international responsibility to protect, it can always authorize military action to redress catastrophic internal wrongs if it is prepared to declare that the situation is a "threat to international peace and security," not especially difficult when breaches of international law are involved.

203. We endorse the emerging norm that there is a collective international responsibility to protect, exercisable by the Security Council authorizing military intervention as a last resort, in the event of genocide and other large scale killing, ethnic cleansing or serious violations of international humanitarian law which sovereign Governments have proved powerless or unwilling to prevent.

204. The effectiveness of the global collective security system, as with any other legal order, depends ultimately not only on the legality of decisions but also on the common perception of their legitimacy—their being made on solid evidentiary grounds, and for the right reasons, morally as well as legally.

205. If the Security Council is to win the respect it must have as the primary body in the collective security system, it is critical that its most important and influential decisions, those with large-scale life-and-death impact, be better made, better substantiated and better communicated. In particular, in deciding whether or not to authorize the use of force, the Council should adopt and systematically address a set of agreed guidelines, going directly not to

whether force can legally be used but whether, as a matter of good conscience and good sense, it should be.

206. The guidelines we propose will not produce agreed conclusions with push-button predictability. The point of adopting them is not to guarantee that the objectively best outcome will always prevail. It is rather to maximize the possibility of achieving Security Council consensus around when it is appropriate or not to use coercive action, including armed force; to maximize international support for whatever the Security Council decides; and to minimize the possibility of individual Member States bypassing the Security Council.

207. In considering whether to authorize or endorse the use of military force, the Security Council should always address—whatever other considerations it may take into account—at least the following five basic criteria of legitimacy:

(a) Seriousness of threat. Is the threatened harm to State or human security of a kind, and sufficiently clear and serious, to justify prima facie the use of military force? In the case of internal threats, does it involve genocide and other large-scale killing, ethnic cleansing or serious violations of international humanitarian law, actual or imminently apprehended?

(b) Proper purpose. Is it clear that the primary purpose of the proposed military action is to halt or avert the threat in question, whatever other purposes or motives may be involved?

(c) Last resort. Has every non-military option for meeting the threat in question been explored, with reasonable grounds for believing that other measures will not succeed?

(d) Proportional means. Are the scale, duration and intensity of the proposed military action the minimum necessary to meet the threat in question?

(e) Balance of consequences. Is there a reasonable chance of the military action being successful in meeting the threat in question, with the consequences of action not likely to be worse than the consequences of inaction?[17]

QUESTIONS

6. Are targets such as those adopted in the Millennium Declaration intended to be binding obligations? If so, how might they be enforced? If not, do they serve any purpose?
7. In his reform document "In Larger Freedom," Secretary-General Kofi Annan wrote that the United Nations had three essential purposes: development, security, and human rights. Are these priorities equally reflected in the UN Charter? If they are not, how and why have they emerged over time?

---

[17]UN Doc. A/59/565 (2 December 2004).

8. What does the "responsibility to protect" entail? Is it a legal obligation or a legal right? Whose obligation or right is it? What means are legally and politically available to pursue and discharge the "responsibility to protect"? Is there a sequence for the implementation of these means?

Further Reading

Goodrich, Leland M. "From League of Nations to United Nations." *International Organization*, vol. 1 (1947), p. 3.

Goodrich, Leland M., Edvard Hambro, and Anne Patricia Simons. *Charter of the United Nations: Commentary and Documents*. 3rd edn. New York: Columbia University Press, 1969.

Meisler, Stanley. *United Nations: The First Fifty Years*. New York: Atlantic Monthly Press, 1995.

Simma, Bruno, ed. *The Charter of the United Nations: A Commentary*, 2nd edn. Oxford: Oxford University Press, 2002.

Schlesinger, Stephen. *Act of Creation: The Founding of the United Nations*. Boulder, CO: Westview, 2003.

chapter two

. . . .

Hard Cases

While the preamble of the UN Charter expressed the collective desire "to save succeeding generations from the scourge of war," the United Nations is today seen increasingly as a body that may authorize the collective use of force. That the use of force should be debated as hotly as it has been during the 1990s and 2000s is historically remarkable: during the Cold War, serious discussion about authorization of force was deflected by the unwillingness of the two contending superpowers to subject themselves to the Council's writ, if necessary threatening or using the veto to maintain their freedom of maneuver. For example, the Vietnam War was mostly avoided by the Council, which adopted only one substantive resolution on the topic—in 1964, deploring Vietnamese military incursions into Cambodia.[1]

It was the Council's unity in 1987 in forging a strategy to end the Iran-Iraq war that signalled the beginning of the end of the Cold War at the United Nations.[2] The Council's ability to unite around a US-led strategy to reverse Iraq's aggression against Kuwait in 1990 led to a renewed belief in collective action in the security sphere. This was initiated by Security Council resolution 660 (1990) on the very day of Iraq's invasion of Kuwait, and ran through the adoption of resolution 688 (1991) (on humanitarian relief) some eight months later. The series of Council resolutions adopted in this period—eighteen of the twenty-nine resolutions related to Iraq—demonstrate a creative and energetic attempt to use the United Nations to assemble international support in confronting Saddam Hussein. This effort was largely successful, with no less than 26 countries supplying troops for Operation Desert Storm, importantly including regional powers such as Egypt, Saudi Arabia, and the United Arab Emirates.

With the success of the US diplomatic and security strategy for Iraq pursued through the Security Council in 1990–1991, following on the Council's

---

[1] SC Res. 189 (1964).
[2] SC Res. 598 (1987).

central role in the independence process of Namibia in 1989, the body's salience in multilateral diplomacy grew markedly. When security challenges arose, the United Nations frequently became the "first stop" in efforts to address them. The Council during the years 1991–1993 addressed conflict in Central America, Haiti, Cambodia, the Balkans, and across Africa (notably Angola, Mozambique, Somalia, Rwanda, Liberia, and the Western Sahara), with varying degrees of success. However, with the exception of Bosnia and Herzegovina, which provoked disagreements between Washington on the one hand and Paris and London on the other, Council unity on strategy in addressing these conflicts was striking. It soon came to be taken for granted.

This was a mistake. Over the course of the 1990s the consensus on Iraq policy frayed, leading ultimately to a second conflict in 2003 without Security Council authorization and without a large coalition of the willing. These two Iraq wars, of 1991 and 2003, bookend a period of unprecedented international cooperation in the management of war and peace. A key question is whether that period of cooperation was the norm, or the exception.

This chapter examines the resolutions surrounding the use of force in Iraq as well as a second situation in which force was used in the name of the international community but without authorization from the Security Council, in NATO's 1999 Kosovo intervention. In different ways, both situations challenged the claim of the United Nations to fulfill its primary purpose of saving succeeding generations from the scourge of war.

Most of the documents in this chapter are Security Council resolutions. When reading such resolutions, note the distinction between *preambular* and *operative* text. Operative paragraphs are typically numbered, though this was not always the case. Preambular paragraphs provide relevant facts and context, often recalling these from earlier resolutions and other documents, in effect setting up the case for action. Operative paragraphs outline the Council's response.

2.1 Iraq, 1990–1991

The resolution below—an unusually short one—was adopted in reaction to the invasion of Kuwait by Iraq in August 1990.

SECURITY COUNCIL RESOLUTION 660 (1990)

The Security Council,
   Alarmed by the invasion of Kuwait on 2 August 1990 by the military forces of Iraq,
   Determining that there exists a breach of international peace and security as regards the Iraqi invasion of Kuwait,

Acting under Articles 39 and 40 of the Charter of the United Nations,

1. *Condemns* the Iraqi invasion of Kuwait;

2. *Demands* that Iraq withdraw immediately and unconditionally all its forces to the positions in which they were located on 1 August 1990;

3. *Calls upon* Iraq and Kuwait to begin immediately intensive negotiations for the resolution of their differences and supports all efforts in this regard, and especially those of the League of Arab States;

4. *Decides* to meet again as necessary to consider further steps to ensure compliance with the present resolution.

Four days later the Security Council imposed a sweeping trade embargo on Iraq. This hastily adopted resolution, among other things, created the Committee that later came to oversee the Oil-for-Food Programme, discussed in chapter 16.

SECURITY COUNCIL RESOLUTION 661 (1990)

The Security Council,

Reaffirming its resolution 660 (1990) of 2 August 1990,

Deeply concerned that that resolution has not been implemented and that the invasion by Iraq of Kuwait continues with further loss of human life and material destruction,

Determined to bring the invasion and occupation of Kuwait by Iraq to an end and to restore the sovereignty, independence and territorial integrity of Kuwait,

Noting that the legitimate Government of Kuwait has expressed its readiness to comply with resolution 660 (1990),

Mindful of its responsibilities under the Charter of the United Nations for the maintenance of international peace and security,

Affirming the inherent right of individual or collective self-defence, in response to the armed attack by Iraq against Kuwait, in accordance with Article 51 of the Charter,

Acting under Chapter VII of the Charter of the United Nations,

1. *Determines* that Iraq so far has failed to comply with paragraph 2 of resolution 660 (1990) and has usurped the authority of the legitimate Government of Kuwait;

2. *Decides*, as a consequence, to take the following measures to secure compliance of Iraq with paragraph 2 of resolution 660 (1990) and to restore the authority of the legitimate Government of Kuwait;

3. *Decides* that all States shall prevent:

(a) The import into their territories of all commodities and products originating in Iraq or Kuwait exported there from after the date of the present resolution;

(b) Any activities by their nationals or in their territories which would promote or are calculated to promote the export or trans-shipment of any commodities or products from Iraq or Kuwait; and any dealings by their nationals or their flag vessels or in their territories in any commodities or products originating in Iraq or Kuwait and exported therefrom after the date of the present resolution, including in particular any transfer of funds to Iraq or Kuwait for the purposes of such activities or dealings;

(c) The sale or supply by their nationals or from their territories or using their flag vessels of any commodities or products, including weapons or any other military equipment, whether or not originating in their territories but not including supplies intended strictly for medical purposes, and, in humanitarian circumstances, foodstuffs, to any person or body in Iraq or Kuwait or to any person or body for the purposes of any business carried on in or operated from Iraq or Kuwait, and any activities by their nationals or in their territories which promote or are calculated to promote such sale or supply of such commodities or products;

4. *Decides* that all States shall not make available to the Government of Iraq or to any commercial, industrial or public utility undertaking in Iraq or Kuwait, any funds or any other financial or economic resources and shall prevent their nationals and any persons within their territories from removing from their territories or otherwise making available to that Government or to any such undertaking any such funds or resources and from remitting any other funds to persons or bodies within Iraq or Kuwait, except payments exclusively for strictly medical or humanitarian purposes and, in humanitarian circumstances, foodstuffs;

5. *Calls upon* all States, including States non-members of the United Nations, to act strictly in accordance with the provisions of the present resolution notwithstanding any contract entered into or licence granted before the date of the present resolution;

6. *Decides* to establish, in accordance with rule 28 of the provisional rules of procedure of the Security Council, a Committee of the Security Council consisting of all the members of the Council, to undertake the following tasks and to report on its work to the Council with its observations and recommendations:

(a) To examine the reports on the progress of the implementation of the present resolution which will be submitted by the Secretary-General;

(b) To seek from all States further information regarding the action taken by them concerning the effective implementation of the provisions laid down in the present resolution;

7. *Calls upon* all States to co-operate fully with the Committee in the fulfilment of its task, including supplying such information as may be sought by the Committee in pursuance of the present resolution;

8. *Requests* the Secretary-General to provide all necessary assistance to the Committee and to make the necessary arrangements in the Secretariat for the purpose;

9. *Decides* that, notwithstanding paragraphs 4 through 8 above, nothing in the present resolution shall prohibit assistance to the legitimate Government of Kuwait, and calls upon all States:

(a) To take appropriate measures to protect assets of the legitimate Government of Kuwait and its agencies;

(b) Not to recognize any regime set up by the occupying Power;

10. *Requests* the Secretary-General to report to the Council on the progress of the implementation of the present resolution, the first report to be submitted within thirty days;

11. *Decides* to keep this item on its agenda and to continue its efforts to put an early end to the invasion by Iraq.

On 29 November 1990, after several further resolutions, the Council adopted a carefully crafted resolution authorizing the use of force against Iraq (coded in UN terms as "all necessary means" to this end) by "member states cooperating with the government of Kuwait" (now exiled). Considerable diplomatic wrangling had characterized drafting of this resolution. Several Council members were unalterably opposed to the use of force against Iraq, others including the Soviet Union, China and France were eager that further diplomacy, leveraged by the serious consequences promised in this resolution, be given a chance to succeed, hence the time-lagged authorization coming into effect only on 15 January 1991. Despite intensive negotiations over the text, it remained unusually concise and clear:

SECURITY COUNCIL RESOLUTION 678 (1990)

The Security Council,

Recalling, and reaffirming its resolutions . . .

Noting that, despite all efforts by the United Nations, Iraq refuses to comply with its obligation to implement resolution 660 (1990) and the above-mentioned subsequent relevant resolutions, in flagrant contempt of the Security Council,

Mindful of its duties and responsibilities under the Charter of the United Nations for the maintenance and preservation of international peace and security,

Determined to secure full compliance with its decisions,

Acting under Chapter VII of the Charter,

1. *Demands* that Iraq comply fully with resolution 660 (1990) and all subsequent relevant resolutions, and decides, while maintaining all its decisions, to allow Iraq one final opportunity, as a pause of goodwill, to do so;

2. *Authorizes* Member States co-operating with the Government of Kuwait, unless Iraq on or before 15 January 1991 fully implements, as set forth in paragraph 1 above, the foregoing resolutions, to use all necessary means to uphold and implement resolution 660 (1990) and all subsequent relevant resolutions and to restore international peace and security in the area;

3. *Requests* all States to provide appropriate support for the actions undertaken in pursuance of paragraph 2 of the present resolution;

4. *Requests* the States concerned to keep the Security Council regularly informed on the progress of actions undertaken pursuant to paragraphs 2 and 3 of the present resolution;

5. *Decides* to remain seized of the matter.

Operative paragraph 2, by referring to member states "cooperating with the Government of Kuwait" was understood to exclude Israel from the authorization to use force.

At the conclusion of the brief but fierce fighting in early 1991, the Security Council adopted an elaborate resolution intended to end hostilities, resolve some issues, and contain Iraq's capacity to threaten the region. What would happen in the event that Iraq failed to comply with these provisions, and how such a determination would be made, was left unstated.

SECURITY COUNCIL RESOLUTION 687 (1991)

The Security Council,

Recalling its resolutions . . .

Welcoming the restoration to Kuwait of its sovereignty, independence and territorial integrity and the return of its legitimate Government,

Affirming the commitment of all Member States to the sovereignty, territorial integrity and political independence of Kuwait and Iraq, and noting the intention expressed by the Member States cooperating with Kuwait under paragraph 2 of resolution 678 (1990) to bring their military presence in Iraq to an end as soon as possible consistent with paragraph 8 of resolution 686 (1991),

Reaffirming the need to be assured of Iraq's peaceful intentions in the light of its unlawful invasion and occupation of Kuwait, . . .

Noting that Iraq and Kuwait, as independent sovereign States, signed at Baghdad on 4 October 1963 "Agreed Minutes Between the State of Kuwait and the Republic of Iraq Regarding the Restoration of Friendly Relations, Recognition and Related Matters," thereby recognizing formally the boundary between Iraq and Kuwait and the allocation of islands, which were registered with the United Nations in accordance with Article 102 of the Charter of the United Nations and in which Iraq recognized the independence and complete sovereignty of the State of Kuwait within its borders as specified and accepted in the letter of the Prime Minister of Iraq dated 21 July 1932, and as accepted by the Ruler of Kuwait in his letter dated 10 August 1932,

Conscious of the need for demarcation of the said boundary,

Conscious also of the statements by Iraq threatening to use weapons in violation of its obligations under the Geneva Protocol for the Prohibition of the Use in War of Asphyxiating, Poisonous or Other Gases, and of Bacteriological Methods of Warfare, signed at Geneva on 17 June 1925, and of its prior use of chemical weapons and affirming that grave consequences would follow any further use by Iraq of such weapons, . . .

Recalling also that Iraq has signed the Convention on the Prohibition of the Development, Production and Stockpiling of Bacteriological (Biological) and Toxin Weapons and on Their Destruction, of 10 April 1972,

Noting the importance of Iraq ratifying this Convention, . . .

Aware of the use by Iraq of ballistic missiles in unprovoked attacks and therefore of the need to take specific measures in regard to such missiles located in Iraq,

Concerned by the reports in the hands of Member States that Iraq has attempted to acquire materials for a nuclear-weapons programme contrary to its obligations under the Treaty on the Non-Proliferation of Nuclear Weapons of 1 July 1968,

Recalling the objective of the establishment of a nuclear-weapons-free zone in the region of the Middle East,

Conscious of the threat that all weapons of mass destruction pose to peace and security in the area and of the need to work towards the establishment in the Middle East of a zone free of such weapons, . . .

Bearing in mind its objective of restoring international peace and security in the area as set out in recent resolutions of the Security Council,

Conscious of the need to take the following measures acting under Chapter VII of the Charter,

1. *Affirms* all thirteen resolutions noted above, except as expressly changed below to achieve the goals of this resolution, including a formal cease-fire;

2. *Demands* that Iraq and Kuwait respect the inviolability of the international boundary and the allocation of islands set out in the "Agreed Minutes Between the State of Kuwait and the Republic of Iraq Regarding the Restoration of Friendly Relations, Recognition and Related Matters," signed by them in the exercise of their sovereignty at Baghdad on 4 October 1963 and registered with the United Nations . . .;

3. *Calls upon* the Secretary-General to lend his assistance to make arrangements with Iraq and Kuwait to demarcate the boundary between Iraq and Kuwait, drawing on appropriate material, including the map transmitted by Security Council document S/22412 and to report back to the Security Council within one month;

4. *Decides* to guarantee the inviolability of the above-mentioned international boundary and to take as appropriate all necessary measures to that end in accordance with the Charter of the United Nations;

5. *Requests* the Secretary-General, after consulting with Iraq and Kuwait, to submit within three days to the Security Council for its approval a plan for the immediate deployment of a United Nations observer unit to monitor the Khor Abdullah and a demilitarized zone, which is hereby established, extending ten kilometres into Iraq and five kilometres into Kuwait from the boundary referred to in the "Agreed Minutes Between the State of Kuwait and the Republic of Iraq Regarding the Restoration of Friendly Relations, Recognition and Related Matters" of 4 October 1963; to deter violations of the boundary through its presence in and surveillance of the demilitarized zone; to observe any hostile or potentially hostile action mounted from the territory of one State to the other; and for the Secretary-General to report regularly to the Security Council on the operations of the unit, and immediately if there are serious violations of the zone or potential threats to peace;

6. *Notes* that as soon as the Secretary-General notifies the Security Council of the completion of the deployment of the United Nations observer unit, the conditions will be established for the Member States cooperating with Kuwait in accordance with resolution 678 (1990) to bring their military presence in Iraq to an end consistent with resolution 686 (1991);

7. *Invites* Iraq to reaffirm unconditionally its obligations under the Geneva Protocol for the Prohibition of the Use in War of Asphyxiating, Poisonous or Other Gases, and of Bacteriological Methods of Warfare, signed at Geneva on 17 June 1925, and to ratify the Convention on the Prohibition of the Development, Production and Stockpiling of Bacteriological (Biological) and Toxin Weapons and on Their Destruction, of 10 April 1972;

8. *Decides* that Iraq shall unconditionally accept the destruction, removal, or rendering harmless, under international supervision, of:

(a) All chemical and biological weapons and all stocks of agents and all related subsystems and components and all research, development, support and manufacturing facilities;

(b) All ballistic missiles with a range greater than 150 kilometres and related major parts, and repair and production facilities;

9. *Decides*, for the implementation of paragraph 8 above, the following:

(a) Iraq shall submit to the Secretary-General, within fifteen days of the adoption of the present resolution, a declaration of the locations, amounts and types of all items specified in paragraph 8 and agree to urgent, on-site inspection as specified below;

(b) The Secretary-General, in consultation with the appropriate Governments and, where appropriate, with the Director-General of the World

Health Organization, within forty-five days of the passage of the present resolution, shall develop, and submit to the Council for approval, a plan calling for the completion of the following acts within forty-five days of such approval:

(i) The forming of a Special Commission, which shall carry out immediate on-site inspection of Iraq's biological, chemical and missile capabilities, based on Iraq's declarations and the designation of any additional locations by the Special Commission itself;

(ii) The yielding by Iraq of possession to the Special Commission for destruction, removal or rendering harmless, taking into account the requirements of public safety, of all items specified under paragraph 8 (a) above, including items at the additional locations designated by the Special Commission under paragraph 9 (b) (i) above and the destruction by Iraq, under the supervision of the Special Commission of all its missile capabilities, including launchers, as specified under paragraph 8 (b) above;

(iii) The provision by the Special Commission of the assistance and cooperation to the Director-General of the International Atomic Energy Agency required in paragraphs 12 and 13 below;

10. *Decides* that Iraq shall unconditionally undertake not to use, develop, construct or acquire any of the items specified in paragraphs 8 and 9 above and requests the Secretary-General, in consultation with the Special Commission, to develop a plan for the future ongoing monitoring and verification of Iraq's compliance with this paragraph, to be submitted to the Security Council for approval within one hundred and twenty days of the passage of this resolution;

11. *Invites* Iraq to reaffirm unconditionally its obligations under the Treaty on the Non-Proliferation of Nuclear Weapons of 1 July 1968;

12. *Decides* that Iraq shall unconditionally agree not to acquire or develop nuclear weapons or nuclear-weapons-usable material or any subsystems or components or any research, development, support or manufacturing facilities related to the above; to submit to the Secretary-General and the Director-General of the International Atomic Energy Agency within fifteen days of the adoption of the present resolution a declaration of the locations, amounts, and types of all items specified above; to place all of its nuclear-weapons-usable materials under the exclusive control, for custody and removal, of the International Atomic Energy Agency, with the assistance and cooperation of the Special Commission as provided for in the plan of the Secretary-General discussed in paragraph 9 (b) above; to accept, in accordance with the arrangements provided for in paragraph 13 below, urgent on-site inspection and the destruction, removal or rendering harmless as appropriate of all items specified above; and to accept the plan discussed in paragraph 13 below for the future ongoing monitoring and verification of its compliance with these undertakings;

13. *Requests* the Director-General of the International Atomic Energy Agency, through the Secretary-General, with the assistance and cooperation of the Special Commission as provided for in the plan of the Secretary-General in paragraph 9 (b) above, to carry out immediate on-site inspection of Iraq's nuclear capabilities based on Iraq's declarations and the designation of any additional locations by the Special Commission; to develop a plan for submission to the Security Council within forty-five days calling for the destruction, removal, or rendering harmless as appropriate of all items listed in paragraph 12 above; to carry out the plan within forty-five days following approval by the Security Council; and to develop a plan, taking into account the rights and obligations of Iraq under the Treaty on the Non-Proliferation of Nuclear Weapons of 1 July 1968, for the future ongoing monitoring and verification of Iraq's compliance with paragraph 12 above, including an inventory of all nuclear material in Iraq subject to the Agency's verification and inspections to confirm that Agency safeguards cover all relevant nuclear activities in Iraq, to be submitted to the Security Council for approval within one hundred and twenty days of the passage of the present resolution;

14. *Takes note* that the actions to be taken by Iraq in paragraphs 8, 9, 10, 11, 12 and 13 of the present resolution represent steps towards the goal of establishing in the Middle East a zone free from weapons of mass destruction and all missiles for their delivery and the objective of a global ban on chemical weapons;

15. *Requests* the Secretary-General to report to the Security Council on the steps taken to facilitate the return of all Kuwaiti property seized by Iraq, including a list of any property that Kuwait claims has not been returned or which has not been returned intact;

16. *Reaffirms* that Iraq, without prejudice to the debts and obligations of Iraq arising prior to 2 August 1990, which will be addressed through the normal mechanisms, is liable under international law for any direct loss, damage, including environmental damage and the depletion of natural resources, or injury to foreign Governments, nationals and corporations, as a result of Iraq's unlawful invasion and occupation of Kuwait;

17. *Decides* that all Iraqi statements made since 2 August 1990 repudiating its foreign debt are null and void, and demands that Iraq adhere scrupulously to all of its obligations concerning servicing and repayment of its foreign debt;

18. *Decides also* to create a fund to pay compensation for claims that fall within paragraph 16 above and to establish a Commission that will administer the fund;

19. *Directs* the Secretary-General to develop and present to the Security Council for decision, no later than thirty days following the adoption of the present resolution, recommendations for the fund to meet the requirement for the payment of claims established in accordance with paragraph 18 above and for a programme to implement the decisions in paragraphs 16, 17 and 18 above, . . .

20. *Decides*, effective immediately, that the prohibitions against the sale or supply to Iraq of commodities or products, other than medicine and health supplies, and prohibitions against financial transactions related thereto contained in resolution 661 (1990) shall not apply to foodstuffs notified to the Security Council Committee established by resolution 661 (1990) concerning the situation between Iraq and Kuwait or, with the approval of that Committee, under the simplified and accelerated "no-objection" procedure, to materials and supplies for essential civilian needs as identified in the report of the Secretary-General dated 20 March 1991, and in any further findings of humanitarian need by the Committee;

21. *Decides* that the Security Council shall review the provisions of paragraph 20 above every sixty days in the light of the policies and practices of the Government of Iraq, including the implementation of all relevant resolutions of the Security Council, for the purpose of determining whether to reduce or lift the prohibitions referred to therein;

22. *Decides* that upon the approval by the Security Council of the programme called for in paragraph 19 above and upon Council agreement that Iraq has completed all actions contemplated in paragraphs 8, 9, 10, 11, 12 and 13 above, the prohibitions against the import of commodities and products originating in Iraq and the prohibitions against financial transactions related thereto contained in resolution 661 (1990) shall have no further force or effect;

23. *Decides* that, pending action by the Security Council under paragraph 22 above, the Security Council Committee established by resolution 661 (1990) shall be empowered to approve, when required to assure adequate financial resources on the part of Iraq to carry out the activities under paragraph 20 above, exceptions to the prohibition against the import of commodities and products originating in Iraq;

24. *Decides* that, in accordance with resolution 661 (1990) and subsequent related resolutions and until a further decision is taken by the Security Council, all States shall continue to prevent the sale or supply, or the promotion or facilitation of such sale or supply, to Iraq by their nationals, or from their territories or using their flag vessels or aircraft, of:

(a) Arms and related materiel of all types, specifically including the sale or transfer through other means of all forms of conventional military equipment, including for paramilitary forces, and spare parts and components and their means of production, for such equipment;

(b) Items specified and defined in paragraphs 8 and 12 above not otherwise covered above;

(c) Technology under licensing or other transfer arrangements used in the production, utilization or stockpiling of items specified in subparagraphs (a) and (b) above;

(d) Personnel or materials for training or technical support services relating to the design, development, manufacture, use, maintenance or support of items specified in subparagraphs (a) and (b) above;

25. *Calls upon* all States and international organizations to act strictly in accordance with paragraph 24 above, notwithstanding the existence of any contracts, agreements, licences or any other arrangements;

26. *Requests* the Secretary-General, in consultation with appropriate Governments, to develop within sixty days, for the approval of the Security Council, guidelines to facilitate full international implementation of paragraphs 24 and 25 above and paragraph 27 below, and to make them available to all States and to establish a procedure for updating these guidelines periodically;

27. *Calls upon* all States to maintain such national controls and procedures and to take such other actions consistent with the guidelines to be established by the Security Council under paragraph 26 above as may be necessary to ensure compliance with the terms of paragraph 24 above, and calls upon international organizations to take all appropriate steps to assist in ensuring such full compliance;

28. *Agrees* to review its decisions in paragraphs 22, 23, 24 and 25 above, except for the items specified and defined in paragraphs 8 and 12 above, on a regular basis and in any case one hundred and twenty days following passage of the present resolution, taking into account Iraq's compliance with the resolution and general progress towards the control of armaments in the region;

29. *Decides* that all States, including Iraq, shall take the necessary measures to ensure that no claim shall lie at the instance of the Government of Iraq, or of any person or body in Iraq, or of any person claiming through or for the benefit of any such person or body, in connection with any contract or other transaction where its performance was affected by reason of the measures taken by the Security Council in resolution 661 (1990) and related resolutions;

30. *Decides* that, in furtherance of its commitment to facilitate the repatriation of all Kuwaiti and third country nationals, Iraq shall extend all necessary cooperation to the International Committee of the Red Cross, . . .

32. *Requires* Iraq to inform the Security Council that it will not commit or support any act of international terrorism or allow any organization directed towards commission of such acts to operate within its territory and to condemn unequivocally and renounce all acts, methods and practices of terrorism;

33. *Declares* that, upon official notification by Iraq to the Secretary-General and to the Security Council of its acceptance of the provisions above, a formal cease-fire is effective between Iraq and Kuwait and the Member States cooperating with Kuwait in accordance with resolution 678 (1990);

34. *Decides* to remain seized of the matter and to take such further steps as may be required for the implementation of the present resolution and to secure peace and security in the area.

QUESTIONS ....

1. What is the threshold for Council authorization of the use of force? When may force be used without Council authorization?
2. Reading resolution 661 (1990), what is the significance of the Council "affirming" the inherent right of self-defense?
3. What is the significance of the Council acting, in resolution 678 (1990), under Chapter VII of the Charter? How does this compare with resolution 660 (1990)? When military measures ensued, were they taken under Article 51 of the Charter, in collective self-defense, or under Articles 39 and 42?
4. What is the significance of the authorization to use force being limited to member states "co-operating with the Government of Kuwait"? (Is there a state in the region that might have been intentionally excluded from the authorization?)
5. Were member states co-operating with the Government of Kuwait obliged to wait until 15 January 1991 before resorting to force against Iraq?
6. Reading resolution 687 (1991), what consequences would follow a breach of Iraq's obligations?
7. Where in the Charter does the Security Council derive its authority to require a state not to develop certain kinds of weapons and to adhere to designated treaties?

2.2 Kosovo, 1999

The Security Council authorized a series of military operations in the 1990s, though resolutions authorizing the use of "all necessary means" or "all means necessary" typically followed the offer of a member state to lead such an action. Kosovo provided the first high-profile example of states making such an offer but being unable to secure a Council resolution to authorize the action.

Kosovo was a predominantly Albanian-Muslim province of Serbia which had long enjoyed a high level of autonomy within the Yugoslav Federation. After the disintegration of this state, the government in Belgrade suspended Kosovo's autonomy in an effort to forestall moves toward secession. Instead, the suspension led to more violence on both sides. This was seen as a potential flashpoint to reignite the Balkan wars of the early 1990s along with their disastrous humanitarian consequences. As tensions escalated in 1998, NATO members sought to avoid the hesitation that, some believed, Slobodan Milosevic's Serbia had brutally exploited in earlier conflicts. Others sought creative means to avoid war.

SECURITY COUNCIL RESOLUTION 1203 (1998)

The Security Council, . . .

Welcoming the agreement signed in Belgrade on 16 October 1998 by the Minister of Foreign Affairs of the Federal Republic of Yugoslavia and the Chairman-in-Office of the Organization for Security and Cooperation in Europe (OSCE) providing for the OSCE to establish a verification mission in Kosovo (S/1998/978) . . .

Welcoming also the agreement signed in Belgrade on 15 October 1998 by the Chief of General Staff of the Federal Republic of Yugoslavia and the Supreme Allied Commander, Europe, of the North Atlantic Treaty Organization (NATO) providing for the establishment of an air verification mission over Kosovo . . .

Reaffirming that, under the Charter of the United Nations, primary responsibility for the maintenance of international peace and security is conferred on the Security Council,

Recalling the objectives of resolution 1160 (1998), in which the Council expressed support for a peaceful resolution of the Kosovo problem which would include an enhanced status for Kosovo, a substantially greater degree of autonomy, and meaningful self-administration,

Condemning all acts of violence by any party, as well as terrorism in pursuit of political goals by any group or individual, and all external support for such activities in Kosovo, including the supply of arms and training for terrorist activities in Kosovo, . . .

Emphasizing the need to ensure the safety and security of members of the Verification Mission in Kosovo and the Air Verification Mission over Kosovo,

Reaffirming the commitment of all Member States to the sovereignty and territorial integrity of the Federal Republic of Yugoslavia,

Affirming that the unresolved situation in Kosovo, Federal Republic of Yugoslavia, constitutes a continuing threat to peace and security in the region,

Acting under Chapter VII of the Charter of the United Nations,

1. *Endorses and supports* the agreements signed in Belgrade on 16 October 1998 between the Federal Republic of Yugoslavia and the OSCE, and on 15 October 1998 between the Federal Republic of Yugoslavia and NATO, concerning the verification of compliance by the Federal Republic of Yugoslavia and all others concerned in Kosovo with the requirements of its resolution 1199 (1998), and demands the full and prompt implementation of these agreements by the Federal Republic of Yugoslavia; . . .

3. *Demands* that the Federal Republic of Yugoslavia comply fully and swiftly with resolutions 1160 (1998) and 1199 (1998) and cooperate fully with the OSCE Verification Mission in Kosovo and the NATO Air Verification Mission over Kosovo according to the terms of the agreements referred to in paragraph 1 above;

4. *Demands also* that the Kosovo Albanian leadership and all other elements of the Kosovo Albanian community comply fully and swiftly with resolutions

1160 (1998) and 1199 (1998) and cooperate fully with the OSCE Verification Mission in Kosovo;

5. *Stresses* the urgent need for the authorities in the Federal Republic of Yugoslavia and the Kosovo Albanian leadership to enter immediately into a meaningful dialogue without preconditions and with international involvement, and to a clear timetable, leading to an end of the crisis and to a negotiated political solution to the issue of Kosovo;

6. *Demands* that the authorities of the Federal Republic of Yugoslavia, the Kosovo Albanian leadership and all others concerned respect the freedom of movement of the OSCE Verification Mission and other international personnel;

7. *Urges* States and international organizations to make available personnel to the OSCE Verification Mission in Kosovo;

8. *Reminds* the Federal Republic of Yugoslavia that it has the primary responsibility for the safety and security of all diplomatic personnel accredited to the Federal Republic of Yugoslavia, including members of the OSCE Verification Mission, as well as the safety and security of all international and non-governmental humanitarian personnel in the Federal Republic of Yugoslavia, . . .

9. *Welcomes* in this context the commitment of the Federal Republic of Yugoslavia to guarantee the safety and security of the Verification Missions as contained in the agreements referred to in paragraph 1 above, notes that, to this end, the OSCE is considering arrangements to be implemented in cooperation with other organizations, and affirms that, in the event of an emergency, action may be needed to ensure their safety and freedom of movement as envisaged in the agreements referred to in paragraph 1 above;

10. *Insists* that the Kosovo Albanian leadership condemn all terrorist actions, demands that such actions cease immediately and emphasizes that all elements in the Kosovo Albanian community should pursue their goals by peaceful means only; . . .

14. *Calls* for prompt and complete investigation, including international supervision and participation, of all atrocities committed against civilians and full cooperation with the International Tribunal for the former Yugoslavia, . . .

17. *Decides* to remain seized of the matter.

The OSCE Mission deployed rapidly in large numbers and verified the spread of human rights violations. In spite of intense diplomacy involving several international organizations, negotiations failed as NATO sought extensive Serbian compromises on autonomy for Kosovo with an international security presence and Russia threatened to veto any Security Council resolution authorizing the use of force. On 24 March 1999, NATO commenced air strikes. Two days later a draft resolution was proposed by Russia, together with Belarus and India (neither sitting on the Council at the time).

DRAFT SECURITY COUNCIL RESOLUTION SPONSORED BY BELARUS, INDIA AND RUSSIA, 26 MARCH 1999[3]

The Security Council,

Recalling its primary responsibility under the United Nations Charter for the maintenance of international peace and security,

Deeply concerned that the North Atlantic Treaty Organization (NATO) used military force against the Federal Republic of Yugoslavia without the authorization by the Council,

Affirming that such unilateral use of force constitutes a flagrant violation of the United Nations Charter, in particular Articles 2 (4), 24 and

Recognizing that the ban by NATO of civil flights in the airspace of a number of countries in the region constitutes a flagrant violation of the principle of complete and exclusive sovereignty of every State over the airspace above its territory in accordance with article 1 of the Chicago Convention on International Civil Aviation,

Recalling all its relevant resolutions and decisions, in particular the Statement of its President of 29 January 1999 (S/PRST/1999/5), in which it, *inter alia*, expressed the intention to be informed by members of the Contact Group about the progress reached in the negotiations on a political settlement of the situation in Kosovo, Federal Republic of Yugoslavia, and awaiting such a report,

Reaffirming its commitment to the sovereignty and territorial integrity of the Federal Republic of Yugoslavia,

Determining that the use of force by NATO against the Federal Republic of Yugoslavia constitutes a threat to international peace and security,

Acting under Chapters VII and VIII of the Charter,

1. *Demands* an immediate cessation of the use of force against the Federal Republic of Yugoslavia and urgent resumption of negotiations;

2. *Decides* to remain actively seized of the matter.

The resolution was defeated by twelve votes to three (Russia, China, Namibia). After seventy-eight days the air campaign concluded with an agreement accepted by the Federal Republic of Yugoslavia (Serbia and Montenegro) and by NATO, which was endorsed by the Council in resolution 1244 (1999). The resolution established an interim administration that put Kosovo effectively under the control of the United Nations, while delegating security responsibilities to NATO. This aspect of the Kosovo situation is considered further in chapter 9.

---

[3] UN Doc. S/1999/328 (1999).

A separate question was how to resolve the tension between the willingness of some states to use force to protect vulnerable populations and the inability of the Security Council to authorize such action. Following a more accepted use of force, authorized by the Council in response to the crisis in East Timor some months later, the Secretary-General took up this topic in his annual address to the General Assembly.

SECRETARY-GENERAL'S ADDRESS TO THE GENERAL ASSEMBLY, 20 SEPTEMBER 1999[4]

On this occasion, I shall like to address the prospects for human security and intervention in the next century. In light of the dramatic events of the past year, I trust that you will understand this decision. . . .

While the genocide in Rwanda will define for our generation the consequences of inaction in the face of mass murder, the more recent conflict in Kosovo has prompted important questions about the consequences of action in the absence of complete unity on the part of the international community.

It has cast in stark relief the dilemma of what has been called humanitarian intervention: on one side, the question of the legitimacy of an action taken by a regional organization without a United Nations mandate; on the other, the universally recognized imperative of effectively halting gross and systematic violations of human rights with grave humanitarian consequences.

The inability of the international community in the case of Kosovo to reconcile these two equally compelling interests—universal legitimacy and effectiveness in defence of human rights—can only be viewed as a tragedy.

It has revealed the core challenge to the Security Council and to the United Nations as a whole in the next century: to forge unity behind the principle that massive and systematic violations of human rights—wherever they may take place—should not be allowed to stand.

The Kosovo conflict and its outcome have prompted a wide debate of profound importance to the resolution of conflicts from the Balkans to Central Africa to East Asia. And to each side in this critical debate, difficult questions can be posed.

---

[4] Kofi A. Annan, Address to the General Assembly (United Nations, UN Press Release SG/SM/7136, New York, 20 September 1999), available at http://www.un.org/news/Press/docs/1999/19990920.sgsm7136.html. This and other speeches on intervention have been collected in Kofi A. Annan, *The Question of Intervention: Statements by the Secretary-General* (New York: UN Department of Public Information, 1999).

To those for whom the greatest threat to the future of international order is the use of force in the absence of a Security Council mandate, one might ask—not in the context of Kosovo—but in the context of Rwanda: If, in those dark days and hours leading up to the genocide, a coalition of States had been prepared to act in defence of the Tutsi population, but did not receive prompt Council authorization, should such a coalition have stood aside and allowed the horror to unfold?

To those for whom the Kosovo action heralded a new era when States and groups of States can take military action outside the established mechanisms for enforcing international law, one might ask: Is there not a danger of such interventions undermining the imperfect, yet resilient, security system created after the Second World War, and of setting dangerous precedents for future interventions without a clear criterion to decide who might invoke these precedents, and in what circumstances? . . .

In response to this turbulent era of crises and interventions, there are those who have suggested that the Charter itself—with its roots in the aftermath of global inter-State war—is ill-suited to guide us in a world of ethnic wars and intra-State violence. I believe they are wrong.

The Charter is a living document, whose high principles still define the aspirations of peoples everywhere for lives of peace, dignity and development. Nothing in the Charter precludes a recognition that there are rights beyond borders.

Indeed, its very letter and spirit are the affirmation of those fundamental human rights. In short, it is not the deficiencies of the Charter which have brought us to this juncture, but our difficulties in applying its principles to a new era; an era when strictly traditional notions of sovereignty can no longer do justice to the aspirations of peoples everywhere to attain their fundamental freedoms.

The sovereign States who drafted the Charter over half a century ago were dedicated to peace, but experienced in war.

They knew the terror of conflict, but knew equally that there are times when the use of force may be legitimate in the pursuit of peace. That is why the Charter's own words declare that "armed force shall not be used, save in the common interest." But what is that common interest? Who shall define it? Who will defend it? Under whose authority? And with what means of intervention? These are the monumental questions facing us as we enter the new century. While I will not propose specific answers or criteria, I shall identify four aspects of intervention which I believe hold important lessons for resolving future conflicts.

First, it is important to define intervention as broadly as possible, to include actions along a wide continuum from the most pacific to the most coercive. . . .

Second, it is clear that sovereignty alone is not the only obstacle to effective action in human rights or humanitarian crises. No less significant are the ways in which the Member States of the United Nations define their national interest in any given crisis.

Of course, the traditional pursuit of national interest is a permanent feature of international relations and of the life and work of the Security Council. But as the world has changed in profound ways since the end of the cold war, I believe our conceptions of national interest have failed to follow suit. . . .

Third, in the event that forceful intervention becomes necessary, we must ensure that the Security Council, the body charged with authorizing force under international law—is able to rise to the challenge. The choice, as I said during the Kosovo conflict, must not be between Council unity and inaction in the face of genocide—as in the case of Rwanda, on the one hand; and Council division, and regional action, as in the case of Kosovo, on the other. In both cases, the Member States of the United Nations should have been able to find common ground in upholding the principles of the Charter, and acting in defence of our common humanity. . . .

The Charter requires the Council to be the defender of the common interest, and unless it is seen to be so—in an era of human rights, interdependence, and globalization—there is a danger that others could seek to take its place. . . .

Finally, after the conflict is over, in East Timor as everywhere, it is vitally important that the commitment to peace be as strong as the commitment to war. . . .

We leave a century of unparalleled suffering and violence. Our greatest, most enduring test remains our ability to gain the respect and support of the world's peoples.

If the collective conscience of humanity—a conscience which abhors cruelty, renounces injustice and seeks peace for all peoples—cannot find in the United Nations its greatest tribune, there is a grave danger that it will look elsewhere for peace and for justice.

If it does not hear in our voices, and see in our actions, reflections of its own aspirations, its needs, and its fears, it may soon lose faith in our ability to make a difference.

Just as we have learned that the world cannot stand aside when gross and systematic violations of human rights are taking place, so we have also learned that intervention must be based on legitimate and universal principles if it is to enjoy the sustained support of the world's peoples.

This developing international norm in favour of intervention to protect civilians from wholesale slaughter will no doubt continue to pose profound challenges to the international community.

Any such evolution in our understanding of State sovereignty and individual sovereignty will, in some quarters, be met with distrust, scepticism, even hostility. But it is an evolution that we should welcome.

Why? Because, despite its limitations and imperfections, it is testimony to a humanity that cares more, not less, for the suffering in its midst, and a humanity that will do more, and not less, to end it.

It is a hopeful sign at the end of the twentieth century.

QUESTIONS ....

8. In the case of Kosovo, how central was the role of the Security Council? What significance, if any, should be attributed to the draft resolution proposed on 26 March 1999 and the Council's response? Was the defeat of the Russian resolution tantamount to *post hoc* authorization of NATO's recourse to force? If you were representing Russia on the Council, would you have advised your government to put this draft resolution to a vote? Why, or why not?

9. A non-governmental commission, created to examine the Kosovo intervention and headed by Richard Goldstone, concluded that NATO's action was "illegal but legitimate."[5] What does this mean?

10. Customary international law develops when state practice is combined with *opinio juris*. What, if anything, does Kosovo stand for?

2.3 Iraq, 2002–2003

While the Council rapidly restored its unity on Kosovo, divergences over Iraq policy only grew with time, particularly after the terrorist attacks on the United States of 11 September 2001, which intensified the views of some in Washington to resolve the Iraq problem once and for all.

By late 2002, the Council was again seized of Iraq's apparent non-compliance with resolution 687 (1991) and its heirs. The United States was prepared to topple Saddam Hussein without Council authorization, but its allies, in particular Britain, pushed for such international legitimation. Following an extraordinarily divisive Council debate, resolution 1441 (2002) was adopted unanimously and hailed as a diplomatic masterpiece by its architects.

SECURITY COUNCIL RESOLUTION 1441 (2002)

The Security Council,
  Recalling all its previous relevant resolutions, . . .
  Recognizing the threat Iraq's non-compliance with Council resolutions and proliferation of weapons of mass destruction and long-range missiles poses to international peace and security,
  Recalling that its resolution 678 (1990) authorized Member States to use all necessary means to uphold and implement its resolution 660 (1990) of 2

---

[5] Independent International Commission on Kosovo, *The Kosovo Report* (Oxford: Oxford University Press, 2000), p. 4.

August 1990 and all relevant resolutions subsequent to resolution 660 (1990) and to restore international peace and security in the area,

Further recalling that its resolution 687 (1991) imposed obligations on Iraq as a necessary step for achievement of its stated objective of restoring international peace and security in the area,

Deploring the fact that Iraq has not provided an accurate, full, final, and complete disclosure, as required by resolution 687 (1991), of all aspects of its programmes to develop weapons of mass destruction and ballistic missiles with a range greater than one hundred and fifty kilometres, and of all holdings of such weapons, their components and production facilities and locations, as well as all other nuclear programmes, including any which it claims are for purposes not related to nuclear-weapons-usable material,

Deploring further that Iraq repeatedly obstructed immediate, unconditional, and unrestricted access to sites designated by the United Nations Special Commission (UNSCOM) and the International Atomic Energy Agency (IAEA), failed to cooperate fully and unconditionally with UNSCOM and IAEA weapons inspectors, as required by resolution 687 (1991), and ultimately ceased all cooperation with UNSCOM and the IAEA in 1998,

Deploring the absence, since December 1998, in Iraq of international monitoring, inspection, and verification, as required by relevant resolutions, of weapons of mass destruction and ballistic missiles, in spite of the Council's repeated demands that Iraq provide immediate, unconditional, and unrestricted access to the United Nations Monitoring, Verification and Inspection Commission (UNMOVIC), established in resolution 1284 (1999) as the successor organization to UNSCOM, and the IAEA, and regretting the consequent prolonging of the crisis in the region and the suffering of the Iraqi people, . . .

Recalling that in its resolution 687 (1991) the Council declared that a ceasefire would be based on acceptance by Iraq of the provisions of that resolution, including the obligations on Iraq contained therein, . . .

Reaffirming the commitment of all Member States to the sovereignty and territorial integrity of Iraq, Kuwait, and the neighbouring States, . . .

Acting under Chapter VII of the Charter of the United Nations,

1. *Decides* that Iraq has been and remains in material breach of its obligations under relevant resolutions, including resolution 687 (1991), in particular through Iraq's failure to cooperate with United Nations inspectors and the IAEA, and to complete the actions required under paragraphs 8 to 13 of resolution 687 (1991);

2. *Decides*, while acknowledging paragraph 1 above, to afford Iraq, by this resolution, a final opportunity to comply with its disarmament obligations under relevant resolutions of the Council; and accordingly decides to set up an enhanced inspection regime with the aim of bringing to full and verified completion the disarmament process established by resolution 687 (1991) and subsequent resolutions of the Council;

3. *Decides* that, in order to begin to comply with its disarmament obligations, in addition to submitting the required biannual declarations, the

Government of Iraq shall provide to UNMOVIC, the IAEA, and the Council, not later than 30 days from the date of this resolution, a currently accurate, full, and complete declaration of all aspects of its programmes to develop chemical, biological, and nuclear weapons, ballistic missiles, and other delivery systems such as unmanned aerial vehicles and dispersal systems designed for use on aircraft, including any holdings and precise locations of such weapons, components, subcomponents, stocks of agents, and related material and equipment, the locations and work of its research, development and production facilities, as well as all other chemical, biological, and nuclear programmes, including any which it claims are for purposes not related to weapon production or material;

4. *Decides* that false statements or omissions in the declarations submitted by Iraq pursuant to this resolution and failure by Iraq at any time to comply with, and cooperate fully in the implementation of, this resolution shall constitute a further material breach of Iraq's obligations and will be reported to the Council for assessment in accordance with paragraphs 11 and 12 below;

5. *Decides* that Iraq shall provide UNMOVIC and the IAEA immediate, unimpeded, unconditional, and unrestricted access to any and all, including underground, areas, facilities, buildings, equipment, records, and means of transport which they wish to inspect, as well as immediate, unimpeded, unrestricted, and private access to all officials and other persons whom UNMOVIC or the IAEA wish to interview in the mode or location of UNMOVIC's or the IAEA's choice pursuant to any aspect of their mandates; further *decides* that UNMOVIC and the IAEA may at their discretion conduct interviews inside or outside of Iraq, may facilitate the travel of those interviewed and family members outside of Iraq, and that, at the sole discretion of UNMOVIC and the IAEA, such interviews may occur without the presence of observers from the Iraqi Government; and instructs UNMOVIC and requests the IAEA to resume inspections no later than 45 days following adoption of this resolution and to update the Council 60 days thereafter; . . .

8. *Decides further* that Iraq shall not take or threaten hostile acts directed against any representative or personnel of the United Nations or the IAEA or of any Member State taking action to uphold any Council resolution;

9. *Requests* the Secretary-General immediately to notify Iraq of this resolution, which is binding on Iraq; demands that Iraq confirm within seven days of that notification its intention to comply fully with this resolution; and demands further that Iraq cooperate immediately, unconditionally, and actively with UNMOVIC and the IAEA;

10. *Requests* all Member States to give full support to UNMOVIC and the IAEA in the discharge of their mandates, including by providing any information related to prohibited programmes or other aspects of their mandates, including on Iraqi attempts since 1998 to acquire prohibited items, and by recommending sites to be inspected, persons to be interviewed, conditions of such interviews, and data to be collected, the results of which shall be reported to the Council by UNMOVIC and the IAEA;

11. *Directs* the Executive Chairman of UNMOVIC and the Director-General of the IAEA to report immediately to the Council any interference by Iraq with inspection activities, as well as any failure by Iraq to comply with its disarmament obligations, including its obligations regarding inspections under this resolution;

12. *Decides* to convene immediately upon receipt of a report in accordance with paragraphs 4 or 11 above, in order to consider the situation and the need for full compliance with all of the relevant Council resolutions in order to secure international peace and security;

13. *Recalls*, in that context, that the Council has repeatedly warned Iraq that it will face serious consequences as a result of its continued violations of its obligations;

14. *Decides* to remain seized of the matter.

Thereafter, the Security Council deadlocked over whether the time was ripe to authorize actual use of force against Saddam Hussein. On 20 March 2003, without having obtained such authorization and claiming that its action was authorized by resolutions 687 (1991) and 1441 (2002), a US-led Coalition initiated military action, soon routing Iraqi forces.

After Saddam Hussein's regime had been overthrown, the Council found itself in a difficult position. The poisonous debate in the Council had meant that any implicit endorsement of the military action was impossible, though there was agreement on the need for Council action in response to the humanitarian consequences of the crisis and a desire to involve the Council in the political process that would follow.

SECURITY COUNCIL RESOLUTION 1483 (2003)

The Security Council,

Recalling all its previous relevant resolutions,

Reaffirming the sovereignty and territorial integrity of Iraq, . . .

Stressing the right of the Iraqi people freely to determine their own political future and control their own natural resources, welcoming the commitment of all parties concerned to support the creation of an environment in which they may do so as soon as possible, and expressing resolve that the day when Iraqis govern themselves must come quickly,

Encouraging efforts by the people of Iraq to form a representative government based on the rule of law that affords equal rights and justice to all Iraqi citizens . . .

Resolved that the United Nations should play a vital role in humanitarian relief, the reconstruction of Iraq, and the restoration and establishment of national and local institutions for representative governance, . . .

Stressing the need for respect for the archaeological, historical, cultural, and religious heritage of Iraq, and for the continued protection of archaeological, historical, cultural, and religious sites, museums, libraries, and monuments,

Noting the letter of 8 May 2003 from the Permanent Representatives of the United States of America and the United Kingdom of Great Britain and Northern Ireland to the President of the Security Council (S/2003/538) and recognizing the specific authorities, responsibilities, and obligations under applicable international law of these states as occupying powers under unified command (the "Authority"),

Noting further that other States that are not occupying powers are working now or in the future may work under the Authority,

Welcoming further the willingness of Member States to contribute to stability and security in Iraq by contributing personnel, equipment, and other resources under the Authority, . . .

Determining that the situation in Iraq, although improved, continues to constitute a threat to international peace and security,

Acting under Chapter VII of the Charter of the United Nations,

1. *Appeals* to Member States and concerned organizations to assist the people of Iraq in their efforts to reform their institutions and rebuild their country, and to contribute to conditions of stability and security in Iraq in accordance with this resolution;

2. *Calls upon* all Member States in a position to do so to respond immediately to the humanitarian appeals of the United Nations and other international organizations for Iraq . . .

3. *Appeals* to Member States to deny safe haven to those members of the previous Iraqi regime who are alleged to be responsible for crimes and atrocities and to support actions to bring them to justice;

4. *Calls upon* the Authority, consistent with the Charter of the United Nations and other relevant international law, to promote the welfare of the Iraqi people through the effective administration of the territory, including in particular working towards the restoration of conditions of security and stability and the creation of conditions in which the Iraqi people can freely determine their own political future;

5. *Calls upon* all concerned to comply fully with their obligations under international law including in particular the Geneva Conventions of 1949 and the Hague Regulations of 1907;

6. *Calls upon* the Authority and relevant organizations and individuals to continue efforts to locate, identify, and repatriate all Kuwaiti and Third-State Nationals . . .

7. *Decides* that all Member States shall take appropriate steps to facilitate the safe return to Iraqi institutions of Iraqi cultural property and other items of archaeological, historical, cultural, rare scientific, and religious importance . . .

8. *Requests* the Secretary-General to appoint a Special Representative for Iraq whose independent responsibilities shall involve reporting regularly to the Council on his activities under this resolution, coordinating activities of the United Nations in post-conflict processes in Iraq, coordinating among United Nations and international agencies engaged in humanitarian assistance and reconstruction activities in Iraq, and, in coordination with the Authority, assisting the people of Iraq through:

(a) coordinating humanitarian and reconstruction assistance by United Nations agencies and between United Nations agencies and non-governmental organizations;

(b) promoting the safe, orderly, and voluntary return of refugees and displaced persons;

(c) working intensively with the Authority, the people of Iraq, and others concerned to advance efforts to restore and establish national and local institutions for representative governance, including by working together to facilitate a process leading to an internationally recognized, representative government of Iraq;

(d) facilitating the reconstruction of key infrastructure, in cooperation with other international organizations;

(e) promoting economic reconstruction and the conditions for sustainable development, including through coordination with national and regional organizations, as appropriate, civil society, donors, and the international financial institutions;

(f) encouraging international efforts to contribute to basic civilian administration functions;

(g) promoting the protection of human rights;

(h) encouraging international efforts to rebuild the capacity of the Iraqi civilian police force; and

(i) encouraging international efforts to promote legal and judicial reform;

9. *Supports* the formation, by the people of Iraq with the help of the Authority and working with the Special Representative, of an Iraqi interim administration as a transitional administration run by Iraqis, until an internationally recognized, representative government is established by the people of Iraq and assumes the responsibilities of the Authority;

10. *Decides* that, with the exception of prohibitions related to the sale or supply to Iraq of arms and related materiel other than those arms and related materiel required by the Authority to serve the purposes of this and other related resolutions, all prohibitions related to trade with Iraq and the provision of financial or economic resources to Iraq established by resolution 661 (1990) and subsequent relevant resolutions, including resolution 778 (1992) of 2 October 1992, shall no longer apply;

11. *Reaffirms* that Iraq must meet its disarmament obligations, . . .

12. *Notes* the establishment of a Development Fund for Iraq to be held by the Central Bank of Iraq and to be audited by independent public accountants . . .

13. *Notes* further that the funds in the Development Fund for Iraq shall be disbursed at the direction of the Authority, in consultation with the Iraqi interim administration, for the purposes set out in paragraph 14 below;

14. *Underlines* that the Development Fund for Iraq shall be used in a transparent manner to meet the humanitarian needs of the Iraqi people, for the economic reconstruction and repair of Iraq's infrastructure, for the continued disarmament of Iraq, and for the costs of Iraqi civilian administration, and for other purposes benefiting the people of Iraq;

15. *Calls upon* the international financial institutions to assist the people of Iraq in the reconstruction and development of their economy and to facilitate assistance by the broader donor community, and welcomes the readiness of creditors, including those of the Paris Club, to seek a solution to Iraq's sovereign debt problems;

16. *Requests* also that the Secretary-General, in coordination with the Authority, continue the exercise of his responsibilities under Security Council resolution 1472 (2003) of 28 March 2003 and 1476 (2003) of 24 April 2003, for a period of six months following the adoption of this resolution, and terminate within this time period, in the most cost effective manner, the ongoing operations of the "Oil-for-Food" Programme (the "Programme"), both at headquarters level and in the field, transferring responsibility for the administration of any remaining activity under the Programme to the Authority . . .

17. *Requests* further that the Secretary-General transfer as soon as possible to the Development Fund for Iraq 1 billion United States dollars from unencumbered funds in the accounts established pursuant to paragraphs 8 (a) and 8 (b) of resolution 986 (1995) . . .

18. *Decides* to terminate effective on the adoption of this resolution the functions related to the observation and monitoring activities undertaken by the Secretary-General under the Programme, including the monitoring of the export of petroleum and petroleum products from Iraq;

19. *Decides* to terminate the Committee established pursuant to paragraph 6 of resolution 661 (1990) at the conclusion of the six month period called for in paragraph 16 above and further *decides* that the Committee shall identify individuals and entities referred to in paragraph 23 below;

20. *Decides* that all export sales of petroleum, petroleum products, and natural gas from Iraq following the date of the adoption of this resolution shall be made consistent with prevailing international market best practices, to be audited by independent public accountants reporting to the International Advisory and Monitoring Board referred to in paragraph 12 above in order to ensure transparency, and *decides further* that, except as provided in paragraph 21 below, all proceeds from such sales shall be deposited into the Development Fund for Iraq until such time as an internationally recognized, representative government of Iraq is properly constituted;

21. *Decides further* that 5 per cent of the proceeds referred to in paragraph 20 above shall be deposited into the Compensation Fund established in accordance with resolution 687 (1991) and subsequent relevant resolutions and that, unless an internationally recognized, representative government

of Iraq and the Governing Council of the United Nations Compensation Commission, in the exercise of its authority over methods of ensuring that payments are made into the Compensation Fund, decide otherwise, this requirement shall be binding on a properly constituted, internationally recognized, representative government of Iraq and any successor thereto;

22. *Noting* the relevance of the establishment of an internationally recognized, representative government of Iraq and the desirability of prompt completion of the restructuring of Iraq's debt as referred to in paragraph 15 above, further *decides* that, until December 31, 2007, unless the Council decides otherwise, petroleum, petroleum products, and natural gas originating in Iraq shall be immune, until title passes to the initial purchaser from legal proceedings against them and not be subject to any form of attachment, garnishment, or execution, and that all States shall take any steps that may be necessary under their respective domestic legal systems to assure this protection, and that proceeds and obligations arising from sales thereof, as well as the Development Fund for Iraq, shall enjoy privileges and immunities equivalent to those enjoyed by the United Nations except that the abovementioned privileges and immunities will not apply with respect to any legal proceeding in which recourse to such proceeds or obligations is necessary to satisfy liability for damages assessed in connection with an ecological accident, including an oil spill, that occurs after the date of adoption of this resolution;

23. *Decides* that all Member States in which there are:

(a) funds or other financial assets or economic resources of the previous Government of Iraq or its state bodies, corporations, or agencies, located outside Iraq as of the date of this resolution, or

(b) funds or other financial assets or economic resources that have been removed from Iraq, or acquired, by Saddam Hussein or other senior officials of the former Iraqi regime and their immediate family members, including entities owned or controlled, directly or indirectly, by them or by persons acting on their behalf or at their direction, shall freeze without delay those funds or other financial assets or economic resources and, unless these funds or other financial assets or economic resources are themselves the subject of a prior judicial, administrative, or arbitral lien or judgement, immediately shall cause their transfer to the Development Fund for Iraq, it being understood that, unless otherwise addressed, claims made by private individuals or nongovernment entities on those transferred funds or other financial assets may be presented to the internationally recognized, representative government of Iraq; and *decides further* that all such funds or other financial assets or economic resources shall enjoy the same privileges, immunities, and protections as provided under paragraph 22;

24. *Requests* the Secretary-General to report to the Council at regular intervals on the work of the Special Representative with respect to the implementation of this resolution and on the work of the International Advisory

and Monitoring Board and encourages the United Kingdom of Great Britain and Northern Ireland and the United States of America to inform the Council at regular intervals of their efforts under this resolution;

25. *Decides* to review the implementation of this resolution within twelve months of adoption and to consider further steps that might be necessary;

26. *Calls upon* Member States and international and regional organizations to contribute to the implementation of this resolution;

27. *Decides* to remain seized of this matter.

QUESTIONS

11. Arguments similar to those concerning Kosovo were made that the 2003 Iraq war might be legitimate, or at least might come to be seen as legitimate. Do you agree? Why, or why not?

12. Did resolution 1441 (2002) authorize the invasion of Iraq? Look back at resolution 687 (1991): what significance should be attributed to the decision of the Council that Iraq was in "material breach" of this earlier resolution?

13. It is generally accepted that the Security Council's failure to unite around a strategy to deal with Iraqi non-compliance in 2003 was damaging to the United Nations. What might have been the consequences of the Council authorizing military action on the basis that Iraq was concealing weapons of mass destruction (later proved to be false)?

14. If the 2003 invasion of Iraq was illegal, did resolution 1483 (2003) provide retrospective legitimacy to that act?

15. What role do the Secretary-General, his agents, and independent actors such as the Organization for Security and Cooperation in Europe (OSCE), the International Atomic Energy Agency (IAEA), UNSCOM and UNMOVIC weapons inspectors, when deployed in the field and reporting their findings, appear to play in shaping Council decisions?

Further Reading

Chesterman, Simon. *Just War or Just Peace? Humanitarian Intervention and International Law.* Oxford: Oxford University Press, 2001.

Franck, Thomas M. *Recourse to Force: State Action Against Threats and Armed Attacks.* Cambridge: Cambridge University Press, 2002.

Gray, Christine. *International Law and the Use of Force*, 2nd edn. Oxford: Oxford University Press, 2004.

Holzgrefe, J.L., and Robert O. Keohane, eds. *Humanitarian Intervention: Ethical, Legal and Political Dilemmas.* Cambridge: Cambridge University Press, 2003.

Malone, David M. ed. *The UN Security Council: From the Cold War to the 21st Century.* Boulder, CO: Lynne Rienner, 2004.

Malone, David M. *The International Struggle for Iraq: Politics in the UN Security Council, 1980–2005.* Oxford: Oxford University Press, 2006.

Schachter, Oscar. "United Nations Law in the Gulf Conflict." *American Journal of International Law*, vol. 85 (1991), p. 452.

Part Two **Capacity**

chapter three
. . . .

Legal Status

As a matter of law, what *is* the United Nations? Is it a thing, like a state, or a place, like the UN Headquarters in Manhattan? Is it a club (such as the Club of Rome), an elaborate conference of diplomats and ministers representing the interests of their countries on the model of the nineteenth-century Concert of Europe, or is it a new sort of supra-national authority?

The Peace of Westphalia, declared in 1648, made clear the position of states as sole actors in international law. In the era following the American and French revolutions in the eighteenth century, states replaced the Universal Church and multinational empires as the principal actors in international relations. For centuries, there was no question of equal recognition being extended to other, lesser entities. Individuals, groups, corporations, etc., were entitled to rights and duties solely under municipal legal systems. International organizations, such as the United Nations or its predecessor, the League of Nations, were inventions of the twentieth century.

Once set up, however, they came to acquire legal status in international law, thereby fitting uncomfortably into the paradigm of the legal system established by the Peace of Westphalia. Already at the time of the League of Nations, it was recognized that such a "universal" organization of states must have an international legal personality, separate from that of its members. This, however, was not necessarily a status equivalent to that which the law accorded to states. For example, it was not clear, at first, whether the international organization enjoyed independent legal capacity with respect to non-members of the Organization. With the establishment of the United Nations, the question of objective legal personality was finally addressed, in an advisory opinion given by the International Court of Justice (ICJ) in the *Reparations* case. Today other supranational organizations and non-governmental organizations vie for similar status. It is now generally understood that, even with limited legal personality, these organizations have the capacity to enter into legally binding relations with non-member states, and that member states by joining the Organization may assume legal obligations not only to other members but also to the Organization, as such.

One of the principal incidents of this newly established legal personality, flowing from the very nature of the Organization's activities, is that the Organization has the capacity, like that of states, to bring independent claims on its own behalf. The *Reparations* case discusses this newly recognized aspect of UN legal personality. Consider why it matters to the capacity of the Organization to perform its tasks whether it is accorded legal personality. Consider also whether, by acquiring this capacity to participate in its own right in the international legal system, the United Nations has become a sort of quasi-state.

The chapter begins with the *Reparations* case and continues the inquiry into UN legal personality by examining the acquisition by international organizations of a traditional power of states: the ability to enter into treaties. The chapter then turns to the question of who interprets the Charter and what happens when there is a clash between two UN organs—such as between the Security Council and the International Court of Justice. The chapter later considers the law-making activities of various bodies: the Security Council, the General Assembly, and the special tribunals established by the Council.

3.1 Legal Personality

The *Reparations* case arose in the form of a request by the General Assembly to the ICJ for an advisory opinion, provision for which is made in Chapter IV of the Statute of the Court and Article 96 of the UN Charter. In this request the Court was asked to determine the legality of a claim brought by the United Nations against Israel for reparations for the killing in Jerusalem of Count Bernadotte, a Swedish national, who had been the chief UN Truce Negotiator in the former Palestinian mandate. It is important to note that, at this time, Israel was not yet a member of the United Nations, only being admitted on 11 May 1949, one month after the Court rendered its opinion.

GENERAL ASSEMBLY RESOLUTION 258(III) (1948): REQUEST FOR ADVISORY OPINION

The General Assembly,

Decides to submit the following legal questions to the International Court of Justice for an advisory opinion:

I. In the event of an agent of the United Nations in the performance of his duties suffering injury in circumstances involving the responsibility of a State, has the United Nations, as an Organization, the capacity to bring an international claim against the responsible *de jure* or *de facto* government with a view to obtaining the reparation due in respect of the damage caused *(a)* to the United Nations, *(b)* to the victim or to persons entitled through him?

II. In the event of an affirmative reply on point I *(b)*, how is action by the United Nations to be reconciled with such rights as may be possessed by the State of which the victim is a national?

In its opinion, the Court affirmed the legal personality of the United Nations; its ability to accord protection to its agents in a manner similar, though not directly analogous, to the right of states to offer diplomatic protection to their nationals; and its ability to bring claims against states.

REPARATION FOR INJURIES SUFFERED IN THE SERVICE OF THE UNITED NATIONS (ADVISORY OPINION) (1949) ICJ REPORTS 174

The questions asked of the Court relate to the "capacity to bring an international claim"; accordingly, we must begin by defining what is meant by that capacity and consider the characteristics of the Organization, so as to determine whether, in general these characteristics do, or do not, include for the Organization a right to present an international claim. ...

[T]he Court must first enquire whether the Charter has given the Organization such a position that it possesses in regard to its Members, rights which it is entitled to ask them to respect. In other words, does the Organization possess international personality? This is no doubt a doctrinal expression, which has sometimes given rise to controversy. But it will be used here to mean that if the Organization is recognized as having that personality, it is an entity capable of availing itself of the obligations incumbent upon its Members.

To answer this question which is not settled by the actual terms of the Charter, we must consider what characteristics it was intended thereby to give to the Organization.

The subjects of law in any legal system are not necessarily identical in their nature or in the extent of their rights, and their nature depends upon the needs of the community. Throughout its history, the development of international law has been influenced by the requirements of international life, and the progressive increase in the collective activities of States has already given rise to instances of action upon the international plane by certain entities which are not States. This development culminated in the establishment in June 1945 of an international organization whose purposes and principles are specified in the Charter of the United Nations. But to achieve these ends the attribution of international personality is indispensable.

The Charter has not been content to make the Organization created by it merely a centre "for harmonizing the actions of nations in the attainment of these common ends" (Article I, para. 4). It has equipped that centre with organs, and has given it special tasks. It has defined the position of the Members in relation to the Organization by requiring them to give it every assistance in any action undertaken by it (Article 2, para. 5), and to accept and carry out the decisions of the Security Council; by authorizing the General Assembly to make recommendations to the Members; by giving the Organization legal capacity and privileges and immunities in the territory of each of its Members; and by providing for the conclusion of agreements between the Organization and its Members. Practice-in particular the conclusion of conventions to which the Organization is a party-has confirmed this character of the Organization, which occupies a position in certain respects in detachment from its Members, and which is under a duty to remind them, if need be, of certain obligations. It must be added that the Organization is a political body, charged with political tasks of an important character, and covering a wide field namely, the maintenance of international peace and security, the development of friendly relations among nations, and the achievement of international co-operation in the solution of problems of an economic, social, cultural or humanitarian character (Article 1); and in dealing with its Members it employs political means. The "Convention on the Privileges and Immunities of the United Nations" of 1946 creates rights and duties between each of the signatories and the Organization (see, in particular, Section 35). It is difficult to see how such a convention could operate except upon the international plane and as between parties possessing international personality.

In the opinion of the Court, the Organization was intended to exercise and enjoy, and is in fact exercising and enjoying, functions and rights which can only be explained on the basis of the possession of a large measure of international personality and the capacity to operate upon an international plane. It is at present the supreme type of international organization, and it could not carry out the intentions of its founders if it was devoid of international personality. It must be acknowledged that its Members, by entrusting certain functions to it, with the attendant duties and responsibilities, have clothed it with the competence required to enable those functions to be effectively discharged.

Accordingly, the Court has come to the conclusion that the Organization is an international person. That is not the same thing as saying that it is a State, which it certainly is not, or that its legal personality and rights and duties are the same as those of a State. Still less is it the same thing as saying that it is "a super-State," whatever that expression may mean. It does not even imply that all its rights and duties must be upon the international plane, any more than all the rights and duties of a State must be upon that plane. What it does mean is that it is a subject of international law and capable of possessing international rights and duties, and that it has capacity to maintain its rights by bringing international claims.

The next question is whether the sum of the international rights of the Organization comprises the right to bring the kind of international claim described in the Request for this Opinion. That is a claim against a State to obtain reparation in respect of the damage caused by the injury of an agent of the Organization in the course of the performance of his duties. Whereas a State possesses the totality of international rights and duties recognized by international law, the rights and duties of an entity such as the Organization must depend upon its purposes and functions as specified or implied in its constituent documents and developed in practice. The functions of the Organization are of such a character that they could not be effectively discharged if they involved the concurrent action, on the international plane, of fifty-eight or more Foreign Offices, and the Court concludes that the Members have endowed the Organization with capacity to bring international claims when necessitated by the discharge of its functions. ...

The damage specified in Question I (*a*) means exclusively damage caused to the interests of the Organization itself, to its administrative machine, its property and assets and to the interests of which it is guardian. It is clear the Organization has the capacity to bring a claim for this damage. As the claim is based on the breach of an international obligation on the part of the Member held responsible by the International Organization, the Member cannot contend that this obligation is governed by municipal law, and the Organization is justified in giving its claim the character of an international claim. ...

The traditional rule that diplomatic protection is exercised by the national State does not involve the giving of a negative answer to Question I (*b*).

In the first place, this rule applies to claims brought by a State. But here we have the different and new case of a claim that would be brought by the Organization.

In the second place, even in inter-State relations, there are important exceptions to the rule, for there are cases in which protection may be exercised by a State on behalf of persons not having its nationality.

In the third place, the rule rests on two bases. The first is that the defendant State has broken an obligation towards the national State in respect of its nationals. The second is that only the party to whom an international obligation is due can bring a claim in respect of its breach. This is precisely what happens when the Organization, in bringing a claim for damage suffered by its agent, does so by invoking the breach of an obligation towards itself. Thus, the rule of the nationality of claims affords no reason against recognizing that the Organization has the right to bring a claim for the damage referred to in Question I (*b*). On the contrary, the principle underlying this rule leads to the recognition of this capacity as belonging to the Organization, when the Organization invokes, as the ground of its claim, a breach of an obligation towards itself.

Nor does the analogy of the traditional rule of diplomatic protection of nationals abroad justify in itself an affirmative reply. It is not possible, by a strained use of the concept of allegiance, to assimilate the legal bond which exists, under Article 100 of the Charter, between the Organization on the one hand, and the Secretary-General and the staff on the other, to the bond of nationality existing between a State and its nationals. ...

The Charter does not expressly confer upon the Organization the capacity to include, in its claim for reparation, damage caused to the victim or to persons entitled through him. The Court must therefore begin by enquiring whether the provisions of the Charter concerning the functions of the Organization, and the part played by its agents in the performance of those functions, imply for the Organization power to afford its agents the limited protection that would consist in the bringing of a claim on their behalf for reparation for damage suffered in such circumstances. Under international law, the Organization must be deemed to have those powers which, though not expressly provided in the Charter, are conferred upon it by necessary implication as being essential to the performance of its duties. ...

Having regard to its purposes and functions already referred to, the Organization may find it necessary, and has in fact found it necessary, to entrust its agents with important missions to be performed in disturbed parts of the world. Many missions, from their very nature, involve the agents in unusual dangers to which ordinary persons are not exposed. For the same reason, the injuries suffered by its agents in these circumstances will sometimes have occurred in such a manner that their national State would not be justified in bringing a claim for reparation on the ground of diplomatic protection, or, at any rate, would not feel disposed to do so. Both to ensure the efficient and independent performance of these missions and to afford effective support to its agents, the Organization must provide them with adequate protection. ...

Upon examination of the character of the functions entrusted to the Organization and of the nature of the missions of its agents, it becomes clear that the capacity of the Organization to exercise a measure of functional protection of its agents arises by necessary intendment out of the Charter.

The obligations entered into by States to enable the agents of the Organization to perform their duties are undertaken not in the interest of the agents, but in that of the Organization. When it claims redress for a breach of these obligations, the Organization is invoking its own right, the right that the obligations due to it should be respected. ...

The question remains whether the Organization has the "capacity to bring an international claim against the responsible *de jure* or *de facto* government with a view to obtaining the reparation due" ... or whether, on the contrary, the defendant State, not being a member, is justified in raising the objection that the Organization lacks the capacity to bring an international claim. On this point the Court's opinion is that fifty States, representing the vast majority of the members of the international community, had the power, in conformity with international law, to bring into being an entity possessing objective international personality and not merely personality recognized by them alone, together with the capacity to bring international claims. ...

The affirmative reply given by the Court on point I (*b*) obliges it now to examine Question II ...

In such a case, there is no rule of law which assigns priority to the one or the other, or which compels either the State or the Organization to refrain from bringing an international claim. The Court sees no reason why the parties concerned should not find solutions inspired by goodwill and common sense, and as between the Organization and its Members it draws attention to their duty to render "every assistance" provided by Article 2, paragraph 5, of the Charter. ...

The question of reconciling action by the Organization with the rights of a national State may arise in another way; that is to say when the agent bears the nationality of the defendant State.

The ordinary practice whereby a State does not exercise protection on behalf of one of its nationals against a State which regards him as its own national, does not constitute a precedent which is relevant here. The action of the Organization is in fact based not upon the nationality of the victim but upon his status as an agent of the Organization. Therefore, it does not matter whether or not the State to which the claim is addressed regards him as its own national. The question of nationality is not pertinent to the admissibility of the claim. ...

FOR THESE REASONS,

The Court is of opinion

On Question I (*a*):

(*i*) unanimously,

That, in the event of an agent of the United Nations in the performance of his duties suffering injury in circumstances involving the responsibility of a Member State, the United Nations as an Organization has the capacity to bring an international claim against the responsible *de jure* or *de facto* government with a view to obtaining the reparation due in respect of the damage caused to the United Nations.

(*ii*) unanimously,

That, in the event of an agent of the United Nations in the performance of his duties suffering injury in circumstances involving the responsibility of a State which is not a member, the United Nations as an Organization has the capacity to bring an international claim against the responsible *de jure* or *de facto* government with a view to obtaining the reparation due in respect of the damage caused to the United Nations.

On Question I (*b*):

(*i*) by eleven votes against four,

That, in the event of an agent of the United Nations in the performance of his duties suffering injury in circumstances involving the responsibility of a Member State, the United Nations as an Organization has the capacity to bring an international claim against the responsible *de jure* or *de facto* government with a view to obtaining the reparation due in respect of the damage caused to the victim or to persons entitled through him.

(*ii*) by eleven votes against four,

That, in the event of an agent of the United Nations in the performance of his duties suffering injury in circumstances involving the responsibility of a State which is not a member, the United Nations as an Organization has the capacity to bring an international claim against the responsible *de jure* or *de facto* government with a view to obtaining the reparation due in respect of the damage caused to the victim or to persons entitled through him.

On Question II:

By ten votes against five,

When the United Nations as an Organization is bringing a claim for reparation of damage caused to its agent, it can only do so by basing its claim upon a breach of obligations due to itself; respect for this rule will usually prevent a conflict between the action of the United Nations and such rights as the agent's national State may possess, and thus bring about a reconciliation between their claims; moreover, this reconciliation must depend upon considerations applicable to each particular case, and upon agreements to be made between the Organization and individual States, either generally or in each case. . . .

Dissenting Opinion of Justice Hackworth

The conclusion that power in the Organization to sponsor private claims is conferred by "necessary implication" is not believed to be warranted under rules laid down by tribunals for filling lacunae in specific grants of power.

There can be no gainsaying the fact that the Organization is one of delegated and enumerated powers ... Powers not expressed cannot freely be implied. Implied powers flow from a grant of expressed powers, and are limited to those that are "necessary" to the exercise of powers expressly granted. No necessity for the exercise of the power here in question has been shown to exist ... The employees are still nationals of their respective countries and the customary methods of handling such claims are still available in full vigour. The prestige and efficiency of the Organization will be safeguarded by an exercise of its undoubted right under point I (*a*) *supra*.

. . . .

A second incident of legal personality is the power to enter into treaties. The United Nations clearly does possess this power, as do many other international organizations. In 1986 the Vienna Convention on the Law of Treaties between States and International Organizations or between International Organizations was adopted.[1] Though this Convention is not yet in force, it draws to a great extent upon the 1969 Vienna Convention on the Law of Treaties and is thus replete with the customary principles of law established

---

[1] UN Doc. A/CONF.129/15 (1986), 25 ILM 543.

in that convention, including the underlying requirement of good faith in interpretation and application of any agreement entered into by the parties. The convention is non-retroactive in application.

Although the Convention still awaits final implementation, there are already many instances of treaties between states and the United Nations. One such is the Agreement between the United States and the United Nations Regarding the Headquarters of the United Nations, which was concluded in 1947.[2] Section 11 provides that "the federal, state or local authorities of the United States shall not impose any impediments to transit to or from the headquarters district of: (1) representatives of Members ... or the families of such representatives ... ; ... (5) other persons invited to the headquarters district by the United Nations on official business." Section 12 provides that "[t]he provisions of section 11 shall be applicable irrespective of the relations existing between the Governments of the persons referred to in that section and the Government of the United States." Section 13 provides that "Laws and regulations in force in the United States regarding the entry of aliens shall not be applied in such manner as to interfere with the privileges referred to in section 11." Acting under these provisions, the United Nations in 1974 invited the Palestine Liberation Organization (PLO) to send a Permanent Observer Mission to the United Nations.[3] The PLO, established in 1964, is an umbrella organization committed to the establishment of an independent Palestinian state.

In the 1980s the legal status of the Headquarters Agreement came into question in two cases—one before the ICJ, the other in a US Federal Court—relating to the closure of the offices of the PLO's Observer Mission to the United Nations. Section 1003 of the US Anti-Terrorism Act (ATA) of 1987[4] provided that "It shall be unlawful, if the purpose is to further the interests of the Palestine Liberation Organization or any of its constitutive groups, any successor to any of those or any agents thereof, on or after the effective date of this chapter ... notwithstanding any provision of the law to the contrary to establish or maintain an office, headquarters, premises or other facilities or establishments within the jurisdiction of the United States at the behest or direction of, or with funds provided by, the Palestine Liberation Organization."

The United States insisted that this legislation superseded the Headquarters Agreement, while the United Nations claimed that international law prevailed over domestic law and asked the United States to enter into arbitration to resolve the issue as specified by the Headquarters Agreement. The first case, an Advisory Opinion of the ICJ, dealt primarily with the capacity of the United States to refuse to enter into arbitration on the ground that the Agreement had been superseded by the US legislation; the second, a District Court judgment, addressed more directly whether US legislation can override international agreements.

---

[2] 11 UNTS 11, No. 147 (1947).
[3] GA Res. 3237(XXIX) (1974).
[4] Pub. L. No. 100-204, Title X, 21 March 1988.

During the debate over the Anti-Terrorism Bill, the Secretary-General and the PLO Observer Mission had repeatedly raised the concern that closure of PLO offices would be contrary to US obligations under Sections 11–13 of the Headquarters Agreement. The Reagan Administration sought to assure the Secretary-General and the General Assembly that it was opposed to the closure of the PLO mission.

Once the Act was passed, the Reagan Administration proposed "to engage with the Congress in an effort to resolve this matter."[5] It could not, however, assure the Secretary-General that the office of the PLO would not be closed.

The Secretary-General thereafter invoked the dispute settlement procedure under Article 21(a) of the Headquarters Agreement, which provides that "[a]ny dispute between the United Nations and the United States concerning the interpretation or application of this agreement or of any supplemental agreement, which is not settled by negotiation or other agreed mode of settlement, shall be referred for final decision to a tribunal of three arbitrators." He proposed negotiations between the United Nations and the United States toward this end. The United States agreed to informal discussions but refused to enter into a formal dispute settlement process.

On 11 March 1988, ten days prior to the date of commencement of the Act, the United States informed the Secretary-General and the PLO that the Attorney General had determined that the Anti-Terrorism Act required the closure of the office of the PLO Observer Mission, and that he would file a suit for compliance in the appropriate domestic court. In such circumstances, the memo stated, it would not be worthwhile to enter into arbitration.[6] On the same day, the Assistant Attorney General also stated that "[t]he Anti-Terrorism Act of 1987 has superseded the requirements of the UN Headquarters Agreement." The suit to require closure of the mission was filed in the District Court of New York the day the Act came into effect.

On 23 March 1988 the General Assembly adopted resolution 42/230 (1988), by which it reaffirmed that "a dispute exists concerning the interpretation or application of the Headquarters Agreement, and that the dispute settlement procedure provided for under section 21 of the Agreement ... should be set in operation." It requested the International Court of Justice to render an opinion as to whether the United States was obliged to go to arbitration, rather than closing the mission. The UN Legal Counsel also stated that the United Nations would submit an amicus curiae brief in the compliance proceedings instituted by the United States against the PLO in the US Federal District Court, asserting the binding nature of the Headquarters Agreement and asserting its legal priority over a domestic US statute.

---

[5] Letter dated 5 January 1988 from the Acting Permanent Representative of the United States to the United Nations addressed to the Secretary-General.
[6] Letter dated 11 March 1988 from the Acting Permanent Representative of the United States to the United Nations addressed to the Secretary-General, UN Doc. A/42/915/Add.2 (Annex I) (1988).

APPLICABILITY OF THE OBLIGATION TO ARBITRATE UNDER SECTION 21 OF THE UNITED NATIONS HEADQUARTERS AGREEMENT OF 26 JUNE 1947 (ADVISORY OPINION) (1988) ICJ REPORTS 12

7. The question upon which the advisory opinion of the Court has been requested is whether the United States ... , as a party to the [Headquarters Agreement], is under an obligation to enter into arbitration ...

There is no question but that the Headquarters Agreement is a treaty in force binding the parties thereto. What the Court has therefore to determine, in order to answer the question put to it, is whether there exists a dispute between the United Nations and the United States of the kind contemplated by section 21 of the Agreement. ...

33. ... the Court is not called upon to decide whether the measures adopted by the United States in regard to the Observer Mission of the PLO to the United Nations do or do not run counter to the Headquarters Agreement. The question put to the Court is not about either the alleged violations of the Headquarters Agreement applicable to that Mission or the interpretation of those provisions. ...

36. In the present case, the Secretary-General informed the Court that, in his opinion, a dispute within the meaning of section 21 of the Headquarters Agreement existed between the United Nations and the United States from the moment the Anti-Terrorism Act was signed into law by the President of the United States and in the absence of adequate assurances to the Organization that the Act would not be applied to the PLO Observer Mission to the United Nations ...

37. The United States has never expressly contradicted the view expounded by the Secretary-General and endorsed by the General Assembly regarding the sense of the Headquarters Agreement. Certain United States authorities have even expressed the same view, but the United States has nevertheless taken measures against the PLO Mission to the United Nations. It has indicated those measures were being taken "irrespective of any obligations the United States may have under the [Headquarters] Agreement" ...

38. In the view of the Court, where one party to a treaty protests against the behaviour or a decision of another party, and claims that such behaviour or decision constitutes a breach of the treaty, the mere fact that the party accused does not advance any argument to justify its conduct under international law does not prevent the opposing attitudes of the parties from giving rise to a dispute concerning the interpretation or application of the treaty ...

39. In the present case, the United States in its public statements has not referred to the matter as a "dispute" ... and it has expressed the view the arbitration would be "premature" ...

40. The Court could not allow considerations as to what might be "appropriate" to prevail over obligations which derive from section 21 of the Headquarters Agreement, as "the Court, being a Court of justice, cannot

disregard rights recognized by it, and base its decision on considerations of pure expediency" (*Free Zones of Upper Savoy and the district of Gex, Order of 6 December 1930, PCIJ Series A, No. 24*, p. 15)

41. The Court must further point out that the alleged dispute relates solely to what the United Nations considers to be its rights under the Headquarters Agreement. The purpose of the arbitration procedure envisaged by that Agreement is precisely the settlement of such disputes as may arise between the Organization and the host country without any prior recourse to municipal courts, and it would be against both the letter and the spirit of the Agreement for the implementation of that procedure to be subjected to such prior recourse. ...

43. ... Although the [ATA] extends to every PLO office situated within the jurisdiction of the United States and contains no express reference to the office of the PLO Mission to the United Nations in New York, its chief, if not its sole, objective was the closure of that office ... [T]he opposing attitudes of the UN and the US show the existence of a dispute between the two parties to the Headquarters Agreement. ...

45. The Court has next to consider whether the dispute was one which concerns the interpretation or application of the Headquarters Agreement ...

46. The Secretary-General and the General Assembly have constantly pointed out that the PLO was invited "to participate in the sessions and the work of the General Assembly in the capacity of Observer" (resolution 3237(XXIX)). In their view therefore, the PLO Observer Mission was as such covered by Sections 11, 12 and 13 of the Headquarters Agreement." ...

48. ... [T]he United States did not dispute that certain provisions of that Agreement applied to the PLO Mission to the United Nations in New York. However ... it gave precedence to the Anti-Terrorism Act over the Headquarters Agreement and this was challenged by the Secretary-General ...

49. To conclude, the United States has taken a number of measures against the PLO Observer Mission to the United Nations in New York. The Secretary-General regarded these as contrary to the Headquarters Agreement. Without expressly disputing that point, the United States stated that the measures in question were taken "irrespective of any obligations the United States may have under the Agreement." Such conduct cannot be reconciled with the position of the Secretary-General. There thus exists a dispute between the United Nations and the United States concerning the application of the Headquarters Agreement, falling within the terms of section 21 thereof.

50. The question might be raised whether in United States domestic law the decisions taken ... by the Attorney General brought about the application of the [ATA], or whether the Act can only be regarded as having received effective application when or if, on completion of the current judicial proceedings, the PLO Mission is in fact closed. This is however not decisive in regard to section 21 of the Headquarters Agreement, which refers to any dispute "concerning the interpretation or application" of the Agreement, and not concerning the application of the measures taken in the municipal law of the United States. ...

55. The Court considers that, taking into account the United States attitude, the Secretary-General had in the circumstances exhausted such possibilities of negotiation as were open to him. ...

56. Nor was any "other agreed mode of settlement" of their dispute contemplated by the United Nations and the United States. In this context the Court should observe that current proceedings brought by the US Attorney General before the United States courts cannot be an "agreed mode of settlement" within the meaning of section 21 of the Headquarters Agreement. The purpose of these proceedings is to enforce the Anti-Terrorism Act of 1987; it is not directed to settling the dispute concerning the application of the Headquarters Agreement ... Furthermore, the United Nations has never agreed to the settlement of the dispute in the American courts; it has taken care to make it clear that it wishes to be admitted only as *amicus curiae* before the District Court ...

57. The Court must therefore conclude that the United States is bound to respect the obligation to have recourse to arbitration under section 21 of the Headquarters Agreement ... It would be sufficient to recall the fundamental principle of international law that international law prevails over domestic law.

Following the determination by the Attorney General that the ATA required the closure of the office of the PLO Observer Mission to the United Nations, the United States commenced action before the District Court for the Southern District of New York, seeking injunctive relief to accomplish closure of the PLO Permanent Observer Mission. As in the advisory opinion, the United States contended that the Act prevailed over the positions of the Headquarters Agreement, which would thus be inapplicable.

UNITED STATES OF AMERICA V. THE PALESTINE LIBERATION ORGANIZATION, ET AL., 695 F. SUPP. 1456 (S.D.N.Y. 1988)

Under our constitutional system, statutes and treaties are both the supreme law of the land, and the Constitution sets forth no order of precedence to differentiate between them ... Wherever possible, both are to be given effect ... Only where a treaty is irreconcilable with a later enacted statute and Congress has clearly evinced an intent to supersede a treaty by enacting a statute does the later enacted statute take precedence ...

The long standing and well-established position of the Mission at the UN, sustained by international agreement, when considered along with the text of the ATA and its legislative history, fails to disclose any clear legislative intent that Congress was directing the Attorney General, the State Department or this

Court to act in contravention of the Headquarters Agreement ... This court acknowledges the validity of the government's position that Congress has the power to enact statutes abrogating prior treaties or international obligations entered into by the US ... However unless this power is clearly and unequivocally exercised, this court is under a duty to interpret statutes in a manner consonant with the existing treaty obligations. This is a rule of statutory construction sustained by an unbroken line of authority for over a century and a half. Recently, the Supreme Court articulated it in *Weinberger v. Rossi* ...:

"It has been maxim of statutory construction since the decision in *Murray v. The Charming Betsy* ... (1804), that "an act of Congress ought never to be construed to violate the law of nations, if any other possible construction remains ..."

The American Law Institute's recently revised Restatement (Third) Foreign Relations Law of the United States (1988) reflects this unbroken line of authority:

> §115. Inconsistency Between International Law or Agreement and Domestic Law: law of the United States.
> (1)(a) An Act of Congress supersedes an earlier rule of international law or a provision of an international agreement as law of the United States *if the purpose of the act to supersede the earlier rule or provision is clear* and if the act and the earlier rule or provision cannot be fairly reconciled. (Emphasis supplied.)

We believe the ATA and the Headquarters Agreement cannot be reconciled except by finding the ATA inapplicable to the PLO Observer Mission.

The obligation of the United States to allow transit, entry and access stems not only from the language of the Headquarters Agreement but also from forty years of practice under it ...

It seemed clear to those in the executive branch that closing the PLO mission would be a departure from the United States' practice in regard to observer missions, and they made their views known to members of Congress who were instrumental in the passage of the ATA. In addition, United States representatives to the United Nations made repeated efforts to allay the concerns of the UN Secretariat by reiterating and reaffirming the obligations of the United States under the Headquarters Agreement.

"Although not conclusive, the meaning attributed to treaty provisions by the Government agencies charged with their negotiation and enforcement is entitled to great weight." *Sumitomo Shoji America, Inc. v. Avagliano* ... (1982). The interpretive statements of the United Nations also carry some weight, especially because they are in harmony with the interpretation given to the Headquarters Agreement by the Department of State. ...

Thus the language, application and interpretation of the Headquarters Agreement lead us to the conclusion that it requires the United States to refrain from interference with the PLO Observer Mission in the discharge of its functions at the United Nations.

... The principles enunciated and applied in *Chew Heong* and its progeny ... require the clearest of expressions on the part of Congress. We are constrained by these decisions to stress the lack of clarity in Congress' action in this instance. Congress' failure to speak with one clear voice on this subject requires us to interpret the ATA as inapplicable to the Headquarters Agreement. This is so, in short, for the reasons which follow.

First, neither the Mission nor the Headquarters Agreement is mentioned in the ATA itself. Such an inclusion would have left no doubt as to Congress' intent on a matter which had been raised repeatedly with respect to this act, and its absence here reflects equivocation and avoidance, leaving the court without clear interpretive guidance in the language of the act. Second, while the section of the ATA prohibiting the maintenance of an office applies "notwithstanding any provision of law to the contrary," 22 USC § 5202(3), it does not purport to apply notwithstanding any *treaty*. The absence of that interpretive instruction is especially relevant because elsewhere in the same legislation Congress expressly referred to "United States law (including any treaty)." 101 Stat. at 1343. Thus Congress failed, in the text of the ATA, to provide guidance for the interpretation of the act, where it became repeatedly apparent before its passage that the prospect of an interpretive problem was inevitable. Third, no member of Congress expressed a clear and unequivocal intent to supersede the Headquarters Agreement by passage of the ATA. In contrast, most who addressed the subject of conflict denied that there would be a conflict: in their view, the Headquarters Agreement did not provide the PLO with any right to maintain an office. Here again, Congress provided no guidance for the interpretation of the ATA in the event of a conflict which was clearly foreseeable ...

In sum, the language of the Headquarters Agreement, the longstanding practice under it, and the interpretation given it by the parties to it leave no doubt that it places an obligation upon the US to refrain from impairing the function of the PLO Observer Mission to the UN. The ATA and its legislative history do not manifest Congress' intent to abrogate this obligation. We are therefore constrained to interpret the ATA as failing to supersede the Headquarters Agreement and inapplicable to the Mission.

. . . .

A further controversy arose concerning US obligations under the Headquarters Agreement when, only a few weeks later, the United States refused to grant a visa to Yasser Arafat, chairman of the PLO. Arafat was scheduled to participate and speak at the General Assembly; a visa request had been personally transferred by the UN Legal Counsel to the Permanent Mission of the United States to the United Nations. The US government claimed that Mr. Arafat was an accessory to terrorism and thus on 26 November 1988 denied him a visa.

The decision was criticized. On 29 November a meeting of the Committee on Relations with the Host Country saw the vast majority of speakers agree with the Secretary-General and the Speaker of the General Assembly that this was a violation of the Headquarters Agreement and asked the United States to review its decision.[7] The United States rejected this view and the General Assembly decided to move its sessions on Palestine-related issues to Geneva, held from 13–15 December 1988.[8] The United States has not subsequently denied a visa to the Chairman of the PLO and Congress did not again legislate to close its Observer Mission to the United Nations.

QUESTIONS

1. How would you describe the United Nations? Is it more like a state, a conference center, or something else entirely?
2. In the *Reparations* case, the ICJ provides an incomplete definition of the term "international personality" insofar as it applies to the United Nations, mentioning only that it has rights and duties on the international plane, and that these include the capacity to bring international claims. It accepts also that the rights and duties associated with such international personality differ for states and international organizations.[9] Can all of these characteristics be ascribed to international organizations? If not, which ones are applicable?
3. Judge Rosalyn Higgins of the ICJ holds the opinion that international organizations, like states, enjoy objective legal personality—that is, personality independent of recognition by other entities, based only on the possession of certain attributes.[10] Is this view reflected in the Advisory Opinion of the Court in the *Reparations* case? Which attributes are necessary for "objective personality"?[11]

---

[7] Report of Committee on Relations with the Host Country, UN Doc. A/43/26/Add.1 (1988). The Committee was established by GA Res. 2819(XXVI) (1971).

[8] GA Res. 43/49 (1988).

[9] Grigory Tunkin defined full legal personality of States as including the following characteristics: (i) rights and duties under international law; (ii) sovereignty, which means supreme power over states' respective territories and population; (iii) sovereign equality of all states; (iv) privileges and immunities of states and their organs; (v) the capacity to participate in the process of creating norms of international law; (vi) the capacity to participate in international legal relations; (vii) the capacity to bring international claims; (viii) the capacity to take enforcement actions under international law; and (ix) the capacity to bear international responsibility: Grigory Tunkin, "International Law in the International System," Receuil des cours, vol. 147(1) (1975), pp. 201-202.

[10] Rosalyn Higgins, Problems and Process: The International Law and How We Use It (Oxford: Oxford University Press, 1995), p. 48.

[11] For a discussion, see Sigmar Stadelmeier, External Security Dimensions of a Non-Entity? Pleading the Legal Personality of the Union, available at http://www.ecsanet .org/ecsaworld6/contributions/others/Stadelmeier.doc.

4. Does the capacity to bring international claims flow directly from the possession of international personality? Are there organizations which have limited international personality that does not include the capacity to bring international claims?

5. The Court's 1949 opinion in the *Reparations* case indicates that an international organization may bring a claim against a state for injury to its own national, if such national is an agent of the Organization. Should this be viewed as an intrusion upon the internal sovereignty of a state? What public policy justifies according a right to the United Nations to bring claims against the state of which a UN civil servant is a national? Under what circumstances might such a right of action arise? What would be the measure of damages?

6. The Secretary-General and the General Assembly relied upon sections 11–13 of the Headquarters Agreement to claim that the United States has an obligation to allow the PLO Observer Mission to maintain an office in New York. These sections make no mention of observer missions. Is it acceptable for the ICJ to have interpreted these provisions, meant for delegations representing states, as applying also to observer missions?

7. The ICJ concluded in its 1988 advisory opinion that "international law prevails over domestic law." What are the implications of this finding for other US Treaty Commitments, such as those in the UN Charter, when they conflict with laws made by Congress or actions authorized by the President?

8. Both the District Court and the International Court of Justice concluded that the United States must respect its obligations under the Headquarters Agreement. It appears however that the ICJ refers to the procedural obligation of the US to enter into arbitration as per section 21 of the Headquarters Agreement, while the District Court is referring to substantive obligations under Articles 13–15 of the Headquarters Agreement. If this reading is correct, how does it affect the maxim "international law prevails over domestic law," subscribed to by the ICJ?

3.2 Who Interprets the Charter?

The United Nations Conference on International Organization was convened in San Francisco in 1945 for the purposes of drafting the Charter of the United Nations. The work was divided between four Commissions that were further divided into twelve technical Committees, each of which was responsible for preparing a separate portion of the Charter.

Among the issues raised for discussion during the course of this Conference was "how and by what organ or organs of the Organization the Charter should be interpreted." This question, originally presented by the Belgian Delegation to Committee II/2, was thereafter referred to Committee IV/2 and was debated upon on 28 May and 7 June 1945.

STATEMENT OF COMMITTEE IV/2 OF THE SAN FRANCISCO CONFERENCE, REPORT OF COMMITTEE IV/2 OF THE UNITED NATIONS CONFERENCE ON INTERNATIONAL ORGANIZATION, SAN FRANCISCO, 12 JUNE 1945[12]

In the course of the operations from day to day of the various organs of the Organization, it is inevitable that each organ will interpret such parts of the Charter as are applicable to its particular functions. The process is inherent in the functioning of any body which operates under an instrument defining its functions and powers. It will be manifested in the functioning of such a body as the General Assembly, the Security Council or the International Court of Justice. Accordingly it is not necessary to include in the Charter a provision either authorizing or approving the normal operation of this principle. ...

Difficulties may conceivably arise in the event that there should be a difference in opinion among the organs of the Organization concerning the correct interpretation of a provision of the charter. Thus, two organs may conceivably hold and may express or even act upon different views. Under unitary forms of national government the final determinations of such a question may be vested in the highest court or in some other national authority. However, the nature of the Organization and of its operation would not seem to be such as to invite the inclusion in the Charter of any provision of this nature. If two member states are at a variance concerning the correct interpretation of the Charter, they are of course free to submit the dispute to the International Court of Justice as in the case of any other treaty. Similarly, it would always be open to the General Assembly or to the Security Council, in appropriate circumstances, to ask the International Court of Justice for an advisory opinion concerning the meaning of a provision of the Charter. Should the General Assembly or the Security Council prefer another course, an ad hoc committee of jurists might be set up to examine the question and report its views, or recourse might be had to a joint conference. In brief, the members or the organs of the Organization might have recourse to various expedients in order to obtain appropriate interpretation. It would appear neither necessary nor desirable to list or to describe in the Charter the various possible expedients.

It is to be understood, of course, that if an interpretation made by any organ of the Organization or by a committee of jurists is not generally acceptable it will be without binding force. In such circumstances, or in cases where it is desired to establish an authoritative interpretation as a precedent for the future, it may be necessary to embody the interpretation in an amendment to the Charter.

---

[12] UNCIO Doc. 933, IV/2/42(2), p.7; 13 UNCIO Documents, p. 703, at 709-710.

The *Lockerbie* case was an example of the overlap in jurisdiction between the ICJ and the Security Council, when seized of the same matter. The issue involved the bombing of Pan Am Flight 103 on 21 December 1988 over Lockerbie, in Scotland. The United States indicted two Libyan nationals on the charge on having placed a bomb on board that flight and demanded they be extradited for prosecution in US courts. In the Security Council resolution 731 (1992) was passed, under Chapter VI of the UN Charter.

SECURITY COUNCIL RESOLUTION 731 (1992)

The Security Council, ...
Deeply concerned over results of investigations which implicate officials of the Libyan Government and which are contained in Security Council documents that include the requests addressed to the Libyan authorities by France, the United Kingdom of Great Britain and Northern Ireland and the United States of America in connection with the legal procedures related to the attacks carried out against Pan Am flight 103 and UTA flight 772 ...
3. *Urges* the Libyan Government immediately to provide a full and effective response to those requests so as to contribute to the elimination of international terrorism ...

Libya instituted proceedings against the United States at the ICJ, claiming that the matter fell under Article 14, paragraph 1 of the Convention for the Suppression of Unlawful Acts Against the Safety of Civil Aviation[13] (the "Montreal Convention"). Both states were parties to the Convention, which provides that "any dispute between two or more contracting states concerning the interpretation or application of this convention which cannot be settled through negotiation, shall, at the request of one of them, be submitted to arbitration. If within six months of the date of the request for arbitration the parties are unable to agree on the organization of the arbitration, any one of those parties may refer the dispute to the International Court of Justice by request in conformity with the Statute of the Court." While under Article 8, the requested state on whose territory the offender was found was not under a duty to extradite in the absence of an extradition treaty if it had made such extradition conditional upon the existence of such a treaty, Article 7 provided that in such a case, that state would "be obliged,

---

[13] 974 UNTS 178, no. 14118 (1971).

without exception whatsoever and whether or not the offence was committed in its territory, to submit the case to its competent authorities for the purpose of prosecution. Those authorities shall take their decision in the same manner as in the case of any ordinary offence of a serious nature under the law of that state." Under Article 11, the governing law would be the law of the requested state; all other states were under obligation to provide it with all possible assistance in the course of the prosecution. Claiming breach of these provisions by the United States, Libya brought this matter before the ICJ. Fearing both economic and military sanctions to force compliance, Libya also requested that the ICJ order "urgent provisional measures" to prevent them.

The United States contended that the ICJ should refrain from exercising jurisdiction, as the Security Council was already seized of the matter. After the close of oral proceedings but before the ICJ had announced its decision, the Security Council passed resolution 748 (1992).

SECURITY COUNCIL RESOLUTION 748 (1992)

The Security Council, ...
   Acting under Chapter VII,
   1. *Decides* that the Libyan Government must now comply without any further delay with [resolution 731 (1992)] ...
   7. *Calls upon* all States, including States not members of the United Nations, and all international organizations, to act strictly in accordance with the provisions of the present resolution, notwithstanding the existence of any rights or obligations conferred or imposed by any international agreement or any contract entered into or any licence or permit granted prior to 15 April 1992.

The ICJ subsequently invited comments from both parties on the significance of this resolution. Libya argued that the resolution did not prejudice Libya's right to request the Court to indicate provisional measures as there is no hierarchy between the ICJ and the Security Council and therefore the risk of contradiction between the resolution and the request for provisional measures did not render the latter inadmissible. The United States claimed that resolution 748 (1992) was framed as a binding decision and irrespective of the right claimed by Libya under the Montreal Convention, Libya had a Charter-based duty to carry out the decisions in the resolution.

QUESTIONS OF INTERPRETATION AND APPLICATION OF THE 1971 MONTREAL CONVENTION ARISING FROM THE AERIAL INCIDENT AT LOCKERBIE (*LIBYAN ARAB JAMAHIRIYA V. UNITED STATES OF AMERICA*) (PROVISIONAL MEASURES) (1992) ICJ REPORTS 114

42. ...[B]oth Libya and the United States, as Members of the United Nations, are obliged to accept and carry out the decisions of the Security Council in accordance with Article 25 of the Charter; whereas the Court, which is at the stage of proceedings on provisional measures, considers that prima facie this obligation extends to the decision contained in resolution 748 (1992); and whereas, in accordance with Article 103 of the Charter, the obligations of the Parties in that respect prevail over their obligations under any other international agreement, including the Montreal Convention;

43. ...[T]he Court, while thus not at this stage called upon to determine definitively the legal effect of Security Council resolution 748 (1992), considers that, whatever the situation previous to the adoption of that resolution, the rights claimed by Libya under the Montreal Convention cannot now be regarded as appropriate for protection by the indication of provisional measures;

44. ...[F]urthermore, an indication of the measures requested by Libya would be likely to impair the rights which appear prima facie to be enjoyed by the United States by virtue of Security Council resolution 748 (1992).

45. ...[I]n order to pronounce on the present request for provisional measures, the Court is not called upon to determine any of the other questions which have been raised before it in the present proceedings, including the question of its jurisdiction to entertain the merits of the case; and whereas the decision given in these proceedings in no way prejudges any such question, and leaves unaffected the rights of the Government of Libya and the Government of the United States to submit arguments in respect of any of these questions;

46. ...The Court by eleven votes to five, [f]inds that the circumstances of the case are not such as to require the exercise of its power under Article 41 of the Statute to indicate provisional measures.

In the above order, the Court did not directly answer the contention of the United States that resolution 748 (1992) had displaced its jurisdiction over the matter. Its position was somewhat clearer in the judgment on preliminary objections, delivered on 27 February 1998.

QUESTIONS OF INTERPRETATION AND APPLICATION OF THE 1971 MONTREAL CONVENTION ARISING FROM THE AERIAL INCIDENT AT LOCKERBIE (*LIBYAN ARAB JAMAHIRIYA V. UNITED STATES OF AMERICA*) (PRELIMINARY OBJECTIONS) (1998) ICJ REPORTS 115

36. In the present case, the United States has contended ... that even if the Montreal Convention did confer on Libya the rights it claims, those rights could not be exercised in this case because they were superseded by Security Council resolutions 748 (1992) and 883 (1993) which, by virtue of Articles 25 and 103 of the United Nations Charter, have priority over all rights and obligations arising out of the Montreal Convention ...

37. The Court cannot uphold this line of argument. Security Council resolutions 748 (1992) and 883 (1993) were in fact adopted after the filing of the Application on 3 March 1992. In accordance with its established jurisprudence, if the Court had jurisdiction on that date, it continues to do so; the subsequent coming into existence of the above-mentioned resolutions cannot affect its jurisdiction once established ...

40. ...The United States further contends that if the Court should see fit to "assert [its] jurisdiction to examine on the merits, by way of objection, the validity of Security Council resolutions 731 (1992), 748 (1992) and 883 (1993), the Libyan Application should nonetheless be dismissed at the preliminary objections stage because it is not admissible." ...

43. ...The date, 3 March 1992, on which Libya filed its Application, is in fact the only relevant date for determining the admissibility of the Application. Security Council resolutions 748 (1992) and 883 (1993) cannot be taken into consideration in this regard, since they were adopted at a later date. As to Security Council resolution 731 (1992), adopted before the filing of the Application, it could not form a legal impediment to the admissibility of the latter because it was a mere recommendation without binding effect, as was recognized moreover by the United States. Consequently, Libya's Application cannot be held inadmissible on these grounds. ...

45. The Court will now consider the third objection raised by the United States. According to that objection, Libya's claims have become moot because Security Council resolutions 748 (1992) and 883 (1993) have rendered them without object; any judgment which the Court might deliver on the said claims would thenceforth be devoid of practical purpose. ...

47. ...What Libya contends is that this objection ... falls within the category of those which Article 79, paragraph 7, of the Rules of Court characterizes as objections "not possess[ing], in the circumstances of the case, an exclusively preliminary character." ...

49. The Court must therefore ascertain whether ... the United States objection considered here contains "both preliminary aspects and other aspects relating to the merits" or not.

That objection relates to many aspects of the dispute ... [B]y requesting such a decision, the United States is requesting, in reality, at least two others ... on the one hand a decision establishing that the rights claimed by Libya under the Montreal Convention are incompatible with its obligations under the Security Council resolutions; and, on the other hand, a decision that those obligations prevail over those rights by virtue of Articles 25 and 103 of the Charter.

The Court therefore has no doubt that Libya's rights on the merits would not only be affected by a decision not to proceed to judgment on the merits, at this stage in the proceedings, but would constitute, in many respects, the very subject-matter of that decision. ...

The Court concludes from the foregoing that the objection of the United States according to which the Libyan claims have become moot as having been rendered without object does not have "an exclusively preliminary character" within the meaning of that Article.

A joint notification was issued by Libya and the United States on 9 September 2003 communicating their decision to discontinue with prejudice the proceedings initiated by Libya. The ICJ was therefore not called upon to decide whether Libya's rights under the Montreal Convention were indeed superseded by its obligations under the Security Council resolutions. The deeper question of what complications could arise if the ICJ were to rule that they were not superseded—that is, that Libya's rights prevailed over its obligations to the Security Council—therefore remained unanswered.

Another incident that highlights the possible conflict of jurisdiction between the Security Council and the ICJ, was the application, filed by Bosnia and Herzegovina, claiming that Yugoslavia (Serbia and Montenegro) was committing acts of genocide in its territory. One of the issues raised pertains directly to the power of the ICJ to interpret and review resolutions of the Security Council.

In September 1991 the Security Council in resolution 713 (1991) had imposed a general and complete embargo on all deliveries of weapons and military equipment to Yugoslavia. Resolution 727 (1992) reaffirmed this arms embargo and clarified that it was applicable to all areas that had been part of Yugoslavia.

Bosnia and Herzegovina, one of the constituent parts of the former Yugoslavia, asked the Court to declare that it could, "as a member of the United Nations and as a party to the Genocide Convention, invoke the right of self-defence under Article 51 of the UN Charter and thereby demand the assistance of the international community in stopping the violations." In this context it claimed also that resolution 713 (1991) adopted by the Security Council pursuant to its powers under Chapter VII of the Charter, should be construed as not applicable to it because it violated Bosnia and Herzegovina's Charter-based and "inherent" right of self-defense.

Note that the following is an *application to the Court by one of the parties*, not a decision by the Court.

APPLICATION OF THE REPUBLIC OF BOSNIA AND HERZEGOVINA IN CASE CONCERNING APPLICATION OF THE CONVENTION ON THE PREVENTION AND PUNISHMENT OF THE CRIME OF GENOCIDE (*BOSNIA AND HERZEGOVINA V. SERBIA AND MONTENEGRO*), 20 MARCH 1993

112. ...Pursuant to United Nations Charter Article 51, Bosnia and Herzegovina has the right to seek and receive support from the other 179 Member States of the United Nations ... including ... from the armed attacks, armed aggressions and acts of genocide currently being perpetrated by Yugoslavia (Serbia and Montenegro) and its agents and surrogates in gross violation of the Genocide Convention as well as of its solemn obligations found in Article 2, paragraphs 2, 3 and 4, and in Article 33, paragraph I, of the United Nations Charter.

115. ...[S]o far the United Nations Security Council has not yet taken effective measures necessary to maintain international peace and security with respect to it and its People within the meaning of United Nations Charter Article 51. Therefore, Bosnia and Herzegovina's inherent right of individual and collective self-defence against the armed attack and armed aggressions by Yugoslavia (Serbia and Montenegro) and its agents and surrogates remains intact. ...

122. Therefore, all subsequent Security Council resolutions that routinely reaffirmed the arms embargo imposed upon the former Yugoslavia by paragraph 6 of resolution 713 (1991), paragraph 5 of resolution 724 (1991), and paragraph 6 of resolution 727 (1992) cannot properly be construed to apply to the Republic of Bosnia and Herzegovina. Rather, all such Security Council resolutions must be construed in a manner consistent with Article 51 of the United Nations Charter. Thereunder, the Republic of Bosnia and Herzegovina has and still has the inherent right of individual and collective self-defence, including the right immediately to seek and receive from other States military weapons, equipment, supplies, troops and financing necessary in order to defend Itself and its People from the armed attacks, armed aggressions, and acts of genocide that have been and are continuously being perpetrated upon Us by Yugoslavia (Serbia and Montenegro) and its agents and surrogates.

123. Therefore, none of these numerous Security Council resolutions imposing or routinely reaffirming an arms embargo upon the former Yugoslavia under Chapter VII of the Charter can be properly interpreted to apply to the Republic of Bosnia and Herzegovina. To do otherwise would "impair the inherent right of individual or collective self-defence" of the Republic of Bosnia and Herzegovina, and thus violate United Nations Charter Article 51, and furthermore render these Security Council resolutions *ultra vires*: "*Nothing* in the present Charter shall impair the inherent right of individual or collective self defence. ... " (Emphasis added.)

124. Furthermore, United Nations Charter Article 24, paragraph 2, provides:

2. In discharging these duties [maintaining international peace and security] the Security Council shall act in accordance with the Purposes and Principles of the United Nations. The specific powers granted to the Security Council for the discharge of these duties are laid clown in Chapters VI, VII, VIII, and XII.

Therefore, even when it acts under Chapter VII of the Charter, the Security Council must "act in accordance with the Purposes and Principles of the United Nations" that are set forth in Chapter I, which consists of Articles I and 2 of the Charter.

125. Bosnia and Herzegovina claims that the arms embargo imposed upon the former Yugoslavia by the Security Council in resolution 713 (1992) and its successors legally did not apply and could not apply to the Republic of Bosnia and Herzegovina at any time. Otherwise, the Security Council would not be acting "in accordance with the Purposes and Principles of the United Nations" and thus would be in breach of Charter Article 24 (2). Such an improper interpretation of resolution 713 (1991) and its successors would render resolution 713 (1991) *ultra vires* the Security Council under both Article 24 (2) and Article 51 of the Charter.

126. In order to avoid these results, Bosnia and Herzegovina claims that this Court must interpret Security Council resolution 713 (1991) and its successors to mean that there is not, has never been, and is still not as of today, a mandatory arms embargo applicable to Bosnia and Herzegovina under Chapter VII of the Charter. This is a straightforward question of interpreting the terms of the United Nations Charter that clearly falls within the powers, competence, and purview of the Court. Indeed, no other organ of the United Nations but this Court can clarify this master and thus vindicate the "inherent right" of Bosnia and Herzegovina under Article 51. According to Charter Article 92, it is the Court—not the Security Council or the General Assembly—that is "the principal judicial organ of the United Nations."

127. Unless and until this Court definitively rules against its claims, Bosnia and Herzegovina remains free under Article 51 and customary international law to defend itself notwithstanding the terms of any Security Council resolutions adopted so far. Thus, Bosnia and Herzegovina has the basic right under international law to immediately seek and receive from other States

military weapons, equipment, supplies, troops and financing in order to defend Itself from armed attacks, armed aggressions, and acts of genocide that are currently being perpetrated upon Us by Yugoslavia (Serbia and Montenegro) and its agents and surrogates, continuously from our date of independence as a sovereign State on 6 March 1992 until today and beyond.

The Court did not make any direct reference to this request. In its Order of 13 September 1993—following a further request for provisional measures by Bosnia and Herzegovina including that it "must have the means" to prevent the commission of genocide and to defend its people against genocide, and "must have the ability to obtain military weapons, equipment, and supplies" from the other parties to the Genocide Convention—the Court stated that it was evident that the intention of the Applicant in requesting these measures was to obtain a declaration of what its rights were that could be invoked before the Security Council. It held that this request was outside the scope of the provisional measures that could be granted under Article 41 of the Statute.

The request relating to the lifting of the arms embargo was not included in the memorial submitted by Bosnia and Herzegovina on 15 April 1994, although it reserved the right to re-invoke various elements of its initial request, including those relating to the lifting of the arms embargo. The ICJ has not since been called upon to address this issue.

The embargo was subsequently lifted in three stages in 1995–96[14] and then re-imposed in 1998, following the crises in Kosovo.[15] Resolution 1367 (2001) finally brought this embargo to an end.

QUESTIONS

9. The conclusions of the Drafting Committee indicate that all organs have the capacity to interpret the provisions of the Charter. Does this also enable these organs to engage in law-making by way of formulating rules guiding their own functioning as well as relations with the other organs and international entities? Does it enable them to make rules at least governing their own procedures? Is it good policy?

10. The Drafting Committee highlights a number of ways in which conflicts of interpretation between two or more organs may be resolved. Is the list exclusive? Which of these means have been invoked in practice?

---

[14] SC Res. 1021 (1995).
[15] SC Res. 1160 (1998).

11. How is Article 103 of the UN Charter relevant (or not) to the implementation of decisions of the UN Security Council? What is the effect of Article 25 of the UN Charter?

12. If you conclude that Security Council resolutions must get priority over other treaty obligations, does this imply that these resolutions are an independent "source of law"? (Compare Article 38(1) of the ICJ Statute.)

13. In the *Lockerbie* advisory opinion, given that the Court has no power to enforce its decisions and must look to the Council for this purpose, what would have been the outcome had the decision gone in Libya's favor?

14. Does the Court, by rejecting the preliminary objections to its jurisdiction advanced by the United States, imply that it has the power to decide whether a resolution of the Security Council exceeds the Council's power under the Charter? Since that question was not to be determined finally until the merits phase—not reached due to the agreement of the parties to settle the case out of court—you are free to speculate as to what the Court might have done with this difficult issue. Should the Court exercise judicial review over Council resolutions?

15. In the *Genocide* case brought by Bosnia and Herzegovina, the ICJ was not required to take a decision that might conflict with a determination of the Security Council. However, assuming that the Court had allowed the provisional measures requested by Bosnia, including affirmations that "it must have the means" to prevent the commission of genocide, and "must have the ability to obtain military weapons, equipment, and supplies" from the other parties to the Genocide Convention, what would be the impact of this ruling? Would it have nullified the effect of the Security Council resolution, such that other states could supply arms to Bosnia?

16. Do you agree with Bosnia's submission that resolution 713 (1992) and its successors were *ultra vires*? Can the ICJ rule upon such a matter? In other words, does the Court have a right to "review" Security Council resolutions?

17. Should the ICJ review Security Council resolutions, even those under Chapter VII?

18. Was the Council's mandatory imposition of an embargo on arms shipments to all parts of the former Yugoslavia a violation of Bosnia's right to "collective self-defence"?

3.3 Law Making by the Security Council

Following the attacks on the World Trade Center in New York and the Pentagon in Washington DC on 11 September 2001, the Security Council passed a series of resolutions hailed as embodying new "law." As Professor Stefan Talmon points out, the hallmark of any international legislation is the general and abstract character of the obligations imposed. These may well be triggered by a particular situation, conflict, or event, but they are not restricted to it. Rather, the obligations are phrased in neutral language, apply to an indefinite number of cases, and are not usually limited in time.[16] The resolutions excerpted in this section conform to this. The first of these resolutions was passed one day after the September 11 attacks.

SECURITY COUNCIL RESOLUTION 1368 (2001)

The Security Council, ...
   Recognizing the inherent right of individual or collective self-defence in accordance with the Charter,
   1. *Unequivocally condemns* in the strongest terms the horrifying terrorist attacks which took place on 11 September 2001 in New York, Washington, D.C. and Pennsylvania and *regards* such acts, like any act of international terrorism, as a threat to international peace and security; ...
   3. *Calls* on all States to work together urgently to bring to justice the perpetrators, organizers and sponsors of these terrorist attacks and *stresses* that those responsible for aiding, supporting or harbouring the perpetrators, organizers and sponsors of these acts will be held accountable;
   4. *Calls also* on the international community to redouble their efforts to prevent and suppress terrorist acts including by increased cooperation and full implementation of the relevant international anti-terrorist conventions and Security Council resolutions, in particular resolution 1269 (1999) of 19 October 1999;
   5. *Expresses* its readiness to take all necessary steps to respond to the terrorist attacks of 11 September 2001, and to combat all forms of terrorism, in accordance with its responsibilities under the Charter of the United Nations;
   6. *Decides* to remain seized of the matter.

Two weeks later, on 28 September 2001, the Security Council, passed resolution 1373 (2001) reaffirming the need to combat threats to international peace and security caused by terrorist acts. Several provisions of this resolution are similar to provisions in the International Convention for the Suppression of the Financing of Terrorism which was not then in force.[17] The resolution calls upon states to become parties to the convention.

---

[16] Stefan A. Talmon, "The Security Council as World Legislature," American Journal of International Law, vol. 99 (2005), p. 175.
[17] GA Res. 54/109 (1999), entered into force 10 April 2002.

SECURITY COUNCIL RESOLUTION 1373 (2001)

The Security Council, ...
   Acting under Chapter VII of the Charter of the United Nations,
   1. *Decides* that all States shall:
   (a) Prevent and suppress the financing of terrorist acts;
   (b) Criminalize the wilful provision or collection, by any means, directly or indirectly, of funds by their nationals or in their territories with the intention that the funds should be used, or in the knowledge that they are to be used, in order to carry out terrorist acts;
   (c) Freeze without delay funds and other financial assets or economic resources of persons who commit, or attempt to commit, terrorist acts or participate in or facilitate the commission of terrorist acts; of entities owned or controlled directly or indirectly by such persons; and of persons and entities acting on behalf of, or at the direction of such persons and entities, including funds derived or generated from property owned or controlled directly or indirectly by such persons and associated persons and entities;
   (d) Prohibit their nationals or any persons and entities within their territories from making any funds, financial assets or economic resources or financial or other related services available, directly or indirectly, for the benefit of persons who commit or attempt to commit or facilitate or participate in the commission of terrorist acts, of entities owned or controlled, directly or indirectly, by such persons and of persons and entities acting on behalf of or at the direction of such persons;
   2. *Decides also* that all States shall:
   (a) Refrain from providing any form of support, active or passive, to entities or persons involved in terrorist acts, including by suppressing recruitment of members of terrorist groups and eliminating the supply of weapons to terrorists;
   (b) Take the necessary steps to prevent the commission of terrorist acts, including by provision of early warning to other States by exchange of information;
   (c) Deny safe haven to those who finance, plan, support, or commit terrorist acts, or provide safe havens;
   (d) Prevent those who finance, plan, facilitate or commit terrorist acts from using their respective territories for those purposes against other States or their citizens;
   (e) Ensure that any person who participates in the financing, planning, preparation or perpetration of terrorist acts or in supporting terrorist acts is brought to justice and ensure that, in addition to any other measures against them, such terrorist acts are established as serious criminal offences in domestic laws and regulations and that the punishment duly reflects the seriousness of such terrorist acts;

(f) Afford one another the greatest measure of assistance in connection with criminal investigations or criminal proceedings relating to the financing or support of terrorist acts, including assistance in obtaining evidence in their possession necessary for the proceedings;

(g) Prevent the movement of terrorists or terrorist groups by effective border controls and controls on issuance of identity papers and travel documents, and through measures for preventing counterfeiting, forgery or fraudulent use of identity papers and travel documents;

3. *Calls upon* all States to:

(a) Find ways of intensifying and accelerating the exchange of operational information, especially regarding actions or movements of terrorist persons or networks; forged or falsified travel documents; traffic in arms, explosives or sensitive materials; use of communications technologies by terrorist groups; and the threat posed by the possession of weapons of mass destruction by terrorist groups;

(b) Exchange information in accordance with international and domestic law and cooperate on administrative and judicial matters to prevent the commission of terrorist acts;

(c) Cooperate, particularly through bilateral and multilateral arrangements and agreements, to prevent and suppress terrorist attacks and take action against perpetrators of such acts;

(d) Become parties as soon as possible to the relevant international conventions and protocols relating to terrorism, including the International Convention for the Suppression of the Financing of Terrorism of 9 December 1999;

(e) Increase cooperation and fully implement the relevant international conventions and protocols relating to terrorism and Security Council resolutions 1269 (1999) and 1368 (2001);

(f) Take appropriate measures in conformity with the relevant provisions of national and international law, including international standards of human rights, before granting refugee status, for the purpose of ensuring that the asylum-seeker has not planned, facilitated or participated in the commission of terrorist acts;

(g) Ensure, in conformity with international law, that refugee status is not abused by the perpetrators, organizers or facilitators of terrorist acts, and that claims of political motivation are not recognized as grounds for refusing requests for the extradition of alleged terrorists;

4. *Notes with concern* the close connection between international terrorism and transnational organized crime, illicit drugs, money-laundering, illegal arms-trafficking, and illegal movement of nuclear, chemical, biological and other potentially deadly materials, and in this regard *emphasizes* the need to enhance coordination of efforts on national, sub-regional, regional and international levels in order to strengthen a global response to this serious challenge and threat to international security;

5. *Declares* that acts, methods, and practices of terrorism are contrary to the purposes and principles of the United Nations and that knowingly financing,

planning and inciting terrorist acts are also contrary to the purposes and principles of the United Nations;

6. *Decides* to establish, in accordance with rule 28 of its provisional rules of procedure, a Committee of the Security Council, consisting of all the members of the Council, to monitor implementation of this resolution, with the assistance of appropriate expertise, and calls upon all States to report to the Committee, no later than 90 days from the date of adoption of this resolution and thereafter according to a timetable to be proposed by the Committee, on the steps they have taken to implement this resolution;

7. *Directs* the Committee to delineate its tasks, submit a work programme within 30 days of the adoption of this resolution, and to consider the support it requires, in consultation with the Secretary-General;

8. *Expresses its determination* to take all necessary steps in order to ensure the full implementation of this resolution, in accordance with its responsibilities under the Charter; ...

Next came resolution 1540 (2004), passed in response to concerns over the proliferation of nuclear, chemical and biological weapons, in particular their acquisition by non-state actors posing terrorist threats.

SECURITY COUNCIL RESOLUTION 1540 (2004): NON-PROLIFERATION OF WEAPONS OF MASS DESTRUCTION

The Security Council, ...

Acting under Chapter VII of the Charter of the United Nations,

1. *Decides* that all States shall refrain from providing any form of support to non-State actors that attempt to develop, acquire, manufacture, possess, transport, transfer or use nuclear, chemical or biological weapons and their means of delivery;

2. *Decides also* that all States, in accordance with their national procedures, shall adopt and enforce appropriate effective laws which prohibit any non-State actor to manufacture, acquire, possess, develop, transport, transfer or use nuclear, chemical or biological weapons and their means of delivery, in particular for terrorist purposes, as well as attempts to engage in any of the foregoing activities, participate in them as an accomplice, assist or finance them;

3. *Decides also* that all States shall take and enforce effective measures to establish domestic controls to prevent the proliferation of nuclear, chemical, or biological weapons and their means of delivery, including by establishing appropriate controls over related materials and to this end shall:

(a) Develop and maintain appropriate effective measures to account for and secure such items in production, use, storage or transport;

(b) Develop and maintain appropriate effective physical protection measures;

(c) Develop and maintain appropriate effective border controls and law enforcement efforts to detect, deter, prevent and combat, including through international cooperation when necessary, the illicit trafficking and brokering in such items in accordance with their national legal authorities and legislation and consistent with international law;

(d) Establish, develop, review and maintain appropriate effective national export and trans-shipment controls over such items, including appropriate laws and regulations to control export, transit, trans-shipment and re-export and controls on providing funds and services related to such export and trans-shipment such as financing, and transporting that would contribute to proliferation, as well as establishing end-user controls; and establishing and enforcing appropriate criminal or civil penalties for violations of such export control laws and regulations;

4. *Decides* to establish, in accordance with rule 28 of its provisional rules of procedure, for a period of no longer than two years, a Committee of the Security Council, consisting of all members of the Council, which will, calling as appropriate on other expertise, report to the Security Council for its examination, on the implementation of this resolution, and to this end calls upon States to present a first report no later than six months from the adoption of this resolution to the Committee on steps they have taken or intend to take to implement this resolution;

5. *Decides* that none of the obligations set forth in this resolution shall be interpreted so as to conflict with or alter the rights and obligations of State Parties to the Nuclear Non-Proliferation Treaty, the Chemical Weapons Convention and the Biological and Toxin Weapons Convention or alter the responsibilities of the International Atomic Energy Agency or the Organization for the Prohibition of Chemical Weapons; ...

8. *Calls upon* all States:

(a) To promote the universal adoption and full implementation, and, where necessary, strengthening of multilateral treaties to which they are parties, whose aim is to prevent the proliferation of nuclear, biological or chemical weapons;

(b) To adopt national rules and regulations, where it has not yet been done, to ensure compliance with their commitments under the key multilateral nonproliferation treaties;

(c) To renew and fulfil their commitment to multilateral cooperation, in particular within the framework of the International Atomic Energy Agency, the Organization for the Prohibition of Chemical Weapons and the Biological and Toxin Weapons Convention, as important means of pursuing and achieving their common objectives in the area of non-proliferation and of promoting international cooperation for peaceful purposes;

(d) To develop appropriate ways to work with and inform industry and the public regarding their obligations under such laws.

This resolution was followed by resolution 1566 (2004), in which the Council proposed further generalized measures for combating terrorism and urged states to become party to the various law-making instruments on this issue. Introduced by Russia and adopted unanimously by the Security Council, it provides a definition of terrorism for the first time and calls on countries to prosecute terrorists and those who aid and abet terrorists. The resolution was inspired by the mass terror attack in Beslan, Ossetia, in which hundreds of students and their teachers were killed by Chechen separatists who had held them hostage in a school. It may have been given further impetus by terror attacks in the Sinai, which killed Israelis, Russians, and Egyptians.

SECURITY COUNCIL RESOLUTION 1566 (2004)

The Security Council, ...
   Acting under Chapter VII of the Charter of the United Nations, ...
   2. *Calls upon* States to cooperate fully in the fight against terrorism, especially with those States where or against whose citizens terrorist acts are committed, in accordance with their obligations under international law, in order to find, deny safe haven and bring to justice, on the basis of the principle to extradite or prosecute, any person who supports, facilitates, participates or attempts to participate in the financing, planning, preparation or commission of terrorist acts or provides safe havens;
   3. *Recalls* that criminal acts, including against civilians, committed with the intent to cause death or serious bodily injury, or taking of hostages, with the purpose to provoke a state of terror in the general public or in a group of persons or particular persons, intimidate a population or compel a government or an international organization to do or to abstain from doing any act, and all other acts which constitute offences within the scope of and as defined in the international conventions and protocols relating to terrorism, are under no circumstances justifiable by considerations of a political, philosophical, ideological, racial, ethnic, religious or other similar nature, and calls upon all States to prevent such acts and, if not prevented, to ensure that such acts are punished by penalties consistent with their grave nature;
   4. *Calls upon* all States to become party, as a matter of urgency, to the relevant international conventions and protocols whether or not they are a party to regional conventions on the matter;
   5. *Calls upon* Member States to cooperate fully on an expedited basis in resolving all outstanding issues with a view to adopting by consensus the draft comprehensive convention on international terrorism and the draft international convention for the suppression of acts of nuclear terrorism;

6. *Calls upon* relevant international, regional and sub-regional organizations to strengthen international cooperation in the fight against terrorism and to intensify their interaction with the United Nations and, in particular, the CTC with a view to facilitating full and timely implementation of resolution 1373 (2001);

7. *Requests* the CTC in consultation with relevant international, regional and sub-regional organizations and the United Nations bodies to develop a set of best practices to assist States in implementing the provisions of resolution 1373 (2001) related to the financing of terrorism;

8. *Directs* the CTC, as a matter of priority and, when appropriate, in close cooperation with relevant international, regional and sub-regional organizations to start visits to States, with the consent of the States concerned, in order to enhance the monitoring of the implementation of resolution 1373 (2001) and facilitate the provision of technical and other assistance for such implementation;

9. *Decides* to establish a working group consisted of all members of the Security Council to consider and submit recommendations to the Council on practical measures to be imposed upon individuals, groups or entities involved in or associated with terrorist activities, other than those designated by the Al-Qaida/Taliban Sanctions Committee, including more effective procedures considered to be appropriate for bringing them to justice through prosecution or extradition, freezing of their financial assets, preventing their movement through the territories of Member States, preventing supply to them of all types of arms and related material, and on the procedures for implementing these measures;

10. *Requests* further the working group, established under paragraph 9 to consider the possibility of establishing an international fund to compensate victims of terrorist acts and their families, which might be financed through voluntary contributions, which could consist in part of assets seized from terrorist organizations, their members and sponsors, and submit its recommendations to the Council; . . .

Concerns about the human rights consequences of counterterrorism measures adopted by the Security Council, in particular targeted financial sanctions, are discussed in chapter 13.

QUESTION

19. Is law making within the competence of the Security Council? If so, what are the limits on this competence? Can a Security Council resolution require UN members to comply with the terms of a treaty? Can it exempt member states from the terms of a treaty?

3.4 Law Making by the General Assembly

The Declaration on the Inadmissibility of Intervention in the Domestic Affairs of States and the Protection of their Independence and Sovereignty, passed in the 1408th plenary meeting, on 21 December 1965, was born out of the concern within the General Assembly at the increasing armed intervention and direct and indirect forms of interference by some states threatening the sovereign personality and political independence of others. It marked the first time that an instrument expressly provided against intervention by states in territories of other states; documents like the UN Charter had provided only against non-intervention by the United Nations in the domestic affairs of States (Article 2(7) of the UN Charter).

GENERAL ASSEMBLY RESOLUTION 2131(XX) (1965): DECLARATION ON THE INADMISSIBILITY OF INTERVENTION IN THE DOMESTIC AFFAIRS OF STATES AND THE PROTECTION OF THEIR INDEPENDENCE AND SOVEREIGNTY

The General Assembly, ...
    ...*solemnly declares*:
    1. No State has the right to intervene, directly or indirectly, for any reason whatever, in the internal or external affairs of any other State. Consequently, armed intervention and all other forms of interference or attempted threats against the personality of the State or against its political, economic and cultural elements, are condemned.
    2. No State may use or encourage the use of economic, political or any other type of measures to coerce another State in order to obtain from it the subordination of the exercise of its sovereign rights or to secure from it advantages of any kind. Also, no State shall organize, assist, foment, finance, incite or tolerate subversive, terrorist or armed activities directed towards the violent overthrow of the regime of another State, or interfere in civil strife in another State.
    3. The use of force to deprive peoples of their national identity constitutes a violation of their inalienable rights and of the principle of non-intervention. ...
    6. All States shall respect the right of self-determination and independence of peoples and nations, to be freely exercised without any foreign pressure, and with absolute respect for human rights and fundamental freedoms. Consequently, all States shall contribute to the complete elimination of racial discrimination and colonialism in all its forms and manifestations.

The principles embodied in this resolution have subsequently been recognized as customary international law (*Nicaragua*), but it is debatable whether the states that voted it into existence had visualized it as creating law. To quote the representative of the United States: "[We] view this declaration as a statement of attitude and policy, as a political declaration with a vital political message, not as a declaration or elaboration of the law governing non-intervention ... the Special Committee of the Assembly on the Principles of International Law concerning Friendly Relations and Cooperation among States has been given the precise job of enunciating that law. Thus, we leave the precise definition of law to the lawyers, and our vote on this resolution is without prejudice to the definition of the law we shall make in the Special Committee."[18]

Rosalyn Higgins, later a judge on the ICJ, saw the resolution as an example of lawmaking by the General Assembly;[19] but many others including Judge Stephen M. Schwebel, who reviewed her book, disagreed.[20]

Interestingly, while the Declaration had been adopted by an almost unanimous vote, with only Britain abstaining, the efforts to give the principles embodied in this Declaration greater legal standing met with opposition even within the Special Committee and negotiations proved unsuccessful for years afterwards.[21]

Note also that while the resolution addressed intervention in the domestic affairs of states, paragraph 3 addresses the rights of "peoples." What rights do "peoples" have in international law and under the charter? Who are the likely perpetrators of such "interventions" and what are the intended remedies available to "peoples"?

QUESTIONS

20. In General Assembly resolution 2131(XX) (1965), how can one reconcile the demand for sovereign inviolability in paragraph 1 with the apparently interventionist language of paragraph 6?

21. Are General Assembly resolutions sources of law? Does article 38(1) of the Statute of the International Court of Justice provide any guidance?

22. Does it matter whether a resolution is called a "resolution" or a "declaration"? Does it matter whether the resolution was passed unani-

---

[18] United Nations General Assembly, Twentieth Session, First Committee, Verbatim Record of the 143rd Meeting, A/C.1/PV. 1423, p. 12.

[19] Rosalyn Higgins, The Development of International Law Through the Political Organs of the United Nations (Oxford: Oxford University Press, 1963).

[20] Stephen M. Schwebel, "Book Review," Yale Law Journal, vol. 75 (1966), p. 677.

[21] See Robert Rosenstock, "The Declaration of Principles of International Law Governing Friendly Relations: A Survey," American Journal of International Law, vol. 65 (1971), p. 713.

mously, by consensus, or only by a majority vote? Do these affect its capacity to be a source of law?

3.5 Special Courts and Tribunals

In 1993 the Security Council used its Chapter VII powers to establish the International Criminal Tribunal for former Yugoslavia (ICTY), an ad hoc judicial forum empowered to prosecute "serious violations of international humanitarian law committed in the territory of the former Yugoslavia between 1 January 1991 and a date to be determined by the Security Council."[22] In 1994, it established a similar International Criminal Tribunal for Rwanda (ICTR).[23]

The establishment of a permanent International Criminal Court had been on the agenda of the United Nations for more than four decades. A 1948 resolution of the General Assembly had called upon the UN International Law Commission to "to study the desirability and possibility of establishing an international judicial organ for the trial of persons charged with genocide."[24] The efforts of the ILC however, bore fruit only in 1998, with the adoption of the Rome Statute of the International Criminal Court, which came into force in 2002.

Both resolutions 827 (1993) and 955 (1994) asserted that the action being taken was exceptional action, necessitated by the "particular circumstance" in these two cases, and the constitutive statutes were thus carefully drafted to limit the material and temporal jurisdiction of the two tribunals. At the same time, for matters falling within their jurisdiction the two tribunals were given primacy over national courts, a feature that has not been repeated in the Rome Statute.

What set the Yugoslav and Rwandan Tribunals apart was that they were established solely by a mandatory resolution of the Security Council. Even though the establishment of the ICTR was preceded by a request for a criminal tribunal from Rwanda,[25] its consent to the actually proposed structure was not required; and indeed resolution 955 (1994) was passed despite Rwanda's vote against it—cast in part because the tribunal was denied the option of imposing the death penalty on convicted offenders. The duty to cooperate was also imposed upon all the other member states of the United Nations.

While these two tribunals have been followed by a number of other international dispute settlement bodies of limited jurisdiction,[26] they continue

---

[22]SC Res. 827 (1993).

[23] SC Res. 955 (1994).

[24] GA Res. 260(III) (1948).

[25] UN Doc. S/1994/1115 (1994).

[26] Even after its establishment, the ICC has jurisdiction only to prosecute violations of humanitarian law committed after 1 July 2002: Statute of the International Criminal Court, art. 11.

to be the only international criminal tribunals based solely upon a Chapter VII resolution.

The other special courts and tribunals, such as the Special Court of Sierra Leone, the Iraqi Special Tribunal, and the Extraordinary Chambers for the Prosecution under Cambodian Law of Crimes Committed during the Period of Democratic Kampuchea, have been established either through agreement between the United Nations and the state government or by decision of occupying powers. Moreover, these bodies usually possess a more hybrid character, mingling international judges and personnel with judges who are citizens of the state whose nationals are being brought to trial.

The following excerpts highlight some important provisions of the Statute of the International Criminal Tribunal for Rwanda.

SECURITY COUNCIL RESOLUTION 955 (1994), ANNEX: STATUTE OF THE INTERNATIONAL TRIBUNAL FOR RWANDA

Article 1—Competence of the International Tribunal for Rwanda

The International Tribunal for Rwanda shall have the power to prosecute persons responsible for serious violations of international humanitarian law committed in the territory of Rwanda and Rwandan citizens responsible for such violations committed in the territory of neighbouring States, between 1 January 1994 and 31 December 1994, in accordance with the provisions of the present Statute. ...

Article 6—Individual Criminal Responsibility

1. A person who planned, instigated, ordered, committed or otherwise aided and abetted in the planning, preparation or execution of a crime referred to in articles 2 to 4 of the present Statute, shall be individually responsible for the crime.

2. The official position of any accused person, whether as Head of State or Government or as a responsible Government official, shall not relieve such person of criminal responsibility nor mitigate punishment.

3. The fact that any of the acts referred to in articles 2 to 4 of the present Statute was committed by a subordinate does not relieve his or her superior of criminal responsibility if he or she knew or had reason to know that the subordinate was about to commit such acts or had done so and the superior failed to take the necessary and reasonable measures to prevent such acts or to punish the perpetrators thereof.

4. The fact that an accused person acted pursuant to an order of a Government or of a superior shall not relieve him or her of criminal responsibility,

but may be considered in mitigation of punishment if the International Tribunal for Rwanda determines that justice so requires. ...

Article 8—Concurrent Jurisdiction

1. The International Tribunal for Rwanda and national courts shall have concurrent jurisdiction to prosecute persons for serious violations of international humanitarian law committed in the territory of Rwanda and Rwandan citizens for such violations committed in the territory of neighbouring States, between 1 January 1994 and 31 December 1994.

2. The International Tribunal for Rwanda shall have primacy over the national courts of all States. At any stage of the procedure, the International Tribunal for Rwanda may formally request national courts to defer to its competence in accordance with the present Statute and the Rules of Procedure and Evidence of the International Tribunal for Rwanda.

Article 9—Non bis in idem

1. No person shall be tried before a national court for acts constituting serious violations of international humanitarian law under the present Statute, for which he or she has already been tried by the International Tribunal for Rwanda.

2. A person who has been tried by a national court for acts constituting serious violations of international humanitarian law may be subsequently tried by the International Tribunal for Rwanda only if:

(a) The act for which he or she was tried was characterized as an ordinary crime; or

(b) The national court proceedings were not impartial or independent, were designed to shield the accused from international criminal responsibility, or the case was not diligently prosecuted.

3. In considering the penalty to be imposed on a person convicted of a crime under the present Statute, the International Tribunal for Rwanda shall take into account the extent to which any penalty imposed by a national court on the same person for the same act has already been served. ...

Article 15—The Prosecutor

1. The Prosecutor shall be responsible for the investigation and prosecution of persons responsible for serious violations of international humanitarian law committed in the territory of Rwanda and Rwandan citizens responsible for such violations committed in the territory of neighbouring States, between 1 January 1994 and 31 December 1994.

2. The Prosecutor shall act independently as a separate organ of the International Tribunal for Rwanda. He or she shall not seek or receive instructions from any Government or from any other source.

3. The Prosecutor of the International Tribunal for the Former Yugoslavia shall also serve as the Prosecutor of the International Tribunal for Rwanda. He or she shall have additional staff, including an additional Deputy Prosecutor, to assist with prosecutions before the International Tribunal for Rwanda. Such staff shall be appointed by the Secretary-General on the recommendation of the Prosecutor. ...

Article 17—Investigation and Preparation of Indictment

1. The Prosecutor shall initiate investigations ex-officio or on the basis of information obtained from any source, particularly from Governments, United Nations organs, intergovernmental and non-governmental organizations.

The Prosecutor shall assess the information received or obtained and decide whether there is sufficient basis to proceed.

2. The Prosecutor shall have the power to question suspects, victims and witnesses, to collect evidence and to conduct on-site investigations. In carrying out these tasks, the Prosecutor may, as appropriate, seek the assistance of the State authorities concerned.

3. If questioned, the suspect shall be entitled to be assisted by counsel of his or her own choice, including the right to have legal assistance assigned to the suspect without payment by him or her in any such case if he or she does not have sufficient means to pay for it, as well as to necessary translation into and from a language he or she speaks and understands.

4. Upon a determination that a prima facie case exists, the Prosecutor shall prepare an indictment containing a concise statement of the facts and the crime or crimes with which the accused is charged under the Statute. The indictment shall be transmitted to a judge of the Trial Chamber. ...

Article 21—Protection of Victims and Witnesses

The International Tribunal for Rwanda shall provide in its rules of procedure and evidence for the protection of victims and witnesses. Such protection measures shall include, but shall not be limited to, the conduct of in camera proceedings and the protection of the victim's identity. ...

Article 26—Enforcement of Sentences

Imprisonment shall be served in Rwanda or any of the States on a list of States which have indicated to the Security Council their willingness to accept convicted persons, as designated by the International Tribunal for Rwanda. Such imprisonment shall be in accordance with the applicable law of the State concerned, subject to the supervision of the International Tribunal for Rwanda.

Article 27—Pardon or Commutation
of Sentences

If, pursuant to the applicable law of the State in which the convicted person is imprisoned, he or she is eligible for pardon or commutation of sentence, the State concerned shall notify the International Tribunal for Rwanda accordingly. There shall only be pardon or commutation of sentence if the President of the International Tribunal for Rwanda, in consultation with the judges, so decides on the basis of the interests of justice and the general principles of law.

Article 28—Cooperation and Judicial Assistance

1. States shall cooperate with the International Tribunal for Rwanda in the investigation and prosecution of persons accused of committing serious violations of international humanitarian law.
2. States shall comply without undue delay with any request for assistance or an order issued by a Trial Chamber, including, but not limited to:
 (a) The identification and location of persons;
 (b) The taking of testimony and the production of evidence;
 (c) The service of documents;
 (d) The arrest or detention of persons;
 (e) The surrender or the transfer of the accused to the International Tribunal for Rwanda.

The resolution establishing the International Tribunal for Rwanda was followed by statements from members of the Security Council explaining the reasons for their positions. All members with the exception of Rwanda and China voted in favor of the resolution. China abstained; Rwanda voted against the resolution.

Many members clarified that they voted for the ICTR because they viewed it as an ad hoc measure justified only by the exceptional nature of the circumstances and the urgency required by the situation in Rwanda. A number stressed that the setting up of this Tribunal and the Tribunal for Yugoslavia should not be seen as constituting precedent for the future.

Article 28(2)(e) Statute of the Tribunal for Rwanda provides that States shall comply without undue delay with any request for assistance or an order issued by a Trial Chamber, including the surrender or the transfer of the accused to the Tribunal. Based on this a request was made to the United States to surrender Mr. Elizaphan Ntakirutimana, a seventy-three-year-old Rwandan Hutu residing in Laredo, Texas. As the former President of the Seventh Day Adventist Church in Rwanda, he was charged with luring several ethnic

Tutsis to his church complex at Mugonero and then organizing and leading an attack to kill these Tutsis. He was also accused of leading armed bands of men into the countryside of the Bisesero region to hunt down and kill those Tutsis who survived the attack at Mugonero. On 26 September 1996, he was provisionally arrested on the above charges. The Clinton Administration requested the District Court for the Southern District of Texas, Laredo Division, to authorize his surrender to the International Criminal Tribunal for Rwanda. The District Court refused to grant this request. J. Marcel C Notzon, who delivered the judgment, held that such surrender was not possible in the absence of an extradition treaty between the United States and the Tribunal. He waived aside all claims that Section 18 USC 3181(b) (1996) allows fugitives other than citizens, nationals, or permanent residents to be extradited without treaty in certain circumstances, holding that in practice this section was always construed as requiring a treaty of extradition to be in existence. Furthermore, he refused to accept the Agreement on Surrender of Persons between the Government of the United States and the International Tribunal, signed in January 1995, as a "treaty" of extradition. Finally, he also found the evidence insufficient to demonstrate to the Court probable cause to believe that Ntakirutimana had participated in the attacks at Mugonero and Bisesero.[27]

Following this decision, the Government filed a second request for surrender in the same court. To address the evidentiary issues raised by the Magistrate Judge, the Government added two declarations. The district court certified the surrender to the International Criminal Tribunal for Rwanda, holding that the Agreement and the act incorporating it into US law provided a constitutional basis for the extradition of Ntakirutimana. Among other reasons, the court found that the Constitution sets forth no specific requirements for extradition, that the Supreme Court has indicated its approval of extraditions made in the absence of a treaty, and that there is precedent wherein fugitives were extradited pursuant to statutes that "filled the gap" left by a treaty provision. The court also held that the evidence sufficed to establish probable cause for the charges against Ntakirutimana. Ntakirutimana filed a petition for a writ of habeas corpus under 28 USC § 2241. The district court denied the petition, after which Ntakirutimana filed the present appeal before the Court of Appeals for the Fifth Circuit alleging that the district court erred because (1) the Constitution of the United States requires an Article II treaty for the surrender of a person to the ICTR, (2) the request for surrender does not establish probable cause, (3) the UN Charter does not authorize the Security Council to establish the ICTR, and (4) the ICTR is not capable of protecting fundamental rights guaranteed by the United States Constitution and international law.

---

[27] In the Matter of Surrender of Elizaphan Ntakirutimana, 988 F. Supp. 1038 (1997).

ELIZAPHAN NTAKIRUTIMANA V. JANET RENO, ATTORNEY GENERAL OF THE UNITED STATES; AND OTHERS, 184 F.3D 419 (5TH CIR., 1999)

... To determine whether a treaty is required to extradite Ntakirutimana, we turn to the text of the Constitution. Ntakirutimana contends that Article II, Section 2, Clause 2 of the Constitution requires a treaty to extradite ... This provision does not refer either to extradition or to the necessity of a treaty to extradite. The Supreme Court has explained, however, that "the power to surrender is clearly included within the treaty-making power and the corresponding power of appointing and receiving ambassadors and other public ministers." *Terlinden v. Ames* ... (1902).

Yet, the Court has found that the Executive's power to surrender fugitives is not unlimited. In *Valentine v. United States* ... (1936), the Supreme Court ... stated that the power to provide for extradition is a national power that "is not confided to the Executive in the absence of treaty or legislative provision." ...

Valentine indicates that a court should look to whether a treaty *or statute* grants executive discretion to extradite. Hence, *Valentine* supports the constitutionality of using the Congressional-Executive Agreement to extradite Ntakirutimana ... Thus, although some authorization by law is necessary for the Executive to extradite, neither the Constitution's text nor *Valentine* require that the authorization come in the form of a treaty.

Notwithstanding the Constitution's text or *Valentine*, Ntakirutimana argues that the intent of the drafters of the Constitution supports his interpretation. He alleges that the delegates to the Constitutional Convention intentionally placed the Treaty power exclusively in the President and the Senate. The delegates designed this arrangement because they wanted a single executive agent to negotiate agreements with foreign powers, and they wanted the senior House of Congress—the Senate—to review the agreements to serve as a check on the executive branch. Ntakirutimana also claims that the rejection of alternative proposals suggests that the framers believed that a treaty is the only means by which the United States can enter into a binding agreement with a foreign nation.

We are unpersuaded by Ntakirutimana's extended discussion of the Constitution's history. Ntakirutimana does not cite to any provision in the Constitution or any aspect of its history that requires a treaty to extradite. Ntakirutimana's argument, which is not specific to extradition, is premised on the assumption that a treaty is required for an international agreement. To the contrary, "the Constitution, while expounding procedural requirements for treaties alone, apparently contemplates alternate modes of international agreements." Laurence H. Tribe, American Constitutional Law § 4-5, at 228-29 (2d edn. 1988); ... "The Supreme Court has recognized that of necessity the President may enter into certain binding agreements with foreign nations not strictly congruent with the formalities required by the Constitution's Treaty Clause;" *United States v. Walczaky*(9th Cir. 1986). . . .

Ntakirutimana next argues that historical practice establishes that a treaty is required to extradite. According to Ntakirutimana, the United States has never surrendered a person except pursuant to an Article II treaty, and the only involuntary transfers without an extradition treaty have been to "a foreign country or territory occupied by or under the control of the United States." *Valentine* . . . This argument fails for numerous reasons. First, *Valentine* did not suggest that this "historical practice" limited Congress's power. Second, the Supreme Court's statements that a statute may confer the power to extradite also reflect a historical understanding of the Constitution. Even if Congress has rarely exercised the power to extradite by statute, a historical understanding exists nonetheless that it may do so. Third, in some instances in which a fugitive would not have been extraditable under a treaty, a fugitive has been extradited pursuant to a statute that "filled the gap" in the treaty. . . . Thus, we are unconvinced that the President's practice of usually submitting a negotiated treaty to the Senate reflects a historical understanding that a treaty is required to extradite.

We are unpersuaded by Ntakirutimana's other arguments. First, he asserts that the failure to require a treaty violates the Constitution's separation of powers. He contends that if a treaty is not required, then "the President alone could make dangerous agreements with foreign governments" or "Congress could legislate foreign affairs." This argument is not relevant to an Executive-Congressional agreement, which involves neither the President acting unilaterally nor Congress negotiating with foreign countries. Second, Ntakirutimana argues that "statutes cannot usurp the Treaty making power of Article II." The Supreme Court, however, has held that statutes can usurp a treaty. This is confirmed by the "last in time" rule that, if a statute and treaty are inconsistent, then the last in time will prevail. This rule explicitly contemplates that a statute and a treaty may at times cover the same subject matter. Third, Ntakirutimana contends that not requiring a treaty reads the treaty-making power out of the Constitution. Yet, the treaty-making power remains unaffected, because the President may still elect to submit a negotiated treaty to the Senate, instead of submitting legislation to Congress. Thus, we conclude that it is not unconstitutional to surrender Ntakirutimana to the ICTR pursuant to the Executive-Congressional Agreement.

Ntakirutimana contends next that the district court erred in dismissing his habeas petition because the request for surrender fails to establish probable cause. The Agreement with the International Criminal Tribunal for Rwanda requires that the Tribunal present "information sufficient to establish that there is a reasonable basis to believe that the person sought has committed the violation or violations for which surrender is requested." . . .

The evidence at the extradition hearing consisted of several documents, all of which were admissible . . . Along with the first request for surrender, the Government included a declaration from Arjen Mostert, who served for six months as a Tribunal investigator. Mostert obtained the declarations of twelve witnesses, labeled A-L to protect their identities, who survived the Mugonero and Bisesero massacres. Mostert declared that the witnesses were ordinary citizens and did not receive consideration for their testimony. The witnesses, all of whom were familiar with Ntakirutimana, described seeing him at the massacre or leading the soldiers in search of Tutsis at Bisesero. The witnesses' statements corroborated one another, and many of the witnesses positively identified a photograph of Ntakirutimana. When the Magistrate Judge denied the first request for surrender, he found Mostert's affidavit alone insufficient to provide probable cause to support the charges. ...

In response to the Magistrate Judge's concerns, the Government added a supplemental declaration of Mostert with its second request for surrender. The second request also included the declaration of Pierre-Richard Prosper, the assistant prosecutor for the International Criminal Tribunal for Rwanda. Prosper further clarified the information in Mostert's initial declaration. The district court stated that the supplemental declarations satisfactorily responded to the Magistrate Judge's earlier objections. The district court concluded that probable cause existed to sustain the charges against Ntakirutimana. ...

Ntakirutimana argues that the district court erred. He contends that the Tribunal has not presented evidence sufficient to show probable cause, because the allegations in Mostert's declarations "lack probative force and are unreliable." Ntakirutimana primarily raises credibility challenges to the evidence against him. Yet, the issue of credibility "is a matter committed to the magistrate and is not reviewable on habeas corpus." *Escobedo*. ...

... In short, the district court resolved the credibility challenges adversely to Ntakirutimana, and we will not review those issues. We hold that, based on Mostert's and Prosper's declarations, there is competent evidence in the record to support the district court's finding that the evidence established probable cause to believe that Ntakirutimana committed the crimes charged. ...

Finally, we turn to Ntakirutimana's remaining arguments. Ntakirutimana argues that the UN Charter does not authorize the Security Council to establish the International Criminal Tribunal for Rwanda, and that the only method for the UN to create an international criminal tribunal is by a multinational treaty. This issue is beyond the scope of habeas review ...

Ntakirutimana contends additionally that the International Criminal Tribunal for Rwanda is incapable of protecting his rights under the United States Constitution and international law. He contends, for example, that the [Tribunal] is incapable of protecting his due process rights and that the [Tribunal] denies the right to be represented by the counsel of one's choice. Due to the limited scope of habeas review, we will not inquire into the procedures that await Ntakirutimana.

For the foregoing reasons, we AFFIRM the order of the district court denying Ntakirutimana's petition for a writ of habeas corpus, and LIFT the stay of extradition.

Special Concurrence of J. Robert M. Parker

I write separately and briefly to invite the Secretary to closely scrutinize the underlying evidence as she makes her decision regarding whether Ntakirutimana should be surrendered to the International Criminal Tribunal for Rwanda. The evidence supporting the request is highly suspect. Affidavits of unnamed Tutsi witnesses acquired during interviews utilizing questionable interpreters in a political environment that has all the earmarks of a campaign of tribal retribution raises serious questions regarding the truth of their content. ...

I fully understand that the ultimate decision in this case may well be a political one that is driven by important considerations of State that transcend the question of guilt or innocence of any single individual. I respect the political process that necessarily is implicated in this case, just as I respect the fact that adherence to precedent compels my concurrence.

Dissenting Opinion of J. Harold R. DeMoss

... A structural reading of the Constitution compels the conclusion that most international agreements must be ratified according to the Treaty Clause of Article II. The history of national and international practice indicate that extradition agreements fall into this category. ...

The Constitution's treaty procedure must be followed in order to ratify an extradition agreement which contractually binds our nation to respect obligations to another nation. The intent of the framers could not be clearer on this point ... The Founders were especially concerned with the possibility that, in the conduct of foreign policy, American officials might become seduced by their foreign counterparts or a President might actually betray the country. Thus, while primary responsibility for foreign affairs was given to the President, a significant restraint and "check" on the use of the treaty power was created by requiring for treaties the advice and consent of two-thirds of the Senate. ... The decision to require approval of two-thirds of Senators was controversial and hotly debated, but it was ultimately decided that sheer importance of the treaty power merited such a treatment. Treaties cannot be accomplished by any means other than the Article II treaty ratification procedure.

Of course, not all agreements with foreign countries require the full Article II "treaty" treatment in order to be effective. The Constitution implicitly recognizes a hierarchy of arrangements with foreign countries, of which treaties are the most sacrosanct ... The Attorney General's primary argument in defense of the enforceability of the extradition agreement with the Tribunal follows this line of thought. She has argued, and the majority echoes ... that the Constitution contains no explicit reference to extradition.

But the fact of the matter is that while the Constitution has no provisions explicitly relating to extradition, it likewise has no provisions explicitly relating to executive agreements. It only mentions treaties. Our national government is one of limited, enumerated powers ... All agree that the Surrender Agreement is not a treaty. We are therefore left to read between the lines to ascertain whether the President and Congress have wrongfully attempted by ordinary legislative procedures, to exercise a power governed by the Treaty Clause or whether some source of power other than the Treaty Clause enables the President and Congress to bind the country to the Surrender Agreement. ...

If the Treaty Clause is to have any meaning there is some variety of agreements which *must* be accomplished through the formal Article II process. Otherwise, the heightened consideration dictated by Article II could be avoided by the President and a majority of Congress simply by substituting the label of "executive agreement" for that of "treaty." ...

Plainly, an extradition agreement is a type of agreement historically found in a treaty and therefore governed by the Treaty Clause. Extradition, which is defined as "the surrender by one nation to another of an individual accused or convicted of an offense outside of its own territory, and within the territorial jurisdiction of the other, which, being competent to try and to punish him, demands the surrender," *Terlinden v. Ames* ... (1902), has usually been regarded as the proper subject of negotiation and treaty. Historically, the United States has not surrendered a person to a foreign authority (excluding countries or territories controlled by the United States) in the absence of a valid extradition treaty. The original extradition statutes, enacted in 1848, required the existence of an extradition treaty, and there was no exception until § 1342 was passed to accommodate the Tribunals for Rwanda and the former Yugoslavia. Furthermore, "the principles of international law recognize no *right* to extradition apart from treaty." *Factor v. Laubenheimer* ... (1933). ...

Notably, the United States has publicly declared to the entire world that it can only enter into an extradition agreement through a treaty. In its fifth reservation to the Convention on the Prevention and Punishment of the Crime of Genocide, Dec. 9, 1948, 78 UNTS 277, the United States proclaimed to the international diplomatic community that it "reserves the right to effect its participation in any such tribunal only by a treaty entered into specifically for that purpose with the advice and consent of the Senate." ...

The Attorney General and my colleagues in the majority place great reliance on *Valentine* ... *Valentine* was a case that did involve a treaty—its stray reference to "legislative provision" is pure dicta, and certainly not a plain holding that extradition may be accomplished by the President simply on the basis of congressional approval. Likewise, in *Terlinden v. Ames* ... (1902), ... there was also a valid extradition treaty, and the reference to a "legislative provision" is again dicta. ...

... The extradition agreement in place between the United States and the Tribunal is unenforceable, as it has not been properly ratified. The agreement's implementing legislation is unconstitutional insofar as it purports to ratify the Surrender Agreement by a means other than that prescribed by the Treaty Clause. The two acts seek impermissibly to evade the mandatory constitutional route for implementing such an agreement. I therefore respectfully dissent.

In February 2003, the International Criminal Tribunal for Rwanda found Ntakirutimana guilty of aiding and abetting genocide. He was sentenced to ten years' imprisonment.

QUESTIONS

23. Do member states of the United Nations have a legal obligation to surrender persons charged with an offense under the Security Council resolution establishing the Yugoslav and Rwandan tribunals? Does this obligation apply whether or not the state voted for these resolutions? Under what provision of the Charter is such an obligation made mandatory?

24. The rules of the tribunals do not permit national courts to review the indictments of the tribunals for adequacy, such power being given exclusively to a panel of the tribunals' judges charged with confirming the indictments after a review for probable cause. The duty to surrender also extends to citizens of the state from which the surrender is sought. Is this an appropriate division of power between international and national judiciaries?

25. In view of the method by which the Yugoslav and Rwandan tribunals were established, why did the Security Council not simply adopt the Rome Statute (establishing the International Criminal Court and its jurisdiction) as a mandatory (Chapter VII) resolution binding on all members, thereby alleviating the problems caused by some states' reluctance to ratify that treaty?

Further Reading

de Wet, Erika. *The Chapter VII Powers of the United Nations Security Council.* Oxford: Hart Publishing, 2004.

Franck, Thomas M. "Collective Security and UN Reform: Between the Necessary and the Possible." *Chicago Journal of International Law,* vol. 6 (2006), p. 597.

Gerber, Michael. "The Anti-Terrorism Act of 1987: Sabotaging the United Nations and Holding the Constitution Hostage." *New York University Law Review,* vol. 53 (1990), p. 364.

Klabbers, Jan. "The Concept of Legal Personality." *Ius Gentium,* vol. 11 (2005), p. 35.

Klarevas, Louis. "The Surrender of Alleged War Criminals to International Tribunals: Examining the Constitutionality of Extradition via Congressional-Executive Agreement." *UCLA Journal of International and Foreign Affairs,* vol. 8 (2003), p. 77.

Malone, David M., ed. *The UN Security Council: From the Cold War to the 21st Century.* Boulder, CO: Lynne Rienner, 2004.

Nijman, Janne Elisabeth. *The Concept of International Legal Personality: An Inquiry into the History and Theory of International Law.* The Hague: TMC Asser, 2004.

Sands, Philippe, and Pierre Klein. *Bowett's Law of International Institutions.* London: Sweet & Maxwell, 2001.

Scott, Craig, et al. "A Memorial For Bosnia: Framework of Legal Arguments Concerning the Lawfulness of the Maintenance of the United Nations Security Council's Arms Embargo on Bosnia and Herzegovina." *Michigan Journal of International Law,* vol. 16 (1994), p. 1.

Talmon, Stefan A. "The Security Council as World Legislature." *American Journal of International Law,* vol. 99 (2005), p. 175.

Vagts, Detlev F. "The United States and Its Treaties: Observance and Breach." *American Journal of International Law,* vol. 95 (2001), p. 313.

chapter four
....

The Secretary-General and the Secretariat[1]

The UN Charter defines the Secretary-General as "chief administrative officer" of the United Nations Organization, a capacity in which he or she serves the Security Council, the General Assembly, and the Economic and Social Council, as well as performing "such other functions as are entrusted to him by these organs."[2] At the same time, the Secretary-General is granted significant institutional and personal independence: the Secretariat he or she leads is itself a principal organ of the United Nations; the Secretary-General and the staff serve as international officials responsible only to the Organization; and member states undertake "to respect the exclusively international character of the responsibilities of the Secretary-General and the staff and not to seek to influence them in the discharge of their responsibilities."[3]

In practice, then, the Secretary-General and the Secretariat are set up to play two distinct roles. One is as a service staff to facilitate the United Nations' effective functioning as a continuously operating interstatal conference of governments. The other function is to administer the Organization in such a way as to effectuate its stated goals—which, at any particular moment, may or may not coincide with the interests of any particular member. These separate functions, combined in a single principal organ of the United Nations, create a dynamic tension. This chapter explores that tension through the original conception of the role of Secretary-General, challenges to the exercise of his discretionary powers in a case decided by the UN Administrative Tribunal, efforts to reform the Secretariat, and the innovative and important role of the Secretary-General's "good offices."

---

[1] Before reading this chapter, it may be helpful to re-read the *Reparations* case advisory opinion in chapter 3. Consider the effect of that opinion on the status and independence of the Secretary–General and Secretariat of the Organization.

[2] UN Charter, arts. 97–98.

[3] UN Charter, art. 100.

4.1 Secretary or General?

The Secretary-General of the United Nations is a unique figure in world politics. At once the world's senior diplomat, servant of the UN Security Council (and member states more generally), and commander-in-chief of up to a hundred thousand peacekeepers, he or she depends on states for both the legitimacy and resources that enable the United Nations to function. The tension between these roles—of being secretary or general—has challenged every incumbent. The first, the Norwegian Trygve Lie (1946–1952), memorably welcomed his successor to New York's Idlewild Airport with the words: "You are about to enter the most impossible job on this earth."

··

REPORT OF THE PREPARATORY COMMISSION OF THE UNITED NATIONS, 23 DECEMBER 1945[4]

8. The principal functions assigned to the Secretary-General, explicitly or by inference, by the Charter, may be grouped under six headings: general administrative and executive functions, technical functions, financial functions, the organization and administration of the International Secretariat, political functions and representational functions.

9. Many of the Secretary-General's duties will naturally be delegated, in greater or lesser degree, to members of his staff and particularly to his higher officials. But the execution of these duties must be subject to his supervision and control; the ultimate responsibility remains his alone.

10. The Secretary-General is the "chief administrative officer of the Organization" (Article 97) and Secretary-General of the General Assembly, the Security Council, the Economic and Social Council and the Trusteeship Council (Article 93). Certain specific duties of a more narrowly administrative character derived from these provisions are indicated in the Charter (for example, in Articles 12 and 20, and in Article 98, the last sentence of which requires the Secretary-General to present an annual report to the General Assembly on the work of the Organization) and in the Statute of the International Court of Justice (Articles 5 and 15).

11. Further specific duties falling under this head, many of which will no doubt be defined in the Rules of Procedure of the various principal organs concerned and their subsidiary bodies, relate to the preparation of the agenda

---

[4] Report of the Preparatory Commission of the United Nations (23 December 1945), Chapter VIII, section 2, paras. 8–17, reprinted in Simon Chesterman (ed.), *Secretary or General? The UN Secretary-General in World Politics* (Cambridge: Cambridge University Press, 2007), pp. 243–245.

and the convocation of sessions, the provision of the necessary staff, and the preparation of the minutes and other documents.

12. The Secretary-General also has administrative and executive duties of a wider character. He is the channel of all communication with the United Nations or any of its organs. He must endeavour, within the scope of his functions, to integrate the activity of the whole complex of United Nations organs and see that the machine runs smoothly and efficiently. He is responsible, moreover, for the preparation of the work of the various organs and for the execution of their decisions, in cooperation with the Members.

13. The last-mentioned functions of the Secretary-General have technical as well as administrative aspects. More particularly as regards the work of the Economic and Social Council and the Trusteeship Council, the expert technical assistance which the Secretary-General is able to provide, and which he himself must control, will clearly affect the degree in which these organs can achieve their purposes.

14. Under the Charter, the Secretary-General has wide responsibilities in connexion with the financial administration of the United Nations; and it may be assumed that, under the financial regulations which will be established by the General Assembly, he will be made primarily responsible for preparing the budget, for allocating funds, for controlling expenditure, for administering such financial and budgetary arrangements as the General Assembly may enter into with specialized agencies, for collecting contributions from Members and for the custodianship of all funds.

15. The Secretary-General is the head of the Secretariat. He appoints all staff under regulations established by the General Assembly (Article 101, paragraphs 1 and 5), and assigns appropriate staff to the various organs of the United Nations (Article 101, paragraph 2). He alone is responsible to the other principal organs for the Secretariat's work; his choice of staff—more particularly of higher staff—and his leadership will largely determine the character and the efficiency of the Secretariat as a whole. It is on him that will mainly fall the duty of creating and maintaining a team spirit in a body of officials recruited from many countries. His moral authority within the Secretariat will depend at once upon the example he gives of the qualities prescribed in Article 100, and upon the confidence shown in him by the Members of the United Nations.

16. The Secretary-General may have an important role to play as a mediator and as an informal adviser of many governments, and will undoubtedly be called upon from time to time, in the exercise of his administrative duties, to take decisions which may justly be called political. Under Article 99 of the Charter, moreover, he has been given a quite special right which goes beyond any power previously accorded to the head of an international organization, viz: to bring to the attention of the Security Council any matter (not merely any dispute or situation) which, in his opinion, may threaten the maintenance of international peace and security. It is impossible to foresee how this Article will be applied; but the responsibility it confers upon the Secretary-General will require the exercise of the highest qualities of political judgement, tact and integrity.

17. The United Nations cannot prosper, nor can its aims be realized, without the active and steadfast support of the peoples of the world. The aims and activities of the General Assembly, the Security Council, the Economic and Social Council and the Trusteeship Council will, no doubt, be represented before the public primarily by the Chairmen of these organs. But the Secretary-General, more than anyone else, will stand for the United Nations as a whole. In the eyes of the world, no less than in the eyes of his own staff, he must embody the principles and ideals of the Charter to which the Organization seeks to give effect.

Article 97 of the UN Charter provides that the Secretary-General shall be appointed by the General Assembly upon the recommendation of the Security Council. The Council has only ever recommended one person and the Assembly has always accepted that recommendation.[5]

GENERAL ASSEMBLY RESOLUTION 11(I) (1946)

Terms of Appointment of the Secretary-General

The General Assembly resolves that, in view of the heavy responsibilities which rest upon the Secretary-General in fulfilling his obligations under the Charter:

1. The terms of the appointment of the Secretary-General shall be such as to enable a man of eminence and high attainment to accept and maintain the position.

2. The Secretary-General shall receive a salary of an amount sufficient to bring him in a net sum of $20,000 (US), together with representation allowance of $20,000 (US), per annum. In addition, he shall be provided with a furnished residence, the repairs and maintenance of which, excluding provision of household staff, shall be borne by the Organization.

3. The first Secretary-General shall be appointed for five years, the appointment being open at the end of that period for a further five-year term.

4. The following observations contained in paragraphs 18–21 of section 2, chapter VIII of the Preparatory Commission's Report be noted and approved:

(a) There being no stipulation on the subject in the Charter, the General Assembly and the Security Council are free to modify the term of office of future Secretaries-General in the light of experience.

(b) Because a Secretary-General is a confident [*sic*] of many governments, it is desirable that no Member should offer him, at any rate immediately on

---

[5] The only exception to this is the 1950 deadlock of the Council that led the General Assembly to decide in a majority vote to extend the term of Secretary-General Trygve Lie without a recommendation from the Council: GA Res. 492(V) (1950).

retirement, any governmental position in which his confidential information might be a source of embarrassment to other Members, and on his part a Secretary-General should refrain from accepting any such position.

(c) From the provisions of Articles 18 and 27 of the Charter, it is clear that, for the nomination of the Secretary-General by the Security Council, an affirmative vote of [nine][6] members, including the concurring votes of the permanent Members, is required; and that for his appointment by the General Assembly, a simple majority of the members of that body present and voting is sufficient, unless the General Assembly itself decides that a two-thirds majority is called for. The same rules apply to a renewal of appointment as to an original appointment; this should be made clear when the original appointment is made.

(d) It would be desirable for the Security Council to proffer one candidate only for the consideration of the General Assembly, and for debate on the nomination in the General Assembly to be avoided. Both nomination and appointment should be discussed at private meetings, and a vote in either the Security Council or the General Assembly, if taken, should be by secret ballot.

QUESTIONS

1. How might one define the job description of the position of Secretary-General?
2. Why did the General Assembly suggest that it would be desirable that the Security Council recommend only one candidate for Secretary-General? What other methods of selection might be possible?
3. The term of office of the Secretary-General is usually five years, with the possibility of a second term of the same length. Would it help protect the independence of the incumbent if his or her term were longer (say, seven years) and not renewable? Why, or why not?
4. The Secretary-General fulfills many of the ceremonial functions of a head of state, together with the policy making and administrative functions of a head of government. Would it be possible and desirable to divide these functions between different positions? Kofi Annan, in his second term, tried to move in this direction by appointing a Deputy Secretary-General to be in charge of the administrative structure of the Secretariat. Would you expect such a reform to succeed?
5. Should the Secretary-General be more of a "secretary" or more of a "general"?

---

[6] Prior to expansion of the Security Council in 1965, decisions of the Council adopted under Article 27 required seven votes.

4.2 The United Nations Administrative Tribunal

The UN Administrative Tribunal (UNAT) was established by the General Assembly through resolution 351A(IV) (1949). It is an independent organ competent to hear and pass judgment upon applications alleging non-observance of contracts or terms of employment by staff members of the UN Secretariat.

The competence of the Tribunal extends to the secretariats of the Programmes and Funds, such specialized agencies and related organizations that have accepted the competence of the Tribunal (the International Maritime Organization (IMO) and the International Civil Aviation Organization (ICAO)), the staff of the Registries of the International Court of Justice, the International Tribunal for the Law of the Sea, and the staff of the International Seabed Authority.

In the *Chinese Translators* case, which dealt with the question of re-appointment of three Chinese Verbatim Reporters ("Applicants") employed in the Department of Conference Services (DCS), the UNAT discusses the appropriate role of the Secretary-General in staffing matters, as well as the considerations relevant for employment in the civil services of the United Nations.

All three Applicants had been recruited for five year terms beginning in September 1984. Their contracts stated as a special condition that they were "on secondment from the Government of China." During these five years, they had "very good" or higher performance reports and had been promoted one level. On 1 May 1989, the Administrative Officer of the DCS had requested the Office of Human Resources Management (OHRM) to grant "probationary appointments" to the Applicants (laying the ground for them to achieve permanent status as UN employees). On 11 August 1989, the Secretary-General instead submitted a request to the Chinese Government to grant the Applicants a two-year extension. The Chinese Government replied on 23 August 1989 that they would extend the three Applicants' secondment only until 31 December 1989, after which successors proposed by the Chinese Government would take over the posts.

In October 1989 the Applicants submitted requests to be considered for career appointments in accordance with General Assembly resolutions 37/126 (1982) and 38/232 (1983), which provide for "reasonable consideration upon completion of five years of continuing good service" and recommend that in such case "the organizations normally dispense with the requirement of a probationary appointment as a precondition for a career appointment." The Secretary-General denied these requests.

The Applicants had taken part in protests against events in China (the Tiananmen Square incident of 4 June 1989) and stated that they were afraid to return to their home country. To this end, they offered to resign from any posts they may have held in their home country. The Applicants wrote to the

Secretary-General stating that the Chinese Government had interfered in the administration of the international civil service and added that China had been forcing them to hand over part of their salaries to the government. They argued that their application for tenured appointment had not been reviewed by the Secretary-General with due consideration for their qualifications.

On 15 January 1990 the Office of the Secretary-General informed the Applicants that during the review all the factors in favor of their appointment had been duly noted:

> On the other hand, it was also necessary to take into account the interests of the Organization and in particular its functional needs. In this connection, it was important to ensure that the Chinese language services continued to function effectively and efficiently. Since the primary users of those services are representatives of the Government of the People's Republic of China, it is of critical importance for the effectiveness of the services that those representatives have confidence that their statements, both oral and written, will be objectively and fairly rendered, interpreted or reported. Furthermore, the efficient functioning of the Chinese language services would not be possible in a situation where staff members were antagonistic to each other because of expressly stated political animosities.
>
> It would also not be in the interests of the Organization to disrupt the rotational system for the staffing of the Chinese language services, which has proven to be most effective. This system has enabled the establishment of a specialized language training programme at the Beijing Institute for Foreign Languages, the termination of which would make it immensely difficult to recruit language staff with the specific qualifications required to fill vacancies appropriately and expeditiously.[7]

The communication also informed the Applicants that the Secretary-General was conducting an examination of the alleged deductions from the salaries of the staff members of the United Nations.

On 28 February 1990 the Applicants filed their appeals with the Administrative Tribunal on the grounds that: (i) the Secretary-General failed to discharge his obligations under Article 100 and 101(3) of the Charter and General Assembly resolutions 37/126 and 38/232 to give the Applicants every reasonable consideration for a career appointment; (ii) under Article 100 staff members do not serve their governments but the United Nations and do not have to agree with the policies of Governments in order to carry out their duties with impartiality; (iii) the Secretary-General's decision was based on illegal considerations; and (iv) the establishment of a training institute does not derogate from Articles 100 and 101 of the Charter or the Staff regulations and rules.

---

[7] UN Doc. AT/DEC/482 (1990), p. 10.

THE CHINESE TRANSLATORS CASE: *QIU, ZHOU, AND YAO V. SECRETARY-GENERAL OF THE UNITED NATIONS* (UNITED NATIONS ADMINISTRATIVE TRIBUNAL JUDGMENT NO. 482, 25 MAY 1990)[8]

Judgment

VII. ... The Tribunal notes that no details concerning the nature and conditions of the employment with the Chinese government from which the Applicants were seconded are given in the letters of appointment submitted by the Administration.

VIII. Neither has the Administration produced any agreement concluded with the Chinese Government ... concerning the secondment of the Applicants nor any document in which the competent authorities define the Applicants'situation in writing and specify the conditions of secondment ... no details are given concerning the Applicants' posts in their own country nor of the conditions governing their reintegration into those posts ... if such agreement did exist, it was not brought to the Applicants, for their consent.

IX. The Applicants have duly taken and signed the oath required of every United Nations staff member:

> ... to exercise in all loyalty, discretion and conscience the functions entrusted to me as an international civil servant of the United Nations, to discharge these functions and regulate my conduct with the interests of the United Nations only in view, and not to seek or accept instructions in regard to the performance of my duties from any Government or other authority external to the organization. ...

XIV. The three Applicants gave complete satisfaction in the performance of their functions in the UN ... there was no allegation of any sign of antagonism towards other colleagues, certainly not Chinese colleagues. There was no sign of political animosity. ...

XXIII. The Tribunal finds that the conditions laid down for an official to be on secondment are not fulfilled in this case ... The Applicants were not on genuine secondment within the meaning given to that term ... established in Judgment No 92, Higgins (1964): "... the term 'secondment' implies that the staff member is posted away from his establishment of origin but has the right to revert to employment in the establishment at the end of the period of secondment and retains the right to promotion and retirement benefits ..."

XXIV. ... [I]t is only when these conditions are fulfilled that "the Secretary-General of the United Nations as the administrative head of the Organization, is obliged to take into account the decision of the Government."

XXV. ... Accordingly the Tribunal considers that it was not for the Respondent either to request authorization of, or to comply with the decision of

---

[8] UN Doc. AT/DEC/482 (1990).

the Government in order to renew the Applicant's contracts. This being so, the Tribunal finds that the decision not to renew the Applicants' fixed term contracts was vitiated by extraneous reasons contrary to the interests of the United Nations, incompatible with Article 100 of the Charter....

XXIX. More generally, the Tribunal considers that the limits of the Secretary-General's discretionary powers are governed by the principle established by the Tribunal's consistent case law: the Secretary-General may not legally take a decision which is contrary to the Charter, in particular to Articles 100 and 101, or to the provisions of the Staff Rules and Regulations.

XXX.... [T]he Secretary-General has the right to consult Governments of Member States, provided such consultation does not contravene the principle referred to in the preceding paragraph ... [I]n the present case, by accepting the position advocated by the Government the Secretary-General has not acted in conformity with the foregoing principles.

XXXI. Nevertheless, the Tribunal does not hold that the Secretary-General could not, in proper circumstances, take into consideration the requirements of the efficient functioning of the Beijing Institute of Foreign Languages. The Secretary-General stressed, in his letter of 15 January 1990, that the termination of the specialized language training programme "would make it immensely difficult to recruit language staff with the specific qualifications required to fill vacancies appropriately and expeditiously." As the Tribunal shows below, in this case, the alleged adverse effect on the efficient functioning of the Institute and on recruitment is pure speculation. It appears to the Tribunal also, that there might be other sources for the recruitment of qualified language staff.

XXXII. The Tribunal notes that there is no evidence in the files to support the existence of a threat to suppress the programme in question if the Applicants receive career appointments. ...

XXXIII. In keeping with the wishes expressed by the Chinese Mission, there is nothing to prevent the maintenance of a rotation system. The Tribunal considers that a rotation system is not unlawful *per se*. ... But in the opinion of the Tribunal, the rotation system must be established on a precise legal basis—through secondment in accordance with the terms governing secondment and without ruling out career appointments pursuant to GA Resolution 37/126.

XXXIV. Accordingly, the Tribunal can only reject the Respondent's contention that the mere existence of the rotation system would prohibit career appointments.

XXXV. The Tribunal appreciates the Administration's concern that "it is of critical importance ... that [the] representatives [of China] have full confidence that their statements both oral and written, will be objectively and fairly rendered, interpreted or reported."

XXXVI. But the Tribunal notes that during the period when the career appointments of the Applicants were considered ... no complaint was levelled against them concerning their performance. The reason invoked by the Administration for denying appointments to the Applicants is based on inaccuracy, if not an error.

XXXVII. The Tribunal has also taken into account the terms of the letter addressed to the Applicants on 15 January 1990, on behalf of the Secretary-General, by the Acting Under-Secretary-General for Administration and Management:

> The efficient functioning of the Chinese language services would not be possible in a situation where staff members were antagonistic to each other because of expressly stated political animosities.

But the Tribunal notes that no act of this nature has been alleged against the Applicants. It notes moreover that the Applicants have never failed to maintain the discretion incumbent upon them as international civil servants. Even during 1989, no such complaint against them was made by their Government. Lastly, the Tribunal notes that nothing has been shown to indicate the possibility of such a problem arising in the future.

XXXVIII. In the opinion of the Tribunal, the Respondent's assumptions in this respect lack any factual basis. The Applicants' record as international civil servants, as recognized by the Administration itself, shows that they are devoid of any substance. They constitute arbitrary suspicions on the future conduct of the Applicants. The Applicants are being disciplined by the denial of appointments, for potential misconduct. The Tribunal considers that the Applicants are being tried for their imputed intentions. An attitude of irresponsibility is ascribed to international civil servants who, during many years of service, have not given the slightest justification for such a charge.

XXXIX. The Tribunal moreover recalls that the Secretary-General has the necessary powers to prevent any irresponsible conduct on the part of the staff under his authority.

XL. The Respondent acknowledges that discussions took place with representatives of the Chinese Mission throughout the period beginning on 1 May 1989. The Tribunal takes note that following those discussions, the Secretary-General denied the Applicants career appointments on 12 December 1989.

XLI. The Tribunal finds that the Secretary-General accepted the Chinese Mission's position that the Applicants should be denied an extension of their fixed-term contracts or be offered career appointments.

The Tribunal has shown that, in the absence of the necessary criteria for secondment consistent with case-law, it was not permissible for the Secretary-General to take into account the Chinese Mission's opposition to the renewal of the fixed-term contracts.

As regards career appointments, the Tribunal considers that these were withheld because of the Chinese Mission's position concerning the rotation system. The Tribunal notes that, in the opinion of the Chinese Mission, the rotation system categorically ruled out career appointments. The Tribunal considers that the Secretary-General could not defer to this opposition by the Chinese Mission without being in breach of his obligations under the Charter and the Staff Rules and Regulations, as well as under General Assembly resolutions 37/126 and 38/232 (see para. XXXIII).

XLII. Consequently, the Tribunal finds that the Secretary-General's decision to refuse the Applicants' request for career appointments exceeds the limits of his discretion. His decision is based on reasons which are contrary to the interests of the United Nations, erroneous or inaccurate as to fact, and specious. It ignores the basic principles of the international civil service, as enunciated in Articles 100 and 101 of the Charter. ...

XLIII. The Tribunal considers that the Secretary-General wrongly refused the Applicants career appointments, contrary to GA Resolutions 37/126 and 38/232. ...

XLVIII. For these reasons, the Tribunal: ...

2. Rescinds the decision taken by the Secretary-General on 12 December 1989, and confirmed on 15 January 1990, not to grant the Applicants career appointments in the circumstances provided for in General Assembly resolutions 37/126 and 38/232, and decides that they should be granted such appointments as from 1 February 1990.

3. Fixes the compensation to be paid to each of the Applicants at three years' net base salary of the Applicants as at the date of their separation from service, if the Secretary-General decides, within 30 days of the notification of the Judgment, in the interest of the United Nations, not to grant the Applicants career appointments.

Declaration by Jerome Ackerman, First Vice President

Having signed the Judgment in this case, of course, I agree with it entirely. I should like to note, in addition, that had the Tribunal thought it necessary to address the Applicants' contentions concerning the procedure established by the Administration ... I would have deemed it axiomatic that such a procedure must observe the requirements of due process including the absence of discrimination ... I believe that the Applicants were not accorded the due process to which they were entitled.

In my view it is also regrettable, to put it mildly, that there should be even so much as an appearance that this entire affair might be related to humanitarian pleas made by them.

QUESTIONS

6. Does the impartiality of the Secretariat require that it be hired without any regard for the opinions regarding the candidates' suitability or political acceptability expressed by the state of their nationality? Is that what the UN Administrative Tribunal decided?

7. Did the Tribunal interpret correctly the requirements of the UN Charter? Does its decision make for good policy? Does UN service require only that

its civil servants be impartial, or that they also be seen to be impartial by the member states?

8. Does the Secretary-General have a right to require his or her staff to maintain a discreet silence as to controversial political issues arising in their home states? Why, or why not?

4.3 Reports on the Reform of the Secretariat

The Millennium Declaration (General Assembly resolution 55/2 (2000)), issued by Heads of Governments and States while meeting as the General Assembly, recognized the "strengthening the United Nations" as a key objective to the attainment of the goals of securing peace, development, preservation of the environment, respect for human rights, protecting vulnerable populations in terms of humanitarian crises and meeting the special needs of Africa. Following this, reports were commissioned at several levels to suggest the reforms needed and the means by which they may be brought about.

One of the most significant initiatives in this regard was the creation of the High-Level Panel on Threats, Challenges and Change by Secretary-General Kofi Annan in 2003. The Report, submitted by this sixteen-member group, outlined "six clusters" of threats—(i) war between states; (ii) violence within states, including civil wars, large-scale human rights abuses and genocide; (iii) poverty, infectious disease and environmental degradation; (iv) nuclear, radiological, chemical and biological weapons; (v) terrorism; and (vi) transnational organized crime.

It emphasized prevention of these threats through greater cooperation between states and a focus on "development" as a primary strategy. Where prevention is not possible the panel supported responses that fall within the framework of the UN Charter. In addition, it endorsed the "responsibility to protect" as an obligation primarily on national governments, but also, if they fail to act, as a further obligation on the international community. This might be fulfilled through humanitarian operations, monitoring missions, and diplomatic pressure—with force to be used if necessary as a last resort. The report also stressed the importance of post-conflict rebuilding of shattered societies.

The main theme of the report is that if all these issues are to be successfully addressed by the United Nations, then its existing institutions must work more effectively. Among other improvements, it recommended strengthening the Secretary-General's role in peace and security. The following excerpts contain the Panel's suggestions toward this end.[9]

---

[9] The Report of the High-Level Panel is also discussed in chapters one, nine, thirteen, and seventeen in this volume.

REPORT OF THE HIGH-LEVEL PANEL ON THREATS, CHALLENGES, AND CHANGE: A MORE SECURE WORLD: OUR SHARED RESPONSIBILITY, 1 DECEMBER 2004[10]

XIX. The Secretariat

292. A strong Secretary-General at the head of a more professional and better organized Secretariat is an essential component of any effective system for collective security in the twenty-first century.

A. Strengthening Support for the Secretary-General

293. The creation of the post of Deputy Secretary-General in 1996 helped bring far greater coherence to the work of the United Nations in the economic, social and development fields and on issues of management reform. Given the enormous increase in the workload of the Secretary-General in the area of peace and security in the 1990s, creating a second Deputy Secretary-General post for peace and security would ensure that the Secretary-General's efforts in this area are equally well supported. To assist the Secretary-General, an additional Deputy Secretary-General position should be created, responsible for peace and security.

294. With one Deputy Secretary-General focusing on the economic and social development work of the United Nations, the additional Deputy Secretary-General and his/her office would assist the Secretary-General in systematically overseeing the work of the United Nations system in the area of peace and security, with the aim of formulating integrated strategies and ensuring concerted action. Such an office should not be operational and would not duplicate, but instead rationalize and make more effective, existing bureaucratic functions. It would integrate inputs from the various departments and agencies and prepare early-warning reports and strategy options for decision by the Secretary-General. It should comprise approximately 15 Professionals able to perform strategic analysis, planning and coordination tasks. It should also provide the Secretary-General with new expertise to deal with new threats—for example, the scientific advice necessary to address questions of environmental and biological security.

B. A Competent and Professional Secretariat

295. The burden of implementing the decisions of Member States and providing them with timely analysis and advice rests not only on the Secretary-General but on the Secretariat as a whole. If the United Nations is to be effective, it needs a professional and well-trained Secretariat whose skills and experiences have been adapted to match the tasks at hand. The last 15 years have witnessed a large expansion in work related to conflict prevention

---

[10] UN Doc. A/59/565 (2004).

and peacekeeping, the negotiation and implementation of peace agreements, and peacebuilding. And yet, despite the increase in demand since the end of the cold war total Secretariat staff has declined since 1990, while only 6 per cent of the staff of the Secretariat are responsible for the entire range of issues that include mediation, the organization and management of peacekeeping operations, support for the Security Council, disarmament, elections support and sanctions. Many of those based at Headquarters have no field experience or training and the existing rules militate against their gaining it. In addition, there is little or no expertise for tackling many of the new or emerging threats addressed in the present report.

296. The Secretary-General should be provided with the resources he requires to do his job properly and the authority to manage his staff and other resources as he deems best. To meet the needs identified in the present report, we recommend that:

(a) Member States recommit themselves to Articles 100 and 101 of the Charter of the United Nations;

(b) Member States review the relationship between the General Assembly and the Secretariat with the aim of substantially increasing the flexibility provided to the Secretary-General in the management of his staff, subject always to his accountability to the Assembly;

(c) The Secretary-General's reform proposals of 1997 and 2002 related to human resources should now, without further delay, be fully implemented;

(d) There should be a one-time review and replacement of personnel, including through early retirement, to ensure that the Secretariat is staffed with the right people to undertake the tasks at hand, including for mediation and peacebuilding support, and for the office of the Deputy Secretary-General for peace and security. Member States should provide funding for this replacement as a cost-effective long-term investment;

(e) The Secretary-General should immediately be provided with 60 posts—less than 1 per cent of the total Secretariat—for the purpose of establishing all the increased Secretariat capacity proposed in the present report.

. . . .

The Secretary-General in turn also prepared a Report for submission to the Heads of State and Governments, as an agenda to be taken up and acted upon, in the World Summit to be held in New York in September 2005 to review the progress since the adoption of the Millennium Declaration in 2000 by all members of the United Nations. In the hope of generating the political will to push through various policy reforms directed toward the fulfillment of the goals of the Millennium Declaration, the report characterized them in the form of various basic freedoms—freedom from want, freedom from fear, and freedom to live in dignity—and highlighted key issues, concerns, and possible steps to be taken toward reform in each of these areas. In addition to this, it focused upon the need to strengthen the United Nations and adapt it to the circumstances of the twenty-first century.

IN LARGER FREEDOM: TOWARDS DEVELOPMENT, SECURITY, AND HUMAN RIGHTS FOR ALL (REPORT OF THE SECRETARY-GENERAL), 21 MARCH 2005[11]

C. The Secretariat

184. A capable and effective Secretariat is indispensable to the work of the United Nations. As the needs of the Organization have changed, so too must the Secretariat. That is why in 1997 I launched a package of structural reforms for the Secretariat and followed up with a further set of managerial and technical improvements in 2002, aimed at giving the Organization a more focused work programme and a simpler system of planning and budgeting and enabling the Secretariat to provide better service.

185. I am glad that the General Assembly has given broad support to these changes and I believe they have improved our ability to do the job the world expects of us. Thanks to changes in budgeting, procurement, human resources management and the way peacekeeping missions are supported, we now do business in a new and different way. But these reforms do not go far enough. If the United Nations is to be truly effective the Secretariat will have to be completely transformed.

186. Those with the power to make decisions—essentially the General Assembly and the Security Council—must take care, when they assign mandates to the Secretariat, that they also provide resources adequate for the task. In return, management must be made more accountable and the capacity of intergovernmental bodies to oversee it must be strengthened. The Secretary-General and his or her managers must be given the discretion, the means, the authority and the expert assistance that they need to manage an organization which is expected to meet fast changing operational needs in many different parts of the world. Similarly, Member States must have the oversight tools that they need to hold the Secretary-General truly accountable for his/her strategy and leadership.

187. Member States also have a central role to play in ensuring that the Organization's mandates stay current. **I therefore ask the General Assembly to review all mandates older than five years to see whether the activities concerned are still genuinely needed or whether the resources assigned to them can be reallocated in response to new and emerging challenges.**

188. Today's United Nations staff must be: (a) aligned with the new substantive challenges of the twenty first century; (b) empowered to manage complex global operations; and (c) held accountable.

189. First, I am taking steps to realign the Secretariat's structure to match the priorities outlined in the present report. This will entail creating a peace-building support office and strengthening support both for mediation (my "good offices" function) and for democracy and the rule of law. In addition,

---

[11] UN Doc. A/59/2005 (2005).

I intend to appoint a Scientific Adviser to the Secretary-General, who will provide strategic forward looking scientific advice on policy matters, mobilizing scientific and technological expertise within the United Nations system and from the broader scientific and academic community.

190. Achieving real progress in new areas requires staff with the skills and experience to address new challenges. It also requires a renewed effort to secure "the highest standards of efficiency, competence and integrity," as required by Article 101.3 of the Charter of the United Nations, while "recruiting the staff on as wide a geographical basis as possible" and, we must add today, ensuring a just balance between men and women. While existing staff must have reasonable opportunities to develop within the Organization we cannot continue to rely on the same pool of people to address all our new needs. **I therefore request the General Assembly to provide me with the authority and resources to pursue a one-time staff buyout so as to refresh and realign the staff to meet current needs.**

191. Second, the Secretariat must be empowered to do its work. The High-level Panel suggested that I appoint a second Deputy Secretary-General to improve the decision-making process on peace and security. Instead, I have decided to create a cabinet-style decision-making mechanism (with stronger executive powers than the present Senior Management Group) to improve both policy and management. It will be supported by a small cabinet secretariat to ensure the preparation and follow-up of decision making. In this way, I expect to be able to ensure more focused, orderly and accountable decision-making. This should help but will not by itself be enough to ensure the effective management of the worldwide operations of such a complex Organization. The Secretary-General, as Chief Administrative Officer of the Organization, must be given a higher level of managerial authority and flexibility. He or she needs to have the ability to adjust the staffing table as necessary and without undue constraint. And our administrative system needs to be thoroughly modernized. **Therefore, I ask Member States to work with me to undertake a comprehensive review of the budget and human resources rules under which we operate.**

192. Third, we must continue to improve the transparency and accountability of the Secretariat. The General Assembly has taken an important step towards greater transparency by making internal audits available to Member States upon request. I am in the process of identifying other categories of information that could be made available routinely. I am establishing a Management Performance Board to ensure that senior officials are held accountable for their actions and the results their units achieve. A number of other internal improvements are under way. These aim to align our management systems and human resource policies with the best practices of other global public and commercial organizations. **In order to further improve accountability and oversight I have proposed that the General Assembly commission a comprehensive review of the Office of Internal Oversight Services with a view to strengthening its independence and authority as well as its expertise and capacity.** I hope the Assembly will act promptly on this proposal.

The World Summit was concluded in New York on 16 September 2005. The Summit was intended as a follow up to the Millennium Summit and was also meant to review the implementation of the goals of the Millennium Declaration and to adopt suggested recommendations toward achieving them.

2005 WORLD SUMMIT OUTCOME DOCUMENT, 16 SEPTEMBER 2005[12]

Secretariat and Management Reform

161. We recognize that in order to effectively comply with the principles and objectives of the Charter, we need an efficient, effective and accountable Secretariat. Its staff shall act in accordance with Article 100 of the Charter, in a culture of organizational accountability, transparency and integrity. Consequently we:

(a) Recognize the ongoing reform measures carried out by the Secretary-General to strengthen accountability and oversight, improve management performance and transparency and reinforce ethical conduct, and invite him to report to the General Assembly on the progress made in their implementation;

(b) Emphasize the importance of establishing effective and efficient mechanisms for responsibility and accountability of the Secretariat;

(c) Urge the Secretary-General to ensure that the highest standards of efficiency, competence, and integrity shall be the paramount consideration in the employment of the staff, with due regard to the principle of equitable geographical distribution, in accordance with Article 101 of the Charter;

(d) Welcome the Secretary-General's efforts to ensure ethical conduct, more extensive financial disclosure for United Nations officials and enhanced protection for those who reveal wrongdoing within the Organization. We urge the Secretary-General to scrupulously apply the existing standards of conduct and develop a system-wide code of ethics for all United Nations personnel. In this regard, we request the Secretary-General to submit details on an ethics office with independent status, which he intends to create, to the General Assembly at its sixtieth session;

(e) Pledge to provide the United Nations with adequate resources, on a timely basis, to enable the Organization to implement its mandates and achieve its objectives, having regard to the priorities agreed by the General Assembly and the need to respect budget discipline. We stress that all Member States should meet their obligations with regard to the expenses of the Organization;

---

[12] GA Res. 60/1 (2005).

(*f*) Strongly urge the Secretary-General to make the best and most efficient use of resources in accordance with clear rules and procedures agreed by the General Assembly, in the interest of all Member States, by adopting the best management practices, including effective use of information and communication technologies, with a view to increasing efficiency and enhancing organizational capacity, concentrating on those tasks that reflect the agreed priorities of the Organization.

162. We reaffirm the role of the Secretary-General as the chief administrative officer of the Organization, in accordance with Article 97 of the Charter. We request the Secretary-General to make proposals to the General Assembly for its consideration on the conditions and measures necessary for him to carry out his managerial responsibilities effectively.

163. We commend the Secretary-General's previous and ongoing efforts to enhance the effective management of the United Nations and his commitment to update the Organization. Bearing in mind our responsibility as Member States, we emphasize the need to decide on additional reforms in order to make more efficient use of the financial and human resources available to the Organization and thus better comply with its principles, objectives and mandates. We call on the Secretary-General to submit proposals for implementing management reforms to the General Assembly for consideration and decision in the first quarter of 2006, which will include the following elements:

(*a*) We will ensure that the United Nations budgetary, financial and human resource policies, regulations and rules respond to the current needs of the Organization and enable the efficient and effective conduct of its work, and request the Secretary-General to provide an assessment and recommendations to the General Assembly for decision during the first quarter of 2006. The assessment and recommendations of the Secretary-General should take account of the measures already under way for the reform of human resources management and the budget process;

(*b*) We resolve to strengthen and update the programme of work of the United Nations so that it responds to the contemporary requirements of Member States. To this end, the General Assembly and other relevant organs will review all mandates older than five years originating from resolutions of the General Assembly and other organs, which would be complementary to the existing periodic reviews of activities. The General Assembly and the other organs should complete and take the necessary decisions arising from this review during 2006. We request the Secretary-General to facilitate this review with analysis and recommendations, including on the opportunities for programmatic shifts that could be considered for early General Assembly consideration;

(*c*) A detailed proposal on the framework for a one-time staff buyout to improve personnel structure and quality, including an indication of costs involved and mechanisms to ensure that it achieves its intended purpose.

164. We recognize the urgent need to substantially improve the United Nations oversight and management processes. We emphasize the importance of ensuring the operational independence of the Office of Internal Oversight Services. Therefore:

(a) The expertise, capacity and resources of the Office of Internal Oversight Services in respect of audit and investigations will be significantly strengthened as a matter of urgency;

(b) We request the Secretary-General to submit an independent external evaluation of the auditing and oversight system of the United Nations, including the specialized agencies, including the roles and responsibilities of management, with due regard to the nature of the auditing and oversight bodies in question. This evaluation will take place within the context of the comprehensive review of the governance arrangements. We ask the General Assembly to adopt measures during its sixtieth session at the earliest possible stage, based on the consideration of recommendations of the evaluation and those made by the Secretary-General;

(c) We recognize that additional measures are needed to enhance the independence of the oversight structures. We therefore request the Secretary-General to submit detailed proposals to the General Assembly at its sixtieth session for its early consideration on the creation of an independent oversight advisory committee, including its mandate, composition, selection process and qualification of experts;

(d) We authorize the Office of Internal Oversight Services to examine the feasibility of expanding its services to provide internal oversight to United Nations agencies that request such services in such a way as to ensure that the provision of internal oversight services to the Secretariat will not be compromised.

165. We insist on the highest standards of behaviour from all United Nations personnel and support the considerable efforts under way with respect to the implementation of the Secretary-General's policy of zero tolerance regarding sexual exploitation and abuse by United Nations personnel, both at Headquarters and in the field. We encourage the Secretary-General to submit proposals to the General Assembly leading to a comprehensive approach to victims' assistance by 31 December 2005.

166. We encourage the Secretary-General and all decision-making bodies to take further steps in mainstreaming a gender perspective in the policies and decisions of the Organization.

167. We strongly condemn all attacks against the safety and security of personnel engaged in United Nations activities. We call upon States to consider becoming parties to the Convention on the Safety of United Nations and Associated Personnel and stress the need to conclude negotiations on a protocol expanding the scope of legal protection during the sixtieth session of the General Assembly.

QUESTIONS ....

9. The Secretary-General serves as the "face" of the UN. What pressure does this place on the office in terms of what is said and done? It been used by several Secretaries-General as a license to lead debate and press for action from the other UN organs and states. Is this appropriate? How independent can and should the Secretary-General be?

10. The Secretariat consists of professionals with life tenure, persons with fixed-year contracts, and persons on secondment from their governments. What, from the perspective of the efficient discharge of its obligations, is the right percentage of each category to create the best mix of tenures and skills?

11. Should the UN Secretariat be used as a short-term training program for civil servants from developing countries?

4.4 Good Offices of the Secretary-General

The use of the Secretary-General's "good offices" refers primarily to mediating and diplomatic functions necessary to resolve conflicts between or within states, but can also include investigation and reporting on human rights abuses as well as fact finding in conflict situations. Though "good offices" is not expressly provided for in the UN Charter, the functions performed under it have acquired prominence and are increasingly recognized as alternative means of dispute settlement. The good offices function of the Secretary-General, although not specifically granted by the Charter, may have a legal basis in Article 99, which authorizes the Secretary-General to "bring to the attention of the Security Council any matter which in his opinion may affect the maintenance of international peace and security." This authority, to be exercised effectively, may be construed also to empower the Secretary-General to investigate a "situation" or crisis and to engage in discussion with the relevant parties. Another basis for "good offices" has been a direct request by one of the two principal political organs (the Assembly and the Council) to the Secretary-General. Yet another basis is a direct request by the parties to a dispute that authorizes the Secretary-General to mediate.

Secretary-General Trygve Lie invoked his good offices for the first time in September 1946 to investigate alleged infiltration across Greece's northern border, again in October 1948 to offer detailed solutions to the Berlin Crisis, and once more to negotiate with China on starting talks on a settlement of the Korean War. His successors during the Cold War years, Dag Hammarskjöld, U Thant, Kurt Waldheim, and Javier Pérez de Cuéllar, expanded this function, asserting their neutrality and the right to act without prior authorization. By the end of the Cold War they had constructed a dispute settlement role that was clearly separate from, and sometimes at variance with, the policy of one or other UN political organ, or important Member States.

The end of the Cold War had contradictory effects on the good offices function. On the one hand, because of greater cooperation among the powers, it received a boost, as did the effectiveness of other organs of the UN system; on the other, the capacity of the Secretary-General to act independently diminished due to increased activism in the Security Council and the General Assembly.

From the late 1980s, the Secretary-General has mediated in a number of civil conflicts—Afghanistan, Cambodia, Mozambique, Nicaragua, El Salvador, the former Yugoslavia, and in parts of the former Soviet Union. The Secretary-General has also sought to mediate in conflicts of a smaller scale, such as the hostage situation in Lebanon in 1991, and arbitrate disputes specifically referred to him by states, as in the "Rainbow Warrior" dispute between France and New Zealand.

While successive Secretaries-General have sometimes been successful in carrying out their good offices functions, on occasion their efforts have been frustrated due to constraints imposed by the Security Council, by the General Assembly, or by member states. Obduracy of the parties has also contributed to failure on some occasions. The failure of the Secretary-General to resolve the Cyprus conflict may be an example of this.

The following excerpts analyze the different applications of the good offices function and make prescriptions for its sustainable evolution in the future.

THOMAS M. FRANCK

THE SECRETARY-GENERAL'S ROLE IN CONFLICT RESOLUTION: PAST, PRESENT AND PURE CONJECTURE[13]

In legal terms, the Secretary-General's diplomatic and peacemaking functions may derive from at least four different kinds of authorization: (1) the agreement of disputatious parties, (2) the penumbra of the Secretary-General's inherent powers, (3) authorization by resolutions of the Security Council, or (4) authorization by the General Assembly. The Secretary-General has undertaken good offices missions in response to requests from parties to a conflict and/or formal or informal invitations from regional groupings. This is how he entered the Guyana-Venezuela boundary mediation, the *Rainbow Warrior* Case and the Liberian and Yugoslav crises. In the Mozambique case, the Secretary-General's role was initiated at the invitation of the parties to an agreement ending a civil war negotiated outside the UN by the Government and its RENAMO adversaries. The Secretary-General has acted on his own authority, at least initially, in respect of civil wars in Greece, Yemen,

---

[13] From *European Journal of International Law*, vol. 6 (1995), pp. 360–387 (notes omitted). Reprinted by permission of Oxford University Press.

Afghanistan, Burundi, Rwanda, Tajikistan, in the Iran-Iraq conflict and regarding hostages in Lebanon. He has undertaken roles in Cyprus, East Timor,
Libya, the Middle East, Namibia, Somalia and Yugoslavia on the basis of
mandates in resolutions of the Security Council. Some of his activities in
connection with Afghanistan and the Western Sahara were authorized by
resolution of the General Assembly. The last two instances, however, also
demonstrate the difficulty in drawing bright lines regarding authorization.
Prior to the Assembly's resolutions, the Secretary-General had already begun
to exercise his good offices on his own authority. Similarly, in Cambodia, the
Falkland Islands, Iran/Iraq, Iraq/Kuwait, Burundi and Somalia he became
active on his own just before the political organs, usually at his suggestion,
gave his efforts formal approval. In other instances, such as those involving
his good offices missions in Abkhazia and Central America he proceeded
entirely on his own and received approval from the Security Council only
many months later. His efforts to resolve the Lebanon hostage crisis occurred
without any involvement of the political organs. Aside from these explicit or
implicit authorizations it is obvious that the Secretary-General, in order to
perform his good offices functions, must retain the confidence of the principle
organs and the major nations and regional groupings which constitute the
Organization. Thus, the Secretary-General is constantly involved in informal
consultations with the Security Council and individual States. As a result, his
discretion as to how to proceed in a given dispute may, in fact, be narrower
than it appears on paper. Once a political organ—or a powerful Member
State—begins to involve itself in a situation, the Secretary-General's inherent
powers, especially in the post cold war era, usually need to be exercised in
compliance with the limits, directions and parameters established by those
actors. In contemporary practice, however, the Secretary-General frequently
insists upon, and gets, the authority to operate within a wide margin of
discretion. Indeed, most resolutions authorizing the Secretary-General to
engage in good offices have accorded him broad leeway as to how to conduct his soundings. If, however, a UN political organ has taken a stridently
adversarial position against the activities of the very State with which the
Secretary-General is trying to negotiate—as the Security Council did with
respect to Afghanistan, Cambodia and South West Africa—he must use all
his diplomatic skill to retain the margin of discretion he needs to act as a
credible intermediary. On the other hand, the Secretary-General is aware that
there are circumstances when it is actually helpful to have [his] hands tied by
the Charter or the UN political organs. A narrow margin of discretion may
sometimes help him resist unacceptable pressures from either side to a conflict. In the Cyprus negotiations, he has had occasion to remind the Turkish-
Cypriot authorities that the "essence of his mandate" was called into question
by their insistence on a unilateral right of secession, which would violate the
parameters for a constitutional settlement set out in the Security Council resolution authorizing his mediation. He has taken the same position in negotiations with the Abkhazi insurgents and the Bosnian Serbs, holding himself
bound by the Security Council's insistence on the principles of territorial

integrity, the repatriation of "ethnically cleansed" populations, the ratification of negotiated changes by referendum, and the rejection of territorial changes effected by force. As mediator, he has tried to use these constraints on his discretion to gain negotiating leverage.

VII. Recent Trends and the Future

... [T]he Secretary-General has had some remarkable successes in the exercise of his conflict-prevention-and-resolution function: both during, and since the end of, the cold war. Nevertheless, there is some reason to believe that his role's expansion may not continue, or that it may evolve into something qualitatively different, or that it may turn to quite a different set of issues, in response to a changing institutional and political context. As we have indicated, the Security Council now seems more ready and able to perform its Charter-envisaged political functions. That has ended the stasis which, paradoxically, gave the Secretary-General his first occasions—and the interstitial space—to manoeuvre as an "honest broker." The Council, now more readily able to make decisions, tends to ask the Secretary-General to go to Tripoli and to Baghdad not to exercise an independent political role but more as a messenger to deliver its own plan of action.

This may not last. If the principal threat to peace, in the foreseeable future, comes from essentially civil strife in places like Afghanistan, Cambodia, Georgia, Honduras, Liberia, Rwanda, Tajikistan, the former Yugoslavia and Somalia, it is far from clear that the Security Council's new found consensus will prevail. Russia and the United States are already in fundamental disagreement over the rights of the parties in the former Yugoslavia. China will be increasingly concerned about spreading UN interventionism on behalf of what it perceives as "domestic" political or human rights disputes. Many States are concerned about UN involvement in wars of secession, seeing them as inherently internal affairs. They feel that all UN military operations in such instances, even if primarily humanitarian, have the effect of giving a degree of international recognition to secessionist forces. Finally, there is growing unrest on the part of States at the cost of burgeoning UN field operations, and at the dominant role played by militarily and fiscally powerful participants.

In the light of these considerations, it is significant that the least intrusive, least expensive and frequently most successful form of UN peacemaking has proven to be the diplomatic role of the Secretary-General, especially when supported by the authority of the Security Council and its permanent members. His mediation is least threatening to States concerned about the prerogatives of their sovereignty. A certain continuity in the practice of the Secretary-General's good offices often avoids the missteps of *ad hoc* operations designed by political organs or by individual States.

The Council's failure to invoke Chapter VII to intervene on behalf of the Kurds in Iraq, to tame the clan-armies of Mogadishu, and its slowness to become embroiled in the political and security dimensions of the Yugoslav crisis all suggest that it may be precisely in these sorts of domestically-generated threats to international peace that the office of the Secretary-General, with its greater experience, flexibility and lower profile, might fill a growing void and fruitfully bring diplomacy back to centre stage. The Secretary-General's comprehensive, yet low key approach to the civil war in El Salvador—arranging a cease-fire, developing modalities for mutually disarming the combatants with their consent, reforming and integrating their armed forces, supervising human rights and negotiating constitutional guarantees—may be an augury of the future, when his good offices become the Organization's instrument not only of peacemaking but primarily of peacebuilding.

A. Determinants of Success and Failure

The extent to which peacemaking and peacekeeping functions of the Secretary-General will adapt and grow is dependent largely on two variables: personal and institutional.

1. Independence, Influence, Outreach   The personal variable has to do with the Secretary-General's ability to project a persona unbeholden to, uninstructed by, and resistant to pressure of the parties to a dispute, or to their allies. This depends on vision, the ability to communicate personal probity, the respect accumulated from previous successes, and the support the Secretary-General receives from members of the Security Council and General Assembly. It also has to do with the quality of the Secretary-General's information and diplomatic creativity.

As a direct result of the creativity of past Secretaries-General and their designated subalterns, the present Secretary-General has available a repertory of practices that aid the perception of his power to pull disputants toward negotiated compromise. The invention of the "Peking formula" by Hammarskjöld is a prime example of this creativity. Other examples include the recent practice of issuing very detailed interim reports to the Security Council on progress in negotiations. These enable the Secretary-General, when progress is blocked, to allocate blame and bring additional pressures to bear. Then there are the innovative "little steps" that make up his diplomatic minuet. Framework agreements, proximity talks, truth commissions, human rights and election monitoring, "confidence building" measures: these have all become established parts of the Secretary-General's diplomatic repertory.

Providing the newly-invigorated Security Council allows him to use these innovative tools, and to supplement them as the occasion demands, the Secretary-General's diplomatic role will continue to have potential for expansion. But much of the potential is still under-utilized. For example, no Secretary-General except Hammarskjöld has ever really used his "bully pulpit" effectively. None has ever succeeded in creating a directorate of public information that utilizes modern marketing skills. A dramatic example of this failure is the September/October 1994 issue of Foreign Affairs, where one article, by Giandomenico Picco, argues passionately that the Secretary-General's office is unsuitable to any deployment of military force, which should be subcontracted to individual States, while the other, by Saadia Touval, argues that, for similar reasons, all mediating functions should no longer be performed by the UN, but, rather, by powerful States. Together, the two articles argue for the total dismantling of the new dimensions of the Secretary-General's office. In the same issue an article by the Secretary-General, instead of defending his functions, addresses the—admittedly important—need to remove landmines at the sites of former wars. The effect of this juxtaposition is to make the Secretary-General appear ineffective and preoccupied with peripheral matters.

If there is painful evidence of the unresolved communications problem, it is not a new dilemma. No Secretary-General has really succeeded in reaching the "peoples" invoked by the Charter's preamble. Perhaps the problem is inherent. The qualities which make for a good bureaucrat or diplomat may be incompatible with those of a charismatic political leader or statesman. Nevertheless, a Secretary-General has three *potential* sources of power to support him in his quests: the important Member States and blocs of States, the world's "invisible college" of opinion-shapers—the media, universities, churches and captains of industry—and "the peoples." The latter two constituencies have barely been touched by any incumbent.

Even in his dealings with the representatives of States, it would be of immeasurable help if the Secretary-General could occasionally take his case, over the heads of the foreign offices, directly to "the peoples." Of course, no Secretary-General has real power, in the sense in which the major Member States have it. He has few means to affect outcomes except to the extent he makes himself indispensable to governments. Yet successive Secretaries-General have proven themselves quite adept at parlaying the perception of their indispensability into genuine influence: quietly, but adamantly pressing for, or opposing, a course of action, the means to an end, or the wording of a draft resolution.

In these interactions, the representatives of governments would be far more vulnerable to the Secretary-General's influence if he were known to speak not only for himself but for a credible global constituency sharing his perspective. Paradoxically, his independence, which is his weakness, is also his strength: his indispensability vanishes if he is seen to be "in the pocket" of one State, or a group of nations. Towards the ends of their careers, Trygve Lie was perceived as a captive of NATO and U Thant of the non-aligned. Article 100 of the Charter insists that the Secretary-General be independent of "any government or ... any authority external to the Organization." But to be independent of States does not require the Secretary-General to be unconnected to "the peoples." In maintaining both the essence and perception of total independence, every Secretary-General needs to build a constituency that is, in a significant sense, transnational and non-governmental.

2. Staffing and Control   The institutional variable has to do with the Secretary-General's ability to use the full potential of the UN and its related family of organizations and agencies to carry out his mission of conflict resolution. For this he needs, above all, a staff recruited on the basis of competence and answerable exclusively to him and his principal advisors. This the Charter has recognized. Article 101 manifestly seeks to give him a staff selected and retained with a view to "securing the highest standards of efficiency, competence, and integrity" while allowing for "recruiting the staff on as wide a geographical basis as possible."

In practice, however, staffing rules imposed by the General Assembly and the practice of Member States have not permitted the Secretary-General to choose the key members even of his own inner core of Secretariat advisers but, rather, made their appointments subject to claims by the major powers and even some influential middling States. Inevitably, top advisers who owe their posts to the lobbying of home governments look there first in discharging their ostensibly independent functions under the aegis of the Secretary-General.

Even at mid-levels, staff promotion and tenure still tends to reflect pressure by States and regions rather than expert qualifications and experience. This affects both the reality and, more important, the perception of UN diplomacy. If the Secretary-General's staff is skilful and shares a global vision as enunciated by its chief executive, the prospects are good; when they are not, failure of a mission or operation, not infrequently, is at least in part attributable to such deficiencies. Realizing this, Secretary-General Boutros Ghali has made more strenuous efforts than his predecessors to wrest his inner bureaucracy from the control of individual Member States and the whim of the principal political organs.

He has, however, been less successful in getting the large and diffuse UN "family" to march in lock step with his efforts. This is no small task, yet no Secretary-General can optimize his chances at peacemaking without being able to deploy all the UN's resources. The Organization can be described as having three parts: the UN proper, the quasi-autonomous subsidiaries (QASs) and the specialized and related agencies which are fully independent global intergovernmental organizations (IGOs). As to the IGOs, the Secretary-General controls neither their policies nor their personnel although, in trying to perform his conflict-resolving tasks, these bodies—the fiscal institutions, World Food Programme, Food and Agriculture Organization, World Health Organization, etc.—often hold the key to those inducements actually capable of moving disputants towards accommodation.

The same is true of the QASs—the UN Development Programme, High Commissioner for Refugees, etc.—which, although theoretically under the control of a principal political organ of the UN, are structured to give them wide autonomy. The Secretary-General does not control even their top appointments, nor are they funded significantly by the central budget of the Organization, as opposed to direct governmental contributions. Thus, he has little influence over their programmatic decisions. It has been suggested to the author by one Assistant Secretary-General that the divergent and mutually contradictory prescriptions of the World Bank and the UN in seeking to resolve the crisis in El Salvador reminded him of two doctors operating on different sides of a single patient with a curtain separating their efforts.

B. Prescriptions

What is needed? The prescription follows from the diagnosis, but its outlines can only be sketched, here. The Secretary-General is at the beck and call of the Security Council and that is as it should be, but he needs a longer leash. For example, he should have at his disposal a trust fund sufficient to embark on credible mediating missions at his own initiative, subject to a requirement that, after six months, authority would have to be extended by the Security Council and renewed funding voted by the General Assembly. He needs a small, all-volunteer multinational force under his command that could similarly be deployed—but only with the full consent of the parties concerned—for a six-month period. Its mandate should be subject to renewal by subsequent action of the Council or, perhaps, the Assembly. He should be able to put together larger military and civilian operations in short order, after they are authorized by the appropriate political organ, by drawing on a global inventory of stand-by contingents and logistical support earmarked for such contingencies by Member States. He should be able to draw on a pool of trained conflict managers of his own choosing, owing their posts exclusively to him. He should be able to mobilize QASs and IGOs, by exercising his influence on the treasuries of Member States at the time they earmark their contributions to these agencies.

There is every reason to believe that the Secretary-General's role will continue to expand because it is invaluable and there are no evident alternatives. This makes it essential that the role should be performed in an institutional and political context which maximizes its disposition for success.

THOMAS M. FRANCK AND GEORG NOLTE

THE GOOD OFFICES FUNCTION OF THE UN SECRETARY-GENERAL[14]

To Delegate or Not to Delegate

The Secretary-General cannot be everywhere at once. He heads a large bureaucracy (the Secretariat), must perform ceremonial and public relations functions, act as an inspirational leader of public opinion, and meet with world leaders. He is expected to attend important public meetings of the principal organs and engage in discussions about their proposed resolutions with the sponsors. He heads numerous field operations and needs to be aware of their activities as also of impending crises in far-flung parts of the

---

[14] From Adam Roberts and Benedict Kingsbury (eds.), *United Nations, Divided World: The UN's Roles in International Relations*, 2nd edn. (Oxford: Clarendon Press, 1993), pp. 143–182 (some notes omitted). Reprinted by permission of Oxford University Press.

world. When he undertakes a good offices task, it is inevitable that his role, at least in some instances, cannot be that of the omnipresent mediator, that this function must be delegated. This has become truer in the post–Cold war era, as the number of tasks has burgeoned. To delegate is sometimes advantageous: more often it is simply unavoidable.

On occasion, however, delegation is specifically excluded. In the Cyprus case, the Security Council entrusted the Secretary-General specifically and personally with the good-offices mandate. Thus, although there is a special representative of the Secretary-General in Cyprus, he himself has met frequently with each of the parties or has brought them together to negotiate in his personal presence. In the case of the *Rainbow Warrior*, too, the arbitral function was assigned to him in his personal capacity and therefore could not be delegated.

In most instances, fortunately, the Secretary-General has discretion to intervene in person or to delegate the good offices task. An imminent threat to the peace may leave him little choice but to assume the role of good officer in person, especially when the fighting has not yet broken out and may be prevented by a dramatic, personal last-ditch intervention. The Secretary-General's efforts in respect of the conflicts over the Falkland Islands and Kuwait are possible examples. In other cases, however, concern to husband the effectiveness of his role has lead the Secretary-General to stay in the background, appointing a Representative drawn from his inner Secretariat circle or utilizing a highly-regarded outsider who brings his or her own prestige to the process.[15]

Such delegation may happen even in situations where a serious breach of the peace has occurred, if, in the Secretary-General's opinion, a protracted commitment of time is required, rather than a dramatic short-term initiative. Examples include the disputes concerning Afghanistan, Iran-Iraq, Libya, Middle East, Yugoslavia, and also the negotiations for the release of the hostages in Lebanon. In these delegated good offices operations, the Secretary-General is involved in the background. Some missions, such as those with respect to Central America and Somalia, concern questions of such a complex nature that the need for delegation is immediately apparent. Also the protracted, complicated, seemingly endless Afghanistan negotiations could not be conducted by the Secretary-General without imperilling the discharge of his many other functions.

Between those cases clearly calling for the Secretary-General's direct conduct of good offices, and those in which only delegation is appropriate, are those instances where the Secretary-General delegates, yet occasionally intervenes personally in order to break a deadlock or accelerate progress. This has happened, in different degree, in the cases of Cambodia, Central America, Namibia, and Western Sahara.

---

[15] When the Secretary-General delegates, it is to Personal or Special Representatives, often trusted members of his Secretariat. The designation "Special Representative" is usually employed when the Secretary-General acts on the basis of a mandate from one of the political organs, "Personal Representative" when he acts on his own authority. However, not infrequently, outsiders are appointed ... [Footnote by the authors.]

Effectiveness

The secrecy of the process ensures that the effectiveness of each good offices mission is hard to assess. The Secretary-General does not always publish mission reports and, when he does, may omit relevant details. Moreover, it is difficult to evaluate his contribution when, as is often the case, he is but one of several players. Hard-nosed realists, for instance, attribute the successful outcome of the El Salvador talks in part to the US Congress's credible threat to reduce aid drastically if the El Salvador government proved too obdurate. This would have undercut the military establishment of that country, a reported stumbling-block to compromise.[16] Even to the extent this view may be true, it does not significantly detract from the Secretary-General's role as a catalyst for compromise, a formulator of structures for their implementation, and a resource that enables the parties, when agreement has been reached, to present it to disaffected parts of their domestic constituencies as the product of an irresistible global consensus.

The Secretary-General can sometimes reinforce this catalytic effect if he makes public certain aspects or preliminary results of the ongoing process. Increasingly, he issues very detailed interim reports on progress in the negotiations while sometimes, when progress it too slow, putting blame on one or both of the parties.[17] Despite the risk that such public finger-pointing will antagonize a party, it has proven a useful device to bring pressure to bear on behalf of closure.

The question of effectiveness is of more than theoretical interest. Failure harms the office. More important, when the secretary-General accepts a doomed good offices mission he may be being set up as a respectable cover for stasis or failure.[18] This may be what has happened in the case of Cyprus and the Western Sahara ... On the other hand, stasis, even UN-facilitated stasis, may be preferable to some alternatives ...

Moreover, even in a deadlock, the Secretary-General's activity keeps an item on the UN's agenda and thus, as in the case of East Timor, vestigially preserves the principle involved, even when the political organs have ceased actively to pursue it. His activity emphasizes the legitimacy issue and preserves options, keeping them open for the future.

[16] See Terry Lyn Karl, "El Salvador's Negotiated Revolution," *Foreign Affairs*, 71 (Spring 1992), pp. 159–60. [Footnote by the authors.]

[17] See, eg, UN Doc. S/21183 (1990), p. 12 (Cyprus); UN Doc. S/23693 (1992), p. 17 (Somalia); UN Doc. S/23900 (1992), p. 2 (Yugoslavia); and the detailed reports on the missions to Central America, Namibia, and Western Sahara mentioned above. [Footnote by the authors.]

[18] Javier Pérez de Cuéllar, "The Role of the UN Secretary-General" in Adam Roberts and Benedict Kingsbury (eds.), *United Nations, Divided World* (Oxford: Clarendon Press, 1993), p. 125. [Footnote by the authors.]

QUESTIONS ....

12. What role does the Secretary-General play in resolving conflicts? Can he or she create, mould, or enhance political will on the part of other states to resolve conflicts?

13. The Secretary-General, by virtue of Article 99 of the UN Charter, has the power to initiate discussions within the Security Council and to recommend action. The Charter is silent as to the authority of the Secretary-General to *discourage* or prevent action by the Council, which he or she regards as unwise policy, or inadequately resourced. Should the Secretary-General ever say "no" to a task the Security Council or General Assembly intend to assign to him or her? What basis in the law of the Charter might support your answer?

Further Reading

Bailey, Sydney D. *The Secretariat of the United Nations*. New York: Carnegie Endowment for International Peace, 1962.

Boutros-Ghali, Boutros. *Unvanquished: A US-UN Saga*. New York: Random House, 1999.

Chesterman, Simon, ed. *Secretary or General? The UN Secretary-General in World Politics*. Cambridge: Cambridge University Press, 2007.

Franck, Thomas M. "The Secretary-General's Role in Conflict Resolution: Past, Present and Pure Conjecture." *European Journal of International Law*, vol. 6 (1995), p. 360.

Franck, Thomas M., and Georg Nolte. "The Good Offices Function of the UN Secretary-General." In *United Nations, Divided World: The UN's Roles in International Relations*, edited by Adam Roberts and Benedict Kingsbury. 2nd edn., Oxford: Clarendon Press, 1993, p. 143.

Gordenker, Leon. *The UN Secretary-General and Secretariat*. New York: Routledge, 2005.

Hammarskjöld, Dag. "The International Civil Servant in Law and in Fact (Lecture Delivered to Congregation at Oxford University, 30 May 1961)." In *Servant of Peace: A Selection of the Speeches and Statements of Dag Hammarskjöld, Secretary-General of the United Nations 1953–1961* Wilder Foote. New York: Harper and Row, 1962, pp. 329–349.

Johnstone, Ian. "The Role of the UN Secretary-General: The Power of Persuasion Based on Law." *Global Governance*, vol. 9 (2003), p. 441.

Newman, Edward. *The UN Secretary-General from the Cold War to the New Era: A Global Peace and Security Mandate*. New York: Palgrave Macmillan, 1998.

Ramcharan, Bertrand G. *Humanitarian Good Offices in International Law: The Good Offices of the United Nations Secretary-General in the Field of Human Rights*. The Hague: Martinus Nijhoff, 1983.

Schwebel, Stephen M. *The Secretary-General of the United Nations: His Political Powers and Practice*. Cambridge, MA: Harvard University Press, 1952.

Szasz, Paul C. "The Role of the UN Secretary-General: Some Legal Aspects." *New York University Journal of International Law and Politics*, vol. 24 (1991), p. 161.

Thant, Myint-U, and Amy Scott. *The UN Secretariat: A Brief History.* New York: International Peace Academy, 2007.

Traub, James, *The Best Intentions: Kofi Annan and the UN in the Era of American World Power* (New York: Farrar, Straus & Giroux, 2006).

Urquhart, Brian, *Hammarskjöld* (New York: Knopf, 1972).

chapter five
....

Membership

Articles 3 to 6 of the Charter deal with membership of the United Nations. Article 4(1) of the UN Charter provides the criteria in the following terms:

> Membership in the United Nations is open to all other peace-loving states which accept the obligations contained in the present Charter and, in the judgment of the Organization, are able and willing to carry out these obligations.

Is this an exhaustive provision, or may a member state, when called upon to vote on an application for membership, make its consent dependent on conditions not expressly provided in this provision? In particular, may a state subject its affirmative vote to the additional condition that other states be admitted to membership in the United Nations together with that state?

This chapter considers criteria for admission, the question of succession to membership (for example, after the dissolution of one state into two or more states), and the issue of credentials—who gets to represent a state if there is more than one delegation that claims to do so.

5.1 Admission

The issue of admission to the United Nations was a major issue in the early years of the Cold War. The Soviet Union, its allies badly outnumbered in the General Assembly by Western states allied with the United States, tried in various ways to prevent the voting majority from blocking its candidates for membership. It tried to do this by exercising its veto in the Security Council (admission requires a majority vote in both bodies) to block Western-sponsored states, and it threatened to continue doing so unless members agreed to vote to admit candidates sponsored by the Eastern (Soviet) bloc.

By its insistence that no new states would be admitted unless all applicants entered together in a "package deal" the Soviet Union precipitated the first crisis regarding membership. In an effort to break the deadlock, the General

Assembly referred the matter to the International Court of Justice (ICJ) for an advisory opinion. Article 96 of the Charter makes provision for this procedure. The Court was asked to address the two questions asked in the introduction to this chapter.[1]

It answered both in the negative by a majority of nine votes to six—a division that reflected the political split in the General Assembly.

CONDITIONS OF ADMISSION OF A STATE TO MEMBERSHIP IN THE UNITED NATIONS (ADVISORY OPINION), 1948 ICJ REPORTS 57

The requisite conditions are five in number: to be admitted to membership in the United Nations an Applicant must 1) be a State; 2) be peace-loving; 3) accept the obligations of the Charter; 4) be able to carry out these obligations; and 5) be willing to do so.

All these conditions are subject to the judgment of the Organization. The judgment of the Organization means the judgment of the two organs mentioned in paragraph 2 of Article 4, and in the last analysis, that of its Members. The question put is concerned with the individual attitude of each Member called upon to pronounce itself on the question of admission.

Having been asked to determine the character, exhaustive or otherwise of the conditions stated in Article 4, the Court must in the first place consider the text of that Article . . . The text of this paragraph, by the enumeration which it contains and the choice of its terms, clearly demonstrates the intention of its authors to establish a legal rule which, while it fixes the conditions of admission, determines also the reasons for which admission may be refused; for the text does not differentiate between these two cases and any attempt to restrict it to one of them would be purely arbitrary.

. . . The natural meaning of the words used [in both the English and the French texts] leads to the conclusion that these conditions constitute an exhaustive enumeration and are not merely stated by way of guidance or ex-

---

[1] The exact question before the Court was as follows: "Is a Member of the United Nations which is called upon, in virtue of Article 4 of the Charter, to pronounce itself by its vote, either in the Security Council or in the General Assembly, on the admission of a State to membership in the United Nations, juridically entitled to make its consent to the admission dependent on conditions not expressly provided by paragraph I of the said Article? In particular, can such a Member, while it recognizes the conditions set forth in that provision to be fulfilled by the State concerned, subject its affirmative vote to the additional condition that other States be admitted to membership in the United Nations together with that State?"

ample. The provision would lose its significance and weight, if other conditions, unconnected with those laid down, could be demanded. The condition stated in paragraph I of Article 4 must therefore be regarded not merely as the necessary conditions, but also as the conditions which suffice.

Nor can it be argued that the conditions enumerated represent only an indispensable minimum, in the sense that political considerations can be superimposed upon them, and prevent the admission of an applicant which fulfils them. Such an interpretation would inconsistent with the terms of paragraph 2 of Article 4, which provide for the admission of . . . "any *such* State." It would lead to conferring upon Members an indefinite and practically unlimited power of discretion in the imposition of new conditions. Such a power would be inconsistent with the very character of paragraph I of Article 4, which, by reason of the close connection it establishes between membership and the observance of the principles and obligations of the Charter, clearly constitutes a legal regulation of the question of the admission of new States. . . .

If the authors of the Charter had meant to leave Members free to import into the application of this provision considerations extraneous to the conditions laid down therein, they would undoubtedly have adopted a different wording.

The Court considers that the text is sufficiently clear, consequently, it does not feel that it should deviate from the consistent practice of the Permanent Court of International Justice, according to which there is no occasion to resort to preparatory work if the text of a convention is sufficiently clear in itself.

The Court furthermore observes that Rule 60 of the Provisional Rules of Procedure of the Security Council is based on this interpretation. The first paragraph of this Rule reads as follows:

> The Security Council shall decide whether in its judgment the applicant is a peace-loving State and is able and willing to carry out the obligations contained in the Charter, and accordingly whether to recommend the applicant State for membership.

It does not, however, follow from the exhaustive character of Article 4 that an appreciation is precluded of such circumstances of fact as would enable the existence of the requisite conditions to be verified.

Article 4 does not forbid the taking into account of any factor which it is possible reasonably and in good faith to connect with the conditions laid down. The taking into account of such factors is implied in the very wide and very elastic nature of the prescribed conditions; no relevant political factor— that is to say, none connected with the conditions of admissions—is excluded.

It has been sought to deduce either from the second paragraph of Article 4, or from the political character of the organ recommending or deciding upon admission, arguments in favour of an interpretation of paragraph 1 of Article 4, to the effect that the fulfillment of the conditions provided for in that Article is necessary before the admission of a State can be recommended or decided upon, but that it does not preclude the Members of the Organization from advancing considerations of political expediency, extraneous to the conditions of Article 4.

But paragraph 2 is concerned only with the procedure for admission . . . the manner in which admission is effected, and not with the subject of the judgment of the Organization nor with the nature of the appreciation involved in that judgment, these two questions being dealt with in the preceding paragraph. . . .

The political character of an organ cannot release it from observance of the treaty provisions established by the Charter when they constitute limitations on its power, or criteria for its judgment . . . In this case, the limits . . . are fixed by Article 4 and allow for a wide liberty appreciation. There is therefore no conflict between the functions of the political organs and the exhaustive character of the prescribed conditions. . . .

It has been sought to base on the political responsibilities assumed by the Security Council, in virtue of Article 24 of the Charter, an argument justifying the necessity for according to the Security Council as well as to the General Assembly complete freedom of appreciation in connection with the admission of new Members. But Article 24, owing to the very general nature of its terms, cannot, in the absence of any provision, affect the special rules for admission which emerge from Article 4. . . .

The second part of the question, concerns a demand on the part of a Member making its consent to the admission of an applicant, dependent on the admission of other applicants.

Judged on the basis of the rule which the Court adopts in its interpretation of Article 4, such a demand constitutes a new condition, since it is entirely unconnected with those prescribed in Article 4. It is also in an entirely different category from those conditions, since it makes admission dependent, not on the conditions required of applicants, qualifications which are supposed to be fulfilled, but on an extraneous consideration concerning States other than the applicant State.

The provisions of Article 4 necessarily imply that every application for admission should be examined and voted on separately and on its own merits; otherwise it would be impossible to determine whether a particular applicant fulfils the necessary conditions. To subject an affirmative vote for the admission of an applicant State to the condition that other States be admitted would prevent Members from exercising their judgment in each case with complete liberty, within the scope of the prescribed conditions. Such a demand is incompatible with the letter and spirit of Article 4 of the Charter.

Dissenting Opinion of Judges Basdevant, Winiarski, Sir Arnold Mcnair, and Read

The provisions of paragraph 2 of Article 4, which fix the respective powers of the General Assembly and the Security Council in this matter, do not treat the admission of new Members as a mere matter of the routine application of rules of admission. It would only be possible to attribute such a meaning to this Article if it had adopted a system of accession and not of admission; and if accession had been the system adopted it would have been better to have placed the Secretary-General in control of the procedure. This Article does not create a system of accession, but the entirely different system of admission. In the working of this system the Charter requires the intervention of the two principal political organs of the United Nations, one for the purpose of making a recommendation and then the other for the purpose of effecting the admission. It is impossible by means of interpretation to regard these organs as mere pieces of procedural machinery like the Committee for Admissions established by the Security Council. In the system adopted by the Charter, admission is effected by the decision of the General Assembly, which can only act upon a recommendation of the Security Council, and after both these organs are satisfied that the applicant State possesses the qualifications required by paragraph 1 of Article 4.

The resolutions which embody either a recommendation or a decision in regard to admission are decisions of a political character; they emanate from political organs; by general consent they involve the examination of political factors, with a view to deciding whether the applicant State possesses the qualifications prescribed by paragraph 1 of Article 4; they produce a political effect by changing the condition of the applicant State in making it a Member of the United Nations. Upon the Security Council, whose duty it is to make the recommendation, there rests by the provisions of Article 24 of the Charter "primary responsibility for the maintenance of international peace and security"—a purpose inscribed in Article 1 of the Charter as the first of the Purposes of the United Nations. The admission of a new Member is preeminently a political act, and a political act of the greatest importance. The main function of a political organ is to examine questions in their political aspect, which means examining them from every point of view. It follows that the Members of such an organ who are responsible for forming its decisions must consider questions from every aspect, and, in consequence, are legally entitled to base their arguments and their vote upon political considerations. That is the position of a member of the Security Council or of the General Assembly who raises an objection based upon reasons other than the lack of one of the qualifications expressly required by paragraph 1 of Article 4.

That does not mean that no legal restriction is placed upon this liberty. We do not claim that a political organ and those who contribute to the formation of its decisions are emancipated from all duty to respect the law. The Security Council, the General Assembly and the Members who contribute by their votes to the decisions of these bodies are clearly bound to respect paragraph 1 of Article 4, and, in consequence, bound not to admit a State which fails to possess the conditions required in this paragraph. . . .

In our opinion, while the Charter makes the qualifications specified in paragraph 1 of Article 4 essential, it does not make them sufficient. If it had regarded them as sufficient, it would not have failed to say so. The point was one of too great importance to be left in obscurity. . . .

A consideration based on the desire that the admission of the State should involve the contemporaneous admission of other States is clearly foreign to the process of ascertaining that the first State possesses the qualifications laid down in Article 4, paragraph 1; it is a political consideration. If a Member of the United Nations is legally entitled to make its refusal to admit depend on political considerations, that is exactly what the Member would be doing in this case.

In 1991, after the dissolution of the Federal Socialist Republic of Yugoslavia, one of the breakaway republics (the former Yugoslav Republic of Macedonia, "FYROM") declared its sovereignty and sought international recognition as the "Republic of Macedonia."[2] This led to outrage on the part of Greece, which claimed that the name pertained to an ancient Greek kingdom and to a large part of the territory of modern Greece. The Greek government officially proclaimed its opposition to the use of this denomination by FYROM/Macedonia.[3]

On 27 June 1992 the European Council decided to recognize FYROM/Macedonia only "under a name which does not include the term Macedonia."[4] In response, a defiant government of FYROM adopted the sixteen-point Star of Vergina, closely associated with ancient Macedonia, as the emblem on its national flag and issued new school textbooks that contained irredentist references to "Greater Macedonia."

On 30 July 1992 the FYROM government applied to the United Nations for recognition. In response, in January 1993 the Greek government submitted a sixteen-point memorandum to the Security Council, denouncing FYROM/Macedonia's intransigence and "destabilising influence in the region." It also contained attachments of the "Greater Macedonia" maps printed in FYROM/Macedonia and of the Vergina Star on its flag. The FYROM/Macedonia government responded with representations of goodwill, but also by insisting that its choice of name should not affect its eligibility for admission to the United Nations. In a compromise the Security Council passed resolution 817 (1993) admitting the new state under the provisional name "Former Yugoslav Republic of Macedonia." It also recommended that the difference over the name be resolved by the parties "in the interest of the maintenance of peaceful and good-neighbourly relations in the region."[5]

---

[2] Constitution of the Republic of Macedonia, 1991, Preamble.

[3] Letter dated 25 January 1993 from the Minister for Foreign Affairs of Greece to the Secretary-General, UN Doc. A/47/877-S/25158 (1993).

[4] European Council, Declaration on the former Yugoslavia, Lisbon, 27 June 1992.

[5] See Demetrius Andreas Floudas, "Pardon? A Conflict for a Name? Fyrom's Dispute with Greece Revisited," available at http://www.intersticeconsulting.com/documents/FYROM.pdf.

The documents that follow represent the position that has been taken on this question by the parties, Greece, FYROM/Macedonia, and, the Security Council.

MEMORANDUM OF GREECE CONCERNING THE APPLICATION OF FORMER YUGOSLAV REPUBLIC OF MACEDONIA FOR ADMISSION TO THE UNITED NATIONS, 21 JANUARY 1993[6]

[Greece opposed the admission of the FYROM to the UN on the grounds that, *inter alia*]

3. . . . past experiences and practices, as well as constituent acts and policies of the new republic raise serious concerns about its willingness to fulfil the obligations arising from the UN Charter.

4. The new republic emerged as successor to the former Yugoslav Federative Republic of Macedonia. The philosophy of its Constitution is based on the principles and constituent declarations . . . endorsed in August 1944 by the Antifascist Assembly of the National Liberation of Macedonia (ASNOM). In these declarations, cited in the preamble of the Constitution, there are direct references to the annexation of the Macedonian provinces of Greece and Bulgaria, and to the establishment eventually of a Greater Macedonian state within the Yugoslav Federation. . . .

8. Since the declaration of independence, a series of initiatives taken by the authorities of Skopje have shown that there is a clear link and continuity of aims and actions in particular against Greece. In the [FYROM] Constitution there are references to the possibility of changing of borders—while FYROM's territory remains "indivisible and inalienable" (Art 3)—and intervening in the internal affairs of neighbouring states on the pretext of issues concerning "the status and rights of alleged minorities (Art 49). There are numerous indications that the expansionist propaganda aimed at the neighbouring Macedonian province of Greece continues unabated. This is shown, in particular, through the wide circulation within FYROM of maps portraying a greater Macedonia i.e. incorporating parts of the territory of all its neighbouring states, and of hostile literature usurping Greek symbols and heritage. As recently as August 1992, the authorities in Skopje affixed on the new flag of the republic the emblem of the ancient Macedonian dynasty found in Greece in the tomb of King Phillip II. . . .

10. The name of a state is a symbol. Thus the fact that the authorities in Skopje have adopted the denomination "Republic of Macedonia" for their

---

[6] UN Doc. A/47/877-S/25158 (1993).

state is of paramount significance. It is important to note that they have explicitly adopted the name of a wider geographical region extending over four neighbouring countries, with only 38.5% to be found in the territory of FYROM. This fact by itself clearly undermines the sovereignty of neighbouring states to their respective Macedonian regions . . .

11. To prevent such destabilizing situations . . . the European Community, to which the FYROM has applied for recognition, has set prerequisites for the recognition of the applicant by the Community and its member states . . . - Briefly they stipulate that FYROM should provide the necessary legal and political guarantees that it will harbor no territorial claims against Greece, that it will abstain from hostile propaganda against this country and that it will no use the term Macedonia in the state's denomination. Unfortunately, FYROM has failed to comply.

12. During the past year, Greece has conveyed to Skopje, on a number of occasions, its sincere determination to proceed with the development of all round economic and political co-operation with the neighbouring republic, as soon as FYROM adopted the foregoing E.C. prerequisites for recognition. Moreover, Greece has taken the initiative so that all neighbouring states of FYROM make public declarations recognizing and guaranteeing as inviolable their respective frontiers. Furthermore, Greece has supported E.C. initiatives to provide humanitarian and economic aid to this republic, while the Greek Prime Minister publicly extended a hand of co-operation to Skopje. In addition, Greece has supported a recent effort by the European Community and individual members of the Community in seeking a peaceful way to settle the problem.

13. Unfortunately, the authorities of Skopje have persisted in pursuing an inflexible and uncooperative attitude by rejecting all proposals aiming at peaceful settlement of the outstanding issues.

14. It is in the competence of the Security Council not only to resolve disputes but also to take necessary actions prevent them as well. This is a clear case were preventive diplomacy is urgently needed. All efforts and all proposals in this direction should be explored. It should be noted that there have been cases in which application to membership has been subjected to prior fulfillment of certain conditions in the interest of peace and security.

15. Greece wishes to point out that the admission of FYROM to UN membership prior to meeting the necessary prerequisites, and in particular abandoning the use of the denomination "Republic of Macedonia," would perpetuate and increase friction and tension and would not be conducive to peace and stability in an already troubled region. Under these circumstances, Greece regretfully would not be able to recognize this republic.

FYROM/Macedonia responded two months later.

LETTER TO THE PRESIDENT OF THE SECURITY COUNCIL
FROM THE PRESIDENT OF MACEDONIA, 24 MARCH 1993[7]

I wish to bring to your attention our disappointment that it has not proved possible for the Security Council to adopt the standard straightforward resolution on admission of new members.

Regardless of our concerns I would like to assure you that the Republic of Macedonia is able and willing to carry obligations under the Charter. We shall proceed with out policy of good neighborly relations and cooperation aiming at establishing our country as a factor of peace and security in the region and in the broader international community.

I would also like to express our willingness to continue to cooperate with the co-chairman of the Steering Committee of the International Conference on the former Yugoslavia in setting up a mechanism to settle the difference that has arisen and to promote confidence building measures with the Republic of Greece, on the clear understanding that his in no way affects the completion of the process of the admission of the Republic of Macedonia to the Membership of the United Nations.

The Republic of Macedonia will in no circumstances be prepared to accept the "former Yugoslav Republic of Macedonia" as the name of the country. We refuse to be associated in any way with the present connotation of the term "Yugoslavia"

On 7 April 1993, the Council adopted resolution 817 (1993).

SECURITY COUNCIL RESOLUTION 817 (1993):
MACEDONIAN MEMBERSHIP

The Security Council, . . .

Noting that the applicant fulfils the criteria for membership in the United Nations laid down in Article 4 of the Charter,

Noting however that a difference has arisen over the name of the State, which needs to be resolved in the interest of the maintenance of peaceful and good-neighbourly relations in the region,

Welcoming the readiness of the Co-Chairmen of the Steering Committee of the International Conference on the Former Yugoslavia, at the request of the Secretary-General, to use their good offices to settle the above-mentioned difference, and to promote confidence-building measures among the parties, . . .

[7] UN Doc. S/25541 (1993).

1. *Urges* the parties to continue to cooperate with the Co-Chairmen of the Steering Committee of the International Conference on the Former Yugoslavia in order to arrive at a speedy settlement of their difference;

2. *Recommends* to the General Assembly that the State whose application is contained in document S/25147 be admitted to membership in the United Nations, this State being provisionally referred to for all purposes within the United Nations as "the former Yugoslav Republic of Macedonia" pending settlement of the difference that has arisen over the name of the State;

3. *Requests* the Secretary-General to report to the Council on the outcome of the initiative taken by the Co-Chairmen of the Steering Committee of the International Conference on the Former Yugoslavia.

Pursuant to this, the General Assembly adopted resolution 47/225 (1993) admitting the country under the provisional name suggested by the Security Council. FYROM/Macedonia was also encouraged to arrive at a settlement with Greece over this matter. For many years thereafter, UN organs and members continued to refer to the "former Yugoslav Republic of Macedonia" while the state itself used "Republic of Macedonia."

The stalemate continues, and international bodies such as the International Criminal Tribunal for the former Yugoslavia have maintained the status quo by continuing to use "FYROM" to refer to the republic.

QUESTIONS

1. An Advisory Opinion rendered by the Court is not binding on the requesting organ of the United Nations or on any other organ. Article 65 of the Statute of the ICJ makes provision for the Court's jurisdiction to give such opinions and to render its "advisory functions" (art. 68). Must the court accede to such a request? May there be circumstances in which it would be wise to refuse to provide such advice? Was it useful for the Court to render the 1948 opinion on conditions of admission? Since states do not have to explain their votes in the principal political organs (the General Assembly and the Security Council) what would be the likely effect of the opinion given by the Court?

2. The deadlock over admissions was resolved in 1955 by an agreement between the Western and the Soviet blocs to admit sixteen nations simultaneously, by the very "package deal" rejected by the Court.[8] Was this a violation of the Charter, or was it a sensible interpretation of the rules by

---

[8] UN Doc. S/13509 (1955); GA Res. 995(X) (1955).

the members of the Security Council? What is the legal effect of such a "reinterpretation" of the Charter by the members of the Security Council?

3. The General Assembly admitted Macedonia under a provisional name, on the recommendation of the Security Council. Igor Janev, a former Special Advisor of the Minister of Foreign Affairs of the Republic of Macedonia, contends that in effect the General Assembly imposed two conditions on Macedonia: first, the acceptance of a provisional name and, second, the obligation to negotiate with another country (Greece) over its final name. This, he argues is *ultra vires* article 4 of the UN Charter.[9] Do you agree?

4. May the choice by an applicant state of a name be taken into consideration by other states in determining whether the applicant is "peace-loving"?

5. Would it be acceptable for a state to vote against the admission of an applicant on the ground that it is not democratic? Is it plausible that a non-democratic state be presumed not to be "peace-loving"?

5.2 Succession (I): The Soviet Union

The formal process of disintegration of the Soviet Union was initiated in Minsk on 8 December 1991, with the signing of the Declaration by the Heads of State of the Republic of Belarus, the Russian Soviet Federative Socialist Republic, and Ukraine, and the Agreement Establishing the Commonwealth of Independent States. These instruments declared that the Soviet Union no longer existed as a subject of international law and a geopolitical reality; they also proclaimed the establishment of the Commonwealth of Independent States (CIS). The CIS constituted by the three signing States would be open for accession to all member states of the Soviet Union, as well as to other states sharing the purposes and principles of the founding agreement.

These instruments, commonly referred to as the Minsk Agreements, were of questionable legality, however. For while the participating states had the right to withdraw from the Soviet Union and to set up another association of sovereign states, they could not, as only three of the twelve states that comprised the Soviet Union, declare that it had ceased to exist.[10]

Soon after, on 21 December 1991, eight other states (Azerbaijan, Armenia, Kazakhstan, Kyrgyzstan, Moldova, Tajikistan, Turkmenistan, and Uzbekistan) met with the signatories to the Minsk Agreements at Alma Ata and issued a declaration supporting the establishment of the CIS and demise of the Soviet Union. The Alma Ata Declaration[11] provided that with the establishment of the CIS, the Soviet Union would cease to exist. As Ukraine,

---

[9] Igor Janev, "Some Remarks of the Legal Status of Macedonia in the United Nations Organization," *Review of International Affairs*, vol. 53(1108) (2002).

[10] See Sergei A. Voitovich, *The Commonwealth of Independent States: An Emerging Institutional Model, European Journal of International Law*, vol. 4 (1993), p. 403.

[11] UN Doc. A/47/60-S/23329 (1991), Annex II.

Russia, and Belarus were among the founder members of the United Nations, and as Ukraine and Belarus had maintained their membership, the Council of the Heads of State of the CIS also took a decision to support Russia's succession to the Soviet Union's seat at the United Nations, including permanent membership of the Security Council and the right to exercise the Soviet veto.

DECISION BY THE COUNCIL OF HEADS OF STATE OF THE COMMONWEALTH OF INDEPENDENT STATES, 21 DECEMBER 1991[12]

The States participating in the Commonwealth, referring to article 12 of the Agreement establishing the Commonwealth of Independent States,

Proceeding from the intention of each State to discharge the obligations under the Charter of the United Nations and to participate in the work of that Organization as full Members,

Bearing in mind that the Republic of Belarus, the Union of Soviet Socialist Republics and Ukraine were founder Members of the United Nations,

Expressing satisfaction that the Republic of Belarus and Ukraine continue to participate in the United Nations as sovereign independent States,

Resolved to promote the strengthening of international peace and security on the basis of the Charter of the United Nations in the interests of their peoples and of the entire international community,

Have decided that:

1. The States of the Commonwealth support Russia's continuance of the membership of the Union of Soviet Socialist Republics in the United Nations, including permanent membership of the Security Council, and other international organizations.

2. The Republic of Belarus, [Russia] and Ukraine will extend their support to the other States of the Commonwealth in resolving issues of their full membership in the United Nations and other international organizations.

LETTER FROM PRESIDENT OF THE RUSSIAN FEDERATION BORIS YELTSIN TO THE SECRETARY-GENERAL OF THE UNITED NATIONS, 24 DECEMBER 1991

I have the honour to inform you that the membership of the Union of Soviet Socialist Republics in the United Nations, including the Security Council and

---

[12] UN Doc. A/47/60-S/23329 (1991), Annex V.

all other organs and organizations of the United Nations system, is being continued by the Russian Federation (RSFSR) with the support of the countries of the Commonwealth of Independent States. In this connection, I request that the name "Russian Federation" should be used in the United Nations in place of the name "the Union of Soviet Socialist Republics."

The Russian Federation maintains full responsibility for all the rights and obligations of the USSR under the Charter of the United Nations, including the financial obligations.

I request that you consider this letter as confirmation of the credentials to represent the Russian Federation in United Nations organs for all the persons currently holding the credentials of representatives of the USSR to the United Nations.

Russia was thereafter confirmed, at least by acquiescence, as the Soviet Union's successor to the United Nations and to the Soviet Union's permanent seat in the Security Council. While this transition had been fairly smooth for Russia, there were some questions raised about the legality of the course adopted. Yehuda Z. Blum argued that "with the demise of the Soviet Union itself, its membership in the United Nations should have automatically lapsed and Russia should have been admitted to membership in the same way as the other newly-independent republics." The issue here was not merely of a change in name, or system of government, it was the termination of the Soviet Union as a legal entity.[13] According to his analysis, the lack of objections by the UN Secretary-General or member states is probably explained by the fact that the elimination of Soviet (and subsequently Russian) membership on the Security Council would have created a constitutional crisis for the United Nations.

Rein Mullerson on the other hand, concluded that the succession was legitimate, for three reasons: first, Russia remains one of the largest States in the world geographically and demographically; secondly, Soviet Russia after 1917 and the Soviet Union after 1922 were treated as continuing the State which existed under the Russian Empire; and thirdly, Russia's continuity of the legal personality of the Soviet Union was recognized by third states.[14]

The Vienna Convention on Succession of States in Respect of Treaties was not in force at this time. In any event it does not appear to envisage a situation where one of the constituent states of a larger entity takes over its identity after its dissolution.

---

[13] Yehuda Z. Blum, "Russia Takes Over the Soviet Union's Seat at the United Nations," *European Journal of International Law*, vol. 3 (1992) p. 360.
[14] Rein Mullerson, "The Continuity and Succession of States, by Reference to the Former USSR and Yugoslavia," *International & Comparative Law Quarterly*, vol. 42(3) (1993), p. 473.

5.3 Succession (II): The Socialist Federal Republic of Yugoslavia

In contrast to the relative smoothness of the Russian transition, the succession of the Federal Republic of Yugoslavia (Serbia and Montenegro) to the seat of the former Socialist Federal Republic of Yugoslavia (SFRY), was a complicated and often bitterly contested affair. The Federal Republic of Yugoslavia (FRY) consisting of two of the SFRY's six republics claimed a right to succeed to its membership of the United Nations, particularly since the breakaway republics of Slovenia, Bosnia and Herzegovina, and Croatia had already been admitted to membership on 22 May 1992 by General Assembly resolutions 236, 237, and 238 respectively. The Security Council, however, opposed this request as did the other constituent units of the former Yugoslavia. Instead on 19 September 1992 the Council passed resolution 777 (1992) by a vote of twelve in favor, with China, India, and Zimbabwe abstaining.

SECURITY COUNCIL RESOLUTION 777 (1992)

The Security Council, . . .
1. *Considers* that the Federal Republic of Yugoslavia (Serbia and Montenegro) cannot continue automatically the membership of the former Socialist Federal Republic of Yugoslavia in the United Nations; and therefore recommends to the General Assembly that it decide that the Federal Republic of Yugoslavia (Serbia and Montenegro) should apply for membership in the United Nations and that it shall not participate in the work of the General Assembly; . . .

At the Security Council meeting held to pass this resolution, various members explained why they had chosen to support the resolution or to abstain. The main reason was the lack of agreement among the six states that had been members of SFRY to allow the FRY to succeed to its membership, as Russia had succeeded to the membership of the former Soviet Union. Another factor was the conflict that was raging between several ethnic groups in this region. Non-admission, especially the bar on participation in the work of the General Assembly was thus seen as an act of condemnation and as leverage to compel the applicant, Belgrade, to desist from coercive acts against Croatia and Bosnia. At the same time, exclusion from the General Assembly but not other UN bodies still allowed the Security Council to engage with the FRY (and hear from its representatives).

The three abstaining states all felt the Security Council was acting in excess of its powers by not conforming to Articles 5 and 6 of the UN Charter re-

garding suspension and expulsion and by attempting to make recommendations to the General Assembly regarding the right of states to participate in
its working.

PROVISIONAL VERBATIM RECORD OF THE MEETING HELD AT HEADQUARTERS, NEW YORK, ON SATURDAY, 19 SEPTEMBER 1992, AT 12.55 PM, S/PV.3116

Mr. Vorontsov (Russian Federation) (interpretation from Russian):
[Russia] is ready to support the draft resolution . . . on the basis of the
prevailing view in the international community that none of the republics that
have emerged in the place of the former [SFRY] can claim automatic continued membership in the United Nations. We agree that the [FRY], like other
former Yugoslav republics, will have to apply for membership in the United
Nations, and we will support such an application.

At the same time, we were unable to agree with the proposal, put forward
by some States, that the FRY should be excluded, formally or de facto, from
membership in the United Nations. We are convinced that such a decision
would have negative consequences for the process of the political settlement
of the Yugoslav crisis . . . and would also be counterproductive with regard
to the London Conference, since the United Nations, through its Secretary-
General, is among the leaders of that process.

The compromise that has been reached—that the FRY should not participate in the work of the General Assembly—may seem unsatisfactory to some.
Frankly, we would have preferred not to have recourse to such a measure to
influence the FRY, because it is already experiencing sufficient pressure from
the international community in the form of economic sanctions. But we agree
to this gesture of condemnation by the world community on the understanding that in order to make a full contribution to the solution of the world
problems discussed in the General Assembly, the FRY must take all possible
measures to bring about an early cessation of the fratricidal conflict in its
region. It must effectively cooperate to promote national reconciliation and
cooperation between the various ethnic groups.

At the same time, the decision to suspend the participation of the FRY in
the work of the General Assembly will in no way affect the possibility of
participation by the FRY in the work of other organs of the UN, in particular
the Security Council, nor will it affect the issuance of documents to it, the
functioning of the Permanent Mission of the FRY to the UN or the keeping of
the nameplate with the name Yugoslavia in the General Assembly Hall and
the rooms in which the Assembly's organs meet.

In short, since the decision of the Security Council does not provide for the
expulsion of the Federal Republic of Yugoslavia from the United Nations, the

measures taken with regard to it must remain strictly within the limits of the decision we are taking today. . . .

Mr. Gharekhan (India):

Regarding the constitutional aspect . . . any action by the Council should be in strict conformity with the provisions of the Charter. That is the only way in which the prestige and credibility of this important organ can be preserved. There are specific provisions in the Charter regarding membership in the Organisation. Questions of membership or rights and privileges of participation are matters of fundamental importance. This makes it all the more essential to adhere to the provisions of the Charter. The draft resolution . . . does not conform to either Article 5 or Article 6 of the Charter, the only two Articles that deal with the issue it is attempting to address.

The Security Council, under the Charter, is competent to recommend either suspension or expulsion of a State. Nowhere in the Charter has the Security Council been given the authority to recommend to the General Assembly that a country's participation in the Assembly be withdrawn or suspended. That authority belongs to the General Assembly, which does not need any recommendation to that effect from the Security Council. Indeed, the General Assembly is under no legal obligation to act on any such recommendation, just as the Security Council is under no legal obligation to comply with the General Assembly's recommendations.

For these reasons, my delegation will not be in a position to support the draft resolution.

Mr. Mumbengegwi (Zimbabwe):

It is significant that the text of the draft resolution before us makes no reference to any provisions of the Charter under which this action is being taken. Strict adherence to the provisions of the Charter has always been a source of protection for small States, and the increasing disregard for, or mutation of, Charter provisions causes us great concern. It would seem that the Charter's provisions are consistently ignored or applied selectively in the deliberations of our Council. My delegation has on previous occasions cautioned against the tendency to equate a majority vote in this Council as constituting international law. This tendency is bound to undermine the prestige and the moral authority of the Security Council. . . .

For these reasons, my delegation will not be able to support the draft resolution before us. . . .

Mr. Merimee (France) (interpretation from French):

This text responds both to the requirements of the Charter and the needs of the moment. Indeed, it respects the apportioning of competence established by the Charter between the Security Council and the General Assembly. Furthermore, it adopts a pragmatic approach in keeping with the political situation following upon the London Conference. In this respect, it confirms and translates into reality the international community's rejection of the automatic continuation in the United Nations of the former SFRY by the FRY. . . .

Mr. Watson (United States of America):

For the first time, the UN is facing the dissolution of one of its Members without agreement by the successor States on the status of the original UN seat. Moreover none of the former republics of the former Yugoslavia is so clearly a predominant portion of the original State as to be entitled to be treated as the continuation of that State. For these reasons, and in the absence of agreement among the former republics on this issue . . . we cannot accept Serbia and Montenegro's claim to the former Yugoslavia's UN Seat.

I would like to comment on the provision of the resolution that Serbia and Montenegro shall not participate in the work of the General Assembly. This provision flows inevitably from the determination by the Council and the General Assembly that Serbia and Montenegro is not the continuation of the former Yugoslavia and must apply for membership in the United Nations. To state the obvious, a country which is not a member of the United Nations cannot participate in the work of the General Assembly.

The resolution's call to have the Security Council review the matter once again before the end of the fall session of the General Assembly simply refers to a willingness on the part of the Council to consider an expected application from Serbia and Montenegro. The resolution makes it clear that, in the view of the Council, Serbia and Montenegro, like any other new state must apply for membership in the United Nations and should be held to the criteria in the United Nations Charter if it does so. The criteria require that the applicant be both willing and able to fulfil United Nations obligations, including compliance with Chapter VII Security Council resolutions.

Following the Security Council resolution, the General Assembly was faced with the questions of admission and of FRY's participation in its working. The following resolution was passed on the 21 September 1992 by a vote of 127 in favor, 6 against and 26 abstentions. A further 19 members were absent.

GENERAL ASSEMBLY RESOLUTION 47/1 (1992)

The General Assembly,

Having received the recommendation of the Security Council of 19 September 1992 . . .

1. *Considers* that the Federal Republic of Yugoslavia (Serbia and Montenegro) cannot continue automatically the membership of the former Socialist Federal Republic of Yugoslavia in the United Nations; and therefore *decides* that the Federal Republic of Yugoslavia (Serbia and Montenegro) should apply for membership in the United Nations and that it shall not participate in the work of the General Assembly;

2. *Takes note* of the intention of the Security Council to consider the matter again before the end of the main part of the forty-seventh session of the General Assembly.

These actions led to considerable confusion as to the actual status of the FRY in the United Nations. The following clarification was issued by the UN Legal Counsel:

UN LEGAL COUNSEL'S OPINION ON GENERAL ASSEMBLY RESOLUTION 47/1 (1992), ADDRESSED TO THE PERMANENT REPRESENTATIVES OF BOSNIA AND HERZEGOVINA AND CROATIA, 29 SEPTEMBER 1992[15]

General Assembly resolution 47/1 deals with a membership issue which is not foreseen in the Charter of the United Nations, namely, the consequences for purposes of membership in the United Nations of the disintegration of a Member State on which there is no agreement among the immediate successors of that state or among the membership of the Organization at large. This explains the fact that resolution 47/1 was not adopted pursuant to Article 5 (suspension) of the Charter nor under Article 6 (expulsion). . . .

The only practical consequence that the resolution draws is the [FRY] shall not participate in the work of the General Assembly. It is clear therefore that the representatives of the [FRY] can no longer participate in the work of the General Assembly, its subsidiary organs, nor conferences and meetings convened by it. . . .

[T]he Resolution neither terminates nor suspends Yugoslavia's membership in the Organization. Consequently the seat and the nameplate remain as before but in Assembly bodies representatives of the [FRY] cannot sit behind the sign 'Yugoslavia'. Yugoslav missions at the United Nations Headquarters and offices may continue to function and may receive and circulate documents. At Headquarters, the Secretariat will continue to fly the flag of the old Yugoslavia as it is the last flag used by the Secretariat. The Resolution does not take away the right of Yugoslavia to participate in the work of organs other than Assembly bodies. The admission to the United Nations of a new Yugoslavia under Article 4 of the Charter will terminate the situation created by resolution 47/1.

The FRY underwent a radical shift in governance with the popular uprising against the Milosevic regime in 2000. The new government decided to abandon the previous claim of automatic succession and to apply *de novo* [from the beginning] for membership in the United Nations. This was granted with General Assembly resolution 55/12 on 1 November 2000. Nevertheless, the status of the FRY during the intervening period (1992–2000) has been an

---

[15] UN Doc. A/47/485 (1992), Annex.

important subject of litigation. Only member states of the United Nations, ordinarily, are eligible to be parties to a case before the ICJ. The FRY was, nevertheless, a respondent in one case[16] and applicant in another.[17] In the course of these proceedings the Court has had the occasion to comment on FRY's status during the 1992–2000 period, when the alleged acts of genocide and the consequent legal actions were begun.

In the first case, the question of FRY's status between 1992 and 2000 arose in the course of an Application for Revision filed by the FRY, against the Judgment on Preliminary Objections delivered by the Court on 11 July 1996. In this Judgment the Court had ruled against the FRY's objections to the Court's jurisdiction and the admissibility of the application made by Bosnia invoking the Genocide Convention.

The FRY, which in 2003 adopted the name Serbia and Montenegro, applied for revision of the judgment on the basis that it had not been a signatory to the Statute of the International Court of Justice nor a signatory to the Genocide Convention prior to its accession to the UN Charter in 2000, and thus, that the court did not have jurisdiction. It claimed this was a "new fact" on the basis of which the judgment was open to revision as per Article 61 of the ICJ Statute.

(Serbia and Montenegro subsequently separated, though with an agreement that Serbia would succeed to the Serbia and Montenegro seat at the United Nations. Montenegro became the 192nd member of the United Nations on 28 June 2006.)

APPLICATION FOR REVISION OF THE JUDGMENT OF 11 JULY 1996 IN THE CASE CONCERNING APPLICATION OF THE CONVENTION ON THE PREVENTION AND PUNISHMENT OF THE CRIME OF GENOCIDE (*BOSNIA AND HERZEGOVINA V. YUGOSLAVIA*) (PRELIMINARY OBJECTIONS) (INTERNATIONAL COURT OF JUSTICE, JUDGMENT OF 3 FEBRUARY 2003)

33. The Court recalls that between the adoption of General Assembly resolution 47/1 of 22 September 1992 and the admission of the FRY to the United Nations on 1 November 2000, the legal position of the FRY remained complex . . .

---

[16] *Case Concerning the Application of the Convention on the Prevention and Punishment of the Crime of Genocide*, brought against the Federal Republic of Yugoslavia by Bosnia Herzegovina on 20 March 1993.

[17] *Case Concerning Legality of Use of Force*, brought against certain members of the North Atlantic Treaty Organization by the Federal Republic of Yugoslavia on 29 April 1999.

66. FRY claims that the facts which existed at the time of the 1996 Judgment and upon the discovery of which its request for revision of that Judgment is based "are that the FRY was *not* a party to the Statute, and that it did *not* remain bound by the Genocide Convention continuing the personality of the former Yugoslavia." It argues that these "facts" were "revealed" by its admission to the United Nations on 1 November 2000 and by the Legal Counsel's letter of 8 December 2000. . . .

71. The Court wishes to emphasize that General Assembly resolution 55/12 of 1 November 2000 cannot have changed retroactively the *sui generis* position which the FRY found itself in vis-à-vis the United Nations over the period 1992 to 2000, or its position in relation to the Statute of the Court and the Genocide Convention. Furthermore, the letter of the Legal Counsel of the United Nations dated 8 December 2000, cannot have affected the FRY's position in relation to treaties.

The Court also observes that, in any event, the said letter did not contain an invitation to the FRY to accede to the relevant conventions, but rather to "undertake treaty actions, as appropriate, . . . as a successor State."

72. It follows from the foregoing that it has not been established that the request of the FRY is based upon the discovery of "some fact" which was "when the judgment was given, unknown to the Court and also to the party claiming revision." The Court therefore concludes that one of the conditions for the admissibility of an application for revision prescribed by paragraph 1 of Article 61 of the Statute has not been satisfied.

In 1999 Yugoslavia (FRY) filed its own genocide action against the member states of the North Atlantic Treaty Organization (NATO), alleging illegal use of force and perpetration of genocide against the Serbs in the Kosovo intervention of 1999.[18] In 2000, while the case was underway, Yugoslavia was admitted to the United Nations as a new state, but it did not withdraw the case. In the course of this decision the ICJ gave another opinion on the status of FRY in the years between 1992 and 2000, and also discussed its claim vis-à-vis membership of the Genocide Convention.

LEGALITY OF USE OF FORCE *(SERBIA AND MONTENEGRO V. UNITED KINGDOM)* (INTERNATIONAL COURT OF JUSTICE, JUDGMENT OF 15 DECEMBER 2004)

44 . . . As the Court observed earlier . . . , the question whether Serbia and Montenegro was or was not a party to the Statute of the Court at the time of

---

[18] This incident is discussed in chapter 2.

the institution of the present proceedings is fundamental; for if it were not such a party, the Court would not be open to it under Article 35, paragraph 1, of the Statute. In that situation, subject to any application of paragraph 2 of that Article, Serbia and Montenegro could not have properly seized the Court, whatever title of jurisdiction it might have invoked, for the simple reason that Serbia and Montenegro did not have the right to appear before the Court. . . .

45. No specific assertion was made in the Application that the Court was open to Serbia and Montenegro under Article 35, paragraph 1, of the Statute of the Court, but it was later made clear that the Applicant claimed to be a Member of the United Nations and thus a party to the Statute of the Court, by virtue of Article 93, paragraph 1, of the Charter, at the time of filing of the Application. . . .

49. The United Kingdom subsequently argued as its first preliminary objection to the jurisdiction of the Court that "the FRY is not qualified to bring these proceedings" on the grounds, *inter alia*, that

> [t]he FRY is not a party to the Statute of the Court, since it is neither a Member of the United Nations nor a non-Member State that has become a party to the Statute under Article 93 (2) of the Charter [of the United Nations].

50. The Court notes that it is, and has always been, common ground between the Parties that Serbia and Montenegro has not claimed to have become a party to the Statute on any other basis than by membership in the United Nations. Therefore the question raised in this first preliminary objection is simply whether or not the Applicant was a Member of the United Nations at the time when it instituted proceedings in the present case. . . .

62. . . . [I]t is the view of the Court that the legal situation that obtained within the United Nations during that eight-year period concerning the status of the Federal Republic of Yugoslavia . . . remained ambiguous and open to different assessments. This was due, *inter alia*, to the absence of an authoritative determination by the competent organs of the United Nations defining clearly the legal status of the Federal Republic of Yugoslavia vis-à-vis the United Nations. . . .

71. To sum up, all these events testify to the rather confused and complex state of affairs that obtained within the United Nations surrounding the issue of the legal status of the Federal Republic of Yugoslavia in the Organization during this period. It is against this background that the Court, in its Judgment of 3 February 2003, referred to the "*sui generis* position which the FRY found itself in" during the period between 1992 to 2000.

72. It must be stated that this qualification of the position of the Federal Republic of Yugoslavia as "*sui generis*," which the Court employed to describe the situation during this period of 1992 to 2000, is not a prescriptive term from which certain defined legal consequences accrue; it is merely descriptive of the amorphous state of affairs in which the Federal Republic of

Yugoslavia found itself during this period. No final and definitive conclusion was drawn by the Court from this descriptive term on the amorphous status of the Federal Republic of Yugoslavia vis-à-vis or within the United Nations during this period. The Court did not commit itself to a definitive position on the issue of the legal status of the Federal Republic of Yugoslavia in relation to the Charter and the Statute in its pronouncements in incidental proceedings, in the cases involving this issue which came before the Court during this anomalous period . . .

73. This situation, however, came to an end with a new development in 2000. On 24 September 2000, Mr. Koštunica was elected President of the Federal Republic of Yugoslavia. In that capacity, on 27 October 2000 he sent a letter to the Secretary-General requesting admission of the Federal Republic of Yugoslavia to membership in the United Nations, in the following terms:

> In the wake of fundamental democratic changes that took place in the Federal Republic of Yugoslavia, in the capacity of President, I have the honour to request the admission of the Federal Republic of Yugoslavia to membership in the United Nations *in light of the implementation of Security Council resolution 777 (1992)*. . . .

74. Acting upon this application by the Federal Republic of Yugoslavia for membership in the United Nations, the Security Council on 31 October 2000 *"recommend[ed]"* to the General Assembly that the Federal Republic of Yugoslavia be admitted to membership in the United Nations" (United Nations doc. S/RES/1326). On 1 November 2000, the General Assembly, by resolution 55/12, *"[h]aving received"* the recommendation of the Security Council of 31 October 2000" and *"[h]aving considered"* the application for membership of the Federal Republic of Yugoslavia," decided to "admit the Federal Republic of Yugoslavia to membership in the United Nations."

75. As the letter of the President of the Federal Republic of Yugoslavia quoted above demonstrates, this action on the part of the Federal Republic of Yugoslavia signified that it had finally decided to act on Security Council resolution 777 (1992) by aligning itself with the position of the Security Council as expressed in that resolution. Furthermore the Security Council confirmed its own position by taking steps for the admission of the Federal Republic of Yugoslavia as a new Member of the United Nations, which, when followed by corresponding steps taken by the General Assembly, completed the procedure for the admission of a new Member under Article 4 of the Charter, rather than pursuing any course involving recognition of continuing membership of the Federal Republic of Yugoslavia in the United Nations.

76. This new development effectively put an end to the *sui generis* position of the Federal Republic of Yugoslavia within the United Nations, which, as the Court has observed in earlier pronouncements, had been fraught with "legal difficulties" throughout the period between 1992 and 2000 . . . The Applicant thus has the status of membership in the United Nations as from

1 November 2000. However, its admission to the United Nations did not have, and could not have had, the effect of dating back to the time when the Socialist Federal Republic of Yugoslavia broke up and disappeared; there was in 2000 no question of restoring the membership rights of the Socialist Federal Republic of Yugoslavia for the benefit of the Federal Republic of Yugoslavia. At the same time, it became clear that the *sui generis* position of the Applicant could not have amounted to its membership in the Organization.

77. In the view of the Court, the significance of this new development in 2000 is that it has clarified the thus far amorphous legal situation concerning the status of the Federal Republic of Yugoslavia vis-à-vis the United Nations. It is in that sense that the situation that the Court now faces in relation to Serbia and Montenegro is manifestly different from that which it faced in 1999. If, at that time, the Court had had to determine definitively the status of the Applicant vis-à-vis the United Nations, its task of giving such a determination would have been complicated by the legal situation, which was shrouded in uncertainties relating to that status. However, from the vantage point from which the Court now looks at the legal situation, and in light of the legal consequences of the new development since 1 November 2000, the Court is led to the conclusion that Serbia and Montenegro was not a Member of the United Nations, and in that capacity a State party to the Statute of the International Court of Justice, at the time of filing its Application to institute the present proceedings before the Court on 29 April 1999. . . .

89. For all these reasons, the Court concludes that, at the time of filing of its Application to institute the present proceedings before the Court on 29 April 1999, the Applicant in the present case, Serbia and Montenegro, was not a Member of the United Nations, and consequently, was not, on that basis, a State party to the Statute of the International Court of Justice. It follows that the Court was not open to Serbia and Montenegro under Article 35, paragraph 1, of the Statute. . . .

· ·

The majority decision based on *ratione personae* [by reason of the person] was criticized by seven judges, who issued a joint declaration:

· ·

LEGALITY OF USE OF FORCE, JOINT DECLARATION OF VICE-PRESIDENT RANJEVA, JUDGES GUILLAUME, HIGGINS, KOOIJMANS, AL-KHASAWNEH, BUERGENTHAL, AND ELARABY

10. We would first observe that the question whether Yugoslavia was a Member of the United Nations and as such a party to the Statute between 1992 and 2000, remained a subject of debate during that period. The Court declined to settle the issue, both in 1993 [in the *Genocide* case] . . . and in 1999

when issuing its Order on Provisional Measures [in the present case] . . . It then confined itself to stating that the solution adopted in this respect by Security Council resolution 757 and General Assembly resolution 47/1 was "not free from legal difficulties" . . .

Subsequent to the admission of Serbia and Montenegro to the United Nations on 1 November 2000, the Court had to consider the question whether that admission clarified the previous position. The Court then found, in its Judgment of 3 February 2003, that "Resolution 47/1 did not *inter alia* affect the Federal Republic of Yugoslavia's right to appear before the Court or to be a party to a dispute before the Court under the conditions laid down by the Statute" . . . The Court added that "General Assembly resolution 55/12 of 1 November 2000 cannot have changed retroactively the *sui generis* position which the Federal Republic of Yugoslavia found itself in vis-à-vis the United Nations over the period 1992 to 2000, or its position in relation to the Statute of the Court" . . . The Court thus previously found in 2003 that the Federal Republic of Yugoslavia could appear before the Court between 1992 and 2000 and that this position was not changed by its admission to the United Nations . . .

12. . . . Nothing has occurred, in the series of cases concerning Kosovo, since the Court's last judgment in 2003, to suggest that the grounds previously chosen have now lost legal credibility. Further, the grounds today selected by the Court are less certain than others open to it. The Court has determined that the admission of the Applicant to the United Nations in November 2000 "did not have and could not have had, the effect of dating back to the time when the Socialist Federal Republic of Yugoslavia broke up and disappeared" (para. 76). The Court has also stated that "the significance of this new development in 2000 is that it has clarified the thus far amorphous legal situation concerning the status of the Federal Republic of Yugoslavia vis-à-vis the United Nations" (para. 77). Without specifying whether this "clarification" refers to the period 1992–2000, the Court asserts that it has now become "clear that the *sui generis* position of the Applicant could not have amounted to its membership in the Organization." We find this proposition far from self-evident and we cannot trace the steps of the reasoning. Such grounds seem to us to be less legally compelling and therefore less certain, and more open to different points of view, than the grounds relied upon by the Court thus far and which are now set aside by the Court.

13. We have referred also to the care that the Court must have, in selecting one among several possible grounds for a decision on jurisdiction, for the implications and possible consequences for other cases. In that sense, we believe that paragraph 38 of the Judgment does not adequately reflect the proper role of the Court as a judicial institution. The Judgment thus goes back on decisions previously adopted by the Court, whereas it was free to choose the ground upon which to base them and was under no obligation to rule in the present case on its jurisdiction *ratione personae*. Moreover, this approach appears to leave some doubt as to whether Yugoslavia was a party, between

1992 and 2000, to the United Nations Genocide Convention. Such an approach could call into question the solutions adopted by the Court with respect to its jurisdiction in the case brought by Bosnia-Herzegovina against Serbia and Montenegro for the application of the Genocide Convention. We regret that the Court has decided to take such a direction.

As the joint declaration warned, dismissing the *Legality of the Use of Force* case in this way cast a shadow over the ongoing *Genocide* case. To follow the ruling in the former would mean finding that over a decade of proceedings in the latter were, essentially, a waste of time. To ignore the ruling would directly contradict one of its own decisions. The Court ultimately held in the *Genocide* case that the jurisdiction issue was *res judicata*—that is, it had already been decided.

CASE CONCERNING THE APPLICATION OF THE CONVENTION ON THE PREVENTION AND PUNISHMENT OF THE CRIME OF GENOCIDE *(BOSNIA AND HERZEGOVINA V. SERBIA AND MONTENEGRO)* (INTERNATIONAL COURT OF JUSTICE, JUDGMENT OF 26 FEBRUARY 2007)

129. The Respondent has contended that the issue whether the [Federal Republic of Yugoslavia (FRY)] had access to the Court under Article 35 of the Statute has in fact never been decided in the present case, so that no barrier of *res judicata* would prevent the Court from examining that issue at the present stage of the proceedings. It has drawn attention to the fact that when commenting on the 1996 Judgment, in its 2004 Judgments in the cases concerning the *Legality of Use of Force*, the Court observed that "[t]he question of the status of the Federal Republic of Yugoslavia in relation to Article 35 of the Statute was not raised and the Court saw no reason to examine it" . . ., and that "in its pronouncements in incidental proceedings" in the present case, the Court "did not commit itself to a definitive position on the issue of the legal status of the Federal Republic of Yugoslavia in relation to the Charter and the Statute" . . .

130. That does not however signify that in 1996 the Court was unaware of the fact that the solution adopted in the United Nations to the question of continuation of the membership of the SFRY "[was] not free from legal difficulties," as the Court had noted in its Order of 8 April 1993 indicating provisional measures in the case . . . The FRY was, at the time of the proceedings

on its preliminary objections culminating in the 1996 Judgment, maintaining that it was the continuator State of the SFRY. . . .

131. The "legal difficulties" referred to were finally dissipated when in 2000 the FRY abandoned its former insistence that it was the continuator of the SFRY, and applied for membership in the United Nations . . . As the Court here recognized, in 1999—and even more so in 1996—it was by no means so clear as the Court found it to be in 2004 that the Respondent was not a Member of the United Nations at the relevant time. The inconsistencies of approach expressed by the various United Nations organs are apparent . . .

132. . . . Since, as observed above, the question of a State's capacity to be a party to proceedings is a matter which precedes that of jurisdiction *ratione materiae*, and one which the Court must, if necessary, raise ex officio (see paragraph 122 above), this finding must as a matter of construction be understood, by necessary implication, to mean that the Court at that time perceived the Respondent as being in a position to participate in cases before the Court. On that basis, it proceeded to make a finding on jurisdiction which would have the force of *res judicata*. The Court does not need, for the purpose of the present proceedings, to go behind that finding and consider on what basis the Court was able to satisfy itself on the point. Whether the Parties classify the matter as one of "access to the Court" or of "jurisdiction *ratione personae*," the fact remains that the Court could not have proceeded to determine the merits unless the Respondent had had the capacity under the Statute to be a party to proceedings before the Court.

133. In the view of the Court, the express finding in the 1996 Judgment that the Court had jurisdiction in the case *ratione materiae*, on the basis of Article IX of the Genocide Convention, seen in its context, is a finding which is only consistent, in law and logic, with the proposition that, in relation to both Parties, it had jurisdiction *ratione personae* in its comprehensive sense, that is to say, that the status of each of them was such as to comply with the provisions of the Statute concerning the capacity of States to be parties before the Court. . . . As regards the FRY, the Court found that it "was bound by the provisions of the Convention," i.e. was a party thereto, "on the date of the filing of the Application" (*ibid.*, p. 610, para 17); in this respect the Court took note of the declaration made by the FRY on 27 April 1992, set out in paragraph 89 above, whereby the FRY "continuing the State, international legal and political personality" of the SFRY, declared that it would "strictly abide by" the international commitments of the SFRY. The determination by the Court that it had jurisdiction under the Genocide Convention is thus to be interpreted as incorporating a determination that all the conditions relating to the capacity of the Parties to appear before it had been met.

134. It has been suggested by the Respondent that the Court's finding of jurisdiction in the 1996 Judgment was based merely upon an assumption: an assumption of continuity between the SFRY and the FRY. It has drawn attention to passages, already referred to above (paragraph 129), in the Judgments in the *Legality of Use of Force* cases, to the effect that in 1996 the Court saw no reason to examine the question of access, and that, in its pro-

nouncements in incidental proceedings, the Court did not commit itself to a definitive position on the issue of the legal status of the Respondent.

135. That the FRY had the capacity to appear before the Court in accordance with the Statute was an element in the reasoning of the 1996 Judgment which can—and indeed must—be read into the Judgment as a matter of logical construction. That element is not one which can at any time be reopened and re-examined, for the reasons already stated above. As regards the passages in the 2004 Judgments relied on by the Respondent, it should be borne in mind that the concern of the Court was not then with the scope of *res judicata* of the 1996 Judgment, since in any event such *res judicata* could not extend to the proceedings in the cases that were then before it, between different parties. It was simply appropriate in 2004 for the Court to consider whether there was an expressly stated finding in another case that would throw light on the matters before it. No such express finding having been shown to exist, the Court in 2004 did not, as it has in the present case, have to go on to consider what might be the unstated foundations of a judgment given in another case, between different parties.

136. The Court thus considers that the 1996 Judgment contained a finding, whether it be regarded as one of jurisdiction *ratione personae*, or as one anterior to questions of jurisdiction, which was necessary as a matter of logical construction, and related to the question of the FRY's capacity to appear before the Court under the Statute. The force of *res judicata* attaching to that judgment thus extends to that particular finding.

137. However it has been argued by the Respondent that even were that so,

> the fundamental nature of access as a precondition for the exercise of the Court's judicial function means that positive findings on access cannot be taken as definitive and final until the final judgment is rendered in proceedings, because otherwise it would be possible that the Court renders its final decision with respect to a party over which it cannot exercise [its] judicial function. In other words, access is so fundamental that, until the final judgment, it overrides the principle of *res judicata*. Thus, even if the 1996 Judgment had made a finding on access, *quod non*, that would not be a bar for the Court to re-examine this issue until the end of the proceedings.

A similar argument advanced by the Respondent is based on the principle that the jurisdiction of the Court derives from a treaty, namely the Statute of the Court; the Respondent questions whether the Statute could have endowed the 1996 Judgment with any effects at all, since the Respondent was, it alleges, not a party to the Statute. Counsel for the Respondent argued that

> Today it is known that in 1996 when the decision on preliminary objections was rendered, the Respondent was not a party to the Statute. Thus, there was no foothold, Articles 36 (6), 59, and 60 did not represent a binding treaty provision providing a possible basis for deciding on jurisdiction with *res judicata* effects.

138. It appears to the Court that these contentions are inconsistent with the nature of the principle of *res judicata*. That principle signifies that once the Court has made a determination, whether on a matter of the merits of a dispute brought before it, or on a question of its own jurisdiction, that determination is definitive both for the parties to the case, in respect of the case (Article 59 of the Statute), and for the Court itself in the context of that case. However fundamental the question of the capacity of States to be parties in cases before the Court may be, it remains a question to be determined by the Court, in accordance with Article 36, paragraph 6, of the Statute, and once a finding in favour of jurisdiction has been pronounced with the force of *res judicata*, it is not open to question or re-examination, except by way of revision under Article 61 of the Statute. There is thus, *as a matter of law*, no possibility that the Court might render "its final decision with respect to a party over which it cannot exercise its judicial function," because the question whether a State is or is not a party subject to the jurisdiction of the Court is one which is reserved for the sole and authoritative decision of the Court.

139. Counsel for the Respondent contended further that, in the circumstances of the present case, reliance on the *res judicata* principle "would justify the Court's *ultra vires* exercise of its judicial functions contrary to the mandatory requirements of the Statute." However, the operation of the "mandatory requirements of the Statute" falls to be determined by the Court in each case before it; and once the Court has determined, with the force of *res judicata*, that it has jurisdiction, then for the purposes of that case no question of *ultra vires* action can arise, the Court having sole competence to determine such matters under the Statute. For the Court *res judicata pro veritate habetur*, and the judicial truth within the context of a case is as the Court has determined it, subject only to the provision in the Statute for revision of judgments. This result is required by the nature of the judicial function, and the universally recognized need for stability of legal relations. . . .

140. The Court accordingly concludes that, in respect of the contention that the Respondent was not, on the date of filing of the Application instituting proceedings, a State having the capacity to come before the Court under the Statute, the principle of *res judicata* precludes any reopening of the decision embodied in the 1996 Judgment. The Respondent has however also argued that the 1996 Judgment is not *res judicata* as to the further question whether the FRY was, at the time of institution of proceedings, a party to the Genocide Convention, and has sought to show that at that time it was not, and could not have been, such a party. The Court however considers that the reasons given above for holding that the 1996 Judgment settles the question of jurisdiction in this case with the force of *res judicata* are applicable *a fortiori* as regards this contention, since on this point the 1996 Judgment was quite specific, as it was not on the question of capacity to come before the Court. The Court does not therefore find it necessary to examine the argument of the Applicant that the failure of the Respondent to advance at the time the reasons why it now contends that it was not a party to the Genocide Convention might raise considerations of estoppel, or *forum prorogatum* (cf. paragraphs 85

and 101 above). The Court thus concludes that, as stated in the 1996 Judgment, it has jurisdiction, under Article IX of the Genocide Convention, to adjudicate upon the dispute brought before it by the Application filed on 20 March 1993. It follows from the above that the Court does not find it necessary to consider the questions, extensively addressed by the Parties, of the status of the Respondent under the Charter of the United Nations and the Statute of the Court, and its position in relation to the Genocide Convention at the time of the filing of the Application.

QUESTIONS

6. Does the Council have the power to do what it purported to do in resolution 777 (1992)? What would have been the effect if the Council had omitted from the quoted section the words "and that it shall not participate in the work of the General Assembly"?

7. The Court's 2004 decision in the *Legality of the Use of Force* case, brought by the FRY, may seem to contradict its own 2002 decision in the *Genocide* case, by removing the ambiguity on the FRY's status between 1992 and 2000. Should the Court have perpetuated this "ambiguous" status of quasi-membership, or was it right to determine that the ambiguity never existed—that is, that the FRY had never been allowed to take up the UN membership of its predecessor, the SFRY?

8. In practical terms, what are the advantages and disadvantages of the Organization being able to place a state in a status that can best be described as "quasi-membership"? Note that Article 5 of the UN Charter envisages a suspension of some rights and privileges of membership by the General Assembly upon the recommendation of the Security Council. Is this what happened to the FRY during the period 1992–2000? If not, should it have happened, in preference to an exclusion of the FRY from membership? Do you think that the interests of some member states on this issue were at odds with those of the UN as an institution?

9. In its 2007 decision, the ICJ applied *res judicata* as to its decision in 1996, preferring that decision as to the status of the Federal Republic of Yugoslavia over its own 2004 Judgment in the *Legality of Use of Force* case. Are you satisfied with the reasoning by which the Court was able to come to this conclusion?

5.4 Credentials

The uncertain status of the FRY between 1992 and 2000 gives rise to the possibility that a state may be a member of the United Nations but not be permitted to exercise all of the privileges of membership. In the materials that follow it will become apparent that, potentially, another form of suspension may be achieved by rejection of the credentials of a state's delegation to the General Assembly. In 1974, this was done with respect to the delegation of South Africa, thereby denying it the right to speak and vote in the General Assembly while the state, under the regime of apartheid, denied its non-white citizens most of the rights of participation in governance.[19]

Each delegation appointed to represent a state at the General Assembly is required to present its credentials to the Secretary-General. These documents are then passed on to a "Credentials Committee," which consists of nine members appointed by the Assembly on the proposal of the President at each session. The Committee studies these credentials and reports on their acceptance or rejection to the Assembly. Usually the acceptance of credentials is a procedural matter; in this sense the acceptance or rejection of credentials does not signify recognition or non-recognition of any particular government. Nevertheless, there have been instances where the acceptance of credentials from one of two rival claimants to governance of a country has been used to indicate which one is considered legitimate by the United Nations. The South African example cited above set an unusual precedent, for as the following statement by the legal counsel indicates, this use of credentials was not envisaged by the UN Charter or the Rules of Procedure of the General Assembly.

STATEMENT BY THE LEGAL COUNSEL: SCOPE OF CREDENTIALS IN RULE 27 OF THE RULES OF PROCEDURE OF THE GENERAL ASSEMBLY, 1970[20]

1. The Rules of procedure of the General Assembly do not contain a definition of credentials. Rule 27, however, provides:

> The credentials of representatives and the names of members of a delegation shall be submitted to the Secretary-General if possible not less than one week before the date fixed for the opening of the session. The credentials shall be issued either by the Head of the State or Government or by the Minister for Foreign Affairs.

2. From this rule one may derive the three essential elements with respect to credentials to the General Assembly:

---

[19] A/PV.2281, pp. 76, 86 (1974).
[20] Scope of "Credentials" in Rule 27 of the Rules of Procedure of the General Assembly: Statement by the Legal Counsel Submitted to the President of the General Assembly at his Request, 25 UN GAOR, Agenda Item 3, at 1 n.1, UN Doc. A/8160 (1970).

(a) "Credentials" designate the representatives of the Member State to the General Assembly;

(b) They are to be submitted to the Secretary-General; and

(c) They are to be issued by the Head of the State or Government or by the Minister for Foreign Affairs.

3. Thus credentials for the General Assembly may be defined as a document issued by the Head of State or Government or by the Minister for Foreign Affairs of a State Member of the UN submitted to the Secretary-General designating the persons entitled to represent that Member at a given session of the General Assembly. Unlike the acceptance of credentials in bilateral relations, the question of recognition of the government of a member state is not involved, and substantive issues concerning the status of Government do not arise except as examined in the following paragraph.

4. While normally the examination of credentials, both in the Credentials Committee and in the General Assembly, is a procedural matter limited to ascertaining that the requirements of Rule 27 have been satisfied, there have nevertheless been a few instances involving rival claimants where the question of which claimant represents the true government of the State has arisen as a substantive issue. This issue of representation may, as in the case of the Republic of Congo (Leopoldville) at the fiftieth session and Yemen at the sixtieth session, be considered in connection with the examination of credentials, or it may, as in the case of China, be dealt with both in connection with credentials and as a separate agenda item.

5. Questions have also been raised in the Credentials Committee with respect to the Representatives of certain Members, notably South Africa and Hungary, where there was no rival claimant. There has, however, been no case where the representatives were precluded from participation in the meetings of the General Assembly. The General Assembly in the case of Hungary from the eleventh to the seventeenth session and in the case of South Africa at the twentieth session decided to take no action on the credentials submitted on behalf of the representatives of Hungary and South Africa. Under rule 29, any representative to whose admission a Member has made objection is seated provisionally with the same rights as other representatives until the Credentials Committee has reported and the General Assembly has given its decision.

6. Should the General Assembly, where there is no question of rival claimants, reject credentials satisfying the requirements of rule 27 for the purpose of excluding a member state from participation in its meetings, this would have the effect of suspending a member state from the exercise of rights and privileges of membership in a manner not foreseen by the Charter. . . . The participation in the meetings of the General Assembly is quite clearly one of the important rights and privileges. Suspension of this right through the rejection of credentials would not satisfy the requirements [of Article 5 of the Charter] and would therefore be contrary to the Charter.

The UN Legal Counsel's opinion regarding challenges to South Africa's credentials was, itself, soon challenged. At the twenty-fifth session a Member requested the Credentials Committee to consider the credentials of the South African delegation to the General Assembly and to make a special report on the matter. The Credentials Committee examined the credentials of South Africa and approved them, deciding, however, to reflect in its report that some delegations had objected. In the Assembly's plenary meeting, two amendments to the draft resolution of the Credentials Committee were proposed: the first to add the words "except with regard to the credentials of the representatives of the Government of South Africa"; the second to note that, "notwithstanding the authenticity of the credentials of the representatives of the Government of South Africa, the authorities of South Africa who issued those credentials do not represent a large segment of the population of South Africa which the said authorities claim to represent." A request to vote first on the second amendment was rejected by sixty-one votes to one, with twenty-one abstentions.[21]

At the request of one representative, the President gave his opinion on the implications of the first amendment proposed.

STATEMENT BY THE PRESIDENT OF THE GENERAL ASSEMBLY, MR. EDVARD HAMBRO, 25TH SESSION, 1901ST PLENARY MEETING, A/PV.1901 (1970)

286 . . . I reach the conclusion that a vote in favour of the Amendment would mean, on the part of this Assembly, a very strong condemnation of the policies pursued by the Government of South Africa. It would also constitute a warning to that Government as solemn as any such warning could be. But that, apart from that, the amendment as it is worded at present would not seem to me to mean that the South African delegation is unseated or cannot continue to sit in this Assembly; if adopted it will not affect the right and privileges of membership of South Africa. That is my understanding.

The first amendment proposed was adopted by sixty votes to forty-two, with twelve abstentions; the second amendment was withdrawn.

Further developments ensued. At the twenty-sixth session an amendment identical to the one adopted by the Assembly at the previous session was adopted by sixty votes to thirty-six, with twenty-two abstentions. At the same meeting, when the representative of South Africa was speaking on another

---

[21] See http://untreaty.un.org/cod/repertory/art9/english/rep_supp5_vol1-art9_e.pdf.

item, a point of order was raised in connection with his right to continue to participate in the debates of the General Assembly. The President stated that his opinion on the amendment adopted was the same as that given by the President of the twenty-fifth session under the same circumstances.[22] Identical amendments were also adopted during the twenty-seventh and twenty-eighth sessions of the General Assembly, as well as in the Sixth Special Session in 1974.

At the twenty-ninth session, in 1974, a proposal was adopted in the in the Credentials Committee itself, to accept all the credentials submitted except those of South Africa by five votes to three, with one abstention. The Committee presented its report to the General Assembly, which approved it by ninety-eight votes to twenty-three, with fourteen abstentions.[23]

A member state requested that the President of the General Assembly explain the effect of the resolution just adopted.

- -

RULING BY THE PRESIDENT OF THE GENERAL ASSEMBLY, MR. ABDELAZIZ BOUTEFLIKA, 29TH SESSION, 2281ST PLENARY MEETING, A/PV.2281 (1974)

153 . . . I am asked to state here my interpretation of the General Assembly's decision to reject the credentials of the delegation of South Africa. . . .

156. It is clear that the opinion of Mr. Hambro . . . was based above all on the exact words of the decision adopted by the General Assembly in the form of an amendment. That opinion did not mean that if the amendment had been worded in some other way it might not have had different consequences for the legal position of the South African delegation in this Assembly. . . .

158. That text [of rule 29] perhaps does not indicate with sufficient clarity what should happen once the General Assembly has taken a decision confirming the objective to the admission of a representative or a delegation. Now, year after year, the General Assembly has decided, by ever-larger majorities, not to recognize the credentials of the South African delegation, and during this session the Credentials Committee itself took the initiative of rejecting those credentials. It has not been necessary for the Assembly to adopt an amendment along these lines to the report submitted by the Credentials Committee.

159. It would therefore be a betrayal of the clearly and repeatedly expressed will of the General Assembly to understand this to mean that it was merely a procedural method of expressing its rejection of the policy of *apartheid*. On the basis of the consistency with which the General Assembly

---

[22] 26 UN GAOR (2027th mtg.) (1971), para. 292–295.
[23] GA Res. 3206(XXIX) (1974).

has regularly refused to accept the credentials of the South African delegation, one may legitimately infer that the General Assembly would in the same way reject the credentials of any other delegation authorized by the Government of the Republic of South Africa to represent it, which is tantamount to saying in explicit terms that the General Assembly refuses to allow the South African delegation to participate in its work.

160. Thus it is, as President of the twenty-ninth session of the General Assembly, that I interpret the decision of the General Assembly, leaving open the question of the status of the Republic of South Africa as a Member of the United Nations which, as we all know, is a matter requiring a recommendation from the Security Council. My interpretation refers exclusively to the position of the South African delegation within the strict framework of the rules of procedure of the General Assembly. That is my belief.

Response by Mr. Scali, Representative
of the United States of America

. . .

162. There is also an obvious conflict, Mr. President, between your ruling and the Legal Opinion given to this Assembly on 11 November 1970 at the 25th Session. Further there is a conflict between your ruling and the practice that the General Assembly has consistently followed since [1970] . . . during the twenty ninth session, South Africa was allowed to vote without objection after the Assembly's decision on its credentials was made.

163. The legal opinion given at the 25th Session remains as valid today, in our view as it was then. It affirms that under the Charter the Assembly may not deprive a Member of any of the rights of membership. The Assembly may be master of its rules of procedure but no majority, no matter how large, can ignore or change the clear provisions of the Charter in this way. We consider it to be a violation of the rules of procedure and of Articles 5 and 6 of the Charter for the assembly to attempt to deny a Member State of the United Nations its right to participate in the Assembly, through this type of unprecedented action . . . The Assembly is not empowered to deprive a Member of the rights and privileges of membership other than in accordance with Articles 5, 6 and 19 of the Charter. In our view, none of these circumstances applies in this case. . . .

The ruling of the President was challenged and upheld by ninety-one votes to twenty-two, with nineteen abstentions.[24]

Another use of credentials, has been to confer legitimacy upon one of two rival claimants to the government of a particular Member State. In the 1990s,

---

[24] A/PV.2281.

for example, the UN General Assembly refused to recognize the credentials of the delegations representing governments of Haiti, Sierra Leone, Cambodia, Liberia, and Afghanistan—representing regimes that had seized effective control of their countries. Instead, the Assembly continued to recognize the representatives of the deposed governments. The following resolution of the General Assembly concerning Haiti is representative.

GENERAL ASSEMBLY RESOLUTION 46/7 (1991): THE SITUATION OF DEMOCRACY AND HUMAN RIGHTS IN HAITI

The General Assembly,
  Bearing in mind that . . . the United Nations system, at the request of the lawful authorities of that country and in cooperation with the Organization of American States, supported the efforts of the people of Haiti to consolidate their democratic institutions and also supported the holding of free elections on 16 December 1990,
  Concerned about the critical events occurring in Haiti since 29 September 1991, which have brought about a sudden and violent interruption of the democratic process in that country, entailing human rights abuses and the loss of human lives, . . .
  1. *Strongly condemns* the attempted illegal replacement of the constitutional President of Haiti, the use of violence and military coercion and the violation of human rights in that country;
  2. *Affirms* as unacceptable any entity resulting from that illegal situation and demands the immediate restoration of the legitimate Government of President Jean-Bertrand Aristide, together with the full application of the National Constitution and hence the full observance of human rights in Haiti;
  3. *Requests* the Secretary-General of the United Nations, in accordance with his functions, to consider providing support sought by the Secretary-General of the Organization of American States in implementing the mandates arising from resolutions MRE/RES.1/91 and MRE/RES.2/91 adopted by that organization;
  4. *Appeals* to the States Members of the United Nations to take measures in support of the resolutions of the Organization of American States referred to in paragraph 3 above;
  5. *Emphasizes* that an increase in technical, economic and financial cooperation, when constitutional order is restored in Haiti, is necessary to support its economic and social development efforts in order to strengthen its democratic institutions

An argument against the use of credentials as determinative of legitimacy appears to be the low reliance placed on them by states. As the following excerpt indicates—concerning the potentially controversial representation of Iraq while under military occupation by the United States and Britain—few states appear to place priority on filing credentials early, the report of the Credentials Committee is not made until several months into the session, and until credentials are approved or disapproved delegations are free to participate in the work of the Assembly.

DAILY PRESS BRIEFING BY THE OFFICES OF THE SPOKESMAN FOR THE SECRETARY-GENERAL AND THE SPOKESWOMAN FOR THE GENERAL ASSEMBLY PRESIDENT, 24 SEPTEMBER 2003[25]

Question: Fred, what can you tell us about the meeting with Annan and the Iraqi delegation this morning? Was there a discussion about the UN's presence there and the future of the UN in Iraq?

Spokesman: He did meet at 8 o'clock this morning with a number of people from Iraq. There was Ahmad [Chalabi], this month's President of the Governing Council. There was also Adnan Pachachi, another member of the Council and Foreign Minister Hoshyar Zebari, and several others. They discussed the current security situation in Iraq. The Secretary-General expressed his concern about the condition of his own staff in that context. They also talked about the prospects for a second Security Council resolution on Iraq, including both the role of the UN and a timetable for an early restoration of Iraqi sovereignty.

Question: Yes. To follow on that, we understand that Chalabi has not presented his credentials for recognition by the United Nations, so we are curious to know why the Secretary-General met with somebody who didn't present their credentials to be, you know, the diplomat representing Iraq in the General Assembly, even though he sat behind that sign yesterday, there was a question of protocol.

Spokesman: First of all, it's not for the Secretary-General to decide who has valid credentials and who doesn't. That's a matter for the General Assembly. Michele can correct me if I'm wrong. But my understanding is that under the rules of the General Assembly, everyone is seated provisionally with the right to participate until the Credentials Committee of the Assembly gets to review all of the credentials letters that are submitted. I was told yesterday that only 45 of 191 Member States had submitted letters of credentials as of yesterday,

---

[25] See http://www.un.org/News/briefings/docs/2003/db092403.doc.htm.

so it is obviously something that comes in slowly, and the Credentials Committee, I don't believe has met yet. And they normally don't submit their report until several months into the session, usually December, giving time for all the other letters to come in and for them to review all those letters. So, unless any Member State, any other delegation, challenges the delegation of Iraq, they can sit there legally. And from the Secretariat point of view, we deal with them as a delegation recognized by the General Assembly, by the Credentials Committee, which hasn't met since about a year ago. It's a little complicated but that's how we work.

QUESTIONS

10. Were the efforts to exclude South Africa from participation in the General Assembly consistent with the UN Charter provisions pertaining to the suspension of membership or expulsion (Articles 5, 6, and 19)?

11. South Africa's credentials were accepted finally in 1994, after apartheid was abolished, and the country's first non-racial elections were held resulting in the installation of Nelson Mandela as president on 10 May 1994. Did the Assembly's exclusion of South Africa from participation in its work contribute to this outcome? Would this precedent have constituted a better way to have dealt with the Federal Republic of Yugoslavia from 1992 to 2000? What is the effect of these precedents on Article 5 and 6 and, by implication, on the prerogatives of the Security Council as set out in those articles?

12. Gregory Fox has suggested adoption of a general practice of using credentials to indicate UN approval of democratically elected regimes over their undemocratic counterparts, even if it is the latter that enjoys effective power.[26] Do you agree with this idea? Would you seek to expand the role of credentials to allow for identification of the legitimate government even when elections have not been monitored by the United Nations, or have not taken place at all, or there is no immediate rival contender? Would you extend the argument regarding democracy to include also racism as a basis for denying accreditation?

13. Matthew Griffin points out some of the complications surrounding the use of credentials as a means of promoting democracy.[27] These include: (i) the lack of representation in the Credentials Committee which is

---

[26] Gregory H. Fox, "The Right to Political Participation in International Law," *Yale Journal of International Law*, vol. 17 (1992), pp. 588–607.

[27] Matthew Griffin, "Accrediting Democracies: Does the Credentials Committee of the United Nations Promote Democracy through its Accreditation Process, and Should It?" *New York University Journal of International Law and Politics*, vol. 32 (2000).

composed of nine members, three of which—the United States, Russia, and China—are permanent; (ii) that especially where there are no rival claimants, the country is deprived of representation altogether; (iii) the fact that there is no provision that appears to provide the use of credentials in such manner to limit the benefits of membership to states; (iv) that many present member states have governments which were not elected democratically, but which are nevertheless allowed to participate, and therefore there may be arbitrariness in deciding who should be barred and who should be allowed to continue; and (v) that democracy cannot be considered a universal entitlement. Do you agree with these arguments?

Further Reading

Fox, Gregory H. "The Right to Political Participation in International Law." *Yale Journal of International Law*, vol. 17 (1992), p. 539.

Griffin, Matthew. "Accrediting Democracies: Does the Credentials Committee of the United Nations Promote Democracy Through Its Accreditation Process, and Should It?" *New York University Journal of International Law and Politics*, vol. 32 (2000), p. 725.

Janev, Igor. "Legal Aspects of the Use of a Provisional Name for Macedonia in the United Nations System." *American Journal of International Law*, vol. 93 (1999), p. 155.

Ratliff, Suellen. "UN Representation Disputes: A Case Study of Cambodia and a New Accreditation Proposal for the Twenty-First Century." *California Law Review*, vol. 87 (1999), p. 1207.

Roth, Brad R. *Governmental Illegitimacy in International Law*. Oxford: Clarendon Press, 1999.

chapter six

·············

Financing

The total budget of the United Nations is approximately equal to that of the Fire Department of the City of Tokyo, or a mere 4 percent of the annual budget of the City of New York.[1] In spite of this, the United Nations has teetered on the brink of financial crises for most of the last forty years.[2] Financial reform has therefore long been a key issue on the agenda of the United Nations.

Articles 17–19 of the Charter address the question of financing. It is notable that the "power of the purse" is lodged not in the Security Council, where it would be subject to the predominant role of the permanent members, but in the General Assembly, where every state has an equal voice. Articles 17(1) and (2) allot power to the General Assembly to approve the budget for the United Nations, and to apportion its expenses between the member states. Article 18(2) specifies the requirement of a two-thirds majority to decide budgetary questions. Article 19 provides that any member of the United Nations two years in arrears of payment of its financial contribution to the United Nations shall not be allowed to vote in the General Assembly, unless the Assembly decides otherwise. These provisions together constitute the basic fiscal law of the Organization.[3]

The General Assembly acts through the Fifth Committee, which, as re-affirmed by General Assembly resolution 45/248B (1990), is the committee with principal jurisdiction over administrative and budgetary matters. It is a

---

[1] These were figures quoted by the Secretary-General in his Millennium Report to the General Assembly in March 2000, UN Doc. A/54/2000.
[2] See Wilfried Koschorreck, "Article 17", in Bruno Simma (ed.), *The Charter of the United Nations: A Commentary*, 2nd edn. (Oxford: Oxford University Press, 2002), vol. 1, p. 348, para. 89.
[3] Ibid., p. 334, para. 1.

committee of the whole, which means that every member of the Organization is entitled to representation. In practice, two smaller committees, the Advisory Committee on Administrative and Budgetary Questions (ACABQ) and the Committee on Contributions (established by resolution 14(I) (1946)) have become the critical foci for fiscal decision making. The Contributions Committee advises the General Assembly on the apportionment among members of the expenses of the United Nations, assessments for new members, appeals by members for a change of assessment, and application of article 19 in cases of arrears in the payment of assessments. Its membership has been expanded a number of times and now stands at 18.[4] The ACABQ will be discussed in greater detail, below.

The UN System is financed from two sources: the assessment of member states and voluntary contributions. Assessments are supposed to be based on the "capacity to pay"—that is, taking into account several factors, primarily the wealth of each state as measured by its Gross National Income (GNI) as a proportion of the global total. The application of this policy has been modified in two principal respects. The first is the ceiling for contributions, applicable only to the United States, whose assessment once amounted to one third of the budget and was later set at 25 percent, lowered in 2001 to 22 percent. The second is a reduction for countries below a specified income threshold. The United States remains the largest absolute contributor, followed by Japan, Germany, Britain, France, Italy, Canada, and Spain.

Expenditures of peacekeeping operations are assessed separately, through a scale that provides larger discounts to poorer countries and transfers the burden to the permanent members of the Council. Expenditures for the International Criminal Tribunals for Rwanda and the former Yugoslavia are assessed through a scale that is the average of the regular budget and peacekeeping scales of assessment.

Assessed contributions also support the UN Specialized Agencies[5] but these are supplemented by voluntary contributions that are approximately equal in total to the assessed contributions. The UN Programmes, Funds, and

---

[4] See, most recently, GA Res. 31/96 (1976).

[5] These include FAO (Food and Agriculture Organisation), ILO (International Labour Organisation), UNESCO (United Nations Educational, Scientific, and Cultural Organisation), UNIDO (United Nations Industrial Development Organisation) since 1986, WHO (World Health Organisation), ICAO (International Civil Aviation Organization), IMO (International Maritime Organisation), ITU (International Telecommunication Union), UPU (Universal Postal Union), WIPO (World Intellectual Property Organization), WMO (World Meteorological Organization) and IAEA (International Atomic Energy Agency). The IAEA although not formally a Specialized Agency, is also financed by assessed contributions. The International Monetary Fund and the World Bank also have Specialized Agency status, but they are not included here due to their separate funding arrangements.

other organs[6] rely solely on voluntary contributions. In 2004, for example, the UN regular budget was $1.3bn, the peacekeeping budget was $3.6bn, the Specialized Agencies received $2bn in assessed contributions and $2.2bn in voluntary contributions, while the programmes and funds received a further $9.5bn in voluntary contributions.[7]

As the *Certain Expenses* case demonstrates, the extent of members' responsibility to contribute to operational expenses, especially those incurred by the General Assembly for peacekeeping, has been a matter of debate. This chapter examines the *Certain Expenses* case before describing the regular budget, assessment of contributions, administrative oversight within the Organization, and some of the challenges that it has confronted. The chapter concludes with a brief discussion of alternative financing arrangements that have been discussed.

6.1 Expenses of the Organization

In the *Certain Expenses* case, the International Court of Justice was asked for its opinion on whether certain expenditures authorized by the General Assembly to cover the costs of the UN Operation in the Congo (ONUC) and of the operations of the UN Emergency Force in the Middle East (UNEF), "constitute 'expenses of the Organization' within the meaning of Article 17, paragraph 2, of the Charter of the United Nations" The issue arose because two members (France and the Soviet Union) refused to pay their assessed share of the UN peacekeeping initiatives in Egypt and the Congo—initiatives taken in whole or in part by the General Assembly over the opposition previously registered by the two permanent members of the Security Council. When the Security Council had deadlocked, the states seeking authorization for a UN Peacekeeping initiative had transferred the issue to the General Assembly, in which authorization was obtained. France and the Soviets based their refusal on the *ultra vires* of these UN operations. The procedure for removing these initiatives from a deadlocked Security Council, the "Uniting for Peace" Resolution—General Assembly resolution 377(V) (1950), discussed in chapter 8—was passed over the vociferous opposition by Moscow and forms the background of this advisory power.

---

[6] These include UNCDF (United Nations Capital Development Fund) since 1973, UNDP (United Nations Development Programme), UNEP (United Nations Environment Program) since 1973, UNFPA (United Nations Population Fund), UNHCR (Office of the United Nations High Commissioner for Refugees), UNICEF (United Nations Children's Fund), UNIDO (United Nations Industrial Development Organization) until 1986, UNITAR (United Nations Institute for Training and Research), UNRWA (UN Relief & Works Agency for Palestinian Refugees in the Near East), UNU (United Nations University) since 1975, and WFP (World Food Programme).
[7] See data compiled by Klaus Hüfner (Senior Research Fellow, Global Policy Forum), Michael Renner (Worldwatch Institute) and Global Policy Forum, available at http://www.globalpolicy.org/finance/tables/system/tabsyst.htm

CERTAIN EXPENSES OF THE UNITED NATIONS (ARTICLE 17, PARAGRAPH 2, OF THE CHARTER) (ADVISORY OPINION) 1962 ICJ REPORTS 151

[I]t should be noted that at least three separate questions might arise in the interpretation of paragraph 2 of this Article. One question is that of identifying what are "the expenses of the Organization"; a second question might concern apportionment by the General Assembly; while a third question might involve the interpretation of the phrase "shall be borne by the Members." It is the second and third questions which directly involve "the financial obligations of the Members," but it is only the first question which is posed by the request for the advisory opinion. ...

If the Court finds that the indicated expenditures are such "expenses," it is not called upon to consider the manner in which, or the scale by which, they may be apportioned. The amount of what are unquestionably "expenses of the Organization within the meaning of Article 17, paragraph 2" is not in its entirety apportioned by the General Assembly and paid for by the contributions of Member States, since the Organization has other sources of income. ...

The text of Article 17, paragraph 2, refers to "the expenses of the Organization" without any further explicit definition of such expenses. It would be possible to begin with a general proposition to the effect that the "expenses" of any organization are the amounts paid out to defray the costs of carrying out its purposes, in this case, the political, economic, social, humanitarian and other purposes of the United Nations. The next step would be to examine, as the Court will, whether the resolutions authorizing the operations here in question were intended to carry out the purposes of the United Nations and whether the expenditures were incurred in furthering these operations. Or, it might simply be said that the "expenses" of an organization are those which are provided for in its budget. ...

It is perhaps the simple identification of "expenses" with the items included in a budget, which has led to linking the interpretation of the word "expenses" in paragraph 2 of Article 17, with the word "budget" in paragraph 1 of that Article; in both cases, it is contended, the qualifying adjective "regular" or "administrative" should be understood to be implied. Since no such qualification is expressed in the text of the Charter, it could be read in only if such qualification must necessarily be implied from the provisions of the Charter considered as a whole, or from some particular provision thereof which makes it unavoidable to do so in order to give effect to the Charter.

In the first place, concerning the word "budget" in paragraph 1 of Article 17, it is clear that the existence of the distinction between "administrative budgets" and "operational budgets" was not absent from the minds of the drafters of the Charter, nor from the consciousness of the Organization even in the early days of its history. In drafting Article 17, the drafters found it suitable to provide in paragraph 1 that "The General Assembly shall consider and approve the budget of the Organization." But in dealing with the function of the General Assembly in relation to the specialized agencies, they provided in paragraph 3 that the General Assembly "shall examine the administrative budgets of such specialized agencies" ... Moreover, had it been contemplated that the Organization would also have had another budget, different from the one which was to be approved by the General Assembly, the Charter would have included some reference to such other budget and to the organ which was to approve it.

Similarly, at its first session, the General Assembly in drawing up and approving the Constitution of the International Refugee Organization, provided that the budget of that Organization was to be divided under the headings "administrative," "operational" and "large-scale resettlement"; but no such distinctions were introduced into the Financial Regulations of the United Nations which were adopted by unanimous vote in 1950 ...

Actually, the practice of the Organization is entirely consistent with the plain meaning of the text. The budget of the Organization has from the outset included items which would not fall within any of the definitions of "administrative budget" which have been advanced in this connection. Thus, for example ... the annual budget of the Organization contains provision for funds for technical assistance [etc]. ...

It is a consistent practice of the General Assembly to include in the annual budget resolutions, provision for expenses relating to the maintenance of international peace and security. Annually, since 1947, the General Assembly has made anticipatory provision for "unforeseen and extraordinary expenses" arising in relation to the "maintenance of peace and security." ...

It is notable that the 1961 Report of the Working Group of Fifteen on the Examination of the Administrative and Budgetary Procedures of the United Nations ... records that the following statement was adopted without opposition:

> 22. Investigations and observation operations undertaken by the Organization to prevent possible aggression should be financed as part of the regular budget of the United Nations.

In the light of what has been stated, the Court concludes that there is no justification for reading into the text of Article 17, paragraph 1, any limiting or qualifying word before the word "budget." ...

Turning to paragraph 2 of Article 17, the Court observes that, on its face, the term "expenses of the Organization" means all the expenses and not just certain types of expenses which might be referred to as "regular expenses." An examination of other parts of the Charter shows the variety of expenses which must inevitably be included within the "expenses of the Organization" just as much as the salaries of staff or the maintenance of buildings.

For example, the text of Chapter IX and X of the Charter with reference to international economic and social cooperation, especially the wording of those articles which specify the functions and powers of the Economic and Social Council, anticipated the numerous and varied circumstances under which expenses of the Organization could be incurred and which have indeed eventuated in practice.

Furthermore, by Article 98 of the Charter, the Secretary-General is obligated to perform such functions as are entrusted to him by the General Assembly, the Security Council, the Economic and Social Council, and the Trusteeship Council. Whether or not expenses incurred in his discharge of this obligation become "expenses of the Organization" cannot depend on whether they be administrative or some other kind of expenses.

The Court does not perceive any basis for challenging the legality of the settled practice of including such expenses as these in the budgetary amounts which the General Assembly apportions among the Members in accordance with the authority which is given to it by Article 17, paragraph 2. ...

... [I]t has been argued before the Court that one type of expenses, namely those resulting from operations for the maintenance of international peace and security, are not "expenses of the Organization" within the meaning of Article 17, paragraph 2, of the Charter, inasmuch as they fall to be dealt with exclusively by the Security Council, and more especially through agreements negotiated in accordance with Article 43 of the Charter.

The argument rests in part upon the view that when the maintenance of international peace and security is involved, it is only the Security Council which is authorized to decide on any action relative thereto. It is argued further that since the General Assembly's power is limited to discussing, considering, studying and recommending, it cannot impose an obligation to pay the expenses which result from the implementation of its recommendations. This argument leads to an examination of the respective functions of the General Assembly and of the Security Council under the Charter, particularly with respect to the maintenance of international peace and security. ...

... [Under Article 24] the responsibility conferred is "primary," not exclusive ... it is the Security Council which is given a power to impose an explicit obligation of compliance if for example it issues an order or command to an aggressor under Chapter VII. It is only the Security Council which can require enforcement by coercive action against an aggressor.

The Charter makes it abundantly clear, however, that the General Assembly is also to be concerned with international peace and security. Article 14 authorizes the General Assembly to "recommend measures for the peaceful adjustment of any situation, regardless of origin, which it deems likely to impair the general welfare or friendly relations among nations, including situations resulting from a violation of the provisions of the present Charter setting forth the purposes and principles of the United Nations." The word "measures" implies some kind of action, and the only limitation which Article 14 imposes on the General Assembly is the restriction found in Article 12, namely, that the Assembly should not recommend measures while the Security Council is dealing with the same matter unless the Council requests it to do so. Thus while it is the Security Council which, exclusively, may order coercive action, the functions and powers conferred by the Charter on the General Assembly are not confined to discussion, consideration, the initiation of studies and the making of recommendations; they are not merely hortatory. Article 18 deals with "decisions" of the General Assembly "on important questions." These "decisions" do indeed include certain recommendations, but others have dispositive force and effect. Among these latter decisions, Article 18 includes suspension of rights and privileges of membership, expulsion of Members, "and budgetary questions." In connection with the suspension of rights and privileges of membership and expulsion from membership under Articles 5 and 6, it is the Security Council which has only the power to recommend and it is the General Assembly which decides and whose decision determines status; but there is a close collaboration between the two organs. Moreover, these powers of decision of the General Assembly under Articles 5 and 6 are specifically related to preventive or enforcement measures.

By Article 17, paragraph 1, the General Assembly is given the power not only to "consider" the budget of the Organization, but also to "approve" it. The decision to "approve" the budget has a close connection with paragraph 2 of Article 17, since thereunder the General Assembly is also given the power to apportion the expenses among the Members and the exercise of the power of apportionment creates the obligation, specifically stated in Article 17, paragraph 2, of each Member to bear that part of the expenses which is apportioned to it by the General Assembly ... The provisions of the Charter which distribute functions and powers to the Security Council and to the General Assembly give no support to the view that such distribution excludes from the powers of the General Assembly the power to provide for the financing of measures designed to maintain peace and security.

The argument supporting a limitation on the budgetary authority of the General Assembly with respect to the maintenance of international peace and security relies especially on the reference to "action" in the last sentence of Article 11, paragraph 2. ...

The Court considers that the kind of action referred to in Article 11, paragraph 2, is coercive or enforcement action. This paragraph, which applies not merely to general questions relating to peace and security, but also to specific cases brought before the General Assembly by a State under Article 35, in its first sentence empowers the General Assembly, by means of recommendations to States or to the Security Council, or to both, to organize peacekeeping operations, at the request, or with the consent, of the States concerned. This power of the General Assembly is a special power which in no way derogates from its general powers under Article 10 or Article 14, except as limited by the last sentence of Article 11, paragraph 2. This last sentence says that when "action" is necessary the General Assembly shall refer the question to the Security Council. The word "action" must mean such action as is solely within the province of the Security Council. It cannot refer to recommendations which the Security Council might make, as for instance under Article 38, because the General Assembly under Article 11 has a comparable power. The "action" which is solely within the province of the Security Council is that which is indicated by the title of Chapter VII of the Charter, namely "Action with respect to threats to the peace, breaches of the peace, and acts of aggression." If the word "action" in Article 11, paragraph 2, were interpreted to mean that the General Assembly could make recommendations only of a general character affecting peace and security in the abstract, and not in relation to specific cases, the paragraph would not have provided that the General Assembly may make recommendations on questions brought before it by States or by the Security Council. Accordingly, the last sentence of Article 11, paragraph 2, has no application where the necessary action is not enforcement action. ...

The Court accordingly finds that the argument which seeks, by reference to Article 11, paragraph 2, to limit the budgetary authority of the General Assembly in respect of the maintenance of international peace and security is unfounded. ...

It has further been argued before the Court that Article 43 of the Charter constitutes a particular rule, a *lex specialis*, which derogates from the general rule in Article 17, whenever an expenditure for the maintenance of international peace and security is involved. ...

The argument is that agreements [under Article 43] were intended to include specifications concerning the allocation of costs of such enforcement actions as might be taken by direction of the Security Council, and that it is only the Security Council which has the authority to arrange for meeting such costs.

With reference to this argument, the Court will state at the outset that, for reasons fully expounded later in this Opinion, the operations known as UNEF and ONUC were not enforcement actions within the compass of Chapter VII of the Charter and that therefore Article 43 could not have any applicability to the cases with which the Court is here concerned. However, even if Article 43 were applicable, the Court could not accept this interpretation of its text for the following reasons.

There is nothing in the text of Article 43 which would limit the discretion of the Security Council in negotiating such agreements ... If, during negotiations under the terms of Article 43, a Member State would be entitled (as it would be) to insist, and the Security Council would be entitled (as it would be) to agree, that some part of the expense should be borne by the Organization, then such expense would form part of the expenses of the Organization and would fall to be apportioned by the General Assembly under Article 17. It is difficult to see how it could have been contemplated that all potential expenses could be envisaged in such agreements concluded perhaps long in advance. ...

Moreover, an argument which insists that all measures taken for the maintenance of international peace and security must be financed through agreements concluded under Article 43, would seem to exclude the possibility that the Security Council might act under some other Article of the Charter. The Court cannot accept so limited a view of the powers of the Security Council under the Charter. It cannot be said that the Charter has left the Security Council impotent in the face of an emergency situation when agreements under Article 43 have not been concluded.

Articles of Chapter VII of the Charter speak of "situations" as well as disputes, and it must lie within the power of the Security Council to police a situation even though it does not resort to enforcement action against a State. The costs of actions which the Security Council is authorized to take constitute "expenses of the Organization within the meaning of Article 17, paragraph 2." ...

... [T]he Court agrees that such expenditures must be tested by their relationship to the purposes of the United Nations in the sense that if an expenditure were made for a purpose which is not one of the purposes of the United Nations, it could not be considered an "expense of the Organization."

The purposes of the United Nations are set forth in Article I of the Charter. The first two purposes as stated in paragraphs 1 and 2, may be summarily described as pointing to the goal of international peace and security and friendly relations. The third purpose is the achievement of economic, social, cultural and humanitarian goals and respect for human rights. The fourth and last purpose is: "To be a center for harmonizing the actions of nations in the attainment of these common ends."

The primary place ascribed to international peace and security is natural, since the fulfillment of the other purposes will be dependent upon the attainment of that basic condition. These purposes are broad indeed, but neither they nor the powers conferred to effectuate them are unlimited. Save as they have entrusted the Organization with the attainment of these common ends, the Member States retain their freedom of action. But when the Organization takes action which warrants the assertion that it was appropriate for the fulfilment of one of the stated purposes of the United Nations, the presumption is that such action is not *ultra vires* the Organization.

If it is agreed that the action in question is within the scope of the functions of the Organization but it is alleged that it has been initiated or carried out in a manner not in conformity with the division of functions among the several organs which the Charter prescribes, one moves to the internal plane, to the internal structure of the Organization. If the action was taken by the wrong organ, it was irregular as a matter of that internal structure, but this would not necessarily mean that the expense incurred was not an expense of the Organization. Both national and international law contemplate cases in which the body corporate or politic may be bound, as to third parties, by an *ultra vires* act of an agent.

In the legal systems of States, there is often some procedure for determining the validity of even a legislative or governmental act, but no analogous procedure is to be found in the structure of the United Nations. Proposals made during the drafting of the Charter to place the ultimate authority to interpret the Charter in the International Court of Justice were not accepted; the opinion which the Court is in the course of rendering is an advisory opinion. As anticipated in 1945, therefore, each organ must, in the first place at least, determine its own jurisdiction. If the Security Council, for example, adopts a resolution purportedly for the maintenance of international peace and security and if, in accordance with a mandate or authorization in such resolution, the Secretary-General incurs financial obligations, these amounts must be presumed to constitute "expenses of the Organization."

The Financial Regulations and Rules of the United Nations, adopted by the General Assembly, provide:

> Regulation 4.1: The appropriations voted by the General Assembly shall constitute an authorization to the Secretary-General to incur obligations and make payments for the purposes for which the appropriations were voted and up to the amounts so voted.

Thus, for example, when the General Assembly in resolution 1619 (XV) included a paragraph reading:

> 3. Decides to appropriate an amount of $100 million for the operations of the United Nations in the Congo from 1 January to 31 October 1961

this constituted an authorization to the Secretary-General to incur certain obligations of the United Nations just as clearly as when in resolution 1590 (XV) the General Assembly used this language:

> 3. Authorizes the Secretary-General ... to incur commitments in 1961 for the United Nations operations in the Congo up to the total of $ 24 million ...:

On the previous occasion when the Court was called upon to consider Article 17 of the Charter, the Court found that an award of the Administrative Tribunal of the United Nations created an obligation of the Organization and with relation thereto the Court said that:

> the function of approving the budget does not mean that the General Assembly has an absolute power to approve or disapprove the expenditure proposed to it; for some part of that expenditure arises out of obligations already incurred by the Organization, and to this extent the General Assembly has no alternative but to honor these engagements. (*Effects of awards of compensation made by the United Nations Administrative Tribunal, I.C.J. Reports 1954, p. 59*)

Similarly, obligations of the Organization may be incurred by the Secretary-General, acting on the authority of the Security Council or of the General Assembly, and the General Assembly "has no alternative but to honour these engagements."

The obligation is one thing: the way in which the obligation is met—that is from what source the funds are secured—is another. The General Assembly may follow any one of several alternatives ... it is of no legal significance whether, as a matter of book-keeping or accounting, the General Assembly chooses to have the item in question included under one of the standard established sections of the "regular" budget or whether it is separately listed in some special account or fund. The significant fact is that the item is an expense of the Organization and under Article 17, paragraph 2, the General Assembly therefore has authority to apportion it.

The reasoning which has just been developed, applied to the resolutions mentioned in the request for the advisory opinion, might suffice as a basis for the opinion of the Court. The Court finds it appropriate, however, to take into consideration other arguments which have been advanced. ...

The expenditures enumerated in the request for an advisory opinion may conveniently be examined first with reference to UNEF and then to ONUC. In each case, attention will be paid first to the operations and then to the financing of the operations.

In considering the operations in the Middle-East, the Court must analyze the functions of UNEF as set forth in resolutions of the General Assembly. ...

[The Court considered General Assembly resolution 998 (ES-I), resolution 1000 (ES-I), paragraphs 9, 10, and 12 of the second and final report of the Secretary-General on the plan for an Emergency International Force of 6 November, and resolution 1001 (ES-I).]

It is not possible to find in this description of the functions of UNEF, as outlined by the Secretary-General and concurred in by the General Assembly without a dissenting vote, any evidence that the Force was to be used for purposes of enforcement. Nor can such evidence be found in the subsequent operations of the Force, operations which did not exceed the scope of the functions ascribed to it. ...

On the other hand, it is apparent that the operations were undertaken to fulfil a prime purpose of the United Nations, that is, to promote and to maintain a peaceful settlement of the situation. This being true, the Secretary-General properly exercised the authority given him to incur financial obligations of the Organization and expenses resulting from such obligations must be considered "expenses of the Organization within the meaning of Article 17, paragraph 2."

Apropos what has already been said about the meaning of the word "action" in Article 11 of the Charter, attention may be called to the fact that resolution 997 (ES-I), which is chronologically the first of the resolutions concerning the operations in the Middle East mentioned in the request for the advisory opinion, provides in paragraph 5:

> *Requests* the Secretary-General to observe and report promptly on the compliance with the present resolution to the Security Council and to the General Assembly, for such further *action as they may deem appropriate in accordance with the Charter.*

The italicized words reveal an understanding that either of the two organs might take "action" in the premises. Actually, as one knows, the "action" was taken by the General Assembly in adopting two days later without a dissenting vote, resolution 998 (ES-I) and, also without a dissenting vote, within another three days, resolutions 1000 (ES-I) and 1001 (ES-I), all providing for UNEF.

The Court notes that these "actions" may be considered "measures" recommended under Article 14, rather than "action" recommended under Article 11. The powers of the General Assembly stated in Article 14 are not made subject to the provisions of Article 11, but only of Article 12. Furthermore, as the Court has already noted, the word "measures" implies some kind of action. So far as concerns the nature of the situations in the Middle East in 1956, they could be described as "likely to impair ... friendly relations among nations," just as well as they could be considered to involve "the maintenance of international peace and security." Since the resolutions of the General Assembly in question do not mention upon which article they are based, and since the language used in most of them might imply reference to either Article 14 or Article 11, it cannot be excluded that they were based upon the former rather than the latter article. ...

The financing of UNEF presented perplexing problems and the debates on these problems have even led to the view that the General Assembly never, either directly or indirectly, regarded the expenses of UNEF as "expenses of the Organization within the meaning of Article 17, paragraph 2, of the Charter." With this interpretation the Court cannot agree. ...

In an oral statement to the plenary meeting of the General Assembly on 26 November 1956, the Secretary-General said:

> ... I wish to make it equally clear that while funds received and payments made with respect to the Force are to be considered as coming outside the regular budget of the Organization, the operation is essentially a United Nations responsibility, and the Special Account to be established must, therefore, be construed as coming within the meaning of Article 17 of the Charter.

At this same meeting, after hearing this statement, the General Assembly in resolution 1122 (XI) noted that it had "provisionally approved the recommendations made by the Secretary-General concerning the financing of the Force." It then authorized the Secretary-General "to establish a United Nations Emergency Force Special Account to which funds received by the United Nations, outside the regular budget, for the purpose of meeting the expenses of the Force shall be credited and from which payments for this purpose shall be made." ...

[The Court then analysed paragraph 15 of the second and final report of the Secretary-General on the plan for an emergency international Force of 6 November 1956 and a series of General Assembly resolutions concerning UNEF]

The Court concludes ... that from year to year the expenses of UNEF have been treated by the General Assembly as expenses of the Organization within the meaning of Article 17, paragraph 2, of the Charter. ...

The operations in the Congo were initially authorized by the Security Council in the resolution of 14 July 1960 which was adopted without a dissenting vote... However, it is argued that that resolution has been implemented in violation of provisions of the Charter inasmuch as under the Charter it is the Security Council that determines which States are to participate in carrying out decisions involving the maintenance of international peace and security, whereas in the case of the Congo the Secretary-General himself determined which States were to participate with their armed forces or otherwise. ...

In the light of ... a record of reiterated consideration, confirmation, approval and ratification by the Security Council and by the General Assembly of the actions of the Secretary-General in implementing the resolution of 14 July 1960, it is impossible to reach the conclusion that the operations in question usurped or impinged upon the prerogatives conferred by the Charter on the Security Council. The Charter does not forbid the Security Council to act through instruments of its own choice: under Article 29 it "may establish such subsidiary organs as it deems necessary for the performance of its functions"; under Article 98 it may entrust "other functions" to the Secretary-General.

It is not necessary for the Court to express an opinion as to which article or articles of the Charter were the basis for the resolutions of the Security Council, but it can be said that the operations of ONUC did not include a use of armed force against a State which the Security Council, under Article 39, determined to have committed an act of aggression or to have breached the peace. The armed forces which were utilized in the Congo were not authorized to take military action against any State. The operation did not involve "preventive or enforcement measures" against any State under Chapter VII and therefore did not constitute "action" as that term is used in Article 11.

For the reasons stated, financial obligations which, in accordance with the clear and reiterated authority of both the Security Council and the General Assembly, the Secretary-General incurred on behalf of the United Nations, constitute obligations of the Organization for which the General Assembly was entitled to make provision under the authority of Article 17, paragraph 2, of the Charter. ...

In relation to ONUC, the first action concerning the financing of the operation was taken by the General Assembly on 20 December 1960 ... This resolution 1583 (XV) of 20 December referred to the report of the Secretary-General on the estimated cost of the Congo operations from 14 July to 31 December 1960, and to the recommendations of the Advisory Committee on Administrative and Budgetary Questions. It decided to establish an ad hoc account for the expenses of the United Nations in the Congo. It also took note of certain waivers of cost claims and then decided to apportion the sum of $ 48.5 million among the Member States "on the basis of the regular scale of assessment" subject to certain exceptions. It made this decision because in the preamble it had already recognized:

that the expenses involved in the United Nations operations in the Congo for 1960 constitute "expenses of the Organization" within the meaning of Article 17, paragraph 2, of the Charter of the United Nations and that the assessment thereof against Member States creates binding legal obligations on such States to pay their assessed shares.

By further resolutions [GA Res. 1619(XV) (1961) and GA Res. 1732(XVI) (1961)] the General Assembly authorized the Secretary-General "to incur commitments [for additional periods and to limited extents] ..."

The conclusion to be drawn ... is that the General Assembly has twice decided that even though certain expenses are "extraordinary" and "essentially different" from those under the "regular budget," they are none the less "expenses of the Organization" to be apportioned in accordance with the power granted to the General Assembly by Article 17, paragraph 2. ...

At the outset of this opinion, the Court pointed out that the text of Article 17, paragraph 2, of the Charter could lead to the simple conclusion that "the expenses of the Organization" are the amounts paid out to defray the costs of carrying out the purposes of the Organization. It was further indicated that the Court would examine the resolutions authorizing the expenditures referred to in the request for the advisory opinion in order to ascertain whether they were incurred with that end in view. The Court has made such an examination and finds that they were so incurred. The Court has also analyzed the principal arguments which have been advanced against the conclusion that the expenditures in question should be considered as "expenses of the Organization within the meaning of Article 17, paragraph 2, of the Charter of the United Nations," and has found that these arguments are unfounded. Consequently, the Court arrives at the conclusion that the questions submitted to it in General Assembly resolution 1731 (XVI) must be answered in the affirmative.

The opinion of the ICJ, though accepted by the General Assembly, was repudiated by France and the Soviet Union, who refused to pay their contribution. Even so, the loss-of-vote sanction provided under Article 19 to deal with non-payment of dues was not applied as many members were uncomfortable with the idea of two major powers being excluded from voting.[8] Indeed many of the other States, members of the Communist bloc and other countries from Latin America, Asia, and Africa also refused to pay their shares. When France and the Soviet Union approached the two-year default level—which would have disqualified them from voting under Article 19—

---

[8] Frederic L Kirgis, United States Dues Arrearages in the United Nations and Possible Loss of Vote in the UN General Assembly, July 1998, http://www.asil.org/insights/insigh21.htm.

the General Assembly members agreed to avoid bringing any matter to a vote, proceeding solely by consensus. Eventually, even the United States gave way and the General Assembly resolved the issue by way of a compromise formula under which the shortfalls caused by the refusals of some of the members were compensated for by voluntary contributions.[9]

To prevent the sort of situation that arose in the *Certain Expenses* case—primarily due to expenditures being incurred despite the objection of some of the permanent members of the Security Council—the normal practice tends to be consensus-based decision making (as opposed to the affirmative vote of a two thirds majority present and voting mandated by Article 18) to ensure money generated through assessed contributions is only directed toward "legitimate expenses."

Nevertheless, a recurrent problem for the United Nations is the withholding or threat of withholding contributions unless certain policies are followed. The United States has been the most prominent actor in this regard, its policy having initially been justified by reference to the Soviet and French position in the *Certain Expenses* case.

Because arrears have been extensive and because non-payment has frequently occurred, a pattern of bloated UN budgeting has emerged, particularly in the peacekeeping field, so that Peter may pay Paul in order to avoid absolute default. We thus see one perverse Secretariat practice (at least in terms of formal accountability) growing up as a response to the vices of member states, all of it leading to a lack of transparency in UN budgeting that only the experts can hope to penetrate.

QUESTIONS

1. Are member states of the United Nations justified in withholding funds from the organization to protest *ultra vires* actions?
2. The *Certain Expenses* case related to peacekeeping operations undertaken with the consent of the host state. Would the same reasoning apply to a General Assembly resolution recommending that states enforce an embargo on sale of material supporting a nuclear program and providing funds to defray costs of member states enforcing such an embargo within their own territory? Why, or why not?
3. Given that the UN has no authority to borrow commercially, what are some of the potential consequences of non-payment by member states? Given the reality of extensive arrears and frequent non-payment of dues by member states, why has the UN never had to shut down? What does

[9] Francesco Franscioni, "Multilateralism à la Carte: The Limits to Unilateral Withholdings of Assessed Contributions to the UN Budget," *European Journal of International Law*, vol. 11 (2000), p. 52.

this tell us about apparently absolute requirements laid down in the Charter (and decisions by the ICJ)?

6.2 The Regular Budget

The regular budget now takes the form of a biennial programme budget, beginning with an even year, a practice that was started in 1974–75. For 2006–2007, the proposed budget was $3.79 billion. However for the first time, a limitation has been imposed on the amount of expenditures the Secretary-General may incur, fixing the sum at $950 million for the first six months of 2006. Remaining funds were to be subject to approval of a later request, which was granted in late June 2006 after an extensive political tussle.[10] To improve accountability within the Organization, the United Nations since 2000 has also followed a system of results-based budgeting,[11] which focuses on the expected accomplishments, before, during and after implementation to measure and evaluate the effectiveness of expenditures.

To illustrate the changes in budgeting over the years, the budgetary arrangements for 1946 and for the 2006–2007 biennium are excerpted below.

GENERAL ASSEMBLY RESOLUTION 14(I) (1946): BUDGETARY AND FINANCIAL ARRANGEMENTS

A

The permanent budgetary and financial arrangements of the United Nations should be so designed as to promote efficient and economical administration and command the confidence of Members.

Therefore the General Assembly resolves that:

1. Arrangements be made on the basis of the general principles set out in Section 2 of Chapter IX of the Report of the Preparatory Commission and of the provisional financial regulations, for budgetary procedures, the collection and custody of funds, the control of disbursements and the auditing of accounts.

2. To facilitate the consideration of administrative and budgetary questions by the General Assembly and its Administrative and Budgetary Committee, there be appointed at the beginning of the second part of the first session of the General Assembly, an Advisory Committee on Administrative and

---

[10] UN Press Release GA/10442 (23 December 2005).
[11] First suggested in the Report of the Secretary-General on "Renewing the United Nations" UN Doc. A/51/950, which was endorsed by the General Assembly in GA Res. 55/231 (2000).

Budgetary Questions of nine members (instead of seven as laid down in rule 37 of the provisional rules of procedure) with the following functions:

(a) To examine and report on the budget submitted by the Secretary-General to the General Assembly;

(b) To advise the General Assembly concerning any administrative and budgetary matters referred to it;

(c) To examine on behalf of the General Assembly the administrative budgets of specialized agencies and proposals for financial arrangements with such agencies;

(d) To consider and report to the General Assembly on the auditors report on the accounts of the United Nations and of the specialized agencies.

The Committee shall deal with personnel matters only in their budgetary aspects, and representatives of the staff shall have the right to be heard by the Committee.

3. A standing expert Committee on Contributions of ten members (instead of seven as laid down in rule 40 of the provisional rules of procedure) be appointed with instructions to prepare a detailed scale of apportionment of expenses, based on the principles set out in paragraph 13 of section 2 of chapter IX of the Report of the Preparatory Commission for consideration at the second part of the first session.

B

With a view to the integration of the administrative and budgetary planning of the Organization,
   the General Assembly:
   4. Recommends that the Secretary-General appoint at an early date a small advisory group of experts, as described in paragraphs 23–26 of section 2 of chapter IX of the Report of the Preparatory Commission to perform the functions suggested by the Preparatory Commission in paragraphs 23–26 of section 2 of chapter IX of its Report, including those specified in the provisional financial regulations.

C

Having made a general examination of the draft provisional financial regulations submitted by the Preparatory Commission,
   the General Assembly:
   5. Adopts the provisional financial regulations, as amended and reproduced in annex I to this report.

D

The opportunities of members to participate in the activities of the United Nations should be equalized as far as possible.
   Therefore the General Assembly resolves that:

6. The actual travelling expenses of representatives and their alternates to and from meetings of the General Assembly shall be borne by the United Nations budget provided that the number of persons whose expenses will be so paid is limited to five in all per member. The maximum travelling allowances shall be restricted to the equivalent of first-class accommodation by recognized public transport *via* an approved route from the capital city of the member to the place where the General Assembly is meeting, and shall not include the payment of subsistence, except where this is included as an integral part of the regular posted schedule for first class accommodation for recognized public transport. Actual travelling expenses to and from the meetings of the General Assembly of representatives or their alternates shall be reimbursed to each Member by means of an adjustment in the Member's annual contribution.

E

The General Assembly resolves that:

7. The Secretary-General after consultation with the Advisory Group referred to above, should be prepared to recommend to the General Assembly during the second part of the first session necessary action on administrative and budgetary questions, including the following:

(a) the form of the budget;

(b) procedure for the examination of the budget by the Advisory Committee on Administrative and Budgetary Questions and for submission of the Committee's report to the General Assembly;

(c) machinery for the control of expenditure;

(d) means of meeting extraordinary expenditure;

(e) provision of working capital;

(f) character and scope of special funds; and

(g) scope and method of audit of accounts and the procedure for the submission of the auditor's report to the Advisory Committee and the General Assembly.

F

The General Assembly:

8. *Notes* the observations made in paragraphs 5, 10 and 11 of section 2 of chapter IX of the report of the Preparatory Commission dealing with the formulation, presentation and execution of the budget, the collection and management of funds and the currency of the account and transmits them to the Secretary-General for his information and consideration.

G

The General Assembly resolves that:

9. An amount of $21,500,000 is hereby appropriated for the following purposes:

Section I—For expenses of the General Assembly and the Councils: US$1,500,000
Section II—For expenses of the Secretariat: US$16,510,750
Section III—For expenses of the International Court of Justice: US$617,250
Section IV—For unforeseen expenses: US$2,000,000
Section V—For the expenses of the Preparatory Commission and the cost of convening the General Assembly for the first part of the first session: US$872,000

10. The above amounts are available for the payment of obligations incurred prior to 1 January 1947. The Secretary-General may transfer by written order credits among or within the above listed classifications.

H

The General Assembly resolves that:
11. A working capital fund is established at the amounts of $ 25,000,000 (US)
12. Members shall make advances to the working capital fund in accordance with [a provisional] scale which is merely a matter of convenience and in no sense a precedent for the assessment of contributions.
13. These advances shall be readjusted at the time of the second part of the first session of the General Assembly in accordance with the scale to be adopted by the General Assembly for contribution of members to the first annual budget.
14. Except for any readjustments which may result from a revision of the scale referred to in paragraph 3, advances to the working capital fund shall not be offset against contribution of members to the first annual budget.
15. The General Assembly at the second part of its first session (September 1946) shall determine the amount at which the working capital fund should be maintained and the method and timing of consequential set-offs against contributions or other adjustments.

GENERAL ASSEMBLY RESOLUTION 60/247 (2005): PROGRAMME BUDGET FOR THE BIENNIUM 2006–2007

The General Assembly
Resolves that, for the biennium 2006–2007:
1. Appropriations totalling 3,798,912,500 United States dollars are hereby approved for the following purposes:

Part I. Overall Policymaking, Direction and Coordination

1. Overall policymaking, direction and coordination: US$74,813,500
2. General Assembly and Economic and Social Council affairs and conference management: US$586,776,200 ...

Part II. Political Affairs

3. Political affairs: US$432,026,900
4. Disarmament: $20,381,100
5. Peacekeeping operations: $94,091,000
6. Peaceful uses of outer space: $5,906,800 ...

Part III. International Justice and Law

7. International Court of Justice 34,956,900
8. Legal affairs: $42,289,400 ...

Part IV. International Cooperation for Development

9. Economic and social affairs 157,930,900
10. Least developed countries, landlocked developing countries and small island developing States 5,056,800
11. United Nations support for the New Partnership for Africa's Development 10,791,900
12. Trade and development 111,091,600
13. International Trade Centre UNCTAD/WTO 25,915,800
14. Environment 11,977,100
15. Human settlements 17,864,500
16. International drug control, crime prevention and criminal justice 31,527,800 ...

Part V. Regional Cooperation for Development

17. Economic and Social Development in Africa 106,011,400
18. Economic and social development in Asia and the Pacific: $71,858,100
19. Economic development in Europe: $54,176,700
20. Economic and social development in Latin America and the Caribbean 94,630,400
21. Economic and social development in Western Asia: $53,416,900
22. Regular programme of technical cooperation: $45,622,000 ...

Part VI. Human rights and humanitarian affairs

23. Human rights 83,088,400
24. Protection of and assistance to refugees: $64,645,200
25. Palestine refugees: $35,184,800
26. Humanitarian assistance: $26,140,500 ...

Part VII. Public Information

27. Public information 177,302,500 ...

Part VIII. Common support services

28. Management and support services: $511,375,800 ...

Part IX. Internal Oversight

29. Internal oversight: $31,330,100 ...

Part X. Jointly Financed Administrative Activities and Special Expenses

30. Jointly financed administrative activities: $11,178,800
31. Special expenses: $92,798,000

Part XI. Capital Expenditures

32. Construction, alteration, improvement and major maintenance: $74,841,300 ...

Part XII. Safety and Security

33. Safety and security $190,131,400 ...

Part XIII. Development Account

34. Development Account: $13,954,100 ...

Part XIV. Staff Assessment

35. Staff assessment: $397,827,900

Total : $3,798,912,500

2. The Secretary-General shall be authorized to transfer credits between sections of the budget with the concurrence of the Advisory Committee on Administrative and Budgetary Questions;

3. The budget for the biennium 2006–2007 amounts to 3,799 million dollars. Expected expenditure in the course of 2006 is 1,899 million dollars. The two-year budget will permit a full assessment on all Member States for 2006, in accordance with Article 17 of the Charter of the United Nations. The Secretary-General, while adhering to the existing procedures regarding the annual assessment on Member States, is authorized to enter into expenditure of a first tranche, limited to 950 million dollars, as an exceptional measure. The General Assembly, in order to ensure the availability of resources for programme delivery, will act in response to a request from the Secretary-General, at an appropriate time, for expenditure of the remaining funds;

4. The total net provision made under the various sections of the budget for contractual printing shall be administered as a unit under the direction of the United Nations Publications Board;

5. In addition to the appropriations approved under paragraph 1 above, an amount of 75,000 dollars is appropriated for each year of the biennium 2006–

2007 from the accumulated income of the Library Endowment Fund for the purchase of books, periodicals, maps and library equipment and for such other expenses of the library at the Palais des Nations in Geneva as are in accordance with the objects and provisions of the endowment.

Separate allocations were made for special subjects including the capital master plan, contingency fund, administrative expenses of the UN Joint Staff Pension fund, the International Trade Centre, special political missions, good offices, and other political initiatives authorized by the General Assembly and/or the Security Council etc. Funds were also set aside to meet "unforeseen and extraordinary expenses" incurred in the maintenance of peace and security and in the operation of the International Court of Justice. In addition, an allocation of $100 million was made towards the Working Capital Fund.

6.3 Assessment of Contributions

Contributions to the regular budget are determined by reference to a scale of assessments approved by the General Assembly on the basis of advice from the Committee on Contributions. In 2000, following the United Nations Millennium Declaration, the Assembly revised this scale substantially, to ensure timely availability of resources to the Organization:

GENERAL ASSEMBLY RESOLUTION 55/5 (2001): SCALE OF ASSESSMENTS FOR THE APPORTIONMENT OF THE EXPENSES OF THE UNITED NATIONS

B

The General Assembly,

1. *Decides* that the scale of assessments for the period 2001–2003 shall be based on the following elements and criteria:

(*a*) Estimates of the gross national product;

(*b*) Average statistical base periods of six and three years;

(*c*) Conversion rates based on market exchange rates, except where that would cause excessive fluctuations and distortions in the income of some Member States, when price-adjusted rates of exchange or other appropriate conversion rates should be employed, taking due account of General Assembly resolution 46/221 B of 21 December 1991;

(d) The debt-burden approach employed in the scale of assessments for the period 1995–1997;

(e) A low per capita income adjustment of 80 per cent, with the threshold per capita income limit of the average per capita gross national product of all Member States for the statistical base periods;

(f) A minimum assessment rate of 0.001 per cent;

(g) A maximum assessment rate for the least developed countries of 0.01 per cent;

(h) A maximum assessment rate of 22 per cent;

2. *Decides also* that the elements of the scale of assessments contained in paragraph 1 above will be fixed until 2006, subject to the provisions of resolution C below, in particular paragraph 2 of that resolution, and without prejudice to rule 160 of the rules of procedure of the General Assembly;

3. *Notes* that the application of the methodology outlined in paragraph 1 above will lead to a substantial increase in the rate of assessment of some Member States;

4. *Decides* to apply transitional measures to address those substantial increases; . . .

8. *Resolves* also that:

(a) Notwithstanding the terms of financial regulation 5.5, the Secretary-General shall be empowered to accept, at his discretion and after consultation with the Chairman of the Committee on Contributions, a portion of the contributions of Member States for the calendar years 2001, 2002 and 2003 in currencies other than United States dollars;

(b) In accordance with financial regulation 5.9, States which are not Members of the United Nations but which participate in certain of its activities shall be called upon to contribute towards the 2001, 2002 and 2003 expenses of the Organization on the basis of the following rates:

Holy See: 0.001
Switzerland[12]: 1.274

These rates represent the basis for the calculation of the flat annual fees to be charged to non-member States in accordance with General Assembly resolution 44/197 B of 21 December 1989.

C

The General Assembly, . . .

1. *Establishes*, as from 1 January 2001, a reduced ceiling of 22 per cent for the assessed contribution of any individual Member State;

2. *Decides* to review the position at the end of 2003 and, depending on the status of contributions and arrears, to determine all appropriate measures to remedy the situation, including adjustments of the ceiling in keeping with its resolution 52/215 A to D of 22 December 1997;

---

[12] Switzerland became a member of the United Nations in 2002.

3. *Stresses* that the reduction of the maximum assessment rate referred to in paragraph 1 of resolution B above shall apply to the apportionment of the expenses of the United Nations and should have no automatic implication for the apportionment of the expenses of the specialized agencies or the International Atomic Energy Agency.

The methodology for the scale of assessments was to remain fixed until 2006.

Since 1992 the peacekeeping budget has surpassed the UN regular budget. In 2003, the peacekeeping budget equalled 67 percent of the assessments available to the United Nations, which are routed in part through the regular budget and in part through special accounts. This has lead to a greater strain upon the resources of the United Nations and brought it closer to financial crisis, as formerly the peacekeeping account was always in surplus, and Secretary-General was able to use these funds to cross subsidize other activities. The 1990s saw the United Nations falling into severe arrears in repayment to troop contributing countries for peacekeeping operations as expenditures on peacekeeping increased from $490 million in 1991 to $3.1 billion in 1993. At the end of the decade, reforms were proposed in the assessment of member contributions for peacekeeping operations.

GENERAL ASSEMBLY RESOLUTION 55/235 (2000): SCALE OF ASSESSMENTS FOR THE APPORTIONMENT OF THE EXPENSES OF UNITED NATIONS PEACEKEEPING OPERATIONS

The General Assembly,

I

. . .

1. *Reaffirms* the following general principles underlying the financing of United Nations peacekeeping operations:

(*a*) The financing of such operations is the collective responsibility of all States Members of the United Nations and, accordingly, the costs of peacekeeping operations are expenses of the Organization to be borne by Member States in accordance with Article 17, paragraph 2, of the Charter of the United Nations;

(*b*) In order to meet the expenditures caused by such operations, a different procedure is required from that applied to meet expenditures under the regular budget of the United Nations;

(c) Whereas the economically more developed countries are in a position to make relatively larger contributions to peacekeeping operations, the economically less developed countries have a relatively limited capacity to contribute towards peacekeeping operations involving heavy expenditures;

(d) The special responsibilities of the permanent members of the Security Council for the maintenance of peace and security should be borne in mind in connection with their contributions to the financing of peace and security operations;

(e) Where circumstances warrant, the General Assembly should give special consideration to the situation of any Member States which are victims of, and those which are otherwise involved in, the events or actions leading to a peacekeeping operation;

2. *Recognizes* the need to reform the current methodology for apportioning the expenses of peacekeeping operations;

3. *Notes with appreciation* voluntary contributions made to peacekeeping operations and, without prejudice to the principle of collective responsibility, invites Member States to consider making such contributions;

II

4. *Decides* that assessment rates for the financing of peacekeeping operations should be based on the scale of assessments for the regular budget of the United Nations, with an appropriate and transparent system of adjustments based on levels of Member States, consistent with the principles outlined above;

5. *Decides also* that the permanent members of the Security Council should form a separate level and that, consistent with their special responsibilities for the maintenance of peace and security, they should be assessed at a higher rate than for the regular budget;

6. *Decides further* that all discounts resulting from adjustments to the regular budget assessment rates of Member States in levels C through J shall be borne on a pro rata basis by the permanent members of the Security Council;

7. *Decides* that the least developed countries should be placed in a separate level and receive the highest rate of discount available under the scale;

8. *Decides also* that the statistical data used for setting the rates of assessment for peacekeeping should be the same as the data used in preparing the regular budget scale of assessments, subject to the provisions of the present resolution;

9. *Decides further* to create levels of discount to facilitate automatic, predictable movement between categories on the basis of the per capita gross national product of Member States; ...

11. *Decides also* that Member States will be assigned to the lowest level of contribution with the highest discount for which they are eligible, unless they indicate a decision to move to a higher level;

12. *Decides further* that for purposes of determining the eligibility of Member States for contribution in particular levels during the 2001–2003 scale period, the average per capita gross national product of all Member States will be 4,797 United States dollars and the per capita gross national product of Member States will be the average of 1993 to 1998 figures;

13. *Decides* that transitions as specified above will occur in equal increments over the transition period as designated above;

14. *Decides also* that after 2001–2003, transition periods of two years will apply to countries moving up by two levels, and that transition periods of three years will apply to countries moving up by three levels or more without prejudice to paragraph 11 above;

15. *Requests* the Secretary-General to update the composition of the levels described above on a triennial basis, in conjunction with the regular budget scale of assessment reviews, in accordance with the criteria established above, and to report thereon to the General Assembly;

16. *Decides* that the structure of levels to be implemented from 1 July 2001 shall be reviewed after nine years;

17. *Decides also* that Member States may agree upon adjustments to their assessment rates under the ad hoc scale in the light of the special transitional circumstances applying during the period 1 January to 30 June 2001

In short, the Assembly decided to adopt a new set of 10 levels (A–J) for Member States for the purposes of apportioning the costs of peacekeeping, to be implemented on a phased basis from 1 July 2001. The apportionments range from a premium payable by permanent Member-States of the Security Council (Level A) to a 90 percent discount for less developed countries (Level J). General Assembly resolution 55/236 (2000) noted the voluntary movement of a number of states to higher levels than had been indicated in the previous resolution.

6.4 The Advisory Committee on Administrative and Budgetary Questions

The Advisory Committee on Administrative and Budgetary Questions (ACABQ) has a key role to play in the budgetary allocations within the United Nations, and its specialized agencies. Initially, it was proposed as a body that would supervise the Secretary-General's financial management. General Assembly resolution 14(I) (1946), quoted earlier, established the committee and outlined four functions for it. The ACABQ's specific program of work is determined by the requirements of the General Assembly and the other legislative bodies to which the Committee reports. Its membership has been expanded since it was first established and presently stands at sixteen.

As General Assembly resolution 32/103 (1977) indicates, the Committee's work involves a detailed, comprehensive and continuous assessment of the Organization's budget, to the point that it, and the Fifth Committee (Administrative and Budgetary), which it advises, have occasionally been accused of "micro-management."

GENERAL ASSEMBLY RESOLUTION 32/103 (1977): ENLARGEMENT OF THE ADVISORY COMMITTEE ON ADMINISTRATIVE AND BUDGETARY QUESTIONS

The General Assembly, ...
  Noting that the membership of the United Nations has increased substantially since the adoption of the Resolutions enlarging the Advisory Committee,
  Mindful of rule 156 of its Rules of procedure and desiring, accordingly, to increase the participation of members from developing countries in the Advisory Committee,
  1. *Decides* to increase the membership of the Advisory Committee on Administrative and Budgetary Questions from thirteen to sixteen members;
  2. *Decides* to amend, with effect from 1 January 1978, rules 155 to 157 of its rules of procedure to read as follows:

Rule 155

The General Assembly shall appoint an Advisory Committee on Advisory and Budgetary Questions consisting of sixteen members, including at least three financial experts of recognized standing.

Rule 156

The members of the Advisory Committee on Advisory and Budgetary Questions, no two of whom shall be nationals of the same State, shall be selected on the basis of broad geographical representations, personal qualifications and experience and shall serve for a period of three years corresponding to three calendar years. Members shall retire by rotation and shall be eligible for reappointment. The three financial experts shall not retire simultaneously. The General Assembly shall appoint the members of the Advisory Committee at the regular session immediately preceding the expiration of the term of office of the members or, in case of vacancies, at the next session.

Rule 157

The Advisory Committee on Administrative and Budgetary Questions shall be responsible for expert examination of the programme budget of the United Nations and shall assist the Administrative and Budgetary Committee (Fifth Committee). At the beginning of each regular session at which the proposed programme budget for the following biennium is to be considered, it shall submit to the General Assembly, a detailed report on the proposed programme budget for that biennium. It shall also submit at such times as shall be specified in the applicable provisions of the Financial Regulations and Rules of the United Nations, a report on the accounts of the United Nations and all United Nations entities for which the Secretary-General has administrative responsibility. It shall examine on behalf of the General Assembly the administrative budgets of specialized agencies and proposals for the financial and budgetary arrangements with such agencies. It shall perform such other duties as may be assigned to it under the Financial Regulations of the United Nations.

Unlike the Fifth Committee, whose appointees are political and diplomatic delegates of their home countries, the ACABQ members operate in their personal capacity and are appointed by the General Assembly (on the recommendation of the Fifth Committee) not only on the basis of geographical representation but also personal qualifications and experience. The working of this committee has a direct bearing on the final assessment with respect to the budget, for its recommendations are almost always adopted by the Fifth Committee and the Assembly. This makes the ACABQ a very powerful, if low profile, body within the United Nations.

The membership of the ACABQ entered into public discussion in 1996 when, for the first time, a national of the United States was denied a place on the Committee. This was seen by many as a sign of UN condemnation of the selective withholding of assessed contributions by the United States. The measure may have been conducive to the Clinton Administration's promising to pay back-dues, conditional on being given their "usual" seat, the next time. However, as it turned out, the $819 million repayment package was vetoed on 21 October 1998 by President Clinton, and the US candidate failed to find a seat on the committee in the elections held on 6 November 1998. On 5 November 1999, the United States was restored to its near permanent seat on the Committee. Soon afterward the United States agreed to repay a part of its arrears to the United Nations.

This episode cast doubt on the independence of the ACABQ members, who are supposed to be appointed in their individual capacity. That states have a direct interest in having their citizens appointed to the Committee was apparent from statements such as that of Bill Richardson, a US Ambassador to the United Nations: "The US considers the work of the ACABQ to be critical to the efforts to make more efficient use of UN resources and to improve the performance of UN programs. Membership of an American on the ACABQ is vitally important for maintaining US confidence in the financial management of the United Nations."[13] It is clear also from the proposals for UN reform in the Senate Report on the Foreign Affairs Reform and Restructuring Act of 1997, which included the creation of a permanent position for a US representative in the ACABQ, or allotment of membership based on the level of contribution[14] (the United States clearly is the biggest contributor). The US position underscores the important role played by the ACABQ in administrative and budgetary matters in the United Nations.

In September 2005, the Committee was again in the news following the arrest of its Chairman Vladimir Kuznetsov, on charges of money laundering.[15] Among other charges, Mr. Kuznetsov was alleged to have connections with the Oil-for-Food scandal.[16] He pleaded not guilty to the charges but in March 2007 was found guilty of helping to launder more than $300,000 in bribes.[17]

6.5 Financial Challenges

Despite its relatively small budget, the United Nations has faced financial crisis with depressing regularity. The primary reason for this is, of course, that the United Nations has no resources of its own and must depend upon member states for contributions. These have not always been forthcoming as member states have withheld both assessed and voluntary contributions on different pretexts. The most significant defaulter in this regard has been the United States, which is responsible for more than 20 percent of the UN Budget.

---

[13] United States Mission to the United Nations Announces its Candidate for Membership on UN Budget Committee, March 12, 1998, USUN Press Release No. 45 (98), available at http://www.un.int/usa/98_45.htm.
[14] Sec. 2231 (5), Senate Report 105-028—Foreign Affairs Reform and Restructuring Act of 1997 states: "The United States must have a seat on the United Nations Committee on Administrative and Budgetary Questions (ACABQ). Until 1997, the United States has served on this committee since the creation of the United Nations. This committee is key to the budgetary decisions at the United Nations and the United States, as the largest contributing nations, should have a seat on this Committee."
[15] Daily Press Briefing by the Office of the Spokesman for the Secretary-General, 02/09/2005, http://www.un.org/News/briefings/docs/2005/db050902.doc.htm. See also Statement by Ambassador John R. Bolton, US Permanent Representative to the United Nations, on the Arrest of the Chairman of the ACABQ Vladimir Kuznetsov, at the Security Council Stakeout, September 2, 2005, USUN Press Release No. 154 (05), 02/09/2005, available at http://www.un.int/usa/05_154.htm.
[16] Betsy Pisik, "FBI Arrests Russian Envoy in UN Corruption Probe", *Washington Times*, 3 September 2005.
[17] Warren Hoge, "United Nations: Russian Ex-Diplomat Guilty In Bribe Case", *New York Times*, 8 March 2007.

The size of its share has allowed the United States to try to impose its own political agenda and policies upon the United Nations. The United States has thus, in the past, put pressure upon UN activities seen as benefiting the Palestine Liberation Organization, the South West Africa's People's Organization, programs for Libya, Iran, Cuba, and for certain Communist countries identified in section 620(f) of the Foreign Assistance Act of 1961. This has typically taken the form of withholding funds from the agencies involved. The US Congress has also denied contributions for UN funds budgeted for the "Second Decade to Combat Racism and Racial Discrimination" and for implementation of General Assembly resolution 3379(XXX) (1975) (the "Zionism is racism" resolution), for the construction of a $73,500,000 conference centre in Addis Ababa, Ethiopia, for the Economic Commission for Africa, for the UN "post adjustment allowance" for employees, and for the Department of Public Information, which at the time was accused of bias. The Executive has withheld contributions for the Preparatory Commission implementing the 1982 Law of the Sea Convention and for alleged "inadequacies" in the UN system to equalize the effect of US income taxation on the salaries of US members of the UN staff.[18]

In June 2005, the UN Reform Act[19] was passed in the US Congress, which provided for the withholding of up to 50 percent of its dues, unless the United Nations committed itself to that has employed withholding to attain its ends. Several of the other major contributors have also used these tactics.

The UN's financial situation has also been affected by the great expansion in its mandate, as well as the mandates of many of its specialized agencies. The number of peacekeeping operations has also increased, to the extent that in the 1990s the peacekeeping budget substantially outstripped the regular budget. Additionally claims of mismanagement and wasteful expenditure have also been made by several countries and, as discussed above, some of the withholdings were directed towards promoting UN reform.

During the Millennium Outcome Summit in September 2005, many states called for greater reforms in the management, accountability and oversight in the UN Secretariat. Secretary-General Kofi Annan issued a follow-up report entitled *Investing in the United Nations: For a Stronger Organization Worldwide*.

The report discusses, *inter alia*, some of the reasons for the financial problems of the United Nations, pointing out factors such as the inflexible budget implementation process that limits the ability of the United Nations to allocate funds strategically for operational needs coupled with the highly restricted authority of the Secretary-General to shift resources to meet emerging needs, the lack of a single, coherent and commonly understood notion of accountability for programme performance, cumbersome practices emerging from the Financial Rules and Regulations, and insufficient trans-

---

[18] José Alvarez, "Legal Remedies and the United Nations a la Carte Problem," *Michigan Journal of International Law*, vol. 12 (1991), pp. 235–237.

[19] H.R. 2745, available at http://wwwa.house.gov/international_relations/109/HR2745.PDF.

parency and availability of relevant financial information to provide clear guidance either to member states or to Secretariat managers on the Organization's financial picture.

INVESTING IN THE UNITED NATIONS: FOR A STRONGER ORGANIZATION WORLDWIDE (REPORT OF THE SECRETARY-GENERAL), 7 MARCH 2006[20]

Proposal 16

In the area of strategic budgetary planning and implementation, I propose that:

- The Member States and the Secretariat work together to find ways to further increase the strategic nature of the budgeting review, reduce duplicative, detailed and labour-intensive processes, and align key inputs across the regular, peacekeeping and extra-budgetary processes.
- The budget cycles be shortened and aligned with the calendar year. Regular budget preparation and adoption should be shortened to 12 months, and all stages of the budget review process should take place during the main part (September through December) of the regular sessions of the General Assembly. The peacekeeping budgetary cycle would be aligned with the calendar year.
- Budget appropriation be consolidated from the current 35 sections into 13 parts.
- Posts be approved in aggregate numbers and grouped into four broad grade categories. The Secretariat would submit an indicative staffing table for information purposes only. The Secretary-General should have the authority to redeploy posts as necessary, and to reclassify up to 10 per cent of posts within each broad category within a given budget period.
- The Secretary-General be given the authority, within a given budget period, to use the savings from vacant posts, with a value not to exceed 10 per cent of the overall post budget, for emerging priorities or unanticipated activities.

Proposal 17

In the area of financial management practices, I propose that:

- Peacekeeping accounts for separate field missions be consolidated into a single set of accounts and reports, starting in 2007, to improve cash management and operational flexibility.

---

[20] UN Doc. A/60/692 (2006)

- A new policy be introduced in July 2006, replacing four existing administrative instructions, to govern the streamlined management of trust funds. Key objectives would include simplified rules and procedures, the introduction of a single, consistent and flexible trust fund category, and the establishment of a new standard for support costs, lower than the current 13 per cent, to bring it more in line with the fee structure in force in the United Nations funds and programmes.
- The ceiling of the commitment authority granted by the General Assembly for peacekeeping operations be increased from $50 million to $150 million and de-linked from a specified number of Security Council decisions.
- The level of the Working Capital Fund for the regular budget be increased from $100 million to $250 million.
- Budget surpluses, including those from peacekeeping operations, be retained for use in subsequent periods, pending Member State approval.
- A separate fund be created to cover unanticipated expenditures arising from exchange rate fluctuations and inflation, to be financed through the transfer of budget surpluses.
- Interest be charged on arrears in a Member State's assessed contributions.

Proposal 18

In the area of performance evaluation and reporting, I propose that:

- United Nations activities in the areas of performance measurement be given increased resources but also rationalized.
- Monitoring and evaluation tools be reformed and synchronized so that their results can be evaluated in the formation of the subsequent budget.The budget and planning process be explicitly linked to the results of performance, work planning and the assessment of managerial performance in order to ensure the effective stewardship of resources provided by Member States.

6.6 Alternative Financing

A number of proposals for alternative means for financing the UN System have been made by independent organizations and think-tanks. These mainly include taxing the activities that link people and enterprises involved in world-wide operations. Included are currency transaction taxes, e-mail taxes, energy taxes, and aviation fuel taxes.[21]

---

[21] See, eg, sources available from www.globalpolicy.org.

It has been suggested that currency and e-mail levies could be imposed on those involved in international transactions facilitated by UN System activities. Global currency trade amounts to approximately $1.3 trillion per day. At least 80 percent of this is exchange rate speculation in the form of short or long term speculation. Cross-border purchase of goods and services accounts for only 2 percent. About 17 percent of foreign exchange trading takes place as a result of hedging against future exchange rate fluctuations. A tax of only 0.25 percent on these transactions could generate about $300 billion, twenty-five times the 2001 UN system-wide budget of $12 billion. An e-mail or internet duty would tax the amount of data sent through the internet. A person sending one hundred e-mails a day, each containing a ten-kilobyte document, might pay a tax of $0.01. The UNDP Development Report 1999 reported that such a tax would have yielded $70 billion in 1996, almost six times the 2001 UN System Budget.[22]

Other suggestions include aviation fuel and energy taxes on those responsible for global carbon emissions. Another idea is to tax carbon dioxide emissions from the combustion of fossil fuels. This proposal would tax carbon emissions from burning of coal, oil, and natural gas. There is active debate on this issue now in the European Union.[23] Some NGOs are pushing for increase in sales taxes on airline tickets and landing fees that could be devoted to financial support of the UN System.[24]

QUESTIONS ....

4. What are the arguments for and against making the United Nations less dependent on state contributions and giving it access to direct funding through various direct taxation schemes?
5. Should UN Members have to pay for operations to which they are opposed?
6. Should UN members have to pay for UN activities that are later found to have been beyond the relevant organ's competence?
7. What was the effect of paragraph three of General Assembly resolution 60/247 (2005)? In fact, it failed to spur meaningful UN reform, and its prime sponsor, the United States, had to back down. Are you surprised?

---

[22] Chadwick F Alger, *The UN System: A Reference Handbook* (Santa Barbara, CA: ABC-CLIO, 2006), pp. 39–40.

[23] Ibid.

[24] Indeed, in 2006, a number of countries, led by France, initiated a new additional tax on airline tickets (the "international solidarity contribution"), the proceeds of which were to benefit international health programming (particularly the fight against malaria, tuberculosis and HIV/Aids) under the umbrella of an international drug purchase facility, UNITAID.

Further Reading

Alvarez, José. "Legal Remedies and the United Nations a la Carte Problem." *Michigan Journal of International Law*, vol. 12 (1991), p. 229.

Cardenas, Emilio J. "Financing the United Nations's Activities: A Matter of Commitment." *University of Illinois Law Review*, vol. 1995 (1995), p. 147.

Koschorreck, Wilfried. "Article 17–19." In *The Charter of the United Nations: A Commentary*, 2nd edn., edited by Bruna Simma. Oxford: Oxford University Press, 2002.

Mangone, Gerard J., and Anand K. Srivastava. "Budgeting for the United Nations." *International Organization*, vol. 12 (1958), p. 473.

Ortiz, Even Fontaine, and Tadanori Inomata. "Evaluation of Results-based Budgeting in Peacekeeping Operations," Report of the Joint Inspection Unit, JIU/REP/2006/1, available at http://www.unsystem.org/JIU/en/reports.htm.

Part Three **Practice**

chapter seven
....

Conflict Prevention

Prevention of conflict is the first promise in the Charter of the United Nations, which begins with the stated determination to "save succeeding generations from the scourge of war." This promise has been broken consistently by local parties, governments, and international organizations such as the United Nations. The ideal of UN action to forestall conflict and resolve the tensions that cause and foster it is, of course, widely shared in the abstract. Practice has been more difficult.

While it functioned imperfectly, the UN Security Council provided a forum that helped avoid the apocalyptic conflicts threatened by the Cold War. The General Assembly also developed some leeway to address conflict when faced with Council deadlock under the "Uniting for Peace" formula.[1] After the Cold War ended, a more activist and creative Security Council suggested that it would do more to prevent and limit conflicts, particularly those occurring primarily within state borders (and therefore outside the scope of traditional international concern). Nevertheless, the Council has proven less effective than the dramatic increase in the number of resolutions passed in the 1990s might initially suggest.

Geostrategic balancing exercises were the hallmark of the Cold War era, and conflict management (both for advantage and when matters threatened to spin out of control) the order of the day. During the Cold War, crises arose frequently between the great powers or their surrogates and were usually the culmination of strategic ventures prepared in secret and executed with stealth. Preventive measures and action of the kind contemplated today, therefore, were rarely an option—partly because such action would have been thwarted by interested powers and partly because the United Nations did not have at its disposal resources sufficient to intervene effectively in conflicts between the great powers or their clients. Even so, the United Nations was able to improvise and develop some specific instruments for preventive action. The

---

[1] See GA Res. 377(V) (1950). See also chapter 8 in this volume.

introduction of peacekeeping forces into various regional and intra-state conflicts, such as the first deployment of UN peacekeepers in the 1956–1957 Suez crisis, were a form of conflict prevention designed, in part, to prevent conflicts from escalating and drawing in the superpowers.[2]

The situation today is very different. Following the collapse of the Soviet Union, the risk that disputes will escalate to the global level greatly diminished. There are also fewer interstate disputes than before, particularly relative to the number of intra-state conflicts. Occasionally a new interstate conflict will surprise the international community, for example the border war between Ethiopia and Eritrea of 1998–2000. But these are relatively rare. A single superpower dominates the global scene. The remaining significant powers have largely refrained from jousting with each other, although certain familiar international "hot spots" (Kashmir, the Arab-Israeli theater, the Korean Peninsula) continue to defy successful mediation and resolution. Today, in stark contrast to the Cold War era, many conflicts are aggravated by a *lack* of interest by large powers in desperately impoverished pockets of the world, notably in Africa. Economic factors play a much larger role in these conflicts, as has been documented in the work of economists and political scientists. These internal crises often unfold in slow motion, following familiar patterns that, given any genuine interest on the part of the outside world and a concomitant willingness to expend resources to support it, might be arrested. It rarely happens.

Such under-emphasis on prevention in the international security system is odd. Preventive action is at the center of international health policy; it is vital to environmental policy (enshrined, for example, in the Montreal Protocol on Substances that Deplete the Ozone Layer); and it is accepted in many human rights treaties and in efforts to reduce the number and scale of natural disasters. In the economic and development field, intensive scrutiny of the most intrusive sort has become the norm and preventive measures are often prescribed by the International Monetary Fund (IMF) (and accepted, however reluctantly, by governments of the affected states). Yet in the security sector, prevention is practiced poorly and piecemeal—if at all.

In this relative vacuum, the Secretary-General has emerged as an important actor, either in his own right or through his ability to mobilize political will of member states. The exercise of such "soft power" has been welcomed on some occasions and dismissed as inappropriate interference on others. The UN Charter gives the Secretary-General the power to bring to the attention of

---

[2] The First United Nations Emergency Force (UNEF I) was authorised by the General Assembly—since the Council was paralyzed on the issue—and was deployed in November 1956 "to secure and supervise the cessation of hostilities, including the withdrawal of the armed forces of France, Israel and the United Kingdom from Egyptian territory and, after the withdrawal, to serve as a buffer between the Egyptian and Israeli forces." See www.un.org/Depts/dpko/dpko/co_mission/unefi.htm and Brian Urquhart, *Ralph Bunche: An American Life* (New York: W.W. Norton, 1993). See also chapter 8.

the Security Council any matter that, in his opinion, threatens international peace and security.[3] Common sense suggests that the Secretary-General's opinion should ideally be an informed one. In practice, however, there has been great reluctance on the part of member states to provide the office with any form of analytical support.

This chapter examines the evolution of conflict prevention as a concept within the United Nations before examining how the Organization responded to indications of the potential for genocide in Rwanda.

7.1 Statements on Conflict Prevention

In a remarkable meeting on 31 January 1992, the Security Council convened for the first time at the level of heads of state and government. The members of the Council affirmed their commitment to the UN Charter system and noted the "new favourable international circumstances" that had enabled the Council to fulfill more effectively its primary responsibility for the maintenance of international peace and security. Among other things, the Council invited the Secretary-General to prepare a report on ways of strengthening the capacity of the United Nations for preventive diplomacy, peacemaking, and peacekeeping.

SECURITY COUNCIL SUMMIT STATEMENT CONCERNING THE COUNCIL'S RESPONSIBILITY IN THE MAINTENANCE OF INTERNATIONAL PEACE AND SECURITY, 31 JANUARY 1992[4]

The members of the Security Council consider that their meeting is a timely recognition of the fact that there are new favourable international circumstances under which the Security Council has begun to fulfil more effectively its primary responsibility for the maintenance of international peace and security. . . .

To strengthen the effectiveness of these commitments, and in order that the Security Council should have the means to discharge its primary responsibility under the Charter for the maintenance of international peace and security, the members of the Council have decided on the following approach.

They invite the Secretary-General to prepare, for circulation to the Members of the United Nations by 1 July 1992, his analysis and recommendations on ways of strengthening and making more efficient within the framework

---

[3] UN Charter, art 99.
[4] UN Doc. S/23500 (1992).

and provisions of the Charter the capacity of the United Nations for preventive diplomacy, for peacemaking and for peacekeeping.

The Secretary-General's analysis and recommendations could cover the role of the United Nations in identifying potential crises and areas of instability as well as the contribution to be made by regional organizations in accordance with Chapter VIII of the United Nations Charter in helping the work of the Council. They could also cover the need for adequate resources, both material and financial. The Secretary-General might draw on lessons learned in recent United Nations peacekeeping missions to recommend ways of making more effective secretariat planning and operations. He could also consider how greater use might be made of his good offices, and of his other functions under the United Nations Charter.

Secretary-General Boutros Boutros-Ghali duly produced his report.

AN AGENDA FOR PEACE: PREVENTIVE DIPLOMACY, PEACEMAKING AND PEACEKEEPING (REPORT OF THE SECRETARY-GENERAL), 17 JUNE 1992[5]

20. The terms preventive diplomacy, peacemaking and peacekeeping are integrally related and as used in this report are defined as follows:

- *Preventive diplomacy* is action to prevent disputes from arising between parties, to prevent existing disputes from escalating into conflicts and to limit the spread of the latter when they occur.
- *Peacemaking* is action to bring hostile parties to agreement, essentially through such peaceful means as those foreseen in Chapter VI of the Charter of the United Nations.
- *Peacekeeping* is the deployment of a United Nations presence in the field, hitherto with the consent of all the parties concerned, normally involving United Nations military and/or police personnel and frequently civilians as well. Peacekeeping is a technique that expands the possibilities for both the prevention of conflict and the making of peace.

21. The present report in addition will address the critically related concept of post-conflict peacebuilding—action to identify and support structures which will tend to strengthen and solidify peace in order to avoid a relapse

---

[5] UN Doc. A/47/277-S/24111 (1992).

into conflict. Preventive diplomacy seeks to resolve disputes before violence breaks out; peacemaking and peacekeeping are required to halt conflicts and preserve peace once it is attained. If successful, they strengthen the opportunity for post-conflict peacebuilding, which can prevent the recurrence of violence among nations and peoples.

22. These four areas for action, taken together, and carried out with the backing of all Members, offer a coherent contribution towards securing peace in the spirit of the Charter. The United Nations has extensive experience not only in these fields, but in the wider realm of work for peace in which these four fields are set. Initiatives on decolonization, on the environment and sustainable development, on population, on the eradication of disease, on disarmament and on the growth of international law—these and many others have contributed immeasurably to the foundations for a peaceful world. The world has often been rent by conflict and plagued by massive human suffering and deprivation. Yet it would have been far more so without the continuing efforts of the United Nations. This wide experience must be taken into account in assessing the potential of the United Nations in maintaining international security not only in its traditional sense, but in the new dimensions presented by the era ahead.

Preventive Diplomacy

23. The most desirable and efficient employment of diplomacy is to ease tensions before they result in conflict—or, if conflict breaks out, to act swiftly to contain it and resolve its underlying causes. Preventive diplomacy may be performed by the Secretary-General personally or through senior staff or specialized agencies and programmes, by the Security Council or the General Assembly, and by regional organizations in cooperation with the United Nations. Preventive diplomacy requires measures to create confidence; it needs early warning based on information gathering and informal or formal fact-finding; it may also involve preventive deployment and, in some situations, demilitarized zones.

Measures to Build Confidence

24. Mutual confidence and good faith are essential to reducing the likelihood of conflict between States. Many such measures are available to Governments that have the will to employ them. Systematic exchange of military missions, formation of regional or subregional risk reduction centres, arrangements for the free flow of information, including the monitoring of regional arms agreements, are examples. I ask all regional organizations to consider what further confidence-building measures might be applied in their areas and to inform the United Nations of the results. I will undertake periodic consultations on confidence-building measures with parties to potential, current or past disputes and with regional organizations, offering such advisory assistance as the Secretariat can provide.

Fact-finding

25. Preventive steps must be based upon timely and accurate knowledge of the facts. Beyond this, an understanding of developments and global trends, based on sound analysis, is required. And the willingness to take appropriate preventive action is essential. Given the economic and social roots of many potential conflicts, the information needed by the United Nations now must encompass economic and social trends as well as political developments that may lead to dangerous tensions.

   (a) An increased resort to fact-finding is needed, in accordance with the Charter, initiated either by the Secretary-General, to enable him to meet his responsibilities under the Charter, including Article 99, or by the Security Council or the General Assembly. Various forms may be employed selectively as the situation requires. A request by a State for the sending of a United Nations fact-finding mission to its territory should be considered without undue delay.

   (b) Contacts with the Governments of Member States can provide the Secretary-General with detailed information on issues of concern. I ask that all Member States be ready to provide the information needed for effective preventive diplomacy. I will supplement my own contacts by regularly sending senior officials on missions for consultations in capitals or other locations. Such contacts are essential to gain insight into a situation and to assess its potential ramifications.

   (c) Formal fact-finding can be mandated by the Security Council or by the General Assembly, either of which may elect to send a mission under its immediate authority or may invite the Secretary-General to take the necessary steps, including the designation of a special envoy. In addition to collecting information on which a decision for further action can be taken, such a mission can in some instances help to defuse a dispute by its presence, indicating to the parties that the Organization, and in particular the Security Council, is actively seized of the matter as a present or potential threat to international security.

   (d) In exceptional circumstances the Council may meet away from Headquarters as the Charter provides, in order not only to inform itself directly, but also to bring the authority of the Organization to bear on a given situation.

Early Warning

26. In recent years the United Nations system has been developing a valuable network of early warning systems concerning environmental threats, the risk of nuclear accident, natural disasters, mass movements of populations, the threat of famine and the spread of disease. There is a need, however, to strengthen arrangements in such a manner that information from these sources can be synthesized with political indicators to assess whether a threat to peace exists and to analyse what action might be taken by the United

Nations to alleviate it. This is a process that will continue to require the close cooperation of the various specialized agencies and functional offices of the United Nations. The analyses and recommendations for preventive action that emerge will be made available by me, as appropriate, to the Security Council and other United Nations organs. I recommend in addition that the Security Council invite a reinvigorated and restructured Economic and Social Council to provide reports, in accordance with Article 65 of the Charter, on those economic and social developments that may, unless mitigated, threaten international peace and security.

27. Regional arrangements and organizations have an important role in early warning. I ask regional organizations that have not yet sought observer status at the United Nations to do so and to be linked, through appropriate arrangements, with the security mechanisms of this Organization.

Preventive Deployment

28. United Nations operations in areas of crisis have generally been established after conflict has occurred. The time has come to plan for circumstances warranting preventive deployment, which could take place in a variety of instances and ways. For example, in conditions of national crisis there could be preventive deployment at the request of the Government or all parties concerned, or with their consent; in inter-State disputes such deployment could take place when two countries feel that a United Nations presence on both sides of their border can discourage hostilities; furthermore, preventive deployment could take place when a country feels threatened and requests the deployment of an appropriate United Nations presence along its side of the border alone. In each situation, the mandate and composition of the United Nations presence would need to be carefully devised and be clear to all.

29. In conditions of crisis within a country, when the Government requests or all parties consent, preventive deployment could help in a number of ways to alleviate suffering and to limit or control violence. Humanitarian assistance, impartially provided, could be of critical importance; assistance in maintaining security, whether through military, police or civilian personnel, could save lives and develop conditions of safety in which negotiations can be held; the United Nations could also help in conciliation efforts if this should be the wish of the parties. In certain circumstances, the United Nations may well need to draw upon the specialized skills and resources of various parts of the United Nations system; such operations may also on occasion require the participation of non-governmental organizations.

30. In these situations of internal crisis the United Nations will need to respect the sovereignty of the State; to do otherwise would not be in accordance with the understanding of Member States in accepting the principles of the Charter. The Organization must remain mindful of the carefully negotiated balance of the guiding principles annexed to General Assembly resolu-

tion 46/182 of 19 December 1991. Those guidelines stressed, inter alia, that humanitarian assistance must be provided in accordance with the principles of humanity, neutrality and impartiality; that the sovereignty, territorial integrity and national unity of States must be fully respected in accordance with the Charter of the United Nations; and that, in this context, humanitarian assistance should be provided with the consent of the affected country and, in principle, on the basis of an appeal by that country. The guidelines also stressed the responsibility of States to take care of the victims of emergencies occurring on their territory and the need for access to those requiring humanitarian assistance. In the light of these guidelines, a Government's request for United Nations involvement, or consent to it, would not be an infringement of that State's sovereignty or be contrary to Article 2, paragraph 7, of the Charter which refers to matters essentially within the domestic jurisdiction of any State.

31. In inter-State disputes, when both parties agree, I recommend that if the Security Council concludes that the likelihood of hostilities between neighbouring countries could be removed by the preventive deployment of a United Nations presence on the territory of each State, such action should be taken. The nature of the tasks to be performed would determine the composition of the United Nations presence.

32. In cases where one nation fears a cross-border attack, if the Security Council concludes that a United Nations presence on one side of the border, with the consent only of the requesting country, would serve to deter conflict, I recommend that preventive deployment take place. Here again, the specific nature of the situation would determine the mandate and the personnel required to fulfil it.

Demilitarized Zones

33. In the past, demilitarized zones have been established by agreement of the parties at the conclusion of a conflict. In addition to the deployment of United Nations personnel in such zones as part of peacekeeping operations, consideration should now be given to the usefulness of such zones as a form of preventive deployment, on both sides of a border, with the agreement of the two parties, as a means of separating potential belligerents, or on one side of the line, at the request of one party, for the purpose of removing any pretext for attack. Demilitarized zones would serve as symbols of the international community's concern that conflict be prevented.

The early 1990s was a period of high—perhaps excessively high—optimism for the United Nations. Evidence that there was some concern of overreach may be found in the more conservative supplement to Boutros-Ghali's *Agenda for Peace* issued two and a half years later.

SUPPLEMENT TO AN AGENDA FOR PEACE: POSITION PAPER OF THE SECRETARY-GENERAL ON THE OCCASION OF THE FIFTIETH ANNIVERSARY OF THE UNITED NATIONS, 3 JANUARY 1995[6]

26. It is evidently better to prevent conflicts through early warning, quiet diplomacy and, in some cases, preventive deployment than to have to undertake major politico-military efforts to resolve them after they have broken out. The Security Council's declaration of 31 January 1992 (S/23500) mandated me to give priority to preventive and peacemaking activities. I accordingly created a Department of Political Affairs to handle a range of political functions that had previously been performed in various parts of the Secretariat. That Department has since passed through successive phases of restructuring and is now organized to follow political developments worldwide, so that it can provide early warning of impending conflicts and analyse possibilities for preventive action by the United Nations, as well as for action to help resolve existing conflicts.

27. Experience has shown that the greatest obstacle to success in these endeavours is not, as is widely supposed, lack of information, analytical capacity or ideas for United Nations initiatives. Success is often blocked at the outset by the reluctance of one or other of the parties to accept United Nations help. This is as true of inter-state conflicts as it is of internal ones, even though United Nations action on the former is fully within the Charter, whereas in the latter case it must be reconciled with Article 2, paragraph 7.

28. Collectively Member States encourage the Secretary-General to play an active role in this field; individually they are often reluctant that he should do so when they are a party to the conflict. It is difficult to know how to overcome this reluctance. Clearly the United Nations cannot impose its preventive and peacemaking services on Member States who do not want them. Legally and politically their request for, or at least acquiescence in, United Nations action is a sine qua non. The solution can only be long-term. It may lie in creating a climate of opinion, or ethos, within the international community in which the norm would be for Member States to accept an offer of United Nations good offices.

29. There are also two practical problems that have emerged in this field. Given Member States' frequently expressed support for preventive diplomacy and peacemaking, I take this opportunity to recommend that early action be taken to resolve them.

30. The first is the difficulty of finding senior persons who have the diplomatic skills and who are willing to serve for a while as special representative or special envoy of the Secretary-General. As a result of the streamlining of the senior levels of the Secretariat, the extra capacity that was there in earlier years no longer exists.

---

[6] UN Doc. A/50/60-S/1995/1 (1995).

31. The second problem relates to the establishment and financing of small field missions for preventive diplomacy and peacemaking. Accepted and well-tried procedures exist for such action in the case of peacekeeping operations. The same is required in the preventive and peacemaking field. Although special envoys can achieve much on a visiting basis, their capacity is greatly enhanced if continuity can be assured by the presence on the ground of a small support mission on a full-time basis. There is no clear view amongst Member States about whether legislative authority for such matters rests with the Security Council or the General Assembly, nor are existing budgetary procedures well-geared to meet this need.

32. Two solutions are possible. The first is to include in the regular budget a contingency provision, which might be in the range of $25 million per biennium, for such activities. The second would be to enlarge the existing provision for unforeseen and extraordinary activities and to make it available for all preventive and peacemaking activities, not just those related to international peace and security strictly defined.

The next Secretary-General, Kofi Annan, sought more modestly to focus not on institutional and doctrinal changes within the United Nations, but on cultural change the better to assist member states.

REPORT OF THE SECRETARY-GENERAL ON THE PREVENTION OF ARMED CONFLICT, 7 JUNE 2001[7]

Executive Summary

Since assuming office, I have pledged to move the United Nations from a culture of reaction to a culture of prevention. In its presidential statement of 20 July 2000, the Security Council invited me to submit a report on the prevention of armed conflict, containing an analysis and recommendations on initiatives within the United Nations, taking into account previous experience and the views and considerations expressed by Member States. My first objective in the present report is to review the progress that has been achieved in developing the conflict prevention capacity of the United Nations, as called for by both the General Assembly and the Security Council. My second aim is to present specific recommendations on how the efforts of the United Nations system in this field could be further enhanced, with the cooperation and active involvement of Member States, who ultimately have the primary responsibility for conflict prevention.

---

[7] UN Doc. A/55/985-S/2001/574 (2001).

In drafting the present report, I have endeavoured to take into account the many different views and considerations of Member States expressed in recent debates of the General Assembly and the Security Council on conflict prevention. It is axiomatic that the active support and cooperation of Member States will be needed for conflict prevention efforts to succeed. The specific contributions that can be made by the General Assembly, the Security Council, the Economic and Social Council, the International Court of Justice and the Secretary-General are explored in the present report, as is the cooperation between the United Nations and outside actors, such as regional organizations, NGOs, civil society and the business community.

The work of the United Nations system in the field of conflict prevention is not new. Many of the development and other programmes and projects of the United Nations system already have preventive effects or at least preventive potential, though they are often disparate and inchoate. My emphasis here is to show how the United Nations family of departments, programmes, offices and agencies (which have all contributed to the present report) interact in the furtherance of the prevention of armed conflict. Of particular importance are United Nations efforts for enhancing the capacity of Member States for conflict prevention. The challenge before us is how to mobilize the collective potential of the United Nations system with greater coherence and focus for conflict prevention, without necessarily requiring major new resources.

The basic premises of the present report are the following:

- Conflict prevention is one of the primary obligations of Member States set forth in the Charter of the United Nations, and United Nations efforts in conflict prevention must be in conformity with the purposes and principles of the Charter. Conflict prevention is also an activity best undertaken under Chapter VI of the Charter.

- The primary responsibility for conflict prevention rests with national Governments, with civil society playing an important role. The main role of the United Nations and the international community is to support national efforts for conflict prevention and assist in building national capacity in this field.

- Preventive action should be initiated at the earliest possible stage of a conflict cycle in order to be most effective. One of the principal aims of preventive action should be to address the deep-rooted socio-economic, cultural, environmental, institutional and other structural causes that often underlie the immediate political symptoms of conflicts.

- An effective preventive strategy requires a comprehensive approach that encompasses both short-term and long-term political, diplomatic, humanitarian, human rights, developmental, institutional and other measures taken by the international community, in cooperation with national and regional actors.

- Conflict prevention and sustainable and equitable development are mutually reinforcing activities. An investment in national and international efforts for conflict prevention must be seen as a simultaneous investment in sustainable development since the latter can best take place in an environment of sustainable peace.

- A successful preventive strategy depends on the cooperation of many United Nations actors, including the Secretary-General, the Security Council, the General Assembly, the Economic and Social Council, the International Court of Justice and United Nations agencies, offices, funds and programmes, as well as the Bretton Woods institutions. The United Nations is not the only actor in prevention and may often not be the actor best suited to take the lead. Therefore, Member States, international, regional and subregional organizations the private sector, non-governmental organizations, and other civil society actors also have very important roles to play in this field.

I am under no illusion that preventive strategies will be easy to implement. The costs of prevention have to be paid in the present, while its benefits lie in the distant future. The main lesson to be drawn from past United Nations experiences in this regard is that the earlier the root causes of a potential conflict are identified and effectively addressed, the more likely it is that the parties to a conflict will be ready to engage in a constructive dialogue, address the actual grievances that lie at the root of the potential conflict and refrain from the use of force to achieve their aims.

Governments that live up to their sovereign responsibility to resolve peacefully a situation that might deteriorate into a threat to international peace and security and call on the United Nations or other international actors for preventive assistance as early as needed, provide the best protection for their citizens against unwelcome outside interference. In this way, preventive action by the international community can contribute significantly to strengthening the national sovereignty of Member States.

In the present report, I have stressed that conflict prevention lies at the heart of the mandate of the United Nations in the maintenance of international peace and security, and that a general consensus is emerging among Member States that comprehensive and coherent conflict prevention strategies offer the greatest potential for promoting lasting peace and creating an enabling environment for sustainable development. The imperative for effective conflict prevention goes beyond creating a culture, establishing mechanisms or summoning political will. The United Nations also has a moral responsibility to ensure that genocides such as that perpetrated in Rwanda are prevented from ever happening again.

The time has come to translate the rhetoric of conflict prevention into concrete action. It is my earnest hope that the United Nations system and Member States will be able to work together in developing a practical road map to implement the specific recommendations contained in the present report. It is axiomatic that effective preventive action will require sustained political will and a long-term commitment of resources by Member States and the United Nations system as a whole if a genuine culture of prevention is to take root in the international community. The present report marks a beginning in that direction.

The Security Council welcomed the report and presented its own view on 30 August 2001.

SECURITY COUNCIL RESOLUTION 1366 (2001)

The Security Council, . . .

Recognizing the essential role of the Secretary-General in the prevention of armed conflict and the importance of efforts to enhance his role in accordance with Article 99 of the Charter of the United Nations,

Recognizing the role of other relevant organs, offices, funds and programmes and the specialized agencies of the United Nations, and other international organizations including the World Trade Organization and the Bretton Woods institutions; as well as the role of non-governmental organizations, civil society actors and the private sector in the prevention of armed conflict,

Stressing the necessity of addressing the root-causes and regional dimensions of conflicts, recalling the recommendations contained in the report of the Secretary-General on Causes of Conflicts and the Promotion of Durable Peace and Sustainable Development in Africa of 13 April 1998 (S/1998/318) and *underlining* the mutually supportive relationship between conflict prevention and sustainable development,

Expressing serious concern over the threat to peace and security caused by the illicit trade in and the excessive and destabilizing accumulation of small arms and light weapons in areas of conflict and their potential to exacerbate and prolong armed conflicts, . . .

Reiterating the shared commitment to save people from the ravages of armed conflicts, acknowledging the lessons to be learned for all concerned from the failure of preventive efforts that preceded such tragedies as the genocide in Rwanda (S/1999/1257) and the massacre in Srebrenica (A/54/549), and resolving to take appropriate action within its competence, combined with the efforts of Member States, to prevent the recurrence of such tragedies,

1. *Expresses its determination* to pursue the objective of prevention of armed conflict as an integral part of its primary responsibility for the maintenance of international peace and security;

2. *Stresses* that the essential responsibility for conflict prevention rests with national Governments, and that the United Nations and the international community can play an important role in support of national efforts for conflict prevention and can assist in building national capacity in this field and recognizes the important supporting role of civil society;

3. *Calls upon* Member States as well as regional and subregional organizations and arrangements to support the development of a comprehensive conflict prevention strategy as proposed by the Secretary-General;

4. *Emphasizes* that for the success of a preventive strategy, the United Nations needs the consent and support of the Government concerned and, if possible the cooperation of other key national actors and underlines in this regard that the sustained political will of neighbouring States, regional allies or other Member States who would be well placed to support United Nations efforts, is necessary;

5. *Expresses* its willingness to give prompt consideration to early warning or prevention cases brought to its attention by the Secretary-General and in this regard, encourages the Secretary-General to convey to the Security Council his assessment of potential threats to international peace and security with due regard to relevant regional and subregional dimensions, as appropriate, in accordance with Article 99 of the Charter of the United Nations;

6. *Undertakes* to keep situations of potential conflict under close review as part of a conflict prevention strategy and expresses its intention to consider cases of potential conflict brought to its attention by any Member State, or by a State not a Member of the United Nations or by the General Assembly or on the basis of information furnished by the Economic and Social Council;

7. *Expresses* its commitment to take early and effective action to prevent armed conflict and to that end to employ all appropriate means at its disposal including, with the consent of the receiving States, its missions to areas of potential conflict;

8. *Reiterates* its call to Member States to strengthen the capacity of the United Nations in the maintenance of international peace and security and in this regard urges them to provide the necessary human, material and financial resources for timely and preventive measures including early warning, preventive diplomacy, preventive deployment, practical disarmament measures and peace-building as appropriate in each case;

9. *Reaffirms* its role in the peaceful settlement of disputes and reiterates its call upon the Member States to settle their disputes by peaceful means as set forth in Chapter VI of the Charter of the United Nations including by use of regional preventive mechanisms and more frequent resort to the International Court of Justice;

10. *Invites* the Secretary-General to refer to the Council information and analyses from within the United Nations system on cases of serious violations of international law, including international humanitarian law and human rights law and on potential conflict situations arising, inter alia, from ethnic, religious and territorial disputes, poverty and lack of development and expresses its determination to give serious consideration to such information and analyses regarding situations which it deems to represent a threat to international peace and security;

11. *Expresses* its intention to continue to invite the Office of the United Nations Emergency Relief Coordinator and other relevant United Nations agencies to brief its members on emergency situations which it deems to represent a threat to international peace and security and supports the im-

plementation of protection and assistance activities by relevant United Nations agencies in accordance with their respective mandates;

12. *Expresses* its willingness to consider preventive deployment upon the recommendation of the Secretary-General and with the consent of the Member States concerned;

13. *Calls upon* all Member States to ensure timely and faithful implementation of the United Nations Programme of Action to Prevent, Combat and Eradicate the Illicit Trade in Small Arms and Light Weapons in All Its Aspects (A/CONF.192/15) adopted on 20 July 2001 and to take all necessary measures at national, regional and global levels to prevent and combat the illicit flow of small arms and light weapons in areas of conflict;

14. *Expresses* its willingness to make full use of information from the Secretary-General provided to him inter alia, under paragraph 33 section II of the Programme of Action in its efforts to prevent armed conflict;

15. *Stresses* the importance of the inclusion, as part of a conflict prevention strategy, of peace-building components including civilian police within peacekeeping operations on a case-by-case basis to facilitate a smooth transition to the post conflict peace-building phase and the ultimate conclusion of the mission;

16. *Decides* to consider inclusion as appropriate, of a disarmament, demobilization and reintegration component in the mandates of United Nations peacekeeping and peace-building operations with particular attention to the rehabilitation of child soldiers;

17. *Reiterates* its recognition of the role of women in conflict prevention and requests the Secretary-General to give greater attention to gender perspectives in the implementation of peacekeeping and peace-building mandates as well as in conflict prevention efforts;

18. *Supports* the enhancement of the role of the Secretary-General in conflict prevention including by increased use of United Nations interdisciplinary fact-finding and confidence-building missions to regions of tension, developing regional prevention strategies with regional partners and appropriate United Nations organs and agencies, and improving the capacity and resource base for preventive action in the Secretariat; . . .

20. *Calls* for the enhancement of the capacity for conflict prevention of regional organizations, in particular in Africa, by extending international assistance to, inter alia, the Organization of African Unity and its successor organization, through its Mechanism of Conflict Prevention, Management and Resolution, as well as to the Economic Community of West African States and its Mechanism for Prevention, Management and Resolution of Conflicts, Peacekeeping and Security;

21. *Stresses* the need to create conditions for durable peace and sustainable development by addressing the root-causes of armed conflict and to this end, calls upon Member States and relevant bodies of the United Nations system to contribute to the effective implementation of the United Nations Declaration and Programme of Action for a Culture of Peace (A/53/243);

22. *Looks forward* to further consideration of the report of the Secretary-General on Prevention of Armed Conflict by the General Assembly and the Economic and Social Council, as well as other actors including the Bretton Woods institutions and supports the development of a system-wide coordinated and mutually supportive approach to prevention of armed conflict;

23. *Decides* to remain actively seized of the matter.

The Secretary-General released a report focused more on operational capacities two years later.

INTERIM REPORT OF THE SECRETARY-GENERAL ON THE PREVENTION OF ARMED CONFLICT, 12 SEPTEMBER 2003[8]

4. Armed conflicts remain the primary source of instability in today's world and the primary concern of the United Nations. The main responsibility for prevention lies with Governments rather than with the international community. However, the United Nations system has increasingly been called upon to work with Member States to develop an integrated response to the threat of armed conflicts. Bearing in mind that the majority of the world's conflicts today take place within States rather than between them, the United Nations system has recently launched a number of efforts to assist Member States in building their capacity for the prevention and peaceful settlement of disputes and for building sustainable peace and development. It has also undertaken initial efforts to strengthen its own capacity for providing such assistance. . . .

II. The State of Our Institutional Responses

6. My report on prevention of armed conflict (A/55/985-S/2001/574 and Corr.1) differentiates between operational prevention, undertaken when violence appears imminent, and relating largely to the realm of diplomacy, and structural prevention, which implies addressing the root causes of potential armed conflict. The United Nations has a tradition of directly addressing operational prevention through preventive diplomacy. That is why present efforts centre on how to move forward on the implementation of a structural prevention strategy—one that would address the political, social, cultural,

---

[8] UN Doc. A/58/365-S/2003/888 (2003).

economic, environmental and other structural causes that often underlie the immediate symptoms of armed conflicts. That approach may be relevant when considering threats to peace and security such as terrorism. Adopting that broader approach to collective security will bring the United Nations back to its roots and strengthen the Organization's role in "the creation of conditions of stability and well-being which are necessary for peaceful and friendly relations among nations . . . " (Article 55 of the Charter of the United Nations). . . .

Coordination and Coherence of United Nations Activities

10. Within the United Nations system, the role of individual agencies and programmes in the prevention of armed conflicts varies from country to country, depending on whether there is potential for an armed conflict of a cross-border nature or a conflict within a State, and on whether there is potential for the recurrence of an armed conflict. Progress in devising an integrated approach to the prevention of armed conflict was made possible by the active involvement of the United Nations System Chief Executives Board for Coordination (CEB), which discussed conflict prevention at its fall 2002 meeting. CEB concluded that the conflict prevention and development agendas should be mutually reinforcing. The imperative to move from a culture of reaction to a culture of prevention should be seen in that perspective. . . .

Capacity-building

12. The responses of the United Nations system are predicated on the belief, shared with many Member States, that the peaceful settlement of disputes is a key element of the day-to-day responsibility of Governments, civil society and other national stakeholders. In other words, efforts by a Member State to acquire capacity in that regard should be seen as a part of a systematic effort to obtain sustainable development by strengthening social cohesion and not necessarily as marking the onset of a crisis. . . .

13. In particular, the United Nations has provided capacity-building assistance in the following areas:

(a) Strengthening the rule of law, including respect for human rights;

(b) Strengthening the ability on the part of public institutions to analyse and identify the potential for conflict and to resolve disputes peacefully;

(c) Establishing processes for generating consensus and dialogue among key stakeholders—through both formal institutions as well as civic forums—on divisive national issues;

(d) Strengthening the ability of Governments and civil society to ensure the delivery of essential services for the most vulnerable elements in society, especially those adversely affected by natural disasters, violent tension, or the shocks of globalization;

(e) Ensuring participation by women, youth and minorities in key national processes;

(f) Building capacity for stopping the illicit trade in small arms and natural resources that often helps to inflame existing tensions;

(g) Building support for diversity and tolerance in media, popular culture and education.

Development Assistance

14. New approaches and methodologies are being developed to ensure that development work is conceived and carried out through a "conflict prevention lens." . . .

16. The prevention of the recurrence of armed conflict is another issue of great concern. Increasingly, it is necessary to understand that the absence of war alone does not constitute peace. Sustainable development and good governance are essential elements in United Nations efforts to build peace. For that reason, a number of country teams have prepared United Nations transitional recovery strategies designed to address the root causes of conflict and minimize the likelihood of conflict recurring in the aftermath of war. . . .

Human Rights

18. As the failure to protect human rights is often a root cause of conflict, the effective promotion and protection of human rights must be seen as a vital element of conflict prevention. . . .

Rule of Law

19. Among the root causes of conflicts are non-compliance with the rule of law as well as the absence of institutional and legal mechanisms to address grievances in a given society. . . .

Regional Dimensions

20. Efforts to bolster national prevention capacity are not always enough. The regional and subregional environment can make the difference between conflict management and conflict mismanagement. All too often, conflicts spill over from one country into another. Regional organizations are often best placed to prevent violent conflicts in their own neighbourhoods and can use a range of conflict prevention tools. For example, the Association of Southeast Asian Nations focuses on economic integration and "quiet dialogue," whereas the Organization for Security and Cooperation in Europe has been successful with confidence-building measures that focus on the question of minorities. . . .

Role of Women

23. The United Nations system is increasingly recognizing the need to prioritize the positive and proactive role that women can play in ensuring lasting peace in crisis situations. . . .

Preventive Action and Terrorism

24. Although there is disagreement on the relation between terrorism and a possible number of enabling factors, early action may be useful to help dissuade groups from embracing terrorism and to deny possibilities for terrorists to take action. Structural prevention, in particular, may help provide an early response to developing conflicts. Managing conflicts in a way that prevents them from becoming entrenched could remove sources that terrorists point to as causes to justify their action. . . .

Disarmament

25. The links between disarmament and the prevention of armed conflict are easy to understand. Instruments such as the Chemical Weapons Convention contain specific provisions relevant to conflict prevention, including in relation to consultations, confidence-building measures and the peaceful resolution of disputes. . . .

International Financial Institutions

27. The Bretton Woods institutions, through their own diverse array of instruments, can add significant value to the United Nations system's collective efforts to prevent violent conflicts. . . .

28. The World Bank has the potential to complement, in a significant way, the United Nations system's efforts to prevent violent conflicts. Recently, it has recognized prevention as central to its mission of eliminating poverty and reaching the Millennium Development Goals. The Bank has also broadened its response from a focus on providing financial capital and rebuilding physical infrastructure to a comprehensive approach including initiatives to support the demobilization and reintegration of ex-combatants, the social and economic reintegration of displaced populations, the promotion of good governance through legal reform and capacity-building, and the alignment of transparent public expenditures. It has also substantively developed its analytical capacity in order to increase its understanding of the root causes of conflict and post-conflict recovery, as well as of the environmental causes and consequences of conflicts. Its initiative to address development priorities of lower-income countries under stress is also an important contribution to the United Nations system's efforts in the area of peace and security. Finally, the Bank is putting increased emphasis on partnerships in supporting war-to-peace transitions, in particular with the United Nations system. Progress has also been made in improving collaboration between the United Nations system and the International Monetary Fund, including in specific country cases. . . .

Civil Society

29. Civil society and non-governmental organizations (NGOs) should be further encouraged to join the United Nations in developing and implementing conflict prevention and recovery strategies and to ensure that their

own mandates focus on the prevention of armed conflicts. . . . In many instances, in tackling the potential conflicts of today, civil society might be best positioned to initiate prevention or warn about dangerous local developments or spillover potential across national borders. . . .

Private Sector

30. There is now increasing awareness of the significance of the role of the private sector. However, while the United Nations generally recognizes that the international private sector can be a powerful player in situations of conflict, the understanding of the precise motivations and interests of the international corporate sector in such situations is still limited. . . .

III. The Way Forward

33. The key task for the United Nations system in the years to come is to agree on practical measures to integrate conflict prevention further into its activities, to build a more structured link between political and socio-economic strategies and to ensure that the prevention of armed conflicts becomes a deliberate component in the planning and coordination arrangements of development programmes. That would help to promote a more comprehensive approach to the prevention of armed conflict, addressing multiple factors in a coordinated fashion and contributing to meeting people's basic economic, social, cultural and humanitarian needs. Each agency, fund and programme, as well as the Bretton Woods institutions, is contributing different approaches which add value and should be built upon in pursuing greater system-wide synergies towards conflict prevention. What is needed therefore is greater coherence and coordination in United Nations efforts in the field of structural prevention at the national, regional and international levels.

34. In addressing those issues, the United Nations system is highly dependent on the political will of national Governments. It is the responsibility of Governments to avoid the risk of conflict through equitable public policies and adherence to the principles of international humanitarian and human rights standards. Sovereignty brings with it the fundamental responsibility to protect not only the physical security of citizens but also, as necessary, their civil, political, social, economic and cultural rights. International assistance for the prevention of armed conflict should not consist of the internationalization of specific issues within a particular country's borders, but rather of discreet support for building local capacity for the peaceful settlement of disputes. In support of national Governments, the United Nations, regional organizations, NGOs, civil society and private sector entities each have a role to play.

35. In addition to the tasks that are already being undertaken and that were described in the previous chapter, I believe that the United Nations system will need to pay additional attention to the following three areas. First, it should strengthen its capacity to help coordinate the international efforts of

all actors, within their mandates, such as States, international financial institutions, regional organizations, NGOs and the private sector, to carry out structural prevention strategies.

36. Secondly, further progress needs to be made in responding to the political economy of armed conflicts. The policy aspects of the issues surrounding resource-based intra-State conflicts and the economic agendas of civil war should be further explored. In addition, the United Nations system will need to devise appropriate instruments to ensure that war economies are addressed at all stages of the conflict, be it conflict prevention, peacemaking, peacekeeping or peace-building.

37. Lastly, in addressing the root causes of armed conflict, the United Nations system will need to devote greater attention to the potential threats posed by environmental problems.

QUESTIONS

1. What can the United Nations system do in order to encourage or coerce states to resolve disputes peacefully before violence breaks out or spreads further? If you were a party to a conflict, would you regard some as more useful than others? If you were representing a member state of the United Nations, would you regard some as more acceptable than others?
2. What is the role of the Secretary-General in conflict prevention? How much of this can be informal? How much of it needs to be, allowing the Council a degree of "deniability" in the event of failure or results it does not like? Conversely, can the Council's explicit backing in some circumstances be helpful?
3. Do member state concerns about sovereignty mean that an early warning capacity will be impossible within the United Nations system?
4. Do essentially internal conflicts (sometimes also involving neighboring states), as opposed to inter-state wars, offer particular challenges to international mediators? Can you think of some

7.2 Rwanda

The failure to prevent or halt the genocide that began in Rwanda in April 1994, which killed approximately 800,000 people in 100 days, is rightly regarded as a failure of political will. It may also be a caution against assuming that improved early warning will necessarily improve international responses to crisis.

In August 1993, a week after the signing of the Arusha Peace Agreement between the Rwandan government and the Rwandese Patriotic Front (RPF), the United Nations published a report by Bacre Waly Ndiaye, the Special Rapporteur on Extrajudicial, Summary, or Arbitrary Executions.

REPORT BY MR. B. W. NDIAYE, SPECIAL RAPPORTEUR, ON HIS MISSION TO RWANDA FROM 8 TO 17 APRIL 1993, 11 AUGUST 1993[9]

1. In recent years, Rwanda has attracted the attention of the human rights protection mechanisms established by the Commission on Human Rights. Reference was thus made to the human rights situation in that country in several reports submitted to the Commission at its forty-ninth session; of particular relevance is the information contained in the report of the Special Rapporteur on the question of torture (E/CN.4/1993/26, paras. 386 to 390), and in that Working Group on Enforced or Involuntary Disappearances. (E/CN.4/1993/25, paras. 441 to 446).

2. Mr. Wako, the previous Special Rapporteur, included allegations of violations of the right to life in Rwanda in his report to the commission at its forty-eighth session (E/CN.4/1992/30, paras. 461 to 467). During 1992, the current Special Rapporteur received reports and allegations relating to extrajudicial, summary or arbitrary executions of unarmed civilians by the Rwandese security forces in connection with the armed conflict between government security forces and the Rwandese Patriotic Front (FPR) since October 1990. He also received information concerning killings of members of the Tutsi minority, in particular the Bagogwe clan, allegedly perpetrated with direct or indirect involvement of the security forces; those alleged violations of the right to life concerned at least 172 persons in 1992. On 25 September 1992, the Special Rapporteur sent an urgent appeal to the Government of Rwanda after receiving reports about death threats and acts of harassment against a member of a human rights group; the latter had conducted inquiries whose findings pointed to the involvement of local government officials in mass killings of members of the Bagogwe clan. These allegations are contained in the report submitted to the Commission on Human Rights at its forty-ninth session (E/CN.4/1993/46, paras. 502 to 504).

3. At the beginning of 1993, Rwandese human rights organizations invited the Special Rapporteur to take part in an international commission of inquiry into violations of human rights in Rwanda. The Special Rapporteur had to decline the invitation in the belief that, since there was a State system in Rwanda, it was for the authorities of that country to conduct inquires and report on measures taken, the Rapporteur's role being confined, in the circumstances, to observing the manner in which the competent authorities were meeting their commitments in regard to protection of human rights. He asked, however, to be kept informed of the findings, conclusions and recommendations of the international commission of inquiry.

---

[9] Commission on Human Rights, 50th Session, Item 12 of the provisional agenda, 11 August 1993, UN Doc. E/CN.4/1994/7/Add.1 (1993).

4. On 8 February 1993, the FPR breached the cease-fire agreement concluded on 12 July 1992 during the Arusha (Tanzania) peace negotiations. It was in that context that serious allegations were brought to the attention of the Special Rapporteur. On 15 February 1993, an urgent appeal was sent to the Rwandese Government following reports of a resumption of the killings and of reprisals and acts of intimidation against persons who had collaborated with or testified before the International Commission of Inquiry on violations of human rights in Rwanda since I October 1990 (referred to hereinafter as "the International Commission of Inquiry"). This Commission, which visited Rwanda from 7 to 21 January 1993, was composed of 10 experts mandated by the International Federation of Human Rights (Paris), Africa Watch (New York), the *Union interafricaine des droits de l'homme et des peuples* (Ouagadougou), and the International Centre for the Rights of the Person and Democratic Development (Montreal). It was these disturbing allegations that prompted the Special Rapporteur, on 1 March 1993, to request an invitation from the President of the Rwandese Republic to visit Rwanda so that he could have personal talks with the Rwandese authorities and with individuals, associations and non-governmental organizations involved in the protection of human rights, and assess the situation at first hand.

5. On 8 March 1993, the President of the Rwandese Republic kindly complied with that request by inviting the Special Rapporteur to visit Rwanda. The report of the International Commission of Inquiry was made public on the same date. . . .

6. Because of the shortage of time and of material and human resources available to the Special Rapporteur (he stayed only about 10 days, from 8 to 17 April 1993), there was no question of undertaking an in-depth fact-finding or verification mission, which would have entailed, *inter alia*, substantial logistic and scientific resources; for example, experts in forensic medicine would have been needed to verify the existence of mass graves.

7. The work of the Special Rapporteur was greatly facilitated by the considerable amount of information which was brought to his attention by various human rights organizations, both Rwandese and international, and which was on the whole sufficiently convincing and precise to be taken into account. Special mention should be made here of the report of the International Commission of Inquiry, which the Special Rapporteur was able to use as his main working document because of its methodical and specific nature and the diversity and consistency of the testimony it contains. The report of the International Commission of Inquiry gives an idea of the scale of Rwanda's problems as regards human rights in general and extrajudicial, summary or arbitrary executions in particular. It goes in detail into the mechanisms behind the massacres and describes the methods used by the perpetrators of violations; it also clearly identifies those responsible for violating the right to life. . . .

22. A climate of mistrust and terror currently prevails in Rwanda. Although rumour is largely responsible for this situation, violence is none the less a feature of everyday life. There is an alarming increase in crime, fuelled

by the profusion of weapons in circulation (in Kigali a grenade can be bought for less than US$2) and the destitute condition of a whole sector of the population, exacerbated by displacements of the population as a result of the war. But the prevalence of crime is also sometimes used to cover up acts of political violence. There are several cases of murder or attempted murder of political opponents, journalists or troublesome witnesses that have been passed off as ordinary crimes. The situation has become particularly explosive with the distribution of weapons to civilians by the authorities, officially to combat the forces of the PPR, an example being in the municipality of Mutura, where 193 guns were distributed in February 1993. This is compounded by the danger of the mines laid by the warring parties, which all too often kill or maim innocent civilians, especially children. . . .

28. Massacres of civilian populations have been perpetrated either by the Rwandese security forces or by certain sectors of the population. Killings have taken place not only in the combat zones during or after clashes, but also in areas situated some distance from the hostilities. In the latter case, it has been shown time and time again that government officials were involved, either directly by encouraging, planning, directing or participating in the violence, or indirectly through incompetence, negligence or deliberate inaction. The number of victims has sometimes reached tragic proportion, as for example in Kibilira, where at least 348 persons were said to have been killed in 48 hours shortly after the outbreak of war in October 1990. Massacres have also been attributed to the FPR.

29. These methods have been used to intimidate or eliminate the regime's opponents (politicians, journalists, etc.), witnesses of human rights violations, or human rights activists. Such violations of the right to life have sometimes been committed by government officials. They can also frequently be attributed to the militias of two parties, the MRND and the Coalition for the Defence of the Republic (CDR), or to clandestine armed groups allegedly close to the party in power. The techniques used include poisoning, faked robbery and death threats. It should be noted that such practices are also aimed at the Hutu and are still being used at the time of writing of the present report. . . .

78. The question whether the massacres described above may be termed genocide has often been raised. It is not for the Special Rapporteur to pass judgement at this stage, but an initial reply may be put forward. Rwanda acceded to the Convention on the Prevention and Punishment of the Crime of Genocide on 15 April 1975. Article II of the Convention reads: "in the present Convention, genocide means any of the following acts committed with intent to destroy, in whole or in part, a national, ethnical, racial or religious group, as such: (a) Killing members of the group; (b) Causing serious bodily or mental harm to members of the group; (c) Deliberately inflicting on the group conditions of life calculated to bring about its physical destruction in whole or in part; (d) Imposing measures intended to prevent births within the group; (e) Forcibly transferring children of the group to another group."

79. The cases of intercommunal violence brought to the Special Rapporteur's attention indicate very clearly that the victims of the attacks, Tutsis in the overwhelming majority of cases, have been targeted solely because of their membership of a certain ethnic group, and for no other objective reason. Article II, paragraphs (a) and (b), might therefore be considered to apply to these cases.

80. The violations of the right to life, as described in this report, could fall within the purview of article III of the convention . . .

A more urgent warning came on 11 January 1994 when the Canadian force commander of the UN mission helping implement the Arusha Agreement (UNAMIR), Major-General Roméo Dallaire, sent a code cable (encrypted fax) to UN Headquarters under the title "Request for Protection for Informant."

CODE CABLE FROM DALLAIRE/UNAMIR/KIGALI TO BARIL/DPKO/UNATIONS (NEW YORK), SUBJECT: REQUEST FOR PROTECTION OF INFORMANT, 11 JANUARY 1994[10]

1. Force commander put in contact with informant by very very important government politician.[11] Informant is a top level trainer in the cadre of interhamwe-armed militia of MRND.

2. He informed us he was in charge of last Saturdays demonstrations which aims were to target deputies of opposition parties coming to ceremonies and Belgian soldiers. They hoped to provoke the RPF BN to engage (being fired upon) the demonstrators and provoke a civil war. Deputies were to be assassinated upon entry or exit from Parliament. Belgian troops were to be provoked and if Belgians soldiers restored [sic] to force a number of them were to be killed and thus guarantee Belgian withdrawal from Rwanda.

3. Informant confirmed 48 RGF PARA CDO and a few members of the gendarmerie participated in demonstrations in plain clothes. Also at least one Minister of the MRND and the sous-prefect of Kigali were in the demonstration. RGF and Interhamwe provided radio communications.

4. Informant is a former security member of the president. He also stated he is paid RF150,000 per month by the MRND party to train Interhamwe. Direct

---

[10] Available at http://www.pbs.org/wgbh/pages/frontline/shows/evil/warning/cable.html.

[11] This was later revealed to be the Prime Minister designate, Faustin Twagiramungu.

link is to chief of staff RGF and president of the MRND for financial and material support.

5. Interhamwe has trained 1700 men in RGF military camps outside the capital. The 1700 are scattered in groups of 40 throughout Kigali. Since UNAMIR deployed he has trained 300 personnel in three week training sessions at RGF camps. Training focus was discipline, weapons, explosives, close combat and tactics.

6. Principal aim of Interhamwe in the past was to protect Kigali from RPF. Since UNAMIR mandate he has been ordered to register all Tutsi in Kigali. He suspects it is for their extermination. Example he gave was that in 20 minutes his personnel could kill up to 1000 Tutsis.

7. Informant states he disagrees with anti-Tutsi extermination. He supports opposition to RPF but cannot support killing of innocent persons. He also stated that he believes the president does not have full control over all elements of his old party/faction.

8. Informant is prepared to provide location of major weapons cache with at least 135 weapons. He already has distributed 110 weapons including 35 with ammunition and can give us details of their location. Type of weapons are G3 and AK47 provided by RGF. He was ready to go to the arms cache tonight-if we gave him the following guarantee. He requests that he and his family (his wife and four children) be placed under our protection.

9. It is our intention to take action within the next 36 hours with a possible H HR of Wednesday at dawn (local). Informant states that hostilities may commence again if political deadlock ends. Violence could take place day of the ceremonies or the day after. Therefore Wednesday will give greatest chance of success and also be most timely to provide significant input to on-going political negotiations.

10. It is recommended that informant be granted protection and evacuated out of Rwanda. This HQ does not have previous UN experience in such matters and urgently requests guidance. No contact has as yet been made to any embassy in order to inquire if they are prepared to protect him for a period of time by granting diplomatic immunity in their embassy in Kigali before moving him and his family out of the country.

11. Force commander will be meeting with the very very important political person tomorrow morning in order to ensure that this individual is conscious of all parameters of his involvement. Force commander does have certain reservations on the suddenness of the change of heart of the informant to come clean with this information. Recce of armed cache and detailed planning of raid to go on late tomorrow. Possibility of a trap not fully excluded, as this may be a set-up against this very very important political person. Force commander to inform SRSG first thing in morning to ensure his support.

13. Peux Ce Que Veux. Allons-y. [Where there's a will, there's a way. Let's do it.]

The response from then Under-Secretary-General for Peacekeeping (later Secretary-General) Kofi Annan, through his chief of staff Iqbal Riza, ruled out any forceful action on the basis that it would have exceeded the mandate given to UNAMIR by the Security Council.

CODE CABLE FROM ANNAN, UNATIONS, NEW YORK TO BOOH-BOOH/DALLAIRE, UNAMIR ONLY (NO DISTRIBUTION), NUMBER: UNAMIR 100, SUBJECT: CONTACTS WITH INFORMANT, 11 JANUARY 1994[12]

1. We have carefully reviewed the situation in the light of your MIR-79. We cannot agree to the operation contemplated in paragraph 7 of your cable, as it clearly goes beyond the mandate entrusted to UNAMIR under resolution 872 (1993).
2. However, on the assumption that you are convinced that the information provided by the informant is absolutely reliable, we request you to undertake the initiatives described in the following paragraphs.
3. SRSG and FC [Force Commander] should request urgent meeting with the President. At that meeting you should inform the President that you have received apparently reliable information concerning the activities of the Interhamwe militia which represents a clear threat to the peace process. You should inform him that these activities include the training and deployment of subversive groups in Kigali as well as the storage and distribution of weapons to these groups.
4. You should inform him that these activities constitute a clear violation of the provisions of the Arusha peace agreement and of the Kigali weapons-secure area. You should assume that he is not aware of these activities, but insist that he must ensure that these subversive activities are immediately discontinued and inform you within 48 hours of the measures taken in this regard, including the recovery of the arms which have been distributed.
5. You should advise the President that, if any violence occurs in Kigali, you would have to immediately bring to the attention of the Security Council the information you have received on the activities of the militia, undertake investigations to determine who is responsible and make appropriate recommendations to the Security Council.
6. Before meeting with the President you should inform the Ambassadors of Belgium, France and the United States of your intentions and suggest to them that they may wish to consider making a similar démarche.
7. For security considerations, we leave it to your discretion to decide whether to inform the PM(D) of your plans before or after the meeting with

the President. When you meet with the PM(D), you should explain to him the limits of your mandate. You should also assure him that, while the mandate of UNAMIR does not allow you to extend protection to the informant, his identity and your contacts with him will not be repeat not be revealed.

8. If you have major problems with the guidance provided above, you may consult us further. We wish to stress, however, that the overriding consideration is the need to avoid entering into a course of action that might lead to the use of force and unanticipated repercussions. Regards.

Five years later, an independent inquiry commissioned by Annan concluded that a major problem in the UN response was the weakness of political analysis in both UNAMIR and at UN Headquarters. UNAMIR lacked a capacity for intelligence analysis; Headquarters lacked the resources for early warning and risk analysis.

REPORT OF THE INDEPENDENT INQUIRY INTO THE ACTIONS OF THE UNITED NATIONS DURING THE 1994 GENOCIDE IN RWANDA, 15 DECEMBER 1999[13]

Only a week after the signing of the Agreement, the United Nations published a report which gave an ominously serious picture of the human rights situation in Rwanda. The report described the visit to Rwanda by the Special Rapporteur of the Commission on Human Rights on extrajudicial, summary or arbitrary executions, Mr. Waly Bacre Ndiaye, from 8 to 17 April 1993. Ndiaye determined that massacres and a plethora of other serious human rights violations were taking place in Rwanda. The targeting of the Tutsi population led Ndiaye to discuss whether the term genocide might be applicable. He stated that he could not pass judgment at that stage, but, citing the Genocide Convention, went on to say that the cases of intercommunal violence brought to his attention indicated "very clearly that the victims of the attacks, Tutsis in the overwhelming majority of cases, have been targeted solely because of their membership of a certain ethnic group and for no other objective reason." Although Ndiaye—in addition to pointing out the serious risk of genocide in Rwanda—recommended a series of steps to prevent further massacres and other abuses, his report seems to have been largely ignored by the key actors within the United Nations system. . . .

---

[13] UN Doc. S/1999/1257 (1999).

A problem in the United Nations response to the situation in Rwanda was the weaknesses apparent in the capacity for political analysis, in particular within UNAMIR, but also at Headquarters. With respect to UNAMIR, a key problem identified by the Force Commander in an interview with the Inquiry was the weak political representation in the reconnaissance mission to Rwanda in August 1993 and the lack of real understanding the team had about the underlying political realities of the Rwandan peace process. Once UNAMIR was set up, there was a lack of capacity for intelligence analysis. At Headquarters there was not sufficient focus or institutional resources for early warning and risk analysis. Much could have been gained by a more active preventive policy aimed at identifying the risks for conflict or tension, including through an institutionalized cooperation with academics, NGOs and better coordination within different parts of the United Nations system dealing with Rwanda.

A key issue in the analysis of the flow of information is whether it should have been possible to predict a genocide in Rwanda. The Inquiry has received very different replies to this question, both from Rwandese and international actors whom it interviewed. As indicated above, early indications of the risk of genocide were contained in NGO and United Nations human rights reports of 1993. The Inquiry is of the view that these reports were not sufficiently taken into account in the planning for UNAMIR. UNAMIR was viewed as a traditional peacekeeping operation under Chapter VI, established at the request of the parties to a two-sided conflict to assist them in the implemention of a peace agreement. Despite warning signs during the Arusha process, in particular related to the lack of commitment by extremists within the President's party to the peace process and to power-sharing, very little if anything seems to have been done in terms of contingency planning for the eventuality that the peace agreement was threatened or challenged. UNAMIR was established without a fall-back position or a worst-case scenario. There were warning signs of the possibility of a genocide in Rwanda, and furthermore clear indications that mass killings were being planned and could take place in Rwanda in early 1994. That failure to formulate a determined response to these warnings is due in part to the lack of correct analysis, both in UNAMIR and within the Secretariat, but also by key Member States.

One of the main tasks of UNAMIR was to monitor the observance of the Arusha Agreement. The delays in this process which were evident already during the first weeks of UNAMIR's presence in Rwanda took place against a backdrop of a steadily worsening security situation. Reports from the field did refer to the rising number of killings, serious ethnic tension, militia activities and the import and distribution of arms. Although the description of these threats in cables to Headquarters seemed at times divorced from the usually separate analysis of the difficulties incurred in the political process, these worrying factors were reported to Headquarters, in increasingly alarming tones.

In his report to the Security Council of 30 December 1993 (S/26927), the Secretary-General mentioned the existence of "a well-armed and reportedly ruthless group" operating in the area of the DMZ "with a view to disrupting or even disrailing [sic] the peace process." After the United States requested more information regarding this group in the Council's consultations of the whole on 5 January 1994, the Special Representative and the Force Commander were asked to provide Headquarters with further details on this score. In a response dated 6 January, Dallaire described massacres on 17–18 and 30 November, in which 55 men, women and children were killed. Dallaire wrote that he did not have definitive proof of who was responsible for the massacres, but continued to say that the "manner in which they were conducted in their execution, in their coordination, in their cover-up, and in their political motives lead us to firmly believe that the perpetrators of these evil deeds were well-organized, well informed, well motivated and prepared to conduct premeditated murder. We have no reason to believe that such occurrences could not and will not be repeated again in any part of this country where arms are prolific and political and ethnic tensions are prevalent."

These are examples which, together with others cited in this report, such as the handling of the Dallaire cable, and the analysis of developments after the genocide began, show an institutional weakness in the analytical capacity of the United Nations. The responsibility for this lack of analytical capacity falls primarily on the Secretariat under the leadership of the Secretary-General.

Even as the report on Rwanda was being written in 1999, the United Nations was preparing for a popular consultation in East Timor (Timor-Leste) that also suffered more from a poverty of analysis than a lack of information. Despite reports of militia preparing for violence in the event of a vote for independence, Indonesia's consent to the process was dependent on retaining responsibility for peace and security. It was therefore not possible to push for international troops on the ground. The Indonesian cabinet, meanwhile, appeared to rely on remarkably bad intelligence of its own that in a free vote the Timorese would choose to remain within Indonesia—or, perhaps, that the result would be close enough to dispute. Officials in the United Nations and concerned governments anticipated precisely the opposite result, but were constrained from planning openly for independence by the delicate political balance that had made a vote possible in the first place. This set the stage for a very swift transition, with little planning for either the logistics of independence or management of the inevitable political crisis it would cause within Indonesia.[14]

A well-documented weakness of the political departments of the UN Secretariat is a lack of in-depth country and regional expertise. Strategies for conflict countries often appear based on past experience of the United Nations, rather than being driven by the specificities of the country or region involved. The results have sometimes been dire. One response has been a much greater willingness of the Secretariat as of the mid-1990s to reach

---

[14] See chapter 9.

out to country experts in the policy research, academic and NGO worlds, with at least one small such organization, the Conflict Prevention and Peace Forum, being created to serve as a knowledge broker for the Secretariat, active on such issues as Nepal, Aceh, and security challenges in the Andean region.

There are many other examples of failed or inadequate early warning. The number of successful cases is harder to establish—as Sherlock Holmes once observed, it is difficult to establish why a dog *didn't* bark on a given night.

QUESTIONS

5. How important is early warning in determining the international response to a crisis? Do worries about "early warning" sometime serve as an alibi for those who do not wish to act? In other words, how often is the outbreak of violence a surprise to academic and other experts on the countries and regions involved (even if, when shooting breaks out, the Security Council frequently portrays itself "shocked, shocked," as in the *Casablanca* script)?
6. How might the United Nations have responded to the situation in Rwanda in 1993?
7. Was Annan's response to Dallaire's cable the correct one? Why, or why not?
8. The Independent Inquiry on Rwanda identifies analysis as a key problem in the response to the signs of impending genocide. If there had been better analysis, what might have been done to prevent or limit the genocide?

Further Reading

Berdal, Mats R., and David M. Malone, eds. *Greed and Grievance: Economic Agendas in Civil Wars*. Boulder, CO: Lynne Rienner, 2000.

Carment, David, and Albrecht Schnabel, eds. *Conflict Prevention: From Rhetoric to Reality*. Lanham, MD: Lexington, 2004.

Carnegie Commission on Preventing Deadly Conflict, *Reports* (1994–1999). Available at http://ccpdc.org

Chesterman, Simon, *Shared Secrets: Intelligence and Collective Security*. Sydney: Lowy Institute for International Policy 2006.

Collier, Paul. *Breaking the Conflict Trap: Civil War and Development Policy*, A World Bank Policy Research Report. New York: Oxford University Press, 2003.

Hampson, Fen, and David M. Malone, eds. *From Reaction to Conflict Prevention: Opportunities for the UN System*. Boulder, CO: Lynne Rienner, 2001.

Peck, Connie. *The United Nations as a Dispute Settlement System: Improving Mechanisms for the Prevention and Resolution of Conflict*. The Hague: Kluwer Law International, 1996.

Sriram, Chandra Lekha, and Karin Wermester, eds. *From Promise to Practice: Strengthening UN Capacities for the Prevention of Violent Conflict*. Boulder, CO: Lynne Rienner, 2003.

chapter eight
....

Peace Operations

The UN Charter foresees activities mandated by the Security Council to maintain peace and security, but it is not expansive on the form such activities should take. With respect to Chapter VI, diplomatic and mediatory activities are principally envisaged, although Article 38, premised on the consent of all relevant member states, provides a degree of latitude to the Council in addressing threats to the peace through unspecified "recommendations" with a view to the pacific settlement of the dispute. In Chapter VII, beyond sanctions and interdiction, most attention is paid to the use of force by member states under Security Council control. (An important role was planned for the Council's Military Staff Committee under Articles 46 and 47, but nothing came of this due to Cold War dynamics, and proposals to create a serious role for the Committee since the end of the Cold War have failed to gain support in part because the Committee's only standing members are the permanent five (P-5) members of the Security Council.)

Very soon afterward, however, the Council deployed personnel to situations of conflict in several configurations that did not fit this neat schema. In 1948, it established a Truce Commission for Palestine, under resolution 48 (1948) that soon evolved into the UN Truce Supervisory Organization (UNTSO), still deployed as an observer force with headquarters in Jerusalem.[1] UNTSO's activities initially related to assistance in supervising observation of a truce between Israeli and Arab forces. As well, the Security Council, seeking to staunch hostilities in Jammu and Kashmir, set up a Commission under resolution 39 (1948) to investigate and mediate the dispute between India and Pakistan.[2] In its resolution 47 (1948), the Council decided to enlarge the Commission in a manner that eventually led to the creation of the UN Military Observer Group in India and Pakistan (UNMOGIP), charged with monitoring cease-fire violations, also still

---

[1] SC Res. 48 (1948). UNTSO was set up under SC Res. 50 (1948).
[2] SC Res. 39 (1948).

on the ground.[3] These developments were linked to the appointment of high-level UN Representatives or Envoys resident in the field, one of whom, Count Folke Bernadotte, was assassinated in Jerusalem on 17 September 1948.[4]

Cold War tensions—epitomized by the 1950 Korean operation, discussed in section one—discouraged further such experimentation by the Security Council. In 1956 the Suez crisis saw the Council deadlocked once again and so it was the General Assembly, acting under the 1950 *Uniting for Peace* resolution, that established "with the consent of the nations concerned," a United Nations Emergency Force (UNEF) to secure and supervise the cessation of hostilities. Target strength of 6,000 troops was attained on the ground in February 1957.

UNEF was a creative approach to interpretation of Chapter VI of the Charter. Further peacekeeping improvisations under the broad heading of Chapter "VI and a half" followed over ensuing years, most notably in the Congo in 1960 and in Cyprus in 1964.[5] The UN Operation in the Congo (ONUC), eventually authorized to enforce its mandate under Chapter VII of the Charter and reaching a strength at its peak of 20,000 troops, proved controversial, with France and the Soviet Union eventually refusing to contribute to its costs, giving rise to the *Certain Expenses* case in the ICJ.[6]

A lot has been said and written about peacekeeping "doctrine," but much of it in fact refers to practice rather than hard and fast rules. Early peacekeeping, sometimes known as "classic" peacekeeping, generally involved UN missions staffed by lightly armed "blue helmets" (as they came to be known), operating under the strict instruction to use force only in self-defense. Falling between Chapter VI (pacific settlement of disputes) and Chapter VII (action with respect to threats to the peace), these were creatively crafted "Chapter VI and a half" peace operations, requiring, in principle, invitation or consent on the part of the recipient state(s). They operated under UN command, primarily undertaking activities agreed on by belligerents, such as the separation of warring parties, border monitoring, overseeing withdrawal of foreign troops, and the cessation of aid to irregular or insurrectionist movements. The guiding principle of early peacekeeping was that it must not give an advantage to either side involved in the conflict. Blue helmets sought to adopt an attitude of strict neutrality and objectivity. It is dangerous, however, to generalize too broadly, as UN "blue helmets" in the UN's first engagement in the Congo of the early 1960s were authorized to and ultimately did use force

---

[3] SC Res. 47 (1948). Other early and important Council resolutions on Kashmir were SC Res. 80 (1950) and SC Res. 91 (1951).

[4] This was the basis for the *Reparations* case, discussed in chapter 3 in this volume.

[5] ONUC in the Congo was created under SC Res. 143 (1960) and UNFICYP was created in Cyprus under SC Res. 186 (1964).

[6] See chapter 6 in this volume.

against one set of belligerents, thus breaching neutrality (albeit in the impartial execution of their mandate).

With the exception of further peacekeeping forces in the Middle East (UNEF II, UNDOF, UNIFIL), however, peacekeeping remained broadly in abeyance until the end of the Cold War. Since then, however, a broad range of peacekeeping operations with ambitious (and widely varying) mandates have been authorized, some extending so broadly beyond the traditional boundaries of UN peacekeeping and some relying so extensively on civilian rather than military components that they came to be known as "peace operations," a term used by Secretary-General Boutros Boutros-Ghali, but resisted then and subsequently by the UN Department of Peacekeeping Operations (DPKO), which may have feared and may still fear encroachment on its turf of other Secretariat units. For our purposes, the term "peace operations," unbounded by UN bureaucratic warfare, seems most appropriate.

"New generation" UN peace operations, as they are frequently known, have relied less on consent of the parties (often shadowy rebel groups and disreputable governments), less on strictly military personnel, and more on civilian components with specific developmental, human rights, policing, humanitarian, and demobilization objectives, with the military contingents providing a degree of security and occasionally the threat of coercion. These complex missions, contending with often very unpromising conflicts, nevertheless often proved quite successful, as was the case in Sierra Leone and in Liberia (where generally free and fair elections were held in late 2005), against the odds. Other complex UN missions, charged with transitional administration of territories in Kosovo and East Timor, are addressed in chapter 9.

Many of these activities go beyond what might have been understood by the drafters of the UN Charter, both in terms of the form and substance of UN-authorized actions. In particular, the line has been blurred between a "classic" peacekeeping operation, where an interposed force creates space for diplomacy, and a new form of "robust" peace operation, sometimes a warfighting one intended to defeat a military rival (as ultimately became the case in Sierra Leone, for example). That being said, the shift toward greater use of force by UN peace operations in order to defend more assertively if impartially ambitious mandates from the Security Council, often in situations in which the United Nations was, in fact, outgunned by belligerents (as in Bosnia and Somalia), greatly exacerbated the risks and costs of failure in terms of casualties and adverse public reaction.

This chapter examines a series of significant episodes in this evolution of the approach of the United Nations to peace operations, focusing on the Security Council's authorization of collective action to defend South Korea in 1950, the birth of peacekeeping in the form of UNEF I, efforts to take advantage of the post–Cold War international environment, and an example of the type of internal conflict with which the United Nations is increasingly faced. The last section considers recent efforts to improve the capacity of the United Nations to respond to these challenges. Questions of what happens when things go wrong—ranging from the failure to prevent genocide to sexual abuse by peacekeepers who are meant to help a vulnerable population—are considered in chapter sixteen 16.

8.1 Enforcement Actions: Korea, 1950

In August–September 1945, by agreement of the Allies, Japanese forces north of the 38th Parallel surrendered to Soviet forces, while those south of the 38th parallel surrendered to American forces. In March 1946, a joint US-Soviet Commission to work out trusteeship proposals for Korea deadlocked. In 1947, the Korean People's Republic was established north of the 38th parallel, with Soviet backing. At the request of the United States, the United Nations assumed responsibility for further efforts to unify Korea and established the United Nations Temporary Commission on Korea (UNTCK). The UNTCK was boycotted by Soviet-bloc nations and barred from entering North Korea. Following the UN-supervised elections in South Korea, the UN General Assembly recognized the Southern "Republic of Korea" as the legal Government of Korea.[7]

On 25 June 1950 the North Korea People's Army invaded South Korea. At the request of the United States, the UN Security Council met on the same day and called for an immediate cease-fire and the withdrawal of North Korean troops to the 38th Parallel.

SECURITY COUNCIL RESOLUTION 82 (1950)   *June 25*

The Security Council,
  Recalling the finding of the General Assembly in its resolution 293 (IV) of 21 October 1949 that the Government of the Republic of Korea is a lawfully established government having effective control and jurisdiction over that part of Korea where the United Nations Temporary Commission on Korea was able to observe and consult and in that which the great majority of the people of Korea reside; that this Government is based on elections which were a valid expression of the free will of the electorate of that part of Korea and which were observed by the Temporary Commission; and that this is the only such Government in Korea,

---

[7] GA Res. 195(III) (1948).

Mindful of the concern expressed by the General Assembly in its resolutions 195 (III) of 12 December 1948 and 293 (IV) of 21 October 1949 about the consequences which might follow unless Member States refrained from acts derogatory to the results sought to be achieved by the United Nations in bringing about the complete independence and unity of Korea; and the concern expressed that the situation described by the United Nations Commission on Korea in its report menaces the safety and well-being of the Republic of Korea and of the people of Korea and might lead to open military conflict there,

Noting with grave concern the armed attack on the Republic of Korea by forces from North Korea,

Determines that this action constitutes a breach of the peace; and

I

Calls for the immediate cessation of hostilities;

Calls upon the authorities in North Korea to withdraw forthwith their armed forces to the 38th parallel;

II

Requests the United Nations Commission on Korea:

(a) To communicate its fully considered recommendations on the situation with the least possible delay;

(b) To observe the withdrawal of North Korean forces from the 38th parallel;

(c) To keep the Security Council informed on the execution of this resolution;

III

Calls upon all Member States to render every assistance to the United Nations in the execution of this resolution and to refrain from giving assistance to the North Korean authorities.

....

The resolution was possible only due to the non-attendance of the Soviet Union, in protest over the refusal to recognize Mao Zedong's regime in Beijing as the government of China. The Soviet representative had withdrawn from the Council on 13 January 1950, stating that he would not participate in the Council's work until "the representative of the Kuomintang group had been removed," and that his government would not recognize as legal any decision of the Council adopted with the participation of that representative. Two days after resolution 82 (1950), another resolution was adopted.

SECURITY COUNCIL RESOLUTION 83 (1950)   *June 27*

The Security Council,

Having determined that the armed attack upon the Republic of Korea by forces from North Korea constitutes a breach of the peace,

Having called for an immediate cessation of hostilities,

Having called upon the authorities in North Korea to withdraw forthwith their armed forces to the 38th parallel,

Having noted from the report of the United Nations Commission on Korea that the authorities in North Korea have neither ceased hostilities nor withdrawn their armed forces to the 38th parallel and that urgent military measures are required to restore international peace and security,

Having noted the appeal from the Republic of Korea to the United Nations for immediate and effective steps to secure peace and security,

Recommends that the Members of the United Nations furnish such assistance to the Republic of Korea as may be necessary to repel the armed attack and to restore international peace and security in the area.

This resolution in turn was followed by yet another, providing a mandate for US leadership of a unified military command (still on the ground today) and requesting reporting from the United States to the Security Council on subsequent developments.

SECURITY COUNCIL RESOLUTION 84 (1950)   *June 27*

The Security Council,

Having determined that the armed attack on the Republic of Korea by forces from North Korea constitutes a breach of the peace,

Having recommended that Members of the United Nations furnish such assistance to the Republic of Korea as may be necessary to repel the armed attack and to restore international peace and security in the area,

1. *Welcomes* the prompt and vigorous support which Governments and peoples of the United Nations have given to its resolutions 82 (1950) and 83 (1950) of 25 and 27 June 1950 to assist the Republic of Korea in defending itself against armed attack and thus to restore international peace and security in the area;

2. *Notes* that Members of the United Nations have transmitted to the United Nations offers of assistance for the Republic of Korea;

3. *Recommends* that all Members providing military forces and other assistance pursuant to the aforesaid Security Council resolutions make such forces and other assistance available to a unified command under the United States of America;

4. *Requests* the United States to designate the commander of such forces;

5. *Authorizes* the unified command at its discretion to use the United Nations flag in the course of operations against North Korean forces concurrently with the flags of the various nations participating;

6. *Requests* the United States to provide the Security Council with reports as appropriate on the course of action taken under the unified command.

The Soviet Union returned to the Council on 1 August 1950 and further such resolutions became subject to its veto threat. The United States and its allies arranged for the General Assembly to adopt a carefully crafted resolution— 377(V) (1950)—known as the *Uniting for Peace* resolution, asserting a role for itself in promoting international peace and security.

Nov. 3, 1950

GENERAL ASSEMBLY RESOLUTION 377(V) (1950): UNITING FOR PEACE

The General Assembly . . .

1. *Resolves* that if the Security Council, because of lack of unanimity of the permanent members, fails to exercise its primary responsibility for the maintenance of international peace and security in any case where there appears to be a threat to the peace, breach of the peace, or act of aggression, the General Assembly shall consider the matter immediately with a view to making appropriate recommendations to Members for collective measures, including in the case of a breach of the peace or act of aggression the use of armed force when necessary, to maintain or restore international peace and security. If not in session at the time, the General Assembly may meet in emergency special session within twenty-four hours of the request therefor. Such emergency special session shall be called if requested by the Security Council on the vote of any seven members, or by a majority of the Members of the United Nations;

On 1 February 1951, in accordance with the *Uniting for Peace* procedures, the Assembly passed a resolution condemning China's armed intervention in

Korea as an act of aggression, and recommended that all states lend every assistance to the UN action in Korea.[8]

The conflict continued for over two years, with direct intervention from American and Chinese forces, as well as the combined forces of fifteen different countries, including the United States, under the UN mandate. In late 1951, cease-fire talks began with agreement being reached on the demarcation line in November but stalled again by May 1952. After the death of Stalin in March 1953, contentious issues connected with the return of prisoners of war were partially resolved. With the UN's support of the proposal for Korean armistice,[9] a cease-fire was finally established on 27 July 1953, by which time the front line of the conflict was back to the 38th parallel. The UN Command Military Armistice Commission—Korea was authorized by the Security Council to supervise the implementation of the Armistice Agreement between North and South Korea, which to this today have not signed a peace treaty. The 151-mile-long Demilitarized Zone (DMZ), a 4,000-meter-wide barrier, remains the most heavily guarded military buffer in the world.[10]

The question of whether the General Assembly was acting *ultra vires* arose again when it requested the International Court of Justice in 2003 to provide an advisory opinion on "the legal consequences arising from the construction of the wall being built by Israel, the occupying Power, in the Occupied Palestinian Territory."

LEGAL CONSEQUENCES OF THE CONSTRUCTION OF A WALL IN THE OCCUPIED PALESTINIAN TERRITORY (ADVISORY OPINION), (2004) ICJ REPORTS 136

26. Under Article 24 of the Charter the Security Council has "primary responsibility for the maintenance of international peace and security." . . . However, the Court would emphasize that Article 24 refers to a primary, but not necessarily exclusive, competence. The General Assembly does have the power, inter alia, under Article 14 of the Charter, to "recommend measures for the peaceful adjustment" of various situations (Certain

---

[8] GA Res. 498(V) (1951).

[9] GA Res. 610(VII) (1952). See also William Whitney Stueck, *The Korean War: An International History* (Princeton: Princeton University Press, 1995), pp. 298–306, cited in Donald W. Boose, Jr., "Fighting While Talking: The Korean War Truce Talks," *Magazine of History*, vol. 14(3) (Spring 2000), pp. 25–31.

[10] Elizabeth D. Scaher, "The Paradoxes of the Demilitarized Zone," *Magazine of History*, vol. 14(3) (Spring 2000).

Expenses of the United Nations, . . . p. 163). "[T]he only limitation which Article 14 imposes on the General Assembly is the restriction found in Article 12, namely, that the Assembly should not recommend measures while the Security Council is dealing with the same matter unless the Council requests it to do so." (Ibid.).

27. As regards the practice of the United Nations, both the General Assembly and the Security Council initially interpreted and applied Article 12 to the effect that the Assembly could not make a recommendation on a question concerning the maintenance of international peace and security while the matter remained on the Council's agenda. Thus the Assembly during its fourth session refused to recommend certain measures on the question of Indonesia, on the ground, inter alia, that the Council remained seized of the matter . . . As for the Council, on a number of occasions it deleted items from its agenda in order to enable the Assembly to deliberate on them . . . In the case of the Republic of Korea, the Council decided on 31 January 1951 to remove the relevant item from the list of matters of which it was seized in order to enable the Assembly to deliberate on the matter. . . .

However, this interpretation of Article 12 has evolved subsequently. Thus the General Assembly deemed itself entitled in 1961 to adopt recommendations in the matter of the Congo (resolutions 1955 (XV) and 1600 (XVI)) and in 1963 in respect of the Portuguese colonies (resolution 1913 (XVIII)) while those cases still appeared on the Council's agenda, without the Council having adopted any recent resolution concerning them. In response to a question posed by Peru during the Twenty-third session of the General Assembly, the Legal Counsel of the United Nations confirmed that the Assembly interpreted the words "is exercising the functions" in Article 12 of the Charter as meaning "is exercising the functions at this moment" . . . Indeed, the Court notes that there has been an increasing tendency over time for the General Assembly and the Security Council to deal in parallel with the same matter concerning the maintenance of international peace and security (see, for example, the matters involving Cyprus, South Africa, Angola, Southern Rhodesia and more recently Bosnia and Herzegovina and Somalia). It is often the case that, while the Security Council has tended to focus on the aspects of such matters related to international peace and security, the General Assembly has taken a broader view, considering also their humanitarian, social and economic aspects.

28. The Court considers that the accepted practice of the General Assembly, as it has evolved, is consistent with Article 12, paragraph 1, of the Charter.

The Court is accordingly of the view that the General Assembly, in adopting resolution ES-10/14, seeking an advisory opinion from the Court, did not contravene the provisions of Article 12, paragraph 1, of the Charter. The Court concludes that by submitting that request the General Assembly did not exceed its competence.

QUESTIONS ....

1. The last paragraph of Security Council resolution 83 (1950) appears to use the language of both article 42 and article 51 of the UN Charter, couched in the language of a "recommendation." What was the legal basis for UN action in Korea?
2. Was the General Assembly acting within its powers in adopting the *Uniting for Peace* resolution?

8.2 Peacekeeping: UNEF I

While observer forces in the Middle East and between Indian and Pakistan had been created in the late 1940s, the birth of large-scale peacekeeping resulted not from decisions of the UN Security Council but from decisions of the General Assembly taken under the authority of the *Uniting for Peace* framework. The UN Emergency Force (UNEF) was established by the General Assembly in 1956 to supervise the cease-fire in the Middle East after the Suez invasion.[11] Soon after the crisis broke out, Canadian Foreign Minister Lester B. Pearson had suggested the need for "a truly international peace and police force . . . large enough to keep these borders at peace while a political settlement is being worked out."[12] The proposal that Secretary-General Dag Hammarskjöld later submitted to the General Assembly did not specifically mention the use of force, but did state that "there was no intent in the establishment of the Force to influence the military balance in the current conflict, and thereby the political balance affecting efforts to settle the conflict."[13] UNEF was later described as a "plate-glass window"—not capable of withstanding assault, but nonetheless "a lightly armed barrier that all see and tend to respect."[14]

---

[11] UNEF was preceded by the unarmed military observers of the UN Truce Supervisory Organization (UNTSO) (1948—) and the UN Military Observer Group in India and Pakistan (UNMOGIP) (1949—).

[12] Brian Urquhart, *Ralph Bunche: An American Life* (New York: W.W. Norton, 1993), p. 265.

[13] Report of the Secretary-General on Basic Points for the Presence and Functioning in Egypt of the United Nations Emergency Force, UN Doc. A/3302 (1956).

[14] Finn Seyersted, *United Nations Forces in the Law of Peace and War* (Leyden: A.W. Sijthoff, 1966), p. 48.

GENERAL ASSEMBLY RESOLUTION 998(ES-I) (1956)

The General Assembly,

Bearing in mind the urgent necessity of facilitating compliance with its resolution 997 (ES-I) of 2 November 1956,

Requests, as a matter of priority, the Secretary-General to submit within forty-eight hours a plan for setting up, with the consent of the nations concerned, of an emergency international United Nations Force to secure and supervise the cessation of hostilities, in accordance with all the terms of the aforementioned resolution.

GENERAL ASSEMBLY RESOLUTION 999(ES-I) (1956)

The General Assembly,

Noting with regret that not all the parties concerned have yet agreed to comply with the provisions of its resolution 997 (ES-I) of 2 November 1956,

Noting the special priority given in that resolution to an immediate cease-fire and, as part thereof, to the halting of the movement of military forces and arms into the area,

Noting further that the resolution urged the parties to the armistice agreements promptly to withdraw all forces behind armistice lines, to desist from raids across the armistice lines into neighbouring territory, and to observe scrupulously the provisions of the armistice agreements,

1. *Reaffirms* its resolution 997 (ES-I), and once again calls upon the parties immediately to comply with the provisions of the said resolution;

2. *Authorizes* the Secretary-General immediately to arrange with the parties concerned for the implementation of the cease-fire and the halting of the movement of military forces and arms into the area, and requests him to report compliance forthwith and, in any case, not later than twelve hours from the time of adoption of the present resolution;

3. *Requests* the Secretary-General, with the assistance of the Chief of Staff and the members of the United Nations Truce Supervision Organization, to obtain compliance of the withdrawal of all forces behind the armistice lines;

4. *Decides* to meet again immediately on receipt of the Secretary-General's report referred to in paragraph 2 of the present resolution.

GENERAL ASSEMBLY RESOLUTION 1000(ES-I) (1956)

The General Assembly,

Having requested the Secretary-General, in its resolution 998 (ES-I) of 4 November 1956, to submit to it a plan for an emergency international United Nations Force, for the purposes stated,

Noting with satisfaction the first report of the Secretary-General on the plan, and having in mind particularly paragraph 4 of that report,

1. *Establishes* a United Nations Command for an emergency international Force to secure and supervise the cessation of hostilities in accordance with all the terms of General Assembly resolution 997 (ES-I) of 2 November 1956;

2. *Appoints*, on an emergency basis, the Chief of Staff of the United Nations Truce Supervision Organization, Major-General E. L. M. Burns, as Chief of the Command;

3. *Authorizes* the Chief of the Command immediately to recruit, from the observer corps of the United Nations Truce Supervision Organization, a limited number of officers who shall be nationals of countries other than those having permanent membership in the Security Council, and further authorizes him, in consultation with the Secretary-General, to undertake the recruitment directly, from various Member States other than the permanent members of the Security Council, of the additional number of officers needed;

4. *Invites* the Secretary-General to take such administrative measures as may be necessary for the prompt execution of the actions envisaged in the present resolution.

GENERAL ASSEMBLY RESOLUTION 1001(ES-I) (1956)

The General Assembly,

Recalling its Resolution 997 (ES-I) of 2 November 1956 concerning the cease-fire, withdrawal of troops and other matters related to the military operations in Egyptian territory, as well as its Resolution 998 (ES-I) of 4 November 1956 concerning the request to the Secretary-General to submit a plan for an emergency international United Nations Force,

Having established by its Resolution 1000 (ES-I) of 5 November 1956 a United Nations Command for an emergency international Force, having appointed the Chief of Staff of the United Nations Truce Supervision Organization as Chief of the Command with authorization to him to begin the recruitment of officers for the Command, and having invited the Secretary-General to take the administrative measures necessary for the prompt execution of that Resolution,

Noting with appreciation the second and final report of the Secretary-General on the plan for an emergency international United Nations Force as requested in General Assembly Resolution 998 (ES-I), and having examined that plan,

1. *Expresses* its approval of the guiding principles for the organization and functioning of the emergency international United Nations Force as expounded in paragraphs 6 to 9 of the Secretary-General's report;

2. *Concurs* in the definition of the functions of the Force as stated in paragraph 12 of the Secretary-General's report;

3. *Invites* the Secretary-General to continue discussions with Governments of member-States concerning offers of participation in the Force, toward the objective of its balanced composition;

4. *Requests* the Chief of the Command, in consultation with the Secretary-General as regards size and composition, to proceed forthwith with the full organization of the Force;

5. *Approves* provisionally the basic rule concerning the financing of the Force laid down in paragraph 15 of the Secretary-General's report;

6. *Establishes* an Advisory Committee composed of one representative from each of the following countries: Brazil, Canada, Ceylon, Colombia, India, Norway and Pakistan, and requests this Committee, whose Chairman shall be the Secretary-General, to undertake the development of those aspects of the planning for the Force and its operation not already dealt with by the General Assembly and which do not fall within the area of the direct responsibility of the Chief of the Command;

7. *Authorizes* the Secretary-General to issue all regulations and instructions which may be essential to the effective functioning of the Force, following consultation with the Committee aforementioned, and to take all other necessary administrative and executive action;

8. *Determines* that, following the fulfilment of the immediate responsibilities defined for it in operative paragraphs 6 and 7 above, the Advisory Committee shall continue to assist the Secretary-General in the responsibilities falling to him under the present and other relevant resolutions;

9. *Decides* that the Advisory Committee, in the performance of its duties, shall be empowered to request, through the usual procedures, the convening of the General Assembly and to report to the Assembly whenever matters arise which, in its opinion, are of such urgency and importance as to require consideration by the General Assembly itself;

10. *Requests* all member-States to afford assistance as necessary to the United Nations Command in the performance of its functions, including arrangements for passage to and from the area involved.

UNEF I came to an end in 1967 when, amidst much tension between Israel and its Arab neighbours, Egyptian President Nasser demanded its withdrawal, a demand with which UN Secretary-General U Thant believed he had no option but to comply. The "Six Days War" of May 1967, during which Israel seized control of the Sinai, ensued. Six years later, following the "Yom Kippur War" and in order to help secure a partial Israeli withdrawal from the Sinai and the Golan Heights, UNEF II and UNDOF were created as forces of interposition of cease-fire monitoring. Following the conclusion of a peace treaty between Egypt and Israel in 1979, UNEF II was replaced by a smaller multinational (non-UN) monitoring force in Sinai.[15] UNDOF is still deployed on the Golan Heights.

QUESTION ....

3. Why did U Thant conclude he had no choice but to withdraw UNEF I when Egypt withdrew its consent? Was he correct as a matter of policy? As a matter of law?

8.3 Post–Cold War Opportunities

The Cold War's end was signalled at the United Nations in subtle and more overt ways. Veiled from public view were consultations among the permanent five in late 1986 on how to address the end of Javier Pérez de Cuéllar's first term as Secretary-General. The P-5 ultimately decided on his re-election, but then faced a challenge from the Secretary-General to tackle cooperatively the ending of the murderous Iran-Iraq war that had been under way since 1980. This they did, with surprising success, initially meeting quietly among themselves away from the United Nations, developing the approach later enshrined in resolution 598 (1987). Later that year, prompted by the opening of the UN General Assembly, Soviet President Mikhail Gorbachev published a lengthy article in *Izvestia* (subsequently submitted to the UN General Assembly and Security Council for consideration) signalling a profound shift in the Soviet Union's approach to conflict (if not to the concept of sovereignty). Perhaps best seen as an effort to withdraw from the Cold War without admitting defeat by pointing to useful new means of conflict resolution, the excerpts below indicate the extent to which Gorbachev's vision embraced a larger role for the United Nations.

---

[15]More information on this force is available from www.mfo.org.

MIKHAIL GORBACHEV

REALITY AND SAFEGUARDS FOR A MORE SECURE WORLD[16]

Objective processes are making our complicated and diverse world ever more interlinked and interdependent, and it is increasingly in need of an apparatus for discussing its common problems responsibly at a representative level, a place for collective efforts to balance the various contradictory but real interests of contemporary society, States and nations. It falls to the United Nations, by conception and descent, to serve as such an apparatus. . . .

Alas, many influential forces still hold to outdated ideas of how to ensure national security. As a result, the world is put in the absurd position of receiving assurances that the route over the precipice is the safest way to go. It is hard to find any other word to describe the view that nuclear weapons make world war avoidable. . . .

Thinking of progress towards a nuclear-free world, now is the time to consider how to maintain security at every stage of the disarmament process; and not just think about it, but agree on machinery for maintaining the peace with sharply reduced quantities of non-nuclear weapons.

All these points are covered in the proposal we and the other socialist countries submitted to the United Nations on the establishment of comprehensive system of international peace and security.

How do we envisage this system?

Our security proposal calls, first of all, for continuity and compatibility with existing institutions for keeping the peace; the system could operate on the basis for the United Nations Charter and within the framework of the United Nations. . . .

Previously unheard-of standards of openness, *glasnost*, and thoroughness in the reciprocal verification and monitoring of undertakings are becoming the norm. . . .

A prerequisite for universal security is unconditional respect for the Charter of the United Nations and the right of peoples to exercise the sovereign choice of the ways and forms of their development, revolutionary or evolutionary. This applies also to the right to the social status quo, for this too is an exclusively internal affair. Any attempts, whether direct or indirect, to influence the development of "other people's" countries and interfere with it must be excluded. Equally impermissible, too, are attempts to destabilize existing Governments from outside.

At the same time, the world community cannot stand aside from inter-State conflicts. A starting point here could be to implement the proposal by the Secretary-General of the Untied Nations for the establishment

---

[16]*Pravda* and *Izvestia*, 17 September 1987. Reprinted as UN Doc. A/42/574-S/19143 (1987).

within the Organization of a multilateral centre for reducing the threat of war. . . .

Our conclusion is that wider use should be made of the United Nations military observers and the United Nations peacekeeping forces for separating the troops of those engaged in hostilities and for monitoring cease-fires and truce agreements. . . .

The permanent members of the Security Council could act as guarantors of regional security, and would for their part assume the obligation to refrain from the use of threat of the use of force and from conspicuous displays of military strength, for this practice is one of the factors in sparking regional conflicts.

A radical strengthening and expansion of co-operation among States in the eradication of international terrorism is of vital importance. Work on this issue should be concentrated within the framework of the United Nations. . . .

The world cannot be regarded as safe if human rights are trampled underfoot—and, I would add, if the elementary conditions for human life in dignity do not exist in a large part of this world . . .

The first requirement of all is for national legislation and administrative rules in the humanitarian field, as well, to be brought everywhere into line with international obligations and standards. . . .

The proposed system of comprehensive security will become operative to the extent that the United Nations, its Security Council and other international institutions and mechanisms function effectively. A decisive increase is required in the authority and role of the United Nations and the International Atomic Energy Agency. . . .

Nor must we forget the possibilities of the International Court of Justice. The General Assembly and the Security Council could address themselves to it more frequently for advisory opinions on disputed international legal issues. Its binding jurisdiction must be acknowledged by all . . .

Special missions of the Council to regions of existing and potential conflict would also help strengthen its authority and enhance the effectives of the decisions it takes.

We are convinced that co-operation between the United Nations and regional organizations can be considerable expanded. The aim would be to promote the political settlement of crisis situations. . . .

And, lastly, with regard to the Secretary-General of the United Nations. The world community elects to this high office an authoritative figure enjoying universal trust. Since the Secretary-General is the representative of every Member of the Organization, all States must extend to him the fullest support and assist him in the discharge of his responsible mission. The world community must encourage the Secretary-General in his missions of good offices, mediation or conciliation. . . .

The idea of the universal system of security is the initial blueprint for the possible restructuring of life in our common planetary home. In other words, it is a gateway to a future in which the security of all is the guarantee of the security of each. We hope this idea will be jointly developed and made reality at the General Assembly session.

In December 1988, Gorbachev amplified on these themes in an intervention at the United Nations calling for "de-ideologizing relations between among States" and advocating a greater role for the Security Council in conflict resolution.[17] The practical implications of these pronouncements were tested not only through the bumpy course of implementation of the Council's decision on how to end the Iran-Iraq war but also in the Council's approach to achieving the independence of Namibia in 1989. These episodes confirmed that while East-West mutual suspicion continued to exist, the desire on both sides to overcome it was greater. A number of Gorbachev's specific suggestions were taken up by Boutros Boutros-Ghali in his *Agenda for Peace* in 1992, also discussed in the previous chapter. The report captured both the promise and the peril inherent in a tectonic shift in international relations following the disappearance of the Berlin Wall.

AN AGENDA FOR PEACE: PREVENTIVE DIPLOMACY, PEACEMAKING AND PEACEKEEPING (REPORT OF THE SECRETARY-GENERAL), 17 JUNE 1992[18]

2. The United Nations is a gathering of sovereign States and what it can do depends on the common ground that they create between them. The adversarial decades of the cold war made the original promise of the Organization impossible to fulfil. The January 1992 Summit[19] therefore represented an unprecedented recommitment, at the highest political level, to the Purposes and Principles of the Charter. . . .

6. The manifest desire of the membership to work together is a new source of strength in our common endeavour. Success is far from certain, however. . . .

I. The Changing Context

8. In the course of the past few years the immense ideological barrier that for decades gave rise to distrust and hostility—and the terrible tools of destruction that were their inseparable companions—has collapsed. Even as the issues between States north and south grow more acute, and call for attention at the highest levels of government, the improvement in relations between States east and west affords new possibilities, some already realized, to meet successfully threats to common security.

---

[17] A/43/PV.72 (8 December 1998).
[18] UN Doc. A/47/277-S/24111 (1992).
[19] See chapter 1 in this volume.

9. Authoritarian regimes have given way to more democratic forces and responsive Governments. The form, scope and intensity of these processes differ from Latin America to Africa to Europe to Asia, but they are sufficiently similar to indicate a global phenomenon. Parallel to these political changes, many States are seeking more open forms of economic policy, creating a world wide sense of dynamism and movement.

10. To the hundreds of millions who gained their independence in the surge of decolonization following the creation of the United Nations, have been added millions more who have recently gained freedom. Once again new States are taking their seats in the General Assembly. . . .

11. [H]owever, fierce new assertions of nationalism and sovereignty spring up, and the cohesion of States is threatened by brutal ethnic, religious, social, cultural or linguistic strife. Social peace is challenged on the one hand by new assertions of discrimination and exclusion and, on the other, by acts of terrorism seeking to undermine evolution and change through democratic means. . . .

15. . . . Our aims must be:

• To seek to identify at the earliest possible stage situations that could produce conflict, and to try through diplomacy to remove the sources of danger before violence results;

• Where conflict erupts, to engage in peacemaking aimed at resolving the issues that have led to conflict;

• Through peacekeeping, to work to preserve peace, however fragile, where fighting has been halted and to assist in implementing agreements achieved by the peacemakers;

• To stand ready to assist in peacebuilding in its differing contexts: rebuilding the institutions and infrastructures of nations torn by civil war and strife; and building bonds of peaceful mutual benefit among nations formerly at war;

• And in the largest sense, to address the deepest causes of conflict: economic despair, social injustice and political oppression. It is possible to discern an increasingly common moral perception that spans the world's nations and peoples, and which is finding expression in international laws, many owing their genesis to the work of this Organization. . . .

17. The foundation-stone of this work is and must remain the State. Respect for its fundamental sovereignty and integrity are crucial to any common international progress. The time of absolute and exclusive sovereignty, however, has passed; its theory was never matched by reality. It is the task of leaders of States today to understand this and to find a balance between the needs of good internal governance and the requirements of an ever more interdependent world. . . . The United Nations has not closed its door. Yet if every ethnic, religious or linguistic group claimed statehood, there would be no limit to fragmentation, and peace, security and economic well-being for all would become ever more difficult to achieve.

18. One requirement for solutions to these problems lies in commitment to human rights with a special sensitivity to those of minorities, whether ethnic, religious, social or linguistic. . . .

19. Globalism and nationalism need not be viewed as opposing trends, doomed to spur each other on to extremes of reaction. The healthy globalization of contemporary life requires in the first instance solid identities and fundamental freedoms. . . . Respect for democratic principles at all levels of social existence is crucial: in communities, within States and within the community of States. Our constant duty should be to maintain the integrity of each while finding a balanced design for all. . . .

Use of Military Force

42. It is the essence of the concept of collective security as contained in the Charter that if peaceful means fail, the measures provided in Chapter VII should be used, on the decision of the Security Council, to maintain or restore international peace and security in the face of a "threat to the peace, breach of the peace, or act of aggression." The Security Council has not so far made use of the most coercive of these measures—the action by military force foreseen in Article 42. In the situation between Iraq and Kuwait, the Council chose to authorize Member States to take measures on its behalf. . . .

43. Under Article 42 of the Charter, the Security Council has the authority to take military action to maintain or restore international peace and security. While such action should only be taken when all peaceful means have failed, the option of taking it is essential to the credibility of the United Nations as a guarantor of international security. This will require bringing into being, through negotiations, the special agreements foreseen in Article 43 of the Charter, whereby Member States undertake to make armed forces, assistance and facilities available to the Security Council for the purposes stated in Article 42, not only on an ad hoc basis but on a permanent basis. Under the political circumstances that now exist for the first time since the Charter was adopted, the long-standing obstacles to the conclusion of such special agreements should no longer prevail. . . .

Peace-Enforcement Units

44. Cease-fires have often been agreed to but not complied with, and the United Nations has sometimes been called upon to send forces to restore and maintain the cease-fire. This task can on occasion exceed the mission of peacekeeping forces and the expectations of peacekeeping force contributors. I recommend that the Council consider the utilization of peace-enforcement units in clearly defined circumstances and with their terms of reference specified in advance. Such units from Member States would be available on call and would consist of troops that have volunteered for such service. They would have to be more heavily armed than peacekeeping forces . . . Deployment and operation of such forces would be under the authorization of the Security Council and would, as in the case of peacekeeping forces, be under the command of the Secretary-General.

V. Peacekeeping

. . .

50. The nature of peacekeeping operations has evolved rapidly in recent years. The established principles and practices of peacekeeping have responded flexibly to new demands of recent years, and the basic conditions for success remain unchanged: a clear and practicable mandate; the cooperation of the parties in implementing that mandate; the continuing support of the Security Council; the readiness of Member States to contribute the military, police and civilian personnel, including specialists, required; effective United Nations command at Headquarters and in the field; and adequate financial and logistic support. . . . [But] a new array of demands and problems has emerged regarding logistics, equipment, personnel and finance . . .

51. Member States are keen to participate in peacekeeping operations. Military observers and infantry are invariably available in the required numbers, but logistic units present a greater problem, as few armies can afford to spare such units for an extended period. Stand-by arrangements should be confirmed. . . .

52. Increasingly, peacekeeping requires that civilian political officers, human rights monitors, electoral officials, refugee and humanitarian aid specialists and police play as central a role as the military. Police personnel have proved increasingly difficult to obtain in the numbers required. As for the United Nations itself, special personnel procedures, including incentives, should be instituted to permit the rapid transfer of Secretariat staff members to service with peacekeeping operations. The strength and capability of military staff serving in the Secretariat should be augmented to meet new and heavier requirements. . . .

54. Member States in a position to do so should make air- and sea-lift capacity available to the United Nations free of cost or at lower than commercial rates, as was the practice until recently. . . .

VII. Cooperation with Regional Arrangements and Organizations

. . .

61. The Charter deliberately provides no precise definition of regional arrangements and agencies, thus allowing useful flexibility for undertakings by a group of States to deal with a matter appropriate for regional action which also could contribute to the maintenance of international peace and security. Such associations or entities could include treaty-based organizations, whether created before or after the founding of the United Nations, regional organizations for mutual security and defence, organizations for general regional development or for cooperation on a particular economic topic or function, and groups created to deal with a specific political, economic or social issue of current concern.

62. In this regard, the United Nations has recently encouraged a rich variety of complementary efforts. . . . The end of the war in Nicaragua involved

a highly complex effort which was initiated by leaders of the region and conducted by individual States, groups of States and the Organization of American States. Efforts undertaken by the European Community and its member States, with the support of States participating in the Conference on Security and Cooperation in Europe, have been of central importance in dealing with the crisis in the Balkans and neighbouring areas. . . .

64. . . . [R]egional arrangements or agencies in many cases possess a potential that should be utilized in serving the functions covered in this report: preventive diplomacy, peacekeeping, peacemaking and post-conflict peacebuilding. Under the Charter, the Security Council has and will continue to have primary responsibility for maintaining international peace and security, but regional action as a matter of decentralization, delegation and cooperation with United Nations efforts could not only lighten the burden of the Council but also contribute to a deeper sense of participation, consensus and democratization in international affairs. . . .

VIII. Safety of Personnel

66. When United Nations personnel are deployed in conditions of strife, whether for preventive diplomacy, peacemaking, peacekeeping, peacebuilding or humanitarian purposes, the need arises to ensure their safety. There has been an unconscionable increase in the number of fatalities. . . . As the variety and scale of threat widens, innovative measures will be required to deal with the dangers facing United Nations personnel. . . .

IX. Financing

69. A chasm has developed between the tasks entrusted to this Organization and the financial means provided to it. . . .

74. Member States wish the Organization to be managed with the utmost efficiency and care. I am in full accord. I have taken important steps to streamline the Secretariat in order to avoid duplication and overlap while increasing its productivity. Additional changes and improvements will take place. . . . The question of assuring financial security to the Organization over the long term is of such importance and complexity that public awareness and support must be heightened.

X. An Agenda for Peace

. . .

80. Power brings special responsibilities, and temptations. The powerful must resist the dual but opposite calls of unilateralism and isolationism if the United Nations is to succeed. For just as unilateralism at the global or regional level can shake the confidence of others, so can isolationism, whether it results from political choice or constitutional circumstance, enfeeble the global un-

dertaking. Peace at home and the urgency of rebuilding and strengthening our individual societies necessitates peace abroad and cooperation among nations. The endeavours of the United Nations will require the fullest engagement of all of its Members, large and small, if the present renewed opportunity is to be seized.

81. Democracy within nations requires respect for human rights and fundamental freedoms, as set forth in the Charter. It requires as well a deeper understanding and respect for the rights of minorities and respect for the needs of the more vulnerable groups of society, especially women and children. . . . [S]trong domestic institutions of participation are essential. Promoting such institutions means promoting the empowerment of the unorganized, the poor, the marginalized. To this end, the focus of the United Nations should be on the "field," the locations where economic, social and political decisions take effect.

Many of Boutros-Ghali's recommendation were ultimately adopted. The Secretary-General's role in promoting the peace, as foreshadowed by Article 99 of the Charter, grew. A preventive deployment of UN peacekeepers occurred in Macedonia in the mid-1990s. His ideas on "peace enforcement units" have found expression in often much more robust peacekeeping mandates and forces. Boutros-Ghali's openness to a greater role for regional organizations (on which he was an academic authority) demonstrated foresight. His stressing of the need for partnership between the United Nations and non-governmental actors was also predictive. His concern over the safety of UN and other international personnel was also validated by many subsequent casualties, of which perhaps the most spectacular were the bombings of UN and International Committee of the Red Cross headquarters in Baghdad in 2003, taking many lives. Indeed, the inviolability of humanitarian staff came increasingly under attack after the Cold War ended. UN focus on the "field," where economic development and conflicts take place has increased (although the very large UN bureaucracies in such comfortable venues as New York, Geneva, and Vienna elicit a degree of cynicism throughout the world).

Other recommendations, for reasons relating to national interest, saw little or no action. For example, in the face of strong opposition from the P-5, it proved impossible for the General Assembly to agree to the Secretary-General's recommendation that he be granted authority to seek advisory opinions from the ICJ. The provisions of Article 42 of the Charter have still not been formally invoked, whereas "coalitions of the willing" authorized by the Security Council but acting under their own command and control procedures have proliferated. His recommendation for "clear" peacekeeping mandates have often been ignored by the Security Council—sometimes with dreadful consequences, as in the case of the "safe areas" in Bosnia and Herzegovina, of which Srebrenica was one. The Department of Peacekeeping Operations at

UN headquarters has been strengthened considerably, but it remains seriously under-resourced relative to national armed forces headquarters often overseeing much smaller contingents.[20]

QUESTIONS ....

4. Did the end of the Cold War present an opportunity to realize the original intent of the UN Charter, or to build on the creative interpretation of its provisions over the subsequent decades?

5. Have recent developments relating to mandates for peace operations and in peacekeeping practice fundamentally changed this instrument for implementation of the Security Council's decisions? How do you assess these developments, particularly their legal implications?

6. Article 43 of the UN Charter provides for agreements by which member states could make armed forces available to the UN Security Council. No such agreements have been concluded. If they were, how might this change the political dynamic concerning the use of force under the Council's auspices?

7. An alternative proposal sometimes floated is to have a volunteer force or, perhaps, a private military force put at the disposal of the Council. Is this realistic? Is it desirable?

8.4 Failing States: Sierra Leone

The complexity of the new wave of peacekeeping operations launched after the end of the Cold War, most often in situations of essentially internal conflict (in which neighboring countries were nevertheless often engaged) was most evident in Africa, where large missions of this nature were deployed in Sierra Leone, Liberia, Ivory Coast, and the Congo early in the twenty-first century. The range of tasks envisaged for these missions involved major civilian as well as military components. They included humanitarian, de-mining, developmental, human rights, and state institution-building objectives. These forces were also increasingly expected to protect civilians from combatants, in ways often very broadly sketched but poorly defined in the mandates granted by the Security Council (see operative paragraph 14 in the resolution below, the only one adopted explicitly under Chapter VII of the Charter, creating an ambitious UN Mission in Sierra Leone in 1999, succeeding a smaller UN observer force). Resolution 1270 reflects many of the tasks routinely assigned to UN peace operations after 1990.

---

[20] For up to date figures on UN peacekeeping deployments, see http://www.un .org/Depts/dpko/dpko/bnote.htm.

SECURITY COUNCIL RESOLUTION 1270 (1999)

The Security Council, . . .

Affirming the commitment of all States to respect the sovereignty, political independence and territorial integrity of Sierra Leone, . . .

Determining that the situation in Sierra Leone continues to constitute a threat to international peace and security in the region,

1. *Welcomes* the important steps taken by the Government of Sierra Leone, the leadership of the Revolutionary United Front of Sierra Leone (RUF), the Military Observer Group (ECOMOG) of the Economic Community of West African States (ECOWAS) and the United Nations Observer Mission in Sierra Leone (UNOMSIL) towards implementation of the Peace Agreement (S/1999/777) since its signing in Lomé on 7 July 1999, and recognizes the important role of the Joint Implementation Committee established by the Peace Agreement under the chairmanship of the President of Togo;

2. *Calls upon* the parties to fulfil all their commitments under the Peace Agreement to facilitate the restoration of peace, stability, national reconciliation and development in Sierra Leone;

3. *Takes note* of the preparations made for the disarmament, demobilization and reintegration of ex-combatants, including child soldiers, by the Government of Sierra Leone through the National Committee for Disarmament, Demobilization and Reintegration, and urges all concerned to make every effort to ensure that all designated centres begin to function as soon as possible;

4. *Calls upon* the RUF, the Civil Defence Forces, former Sierra Leone Armed Forces/Armed Forces Revolutionary Council (AFRC) and all other armed groups in Sierra Leone to begin immediately to disband and give up their arms in accordance with the provisions of the Peace Agreement, and to participate fully in the disarmament, demobilization and reintegration programme;

5. *Welcomes* the return to Freetown of the leaders of the RUF and AFRC, and calls upon them to engage fully and responsibly in the implementation of the Peace Agreement and to direct the participation of all rebel groups in the disarmament and demobilization process without delay;

6. *Deplores* the recent taking of hostages, including UNOMSIL and ECOMOG personnel, by rebel groups and calls upon those responsible to put an end to such practices immediately and to address their concerns about the terms of the Peace Agreement peacefully through dialogue with the parties concerned;

7. *Reiterates* its appreciation for the indispensable role which ECOMOG forces continue to play in the maintenance of security and stability in and the protection of the people of Sierra Leone, and approves the new mandate for ECOMOG (S/1999/1073, annex) adopted by ECOWAS on 25 August 1999;

8. *Decides* to establish the United Nations Mission in Sierra Leone (UN-AMSIL) with immediate effect for an initial period of six months and with the following mandate:

(a) To cooperate with the Government of Sierra Leone and the other parties to the Peace Agreement in the implementation of the Agreement;

(b) To assist the Government of Sierra Leone in the implementation of the disarmament, demobilization and reintegration plan;

(c) To that end, to establish a presence at key locations throughout the territory of Sierra Leone, including at disarmament/reception centres and de- and demobilization centres;

(d) To ensure the security and freedom of movement of United Nations personnel;

(e) To monitor adherence to the ceasefire in accordance with the ceasefire agreement of 18 May 1999 (S/1999/585, annex) through the structures provided for therein;

(f) To encourage the parties to create confidence-building mechanisms and support their functioning;

(g) To facilitate the delivery of humanitarian assistance;

(h) To support the operations of United Nations civilian officials, including the Special Representative of the Secretary-General and his staff, human rights officers and civil affairs officers;

(i) To provide support, as requested, to the elections, which are to be held in accordance with the present constitution of Sierra Leone;

9. *Decides also* that the military component of UNAMSIL shall comprise a maximum of 6,000 military personnel, including 260 military observers, subject to periodic review in the light of conditions on the ground and the progress made in the peace process, in particular in the disarmament, demobilization and reintegration programme, and takes note of paragraph 43 of the report of the Secretary-General of 23 September 1999;

10. *Decides further* that UNAMSIL will take over the substantive civilian and military components and functions of UNOMSIL as well as its assets, and to that end decides that the mandate of UNOMSIL shall terminate immediately on the establishment of UNAMSIL;

11. *Commends* the readiness of ECOMOG to continue to provide security for the areas where it is currently located, in particular around Freetown and Lungi, to provide protection for the Government of Sierra Leone, to conduct other operations in accordance with their mandate to ensure the implementation of the Peace Agreement, and to initiate and proceed with disarmament and demobilization in conjunction and full coordination with UNAMSIL;

12. *Stresses* the need for close cooperation and coordination between ECOMOG and UNAMSIL in carrying out their respective tasks, and welcomes the intended establishment of joint operations centres at headquarters and, if necessary, also at subordinate levels in the field;

13. *Reiterates* the importance of the safety, security and freedom of movement of United Nations and associated personnel, notes that the Government of Sierra Leone and the RUF have agreed in the Peace Agreement to provide guarantees in this regard, and calls upon all parties in Sierra Leone to respect fully the status of United Nations and associated personnel;

14. *Acting* under Chapter VII of the Charter of the United Nations, *decides* that in the discharge of its mandate UNAMSIL may take the necessary action to ensure the security and freedom of movement of its personnel and, within its capabilities and areas of deployment, to afford protection to civilians under imminent threat of physical violence, taking into account the responsibilities of the Government of Sierra Leone and ECOMOG;

15. *Underlines* the importance of including in UNAMSIL personnel with appropriate training in international humanitarian, human rights and refugee law, including child and gender-related provisions, negotiation and communication skills, cultural awareness and civilian-military coordination;

16. *Requests* the Government of Sierra Leone to conclude a status-of-forces agreement with the Secretary-General within 30 days of the adoption of this resolution, and recalls that pending the conclusion of such an agreement the model status-of-forces agreement dated 9 October 1990 (A/45/594) should apply provisionally;

17. *Stresses* the urgent need to promote peace and national reconciliation and to foster accountability and respect for human rights in Sierra Leone, underlines in this context the key role of the Truth and Reconciliation Commission, the Human Rights Commission and the Commission for the Consolidation of Peace established under the Peace Agreement, and urges the Government of Sierra Leone to ensure the prompt establishment and effective functioning of these bodies with the full participation of all parties and drawing on the relevant experience and support of Member States, specialized bodies, other multilateral organizations and civil society;

18. *Emphasizes* that the plight of children is among the most pressing challenges facing Sierra Leone, welcomes the continued commitment of the Government of Sierra Leone to work with the United Nations Children's Fund, the Office of the Special Representative of the Secretary-General for Children and Armed Conflict and other international agencies to give particular attention to the long-term rehabilitation of child combatants in Sierra Leone, and reiterates its encouragement of those involved to address the special needs of all children affected by the conflict;

19. *Urges* all parties concerned to ensure that refugees and internally displaced persons are protected and are enabled to return voluntarily and in safety to their homes, and encourages States and international organizations to provide urgent assistance to that end;

20. *Stresses* the urgent need for substantial additional resources to finance the disarmament, demobilization and reintegration process, and calls upon all States, international and other organizations to contribute generously to the multidonor trust fund established by the International Bank for Reconstruction and Development for this purpose;

21. *Stresses* also the continued need for urgent and substantial humanitarian assistance to the people of Sierra Leone, as well as for sustained and generous assistance for the longer term tasks of peacebuilding, reconstruction, economic and social recovery and development in Sierra Leone, and

urges all States and international and other organizations to provide such assistance as a priority;

22. *Calls upon* all parties to ensure safe and unhindered access of humanitarian assistance to those in need in Sierra Leone, to guarantee the safety and security of humanitarian personnel and to respect strictly the relevant provisions of international humanitarian and human rights law;

23. *Urges* the Government of Sierra Leone to expedite the formation of professional and accountable national police and armed forces, including through their restructuring and training, without which it will not be possible to achieve long-term stability, national reconciliation and the reconstruction of the country, and underlines the importance of support and assistance from the international community in this regard;

24. *Welcomes* the continued work by the United Nations on the development of the Strategic Framework for Sierra Leone aimed at enhancing effective collaboration and coordination within the United Nations system and between the United Nations and its national and international partners in Sierra Leone;

25. *Notes* the intention of the Secretary-General to keep the situation in Sierra Leone under close review and to revert to the Council with additional proposals if required;

26. *Requests* the Secretary-General to report to the Council every 45 days to provide updates on the status of the peace process, on security conditions on the ground and on the continued level of deployment of ECOMOG personnel, so that troop levels and the tasks to be performed can be evaluated as outlined in paragraphs 49 and 50 of the report of the Secretary-General of 23 September 1999;

27. *Decides* to remain actively seized of the matter.

This Mission encountered significant difficulties in its early months, with large numbers of its peacekeepers taken hostage by rebels. Force numbers needed to be more than doubled. Later, it took intervention by a large British military task force to stabilize the volatile security situation, culminating in a clash between British paratroopers operating outside the UN mandate and a local militia, the West Side Boys, on 10 September 2000 that decimated this gang and intimidated others. UNAMSIL completed its mission with a considerable degree of success on 31 December 2005, yielding to a much smaller UN Integrated Office in Sierra Leone (UNIOSIL), mandated to support the Government's efforts to ensure peace and security, consolidate State authority, promote good governance and human rights, address cross-border issues, and advance national recovery as well as economic and social development. At that time, the Special Court for Sierra Leone, set up jointly by the Government of Sierra Leone and the United Nations to try those bearing greatest responsibility for the most serious crimes committed during the Sierra Leone's successive conflicts after 30 November 1996, was still hearing cases.

QUESTIONS ....

8. Many UN peace operations now blend military and civilian responsibilities, encompassing a great many different spheres of potential action. How would you prioritize the various tasks mandated to UNAMSIL in resolution 1270 (1999)? What rationale guides your answer?
9. With an eye to the next section, which discusses reform, what are the principal challenges for UN peace operations you see arising from evolving Security Council mandates and peace operation practices?

8.5 Reform

Through the 1990s expectations of what the United Nations might achieve in the field of peace operations outstripped what it could actually deliver. In the wake of serious setbacks in Bosnia and Herzegovina and Somalia, and paralysis in Rwanda, the number of peacekeepers deployed began to drop from the mid-1990s. These developments and the unvarnished findings of the Rwanda and Srebrenica inquiries (discussed in chapter 16) led to an in-house study on the principles and operational imperatives that should underpin UN peace operations in the future. It was led by UN negotiator Lakhdar Brahimi, who had himself overseen several such UN operations, notably in Haiti. It came to be known as the Brahimi Report.

....

REPORT OF THE PANEL ON UN PEACE OPERATIONS (BRAHIMI REPORT), 21 AUGUST 2000[21]

Summary of Recommendations

1. Preventive Action

(a) The Panel endorses the . . . appeal to "all who are engaged in conflict prevention and development—the United Nations, the Bretton Woods institutions, Governments and civil society organizations—[to] address these challenges in a more integrated fashion";

(b) The Panel supports the Secretary-General's more frequent use of fact-finding missions to areas of tension, and stresses Member States' obligations, under Article 2(5) of the Charter, to give "every assistance" to such activities of the United Nations.

---

[21] UN Doc. A/55/305-S/2000/809 (2000).

2. Peacebuilding strategy

(a) A small percentage of a mission's first-year budget should be made available . . . to fund quick impact projects in its area of operations, with the advice of the United Nations country team's resident coordinator;

(b) The Panel recommends a doctrinal shift in the use of civilian police, other rule of law elements and human rights experts in complex peace operations to reflect an increased focus on strengthening rule of law institutions and improving respect for human rights in post-conflict environments;

(c) The Panel recommends that the legislative bodies consider bringing demobilization and reintegration programmes into the assessed budgets of complex peace operations . . . ;

(d) The Panel recommends . . . a plan to strengthen the permanent capacity of the United Nations to develop peacebuilding strategies and to implement programmes in support of those strategies.

3. Peacekeeping Doctrine and Strategy

Once deployed, United Nations peacekeepers must be able to carry out their mandates professionally and successfully and be capable of defending themselves, other mission components and the mission's mandate, with robust rules of engagement, against those who renege on their commitments to a peace accord or otherwise seek to undermine it by violence.

4. Clear, Credible and Achievable Mandates

(a) The Panel recommends that, before the Security Council agrees to implement a ceasefire or peace agreement with a United Nations-led peacekeeping operation, the Council assure itself that the agreement meets threshold conditions, such as consistency with international human rights standards and practicability of specified tasks and timelines;

(b) The Security Council should leave in draft form resolutions authorizing missions with sizeable troop levels until such time as the Secretary-General has firm commitments of troops and other critical mission support elements, including peacebuilding elements, from Member States; . . .

(d) The Secretariat must tell the Security Council what it needs to know, not what it wants to hear, when formulating or changing mission mandates, and countries that have committed military units to an operation should have access to Secretariat briefings to the Council on matters affecting the safety and security of their personnel, especially those meetings with implications for a mission's use of force.

5. Information and Strategic Analysis

The Secretary-General should establish an entity . . . which would support the information and analysis needs of all [relevant senior Secretariat officials].

6. Transitional Civil Administration

The Panel recommends that the Secretary-General . . . evaluate the feasibility and utility of developing an interim criminal code, including any regional adaptations potentially required, for use by such operations pending the re-establishment of local rule of law and local law enforcement capacity. . . .

8. Mission Leadership

(a) The Secretary-General should systematize the method of selecting mission leaders, beginning with the compilation of a comprehensive list of potential representatives or special representatives of the Secretary-General, force commanders, civilian police commissioners, and their deputies and other heads of substantive and administrative components, within a fair geographic and gender distribution and with input from Member States;

(b) The entire leadership of a mission should be selected and assembled at Headquarters as early as possible in order to enable their participation in key aspects of the mission planning process, for briefings on the situation in the mission area and to meet and work with their colleagues in mission leadership;

(c) The Secretariat should routinely provide the mission leadership with strategic guidance and plans for anticipating and overcoming challenges to mandate implementation, and whenever possible should formulate such guidance and plans together with the mission leadership.

9. Military Personnel

(a) Member States should be encouraged, where appropriate, to enter into partnerships with one another, within the context of the United Nations Standby Arrangements System (UNSAS), to form several coherent brigade-size forces, with necessary enabling forces, ready for effective deployment within 30 days of the adoption of a Security Council resolution establishing a traditional peacekeeping operation and within 90 days for complex peace-keeping operations;

(b) The Secretary-General should be given the authority to formally can-vass Member States participating in UNSAS regarding their willingness to contribute troops to a potential operation, once it appeared likely that a ceasefire accord or agreement envisaging an implementing role for the United Nations, might be reached; . . .

10. Civilian Police Personnel

(a) Member States are encouraged to each establish a national pool of civilian police officers that would be ready for deployment to United Nations peace operations . . .;

(b) Member States are encouraged to enter into regional training partner-ships for civilian police . . .; . . .

(d) The Panel recommends that a revolving on-call list of about 100 police officers and related experts be created in UNSAS to be available on seven days' notice with teams trained to create the civilian police component of a new peacekeeping operation, train incoming personnel and give the component greater coherence at an early date; .

(e) The Panel recommends that parallel arrangements to recommendations (a), (b) and (c) above be established for judicial, penal, human rights and other relevant specialists, who with specialist civilian police will make up collegial "rule of law" teams.

11. Civilian Specialists

(a) The Secretariat should establish a central Internet/Intranet-based roster of pre-selected civilian candidates available to deploy to peace operations on short notice. . . .

(c) Conditions of service for externally recruited civilian staff should be revised to enable the United Nations to attract the most highly qualified candidates, and to then offer those who have served with distinction greater career prospects;

(d) DPKO should formulate a comprehensive staffing strategy for peace operations, outlining, among other issues, the use of United Nations Volunteers, [and] standby arrangements for the provision of civilian personnel on 72 hours' notice to facilitate mission start-up . . .

12. Rapidly Deployable Capacity for Public Information

Additional resources should be devoted in mission budgets to public information and the associated personnel and information technology required to get an operation's message out and build effective internal communications links.

13. Logistics support and expenditure management:

(a) The Secretariat should prepare a global logistics support strategy to enable rapid and effective mission deployment . . . ;

(b) The General Assembly should authorize and approve a one-time expenditure to maintain at least five mission start-up kits . . . , which should include rapidly deployable communications equipment. . . . ;

(c) The Secretary-General should be given authority to draw up to US$50 million from the Peacekeeping Reserve Fund, once it became clear that an operation was likely to be established . . . ;

(d) The Secretariat should undertake a review of the entire procurement policies and procedures . . . , to facilitate in particular the rapid and full deployment of an operation within the proposed timelines;

(e) The Secretariat should conduct a review of the policies and procedures governing the management of financial resources in the field missions with a view to . . . much greater flexibility in the management of their budgets; . . .

14. Funding Headquarters Support for Peacekeeping Operations

(a) The Panel recommends a substantial increase in resources for Headquarters support of peacekeeping operations . . . ;

(b) Headquarters support for peacekeeping should be treated as a core activity of the United Nations, and as such the majority of its resource requirements for this purpose should be funded through . . . the regular . . . budget of the Organization; . . .

15. Integrated Mission Planning and Support

Integrated Mission Task Forces (IMTFs), with members seconded from throughout the United Nations system, as necessary, should be the standard vehicle for mission-specific planning and support. . . .

16. Other Structural Adjustments in DPKO

(a) The current Military and Civilian Police Division should be restructured, moving the Civilian Police Unit out of the military reporting chain. . . . ; . . .

(c) A new unit should be established in DPKO and staffed with the relevant expertise for the provision of advice on criminal law issues that are critical to the effective use of civilian police in the United Nations peace operations; . . .

(e) The Lessons Learned Unit should be substantially enhanced and moved into a revamped DPKO Office of Operations; . . .

18. Peacebuilding Support in the Department of Political Affairs

(a) The Panel supports the Secretariat's effort to create a pilot Peace-building Unit . . .

(b) The Panel recommends that regular budget resources for Electoral Assistance Division programmatic expenses be substantially increased to meet the rapidly growing demand for its services, in lieu of voluntary contributions; . . .

19. Peace Operations Support in the Office of the United Nations High Commissioner for Human Rights

The Panel recommends substantially enhancing the field mission planning and preparation capacity of the Office of the United Nations High Commissioner for Human Rights, with funding partly from the regular budget and partly from peace operations mission budgets.

20. Peace Operations and the Information Age

(a) Headquarters peace and security departments need a responsibility centre to devise and oversee the implementation of common information technology strategy and training for peace operations . . .

QUESTIONS ....

10. From the texts provided above and from earlier readings, what do you perceive as the greatest innovations introduced into peace operations over the years?

11. How has the involvement of the United Nations in a growing number of internal conflicts affected peace operations?

12. What are the legal responsibilities of the United Nations and of individuals and groups acting under its authority arising from their service in peace operations? What legal risks do peace operations create for these international actors?

Further Reading

Bowett, Derek W. *United Nations Forces: A Legal Study of United Nations Practice.* London: Stevens, 1964.

Brownlie, Ian. *International Law and the Use of Force by States.* Oxford: Clarendon Press, 1963.

Center on International Cooperation. *Annual Review of Global Peace Operations.* Boulder, CO: Lynne Rienner, 2006.

Chesterman, Simon, *Just War or Just Peace? Humanitarian Intervention and International Law.* Oxford: Oxford University Press, 2001, chapter 4.

Cockayne, James, and David M. Malone. "The Ralph Bunche Centennial: Peace Operations Then and Now." *Global Governance,* vol. 11 (2005), p. 331.

Doyle, Michael W., and Nicholas Sambanis. *Making War & Building Peace: United Nations Peace Operations.* Princeton, NJ: Princeton University Press, 2006, particularly pp. 1–26 and 334–352.

Durch, William J., ed. *Twenty-First-Century Peace Operations.* Washington, DC: USIP Press, 2006.

Findlay, Trevor. *The Use of Force in UN Peace Operations.* Oxford: SIPRI & Oxford University Press, 2002.

Franck, Thomas M. *Recourse to Force: State Action Against Threats and Armed Attacks.* Cambridge: Cambridge University Press, 2002.

Goulding, Marrack. *Peacemonger.* London: John Murray, 2002.

Gray, Christine. *International Law and the Use of Force.* 2nd edn. Oxford: Oxford University Press, 2004.

Malone, David M., ed. *The UN Security Council: From the Cold War to the 21st Century.* Boulder, CO: Lynne Rienner, 2004.

Smith, Rupert. *The Utility of Force: The Art of War in the Modern World.* London: Allen Lane, 2005.

Stedman, Stephen John, Donald Rothchild, and Elizabeth M. Cousens, eds. *Ending Civil Wars: The Implementation of Peace Agreements.* Boulder, CO: Lynne Rienner, 2002.

Urquhart, Brian. *Hammarskjöld.* New York: Knopf, 1972.

chapter nine
....

Peacebuilding

In early 1995, chastened by the failed operation in Somalia, the failing operation in Bosnia and Herzegovina and inaction in the face of genocide in Rwanda, UN Secretary-General Boutros Boutros-Ghali issued a conservative supplement to his more optimistic 1992 *Agenda for Peace*. The *Supplement* noted that a new breed of intra-state conflicts presented the United Nations with challenges not encountered since the Congo operation of the early 1960s. A feature of these conflicts was the collapse of state institutions, especially the police and judiciary, meaning that international intervention had to extend beyond military and humanitarian tasks to include the "promotion of national reconciliation and the re-establishment of effective government." Nevertheless, he expressed caution against the United Nations assuming responsibility for law and order, or attempting to impose state institutions on unwilling combatants. General Sir Michael Rose, then commander of the UN Protection Force in Bosnia (UNPROFOR), termed this form of mission creep crossing "the Mogadishu line."[1]

Despite such cautious words, by the end of 1995 the United Nations had assumed responsibility for policing in Bosnia under the Dayton Peace Agreement. The following January, a mission was established with temporary civil governance functions over the last Serb-held region of Croatia in Eastern Slavonia. In June 1999, the Security Council authorized an "interim" administration in Kosovo to govern part of what remained technically Serbian territory for an indefinite period; four months later a transitional administration was created with effective sovereignty over East Timor until independence. These expanding mandates continued a trend that began with the operations in Namibia in 1989 and Cambodia in 1993, where the United Nations exercised varying degrees of civilian authority in addition to supervising elections.

---

[1] Michael Rose, "The Bosnia Experience," in Ramesh Thakur (ed.), *Past Imperfect, Future Uncertain: The United Nations at Fifty* (New York: St. Martin's Press, 1998).

Efforts to construct or reconstruct institutions of the state are hardly new: state-building and nation-building were important parts of dismantling colonial structures in the 1960s, notably the Congo operation from 1960–1964.[2] In addition, efforts to support weak governance have long been a feature of UN post-conflict reconstruction, as seen in the missions in Namibia (1989–1990) and Mozambique (1992–1994). What was novel about the missions undertaken in Kosovo and East Timor was the amount of executive authority assumed by the United Nations itself, placing it in the effective position of a government.

Such operations are sometimes referred to as "state-building" or "nation-building." "State-building" refers to extended international involvement (primarily, though not exclusively, through the United Nations) that goes beyond traditional peacekeeping and peacebuilding mandates, and is directed at constructing or reconstructing institutions of governance capable of providing citizens with physical and economic security. This includes quasi-governmental activities such as electoral assistance, human rights and rule of law technical assistance, security sector reform, and certain forms of development assistance. Within this class of operations, *transitional* or *international administration* denotes the less common type of operation in which these ends have been pursued by assuming some or all of the powers of the state on a temporary basis.

"Nation-building," sometimes used in this context, is a broad, vague, and often pejorative term. In the course of the 2000 US presidential campaign, Governor George W. Bush used it as a dismissive reference to the application of US military resources beyond traditional mandates. The term was also used to conflate the circumstances in which US forces found themselves in conflict with the local population—most notably in Somalia—with complex and time-consuming operations such as those underway in Bosnia, Kosovo, and East Timor. Although it continues to be used in this context, nation-building also has a more specific meaning in the post-colonial context, in which new leaders attempted to rally a population within sometimes arbitrary territorial frontiers. The focus here is on the *state* (that is, the highest institutions of governance in a territory) rather than the *nation* (a people who share common customs, origins, history, and frequently language) as such.

Within the United Nations, "peacebuilding" is generally preferred. This has been taken to mean, among other things, "reforming or strengthening governmental institutions"[3] or "the creation of structures for the in-

---

[2] See the discussion of the Congo operation in chapter 6. On decolonization, see further the discussion of self-determination in chapter 12 in this volume.

[3] An Agenda for Peace: Preventive Diplomacy, Peacemaking, and Peace-keeping (Report of the Secretary-General pursuant to the statement adopted by the Summit Meeting of the Security Council on 31 January 1992), UN Doc. A/47/277-S/24111 (17 June 1992), para. 55.

stitutionalization of peace."[4] It tends, however, to embrace a far broader range of activities—at times being used to describe virtually all forms of international assistance to countries that have experienced or are at risk of armed conflict.[5]

This chapter first examines the gradual acceptance that "peacebuilding" was a task appropriate for the United Nations—and the recognition of limitations in its capacity to fulfill such tasks. Sections 2 and 3 consider the most elaborate operations undertaken by the United Nations in this area: Kosovo and East Timor. Section 4 turns to the efforts to develop an institutional capacity to respond to future such crises by creating a Peacebuilding Commission.

9.1 Policies

At the first meeting held by the Security Council at the level of heads of state and government on 31 January 1992, the Council invited the Secretary-General to prepare an "analysis and recommendations on ways of strengthening and making more efficient . . . the capacity of the United Nations for preventive diplomacy, for peacemaking and for peacekeeping."[6] In response, Boutros-Ghali offered *An Agenda for Peace*, which called for a more proactive, assertive approach to peacekeeping, declaring famously that "the time of absolute and exclusive sovereignty has passed."[7]

---

[4] Supplement to An Agenda for Peace: Position Paper of the Secretary-General on the Occasion of the Fiftieth Anniversary of the United Nations, UN Doc. A/50/60-S/1995/1 (3 January 1995), para. 49. From a UN development perspective, peacebuilding aims "to build and enable durable peace and sustainable development in post-conflict situations." See, eg, Role of UNDP in Crisis and Post-Conflict Situations (Policy Paper Distributed to the Executive Board of the United Nations Development Programme and of the United Nations Population Fund), DP/2001/4 (UNDP, New York, 27 November 2000), available at http://www.undp.org, para. 51. The Development Assistance Committee (DAC) of the OECD maintains that peacebuilding and reconciliation focuses "on long-term support to, and establishment of, viable political and socio-economic and cultural institutions capable of addressing the root causes of conflicts, as well as other initiatives aimed at creating the necessary conditions for sustained peace and stability:" OECD, Helping Prevent Violent Conflict, Development Assistance Committee Guidelines (OECD, Paris, 2001), available at http://www.oecd.org, 86.
[5] Elizabeth M. Cousens, "Introduction," in Elizabeth M. Cousens and Chetan Kumar (eds.), *Peacebuilding as Politics* (Boulder, CO: Lynne Rienner, 2001), pp. 5–10.
[6] UN Doc. S/23500 (1992).
[7] UN Doc. A/47/277-S/24111 (1992), para. 17.

AN AGENDA FOR PEACE: PREVENTIVE DIPLOMACY, PEACEMAKING AND PEACEKEEPING (REPORT OF THE SECRETARY-GENERAL), 17 JUNE 1992[8]

49. The demands on the United Nations for peacekeeping, and peacebuilding, operations will in the coming years continue to challenge the capacity, the political and financial will and the creativity of the Secretariat and Member States. Like the Security Council, I welcome the increase and broadening of the tasks of peacekeeping operations. . . .

55. Peacemaking and peacekeeping operations, to be truly successful, must come to include comprehensive efforts to identify and support structures which will tend to consolidate peace and advance a sense of confidence and well-being among people. Through agreements ending civil strife, these may include disarming the previously warring parties and the restoration of order, the custody and possible destruction of weapons, repatriating refugees, advisory and training support for security personnel, monitoring elections, advancing efforts to protect human rights, reforming or strengthening governmental institutions and promoting formal and informal processes of political participation.

56. In the aftermath of international war, post-conflict peacebuilding may take the form of concrete cooperative projects which link two or more countries in a mutually beneficial undertaking that can not only contribute to economic and social development but also enhance the confidence that is so fundamental to peace. I have in mind, for example, projects that bring States together to develop agriculture, improve transportation or utilize resources such as water or electricity that they need to share, or joint programmes through which barriers between nations are brought down by means of freer travel, cultural exchanges and mutually beneficial youth and educational projects. Reducing hostile perceptions through educational exchanges and curriculum reform may be essential to forestall a re-emergence of cultural and national tensions which could spark renewed hostilities.

57. In surveying the range of efforts for peace, the concept of peacebuilding as the construction of a new environment should be viewed as the counterpart of preventive diplomacy, which seeks to avoid the breakdown of peaceful conditions. When conflict breaks out, mutually reinforcing efforts at peacemaking and peacekeeping come into play. Once these have achieved their objectives, only sustained, cooperative work to deal with underlying economic, social, cultural and humanitarian problems can place an achieved peace on a durable foundation. Preventive diplomacy is to avoid a crisis; post-conflict peacebuilding is to prevent a recurrence.

---

[8] UN Doc. A/47/277-S/24111 (1992).

58. Increasingly it is evident that peacebuilding after civil or international strife must address the serious problem of land mines, many tens of millions of which remain scattered in present or former combat zones. De-mining should be emphasized in the terms of reference of peacekeeping operations and is crucially important in the restoration of activity when peacebuilding is under way: agriculture cannot be revived without de-mining and the restoration of transport may require the laying of hard surface roads to prevent re-mining. In such instances, the link becomes evident between peacekeeping and peacebuilding. Just as demilitarized zones may serve the cause of preventive diplomacy and preventive deployment to avoid conflict, so may demilitarization assist in keeping the peace or in post-conflict peacebuilding, as a measure for heightening the sense of security and encouraging the parties to turn their energies to the work of peaceful restoration of their societies.

59. There is a new requirement for technical assistance which the United Nations has an obligation to develop and provide when requested: support for the transformation of deficient national structures and capabilities, and for the strengthening of new democratic institutions. The authority of the United Nations system to act in this field would rest on the consensus that social peace is as important as strategic or political peace. There is an obvious connection between democratic practices—such as the rule of law and transparency in decision-making—and the achievement of true peace and security in any new and stable political order. These elements of good governance need to be promoted at all levels of international and national political communities.

Boutros-Ghali was seen by some as having overreached in his *Agenda for Peace*. In 1995 he offered a significantly less ambitious framework for developing peace operations.

SUPPLEMENT TO AN AGENDA FOR PEACE: POSITION PAPER OF THE SECRETARY-GENERAL ON THE OCCASION OF THE FIFTIETH ANNIVERSARY OF THE UNITED NATIONS, 3 JANUARY 1995[9]

12. The new breed of intra-state conflicts have certain characteristics that present United Nations peacekeepers with challenges not encountered since the Congo operation of the early 1960s. They are usually fought not only by

---

[9]UN Doc. A/50/60-S/1995/1 (1995).

regular armies but also by militias and armed civilians with little discipline and with ill-defined chains of command. They are often guerrilla wars without clear front lines. Civilians are the main victims and often the main targets. Humanitarian emergencies are commonplace and the combatant authorities, in so far as they can be called authorities, lack the capacity to cope with them. The number of refugees registered with the Office of the United Nations High Commissioner for Refugees (UNHCR) has increased from 13 million at the end of 1987 to 26 million at the end of 1994. The number of internally displaced persons has increased even more dramatically.

13. Another feature of such conflicts is the collapse of state institutions, especially the police and judiciary, with resulting paralysis of governance, a breakdown of law and order, and general banditry and chaos. Not only are the functions of government suspended, its assets are destroyed or looted and experienced officials are killed or flee the country. This is rarely the case in inter-state wars. It means that international intervention must extend beyond military and humanitarian tasks and must include the promotion of national reconciliation and the re-establishment of effective government.

14. The latter are tasks that demand time and sensitivity. The United Nations is, for good reasons, reluctant to assume responsibility for maintaining law and order, nor can it impose a new political structure or new state institutions. It can only help the hostile factions to help themselves and begin to live together again. All too often it turns out that they do not yet want to be helped or to resolve their problems quickly. . . .

47. The validity of the concept of post-conflict peacebuilding has received wide recognition. The measures it can use—and they are many—can also support preventive diplomacy. Demilitarization, the control of small arms, institutional reform, improved police and judicial systems, the monitoring of human rights, electoral reform and social and economic development can be as valuable in preventing conflict as in healing the wounds after conflict has occurred.

48. The implementation of post-conflict peacebuilding can, however, be complicated. It requires integrated action and delicate dealings between the United Nations and the parties to the conflict in respect of which peacebuilding activities are to be undertaken.

49. Two kinds of situation deserve examination. The first is when a comprehensive settlement has been negotiated, with long-term political, economic and social provisions to address the root causes of the conflict, and verification of its implementation is entrusted to a multifunctional peacekeeping operation. The second is when peacebuilding, whether preventive or post-conflict, is undertaken in relation to a potential or past conflict without any peacekeeping operation being deployed. In both situations the essential goal is the creation of structures for the institutionalization of peace.

50. The first situation is the easier to manage. The United Nations already has an entree. The parties have accepted its peacemaking and peacekeeping role. The peacekeeping operation will already be mandated to launch various peacebuilding activities, especially the all-important reintegration of former combatants into productive civilian activities.

51. Even so, political elements who dislike the peace agreement concluded by their Government (and the United Nations verification provided for therein) may resent the United Nations presence and be waiting impatiently for it to leave. Their concerns may find an echo among Member States who fear that the United Nations is in danger of slipping into a role prejudicial to the sovereignty of the country in question and among others who may be uneasy about the resource implications of a long-term peacebuilding commitment.

52. The timing and modalities of the departure of the peacekeeping operation and the transfer of its peacebuilding functions to others must therefore be carefully managed in the fullest possible consultation with the Government having invested much effort in helping to end the conflict, can legitimately express views and offer advice about actions the Government could take to reduce the danger of losing what has been achieved. The timing and modalities also need to take into account any residual verification for which the United Nations remains responsible.

53. Most of the activities that together constitute peacebuilding fall within the mandates of the various programmes, funds, offices and agencies of the United Nations system with responsibilities in the economic, social, humanitarian and human rights fields. In a country ruined by war, resumption of such activities may initially have to be entrusted to, or at least coordinated by, a multifunctional peacekeeping operation, but as that operation succeeds in restoring normal conditions, the programmes, funds, offices and agencies can re-establish themselves and gradually take over responsibility from the peacekeepers, with the resident coordinator in due course assuming the coordination functions temporarily entrusted to the special representative of the Secretary-General.

54. It may also be necessary in such cases to arrange the transfer of decision-making responsibility from the Security Council, which will have authorized the mandate and deployment of the peacekeeping operation, to the General Assembly or other inter-governmental bodies with responsibility for the civilian peacebuilding activities that will continue. The timing of this transfer will be of special interest to certain Member States because of its financial implications. Each case has to be decided on its merits, the guiding principle being that institutional or budgetary considerations should not be allowed to imperil the continuity of the United Nations efforts in the field.

55. The more difficult situation is when post-conflict (or preventive) peacebuilding activities are seen to be necessary in a country where the United Nations does not already have a peacemaking or peacekeeping mandate. Who then will identify the need for such measures and propose them to the Government? If the measures are exclusively in the economic, social and humanitarian fields, they are likely to fall within the purview of the resident coordinator. He or she could recommend them to the Government. Even if the resident coordinator has the capacity to monitor and analyse all the indicators of an impending political and security crisis, however, which is rarely the case, can he or she act without inviting the charge of exceeding his or her

mandate by assuming political functions, especially if the proposed measures relate to areas such as security, the police or human rights?

56. In those circumstances, the early warning responsibility has to lie with United Nations Headquarters, using all the information available to it, including reports of the United Nations Development Programme (UNDP) resident coordinator and other United Nations personnel in the country concerned. When analysis of that information gives warning of impending crisis, the Secretary-General, acting on the basis of his general mandate for preventive diplomacy, peacemaking and peacebuilding, can take the initiative of sending a mission, with the Government's agreement, to discuss with it measures it could usefully take. . . .

81. Just as the United Nations does not claim a monopoly of the instruments discussed above, neither can it alone apply them. All the efforts of the Security Council, the General Assembly and the Secretary-General to control and resolve conflicts need the cooperation and support of other players on the international stage: the Governments that constitute the United Nations membership, regional and non-governmental organizations, and the various funds, programmes, offices and agencies of the United Nations system itself. If United Nations efforts are to succeed, the roles of the various players need to be carefully coordinated in an integrated approach to human security.

82. Governments are central to all the activities discussed in the present position paper. It is they who authorize the activities and finance them. It is they who provide directly the vast majority of the personnel required, as well as most of the equipment. It is they who set the policies of the specialized agencies of the United Nations system and of the regional organizations. It is they whose continuing support, and, as necessary, intervention with the parties, is essential if the Secretary-General is to succeed in carrying out the mandates entrusted to him. It is they who are parties, or at least one of the parties, to each conflict the United Nations is trying to control and resolve.

By the end of the 1990s it was clear that United Nations needed a more thorough review of what came to be known collectively as "peace operations." In the course of the decade, important functions in the Department of Peacekeeping Operations had been filled by "gratis military officers," on loan from member states from Australia to Zimbabwe but disproportionately drawn from Western countries. This led to considerable suspicion on the part of developing countries and protests under the auspices of the Non-Aligned Movement. By the late 1990s this had become a politically contentious issue and the United Nations began phasing out the practice in the period 1998–1999. The reduction in capacity coincided with a resurgence in peace operations, as the United Nations assumed civilian responsibilities in Kosovo and temporary sovereign responsibilities for East Timor in the same year (discussed in sections 2 and 3). A major review of UN peace operations was commissioned for the following year, its first meeting coinciding with the near collapse of a third mission in Sierra Leone as a result of poor planning, under-equipped and badly trained personnel, inadequate communication, weak to the point of mutinous command and control, and determined local spoilers.

The Report of the Panel on UN Peace Operations, known as the Brahimi Report after the panel's Algerian chairman, was established in part to justify the expansion of the Department of Peacekeeping Operations to compensate for the lost gratis personnel. It also touched on many other aspects of peace operations, including peacebuilding and the contentious question of whether the United Nations should develop a capacity to respond to crises like Kosovo and East Timor in future.

REPORT OF THE PANEL ON UN PEACE OPERATIONS (BRAHIMI REPORT), 21 AUGUST 2000[10]

76. Until mid-1999, the United Nations had conducted just a small handful of field operations with elements of civil administration conduct or oversight. In June 1999, however, the Secretariat found itself directed to develop a transitional civil administration for Kosovo, and three months later for East Timor. The struggles of the United Nations to set up and manage those operations are part of the backdrop to the narratives on rapid deployment and on Headquarters staffing and structure in the present report.

77. These operations face challenges and responsibilities that are unique among United Nations field operations. No other operations must set and enforce the law, establish customs services and regulations, set and collect business and personal taxes, attract foreign investment, adjudicate property disputes and liabilities for war damage, reconstruct and operate all public utilities, create a banking system, run schools and pay teachers and collect the garbage—in a war-damaged society, using voluntary contributions, because the assessed mission budget, even for such "transitional administration" missions, does not fund local administration itself. In addition to such tasks, these missions must also try to rebuild civil society and promote respect for human rights, in places where grievance is widespread and grudges run deep.

78. Beyond such challenges lies the larger question of whether the United Nations should be in this business at all, and if so whether it should be considered an element of peace operations or should be managed by some other structure. Although the Security Council may not again direct the United Nations to do transitional civil administration, no one expected it to do so with respect to Kosovo or East Timor either. Intra-State conflicts continue

[10]UN Doc. A/55/305-S/2000/809 (2000).

and future instability is hard to predict, so that despite evident ambivalence about civil administration among United Nations Member States and within the Secretariat, other such missions may indeed be established in the future and on an equally urgent basis. Thus, the Secretariat faces an unpleasant dilemma: to assume that transitional administration is a transitory responsibility, not prepare for additional missions and do badly if it is once again flung into the breach, or to prepare well and be asked to undertake them more often because it is well prepared. Certainly, if the Secretariat anticipates future transitional administrations as the rule rather than the exception, then a dedicated and distinct responsibility centre for those tasks must be created somewhere within the United Nations system. In the interim, DPKO has to continue to support this function.

79. Meanwhile, there is a pressing issue in transitional civil administration that must be addressed, and that is the issue of "applicable law." In the two locales where United Nations operations now have law enforcement responsibility, local judicial and legal capacity was found to be non-existent, out of practice or subject to intimidation by armed elements. Moreover, in both places, the law and legal systems prevailing prior to the conflict were questioned or rejected by key groups considered to be the victims of the conflicts.

80. Even if the choice of local legal code were clear, however, a mission's justice team would face the prospect of learning that code and its associated procedures well enough to prosecute and adjudicate cases in court. Differences in language, culture, custom and experience mean that the learning process could easily take six months or longer. The United Nations currently has no answer to the question of what such an operation should do while its law and order team inches up such a learning curve. Powerful local political factions can and have taken advantage of the learning period to set up their own parallel administrations, and crime syndicates gladly exploit whatever legal or enforcement vacuums they can find.

81. These missions' tasks would have been much easier if a common United Nations justice package had allowed them to apply an interim legal code to which mission personnel could have been pre-trained while the final answer to the "applicable law" question was being worked out. Although no work is currently under way within Secretariat legal offices on this issue, interviews with researchers indicate that some headway toward dealing with the problem has been made outside the United Nations system, emphasizing the principles, guidelines, codes and procedures contained in several dozen international conventions and declarations relating to human rights, humanitarian law, and guidelines for police, prosecutors and penal systems.

82. Such research aims at a code that contains the basics of both law and procedure to enable an operation to apply due process using international jurists and internationally agreed standards in the case of such crimes as murder, rape, arson, kidnapping and aggravated assault. Property law would probably remain beyond reach of such a "model code," but at least an operation would be able to prosecute effectively those who burned their neighbours' homes while the property law issue was being addressed.

83. Summary of key recommendation on transitional civil administration: the Panel recommends that the Secretary-General invite a panel of international legal experts, including individuals with experience in United Nations operations that have transitional administration mandates, to evaluate the feasibility and utility of developing an interim criminal code, including any regional adaptations potentially required, for use by such operations pending the re-establishment of local rule of law and local law enforcement capacity.

QUESTIONS

1. What does "peacebuilding" mean? Is the flexibility of the term helpful or unhelpful?
2. Can and should the United Nations build or rebuild institutions of the state by assuming governmental powers on a temporary basis? What legal basis can be found for such activities?
3. How do you assess the concrete recommendations maunde by the Brahimi Report? Were they adequate to the scale of the challenge, and do they appear to have been implemented, based on your reading of case material to date?
4. Are any of these recommendations particularly sensitive from a legal perspective?

9.2 Kosovo, 1999–

Security Council resolution 1244 (1999) was adopted just hours after the last bomb was dropped in the course of NATO's Operation Allied Force.[11] The resolution built upon principles adopted by the G8 Foreign Ministers a month earlier, which in turn had been "elaborated" in a document finally agreed to by Belgrade. The military aspects authorized the deployment of the Kosovo Force (KFOR)—an international security presence with "substantial" NATO participation. But the central contradiction of UNMIK's mandate was that it avoided taking a position on the key political question of Kosovo's relationship to Serbia. With Milosevic in power, it was long an open secret within UNMIK that Kosovo would eventually be granted independence. Nevertheless, the authorizing resolutions and official statements continued to emphasize respect for the territorial integrity and political independence of the Federal Republic of Yugoslavia. One commentator referred to this at the time as "virginity and motherhood combined."[12]

---

[11] See also chapter 2.
[12] Timothy Garton Ash, "Anarchy and Madness," *New York Review*, 10 February 2000, 48.

SECURITY COUNCIL RESOLUTION 1244 (1999)

The Security Council, . . .

Determined to resolve the grave humanitarian situation in Kosovo, Federal Republic of Yugoslavia, and to provide for the safe and free return of all refugees and displaced persons to their homes,

Condemning all acts of violence against the Kosovo population as well as all terrorist acts by any party, . . .

Recalling the jurisdiction and the mandate of the International Tribunal for the Former Yugoslavia,

Welcoming the general principles on a political solution to the Kosovo crisis adopted on 6 May 1999 (S/1999/516, annex 1 to this resolution) and welcoming also the acceptance by the Federal Republic of Yugoslavia of the principles set forth in points 1 to 9 of the paper presented in Belgrade on 2 June 1999 (S/1999/649, annex 2 to this resolution), and the Federal Republic of Yugoslavia's agreement to that paper,

Reaffirming the commitment of all Member States to the sovereignty and territorial integrity of the Federal Republic of Yugoslavia and the other States of the region, as set out in the Helsinki Final Act and annex 2,

Reaffirming the call in previous resolutions for substantial autonomy and meaningful self-administration for Kosovo,

Determining that the situation in the region continues to constitute a threat to international peace and security,

Determined to ensure the safety and security of international personnel and the implementation by all concerned of their responsibilities under the present resolution, and *acting* for these purposes under Chapter VII of the Charter of the United Nations,

1. *Decides* that a political solution to the Kosovo crisis shall be based on the general principles in annex 1 and as further elaborated in the principles and other required elements in annex 2;

2. *Welcomes* the acceptance by the Federal Republic of Yugoslavia of the principles and other required elements referred to in paragraph 1 above, and *demands* the full cooperation of the Federal Republic of Yugoslavia in their rapid implementation;

3. *Demands* in particular that the Federal Republic of Yugoslavia put an immediate and verifiable end to violence and repression in Kosovo, and begin and complete verifiable phased withdrawal from Kosovo of all military, police and paramilitary forces according to a rapid timetable, with which the deployment of the international security presence in Kosovo will be synchronized;

4. *Confirms* that after the withdrawal an agreed number of Yugoslav and Serb military and police personnel will be permitted to return to Kosovo to perform the functions in accordance with annex 2;

5. *Decides* on the deployment in Kosovo, under United Nations auspices, of international civil and security presences, with appropriate equipment and

personnel as required, and welcomes the agreement of the Federal Republic of Yugoslavia to such presences;

6. *Requests* the Secretary-General to appoint, in consultation with the Security Council, a Special Representative to control the implementation of the international civil presence, and *further requests* the Secretary-General to instruct his Special Representative to coordinate closely with the international security presence to ensure that both presences operate towards the same goals and in a mutually supportive manner;

7. *Authorizes* Member States and relevant international organizations to establish the international security presence in Kosovo as set out in point 4 of annex 2 with all necessary means to fulfil its responsibilities under paragraph 9 below;

8. *Affirms* the need for the rapid early deployment of effective international civil and security presences to Kosovo, and *demands* that the parties cooperate fully in their deployment;

9. *Decides* that the responsibilities of the international security presence to be deployed and acting in Kosovo will include:

(a) Deterring renewed hostilities, maintaining and where necessary enforcing a ceasefire, and ensuring the withdrawal and preventing the return into Kosovo of Federal and Republic military, police and paramilitary forces, except as provided in point 6 of annex 2;

(b) Demilitarizing the Kosovo Liberation Army (KLA) and other armed Kosovo Albanian groups as required in paragraph 15 below;

(c) Establishing a secure environment in which refugees and displaced persons can return home in safety, the international civil presence can operate, a transitional administration can be established, and humanitarian aid can be delivered;

(d) Ensuring public safety and order until the international civil presence can take responsibility for this task;

(e) Supervising demining until the international civil presence can, as appropriate, take over responsibility for this task;

(f) Supporting, as appropriate, and coordinating closely with the work of the international civil presence;

(g) Conducting border monitoring duties as required;

(h) Ensuring the protection and freedom of movement of itself, the international civil presence, and other international organizations;

10. *Authorizes* the Secretary-General, with the assistance of relevant international organizations, to establish an international civil presence in Kosovo in order to provide an interim administration for Kosovo under which the people of Kosovo can enjoy substantial autonomy within the Federal Republic of Yugoslavia, and which will provide transitional administration while establishing and overseeing the development of provisional democratic self-governing institutions to ensure conditions for a peaceful and normal life for all inhabitants of Kosovo;

11. *Decides* that the main responsibilities of the international civil presence will include:

(a) Promoting the establishment, pending a final settlement, of substantial autonomy and self-government in Kosovo, taking full account of annex 2 and of the Rambouillet accords (S/1999/648);

(b) Performing basic civilian administrative functions where and as long as required;

(c) Organizing and overseeing the development of provisional institutions for democratic and autonomous self-government pending a political settlement, including the holding of elections;

(d) Transferring, as these institutions are established, its administrative responsibilities while overseeing and supporting the consolidation of Kosovo's local provisional institutions and other peacebuilding activities;

(e) Facilitating a political process designed to determine Kosovo's future status, taking into account the Rambouillet accords (S/1999/648);

(f) In a final stage, overseeing the transfer of authority from Kosovo's provisional institutions to institutions established under a political settlement;

(g) Supporting the reconstruction of key infrastructure and other economic reconstruction;

(h) Supporting, in coordination with international humanitarian organizations, humanitarian and disaster relief aid;

(i) Maintaining civil law and order, including establishing local police forces and meanwhile through the deployment of international police personnel to serve in Kosovo;

(j) Protecting and promoting human rights;

(k) Assuring the safe and unimpeded return of all refugees and displaced persons to their homes in Kosovo;

12. *Emphasizes* the need for coordinated humanitarian relief operations, and for the Federal Republic of Yugoslavia to allow unimpeded access to Kosovo by humanitarian aid organizations and to cooperate with such organizations so as to ensure the fast and effective delivery of international aid;

13. *Encourages* all Member States and international organizations to contribute to economic and social reconstruction as well as to the safe return of refugees and displaced persons, and *emphasizes* in this context the importance of convening an international donors' conference, particularly for the purposes set out in paragraph 11 (g) above, at the earliest possible date;

14. *Demands* full cooperation by all concerned, including the international security presence, with the International Tribunal for the Former Yugoslavia;

15. *Demands* that the KLA and other armed Kosovo Albanian groups end immediately all offensive actions and comply with the requirements for demilitarization as laid down by the head of the international security presence in consultation with the Special Representative of the Secretary-General;

16. *Decides* that the prohibitions imposed by paragraph 8 of resolution 1160 (1998) shall not apply to arms and related *matériel* for the use of the international civil and security presences;

17. *Welcomes* the work in hand in the European Union and other international organizations to develop a comprehensive approach to the economic development and stabilization of the region affected by the Kosovo crisis, including the implementation of a Stability Pact for South Eastern Europe with broad international participation in order to further the promotion of democracy, economic prosperity, stability and regional cooperation;

18. *Demands* that all States in the region cooperate fully in the implementation of all aspects of this resolution;

19. *Decides* that the international civil and security presences are established for an initial period of 12 months, to continue thereafter unless the Security Council decides otherwise;

20. *Requests* the Secretary-General to report to the Council at regular intervals on the implementation of this resolution, including reports from the leaderships of the international civil and security presences, the first reports to be submitted within 30 days of the adoption of this resolution;

21. *Decides* to remain actively seized of the matter.

Annex 1: Statement by the Chairman on the Conclusion of the Meeting of the G8 Foreign Ministers Held at the Petersberg Centre on 6 May 1999

The G8 Foreign Ministers adopted the following general principles on the political solution to the Kosovo crisis:

- Immediate and verifiable end of violence and repression in Kosovo;
- Withdrawal from Kosovo of military, police and paramilitary forces;
- Deployment in Kosovo of effective international civil and security presences, endorsed and adopted by the United Nations, capable of guaranteeing the achievement of the common objectives;
- Establishment of an interim administration for Kosovo to be decided by the Security Council of the United Nations to ensure conditions for a peaceful and normal life for all inhabitants in Kosovo;
- The safe and free return of all refugees and displaced persons and unimpeded access to Kosovo by humanitarian aid organizations;
- A political process towards the establishment of an interim political framework agreement providing for a substantial self-government for Kosovo, taking full account of the Rambouillet accords and the principles of sovereignty and territorial integrity of the Federal Republic of Yugoslavia and the other countries of the region, and the demilitarization of the KLA;
- Comprehensive approach to the economic development and stabilization of the crisis region.

Annex 2: Agreement Should Be Reached on the Following Principles to Move Towards a Resolution of the Kosovo Crisis

1. An immediate and verifiable end of violence and repression in Kosovo.

2. Verifiable withdrawal from Kosovo of all military, police and paramilitary forces according to a rapid timetable.

3. Deployment in Kosovo under United Nations auspices of effective international civil and security presences, acting as may be decided under Chapter VII of the Charter, capable of guaranteeing the achievement of common objectives.

4. The international security presence with substantial North Atlantic Treaty Organization participation must be deployed under unified command and control and authorized to establish a safe environment for all people in Kosovo and to facilitate the safe return to their homes of all displaced persons and refugees.

5. Establishment of an interim administration for Kosovo as a part of the international civil presence under which the people of Kosovo can enjoy substantial autonomy within the Federal Republic of Yugoslavia, to be decided by the Security Council of the United Nations. The interim administration to provide transitional administration while establishing and overseeing the development of provisional democratic self-governing institutions to ensure conditions for a peaceful and normal life for all inhabitants in Kosovo.

6. After withdrawal, an agreed number of Yugoslav and Serbian personnel will be permitted to return to perform the following functions:

- Liaison with the international civil mission and the international security presence;
- Marking/clearing minefields;
- Maintaining a presence at Serb patrimonial sites;
- Maintaining a presence at key border crossings.

7. Safe and free return of all refugees and displaced persons under the supervision of the Office of the United Nations High Commissioner for Refugees and unimpeded access to Kosovo by humanitarian aid organizations.

8. A political process towards the establishment of an interim political framework agreement providing for substantial self-government for Kosovo, taking full account of the Rambouillet accords and the principles of sovereignty and territorial integrity of the Federal Republic of Yugoslavia and the other countries of the region, and the demilitarization of UCK. Negotiations between the parties for a settlement should not delay or disrupt the establishment of democratic self-governing institutions.

9. A comprehensive approach to the economic development and stabilization of the crisis region. This will include the implementation of a stability pact for South-Eastern Europe with broad international participation in

order to further promotion of democracy, economic prosperity, stability and regional cooperation.

10. Suspension of military activity will require acceptance of the principles set forth above in addition to agreement to other, previously identified, required elements, which are specified in the [notes] below. A military-technical agreement will then be rapidly concluded that would, among other things, specify additional modalities, including the roles and functions of Yugoslav/Serb personnel in Kosovo:

Withdrawal

• Procedures for withdrawals, including the phased, detailed schedule and delineation of a buffer area in Serbia beyond which forces will be withdrawn;

Returning Personnel

• Equipment associated with returning personnel;
• Terms of reference for their functional responsibilities;
• Timetable for their return;
• Delineation of their geographical areas of operation;
• Rules governing their relationship to the international security presence and the international civil mission.

Notes

* Other required elements:

• A rapid and precise timetable for withdrawals, meaning, e.g., seven days to complete withdrawal and air defence weapons withdrawn outside a 25 kilometre mutual safety zone within 48 hours;
• Return of personnel for the four functions specified above will be under the supervision of the international security presence and will be limited to a small agreed number (hundreds, not thousands);
• Suspension of military activity will occur after the beginning of verifiable withdrawals;
• The discussion and achievement of a military-technical agreement shall not extend the previously determined time for completion of withdrawals.

A measure of the speed with which the UN Interim Administration Mission in Kosovo was established is the name itself. UN operations typically operate under an acronym, but "UNIAMIK" was dismissed as too much of a mouthful. "UNIAK" sounded like a cross between "eunuch" and "maniac"—associations judged unlikely to help the mission. "UNMIK" was the final choice, having the benefits of being short, punchy, and clear. Only in English, however. Once the operation was on the ground, it was discovered that *anmik*, in the dialect of Albanian spoken in Kosovo, meant "enemy." No one within the United Nations was aware of the problem until it was too late, at which point instructions went out to pronounce the acronym "oon-mik."

REPORT OF THE SECRETARY-GENERAL PURSUANT TO PARAGRAPH 10 OF SECURITY COUNCIL RESOLUTION 1244, 12 JUNE 1999[13]

16. It is clearly an essential requirement for the success of UNMIK that the people of Kosovo be included fully and effectively in its work, in particular that of the interim administration, so that the transition to self-governing institutions is both smooth and timely. Community leaders and professionals can make immediate and significant contributions in judicial affairs, governance and the provision of public services. UNMIK intends to establish from the start a system of advisory mechanisms and implementation committees which will fully engage the local population.

Security Council resolution 1244 (1999) established the civilian authority of UNMIK. Shortly after its establishment on the ground, the first of many regulations was passed.

REGULATION 1999/1, ON THE AUTHORITY OF THE INTERIM ADMINISTRATION IN KOSOVO, 25 JULY 1999

Section 1—Authority of the Interim Administration

1.1 All legislative and executive authority with respect to Kosovo, including the administration of the judiciary, is vested in UNMIK and is exercised by the Special Representative of the Secretary-General.

1.2 The Special Representative of the Secretary-General may appoint any person to perform functions in the civil administration in Kosovo, including the judiciary, or remove such person. Such functions shall be exercised in accordance with the existing laws, as specified in section 3, and any regulations issued by UNMIK.

---

[13] UN Doc. S/1999/672.

Section 2—Observance of Internationally Recognized Standards

In exercising their functions, all persons undertaking public duties or holding public office in Kosovo shall observe internationally recognized human rights standards and shall not discriminate against any person on any ground such as sex, race, colour, language, religion, political or other opinion, national, ethnic or social origin, association with a national community, property, birth or other status.

Section 3—Applicable Law in Kosovo

The laws applicable in the territory of Kosovo prior to 24 March 1999 shall continue to apply in Kosovo insofar as they do not conflict with standards referred to in section 2, the fulfillment of the mandate given to UNMIK under United Nations Security Council resolution 1244 (1999), or the present or any other regulation issued by UNMIK.

Section 4—Regulations Issued by UNMIK

In the performance of the duties entrusted to the interim administration under United Nations Security Council resolution 1244 (1999)), UNMIK will, as necessary, issue legislative acts in the form of regulations. Such regulations will remain in force until repealed by UNMIK or superseded by such rules as are subsequently issued by the institutions established under a political settlement, as provided for in United Nations Security Council resolution 1244 (1999)

Section 5—Entry into Force and Promulgation of Regulations Issued by UNMIK

5.1 UNMIK regulations shall be approved and signed by the Special Representative of the Secretary-General. They shall enter into force upon the date specified therein.

5.2 UNMIK regulations shall be issued in Albanian, Serbian and English. In case of divergence, the English text shall prevail. The regulations shall be published in a manner that ensures their wide dissemination by public announcement and publication.

5.3 UNMIK regulations shall bear the symbol UNMIK/REG/, followed by the year of issuance and the issuance number of that year. A register of the regulations shall indicate the date of promulgation, the subject matter and amendments or changes thereto or the repeal or suspension thereof.

Section 6—State Property

UNMIK shall administer movable or immovable property, including monies, bank accounts, and other property of, or registered in the name of the Federal Republic of Yugoslavia or the Republic

Section 7—Entry into Force

The present regulation shall be deemed to have entered into force as of 10 June 1999, the date of adoption by the United Nations Security Council of resolution 1244 (1999).

Dr. Bernard Kouchner
Special Representative of the Secretary-General

Periodic reports were provided to the Council on progress towards achieving the mandate established by the Council.

REPORT OF THE SECRETARY-GENERAL ON THE UNITED NATIONS INTERIM ADMINISTRATION MISSION IN KOSOVO, 22 APRIL 2002[14]

54. The international community has invested a great deal of energy and resources to create a functioning political system, a viable and legitimate economy and a peaceful society that upholds the rule of law. It is understood that the Mission will not stay in Kosovo indefinitely, but in order to consolidate the provisional institutions of self-government and avoid undercutting the achievements made so far, continued political, technical and financial support will be necessary. Although the current level of support cannot continue indefinitely, premature disengagement could lead to a vacuum of power and instability that could be filled by organized crime and extremism. It is clear that a political roadmap is needed, both for UNMIK and for the provisional institutions of self-government. To this end, I have asked my Special Representative to develop benchmarks against which progress can be measured in the critical areas of the rule of law, functioning democratic institutions, the economy, freedom of movement, the return of internally displaced persons and refugees and contributions to regional stability.

An Ombudsperson for Kosovo was established by the Organization for Security and Cooperation in Europe (OSCE) on 21 November 2000. It was intended to "promote and protect the rights and freedoms of individuals and legal entities and ensure that all persons in Kosovo are able to exercise effectively the human rights and fundamental freedoms safeguarded by in-

---

[14] UN Doc. S/2002/436.

ternational human rights standards, in particular the European Convention on Human Rights and its Protocols and the International Covenant on Civil and Political Rights." The Ombudsperson was to act independently and without charge; the office had wide jurisdiction to receive and investigate complaints from any person in Kosovo concerning human rights violations and actions constituting an abuse of authority by UNMIK or any emerging central or local institution. This jurisdiction was limited to cases within Kosovo arising after 30 June 2000, and excluded cases involving the NATO-led Kosovo Force (KFOR) and disputes between UNMIK and its staff. During or following an investigation, the Ombudsperson's powers were essentially limited to making recommendations, including recommendations that disciplinary or criminal proceedings be instituted against a person. If the officials concerned did not take appropriate measures within a reasonable time, the Ombudsperson could draw the Special Representative's attention to the matter or make a public statement.[15]

OMBUDSPERSON INSTITUTION IN KOSOVO, SECOND ANNUAL REPORT 2001–2002, 10 JULY 2002[16]

The human rights situation in Kosovo is distinct from the human rights situation in other parts of post-conflict Yugoslavia, in part due to the unique role of the United Nations Mission in Kosovo (UNMIK) as the surrogate state. As the state, however, UNMIK is not structured according to democratic principles, does not function in accordance with the rule of law, and does not respect important international human rights norms. The people of Kosovo are therefore deprived of protection of their basic rights and freedoms three years after the end of the conflict by the very entity set up to guarantee them.

On its establishment as the surrogate state in Kosovo, in 1999, UNMIK gave no cognizance to one of the founding principles of democracy, the separation of governmental powers. Amongst the earliest actions of the Special Representative of the Secretary-General of the United Nations (SRSG) was the promulgation of an UNMIK Regulation vesting total executive and legislative powers in himself. In the same Regulation, he also accorded himself administrative authority over the judiciary. The SRSG can and does act outside the bounds of judicial control to restrict or deny fundamental

---

[15] UNMIK Regulation 2000/38 (30 June 2000), On the Establishment of the Ombudsperson Institution in Kosovo. The Ombudsperson Institution was formally inaugurated on 21 November 2000.
[16] Available at http://www.ombudspersonkosovo.org.

human rights to individuals in Kosovo. For example, he has exercised this power to remove individuals from electoral lists and to override the decision of international judges and international prosecutors to release certain individuals from detention. The effects of the failure of the SRSG to respect the principle of the separation of powers continue to have extremely negative ramifications for the rule of law and human rights in the territory.

Since the establishment of the United Nations regime in Kosovo, UNMIK has both perpetuated and created obstacles to the full protection of human rights, issuing Regulations granting themselves and the international military presence (KFOR) total immunity from legal process in Kosovo, removing decision-making authority over important civil rights from the courts and placing it in administrative bodies under the direct control of UNMIK, and pursuing similar courses of action that serve to eliminate or severely restrict the rights of individuals from Kosovo. The applicable law is often unclear, with UNMIK Regulations and subsidiary legal acts declared as the supreme law of the land, prevailing over any domestic laws in force. Whatever law a court in Kosovo may apply is of little importance, however, as UNMIK will choose whether or not to permit the execution of any resulting judgment. It has refused to do so, for instance, in a case relating to a job recruitment conducted under direct UNMIK control and authority.

QUESTIONS

5. What powers did Security Council resolution 1244 give to the Special Representative of the Secretary-General (SRSG) in Kosovo? Did the SRSG exceed these powers in passing Regulation 1999/1? If so, what remedy should be available? If not, what limits (if any) are there on the SRSG's powers?

6. Paragraph 19 of resolution 1244 (1999) established UNMIK "for an initial period of 12 months." Normal practice is to require the Council to approve an extension of a mandate. What was to happen to UNMIK after those twelve months if the Council did nothing?

7. UNMIK was intended to be a temporary solution. How did the passage of time affect this solution?

8. Should a transitional administration such as UNMIK or UNTAET (discussed in the next section) be democratically accountable? Should it be subject to the rule of law?

9.3 East Timor, 1999–2002

The origins of the complex role played by the United Nations in East Timor lie in Indonesia's 1975 invasion of the former Portuguese colony. Since the purported annexation of East Timor by Indonesia was never explicitly recognized by the vast majority of governments, it is questionable what legitimate interest Indonesia had in the territory's transition. In practice, however, East Timor's independence only became possible following the replacement of Indonesian President Suharto by B.J. Habibie, who offered to hold a plebiscite on the territory's future. An agreement dated 5 May 1999, between Indonesia and Portugal (as the administering power of a non-self-governing territory), provided for a "popular consultation" to be held on East Timor's future on 8 August of the same year.

Crucially, the agreement left security arrangements in the hands of Indonesia's military—the very forces that had actively suppressed the East Timorese population for twenty-four years. On 11 June 1999, the Security Council established the UN Mission in East Timor (UNAMET) to organize and conduct the consultation.[17] A month later, with the consultation postponed until the end of August, the Secretary-General reported to the Council that "the situation in East Timor will be rather delicate as the Territory prepares for the implementation of the result of the popular consultation, whichever it may be."[18] Despite threats of violence, 98 percent of registered East Timorese voted in the referendum, with 78.5 percent choosing independence.

The violence that followed took place under the direction of the Indonesian military, if not the government itself. At the time there was great reluctance within the international community to intervene, despite the apparent double standard given the international response to the situation in Kosovo. There seems to have been no legal basis for requiring Indonesia's consent to such an operation. Nevertheless, as a practical matter, it was clear that no form of enforcement action would have been possible without it. A fortuitously timed meeting of the Asia Pacific Economic Cooperation Forum (APEC) in Auckland, New Zealand, and a Security Council mission to Jakarta enabled political and economic pressure to be brought to bear on Indonesia, and resolution 1264 (1999) welcomed a 12 September statement by the Indonesian President that expressed the readiness of Indonesia to accept an international peacekeeping force through the United Nations in East Timor. Australia offered to lead the force and on 15 September the Security Council authorized the International Force in East Timor (INTERFET) to restore peace and security to the territory.[19]

Six weeks later, the Council established a transitional administration to prepare the territory for independence.

---

[17] SC Res. 1246 (1999).
[18] Question of East Timor: Report of the Secretary-General, UN Doc. S/1999/862 (1999), para. 5.
[19] SC Res. 1264 (1999).

SECURITY COUNCIL RESOLUTION 1272 (1999)

The Security Council, . . .

Reiterating its welcome for the successful conduct of the popular consultation of the East Timorese people of 30 August 1999, and *taking note* of its outcome through which the East Timorese people expressed their clear wish to begin a process of transition under the authority of the United Nations towards independence, which it regards as an accurate reflection of the views of the East Timorese people,

Welcoming the decision of the Indonesian People's Consultative Assembly on 19 October 1999 concerning East Timor, . . .

Welcoming the deployment of a multinational force to East Timor pursuant to resolution 1264 (1999), and *recognizing* the importance of continued co-operation between the Government of Indonesia and the multinational force in this regard, . . .

Reaffirming respect for the sovereignty and territorial integrity of Indonesia,

Noting the importance of ensuring the security of the boundaries of East Timor, and *noting* in this regard the expressed intention of the Indonesian authorities to cooperate with the multinational force deployed pursuant to resolution 1264 (1999) and with the United Nations Transitional Administration in East Timor,

Expressing its concern at reports indicating that systematic, widespread and flagrant violations of international humanitarian and human rights law have been committed in East Timor, *stressing* that persons committing such violations bear individual responsibility, and *calling* on all parties to cooperate with investigations into these reports, . . .

Determining that the continuing situation in East Timor constitutes a threat to peace and security,

Acting under Chapter VII of the Charter of the United Nations,

1. *Decides* to establish, in accordance with the report of the Secretary-General, a United Nations Transitional Administration in East Timor (UN-TAET), which will be endowed with overall responsibility for the administration of East Timor and will be empowered to exercise all legislative and executive authority, including the administration of justice;

2. *Decides also* that the mandate of UNTAET shall consist of the following elements:

(a) To provide security and maintain law and order throughout the territory of East Timor;

(b) To establish an effective administration;

(c) To assist in the development of civil and social services;

(d) To ensure the coordination and delivery of humanitarian assistance, rehabilitation and development assistance;

(e) To support capacity-building for self-government;

(f) To assist in the establishment of conditions for sustainable development;

3. *Decides further* that UNTAET will have objectives and a structure along the lines set out in part IV of the report of the Secretary-General, and in particular that its main components will be:

(a) A governance and public administration component, including an international police element with a strength of up to 1,640 officers;

(b) A humanitarian assistance and emergency rehabilitation component;

(c) A military component, with a strength of up to 8,950 troops and up to 200 military observers;

4. *Authorizes* UNTAET to take all necessary measures to fulfil its mandate;

5. *Recognizes* that, in developing and performing its functions under its mandate, UNTAET will need to draw on the expertise and capacity of Member States, United Nations agencies and other international organizations, including the international financial institutions;

6. *Welcomes* the intention of the Secretary-General to appoint a Special Representative who, as the Transitional Administrator, will be responsible for all aspects of the United Nations work in East Timor and will have the power to enact new laws and regulations and to amend, suspend or repeal existing ones;

7. *Stresses* the importance of cooperation between Indonesia, Portugal and UNTAET in the implementation of this resolution;

8. *Stresses* the need for UNTAET to consult and cooperate closely with the East Timorese people in order to carry out its mandate effectively with a view to the development of local democratic institutions, including an independent East Timorese human rights institution, and the transfer to these institutions of its administrative and public service functions;

9. *Requests* UNTAET and the multinational force deployed pursuant to resolution 1264 (1999) to cooperate closely with each other, with a view also to the replacement as soon as possible of the multinational force by the military component of UNTAET, as notified by the Secretary-General having consulted the leadership of the multinational force, taking into account conditions on the ground;

10. *Reiterates* the urgent need for coordinated humanitarian and reconstruction assistance, and *calls upon* all parties to cooperate with humanitarian and human rights organizations so as to ensure their safety, the protection of civilians, in particular children, the safe return of refugees and displaced persons and the effective delivery of humanitarian aid;

11. *Welcomes* the commitment of the Indonesian authorities to allow the refugees and displaced persons in West Timor and elsewhere in Indonesia to choose whether to return to East Timor, remain where they are or be resettled in other parts of Indonesia, and *stresses* the importance of allowing full, safe and unimpeded access by humanitarian organizations in carrying out their work;

12. *Stresses* that it is the responsibility of the Indonesian authorities to take immediate and effective measures to ensure the safe return of refugees in

West Timor and other parts of Indonesia to East Timor, the security of refugees, and the civilian and humanitarian character of refugee camps and settlements, in particular by curbing the violent and intimidatory activities of the militias there;

13. *Welcomes* the intention of the Secretary-General to establish a Trust Fund available for, *inter alia*, the rehabilitation of essential infrastructure, including the building of basic institutions, the functioning of public services and utilities, and the salaries of local civil servants;

14. *Encourages* Member States and international agencies and organizations to provide personnel, equipment and other resources to UNTAET as requested by the Secretary-General, including for the building of basic institutions and capacity, and *stresses* the need for the closest possible coordination of these efforts;

15. *Underlines* the importance of including in UNTAET personnel with appropriate training in international humanitarian, human rights and refugee law, including child- and gender-related provisions, negotiation and communication skills, cultural awareness and civilian-military coordination;

16. *Condemns* all violence and acts in support of violence in East Timor, *calls* for their immediate end, and *demands* that those responsible for such violence be brought to justice;

17. *Decides* to establish UNTAET for an initial period until 31 January 2001;

18. *Requests* the Secretary-General to keep the Council closely and regularly informed of progress towards the implementation of this resolution, including, in particular, with regard to the deployment of UNTAET and possible future reductions of its military component if the situation in East Timor improves, and to submit a report within three months of the date of adoption of this resolution and every six months thereafter;

19. *Decides* to remain actively seized of the matter.

As in the case of Kosovo, the Secretary-General prepared regular reports for the Council on progress in East Timor.

REPORT OF THE SECRETARY-GENERAL ON UNTAET, 26 JANUARY 2000[20]

41. A key objective is to ensure that the East Timorese themselves become the major stakeholders in their own system of governance and public administration, first by intensive consultation through [National Consultative

[20] UN Doc. S/2000/53 (2000).

Council] and district advisory councils, and then through the early and progressive development of their capacity to carry out all necessary functions. In all its current activities, the Governance and Public Administration Component has been in close touch with all sectors of East Timorese society, keeping them informed about major initiatives and soliciting their input. A community empowerment project, supported by the World Bank, is currently under discussion. Its aim is to establish a grass-roots community governance system to ensure that all communities have a degree of decision-making power over the allocation of public resources in their area. . . .

69. The first three months of the operation of UNTAET have seen strenuous efforts to move forward on a broad range of problems, each important and very urgent, while still in the process of establishing the operation in extremely difficult conditions.

70. From the start, UNTAET has sought to establish close consultation with the East Timorese. The National Consultative Council has been a unique means for UNTAET to hear and to respond to the needs of the East Timorese and for the latter to participate in important policy decisions, whose consequences will be with the people of East Timor well beyond UNTAET's limited presence in the Territory.

- -

In contrast to the mission in Kosovo, East Timor had a uniquely clear political endpoint. The outcome of independence was never really questioned after the UN Transitional Administration was established, but the timing and the manner in which power was to be exercised in the meantime soon became controversial.

The widespread assumption that East Timor in late 1999 was a political and economic vacuum was perhaps half true. Even before the vote to separate from Indonesia, East Timor was one of the poorest parts of the archipelago; in the violence that followed, the formal economy simply ceased to function. Unemployment during the period of transitional administration remained at around 80 percent, with much economic activity being parasitic on the temporary market for expatriate food and entertainment. The political situation was far more complex.

Some of these problems were referable to a contradiction within Security Council resolution 1272 (1999). It established UNTAET in order to give the East Timorese eventual control over their country, stressing the need for UNTAET to "consult and cooperate closely with the East Timorese people." At the same time, however, UNTAET followed the Kosovo model of concentrating all political power in UNTAET and the Special Representative, while endowing the administration with all the institutional and bureaucratic baggage that the United Nations carries. The failure to elaborate on the meaning of "consult and cooperate closely" gave UNTAET considerable latitude in its interpretation of the mandate. The initial approach was to establish a non-elected council, comprising representatives of UNTAET and local political factions. Created in December 1999, the fifteen-member National Consultative Council (NCC) was a purely advisory body, though it reviewed (and endorsed) all UNTAET regulations.[21] Nevertheless, as the situation in East Timor became more stable, there were calls for wider and more direct participation in political life.

REPORT OF THE SECRETARY-GENERAL ON UNTAET, 26 JULY 2000[22]

2. The 15-member National Consultative Council (NCC), which was established in December 1999, played a crucial role as the primary mechanism through which the East Timorese participated in UNTAET's decision-making. However, it became clear over time that its membership needed to be expanded to facilitate broader participation in policy-making. After intensive consultation, the National Council (NC) was created on 14 July to replace NCC. It will have 33 members, all Timorese, appointed by the Transitional Administrator as follows: one from each of the 13 districts, 7 from political parties within the National Council of Timorese Resistance (CNRT), three from other parties, and one each representing youth, students, non-governmental organizations, the professions, farmers, labour, business, the Catholic Church, the Protestant Church and the Muslim community. Consultations are under way regarding the selection of the Council's members.

3. At the same time, UNTAET reorganized itself to resemble more closely the future government and to increase the direct participation of the Timorese, who thus assume a greater share of the political responsibility. Eight portfolios were created: internal administration, infrastructure, economic affairs, social affairs, finance, justice, police and emergency services, and political affairs. The first four have been entrusted to East Timorese, the other four to senior UNTAET staff members. They were sworn in on 15 and 17 July. The eight officials form a Cabinet chaired by the Special Representative of the Secretary-General. It is responsible for formulating policies and recommending regulations and directives for consideration by the National Council. The Special Representative of the Secretary-General retains full responsibility as Transitional Administrator in accordance with Security Council resolution 1272 (1999). . . .

63. When I reported to the Security Council last January, UNTAET was a fledgling operation, still building its own capacity while trying to advance as

---

[21] UNTAET Regulation 1999/2 (2 December 1999). See *S/2000/53*, para. 4.
[22] UN Doc. S/2000/738 (2000).

fast as possible on a broad range of issues. Today, although it has not yet reached its full designated capacity, UNTAET can look with satisfaction on what it has achieved so far. It has contributed to the alleviation of the emergency brought about by the violence and destruction that followed the popular consultation last year; it has maintained a secure environment; it has established the foundations of an effective administration; and, above all, it has established a relationship of mutual respect and trust with the East Timorese.

64. The last six months have also made clearer how daunting the task is that the United Nations has undertaken in East Timor. The Organization had never before attempted to build and manage a State. Nor did it have an opportunity to prepare for this assignment; the team in East Timor had to be assembled ad hoc and still lacks important expertise in a number of fields.

65. The relationship between UNTAET and the East Timorese is obviously crucial for the attainment of the mandate. While Security Council resolution 1272 (1999) gives the United Nations exclusive authority, my Special Representative has chosen to proceed only in the closest possible consultation with the East Timorese and with their full consent. The appointment of Timorese as heads of department is a further step towards the increased sharing of political responsibility.

66. UNTAET has maintained close contact with the different political groupings, notably with CNRT and its President, Mr. Xanana Gusmão, who is the most respected Timorese leader and commands great personal authority. However, signs of intolerance of other political groups that have surfaced in recent weeks are cause for concern. I trust that CNRT will defend the political freedom for which it has fought and will welcome and encourage the broader participation in the political process that the creation of the National Council was intended to promote.

67. East Timor's best assurance of a secure future lies in healthy relations with the countries in the region, particularly Indonesia, its closest neighbour. Great progress has been made in this regard, owing in no small measure to the personal efforts of President Wahid and Mr. Gusmão. However, the unresolved issue of the East Timorese refugees in West Timor, the activities of pro-integration militias, who exercise control over the refugees, and continuing cross-border attacks by groups based in West Timor are very disturbing, as highlighted by the fatal shooting of a United Nations soldier. I expect that effective steps will be taken by the Indonesian authorities to bring the situation fully under control.

68. When I visited East Timor last February, I asked my Special Representative to establish benchmarks to guide the activities of the mission towards achieving minimum goals in East Timor that would provide the East Timorese with a sound platform for governing their country when independence was achieved. The key areas are: to ensure security during the transitional period and arrangements for East Timor's security once it is independent; to establish a credible system of justice in which fundamental human rights are respected; to achieve a reasonable level of

reconstruction of public services and infrastructure; to establish an administration that is financially sustainable; and to manage a political transition to independence, culminating in the adoption of a constitution and democratic elections.

69. The last objective is, no doubt, the most important, since it entails the establishment of a political system that is responsive to the citizens and a political leadership that is responsible in its decisions. The East Timorese are increasingly impatient to take responsibility for their affairs and do not wish the transition period to continue for too long. Indeed, many would hope to reach independence by the end of next year, in the full knowledge that East Timor, as one of the least developed countries, will require international support for some time to come.

....

Xanana Gusmão, leader of the Timorese resistance for many years, released his own report on UNTAET more than a year after it arrived in East Timor.

....

JOSE "KAY RALA XANANA" GUSMÃO

NEW YEAR'S MESSAGE: THE RIGHT TO LIVE IN PEACE AND HARMONY, 31 DECEMBER 2000[23]

Compatriots! Timorese!

Today, in East Timor, we are witnessing a move by politicians to affirm, or re-affirm, their position in society. Some try to defend points of view that are almost contrary to common sense just to recruit some followers because they claim to be the defenders of the "underprivileged."

Others, resort to past memories, become untouchable and, because of this, become insensitive to the (real) facts of history. They live in and revisit the past as an alternative to confronting common sense and reality. They claim historic impunity, they surround themselves by angels of peace and heroes of a revolution . . . that brought grief and left scars in our souls.

Others, living thousands of kilometres away from Dili, spout forth points of view as if they own a knowledge of their own, in a remote-control-style

---

[23] *The Guardian* (London), 31 January 2001. Available at http://www.etan.org/et2001a/january/01-06/01xanan.htm

very much in line with the globalisation that turned each country into a larger or smaller village in this world.

Timorese Reality

We are witnessing another phenomenon in East Timor; that of an obsessive acculturation to standards that hundreds of international experts try to convey to the East Timorese, who are hungry for values:

- democracy (many of those who teach us never practised it in their own countries because they became UN staff members);
- human rights (many of those who remind us of them forget the situation in their own countries);
- gender (many of the women who attend the workshops know that in their countries this issue is no example for others);
- NGOs (numerous NGOs live off the aid "business" to poor countries);
- youth (all those who remind us of this issue know that in their countries most of the youth are unemployed and that experience is the main employment drive apart from some exceptions based on intellectual skills).

It might sound as though I am speaking against these noble values of democratic participation. I do not mind if it happens in the democratic minds of people.

What seems to be absurd is that we absorb standards just to pretend we look like a democratic society and please our masters of independence.

What concerns me is the non-critical absorption of (universal) standards given the current stage of the historic process we are building.

Old democracies are no longer like a smooth pavement or a linear social process where such standards slide along without the slightest friction.

What concerns me is that the Timorese may become detached from their reality and, above all, try to copy something which is not yet clearly understood by them.

It is necessary that we are sincere and humble so that we do not lose track of the highest interests of our People.

Democracy

Democracy is not built overnight and it is by experiencing the system that democracy can be shaped.

Some think that mere political party membership is a synonym of democracy and, therefore, it does not need to be cared for.

School-aged youths think democracy empowers them with the right to protest, criticise and insult the teachers, to skip or disturb classes.

Some adults share the opinion that democracy demands that everyone must decide on everything.

This process of preparation for independence is not an easy one when we discuss issues such as democracy, human rights and freedom.

There is some anxiety for self-affirmation which the international staff currently in East Timor try to enhance; they forget how unaware they are of the whole process of our people's struggle and, therefore, encourage the expression of various forms of difference as if this was the only way of ensuring democracy.

This natural need for self-affirmation, of parties and individuals, whether politicians or not, leads to a strong ill-feeling against the CNRT as if the CNRT was the main enemy of political parties and civil society.

To a certain extent, this situation is encouraged by the perception shared by many international organizations that the CNRT is a political party.

It is hard for us to believe that foreigners who come to East Timor to work do not have some knowledge of Timorese political reality.

Foreigners should bear in mind that the essential condition for their operational success is to be aware that they do not come to save East Timor but rather to fulfill a mission of support; therefore, if they are not aware of this reality they will face the ungrateful mission of earning money for six months and returning to their homes, as so many have done, often revealing themselves to be less skilled than the East Timorese who can not find a job.

On 14 April 2002 Xanana Gusmão won East Timor's first presidential elections with 83 percent of the vote.

REPORT OF THE SECRETARY-GENERAL ON UNTAET, 17 APRIL 2002[24]

2. The present report marks the end of a significant stage in the process towards independence which has enabled East Timor to move during the past two and a half years from widespread devastation to the establishment of the foundations for the administration of a new country and to the rehabilitation of a basic infrastructure that can support economic and social activity. Over the past three months, further progress has been achieved in consolidating the political and institutional structure of the new nation, with the adoption of a Constitution, the election of the country's first President and the hand-over of most executive and operational functions to the East

---

[24] UN Doc. S/2002/432 (2002).

Timorese, thus paving the way for the country's independence on 20 May 2002.

3. Nevertheless, . . . a number of issues that present challenges to the short and longer-term security and stability of the new State have not yet and could not have been fully resolved. These range from border demarcation, return of refugees and regulation of commercial activity in the border area, to strengthening of nascent governmental structures, including law enforcement and the judicial system, as well as the consolidation of the framework for economic and social development. It is therefore essential for the international community to remain engaged in East Timor for some time beyond independence, to ensure stability and to build upon the achievements of UNTAET. . . .

107. Two and a half years ago, East Timor was devastated. As UNTAET draws to an end, East Timor is at peace, fundamental government structures are in place, and the independence that it has struggled for over so many years is very close. However, all of these are at risk if they are not reinforced through a continued international presence and commitment. The United Nations had a truly historic mandate in East Timor. Few would have imagined that a de novo public administration could have been established within just 30 months. The East Timorese people, in partnership with the United Nations, have advanced on their path to independence and self-government. But, the East Timorese and members of the international community must be careful not to allow that process to lose momentum. East Timor is desperately poor and will remain so over the immediate future. However, its people are now in a position to determine their own fate and the country can enter into peaceful cooperation with its neighbours. I welcome, in this regard, the initiation of bilateral and trilateral discussions between East Timor, Indonesia and Australia.

108. Despite the considerable efforts made over the past 30 months, a number of critical elements of the State will remain fragile at independence. While the responsibility to establish and maintain a viable State in East Timor clearly belongs to its people and its leaders, assistance from the international community will remain essential for continued stability and the development of the country for some time. . . .

115. Finally, I wish to express my deep appreciation to the Security Council and to the Member States that have provided unwavering support for East Timor. I also wish to pay a special tribute to Sergio Vieira de Mello, my Special Representative, for his exceptional leadership and commitment, and to all the men and women of UNTAET and its partner organizations, for their outstanding contribution in helping East Timor to overcome its tragic past and preparing it to join the community of nations.

East Timor attained its independence on 20 May 2002. The Council issued a statement.

STATEMENT BY THE PRESIDENT OF THE SECURITY
COUNCIL, 20 MAY 2002[25]

The Security Council welcomes the attainment of independence by East Timor on 20 May 2002, which marks the culmination of a process of self-determination and transition that began in May 1999. The Council pays tribute to the people and leadership of East Timor for their efforts in achieving the goal of independence.

The Security Council affirms its commitment to the sovereignty, political independence, territorial integrity and national unity of East Timor within its internationally recognized boundaries. . . .

The Security Council expresses its strong support for the leadership of East Timor as it assumes authority for governing the new, sovereign State of East Timor. The Council recognizes that the people and democratically elected Government of East Timor bear the ultimate responsibility for the establishment and maintenance of a viable State. It expresses its confidence that the people and leadership of East Timor will demonstrate the necessary political will and determination to fulfil their aspirations.

The Security Council appreciates the efforts made by the General Assembly and the Special Committee on the Situation with regard to the Implementation of the Declaration on the Granting of Independence to Colonial Countries and Peoples towards East Timor's achievement of independence. The Council expresses its appreciation to the Government of Indonesia and the Government of Portugal for their cooperation with the United Nations in concluding the 5 May 1999 Agreement which led to the establishment of the United Nations Mission in East Timor (UNAMET) to conduct the popular consultation. It also expresses its appreciation to Australia and all other countries that contributed troops to the International Force in East Timor (INTERFET) and the UNTAET, which helped restore stability following the post-referendum violence.

The Security Council welcomes the Government of East Timor's commitment to develop close and strong relations with Indonesia, and the Government of Indonesia's stated readiness to cooperate with East Timor towards building a peaceful, unified and sustainable society in East Timor. The Council stresses that good relations with neighbouring States will be essential to East Timor's future stability and that of the region, which are inextricably linked.

The Security Council is concerned that challenges to the security and stability of East Timor remain after independence. It notes with concern that shortcomings exist in a number of critical public administration elements of East Timor in the post-independence period. The Council reaffirms that a strong international commitment will be required in East Timor to ensure

---

[25]UN Doc. S/PRST/2002/13 (2002).

continued stability and development of the country for some time after independence. The Council expresses its confidence that the United Nations Mission of Support in East Timor (UNMISET) established through resolution 1410 (2002) on 17 May 2002 will help consolidate and strengthen a stable environment in East Timor.

The Security Council reaffirms the importance of complementing the United Nations peacekeeping contribution with other United Nations funds, programmes and specialized agencies, international financial institutions, bilateral donors and non-governmental organizations to assist the people of East Timor to develop a sustainable social system and economy. It also reaffirms the continued need for effective and close coordination among these programmes and donors to ensure a smooth transition towards a normal development assistance framework. The Council appeals to Member States to respond positively to the urgent appeal of the Secretary-General to fill vacancies in the Civilian Support Group. It also urges Member States and other actors to respond positively to the appeals for assistance in the development of the East Timor defence force, police service and justice sector; and in supporting social and economic development and poverty reduction.

The Security Council looks forward to the day in the near future when East Timor will join us as a Member of the United Nations and to working closely with its representatives. The Council notes that the East Timor Government today submitted a letter to the Secretary-General requesting the admission of East Timor as a Member of the United Nations.

The Security Council will remain actively seized of the matter.

....

Following a recommendation by the Council,[26] the General Assembly considered the application of East Timor (under its preferred name of Timor-Leste) for membership of the United Nations.

....

GENERAL ASSEMBLY RESOLUTION 57/3 (2002)

The General Assembly,
   Having received the recommendation of the Security Council of 23 May 2002 that the Democratic Republic of Timor-Leste should be admitted to membership in the United Nations,
   Having considered the application for membership of the Democratic Republic of Timor-Leste,
   Decides to admit the Democratic Republic of Timor-Leste to membership in the United Nations.

....

---

[26]SC Res. 1414 (2002).

QUESTION ··

9. Were Xanana Gusmão's criticisms of UNTAET accurate? Were they fair?

9.4 Institutions

The High-Level Panel on Threats, Challenges, and Change rightly criticized the UN experience of post-conflict operations as characterized by "countless ill-coordinated and overlapping bilateral and United Nations programmes, with inter-agency competition preventing the best use of scarce resources." Its key recommendation to remedy this situation was the call for a Peacebuilding Commission to be established as a subsidiary organ of the UN Security Council under article 29 of the UN Charter. It also provided for the creation of a Peacebuilding Support Office.[27]

REPORT OF THE HIGH-LEVEL PANEL ON THREATS, CHALLENGES, AND CHANGE: A MORE SECURE WORLD: OUR SHARED RESPONSIBILITY, 1 DECEMBER 2004[28]

38. . . . Post-conflict operations . . . have too often been characterized by countless ill-coordinated and overlapping bilateral and United Nations programmes, with inter-agency competition preventing the best use of scarce resources. . . .

261. Our analysis has identified a key institutional gap: there is no place in the United Nations system explicitly designed to avoid State collapse and the slide to war or to assist countries in their transition from war to peace. That this was not included in the Charter of the United Nations is no surprise since the work of the United Nations in largely internal conflicts is fairly recent. But today, in an era when dozens of States are under stress or recovering from conflict, there is a clear international obligation to assist States in developing their capacity to perform their sovereign functions effectively and responsibly.

262. The United Nations' unique role in this area arises from its international legitimacy; the impartiality of its personnel; its ability to draw on personnel with broad cultural understanding and experience of a wide range of administrative systems, including in the developing world; and its recent

---

[27] The Report of the High-Level Panel is also discussed in chapters 1, 4, 13, and 17.
[28] UN Doc. A/59/565 (2004).

experience in organizing transitional administration and transitional authority operations.

263. Strengthening the United Nations' capacity for peacebuilding in the widest sense must be a priority for the organization. The United Nations needs to be able to act in a coherent and effective way throughout a whole continuum that runs from early warning through preventive action to post-conflict peacebuilding. We recommend that the Security Council, acting under Article 29 of the Charter of the United Nations and after consultation with the Economic and Social Council, establish a Peacebuilding Commission.

264. The core functions of the Peacebuilding Commission should be to identify countries which are under stress and risk sliding towards State collapse; to organize, in partnership with the national Government, proactive assistance in preventing that process from developing further; to assist in the planning for transitions between conflict and post-conflict peacebuilding; and in particular to marshal and sustain the efforts of the international community in post-conflict peacebuilding over whatever period may be necessary.

265. While the precise composition, procedures, and reporting lines of the Peacebuilding Commission will need to be established, they should take account of the following guidelines:

(a) The Peacebuilding Commission should be reasonably small;

(b) It should meet in different configurations, to consider both general policy issues and country-by-country strategies;

(c) It should be chaired for at least one year and perhaps longer by a member approved by the Security Council;

(d) In addition to representation from the Security Council, it should include representation from the Economic and Social Council;

(e) National representatives of the country under consideration should be invited to attend;

(f) The Managing Director of the International Monetary Fund, the President of the World Bank and, when appropriate, heads of regional development banks should be represented at its meetings by appropriate senior officials;

(g) Representatives of the principal donor countries and, when appropriate, the principal troop contributors should be invited to participate in its deliberations;

(h) Representatives of regional and subregional organizations should be invited to participate in its deliberations when such organizations are actively involved in the country in question.

Peacebuilding Support Office

266. A Peacebuilding Support Office should be established in the Secretariat to give the Peacebuilding Commission appropriate Secretariat support and to ensure that the Secretary-General is able to integrate system-wide

peacebuilding policies and strategies, develop best practices and provide cohesive support for field operations.

267. The Office should comprise about 20 or more staff of different backgrounds in the United Nations system and with significant experience in peacebuilding strategy and operations. In addition to supporting the Secretary-General and the Peacebuilding Commission, the Office could also, on request, provide assistance and advice to the heads of peace operations, United Nations resident coordinators or national Governments—for example in developing strategies for transitional political arrangements or building new State institutions. It should submit twice-yearly early warning analyses to the Peacebuilding Commission to help it in organizing its work.

268. The Peacebuilding Support Office should also maintain rosters of national and international experts, particularly those with experience in post-conflict cases.

269. The Office should have an inter-agency advisory board, headed by the Chair of the United Nations Development Group, that would ensure that the Office worked in effective cooperation with other elements of the system that provide related support.

The Commission was generally considered to be one of the more positive ideas to come from the High-Level Panel and appeared likely to be adopted by the membership of the United Nations. When the Secretary-General drew upon this to present his own vision of the Peacebuilding Commission in his "In Larger Freedom" report of March 2005, he significantly reduced the mandate of the new body but elaborated how it might work in practice.

IN LARGER FREEDOM: TOWARDS DEVELOPMENT, SECURITY, AND HUMAN RIGHTS FOR ALL (REPORT OF THE SECRETARY-GENERAL), 21 MARCH 2005[29]

115. A Peacebuilding Commission could perform the following functions: in the immediate aftermath of war, improve United Nations planning for sustained recovery, focusing on early efforts to establish the necessary institutions; help to ensure predictable financing for early recovery activities, in part by providing an overview of assessed, voluntary and standing funding mechanisms; improve the coordination of the many post-conflict activities of the United Nations funds, programmes and agencies; provide a forum in

---

[29] UN Doc. A/59/2005 (2005).

which the United Nations, major bilateral donors, troop contributors, relevant regional actors and organizations, the international financial institutions and the national or transitional Government of the country concerned can share information about their respective post-conflict recovery strategies, in the interests of greater coherence; periodically review progress towards medium-term recovery goals; and extend the period of political attention to post-conflict recovery. I do not believe that such a body should have an early warning or monitoring function, but it would be valuable if Member States could at any stage make use of the Peacebuilding Commission's advice and could request assistance from a standing fund for peacebuilding to build their domestic institutions for reducing conflict, including through strengthening the rule-of-law institutions.

Two essential aspects of how the commission would function were left unresolved: what its membership would be and to whom it would report—the Security Council or the Economic and Social Council. These issues ended up paralyzing debate on the Commission in the lead up to the September 2005 World Summit and were deferred for later consideration. The World Summit Outcome document broadly endorsed the Secretary-General's view of the Peacebuilding Commission as essentially limited to mobilizing resources for post-conflict reconstruction. The Peacebuilding Support Office was also endorsed, but also with a reduced mandate.

2005 WORLD SUMMIT OUTCOME DOCUMENT, 16 SEPTEMBER 2005[30]

98. The main purpose of the Peacebuilding Commission is to bring together all relevant actors to marshal resources and to advise on and propose integrated strategies for post-conflict peacebuilding and recovery. The Commission should focus attention on the reconstruction and institution-building efforts necessary for recovery from conflict and support the development of integrated strategies in order to lay the foundation for sustainable development. In addition, it should provide recommendations and information to improve the coordination of all relevant actors within and outside the United Nations, develop best practices, help to ensure predictable financing for early recovery activities and extend the period of attention by the international community to post-conflict recovery. The Commission should act in all matters on the basis of consensus of its members. . . .

---

[30] GA Res. 60/1 (2005).

104. We also request the Secretary-General to establish, within the Secretariat and from within existing resources, a small peacebuilding support office staffed by qualified experts to assist and support the Peacebuilding Commission. The office should draw on the best expertise available.

Three months later, on 20 December 2005, the Peacebuilding Commission was established.

GENERAL ASSEMBLY RESOLUTION 60/180 (2005): THE PEACEBUILDING COMMISSION

Recognizing the need for a dedicated institutional mechanism to address the special needs of countries emerging from conflict towards recovery, reintegration and reconstruction and to assist them in laying the foundation for sustainable development, . . .

1. *Decides*, acting concurrently with the Security Council, in accordance with Articles 7, 22 and 29 of the Charter of the United Nations, with a view to operationalizing the decision by the 2005 World Summit, to establish the Peacebuilding Commission as an intergovernmental advisory body;

2. *Also decides* that the following shall be the main purposes of the Commission:

(*a*) To bring together all relevant actors to marshal resources and to advise on and propose integrated strategies for post-conflict peacebuilding and recovery;

(*b*) To focus attention on the reconstruction and institution-building efforts necessary for recovery from conflict and to support the development of integrated strategies in order to lay the foundation for sustainable development;

(*c*) To provide recommendations and information to improve the coordination of all relevant actors within and outside the United Nations, to develop best practices, to help to ensure predictable financing for early recovery activities and to extend the period of attention given by the international community to post-conflict recovery; . . .

23. *Reaffirms its request* to the Secretary-General to establish, within the Secretariat, from within existing resources, a small peacebuilding support office staffed by qualified experts to assist and support the Commission, and recognizes in that regard that such support could include gathering and analysing information relating to the availability of financial resources, relevant United Nations in-country planning activities, progress towards meeting short and medium-term recovery goals and best practices with respect to cross-cutting peacebuilding issues;

QUESTIONS ....

10. How did the post-conflict responsibilities of the Peacebuilding Commission and the Peacebuilding Support Office change in the various documents excerpted here? If you were advising the Secretary-General on the best instrument to support the purposes and principles of the United Nations, would you have approved of such changes? If you were advising a member state might your answer be different?

11. What role might the Peacebuilding Commission best play in post-conflict situations? Do you think it is likely to do so? If not, what do you see as the principle hurdles needing to be overcome?

Further Reading

Caplan, Richard. *International Governance of War-Torn Territories: Rule and Reconstruction*. Oxford: Oxford University Press, 2005.

Chesterman, Simon. *You, the People: The United Nations, Transitional Administration, and State-Building*. Oxford: Oxford University Press, 2004.

Cousens, Elizabeth M., and Chetan Kumar, eds. *Peacebuilding as Politics*. Boulder, CO: Lynne Rienner, 2001.

Dobbins, James, et al. *The UN's Role in Nation-Building: From the Congo to Iraq*. Santa Monica, CA: RAND, 2005.

Doyle, Michael W., Ian Johnstone, and Robert C. Orr, eds. *Keeping the Peace: Multidimensional UN Operations in Cambodia and El Salvador*. Cambridge: Cambridge University Press, 1997.

Doyle, Michael W., and Nicholas Sambanis. *Making War & Building Peace: United Nations Peace Operations*. Princeton, NJ: Princeton University Press, 2006.

Fukuyama, Francis. *State-Building: Governance and World Order in the 21st Century*. Ithaca, NY: Cornell University Press, 2004.

Mazurana, Dyan E., and Susan R. McKay. *Women and Peacebuilding*. Montreal: International Centre for Human Rights and Democratic Development, 1999.

Paris, Roland. *At War's End: Building Peace After Civil Conflict*. Cambridge: Cambridge University Press, 2004.

Ratner, Steven R. *The New UN Peacekeeping: Building Peace in Lands of Conflict After the Cold War*. New York: St Martin's Press, 1996.

Stromseth, Jane, David Wippman, and Rosa Brooks. *Can Might Make Rights? Building the Rule of Law After Military Interventions*. Cambridge: Cambridge University Press, 2006.

chapter ten

....

Sanctions

Sanctions, it has often been said, stand between statements and soldiers. In situations where something more than a diplomatic dressing down is required, but where a military response is either inappropriate or impossible, sanctions are frequently turned to as a third option. As a result, sanctions are sometimes used as a default policy option, reflecting the seriousness of the problem rather than the seriousness of engagement with it. As UN Secretary-General Kofi Annan once stated, "getting sanctions right has [often] been a less compelling goal than getting sanctions adopted."[1]

Sanctions are among the few instruments cited in the UN Charter to induce compliance with Security Council decisions. Article 41 of the Charter, under Chapter VII, envisages "complete or partial interruption of economic relations and of rail, sea, air, postal, telegraphic, radio, and other means of communication, and the severance of diplomatic relations." The Charter requires all member states to implement such sanctions adopted under Chapter VII.

This instrument was little used during the Cold War years. An oil embargo was adopted against break-away racist Southern Rhodesia in April 1966, widened to more comprehensive sanctions in December of that year.[2] In 1977, under tremendous pressure from the General Assembly (which had adopted sweeping non-binding sanctions of its own), the Security Council imposed a mandatory arms embargo against apartheid South Africa.[3]

Sanctions were not invoked again until Security Council resolution 661 of August 1990 against Iraq, discussed in chapter 2. Sanctions soon became

---

[1] UN Press Release SG/SM/7360 (2000).
[2] See SC Res. 221 (1966) and SC Res. 232 (1966). These measures were lifted by the Council in SC Res. 460 (1979) after conclusion of the Lancaster House agreement ushering the way for an independent Zimbabwe.
[3] See SC Res. 418 (1977). This measure was lifted in SC Res. 919 (1994) upon the attainment of majority rule in South Africa.

almost routine. In the early 1990s sanctions were sometimes viewed as a magic bullet that could achieve a degree of coercion without the dangers inherent in the use of force. Comprehensive and partial sanctions were imposed during this period on Iraq, the former Yugoslavia, Libya, Liberia, Somalia, parts of Cambodia, Haiti, parts of Angola, Rwanda, Sudan, Sierra Leone, and Afghanistan. (In addition, regional organizations and individual states also imposed sanctions numerous times.)

But the cost of comprehensive sanctions, notably in Iraq, was at times unacceptable. When stringent sanctions were imposed against Iraq in resolution 661 (1990) and reconfirmed in resolution 687 (1991),[4] it was widely assumed that the purposes of the Security Council in Iraq—complete disarmament of weapons of mass destruction—would be achieved rapidly. There was initially little concern over collateral damage from the sanctions, including in the humanitarian sphere. Nevertheless, growing evidence of significant humanitarian distress resulting from the sanctions created pressure on a reluctant Saddam Hussein to agree to the UN's Oil-for-Food Programme in the mid-1990s. The program did help feed a large part of the population and provided other vital support to the Iraqi civilian population caught between a hideous regime and the sanctions, but it could not sustain the Iraqi health system and many other elements of Iraq's social safety net. The growing disaffection among some Council members with continued application of the sanctions as of 1995–1996 also produced a rare outright split among the permanent members, with China, France, and Russia demanding their removal, while Britain and the United States insisted on their maintenance. The plight of Iraqi civilians, publicized by the Iraqi government, NGOs, and some UN staff, created serious hostility against the sanctions regime in most of the UN's member states, and a degree of skepticism about the use of sanctions more generally.

Criticism of the Iraqi sanctions regime led to growing calls for sanctions to be better targeted, designed better to achieve specific political ends rather than as a blunt tool with which to punish a recalcitrant state or non-state actor. This trend was epitomized by the Stockholm Process, an important step toward the embrace of "smart sanctions."

A further aspect of the Iraq sanctions debate concerned the open-ended nature of resolutions such as 661 (1990). Such resolutions impose restrictions that require a further Council resolution to modify or lift them; this effectively gives any permanent member of the Council a power of veto over termination of such punishment, sometimes called a "reverse veto."[5] Although occasionally yielding to pressure to modify certain dimensions of the sanctions regime, Britain and the US relied on this dynamic to sustain the "sanctions

---

[4] See chapter 2 in this volume.
[5] David D. Caron, "The Legitimacy of the Collective Authority of the Security Council," *American Journal of International Law*, vol. 87 (1993), p. 552.

plus inspections" strategy embodied in resolution 687 (1991) until March 2003, and the US-led invasion of Iraq.[6]

A particular form of targeted sanctions goes so far as to list individuals or entities whose assets are to be frozen. Such activities by the Security Council have been criticized on human rights grounds and will be discussed in chapter 13.

The present chapter first reviews the Cold War–era sanctions on Rhodesia and South Africa, which contributed over time to the failure of Rhodesia's Unilateral Declaration of Independence and to the dismantling of apartheid in South Africa. Taken together, these stand out among the UN's most signal accomplishments. The chapter then considers the sanctions regime imposed on Iraq and the Oil-for-Food program. There is a brief discussion of the unfilled promise of Article 50 of the Charter, which is intended to allow for compensation for the effects of sanctions. The chapter next surveys a series of targeted sanctions regimes: in Haiti, where the imposition of sanctions on the import of petroleum and related products in 1993 was intended to bring a recalcitrant de facto military regime to the negotiating table; in Sudan, where the sanctions were political or diplomatic, largely of a symbolic nature; and in Angola, where a non-State actor, the rebel movement UNITA, was the target. The final section discusses the move toward more targeted sanctions.

10.1 Cold War Sanctions (I): Southern Rhodesia

The resolution below was the first adopted by the Security Council imposing mandatory sanctions. The resolution was not adopted against a member state but against a large portion of a rebellious colony of the United Kingdom, with the United Kingdom's support. In the final operative paragraph, note the authorization of a naval blockade against the Mozambican port of Beira, then a Portuguese colony, through which most imports to Rhodesia travelled, to be enforced by the United Kingdom.

SECURITY COUNCIL RESOLUTION 221 (1966)

The Security Council,

Recalling its resolutions . . . and in particular its call to all States to do their utmost to break off economic relations with Southern Rhodesia, including an embargo on oil and petroleum products,

Gravely concerned at reports that substantial supplies of oil may reach Southern Rhodesia as the result of an oil tanker having arrived at Beira and the approach of a further tanker which may lead to the resumption of

---

[6]See chapter 2 in this volume.

pumping through the Companhia do Pipeline Mocambique Rodésias pipeline with the acquiescence of the Portuguese authorities,

Considering that such supplies will afford great assistance and encouragement to the illegal regime in Southern Rhodesia, thereby enabling it to
remain longer in being,

1. *Determines* that the resulting situation constitutes a threat to the peace;
2. *Calls upon* the Portuguese Government not to permit oil to be pumped
through the pipeline from Beira to Southern Rhodesia;
3. *Calls upon* the Portuguese Government not to receive at Beira oil destined
for Southern Rhodesia;
4. *Calls upon* all States to ensure the diversion of any of their vessels reasonably believed to be carrying oil destined for Southern Rhodesia which
may be en route for Beira;
5. *Calls upon* the Government of the United Kingdom of Great Britain and
Northern Ireland to prevent, by the use of force if necessary, the arrival at
Beira of vessels reasonably believed to be carrying oil destined for Southern Rhodesia, and empowers the United Kingdom to arrest and detain the
tanker known as the *Joanna V* upon her departure from Beira in the event her
oil cargo is discharged there.[7]

QUESTIONS

1. Is there a requirement to exhaust other peaceful remedies before the
Council may impose sanctions? Must sanctions be tried before authorizing the use of force? Did resolution 221 (1966) authorize the use of
force?
2. Did Britain require authorization to use force within Southern Rhodesia?

10.2 Cold War Sanctions (II): South Africa

The obduracy of the apartheid government of South Africa in refusing to
engage with the need for majority rule created growing pressure from the UN
membership, now much enlarged by newly de-colonized states, both to
punish Pretoria and to induce it to change its approach. As early as 1963, the
General Assembly recommended to all member states in its resolution 1899 to
refrain from exporting to it both oil and weapons. The operative relevant
paragraphs in this resolution appear below.

---

[7] This first sanctions resolution attracted ten affirmative votes, but also five abstentions, including France and the USSR.

GENERAL ASSEMBLY RESOLUTION 1899(XVIII) (1963)

The General Assembly,
Having considered the question of South West Africa [Namibia] . . .
6. *Decides* to draw the attention of the Security Council to the present critical situation in South West Africa, the continuation of which constitutes a serious threat to international peace and security;
7. *Urges* all States which have not yet done so to take, separately or collectively, the following measures with reference to the question of South West Africa:
(a) Refrain forthwith from supplying in any manner or form any arms or military equipment to South Africa;
(b) Refrain also from supplying in any manner or form any petroleum or petroleum products to South Africa;
(c) Refrain from any action which might hamper the implementation of the present resolution and of the previous General Assembly resolutions on South West Africa;

This resolution and others that followed in the General Assembly had the effect of stigmatizing South Africa, but the effectiveness of these sanctions was limited. The Security Council had not followed up on the reference by the General Assembly expressed in operative paragraph 6 above, but the pressure on it to do so remained unrelenting in ensuing years. Finally, in 1977, the Council acted, making the arms (but not oil) embargo mandatory.

SECURITY COUNCIL RESOLUTION 418 (1977)

The Security Council,
Recalling its resolution . . . strongly condemning the South African Government for its resort to massive violence against and killings of the African people, including schoolchildren and students and others opposing racial discrimination, and calling upon that Government urgently to end violence against the African people and to take urgent steps to eliminate apartheid and racial discrimination,
Recognizing that the military build-up by South Africa and its persistent acts of aggression against the neighbouring States seriously disturb the security of those States,
Further recognizing that the existing arms embargo must be strengthened and universally applied, without any reservations or qualifications whatso-

ever, in order to prevent a further aggravation of the grave situation in South Africa,

Taking note of the Lagos Declaration for Action against Apartheid,

Gravely concerned that South Africa is at the threshold of producing nuclear weapons,

Strongly condemning the South African Government for its acts of repression, its defiant continuance of the system of apartheid and its attacks against neighbouring independent States,

Considering that the policies and acts of the South African Government are fraught with danger to inter-national peace and security,

Recalling . . . other resolutions concerning a voluntary arms embargo against South Africa,

Convinced that a mandatory arms embargo needs to be universally applied against South Africa in the first instance,

Acting therefore under Chapter VII of the Charter of the United Nations,

1. *Determines*, having regard to the policies and acts of the South African Government, that the acquisition by South Africa of arms and related *matériel* constitutes a threat to the maintenance of international peace and security;

2. *Decides* that all States shall cease forthwith any provision to South Africa of arms and related *matériel* of all types, including the sale or transfer of weapons and ammunition, military vehicles and equipment, paramilitary police equipment, and spare parts for the afore-mentioned, and shall cease as well the provision of all types of equipment and supplies and grants of licensing arrangements for the manufacture or maintenance of the aforementioned;

3. *Calls upon* all States to review, having regard to the objectives of the present resolution, all existing contractual arrangements with and licences granted to South Africa relating to the manufacture and maintenance of arms, ammunition of all types and military equipment and vehicles, with a view to terminating them;

4. *Further decides* that all States shall refrain from any co-operation with South Africa in the manufacture and development of nuclear weapons;

5. *Calls upon* all States, including States non-members of the United Nations, to act strictly in accordance with the provisions of the present resolution;

6. *Requests* the Secretary-General to report to the Security Council on the progress of the implementation of the present resolution, the first report to be submitted not later than 1 May 1978;

7. *Decides* to keep this item on its agenda for further action, as appropriate, in the light of developments.

. . . .

The arms embargo itself probably exerted little pressure on South Africa, but the opprobrium associated with UN sanctions through the "pariah state" effect they created undoubtedly contributed the isolation suffered by South Africa throughout ensuing years brought home more strikingly to many of its inhabitants by sporting bans and other forms of shunning. This in turn encouraged the breakthrough in the early 1990s that created the conditions for majority rule in 1994 after negotiations involving President F. W. de Klerk and African National Congress Chair Nelson Mandela. South Africa's first all-race elections, held on 26–29 April 1994, opened a new era in the country's history. A new interim constitution came into effect on the first day of voting, under which all South Africans enjoy for the first time the protection of a bill of rights enforced by a constitutional court. The UN Security Council lifted sanctions in May 1994. In October of that year, newly elected President Nelson Mandela became the first South African head of state to address the UN General Assembly.

The end of white rule in Southern Rhodesia (which became Zimbabwe upon its independence in April 1980, further to the Lancaster House agreement of 21 greatest successes of the UN, uniting virtually the entire membership of the Organization to fight the scourge of organized state racism.

QUESTION

3. This was the first occasion on which the Security Council determined the South African regime posed a threat to international peace and security. It followed riots in Soweto in which schoolchildren had been killed, and was adopted less than two months after anti-apartheid activist Steve Biko was arrested and beaten to death. Reading the text of the resolution, was it primarily intended to respond to South Africa's internal or external policies? Can you think of reasons why the text was crafted as adopted?

10.3 Comprehensive Sanctions: Iraq

As noted in the introduction to this chapter, the humanitarian dimension of the comprehensive sanctions on Iraq, maintained after Operation Desert Storm, was immediately controversial. Early on, the Secretary-General had dispatched a team, headed by Martti Ahtisaari, to assess the humanitarian situation in Iraq. His report of 20 March 1991 described conditions in Iraq as "near-apocalyptic." Dire shortage of medicine and other humanitarian supplies was widespread. Iraq's industrial infrastructure, particularly power plants, oil refineries, water treatment plants, and pumping stations, had been destroyed by Coalition bombing. The sanctions regime imposed by resolution 661 (1990) exacerbated the situation. It was clear that Iraq's humanitarian needs could not be met while the comprehensive sanctions regime remained, and that some relaxation or alteration would be necessary.[8]

---

[8] For a discussion of humanitarian considerations in Security Council decision making see Thomas Weiss, "The Humanitarian Impulse" and Joanna Wechsler, "Human Rights," in David M. Malone (ed.), *The UN Security Council: From the Cold War to the 21st Century* (Boulder, CO: Lynne Rienner: 2004).

Independently of minor relaxations contained in resolution 687 (1991), Secretary-General Pérez de Cuéllar therefore dispatched a further mission to assess Iraq's civilian needs, led by his Executive Delegate, Sadruddin Aga Khan, in July.[9]

Sadruddin Aga Khan's report noted the folly of seeking funds from other states to reconstruct infrastructure in one of the world's largest oil-producing states: "With considerable oil reserves in the ground, Iraq should not have to compete for scarce aid funds with a famine-ravaged Horn of Africa, with a cyclone-hit Bangladesh." Instead, he proposed that "Iraq's 'essential civilian needs' be met urgently and that rapid agreement be secured on the mechanism whereby Iraq's own resources be used to fund them to the satisfaction of the international community."[10]

An "oil-for-food" formula (as it came to be known) was quickly adopted by the Security Council. In resolution 706 (1991), reproduced below, the Council established an elaborate program allowing Iraq to export a quota of oil and to use the resulting export revenues to purchase humanitarian supplies, all under the controlling eye of the United Nations. Resolution 706 (1991) established an escrow account to hold the revenues from sales of Iraqi petroleum, and a mechanism whereby those revenues would be spent on humanitarian requirements such as "the purchase of foodstuffs, medicines and materials and supplies for essential civilian needs."[11] The Council was here taking the unprecedented step of controlling a sovereign state's revenues and directing its expenditures—not only to benefit its own population, but also for other purposes including the payment of costs incurred by the United Nations in the destruction of Iraqi arms in accordance with resolution 687 (1991), of compensation, and of the boundary settlement process.

Since the proposal depended on Iraqi cooperation for both the production of oil and the distribution of humanitarian commodities, the proposal could not be enforced upon Iraq. Unsurprisingly, it refused to cooperate. In response, the United States and Britain sponsored resolution 778 (1992), which authorized states to seize revenues from Iraqi petroleum sales and transfer them to the escrow account provided for in resolution 706 (1991), providing short-term funding for the UN relief program in northern Iraq.[12] Following that unprecedented international expropriation, the UN aid program depended from 1991 to 1995 largely on donations, beset by all of the problems of donor-funded aid programs the United Nations has confronted before and since.

---

[9] Paragraph 20 of SC Res. 687 (1991) provided for expedited import of foodstuffs on the basis of notification to and no objection by the Sanctions Committee.
[10] See Letter dated 15 July 1991 from the Secretary-General addressed to the President of the Security Council (Annex), UN Doc. S/22799 (1991), Annex.
[11] See SC Res. 706 (1991), paras. 1, 2.
[12] SC Res. 778 (1992), para. 1.

SECURITY COUNCIL RESOLUTION 706 (1991)

The Security Council, . . .

Concerned by the serious nutritional and health situation of the Iraqi civilian population as described in this report, and by the risk of a further deterioration of this situation, . . .

Taking note of the conclusions of the above-mentioned report, and in particular of the proposal for oil sales by Iraq to finance the purchase of foodstuffs, medicines and materials and supplies for essential civilian needs for the purpose of providing humanitarian relief, . . .

Convinced of the need for equitable distribution of humanitarian relief to all segments of the Iraqi civilian population through effective monitoring and transparency, . . .

Recalling that . . . Iraq is required to pay the full costs of the Special Commission and the IAEA in carrying out the tasks authorized by section C of resolution 687 (1991), and that the Secretary-General . . . expressed the view that the most obvious way of obtaining financial resources from Iraq to meet the costs of the Special Commission and the IAEA would be to authorize the sale of some Iraqi petroleum and petroleum products; recalling further that Iraq is required to pay its contributions to the Compensation Fund and half the costs of the Iraq-Kuwait Boundary Demarcation Commission; . . .

Acting under Chapter VII of the Charter,

1. *Authorizes* all States, subject to the decision to be taken by the Security Council pursuant to paragraph 5 below and notwithstanding the provisions of [sanctions imposed by] resolution 661 (1990), to permit the import, during a period of 6 months from the date of passage of the resolution pursuant to paragraph 5 below, of petroleum and petroleum products originating in Iraq sufficient to produce a sum to be determined by the Council following receipt of the report of the Secretary-General requested in paragraph 5 of this resolution but not to exceed 1.6 billion United States dollars for the purposes set out in this resolution and subject to the following conditions:

(a) Approval of each purchase of Iraqi petroleum and petroleum products by the Security Council Committee established by resolution 661 (1990) following notification to the Committee by the State concerned;

(b) Payment of the full amount of each purchase of Iraqi petroleum and petroleum products directly by the purchaser in the State concerned into an escrow account to be established by the United Nations and to be administered by the Secretary-General, exclusively to meet the purposes of this resolution;

(c) Approval by the Council, following the report of the Secretary-General requested in paragraph 5 of this resolution, of a scheme for the purchase of foodstuffs, medicines and materials and supplies for essential civilian needs as referred to in paragraph 20 of resolution 687 (1991), in particular health related materials, all of which to be labelled to the extent possible as being supplied under this scheme, and for all feasible and appropriate United

Nations monitoring and supervision for the purpose of assuring their equitable distribution to meet humanitarian needs in all regions of Iraq and to all categories of the Iraqi civilian population as well as all feasible and appropriate management relevant to this purpose, such a United Nations role to be available if desired for humanitarian assistance from other sources;

(d) The sum authorized in this paragraph to be released by successive decisions of the Committee established by resolution 661 (1990) in three equal portions after the Council has taken the decision provided for in paragraph 5 below on the implementation of this resolution, and notwithstanding any other provision of this paragraph, the sum to be subject to review concurrently by the Council on the basis of its ongoing assessment of the needs and requirements;

2. *Decides* that a part of the sum in the account to be established by the Secretary-General shall be made available by him to finance the purchase of foodstuffs, medicines and materials and supplies for essential civilian needs, as referred to in paragraph 20 of resolution 687, and the cost to the United Nations of its roles under this resolution and of other necessary humanitarian activities in Iraq;

3. *Decides also* that a part of the sum in the account to be established by the Secretary-General shall be used by him for appropriate payments to the United Nations Compensation Fund, the full costs of carrying out the tasks authorized by Section C of resolution 687 (1991), the full costs incurred by the United Nations in facilitating the return of all Kuwaiti property seized by Iraq, and half the costs of the Boundary Commission;

4. *Decides further* that the percentage of the value of exports of petroleum and petroleum products from Iraq, authorized under this resolution to be paid to the United Nations Compensation Fund, as called for in paragraph 19 of resolution 687 (1991), and as defined in paragraph 6 of resolution 692 (1991), shall be the same as the percentage decided by the Security Council in paragraph 2 of resolution 705 (1991) for payments to the Compensation Fund, until such time as the Governing Council of the Fund decides otherwise;

5. *Requests* the Secretary-General to submit within 20 days of the date of adoption of this resolution a report to the Security Council for decision on measures to be taken in order to implement paragraphs 1 (a), (b), (c), estimates of the humanitarian requirements of Iraq set out in paragraph 2 above and of the amount of Iraq's financial obligations set out in paragraph 3 above up to the end of the period of the authorization in paragraph 1 above, as well as the method for taking the necessary legal measures to ensure that the purposes of this resolution are carried out and the method for taking account of the costs of transportation of such Iraqi petroleum and petroleum products, . . .

7. *Requires* the Government of Iraq to provide to the Secretary-General and appropriate international organizations on the first day of the month immediately following the adoption of the present resolution and on the first day of each month thereafter until further notice, a statement of the gold and foreign currency reserves it holds whether in Iraq or elsewhere.

By early 1995, opposition to continuation of the sanctions regime had developed on three fronts: within the Council, from France and Russia, and to a lesser extent, China; from Arab (and some other Muslim) countries, increasingly restless about the humanitarian situation in Iraq; and from domestic constituents in the United States and Britain.[13] Increasingly, the United States and Britain were under pressure to compromise. On 14 April 1995, the Council passed resolution 986 (1995), providing a rare concession to Baghdad. It gave Iraq the primary responsibility for the distribution of humanitarian goods under the oil-for-food formula, except in the north, where distribution would be kept under direct UN control. The launch of the Oil-for-Food Programme (OFFP) is thus best understood as a product of the growing divide between the P-5 over the Iraq sanctions regime, matched by a desire to ward off a full-scale disagreement.

SECURITY COUNCIL RESOLUTION 986 (1995) ON AUTHORIZATION TO PERMIT THE IMPORT OF PETROLEUM AND PETROLEUM PRODUCTS ORIGINATING IN IRAQ, AS A TEMPORARY MEASURE TO PROVIDE FOR HUMANITARIAN NEEDS OF THE IRAQI PEOPLE

The Security Council, . . .
Convinced of the need as a temporary measure to provide for the humanitarian needs of the Iraqi people until the fulfilment by Iraq of the relevant Security Council resolutions, including notably resolution 687 (1991) of 3 April 1991, allows the Council to take further action with regard to the prohibitions referred to in resolution 661 (1990) of 6 August 1990, in accordance with the provisions of those resolutions, . . .
Acting under Chapter VII of the Charter of the United Nations,
1. *Authorizes* States, notwithstanding [sanctions imposed by the Council] to permit the import of petroleum and petroleum products originating in Iraq, including financial and other essential transactions directly relating thereto, sufficient to produce a sum not exceeding a total of one billion United States dollars every 90 days for the purposes set out in this resolution and subject to the following conditions:
(a) Approval by the Committee established by resolution 661 (1990), in order to ensure the transparency of each transaction and its conformity with the other provisions of this resolution, after submission of an application by the State concerned, endorsed by the Government of Iraq, for each proposed purchase of Iraqi petroleum and petroleum products, including details of the

---

[13] See Madeleine K. Albright, "A Humanitarian Exception to the Iraqi Sanctions," US Department of State Dispatch 6/17, 24 April 1995.

purchase price at fair market value, the export route, the opening of a letter of credit payable to the escrow account to be established by the Secretary-General for the purposes of this resolution, and of any other directly related financial or other essential transaction;

(b) Payment of the full amount of each purchase of Iraqi petroleum and petroleum products directly by the purchaser in the State concerned into the escrow account to be established by the Secretary-General for the purposes of this resolution; . . .

4. *Further decides* to conduct a thorough review of all aspects of the implementation of this resolution 90 days after the entry into force of paragraph 1 above and again prior to the end of the initial 180 day period, on receipt of the reports referred to in paragraphs 11 and 12 below, and *expresses its intention*, prior to the end of the 180 day period, to consider favourably renewal of the provisions of this resolution, provided that the reports referred to in paragraphs 11 and 12 below indicate that those provisions are being satisfactorily implemented; . . .

7. *Requests* the Secretary-General to establish an escrow account for the purposes of this resolution, to appoint independent and certified public accountants to audit it, and to keep the Government of Iraq fully informed;

8. *Decides* that the funds in the escrow account shall be used to meet the humanitarian needs of the Iraqi population and for the following other purposes, and *requests* the Secretary-General to use the funds deposited in the escrow account:

(a) To finance the export to Iraq, in accordance with the procedures of the Committee established by resolution 661 (1990), of medicine, health supplies, foodstuffs, and materials and supplies for essential civilian needs, . . .

(b) To complement, in view of the exceptional circumstances prevailing in the three [Kurdish] Governorates mentioned below, the distribution by the Government of Iraq of goods imported under this resolution, in order to ensure an equitable distribution of humanitarian relief to all segments of the Iraqi population throughout the country, . . .

(d) To meet the costs to the United Nations of the independent inspection agents and the certified public accountants and the activities associated with implementation of this resolution; . . .

(f) To meet any reasonable expenses, other than expenses payable in Iraq, which are determined by the Committee established by resolution 661 (1990) to be directly related to the export by Iraq of petroleum . . .

11. *Requests* the Secretary-General to report to the Council 90 days after the date of entry into force of paragraph 1 above, and again prior to the end of the initial 180 day period, on the basis of observation by United Nations personnel in Iraq, and on the basis of consultations with the Government of Iraq, on whether Iraq has ensured the equitable distribution of medicine, health supplies, foodstuffs, and materials and supplies for essential civilian needs, financed in accordance with paragraph 8 (a) above, including in his reports any observations he may have on the adequacy of the revenues to meet Iraq's humanitarian needs, and on Iraq's capacity to export sufficient quantities of

petroleum and petroleum products to produce the sum referred to in paragraph 1 above; . . .

13. *Requests* the Secretary-General to take the actions necessary to ensure the effective implementation of this resolution, authorizes him to enter into any necessary arrangements or agreements, and *requests* him to report to the Council when he has done so;

14. *Decides* that petroleum and petroleum products subject to this resolution shall while under Iraqi title be immune from legal proceedings and not be subject to any form of attachment, garnishment or execution, and that all States shall take any steps that may be necessary under their respective domestic legal systems to assure this protection, and to ensure that the proceeds of the sale are not diverted from the purposes laid down in this resolution;

15. *Affirms* that the escrow account established for the purposes of this resolution enjoys the privileges and immunities of the United Nations;

16. *Affirms* that all persons appointed by the Secretary-General for the purpose of implementing this resolution enjoy privileges and immunities as experts on mission for the United Nations in accordance with the Convention on the Privileges and Immunities of the United Nations, and *requires* the Government of Iraq to allow them full freedom of movement and all necessary facilities for the discharge of their duties in the implementation of this resolution;

17. *Affirms* that nothing in this resolution affects Iraq's duty scrupulously to adhere to all of its obligations concerning servicing and repayment of its foreign debt, in accordance with the appropriate international mechanisms;

18. *Also affirms* that nothing in this resolution should be construed as infringing the sovereignty or territorial integrity of Iraq.

Over its lifetime, the OFFP handled $64 billion worth of Iraqi oil revenues, and served as the main source of sustenance for 60 percent of Iraq's estimated twenty-seven million people, reducing malnutrition amongst Iraqi children by 50 percent. It underpinned national vaccination campaigns reducing child mortality and eradicating polio throughout Iraq. In addition, it employed more than 2,500 Iraqis.[14]

But it became clear over time that the sanctions regime generally was being turned by the Baghdad authorities to their advantage, through the creation of black markets they controlled. The costs of sanctions were borne by the most vulnerable sections of Iraqi society, while illegal rents were devised and ex-

---

[14] Oil-For-Food Facts, "Oil-For-Food: FAQ," www.oilforfoodfacts.com/faq.aspx. See especially Independent Inquiry Committee into the United Nations Oil-for-Food Programme, The Impact of the Oil-for-Food Programme on the Iraqi People: Report of an independent Working Group established by the Independent Inquiry Committee (7 September 2005), 177, 179.

tracted by a cynical but still all-powerful clique in government under the initially guileless gaze of UN officials (and of the Security Council).[15] As the later Independent Inquiry Committee under the leadership of former Chairman of the US Federal Reserve, Paul Volcker (the "Volcker Inquiry"), would make clear, over time, UN officials, too, became entangled in the corruption of the OFFP. Excerpts of the Volcker Report are provided in chapter 16.

QUESTIONS ....

4. Who was responsible for oversight of the Oil-for-Food Programme? (See further chapter 16.)
5. If the humanitarian consequences of sanctions were unacceptable, why did the Council not simply replace comprehensive sanctions with a more targeted regime?
6. The Oil-for-Food Programme saw the Security Council making decisions requiring complex administrative machinery and management, and extensive delegation of authority and discretion to agents. Should the Council avoid such decisions in the future or should it seek to build up its regulatory and administrative oversight capacity? What might be the legal implications?

10.4 Article 50 of the UN Charter

One dimension of sanctions that came to the fore shortly after resolution 661 (1990) was adopted in August 1990 imposing a comprehensive blockade was costs to trading partners of the targeted state. Article 50 of the Charter states: "If preventive or enforcement measures against any state are taken by the Security Council, any other state, whether a Member of the United Nations or not, which finds itself confronted with special economic problems arising from the carrying out of those measures shall have the right to consult the Security Council with regard to a solution of those problems." In fact, this article has never been satisfactorily applied, as noted by Boutros Boutros-Ghali in an Agenda for Peace (see chapter 8). Given the absence of compensation for losses sustained during the implementation of sanctions against

---

[15] See Adverse Consequences of Economic Sanctions on the Enjoyment of Human Rights, UN Doc. E/CN.4/Sub.2/RES/1997/35 (1997); Peter van Walsum, "The Iraq Sanctions Committee" in Malone (ed.), *The UN Security Council*; Richard Garfield, "Health and Well-Being in Iraq: Sanctions and the Impact of the Oil-for-Food Program," *Transnational Law & Contemporary Problems*, vol. 11(2) (2001); Christopher C. Joyner, "United Nations Sanctions After Iraq: Looking Back to See Ahead," *Chicago Journal of International Law*, vol. 4 (2003), pp. 341–342.

a major trading partner or geographic neighbor, the temptations of sanctions-busting are intense in some cases, and sometimes winked at by the Security Council (as was the case with large-scale smuggling by Jordan and Turkey in relations to the Iraq sanctions regime). This dimension of sanctions as an instrument for the Council, obviously foreseen at the San Francisco conference, and unresolved today, remains an Achilles heel for the adoption of comprehensive sanctions regimes.

10.5 Sanctions as Leverage: Haiti

While Somalia is a case where UN sanctions had little effect, Haiti provides an example of the opposite. After the overthrow of democratically elected President Jean-Bertrand Aristide in October 1991, the Organization of American States (OAS) initially assumed the lead in seeking to ensure his restoration to power, imposing a trade embargo against the country endorsed by all of its members and also by the UN General Assembly. Because these sanctions were not mandatory in law, and because they involved only OAS members not including a number of European countries that had traditionally been important trading partners of Haiti, they proved leaky and ineffective. Negotiations to return Aristide, now in exile, to Haiti went nowhere, in spite of joint sponsorship by the United Nations and the OAS. The OAS turned to the UN in mid-1993 to seek stronger, mandatory sanctions against the military regime in Haiti, resulting in an embargo on weapons, oil and petroleum products.

SECURITY COUNCIL RESOLUTION 841 (1993)

The Security Council,

Having received a letter dated 7 June 1993 from the Permanent Representative of Haiti to the United Nations . . . requesting that the Council make universal and mandatory the trade embargo on Haiti recommended by the Organization of American States, . . .

Strongly supportive of the continuing leadership of the Secretary-General of the United Nations and the Secretary-General of the Organization of American States and of the efforts of the international community to reach a political solution to the crisis in Haiti,

Commending the efforts undertaken by the Special Representative for Haiti of the Secretary-General of the United Nations and the Secretary-General of the Organization of American States, Mr. Dante Caputo, to establish a political dialogue with the Haitian parties with a view to resolving the crisis in Haiti,

Recognizing the urgent need for an early, comprehensive and peaceful settlement of the crisis in Haiti in accordance with the provisions of the Charter of the United Nations and international law, . . .

Deploring the fact that, despite the efforts of the international community, the legitimate Government of President Jean-Bertrand Aristide has not been reinstated,

Concerned that the persistence of this situation contributes to a climate of fear of persecution and economic dislocation, which could increase the number of Haitians seeking refuge in neighbouring Member States, and convinced that a reversal of this situation is needed to prevent its negative repercussions on the region,

Recalling, in this respect, the provisions of Chapter VIII of the Charter, and stressing the need for effective cooperation between regional organizations and the United Nations,

Considering that the above-mentioned request of the representative of Haiti, made within the context of the related actions previously taken by the Organization of American States and by the General Assembly of the United Nations, defines a unique and exceptional situation warranting extraordinary measures by the Council in support of the efforts undertaken within the framework of the Organization of American States,

Determining that, in these unique and exceptional circumstances, the continuation of this situation threatens international peace and security in the region,

Acting, therefore, under Chapter VII of the Charter,

1. *Affirms* that the solution of the crisis in Haiti should take into account the above-mentioned resolutions of the Organization of American States and of the General Assembly of the United Nations;

2. *Welcomes* the request of the General Assembly that the Secretary-General take the necessary measures in order to assist, in cooperation with the Organization of American States, in the solution of the crisis in Haiti;

3. *Decides* that the provisions set forth in paragraphs 5 to 14 below, which are consistent with the trade embargo recommended by the Organization of American States, shall come into force at 0001 hours eastern standard time on 23 June 1993, unless the Secretary-General, having regard for the views of the Secretary-General of the Organization of American States, has reported to the Council that, in the light of the results of the negotiations conducted by the Special Representative for Haiti of the Secretary-General of the United Nations and Secretary-General of the Organization of American States, the imposition of such measures is not warranted at that time;

4. *Decides also* that if at any time after the submission of the above-mentioned report of the Secretary-General, the Secretary-General, having regard for the views of the Secretary-General of the Organization of American States, reports to the Council that the de facto authorities in Haiti have failed to comply in good faith with their undertakings in the above-mentioned negotiations, the provisions set forth in paragraphs 5 to 14 below shall come into force immediately;

5. *Decides further* that all States shall prevent the sale or supply, by their nationals or from their territories or using their flag vessels or aircraft, of petroleum or petroleum products or arms and related matériel of all types, including weapons and ammunition, military vehicles and equipment, police equipment and spare parts for the aforementioned, whether or not originating in their territories, to any person or body in Haiti or to any person or body for the purpose of any business carried on in or operated from Haiti, and any activities by their nationals or in their territories which promote or are calculated to promote such sale or supply;

6. *Decides* to prohibit any and all traffic from entering the territory or territorial sea of Haiti carrying petroleum or petroleum products, or arms and related matériel of all types, including weapons and ammunition, military vehicles and equipment, police equipment and spare parts for the aforementioned, in violation of paragraph 5 above;

7. *Decides* that the Committee of the Security Council established by paragraph 10 below may authorize, on an exceptional case-by-case basis under a no-objection procedure, the importation, in non-commercial quantities and only in barrels or bottles, of petroleum or petroleum products, including propane gas for cooking, for verified essential humanitarian needs, subject to acceptable arrangements for effective monitoring of delivery and use,

8. *Decides* that States in which there are funds, including any funds derived from property, (a) of the Government of Haiti or of the de facto authorities in Haiti, or (b) controlled directly or indirectly by such Government or authorities or by entities, wherever located or organized, owned or controlled by such Government or authorities, shall require all persons and entities within their own territories holding such funds to freeze them to ensure that they are not made available directly or indirectly to or for the benefit of the de facto authorities in Haiti;

9. *Calls upon* all States and all international organizations to act strictly in accordance with the provisions of the present resolution, notwithstanding the existence of any rights or obligations conferred or imposed by any international agreement or any contract entered into or any licence or permit granted prior to 23 June 1993;

10. *Decides* to establish, in accordance with rule 28 of its provisional rules of procedure, a committee of the Security Council consisting of all the members of the Council to undertake the following tasks and to report on its work to the Council with its observations and recommendations:

(a) To examine the reports submitted pursuant to paragraph 13 below,

(b) To seek from all States further information regarding the action taken by them concerning the effective implementation of the present resolution;

(c) To consider any information brought to its attention by States concerning violations of the measures imposed by the present resolution and to recommend appropriate measures in response thereto;

(d) To consider and decide expeditiously requests for the approval of imports of petroleum and petroleum products for essential humanitarian needs in accordance with paragraph 7 above;

(e) To make periodic reports to the Security Council on information submitted to it regarding alleged violations of the present resolution, identifying where possible persons or entities, including vessels, reported to be engaged in such violations;

(f) To promulgate guidelines to facilitate implementation of the present resolution;

11. *Calls upon* all States to cooperate fully with the Committee in the fulfilment of its tasks, including supplying such information as may be sought by the Committee in pursuance of the present resolution;

12. *Calls upon* States to bring proceedings against persons and entities violating the measures imposed by the present resolution and to impose appropriate penalties;

13. *Requests* all States to report to the Secretary-General by 16 July 1993 on the measures they have initiated for meeting the obligations set out in paragraphs 5 to 9 above;

14. *Requests* the Secretary-General to provide all necessary assistance to the Committee, and to make the necessary arrangements in the Secretariat for that purpose;

15. *Requests* the Secretary-General to report to the Security Council, not later than 15 July 1993, and earlier if he considers it appropriate, on progress achieved in the efforts jointly undertaken by him and the Secretary-General of the Organization of American States with a view to reaching a political solution to the crisis in Haiti;

16. *Expresses its readiness* to review all the measures in the present resolution with a view to lifting them if, after the provisions set forth in paragraphs 5 to 14 above have come into force, the Secretary-General, having regard for the views of the Secretary-General of the Organization of American States, reports to the Council that the de facto authorities in Haiti have signed and have begun implementing in good faith an agreement to reinstate the legitimate Government of President Jean-Bertrand Aristide;

17. *Decides* to remain seized of the matter.

The sanctions came into effect and produced such consternation and crisis within Haiti that negotiations between Aristide and the *de facto* regime in Haiti took place later that month at Governor's Island. This led to an accord that foresaw Aristide's restoration to power in October, supported by various international measures including a small UN peacekeeping operation to deploy in Haiti. Sanctions were suspended in August 1993, but re-imposed in October after violence instigated by the *de facto* government prevented the UN peacekeeping operation from deploying. The sanctions were strengthened by the authorization of enforcement measures (essentially a naval blockade) to give them teeth in resolution 875 (1993). However, as would also prove to be the case in Iraq, the *de facto* regime soon adapted profitably to the sanctions, cornering the black market in petroleum, with the Dominican

Republic border allowing contraband across unfettered by the naval blockade off Haiti's shores. It took the threat of force by a US-led "coalition of the willing," authorized by the UN Security Council in July 1994, to dislodge the *de facto* authorities in September 1994, with Aristide resuming power the following month. Meanwhile, however, the economic sanctions, in place for little more than a year, had devastated Haiti's economy, already the poorest of the Western Hemisphere. The damage has proved lasting and stands as a cautionary tale for the Council to consider before imposing stringent economic sanctions on poor countries. In Haiti, the credible threat of the use of force, as early as 1991, might have represented a better strategy for restoring President Aristide than the incremental measures, including ultimately devastating economic sanctions, adopted.

QUESTIONS ....

7. Why does the preamble to resolution 841 (1993) twice refer to the situation in Haiti as "unique and exceptional"? Is this legally significant?
8. Were sanctions on Haiti intended as punishment or as a means of persuasion? What elements of resolution 841 (1993) support your answer?
9. What powers are given to the Secretary-General in paragraphs 3 and 4 of resolution 841 (1993)? Does this suggest a way of avoiding capricious resort to the veto by permanent members of the Council?

10.6 Sanctions as Symbol: Sudan

So far, we have considered arms and economic sanctions. However, a less drastic form of action, beyond the warnings often issued by the Council but short of the practical (and sometimes unintended) consequences any economic sanctions may have, is available to the Council in the form of diplomatic sanctions. These were invoked following an assassination attempt against President Mubarak of Egypt while visiting Ethiopia in 1995. Investigations in to the incident suggested involvement of the Sudanese government.

SECURITY COUNCIL RESOLUTION 1054 (1996)

The Security Council, . . .

Gravely alarmed at the terrorist assassination attempt on the life of the President of the Arab Republic of Egypt, in Addis Ababa, Ethiopia, on 26 June 1995, and convinced that those responsible for that act must be brought to justice,

Taking note that the statements of the Organization of African Unity (OAU) Mechanism for Conflict Prevention, Management and Resolution of 11 September 1995, and of 19 December 1995 (S/1996/10, annexes I and II) considered the attempt on the life of President Mubarak as aimed, not only at the President of the Arab Republic of Egypt, and not only at the sovereignty, integrity and stability of Ethiopia, but also at Africa as a whole,

Regretting the fact that the Government of Sudan has not yet complied with the requests of the Central Organ of the OAU set out in those statements,

Taking note of the continued effort of the OAU Secretary-General to ensure Sudan's compliance with the requests of the Central Organ of the OAU,

Taking note also, with regret, that the Government of Sudan has not responded adequately to the efforts of the OAU,

Deeply alarmed that the Government of Sudan has failed to comply with the requests set out in paragraph 4 of resolution 1044 (1996),

Reaffirming that the suppression of acts of international terrorism, including those in which States are involved is essential for the maintenance of international peace and security,

Determining that the non-compliance by the Government of Sudan with the requests set out in paragraph 4 of resolution 1044 (1996) constitutes a threat to international peace and security,

Determined to eliminate international terrorism and to ensure effective implementation of resolution 1044 (1996) and to that end *acting* under Chapter VII of the Charter of the United Nations,

1. *Demands* that the Government of Sudan comply without further delay with the requests set out in paragraph 4 of resolution 1044 (1996) by:

(a) Taking immediate action to ensure extradition to Ethiopia for prosecution of the three suspects sheltered in Sudan and wanted in connection with the assassination attempt of 26 June 1995 on the life of the President of the Arab Republic of Egypt in Addis Ababa, Ethiopia; and

(b) Desisting from engaging in activities of assisting, supporting and facilitating terrorist activities and from giving shelter and sanctuary to terrorist elements; and henceforth acting in its relations with its neighbours and with others in full conformity with the Charter of the United Nations and with the Charter of the OAU;

2. *Decides* that the provisions set out in paragraph 3 below shall come into force at 00.01 Eastern Standard Time on 10 May 1996, and shall remain in force until the Council determines that the Government of Sudan has complied with paragraph 1 above;

3. *Decides* that all States shall:

(a) Significantly reduce the number and the level of the staff at Sudanese diplomatic missions and consular posts and restrict or control the movement within their territory of all such staff who remain;

(b) Take steps to restrict the entry into or transit through their territory of members of the Government of Sudan, officials of that Government and members of the Sudanese armed forces;

4. *Calls upon* all international and regional organizations not to convene any conference in Sudan;

5. *Calls upon* all States, including States not members of the United Nations and the United Nations specialized agencies to act strictly in conformity with this resolution, notwithstanding the existence of any rights granted or obligations conferred or imposed by any international agreement or of any contract entered into or any licence or permit granted prior to the entry into force of the provisions set out in paragraph 3 above;

6. *Requests* States to report to the Secretary-General of the United Nations within 60 days from the adoption of this resolution on the steps they have taken to give effect to the provisions set out in paragraph 3 above;

7. *Requests* the Secretary-General to submit an initial report to the Council within 60 days of the date specified in paragraph 2 above on the implementation of this resolution;

8. *Decides* to re-examine the matter, 60 days after the date specified in paragraph 2 above and to consider, on the basis of the facts established by the Secretary-General, whether Sudan has complied with the demands in paragraph 1 above and, if not, whether to adopt further measures to ensure its compliance;

9. *Decides* to remain seized of the matter.

These measures, while far from dramatic or even very convincing at first glance, nevertheless introduced the element of "pariah state" that had so rankled apartheid South Africa during its years under UN sanctions. Accordingly, Sudan took a number of steps to cooperate with the particular inquiries relating to the Mubarak assassination attempt and more broadly to moderate its international behaviour, notably by working with other UN member states in the fight against terrorism. These sanctions were lifted in September 2001, soon after the 11 September 2001 attacks on the United States.

QUESTIONS

10. Why were stronger measures not imposed on Sudan? What action was required for Sudan to comply with the sanctions? How would the Security Council make the determination in paragraph 2 of resolution 1054 (1996)?

11. Compare paragraph 2 with paragraphs 3 and 4 of resolution 841 (1993) on Haiti. Which "trigger" is likely to be more effective in compelling compliance?

10.7 Sanctions Against a Non-State Actor: Angola's UNITA

While earlier UN sanctions had targeted individuals within countries struck by sanctions, the case of UNITA in Angola was strikingly innovative in targeting an entire rebel movement. The UN had been involved in mediating Angola's civil war since 1988 and had deployed three different peacekeeping missions to little avail. As the political calculus in South Africa shifted toward majority rule in Pretoria, the Angolan rebel force UNITA, deprived of earlier support from a wide range of actors (including a degree of diplomatic support from the United States) became more vulnerable to international pressure. Some was applied in resolution 684 (1993), imposing a range of sanctions on UNITA. Due to energetic sanctions-busting across many borders, these did not prove effective. In 1997, the Council was more specific.

SECURITY COUNCIL RESOLUTION 1127 (1997): THE SITUATION IN ANGOLA

Security Council, . . .
Expressing its grave concern at the serious difficulties in the peace process, which are mainly the result of delays by UNITA in the implementation of its obligations under the Lusaka Protocol,
Expressing its firm commitment to preserve the unity, sovereignty and territorial integrity of Angola, . . .
Strongly deploring the failure by UNITA to comply with its obligations under the "Acordos de Paz" (S/22609, annex), the Lusaka Protocol and with relevant Security Council resolutions, in particular resolution 1118 (1997),

A

1. *Demands* that the Government of Angola and in particular UNITA complete fully and without further delay the remaining aspects of the peace process and refrain from any action which might lead to renewed hostilities;
2. *Demands also* that UNITA implement immediately its obligations under the Lusaka Protocol, including demilitarization of all its forces, transformation of its radio station Vorgan into a non-partisan broadcasting facility and full cooperation in the process of the normalization of State administration throughout Angola;
3. *Demands* further that UNITA provide immediately to the Joint Commission, as established under the Lusaka Protocol, accurate and complete information with regard to the strength of all armed personnel under its control, including the security detachment of the Leader of UNITA, the so-called "mining police," armed UNITA personnel returning from outside the

national boundaries, and any other armed UNITA personnel, not previously reported to the United Nations, in order for them to be verified, disarmed and demobilized in accordance with the Lusaka Protocol and agreements between the parties in the context of the Joint Commission, and condemns any attempts by UNITA to restore its military capabilities;

B

Determining that the resulting situation in Angola constitutes a threat to international peace and security in the region,

Acting under Chapter VII of the Charter of the United Nations,

4. *Decides* that all States shall take the necessary measures:

(a) To prevent the entry into or transit through their territories of all senior officials of UNITA and of adult members of their immediate families, as designated in accordance with paragraph 11 (a) below, except those officials necessary for the full functioning of the Government of Unity and National Reconciliation, the National Assembly, or the Joint Commission, provided that nothing in this paragraph shall oblige a State to refuse entry into its territory to its own nationals;

(b) To suspend or cancel all travel documents, visas or residence permits issued to senior UNITA officials and adult members of their immediate families, as designated in accordance with paragraph 11 (a) below, with the exceptions referred to in subparagraph (a) above;

(c) To require the immediate and complete closure of all UNITA offices in their territories; . . .

5. *Further decides* that the measures set out in paragraph 4 above shall not apply to cases of medical emergency or to flights of aircraft carrying food, medicine, or supplies for essential humanitarian needs, as approved in advance by the Committee created pursuant to resolution 864 (1993);

6. *Urges* all States and international and regional organizations to stop travel by their officials and official delegations to the central headquarters of UNITA, except for the purposes of travel to promote the peace process and humanitarian assistance;

7. *Decides also* that the provisions of paragraph 4 above shall come into force without any further notice at 00.01 EST on 30 September 1997, unless the Security Council decides, on the basis of a report by the Secretary-General, that UNITA has taken concrete and irreversible steps to comply with all the obligations set out in paragraphs 2 and 3 above;

8. *Requests* the Secretary-General to submit by 20 October 1997, and every ninety days thereafter, a report on the compliance of UNITA with all the obligations set out in paragraphs 2 and 3 above, and expresses its readiness to review the measures set out in paragraph 4 above if the Secretary-General reports at any time that UNITA has fully complied with these obligations;

9. *Expresses* its readiness to consider the imposition of additional measures, such as trade and financial restrictions, if UNITA does not fully comply with

its obligations under the Lusaka Protocol and all relevant Security Council resolutions; . . .

11. *Requests* the Committee created pursuant to resolution 864 (1993):

(a) To draw up guidelines expeditiously for the implementation of paragraph 4 of this resolution, including the designation of officials and of adult members of their immediate families whose entry or transit is to be prevented and whose travel documents, visas or residence permits are to be suspended or cancelled in accordance with paragraphs 4 (a) and 4 (b) above;

(b) To give favourable consideration to, and decide upon, requests for the exceptions set out in paragraph 5 above;

(c) To report to the Council by 15 November 1997 regarding the actions taken by States to implement the measures set out in paragraph 4 above; . . .

13. *Requests* also Member States to provide to the Committee created pursuant to resolution 864 (1993) information on the measures they have adopted to implement the provisions of paragraph 4 above no later than 1 November 1997.

This resolution, imposing sanctions of a detailed and confining sort on UNITA, exhibits several characteristics that would come to be important for the Council. First, its concern with compliance not just by UNITA but also by many other actors on the ground and in neighboring countries in touch with it reveals the sorry experience of the Council in addressing sanctions-busting in other cases. Secondly, the resolution focuses a great deal on air traffic to rebel-held areas because these were particularly rich in diamonds, the sale of which had sustained UNITA for many years. Diamonds were easy to carry out of the country in small aircraft and then easy to market in Europe and beyond. The following year, in resolution 1173 (1998), the Council was still more specific with respect to financial transactions and prescribing a certification process for all Angolan diamonds. But the sanctions continued to prove leaky.

In a departure for the United Nations, the Security Council's sanctions committee responsible for Angola became a focal point for effective research and diplomatic action to trace and publicize the sources of UNITA's support and to choke its access to international diamond markets in 1999 and 2000. In resolution 1237 (1999), the Council took steps that resulted in an expert panel whose report, in March 2000 "named and shamed" a number of governments and private sector interests, creating significant distress in some UN circles, but greatly increasing the pressure on UNITA's external sources of funds and other support. (Efforts to create a permanent sanctions monitoring capacity at the United Nations foundered, however, on concerns by member states that such a body could produce a raft of inconvenient findings.) This exercise increased the focus on "conflict diamonds," eventually leading to the Kimberley Process, which brought together governments, the diamond industry, and non-governmental actors to prevent the trade in diamonds from war zones such as Sierra Leone. It also greatly increased attention to complex economic factors at play in many of the wars with which the Security Council was at grips, notably in the Democratic Republic of the Congo and generating a debate in the research community centred on the "greed or grievance" dichotomy at the root of many conflicts.

While the efforts of the UN to strengthen implementation of its sanctions against UNITA doubtless played a role in the movement's collapse, it was the death of its leader, Jonas Savimbi, in an ambush, in February 2002 that led to an end of fighting and an initiation of national reconciliation. The Security Council lifted sanctions on 9 December 2002 in resolution 1448 (2002).

QUESTION ....

12. What concerns, if any, are raised by the imposition of sanctions on a non-state actor? On an individual? (See also chapter 13.)

10.8 Targeted Sanctions

Concerns about the humanitarian consequences of comprehensive economic sanctions, in particular those imposed on Iraq from 1990, led to efforts to make them "smarter" by targeting sectors of the economy or specific individuals more likely to influence policies—or at least confining sanctions to ensure that those who bore the brunt of their consequences were also those perceived as most responsible for the situation that led to their imposition. This utilitarian approach to minimizing suffering gave rise to different concerns, however, as the identification of individuals (and, in some cases, their immediate families)[16] for freezing of their assets suggested a shift in the way that sanctions were being used.

SECURITY COUNCIL RESOLUTION 1267 (1999)

The Security Council, . . .
    Noting the indictment of Usama bin Laden and his associates by the United States of America for, inter alia, the 7 August 1998 bombings of the United States embassies in Nairobi, Kenya, and Dar es Salaam, Tanzania and for conspiring to kill American nationals outside the United States, and noting

---

[16] See, eg, SC Res. 1173 (1998) (requiring the freezing of assets belonging to "senior officials of UNITA or adult members of their immediate families").

also the request of the United States of America to the Taliban to surrender them for trial (S/1999/1021),

Determining that the failure of the Taliban authorities to respond to [Council demands that it stop providing sanctuary and training for international terrorists and their organizations, and that all Afghan factions cooperate with efforts to bring indicted terrorists to justice] constitutes a threat to international peace and security,

Stressing its determination to ensure respect for its resolutions,

Acting under Chapter VII of the Charter of the United Nations,

1. *Insists* that the . . . Taliban . . . comply promptly with its previous resolutions and in particular cease the provision of sanctuary and training for international terrorists and their organizations, take appropriate effective measures to ensure that the territory under its control is not used for terrorist installations and camps, or for the preparation or organization of terrorist acts against other States or their citizens, and cooperate with efforts to bring indicted terrorists to justice;

2. *Demands* that the Taliban turn over Usama bin Laden without further delay to appropriate authorities in a country where he has been indicted, or to appropriate authorities in a country where he will be returned to such a country, or to appropriate authorities in a country where he will be arrested and effectively brought to justice; . . .

4. *Decides further* that, in order to enforce paragraph 2 above, all States shall:

(a) Deny permission for any aircraft to take off from or land in their territory if it is owned, leased or operated by or on behalf of the Taliban as designated by the Committee established by paragraph 6 below, unless the particular flight has been approved in advance by the Committee on the grounds of humanitarian need, including religious obligation such as the performance of the Hajj;

(b) Freeze funds and other financial resources, including funds derived or generated from property owned or controlled directly or indirectly by the Taliban, or by any undertaking owned or controlled by the Taliban, as designated by the Committee established by paragraph 6 below, and ensure that neither they nor any other funds or financial resources so designated are made available, by their nationals or by any persons within their territory, to or for the benefit of the Taliban or any undertaking owned or controlled, directly or indirectly, by the Taliban, except as may be authorized by the Committee on a case-by-case basis on the grounds of humanitarian need; . . .

6. *Decides* to establish, in accordance with rule 28 of its provisional rules of procedure, a Committee of the Security Council consisting of all the members of the Council to undertake the following tasks and to report on its work to the Council with its observations and recommendations:

(a) To seek from all States further information regarding the action taken by them with a view to effectively implementing the measures imposed by paragraph 4 above;

(b) To consider information brought to its attention by States concerning violations of the measures imposed by paragraph 4 above and to recommend appropriate measures in response thereto;

(c) To make periodic reports to the Council on the impact, including the humanitarian implications, of the measures imposed by paragraph 4 above;

(d) To make periodic reports to the Council on information submitted to it regarding alleged violations of the measures imposed by paragraph 4 above, identifying where possible persons or entities reported to be engaged in such violations;

(e) To designate the aircraft and funds or other financial resources referred to in paragraph 4 above in order to facilitate the implementation of the measures imposed by that paragraph;

(f) To consider requests for exemptions from the measures imposed by paragraph 4 above as provided in that paragraph, and to decide on the granting of an exemption to these measures in respect of the payment by the International Air Transport Association (IATA) to the aeronautical authority of Afghanistan on behalf of international airlines for air traffic control services;

(g) To examine the reports submitted pursuant to paragraph 9 below;

7. *Calls upon* all States to act strictly in accordance with the provisions of this resolution, notwithstanding the existence of any rights or obligations conferred or imposed by any international agreement or any contract entered into or any licence or permit granted prior to the date of coming into force of the measures imposed by paragraph 4 above;

8. *Calls upon* States to bring proceedings against persons and entities within their jurisdiction that violate the measures imposed by paragraph 4 above and to impose appropriate penalties;

9. *Calls upon* all States to cooperate fully with the Committee established by paragraph 6 above in the fulfilment of its tasks, including supplying such information as may be required by the Committee in pursuance of this resolution;

10. *Requests* all States to report to the Committee established by paragraph 6 above within 30 days of the coming into force of the measures imposed by paragraph 4 above on the steps they have taken with a view to effectively implementing paragraph 4 above;

11. *Requests* the Secretary-General to provide all necessary assistance to the Committee established by paragraph 6 above and to make the necessary arrangements in the Secretariat for this purpose;

12. *Requests* the Committee established by paragraph 6 above to determine appropriate arrangements, on the basis of recommendations of the Secretariat, with competent international organizations, neighbouring and other States, and parties concerned with a view to improving the monitoring of the implementation of the measures imposed by paragraph 4 above;

13. *Requests* the Secretariat to submit for consideration by the Committee established by paragraph 6 above information received from Governments and public sources on possible violations of the measures imposed by paragraph 4 above;

14. *Decides* to terminate the measures imposed by paragraph 4 above once the Secretary-General reports to the Security Council that the Taliban has fulfilled the obligation set out in paragraph 2 above;

15. *Expresses* its readiness to consider the imposition of further measures, in accordance with its responsibility under the Charter of the United Nations, with the aim of achieving the full implementation of this resolution;

16. *Decides* to remain actively seized of the matter.

SECURITY COUNCIL RESOLUTION 1333 (2000)

The Security Council, . . .

Acting under Chapter VII of the Charter of the United Nations,

1. *Demands* that the Taliban comply with resolution 1267 (1999) and, in particular, cease the provision of sanctuary and training for international terrorists and their organizations, take appropriate effective measures to ensure that the territory under its control is not used for terrorist installations and camps, or for the preparation or organization of terrorist acts against other States or their citizens, and cooperate with international efforts to bring indicted terrorists to justice;

2. *Demands also* that the Taliban comply without further delay with the demand of the Security Council in paragraph 2 of resolution 1267 (1999) that requires the Taliban to turn over Usama bin Laden to appropriate authorities in a country where he has been indicted, or to appropriate authorities in a country where he will be returned to such a country, or to appropriate authorities in a country where he will be arrested and effectively brought to justice; . . .

8. *Decides* that all States shall take further measures:

(a) To close immediately and completely all Taliban offices in their territories;

(b) To close immediately all offices of Ariana Afghan Airlines in their territories;

(c) To freeze without delay funds and other financial assets of Usama bin Laden and individuals and entities associated with him as designated by the Committee, including those in the Al-Qaida organization, and including funds derived or generated from property owned or controlled directly or indirectly by Usama bin Laden and individuals and entities associated with him, and to ensure that neither they nor any other funds or financial resources are made available, by their nationals or by any persons within their territory, directly or indirectly for the benefit of Usama bin Laden, his associates or any entities owned or controlled, directly or indirectly, by Usama bin Laden or individuals and entities associated with him including the Al-Qaida organization and *requests* the Committee to maintain an updated list, based on information provided by States and regional organizations, of the individuals and entities designated as being associated with Usama bin Laden, including those in the Al-Qaida organization.

QUESTIONS

13. The human rights consequences of targeted financial sanctions are considered in chapter 13. What challenges do such regimes pose for the Council as a decision-making body? Are decisions made in this context in keeping with the political character of the Council? (Compare the discussion of factors to be taken into account in the *Admissions* case in chapter 5.)

14. Several of the sanctions regimes imposed by the Security Council produced adverse humanitarian effects, sometimes said to amount to international crimes. Who might be held responsible for these consequences? How?

15. Given the limited *repertoire* of Security Council instruments to encourage or coerce compliance with its decisions, sanctions are important to the Council. They tend to follow very established patterns (weapons, economic, financial, travel, diplomatic). Can you think of others that might work well? If so, what would be their strengths and weaknesses?

16. Are sanctions meant to work? That is, are they imposed because of a belief that they impact on policy choices of key actors or because more than words but less than war is required by an international crisis?

Further Reading

Strengthening UN Targeted Sanctions Through Fair and Clear Procedures. Providence, RI: Watson Institute for International Studies, 30 March 2006. Available at http://www.watsoninstitute.org/TFS.

Angell, David J.R. "The Angola Sanctions Committee." In *The UN Security Council: From the Cold War to the 21st Century*, edited by David M. Malone. Boulder, CO: Lynne Rienner, 2004, pp. 195–204.

Bailey, Sydney D., and Sam Daws. *The Procedure of the UN Security Council.* 3rd edn. Oxford: Oxford University Press, 1998, pp. 365–378 (on Security Council Sanctions Committees and some related organs).

Chesterman, Simon, and Béatrice Pouligny. "Are Sanctions Meant to Work? The Politics of Creating and Implementing Sanctions Through the United Nations." *Global Governance*, vol. 9 (2003), p. 503.

Cortright, David, and George A. Lopez, *Sanctions and the Search for Security: Challenges to UN Action*, Boulder, CO: Lynne Rienner, 2002, particularly pp. 201–224.

Cortright, David, and George A. Lopez. *The Sanctions Decade: Assessing UN Strategies in the 1990s,* Boulder, CO: Lynne Rienner, 2000.

Keen, David. *Conflict & Collusion in Sierra Leone.* Oxford: James Currey, 2005, pp. 212–217.

Mack, Andrew, and Asif Khan. "UN Sanctions: A Glass Half-Full." In *The United Nations and Global Security,* edited by Richard M. Price and Mark W. Zacher. New York: Palgrave Macmillan, 2004.

Malone, David M. *Decision-Making in the UN Security Council: The Case of Haiti, 1990–1997.* Oxford: Clarendon Press, 1998, pp. 78–97 and 155–184.

Malone, David M. *The International Struggle for Iraq: Politics in the UN Security Council.* Oxford: Oxford University Press, 2006, pp. 114–151.

Walsum, Peter van. "The Iraq Sanctions Committee." In *The UN Security Council: From Cold War to 21st Century,* edited by David M. Malone. Boulder, CO: Lynne Rienner, 2004, pp. 181–194.

chapter eleven
....

Development

The work of the United Nations on development issues has increased significantly over the years. Chapters IX and X of the UN Charter provide a solid foundation for attention to development issues, but this has sometimes been hampered by the sprawling nature of the UN system that evolved around this mandate—with many agencies, funds, and programs aiming to promote development often in parallel to (when not in outright competition with) the World Bank, regional development banks, and other non-UN institutions. While the efforts of the UN were initially uncontroversial, industrialized countries eventually became disenchanted with being potentially outvoted on development financing in the UN General Assembly by the much larger group of developing countries organized under the umbrella of the "Group of 77" (the G-77, now in fact numbering over 130 members). Wealthy countries today prefer to channel their development funding through the World Bank or regional development banks, where weighted voting ensured control of both the agenda and proposed loans; many developing countries prefer the UN route.

Even following the excitement of the Millennium Summit of 2000, the Millennium Development Goals, and the successful Monterrey Conference on the Financing of Development in 2002, the United Nations remains a junior partner in development financing (although it is frequently the lead international actor in responding to natural and man-made humanitarian emergencies, discussed in chapter 14). In addition to concerns about control by donors, the manner in which funding is provided creates its own problems. Whereas the general running of the United Nations and its peacekeeping operations are supported through assessed contributions (discussed in chapter 6), development assistance, like humanitarian relief, relies upon voluntary contributions. This leads to support for favored programs at the expense of systematic planning, while UN agencies have learned to compete with one another for scarce resources.

Some UN agencies flourished for a time on development policy, displaying real intellectual leadership, for example the Economic Commission for Latin

America and the Caribbean (ECLAC) in the 1960s, and UNICEF in the 1990s—the latter successfully challenging prescriptions of the World Bank and IMF that advocated structural adjustment without any regard for social policy. But the UN system and its agencies were simply never trusted by the donor community to the extent that the Bank and the Fund were.

Thus, while rafts of resolutions were debated and adopted within the United Nations on the serial debt crises afflicting many developing countries in the 1980s and 1990s, solutions were negotiated elsewhere, often under G-7 leadership in close cooperation with the IMF, World Bank and Paris Club (of official creditors). Similarly, the role of the UN on trade liberalization and disputes was consistently minor, in spite of early high hopes for the UN Conference on Trade and Development (UNCTAD) that today limps on alongside the more meaningful World Trade Organization (independent of the UN). One reason for this may lie in the UN's often highly ideological debates on questions involving dollars and cents, which tend to result in pragmatic compromises rather than principled strategies. Debates in the UN's Economic and Social Council (ECOSOC) have been characterized by the rhetoric of diplomats with questionable economic credentials, while the real economic policy and development action unfolds elsewhere.

The UN's failure to matter all that much on development issues, beyond important normative efforts such as the setting of the Millennium Development Goals, has been a source of considerable unhappiness within the Organization. Other efforts to expand the role include the *Global Compact*, which involved private sector companies and non-governmental organizations in the UN's debates, proving controversial in its own right with some delegations.

This chapter begins with an examination of how thinking about development policy has evolved at the United Nations, before considering two of the key efforts to operationalize this rhetoric: the move to articulate a right to development in the 1970s and 1980s, and more recent efforts to set quantifiable goals for development, notably at the Millennium Summit. It then sketches out the early history of an issue certain to be a major one on the international agenda in decades to come: how to ensure that development activities of one generation do not irreparably harm the environment for those generations yet to come.

11.1 The Evolution of Development Policy at the United Nations

The United Nations Intellectual History Project has, among other projects, surveyed the emergence of the present understanding of development and the role of the United Nations in promoting it. It is important to bear in mind the ultimately marginal role of the United Nations in development programming, as opposed to its episodically important role in intellectual leadership on development policy.

RICHARD JOLLY, LOUIS EMMEREIJ, AND THOMAS G. WEISS

THE POWER OF UN IDEAS: LESSONS FROM THE FIRST 60 YEARS[1]

Beginning with its Charter, the United Nations has pursued a vision. And over the years, it has set out ideas and policy proposals that constitute an agenda to achieve that vision. . . . The Charter incorporates four pillars, breathtaking in their boldness and universality:

- Peace—the idea that sovereign states could create an international organization and procedures that would replace military aggression and war by negotiation and collective security.
- Development—the idea that all countries, long independent or newly so, could purposefully pursue policies of economic and social advance, which over time would improve the welfare and living standards of their people.
- Human rights—the idea that every individual in every country throughout the world shared an equal claim not only to such individual civil and political rights as life, liberty, and the pursuit of happiness but also to a core of economic and social freedoms.
- Independence—the idea that people in all countries had rights to be politically independent and sovereign and make whatever national and international agreements that their citizens might choose.

Initially, these four pillars were pursued more in parallel than in an integrated fashion. Development was taken to be *economic* development. . . . Today, the UN gives great emphasis to poverty reduction and, since the 147 heads of state and government met in 2000, to the Millennium Development Goals (MDGs).

The UN's initial focus on an economic process was in line with thinking of the time. The UN issued three major reports on economic development in 1949 and 1951. The starting point for each report was how to achieve or maintain full employment, a preoccupation fired by the memories of the Great Depression in the 1930s and by Keynesianism. Soon though, this initial frame of reference gave way to a perspective more in line with the economic priorities and realities of developing countries. The second report was especially clear; *Measures for Economic Development of the Under-developed Countries* identified the rapid creation of employment as a fundamental goal, but then focused on long-term economic development as the condition for achieving it. The priority for poor countries was seen as raising savings, investment, and

---

[1] Excerpted from Richard Jolly, Louis Emmereij, and Thomas G. Weiss, The Power of UN Ideas: Lessons from the First 60 Years (New York: United Nations Intellectual History Project, 2005). Reprinted with permission. This document and others are available from www.unhistory.org.

thus the rate of economic growth. The issue of diminishing income gaps between rich and poor countries was explicitly taken into account. Although the analysis was subtle and rich, the goal was narrow and in the end incomplete.

By the 1960s the importance of economic development was rising on the UN agenda, greatly stimulated by the many newly independent countries that had or were about to become member states. In 1961 US President John F. Kennedy proposed, in a powerful speech to the General Assembly, that there should be a "development decade." His words even today ring fresh with insight:

> Political sovereignty is but a mockery without the means of meeting poverty and illiteracy and disease. Self-determination is but a slogan if the future holds no hope. This is why my Nation, which has freely shared its capital and technology to help others help themselves, now proposes officially designating the decade of the 1960s as the United Nations Decade of Development.[2]

Almost all parts of the world organization became involved in elaborating what the First Development Decade should include. Inputs came from some of the world's most prominent economists and other experts, including Arthur Lewis, Jan Tinbergen, Paul Hoffman, Barbara Ward, and Walt Rostow. *The UN Development Decade: Proposals for Action* was published in 1962. The "Foreword" by U Thant, then acting Secretary-General [after Dag Hammarskjöld's death], makes clear that even then a more subtle perspective was beginning to emerge. "Development is not just economic growth, it is growth plus change."

The same report quoted the Economic and Social Council (ECOSOC):

> One of the greatest dangers in development policy lies in the tendency to give the more material aspects of growth an overriding and disproportionate emphasis. The end may be forgotten in preoccupation with the means. Human rights may be submerged and human beings seen only as instruments of production rather than as free entities for whose welfare and cultural advance the increased production is intended. The recognition of this issue has a profound bearing upon the formulation of the objectives of economic development and the methods employed in attaining them.[3]

In the 1970s the [International Labour Organization (ILO)] led the way in shifting the focus to employment, but it was embedded in a much broader exploration of the development conundrum. Underlying an apparent "lack of jobs," the ILO pointed to three distinct types of employment problems: open unemployment in the Western sense; the frustration of job-seekers unable to

---

[2] Public Papers of the President of the United States, J.F. Kennedy, January 20 to December 31, 1961 (Washington, DC: US Government Printing Office, 1962), p. 623.
[3] The United Nations Development Decade: Proposals for Action (New York: United Nations, 1962), pp. 10-11.

obtain the type of work or the remuneration which they judged reasonable; and most important, a low level of incomes—in fact, poverty—obtained by many producers and their families, reflecting the under-utilization and low productivity of the labor force, both male and female. This definition of the employment problem created the link between employment, poverty, income distribution, and development.

Over the 1970s, the path led to greater analysis and concern for poverty and to the ideas of redistribution with growth and basic needs. These formed the cutting edge for national development strategies, formally endorsed in the resolutions of the World Employment Conference in 1976. These ideas also had an important impact on the World Bank, where its president, Robert McNamara, and his chief economist, Hollis Chenery, strongly emphasized poverty reduction and, later in the 1970s, basic needs.

Within the UN the development agenda was being broadened further by a series of pioneering world conferences. These focused on environment and development (1972), hunger and world food problems (1974), population growth (1974), employment and basic needs (1976), human settlements (1976), and science and technology (1979). The first of the world conferences on women, in Mexico City in 1975, had an institutional and legal impact, creating two important UN institutions for women—UNIFEM (UN Development Fund for Women) and INSTRAW (International Research and Training Institute for the Advancement of Women). It also set in motion actions that led four years later to the Convention on the Elimination of All Forms of Discrimination against Women (CEDAW).

In contrast to the consensus of these global conferences and the substantive ideas coming out of them, the sixth and seventh special sessions of the General Assembly in 1974 and 1975 led to fireworks. These responded to Third World calls for a New International Economic Order (NIEO). A stalemate on this theme continued until the end of the 1970s, when strong opposition from the industrial countries effectively removed it from the international agenda.

In the early 1980s, with rising debt and world recession, action on many of these broader perspectives came to a shuddering halt. Thus began what Enrique Iglesias, the president of the Inter-American Development Bank, called the "lost decade" for Latin America and Africa. The economic role of the UN diminished. From this point forward, [the International Monetary Fund (IMF)] and the World Bank, with strong support from the West, set the core international agenda for economic development, with a dominant focus, initially on stabilization, later on structural adjustment. These gave overwhelming priority to reducing inflation, correcting imbalances in deficits, and restoring economic growth, in that order of priority and often with space only for the first two. The development agenda narrowed once again.

In the 1980s the United Nations was left to take on the role of constructive dissent. In 1985 UNICEF began promoting the need for "adjustment with a human face." In parallel [the Economic Commission for Africa (ECA)] promoted calls for an African Alternative Framework for Structural Adjustment Programs. By 1990 the world organization put forward a more active and comprehensive strategy, with the publication by the UN Development Programme of its first annual *Human Development Report*, setting out a fundamental alternative to Bretton Woods orthodoxy.

Successive reports broadened the development agenda by exploring what a truly human development approach would mean for several priority areas: the concept and measurement of development, development financing, global income distribution, human security, women's equality and gender, economic growth, poverty, consumption, globalization, human rights, and cultural diversity. Each of these became less an add-on to economic development than an enrichment of the concept of human development.

In the 1990s after the end of the Cold War came the second round of global conferences and summits, reinforcing earlier priorities for environment, human rights, population, social development, gender equality, food security, and urban development. These culminated in 2000 in the Millennium Summit, which adopted a program focused on poverty reduction and the achievement of the Millennium Development Goals by 2015. By this stage, new efforts had been made to establish closer links between the UN and the Bretton Woods institutions, which accepted the MDGs.

Over more than half a century, the four original pillars of the Charter (peace, development, human rights, and independence), largely pursued in parallel in the first few decades, came closer together, a remarkable and underemphasized advance. The integration of these important facets of the human challenge may be the most under-recognized achievement of the world organization. Fernando Henrique Cardoso, Brazil's former president and a distinguished social scientist, told us that the broadening of the concept of development to include social aspects was "a consequence of United Nations presence across the world in order to enlarge views on what the government role is, and also the concept of equitable development . . . All this, I think, has a direct effect on social science in general, even when the persons are not aware of the fact. But the renewal of the issues and themes was very important, a subject matter to be taken up by universities, and by political parties. I think this was a very important role played by the United Nations."

An Agenda for Development, issued in 1995, received little attention at the time but demonstrates the new integration within a formal definition of development:

> The goal of development is the improvement of human wellbeing and the quality of life. This involves the eradication of poverty, the fulfilment of basic needs of all people, and the protection of all human rights and fundamental freedoms, including the right to development. It requires that governments apply active social and environmental policies and that they promote and

protect all human rights and fundamental freedoms on the basis of democratic and widely participatory institutions.[4]

Despite these positive moves to a fuller and more rounded perspective on development, several key issues, identified as major priorities in the early years of the United Nations, appear to have dropped out or faded away. These include moderating the causes of extreme instability in developing countries, especially those linked to fluctuations in commodity prices and other factors in international trade and finance; disarmament and development; and narrowing extreme gaps between the richest and poorest countries. Strong and decisive action on any one of these three, let alone on two or three of them, might have changed the entire *problématique* of the poorest countries and of the global economy. For these reasons, ways need to be found to put these three issues, and no doubt others, back on the agenda. But before turning to the future, we provide some of the highlights of the UN's past contributions.

Many of the UN's pioneering contributions are so readily accepted today that it is often difficult to recall the extent of the controversy and the passion that accompanied their launch and adoption. Most important, the United Nations has been instrumental in widening the concept of development, making it more complicated—and more realistic. Development now includes human rights, human security, gender, environmental issues, population, sustainability, and culture. Measuring concretely the dimensions of the world has been another UN contribution. This chapter explores ideas and issues that made a difference and altered the way we conceive and quantify aspects of economic and social development.

Quantifying the World

National and international statistics are an arena of action that many non-specialists take for granted. Moreover, many are quite unaware of the leading role of the UN over the years. In fact, the world organization's contribution to statistics has often been crucial in ensuring that necessary information is available for analyzing problems and making policies, nationally and internationally. The UN's work in this area often sets the frame for assessing the world's economic and social progress—or the lack of it.

The Statistical Commission was established in 1945, in the UN's first few months. Its work soon achieved worldwide significance and had a global impact. A mass of common information became available to guide national and international action and policymaking. It is these data sets that make possible the assessment of comparative progress and performance, between countries or regions. What a contrast with the situation before the creation of the United Nations! A glance at statistical reports from the 1930s reminds

---

[4] Boutros Boutros-Ghali, An Agenda for Development (New York: United Nations, 1995).

one of maps of the 16th and 17th century, with vast blank areas marked *terra incognita*. Today, a range of comparable data is available for almost all countries.

Setting Global Goals

Achievements must be judged by results—and for most purposes, goals for outputs are even more important than goals for inputs. One essential contribution of the world organization has been formulating, adopting, and promoting global development goals. Beginning with goals for education set around 1960 in three major regional conferences organized by [the United Nations Educational, Scientific and Cultural Organization (UNESCO)], the United Nations has formulated some 50 goals across the whole field of development. This contrasts sharply with the World Bank and the IMF, which not only have shied away from formulating global goals but, until the last few years, have not formally recognized them, even after their adoption by the international community of states. Moreover, in the case of the controversial structural adjustment programs in the 1980s, the Bretton Woods institutions resisted outcome goals country-by-country. Instead, they prioritized general economic indicators, such as the reduction in inflation and budgetary imbalances and the extent of liberalization and privatization.

In 1961 the UN took up John F. Kennedy's challenge for a development decade and formulated the first two global economic goals—an output goal that economic growth in developing countries should increase to 5 percent a year by 1970, and an input goal that total transfers (aid and private capital flows combined) from developed to developing countries should increase to 1 percent of the GNP of industrial countries. The goal for economic growth was exceeded—growth averaged 5.5 percent over the 1960s—even though it was thought by many to be excessively optimistic. The goal for transfers, though not fully achieved, had a considerable impact: total transfers reached almost 0.8 percent of industrial country GNP by 1970, four-fifths of the goal.

Over the 1960s other goals were set—most notably, eradicating smallpox within 10 years, adopted by the World Health Assembly in 1966. This goal was achieved within 11 years. Over the 1970s, 1980s, and 1990s various UN bodies set other global goals with quantitative targets. The MDGs are the latest in a sequence that has extended over four decades. The elaboration of a strategy to accelerate progress by the Millennium Project under Jeffrey Sachs's direction marks a further step.

The value of setting goals is often questioned by those who see them as empty vessels. However, the record of achievement is more positive than this. . . . The 50 or so goals cover a wide range: faster economic growth, higher life expectancy, lower child and maternal mortality, better health, broader access to safe water and sanitation, greater access to education, less hunger and malnutrition, moves to sustainable development—and support for these efforts by the expansion of aid. Most of the goals were adopted after long and vigorous debate and careful scrutiny.

Of course, achieving goals or falling short is only indirectly a reflection of the UN's efforts—but the goals have provided a spur to national policies and a benchmark for success or failure. The record of achievement is better than many believe. Success with the economic growth goal in the First Development Decade led to a higher goal of 6 percent a year in the 1970s for the Second Development Decade. This goal was achieved by 35 countries, and the average growth was 5.6 percent, a bit higher than in the 1960s. After 1980 economic performance largely deteriorated, with the notable exception of China and several other East Asian countries and, in the 1990s, of India. Though the UN continued to set goals for economic growth, it averaged only 4 percent in developing countries in the 1980s and 4.7 percent in the 1990s, in both cases pulled up by the exceptional performance of the two giants, China and India.

The record for the key goals for human development has been considerably better. In 1980, the goal was set that life expectancy should reach 60 years at a minimum—a goal achieved in 124 of 173 countries. At the same time, the goal for reducing infant mortality by 2000 was set at 120 per 1,000 live births in the poorest countries and 50 in all others. By 2000, after impressive acceleration of immunization and other child survival measures, 138 developing countries had attained this goal. Progress in other areas has been considerable. Reductions in malnutrition, iron deficiency anaemia, and vitamin A deficiency advanced over the 1990s. Expansions of water and sanitation facilities over the 1980s more than doubled access in the decade.

The most serious failures have been in Sub-Saharan Africa and the least developed countries. But even here, performance on the human goals has often been considerably better than on the targets for economic growth or international aid. The least developed countries, today numbering 49, were set the target of doubling their national income over each of the last century's two closing decades. In support, developed countries were set the goal of providing aid amounting to 0.15 to 0.20 percent of their GNP. The failure in economic performance was the most serious of all the goals. Only three least developed countries, with only 1 percent of their total population, achieved the growth target. Only eight donor countries achieved the aid target in the 1980s, only five in the 1990s. Total aid to the least developed countries had fallen to 0.05 percent of individual country GNP in the 1990s, down from 0.09 percent in the 1980s (pp. 259–67). Fortunately, in the new millennium there are signs of some recovery in the allocation of aid to these countries.

Sustainability

Sustainable development became a leading theme in 1987 when the World Commission on Environment and Development published *Our Common Future*.[5] Three parts of the equation for the sustainability of the planet—resource management, environment, and population—have been topics in which UN ideas have contributed in essential ways to our ways of conceiving global

---

[5] UN Doc. A/42/427 (1987); Oxford: Oxford University Press, 1987.

responses. A key document in the debate about global resource management is the 1962 UN Declaration on Permanent Sovereignty over Natural Resources, also referred to as the economic pendant of the decolonization declaration.[6] This and subsequent resolutions detail the rights of countries, including the right to manage freely natural resources for the benefit of the population and national economic development. The next step was to extend the resource sovereignty over marine resources as well. This resulted in a thorough revision of the traditional law of the sea.

The Third UN Conference on the Law of the Sea (1973–82) gave rise to an international deep-sea-bed regime based on the nascent principle of common heritage of humankind, as opposed to "first come, first served."[7] The new international resource regime of the law of the sea has proven irreversible and is providing coastal developing countries with considerable protection against distant fishing fleets and mining companies.

The capacity of the world to achieve and sustain development depends very much on dealing with *environmental* problems, little mentioned until the 1970s. As early as 1969 the Secretary-General had alerted the General Assembly to the problems of the human environment: "For the first time in the history of mankind, there is arising a crisis of worldwide proportion involving developed and developing countries—the crisis of the human environment."[8] In 1972 the UN organized in Stockholm the Conference on the Human Environment—it was path-breaking, politically and conceptually. . . . Plans for the conference were initially met with massive criticism from several industrial countries and strong scepticism from developing countries. To lead and organize its work, Maurice Strong, the Canadian industrialist who championed environment and development issues in a number of UN assignments, was appointed secretary-general of the conference. He gathered a group of experts from both North and South at Founex (near Geneva) to explore the issues. The group in Founex focused on squaring the circle—the big differences between the environmental and development priorities of developed and developing countries.

Common ground in this conflict was found by shifting the emphasis to the need for a new strategy that combined priorities for environment *and* development. These were included in the conference declaration, which called for the elimination of mass poverty and the creation of a decent and human environment. Some environmental problems would inevitably arise as a consequence of industrialization, but they should and could be minimized through appropriate policies. This was a major advance in thinking and political agreement. To carry the ideas forward, the conference agreed that a new body, the UN Environment Programme, be established.

---

[6] GA Res. 1803(XVII) (1962).

[7] The Convention, agreed at Montego Bay, 10 December 1982, came into force 16 November 1996.

[8] Problems of the Human Environment: Report of the Secretary-General (New York: United Nations, 1969), p. 4

Through the establishment of the World Commission on Environment and Development, the UN made an effort to develop a more integrated approach to this issue. Building on an earlier notion of sustainable use of natural resources, the world organization defined sustainable development as "development which meets the needs of the present without compromising the ability of future generations to meet their own needs." All this was carried through to the Earth Summit in Rio in 1992 and the World Summit on Sustainable Development in Johannesburg in 2002.

By this time, a better understanding of environmental problems had emerged. The emphasis had shifted from absolute scarcity of certain nonrenewable resources to the pollution or destruction of *renewable* resources, especially water and air, soil, and forests. As ever more evidence of climate change emerged, global warming became one of the world's most recognized and serious environmental problems. Until then, environmental problems were seen as those of how to survive in a global fish bowl. In 1997 the UN conference in Kyoto introduced the problem of what to do when the goldfish bowl is put into a microwave. Kyoto came into force in early 2005.

In 1945 the world's people numbered just under 2.5 billion—today, well over 6 billion, by far the largest and fastest expansion in human history. Even so, population growth was not treated as a major policy issue for the UN's first two decades. Analytically, the world organization issued a comprehensive and pioneering volume in 1953, *The Determinants and Consequences of Population Trends*, which contained data and analysis far ahead of the time. Indeed, in those years many countries lacked even a basic census, let alone population forecasts or policy analyses. The UN's volume also included wildly inaccurate projections that the world population would reach between 3.3 and 3.8 billion by the year 2000. But policy discussion on matters of population was played down as highly sensitive and essentially kept off the international agenda.

A slow awakening occurred in the 1960s. In 1966 the Economic and Social Commission for Asia and the Pacific (ESCAP) organized a meeting on the management of family planning. ECOSOC devoted two sessions in the late 1960s to the issues. The United Nations Fund for Population Activities was established in 1969. Then in 1974 the UN organized its first World Population Conference in Bucharest. After this, concrete action embedding ideas in new institutions and policy measures became commonplace. Within less than 10 years, about 70 percent of the participating countries had established high-level units to deal with population issues. By 1994 fertility rates were falling in most countries outside the poorest, and the UN organized a further conference—the International Conference on Population and Development in Cairo. This put the emphasis on a much broader agenda, shifting it from family planning to women's empowerment, gender equality, the right to choose, and improving maternal and reproductive health. Although the world's population is now projected to grow to about 8.5 billion by 2050, fertility rates in countries with almost half the world's population have now fallen to below replacement levels.

Three points should be noted. First, the UN has been instrumental in generating widespread interest in national resource management by taking account of economic, social, and environmental dimensions. Second, new concepts of resource management have been introduced, such as resource sovereignty, the global commons, sustainable use of natural resources, and sustainable development. Third, the UN has given a major push to put population and environment problems high on the national agendas through the world conferences of the 1970s and 1990s.

Many practical initiatives have followed from these conferences, and progress has been considerable, including the adoption of UN conventions on the Law of the Sea and the Prevention of Marine Pollution by Dumping, and the protection of the ozone layer (1985). The 1992 Rio conference led to further conventions on climate change, biodiversity, and desertification, along with the creation of the Global Environment Facility, to provide funding and technical assistance for projects to preserve biodiversity, protect forests, and improve soils. In 1997, with ever more evidence of global warming, the Kyoto Protocol was adopted to strengthen the provisions of the convention on climate change. Despite the progress, almost all evidence suggests that global warming is advancing fast, with governments still unwilling to provide the support and funding to deal with the damage and degradation to many of the world's critical renewable resources, in both developed and developing countries.

Gender Equality

Four women were among the 160 or so delegates in San Francisco in 1945. Though miniscule in numbers, this group parlayed its influence into ensuring that equality between the sexes was part of the founding ideas of the new world organization. The Charter uses the phrase "men and women" 10 times. . . . The Charter is considerably more straightforward about gender equality in its language than the international conventions that preceded it, even though only about half the UN member states then gave women unrestricted rights to vote and hold public office.

Almost immediately, the UN established the Commission on the Status of Women (CSW) as a separate body for advancing women's rights within the organization. Created as a sub-commission of ECOSOC, it was led by a Danish woman, Bodil Begtrup, who argued that having such a commission would enable women's problems for the first time to be studied at an international level. Many member states were hesitant to internationalize the issue of women's inequality, arguing that this was to intrude into sovereignty. In sharp contrast, a handful of daring women argued that women be given full political suffrage world-wide, entering what was till then distant, if not taboo, political territory. Their founding belief was that "political rights and development are fundamental." They succeeded. By 1952, the UN had adopted the Convention on Political Rights of Women and put the campaign for suffrage for women on a legal footing. This convention stated that women should be entitled to vote in all elections, be eligible for election to all publicly elected bodies, and be entitled to hold public office. The CSW had already been active in calling for the United Nations to collect the facts, which it did in a survey of 74 countries.

Even with this progress on political rights, the situation of women was ignored in most of the UN's work on economic and social development. The declaration on the UN's First Development Decade and its proposals for action made no mention of women—though in 1962 the General Assembly instructed the CSW "to prepare a report on the role of women in the social and economic development plans of member governments." Even within the CSW, there was an opinion that development was not really a women's issue and that too much attention to economic development would divert the commission from its primary goal of securing women's rights. . . .

The big changes for women in economic and social development started in the 1960s. In 1963 the General Assembly asked the CSW and ECOSOC to draft a Declaration on the Elimination of Discrimination against Women—and DEDAW was adopted four years later, the first comprehensive legal measure on women's rights. Among the regional commissions, the Economic Commission for Africa (ECA) was in the lead, supporting several path-breaking seminars and conferences on women in development and in 1967 issuing the *Status and Role of Women in East Africa*.

The publication in 1970 of *Women's Role in Economic Development* by the Danish economist Esther Boserup—who worked in the Economic Commission for Europe—marked an intellectual breakthrough, launching the field of women in development. Her view that women's contributions, both domestic and in the paid workforce, constituted crucial contributions to national economies electrified women scholars and gave birth to a new development approach in the UN and other development agencies.

The four world conferences on women—1975 in Mexico City, 1980 in Copenhagen, 1985 in Nairobi, and 1995 in Beijing—raised awareness and mobilized action at a new level, especially by establishing or extending networks and alliances in novel ways. The Mexico conference in 1975 led to the adoption of CEDAW and in 1976 of UNIFEM and INSTRAW. However significant the contributions of these institutions, *Women, Development, and the UN* shows that the four UN women's conferences have strengthened the worldwide women's movement and given it a new level of impact, influence, and focus.

The changing focus on women also brought changes in thinking about development. The conceptualization of women's work shifted—to incorporate work outside the marketplace and care as key though often forgotten elements of family and community life. This raised questions and challenged how economic and social contributions should be valued. It brought the need to rethink rights to development, not just of women but rights more generally.

Human Development

UNDP's annual *Human Development Report* came on the scene in 1990, elaborating the approach inspired by Mahbub ul Haq, an economic visionary and former minister of finance of Pakistan. There had been much general talk of "human development" in the 1980s and of "putting people at the center of development." But it was the creative economic thinking and philosophy of Amartya Sen, who received the 1998 Nobel Prize in economic sciences, that gave the human development approach its robust theoretical foundations. "Human development" was defined analytically as a process of strengthening human capabilities and expanding human choices. Though deceptively simple, the concept marked a fundamental contrast to the utilitarianism underlying neoclassical economics. Moreover, it provided a frame of reference that could be elaborated and applied to a wide range of development issues, as successive reports have demonstrated.

The importance of the idea of human development is central to the stories told in almost all of the [United Nations International History Project's] volumes. Why? Human development built on the priorities of basic needs thinking in the 1970s but went substantively beyond them by adopting Sen's framework of capabilities and freedom.[9] In addition, human development provided a frame of analysis that brought human rights and development closer together. As the 2000 report showed, human development adds value to human rights by setting rights in a frame of dynamic economic and social advance. In turn, human rights adds value to human development by bringing in legal precision and legitimacy.

In addition to elaborating on the idea of basic needs, human development provided a framework for many UN institutions and governments to change policies and take practical steps. Examples abound. There is now, once again, central emphasis on poverty reduction in development policies, including those of the World Bank and IMF. We observe a growing diversification in development strategies with more emphasis on cultural factors. Social policies—education, health, nutrition—are getting more attention. The adoption of the Millennium Development Goals in 2000 and the revisiting of progress at the summit preceding the 60th session of the General Assembly in 2005 are perhaps the most prominent indications. Human development has been a successful UN counter-offensive to the Washington Consensus, after the hesitations during the 1980s. It redefines the idea of development broadly yet realistically. Development is seen as a complex challenge, one that embraces far more than economic variables and faster growth. These are important factors, but far from the whole story. Development is a process that advances human rights, human capabilities, and human choices, with people at the center.

Human Security

Possibilities for creatively linking development and disarmament have been recognized and recommended over every decade of the world organization's existence. In 1955 France made the first proposal at the United Nations. Participating states should agree to reduce their military spending each year by a fixed percentage, with the resources released paid into an international

---

[9] Amartya Sen, Development as Freedom (Oxford: Oxford University Press, 1999).

fund, a quarter allocated to development and the remainder left at the disposal of the government. Variants of this proposal emerged from other governments in subsequent decades, including the First Development Decade in the 1960s. . . .

[The] long and outspoken concern of the UN for disarmament and development contrasts with the years of silence from the World Bank and the IMF. As the World Bank historians commented, "Arms reduction . . . is sensitive as well as political and was typically avoided by the Bank until . . . the aftermath of the Cold War."[10] Interestingly, the Bank's former president and US secretary of defense, Robert McNamara, became a fervent advocate for tying investments to disarmament. The 1980 Nobel laureate in economics, Lawrence Klein, has long been involved in analyzing the waste of arms expenditures and emphasized the world organization's efforts in his interview with us, including the quest for the elusive "peace dividend."

A major conceptual shift came in 1994, when UNDP's *Human Development Report* articulated the concept of human security: "[F]or too long, the concept of security has been shaped by the potential for conflict between nations . . . equated with the threats to a country's borders . . . [with nations seeking] arms to protect their security." In contrast, the report argued for "human security" to become the focus, shifting priorities to the protection of people rather than borders, to the use of police, health, and other community workers rather than armies and weapons, and to prevention rather than cure. A human security approach should tackle a diversity of threats to people's lives—the threats from disease and famine, from drugs and urban crime, from terrorism and ethnic conflict. The report also covered freedom from job insecurity and environmental threats. . . .

Notwithstanding [some] controversy, human security is an idea that appears to be gaining ground. For instance, the High-level Panel on Threats, Challenges and Change incorporated many of these ideas in its call for "comprehensive, collective security." The panel identified six clusters of threats—beginning with economic and social threats (including poverty, infectious diseases, and environmental degradation) and listing five others: interstate conflict, internal conflict (including civil war and genocide), weapons (nuclear, radiological, chemical, and biological), terrorism, and transnational organized crime. These are all cases, the panel argued, where threats today required collective international action, preventive and reactive. Human security, it concluded, should be a central focus of actions for strengthening the UN in the world of the 21st century. . . .

From the beginning, the United Nations has emphasized that international action must accompany and complement national efforts if development is to be equitable and global poverty reduced. An enabling international environment is required for alternative trade and finance measures to work and for other areas of economic interactions to improve between poorer and richer

---

[10] Devesh Kapur, John P. Lewis and Richard Webb, Eds., The World Bank: Its First Half Century (Washington, DC: Brookings, 1997), p. 533.

countries. Some of the UN's ideas in this area, though often controversial and challenging to conventional thinking, have been among its most creative.

Fresh thinking on trade and finance distinguishes the UN's contributions from the views of the Bretton Woods institutions and the dominant policies of the developed countries over the last half-century. It has been and remains an area of almost continuous tension. Typically, the world organization produces analysis and proposals to accelerate economic and social progress in developing countries. Meanwhile, the developed countries argue for free trade but use their political and economic power to practice something charitably described as "fair trade with important exceptions," or more simply as "unfair trade."

Long-run trends and fluctuations in exports, imports, and international trade were among the first areas for UN scrutiny.

One of the crucial parts of their tale includes the origins of what has become known as the Prebisch-Singer thesis: the tendency over the long run for the prices of coffee, tea, copper, cotton, and other primary product exports to decline relative to the prices of manufactures. Hans Singer, one of the pioneering economists of the UN . . . , investigated the changes in prices of primary product exports relative to manufactured imports for underdeveloped countries. . . .

The scene then moved to Latin America, where Raúl Prebisch . . . [presented] a manifesto urging Latin American countries to launch into industrialization. . . . In 1962 Prebisch headed the preparations for the UN Conference on Trade and Development. He became its first secretary- general in 1964 after the completion of the largest international conference on trade ever convened. Cast as a drama of "global collective bargaining" between rich and poor, the "conference" became a permanent fixture in North-South relations, and UNCTAD itself became a permanent part of the UN's institutional structure.

Since these early days of hope, UNCTAD has continued, although somewhat weakened. This was especially so during the late 1980s after efforts, led by the West, to close it down. UNCTAD has filled an important and often pioneering gap in international analyses of trade and finance, producing significant reports and, at times, innovative proposals, albeit with much less success than hoped for. Unlike the General Agreement on Tariffs and Trade (GATT) and more recently the World Trade Organization (WTO), its focus has been on actions in trade and finance that aim to accelerate progress in the developing countries, with increasing emphasis in the last two decades on the special needs of the least developed countries. . . .

[A] major date for international development assistance was December 1948, when the UN General Assembly passed resolution 198 (III) that recommended "to give further and urgent consideration to the whole problem of economic development of underdeveloped countries in *all* aspects." It passed another resolution dealing more particularly with the role of technical assistance in promoting economic development, the field in which the UN came to put strongest emphasis during the following years.

As was the case so often in those early years, the response with the greatest impact came from Washington. President Harry Truman, in his inaugural address on 20 January 1949, announced a program "for peace and freedom in four major courses of action." . . .

Soon afterward, the United Nations established the Expanded Program for Technical Assistance. It was recognized early on that economic development required not only technical assistance (or "human investment" as it came to be called), but also major additions to capital, that is physical investment. In the end, a soft window was established in 1960 within the World Bank— where donor countries were at the helm—the International Development Association. The UN was left with a small kitty for pre-investment activities, and in 1965 this Special Fund merged with the Expanded Program of Technical Assistance to become the UN Development Programme. . . .

In the Second Development Decade, . . . the famous 0.7 percent target for official development assistance [emerged].

In the field of aid and technical assistance, the UN has consistently emphasized . . . social development and poverty eradication. This emphasis became particularly important in the 1980s when the Washington Consensus and structural adjustment became the leading policy, orchestrated by the World Bank and IMF. Today the Millennium Project has formulated a plan that sets out an economic strategy as well as a calculation of the necessary inputs to achieve the MDGs by 2015.

The creation of the UN provided the forum to take up foreign [direct] investment [FDI]. The attitude toward FDI and transnational corporations (TNCs) has changed dramatically—from critical in the 1970s to benevolent in the 1990s. The ideas of the UN on the subject have seen a parallel evolution, from confrontation and a focus on a code of conduct to cooperation and voluntary agreements. The world organization has been instrumental in bringing to the attention of the international policy arena the need for a multilateral approach to harness the activities of TNCs toward the betterment of all stakeholders. Although the centerpiece of this policy initiative, the Code of Conduct discussed during the 1970s, did not come to pass, ideas within it—on competition, pricing, marketing, resource allocation, labor relations, the environment, and corruption—survived.

Ideas are rarely realized without a battle. From early on the UN struggled against the orthodoxy of the day. The world organization's contributions have often stood in sharp contrast to the reigning orthodoxy of the financially well-heeled World Bank and IMF. Partly this reflected the different political base of the two institutions, with the UN having equal representation of all countries and the Bretton Woods institutions a voting system weighted to reflect financial contributors.

Not surprisingly, the Bretton Woods institutions have tended to produce analyses and policy recommendations that reflected the interests and perspectives of developed countries while the UN has tended in another direction— namely analyses, ideas, and recommendations more in tune with those of developing countries that constitute the bulk of member states.

QUESTIONS ....

1. What role can and should the United Nations plan in development policy and programming? How does this differ from the role it can and should play in the areas of peace and security or human rights?
2. Some member states complain that Security Council resolutions on peace and security are binding, while General Assembly resolutions on development are not. Should development issues be addressed differently at the United Nations?

11.2 The Right to Development

The language of "rights" in the area of development was long resisted by industrialized countries, concerned that its acceptance could create enormous financial obligations in order to realize that right in poor countries. In extended negotiations, stretching over many years, industrialized and developing countries came to a kind of agreement. The rhetoric was settled in a few concepts enshrined in the preambular paragraphs of the Declaration on the Right to Development, adopted in 1986. Consensus was also achieved on a few important operative paragraphs in which obligations of both developed and developing states complement one another and are carefully crafted to avoid supporting expansive claims aiming for a redistributive re-structuring of international economic relations. This became possible only after proponents of a New International Economic Order (NIEO) met their Waterloo in the early 1980s when their claims-based approach ran into determined rejection from the Reagan Administration and the British government under Margaret Thatcher.

DECLARATION ON THE RIGHT TO DEVELOPMENT: GENERAL ASSEMBLY RESOLUTION 41/128 (1986)

The General Assembly,

Bearing in mind the purposes and principles of the Charter of the United Nations relating to the achievement of international co-operation in solving international problems of an economic, social, cultural or humanitarian nature, and in promoting and encouraging respect for human rights and fundamental freedoms for all without distinction as to race, sex, language or religion,

Recognizing that development is a comprehensive economic, social, cultural and political process, which aims at the constant improvement of the well-being of the entire population and of all individuals on the basis of their active, free and meaningful participation in development and in the fair distribution of benefits resulting therefrom,

Considering that under the provisions of the Universal Declaration of Human Rights everyone is entitled to a social and international order in which the rights and freedoms set forth in that Declaration can be fully realized,

Recalling the provisions of the International Covenant on Economic, Social and Cultural Rights and of the International Covenant on Civil and Political Rights,

Recalling further the relevant agreements, conventions, resolutions, recommendations and other instruments of the United Nations and its specialized agencies concerning the integral development of the human being, economic and social progress and development of all peoples, including those instruments concerning decolonization, the prevention of discrimination, respect for and observance of, human rights and fundamental freedoms, the maintenance of international peace and security and the further promotion of friendly relations and co-operation among States in accordance with the Charter,

Recalling the right of peoples to self-determination, by virtue of which they have the right freely to determine their political status and to pursue their economic, social and cultural development,

Recalling also the right of peoples to exercise, subject to the relevant provisions of both International Covenants on Human Rights, full and complete sovereignty over all their natural wealth and resources,

Mindful of the obligation of States under the Charter to promote universal respect for and observance of human rights and fundamental freedoms for all without distinction of any kind such as race, colour, sex, language, religion, political or other opinion, national or social origin, property, birth or other status,

Considering that the elimination of the massive and flagrant violations of the human rights of the peoples and individuals affected by situations such as those resulting from colonialism, neo-colonialism, apartheid, all forms of racism and racial discrimination, foreign domination and occupation, aggression and threats against national sovereignty, national unity and territorial integrity and threats of war would contribute to the establishment of circumstances propitious to the development of a great part of mankind,

Concerned at the existence of serious obstacles to development, as well as to the complete fulfilment of human beings and of peoples, constituted, inter alia, by the denial of civil, political, economic, social and cultural rights, and considering that all human rights and fundamental freedoms are indivisible and interdependent and that, in order to promote development, equal attention and urgent consideration should be given to the implementation, promotion and protection of civil, political, economic, social and cultural rights and that, accordingly, the promotion of, respect for and enjoyment of certain human rights and fundamental freedoms cannot justify the denial of other human rights and fundamental freedoms,

Considering that international peace and security are essential elements for the realization of the right to development,

Reaffirming that there is a close relationship between disarmament and development and that progress in the field of disarmament would considerably promote progress in the field of development and that resources released through disarmament measures should be devoted to the economic and social development and well-being of all peoples and, in particular, those of the developing countries,

Recognizing that the human person is the central subject of the development process and that development policy should therefore make the human being the main participant and beneficiary of development,

Recognizing that the creation of conditions favourable to the development of peoples and individuals is the primary responsibility of their States,

Aware that efforts at the international level to promote and protect human rights should be accompanied by efforts to establish a new international economic order,

Confirming that the right to development is an inalienable human right and that equality of opportunity for development is a prerogative both of nations and of individuals who make up nations,

Proclaims the following Declaration on the Right to Development:

Article 1

1. The right to development is an inalienable human right by virtue of which every human person and all peoples are entitled to participate in, contribute to, and enjoy economic, social, cultural and political development, in which all human rights and fundamental freedoms can be fully realized.

2. The human right to development also implies the full realization of the right of peoples to self-determination, which includes, subject to the relevant provisions of both International Covenants on Human Rights, the exercise of their inalienable right to full sovereignty over all their natural wealth and resources.

Article 2

1. The human person is the central subject of development and should be the active participant and beneficiary of the right to development.

2. All human beings have a responsibility for development, individually and collectively, taking in to account the need for full respect for their human rights and fundamental freedoms as well as their duties to the community,

which alone can ensure the free and complete fulfilment of the human being, and they should therefore promote and protect an appropriate political, social and economic order for development.

3. States have the right and the duty to formulate appropriate national development policies that aim at the constant improvement of the well-being of the entire population and of all individuals, on the basis of their active, free and meaningful participation in development and in the fair distribution of the benefits resulting therefrom.

Article 3

1. States have the primary responsibility for the creation of national and international conditions favourable to the realization of the right to development.

2. The realization of the right to development requires full respect for the principles of international law concerning friendly relations and cooperation among States in accordance with the Charter of the United Nations.

3. States have the duty to co-operate with each other in ensuring development and eliminating obstacles to development. States should realize their rights and fulfil their duties in such a manner as to promote a new international economic order based on sovereign equality, interdependence, mutual interest and co-operation among all States, as well as to encourage the observance and realization of human rights.

Article 4

1. States have the duty to take steps, individually and collectively, to formulate international development policies with a view to facilitating the full realization of the right to development.

2. Sustained action is required to promote more rapid development of developing countries. As a complement to the efforts of developing countries, effective international co-operation is essential in providing these countries with appropriate means and facilities to foster their comprehensive development.

Article 5

States shall take resolute steps to eliminate the massive and flagrant violations of the human rights of peoples and human beings affected by situations such as those resulting from apartheid, all forms of racism and racial discrimination, colonialism, foreign domination and occupation, aggression, foreign interference and threats against national sovereignty, national unity and territorial integrity, threats of war and refusal to recognize the fundamental right of peoples to self-determination.

Article 6

1. All States should co-operate with a view to promoting, encouraging and strengthening universal respect for and observance of all human rights and fundamental freedoms for all without any distinction as to race, sex, language or religion.

2. All human rights and fundamental freedoms are indivisible and interdependent; equal attention and urgent consideration should be given to the implementation, promotion and protection of civil, political, economic, social and cultural rights.

3. States should take steps to eliminate obstacles to development resulting from failure to observe civil and political rights, as well as economic social and cultural rights.

Article 7

All States should promote the establishment, maintenance and strengthening of international peace and security and, to that end, should do their utmost to achieve general and complete disarmament under effective international control, as well as to ensure that the resources released by effective disarmament measures are used for comprehensive development, in particular that of the developing countries.

Article 8

1. States should undertake, at the national level, all necessary measures for the realization of the right to development and shall ensure, inter alia, equality of opportunity for all in their access to basic resources, education, health services, food, housing, employment and the fair distribution of income. Effective measures should be undertaken to ensure that women have an active role in the development process. Appropriate economic and social reforms should be carried out with a view to eradicating all social injustices.

2. States should encourage popular participation in all spheres as an important factor in development and in the full realization of all human rights.

Article 9

1. All the aspects of the right to development set forth in the present Declaration are indivisible and interdependent and each of them should be considered in the context of the whole.

2. Nothing in the present Declaration shall be construed as being contrary to the purposes and principles of the United Nations, or as implying that any State, group or person has a right to engage in any activity or to perform any act aimed at the violation of the rights set forth in the Universal Declaration of Human Rights and in the International Covenants on Human Rights.

Article 10

Steps should be taken to ensure the full exercise and progressive enhancement of the right to development, including the formulation, adoption and implementation of policy, legislative and other measures at the national and international levels.

QUESTIONS

3. For many activists, the debate at the United Nations on the "right to development" crystallized different visions of the UN's core purpose. How important is development to the role and function of the United Nations?
4. Does the language of "rights" make sense in the context of development? Why, or why not? What obligations, if any, were agreed to in the Declaration on the Right to Development?

11.3 Quantifying the Goals of Development

With the collapse of "global negotiations" toward an NIEO in the 1980s, followed by the failure to produce more than very soft law on a "right to development," pressure for priority focus on development issues weakened at the United Nations. This was compounded by the end of the Cold War and the growth in the peace operations of the UN, as well as by significant donor government cutbacks in development assistance budgets in the 1990s. By 2000, and the renewed focus on development issues referred to in chapter 1, much of the debate crystallized around advocacy for the 0.7 percent target for Official Development Assistance relative to gross national product (GNP) in donor countries. (Only a very few Scandinavian countries and the Netherlands had reached or surpassed this target, while many others had dropped away from the high point in their aid contributions of the late 1980s and early 1990s.)

In tandem with agreement on the Millennium Development Goals formulated in 2000 and 2001, a renewed push for growth in development assistance thus arose, centered on the United Nations (although with a clear understanding that much of the funding would be channelled bilaterally and through other international institutions, including the World Bank and the Regional Development Banks). Central to this campaign, beyond public personalities such as the U2 singer Bono, was the economist Jeffrey Sachs, who served as Secretary-General Kofi Annan's special adviser on development issues and as Director of the United Nations Millennium Project. In parallel with the High Level Panel on Threats, Challenges and Change, this project reported in early 2005 on implementation of the MDGs, reinforcing calls for increased development funding.

MILLENNIUM DEVELOPMENT GOALS, TEN KEY RECOMMENDATIONS, 17 JANUARY 2005[11]

Recommendation 1

Developing country governments should adopt development strategies bold enough to meet the Millennium Development Goal (MDG) targets for 2015. We term them MDG-based poverty reduction strategies. To meet the 2015 deadline, we recommend that all countries have these strategies in place by 2006. Where Poverty Reduction Strategy Papers (PRSPs) already exist, those should be aligned with the MDGs.

Recommendation 2

The MDG-based poverty reduction strategies should anchor the scaling up of public investments, capacity building, domestic resource mobilization, and official development assistance. They should also provide a framework for strengthening governance, promoting human rights, engaging civil society, and promoting the private sector. The MDG-based poverty reduction strategies should:

- Be based on an assessment of investments and policies needed to reach the Goals by 2015.
- Spell out the detailed national investments, policies, and budgets for the coming three to five years.
- Focus on rural productivity, urban productivity, health, education, gender equality, water and sanitation, environmental sustainability, and science, technology, and innovation.
- Focus on women's and girls' health (including reproductive health) and education outcomes, access to economic and political opportunities, right to control assets, and freedom from violence.
- Promote mechanisms for transparent and decentralized governance.
- Include operational strategies for scale-up, such as training and retaining skilled workers.
- Involve civil society organizations in decision-making and service delivery, and provide resources for monitoring and evaluation.
- Outline a private sector promotion strategy and an income generation strategy for poor people.

---

[11] Investing in Development: A Practical Plan to Achieve the Millennium Development Goals (Report of the UN Millennium Project to the Secretary-General) (17 January 2005), available at http://www.unmillenniumproject.org/reports.

- Be tailored, as appropriate, to the special needs of landlocked, small island developing, least developed, and fragile states.
- Mobilize increased domestic resources by up to four percentage points of GNP by 2015.
- Calculate the need for official development assistance. Describe an "exit strategy" to end aid dependency, appropriate to the country's situation.

Recommendation 3

Developing country governments should craft and implement the MDG-based poverty reduction strategies in transparent and inclusive processes, working closely with civil society organizations, the domestic private sector, and international partners.

- Civil society organizations should contribute actively to designing policies, delivering services, and monitoring progress.
- Private sector firms and organizations should contribute actively to policy design, transparency initiatives and, where appropriate, public-private partnerships.

Recommendation 4

International donors should identify at least a dozen MDG "fast-track" countries for a rapid scaleup of official development assistance (ODA). In 2005, recognizing that many countries are already in a position for a massive scaleup on the basis of their good governance and absorptive capacity.

Recommendation 5

Developed and developing countries should jointly launch, in 2005, a group of Quick Win actions to save and improve millions of lives and to promote economic growth. They should also launch a massive effort to build expertise at the community level.

The Quick Wins include but are not limited to:

- Free mass distribution of malaria bed-nets and effective antimalaria medicines for all children in regions of malaria transmission by the end of 2007.
- Ending user fees for primary schools and essential health services, compensated by increased donor aid as necessary, no later than the end of 2006.
- Successful completion of the 3 by 5 campaign to bring 3 million AIDS patients in developing countries onto antiretroviral treatment by the end of 2005.
- Expansion of school meals programs to cover all children in hunger hotspots using locally produced foods by no later than the end of 2006.

- A massive replenishment of soil nutrients for smallholder farmers on lands with nutrient-depleted soils, through free or subsidized distribution of chemical fertilizers and agroforestry, by no later than the end of 2006.

The massive training program of community-based workers should aim to ensure, by 2015, that each local community has:

- Expertise in health, education, agriculture, nutrition, infrastructure, water supply and sanitation, and environmental management.
- Expertise in public sector management.
- Appropriate training to promote gender equality and participation.

Recommendation 6

Developing country governments should align national strategies with such regional initiatives as the New Partnership for Africa's Development and the Caribbean Community (and Common Market), and regional groups should receive increased direct donor support for regional projects. Regional development groups should:

- Be supported to identify, plan, and implement high-priority cross-border infrastructure projects (roads, railways, watershed management).
- Receive direct donor support to implement cross-border projects.
- Be encouraged to introduce and implement peer-review mechanisms to promote best practices and good governance.

Recommendation 7

High-Income countries should increase official development assistance (ODA) from 0.25 percent of donor GNP In 2003 to around 0.44 percent in 2006 and 0.54 percent in 2015 to support the Millennium Development Goals, particularly in low-income countries, with improved ODA quality (including aid that is harmonized, predictable, and largely In the form of grants-based budget support). Each donor should reach 0.7 percent no later than 2015 to support the Goals and other development assistance priorities. Debt relief should be more extensive and generous.

- ODA should be based on actual needs to meet the Millennium Development Goals and on countries' readiness to use the ODA effectively.
- Criteria for evaluating the sustainability of a country's debt burden must be consistent with the achievement of the Goals.
- Aid should be oriented to support the MDG-based poverty reduction strategy, rather than to support donor-driven projects.
- Donors should measure and report the share of their ODA that supports the actual scale-up of MDG-related investments.
- Middle-Income countries should also seek opportunities to become providers of ODA and give technical support to low-income countries.

Recommendation 8

High-income countries should open their markets to developing country exports through the Doha trade round and help Least Developed Countries raise export competitiveness through investments in critical trade-related infrastructure, including electricity, roads, and ports. The Doha Development Agenda should be fulfilled and the Doha Round completed no later than 2006.

Recommendation 9

International donors should mobilize support for global scientific research and development to address special needs of the poor in areas of health, agriculture, natural resource and environmental management, energy, and climate. We estimate the total needs to rise to approximately $7 billion a year by 2015.

Recommendation 10

The UN Secretary-General and the UN Development Group should strengthen the coordination of UN agencies, funds, and programs to support the MDGs at headquarters and country level. The UN Country Teams should be strengthened and should work closely with the International financial institutions to support the Goals.

• The UN Country Teams should be properly trained, staffed, and funded to support program countries to achieve the Goals.
• The UN Country Team and the international financial institutions (World Bank, International Monetary Fund, regional development banks) should work closely at country level to improve the quality of technical advice.

Several events and processes in 2005 helped focus attention on the role of the UN in managing key threats to the global commons, the most important of which was the determination of Prime Minister Blair of the United Kingdom to focus in the Gleneagles G8 Summit squarely on two issues: climate change and Africa.

CHAIRMAN'S SUMMARY OF THE G8 GLENEAGLES SUMMIT, 8 JULY 2005[12]

We were joined for our discussion on climate change and the global economy by the leaders of Brazil, China, India, Mexico, and South Africa and by the

---

[12] For full text, see www.g8.gov.uk.

heads of the International Energy Agency, International Monetary Fund, United Nations, World Bank, and the World Trade Organization.

We have issued a statement setting out our common purpose in tackling climate change, promoting clean energy and achieving sustainable development.

All of us agreed that climate change is happening now, that human activity is contributing to it, and that it could affect every part of the globe.

We know that, globally, emissions must slow, peak and then decline, moving us towards a low-carbon economy. This will require leadership from the developed world.

We resolved to take urgent action to meet the challenges we face. The Gleneagles Plan of Action which we have agreed demonstrates our commitment. We will take measures to develop markets for clean energy technologies, to increase their availability in developing countries, and to help vulnerable communities adapt to the impact of climate change.

We warmly welcomed the involvement of the leaders of the emerging economy countries in our discussions, and their ideas for new approaches to international co-operation on clean energy technologies between the developed and developing world.

Our discussions mark the beginning of a new Dialogue between the G8 nations and other countries with significant energy needs, consistent with the aims and principles of the UN Framework Convention on Climate Change. This will explore how best to exchange technology, reduce emissions, and meet our energy needs in a sustainable way, as we implement and build on the Plan of Action.

We will advance the global effort to tackle climate change at the UN Climate Change Conference in Montreal later this year. Those of us who have ratified the Kyoto Protocol remain committed to it, and will continue to work to make it a success.

Africa and Development

We were joined for our discussion on Africa and development by the leaders of Algeria, Ethiopia, Ghana, Nigeria, Senegal, South Africa and Tanzania and by the heads of the African Union Commission, International Monetary Fund, United Nations and the World Bank.

We discussed how to accelerate progress towards the Millennium Goals, especially in Africa which has the furthest to go to achieve these goals by 2015.

We welcomed the substantial progress Africa has made in recent years. More countries have held democratic elections. Economic growth is accelerating. Long running conflicts are being brought to an end.

We agreed that we and our African partners had a common interest in building on that progress to create a strong, peaceful and prosperous Africa; we share a strong moral conviction that this should be done, and have agreed the actions that we will take.

The African leaders set out their personal commitment, reaffirmed strongly at this week's African Union summit, to drive forward plans to reduce poverty and promote economic growth; deepen transparency and good governance; strengthen democratic institutions and processes; show zero tolerance for corruption; remove all obstacles to intra-African trade; and bring about lasting peace and security across the continent.

The G8 in return agreed a comprehensive plan to support Africa's progress. This is set out in our separate statement today. We agreed:

- to provide extra resources for Africa's peacekeeping forces so that they can better deter, prevent and resolve conflicts in Africa
- to give enhanced support for greater democracy, effective governance and transparency, and to help fight corruption and return stolen assets
- to boost investment in health and education, and to take action to combat HIV/AIDS, malaria, TB and other killer diseases
- to stimulate growth, to improve the investment climate and to make trade work for Africa, including by helping to build Africa's capacity to trade and working to mobilise the extra investment in infrastructure which is needed for business.

The G8 leaders agreed to back this plan with substantial extra resources for countries which have strong national development plans and are committed to good governance, democracy and transparency. We agreed that poor countries must decide and lead their own development strategies and economic policies.

We have agreed to double aid for Africa by 2010. Aid for all developing countries will increase, according to the OECD, by around $50bn per year by 2010, of which at least $25bn extra per year for Africa [sic]. A group of G8 and other countries will also take forward innovative financing mechanisms including the IFF for immunisation, an air-ticket solidarity levy and the IFF to deliver and bring forward the financing, and a working group will consider the implementation of these mechanisms. We agreed that the World Bank should have a leading role in supporting the partnership between the G8, other donors and Africa, helping to ensure that additional assistance is effectively co-ordinated.

The G8 has also agreed that all of the debts owed by eligible heavily indebted poor countries to IDA, the International Monetary Fund and the African Development Fund should be cancelled, as set out in our Finance Ministers agreement on 11 June. We also welcomed the Paris Club decision to write off around $17 billion of Nigeria's debt.

The G8 and African leaders agreed that if implemented these measures and the others set out in our comprehensive plan could:

- double the size of Africa's economy and trade by 2015
- deliver increased domestic and foreign investment
- lift tens of millions of people out of poverty every year

- save millions of lives a year
- get all children into primary school
- deliver free basic health care and primary education for all
- provide as close as possible to universal access to treatment for AIDS by 2010
- generate employment and other opportunities for young people bring about an end to conflict in Africa.

In order to ensure delivery, we agreed to strengthen the African Partners Forum and that it should establish a Joint Action Plan.

But we know this is only the beginning. We must build on the progress we have made today. We must take this spirit forward to the UN Millennium Review Summit in New York in September, and ensure a successful conclusion to the Doha Development Agenda.

Note that the commitment to act on these critical challenges may have been entered into with varying degrees of enthusiasm by the G8 governments. Development assistance levels among the G8 remain highly uneven (with the United States and Japan near the bottom of the pack, France, Britain, and Germany near the top). Further, on climate change, while most G8 countries subscribed to the Kyoto Protocol and its targets for greenhouse gas emission reductions, the United States did not. Thus, while consensus often occurs in UN negotiations on ambitious goals, it is considerably more difficult in many countries to generate political will—and expensive policy measures—to make significant progress toward attaining them.

QUESTIONS

5. The Millennium Development Goals (discussed also in chapter 1) have had a powerful mobilizing effect globally. But it is generally accepted that they are unlikely to be fully or evenly reached. Is this the best way for the United Nations to promote development, with implementation left to national agencies, international institutions such as the World Bank and Regional Development Banks, and a number of diverse UN programs, often in competition with each other? If not, what alternatives would you propose?

6. As with many development "agreements," the Gleneagles Summit text provided suggests reciprocal commitments of G8 and African leaders. Who should act first? Would failure by one side to live up to undertakings justify abandonment of obligations by the other?

7. Unilateral acts, such as a statement, may in some cases be binding (see the ICJ's *Nuclear Tests* case of 1974). Would this apply to the Gleneagles statement?

11.4 Sustainable Development

The environmental consequences of growth whether parallel or in tension with the push for more equitable development have led to concerns that development should also be sustainable. The term "sustainable development" has been variously defined but is generally traced to the Report of the World Commission on Environment and Development, "Our Common Future," also known as the Brundtland Report, which stated that sustainable development that "meets the needs of the present without compromising the ability of future generations to meet their own needs." With increasing evidence of the long-term impact of human activity on the environment, this modern tragedy of the commons will become a major issue for the United Nations over the coming years.

GENERAL ASSEMBLY RESOLUTION A/38/161 (1983) PROCESS OF PREPARATION OF THE ENVIRONMENTAL PERSPECTIVE TO THE YEAR 2000 AND BEYOND

The General Assembly, . . .

2. *Welcomes* the desire of the Governing Council [of the United Nations Environment Programme] to develop the Environmental Perspective and transmit it to the General Assembly for adoption, benefiting in carrying out that function from its consideration of the relevant proposals made by a special commission; . . .

6. *Expresses* its view that the Chairman and the Vice-Chairman, in selecting the members of the Special Commission, should take fully into account the need for appropriate geographical distribution and regional balance in membership and the importance of ensuring that at least half of the members of the Commission are from the developing countries, as well as the need to consult as appropriate with representatives of Governments, intergovernmental and non-governmental organizations, industry, the scientific community and others concerned with the environment; . . .

8. *Suggests* that the Special Commission, when established, should focus mainly on the following terms of reference for its work:

(a) To propose long-term environmental strategies for achieving sustainable development to the year 2000 and beyond;

(b) To recommend ways in which concern for the environment may be translated into greater co-operation among developing countries and between countries at different stages of economic and social development and lead to the achievement of common and mutually supportive objectives which take account of the interrelationships between people, resources, environment and development;

(c) To consider ways and means by which the international community can deal more effectively with environmental concerns, in the light of the other recommendations in its report;

(d) To help to define shared perceptions of long-term environmental issues and of the appropriate efforts needed to deal successfully with the problems of protecting and enhancing the environment, a long-term agenda for action during the coming decades, and aspirational goals for the world community, taking into account the relevant resolutions of the session of a special character of the Governing Council in 1982;

REPORT OF THE WORLD COMMISSION ON ENVIRONMENT AND DEVELOPMENT, "OUR COMMON FUTURE" (BRUNDTLAND REPORT)[13]

1. In the middle of the 20th century, we saw our planet from space for the first time. Historians may eventually find that this vision had a greater impact on thought than did the Copernican revolution of the 16th century, which upset the human self-image by revealing that the Earth is not the centre of the universe. From space, we see a small and fragile ball dominated not by human activity and edifice but by a pattern of clouds, oceans, greenery, and soils. Humanity's inability to fit its activities into that pattern is changing planetary systems, fundamentally. Many such changes are accompanied by life-threatening hazards. This new reality, from which there is no escape, must be recognized—and managed.

2. Fortunately, this new reality coincides with more positive developments new to this century. We can move information and goods faster around the globe than ever before; we can produce more food and more goods with less investment of resources; our technology and science give us at least the potential to look deeper into and better understand natural systems. From space, we can see and study the Earth as an organism whose health depends on the health of all its parts. We have the power to reconcile human affairs with natural laws and to thrive in the process. In this our cultural and spiritual heritages can reinforce our economic interests and survival imperatives.

---

[13] UN Doc. A/42/427 (1987), Annex.

3. This Commission believes that people can build a future that is more prosperous, more just, and more secure. Our report, Our Common Future, is not a prediction of ever increasing environmental decay, poverty, and hardship in an ever more polluted world among ever decreasing resources. We see instead the possibility for a new era of economic growth, one that must be based on policies that sustain and expand the environmental resource base. And we believe such growth to be absolutely essential to relieve the great poverty that is deepening in much of the developing world.

4. But the Commission's hope for the future is conditional on decisive political action now to begin managing environmental resources to ensure both sustainable human progress and human survival. We are not forecasting a future; we are serving a notice—an urgent notice based on the latest and best scientific evidence—that the time has come to take the decisions needed to secure the resources to sustain this and coming generations. . . .

27. Humanity has the ability to make development sustainable to ensure that it meets the needs of the present without compromising the ability of future generations to meet their own needs. The concept of sustainable development does imply limits—not absolute limits but limitations imposed by the present state of technology and social organization on environmental resources and by the ability of the biosphere to absorb the effects of human activities. But technology and social organization can be both managed and improved to make way for a new era of economic growth. The Commission believes that widespread poverty is no longer inevitable. Poverty is not only an evil in itself, but sustainable development requires meeting the basic needs of all and extending to all the opportunity to fulfil their aspirations for a better life. A world in which poverty is endemic will always be prone to ecological and other catastrophes.

28. Meeting essential needs requires not only a new era of economic growth for nations in which the majority are poor, but an assurance that those poor get their fair share of the resources required to sustain that growth. Such equity would be aided by political systems that secure effective citizen participation in decision making and by greater democracy in international decision making.

29. Sustainable global development requires that those who are more affluent adopt life-styles within the planet's ecological means—in their use of energy, for example. Further, rapidly growing populations can increase the pressure on resources and slow any rise in living standards; thus sustainable development can only be pursued if population size and growth are in harmony with the changing productive potential of the ecosystem.

30. Yet in the end, sustainable development is not a fixed state of harmony, but rather a process of change in which the exploitation of resources, the direction of investments, the orientation of technological development, and institutional change are made consistent with future as well as present needs. We do not pretend that the process is easy or straightforward. Painful choices have to be made. Thus, in the final analysis, sustainable development must rest on political will.

A key challenge to the language of sustainable development has come from the developing world. It is sometimes argued that imposing environmental controls unfairly prevents developing countries from passing through a stage of development that many industrialized countries have already reached, at which point it is possible to use technology and other resources to scale back the environmental consequences of development. This led to the embrace of differentiated responsibility as between developed and developing states.

UNITED NATIONS FRAMEWORK CONVENTION ON CLIMATE CHANGE, ADOPTED 9 MAY 1992, ENTERED INTO FORCE ON 21 MARCH 1994[14]

Article 3: Principles

In their actions to achieve the objective of the Convention and to implement its provisions, the Parties shall be guided, *inter alia*, by the following:

1. The Parties should protect the climate system for the benefit of present and future generations of humankind, on the basis of equity and in accordance with their common but differentiated responsibilities and respective capabilities. Accordingly, the developed country Parties should take the lead in combating climate change and the adverse effects thereof.

2. The specific needs and special circumstances of developing country Parties, especially those that are particularly vulnerable to the adverse effects of climate change, and of those Parties, especially developing country Parties, that would have to bear a disproportionate or abnormal burden under the Convention, should be given full consideration.

3. The Parties should take precautionary measures to anticipate, prevent or minimize the causes of climate change and mitigate its adverse effects. Where there are threats of serious or irreversible damage, lack of full scientific certainty should not be used as a reason for postponing such measures, taking into account that policies and measures to deal with climate change should be cost-effective so as to ensure global benefits at the lowest possible cost. To achieve this, such policies and measures should take into account different socio-economic contexts, be comprehensive, cover all relevant sources, sinks and reservoirs of greenhouse gases and adaptation, and comprise all economic sectors. Efforts to address climate change may be carried out cooperatively by interested Parties.

---

[14] Available at unfccc.int.

4. The Parties have a right to, and should, promote sustainable development. Policies and measures to protect the climate system against human-induced change should be appropriate for the specific conditions of each Party and should be integrated with national development programmes, taking into account that economic development is essential for adopting measures to address climate change.

5. The Parties should cooperate to promote a supportive and open international economic system that would lead to sustainable economic growth and development in all Parties, particularly developing country Parties, thus enabling them better to address the problems of climate change. Measures taken to combat climate change, including unilateral ones, should not constitute a means of arbitrary or unjustifiable discrimination or a disguised restriction on international trade.

RIO DECLARATION ON ENVIRONMENT AND DEVELOPMENT, ADOPTED 14 JUNE 1992[15]

Principle 7

States shall cooperate in a spirit of global partnership to conserve, protect and restore the health and integrity of the Earth's ecosystem. In view of the different contributions to global environmental degradation, States have common but differentiated responsibilities. The developed countries acknowledge the responsibility that they bear in the international pursuit of sustainable development in view of the pressures their societies place on the global environment and of the technologies and financial resources they command.

The principle of differentiated responsibility is reflected in the embrace of market-based mechanisms to seek efficient methods of achieving global emission reductions, such as the Kyoto Protocol's clean development mechanism (CDM).

[15] UN Doc. A/CONF.151/26 (1992), Annex.

KYOTO PROTOCOL TO THE UNITED NATIONS FRAMEWORK CONVENTION ON CLIMATE CHANGE, ADOPTED 11 DECEMBER 1997, ENTERED INTO FORCE 16 FEBRUARY 2005[16]

Article 12

1. A clean development mechanism is hereby defined.

2. The purpose of the clean development mechanism shall be to assist Parties not included in Annex I [i.e., developing countries] in achieving sustainable development and in contributing to the ultimate objective of the Convention, and to assist Parties included in Annex I [i.e., developed countries] in achieving compliance with their quantified emission limitation and reduction commitments under Article 3.

3. Under the clean development mechanism:

(a) Parties not included in Annex I will benefit from project activities resulting in certified emission reductions; and

(b) Parties included in Annex I may use the certified emission reductions accruing from such project activities to contribute to compliance with part of their quantified emission limitation and reduction commitments under Article 3, as determined by the Conference of the Parties serving as the meeting of the Parties to this Protocol.

4. The clean development mechanism shall be subject to the authority and guidance of the Conference of the Parties serving as the meeting of the Parties to this Protocol and be supervised by an executive board of the clean development mechanism.

5. Emission reductions resulting from each project activity shall be certified by operational entities to be designated by the Conference of the Parties serving as the meeting of the Parties to this Protocol, on the basis of:

(a) Voluntary participation approved by each Party involved;

(b) Real, measurable, and long-term benefits related to the mitigation of climate change; and

(c) Reductions in emissions that are additional to any that would occur in the absence of the certified project activity.

6. The clean development mechanism shall assist in arranging funding of certified project activities as necessary.

7. The Conference of the Parties serving as the meeting of the Parties to this Protocol shall, at its first session, elaborate modalities and procedures with the objective of ensuring transparency, efficiency and accountability through independent auditing and verification of project activities.

8. The Conference of the Parties serving as the meeting of the Parties to this Protocol shall ensure that a share of the proceeds from certified project activities is used to cover administrative expenses as well as to assist developing

---

[16] Available at unfccc.int.

country Parties that are particularly vulnerable to the adverse effects of climate change to meet the costs of adaptation.

9. Participation under the clean development mechanism, including in activities mentioned in paragraph 3(a) above and in the acquisition of certified emission reductions, may involve private and/or public entities, and is to be subject to whatever guidance may be provided by the executive board of the clean development mechanism.

10. Certified emission reductions obtained during the period from the year 2000 up to the beginning of the first commitment period can be used to assist in achieving compliance in the first commitment period.

QUESTIONS

8. Is "sustainable development" sufficiently clear to be actionable in terms of concrete policies, or sufficiently vague to be agreeable to many different countries? Which is more important?

9. If the goal of the Kyoto Protocol was to reduce emissions contributing to climate change, why does it not simply commit all countries to reducing absolute emissions?

10. "The clean development mechanism simply allows developed countries to pay for the right to pollute, while developing countries profit from threatening to pollute." Do you agree?

Further Reading

Alston, Philip, and Mary Robinson. *Human Rights and Development: Toward Mutual Reinforcement*. Oxford: Oxford University Press, 2005.

Center for Development and Human Rights. *The Right to Development: A Primer*. London: Sage, 2004.

Cheru, Fantu, and Colin Bradford, eds. *The Millennium Development Goals: Raising the Resources to Tackle World Poverty*. London: Zed Books, 2006.

International Panel on Climate Change. Summary for Policymakers of "Climate Change 2007," also known as the Fourth Assessment Report (AR4). Available at www.ipcc.ch.

Sachs, Jeffrey. *The End of Poverty: Economic Possibilities for Our Time*. New York: Penguin, 2005.

Weiss, Thomas G., Tatiana Carayannis, Louis Emmerij, and Richard Jolly. *UN Voices: The Struggle for Development and Social Justice*. Bloomington, IN: Indiana University Press, 2005.

See also the UN Development Programme's annual *Human Development Reports*, available at www.undp.org.

chapter twleve
....

Self-Determination

The first use of the term "self-determination" in a public document is generally ascribed to President Woodrow Wilson's "Fourteen Points" issued in 1918, in which he affirmed a right of peoples to self-government.[1] The original invocation of this idea, however, dates back further, to the two early freedom struggles: the American War of Independence and the French Revolution, both of which were targeted toward safeguarding for the people the freedom to participate in the exercise of state power, and the prohibition of intervention by foreign powers. Furthermore, by 1917 the concept of self-determination had already been embraced by the Soviet Union's peace proposals, which expanded it in meaning to endorse, in addition, a people's right of secession.[2]

Following President Wilson's proposals, the Treaty of Versailles adopted a three-pronged approach to determining the claims of statehood of territories that had been subjugated by the Triple Alliance. Under this scheme statehood was accorded to identifiable peoples, the fate of disputed border areas was to be determined by plebiscite, and ethnic groups too small or dispersed for either course of action were to be accorded the protection of special minorities regimes, supervised by the Council of the League of Nations.[3]

This approach however was restricted to territories belonging to the defeated powers; no move to apply this was made to the colonies of the victors. The concept in fact, did not otherwise appear in the League of Nations Covenant. In effect, therefore, self-determination was at best only a procedural

---

[1] Frederic L Kirgis Jr, "The Degrees of Self-Determination in the United Nations Era," *American Journal of International Law*, vol. 88 (1994), p. 304.

[2] This right was in fact preserved in the Constitution of the Soviet Union right up to the time of its dissolution in 1991.

[3] Anthony Whelan, "Wilsonian Self-Determination and the Versailles Settlement," *International & Comparative Law Quarterly*, vol. 43 (1994), p. 99.

right; it did not provide a legal basis to all populations seeking more than a certain degree of participation in the governance of their territories.[4]

The status and content of the principle of self-determination was revisited during the drafting of the UN Charter in 1945, where a move was made to include it within Articles 1 and 55 of the charter. At the San Francisco Conference, the US delegation expressed misgivings about fleshing out the principle in binding treaty form.[5] Even after its inclusion in these articles the debate continued on whether it was to be understood as a political principle or directly applicable law. On the one hand, under Article 1(2) respect for self-determination is classified as a *principle* which advances the purpose of the UN to develop friendly relations among nations, and under Article 55, self-determination is identified as one of the objectives to be promoted in order to create "conditions of stability" necessary for "peaceful and friendly relations among nations." These provisions may be thought to be merely of hortatory value. On the other hand, it is argued by a number of leading scholars that the statute of an international organization, like the constitution of a state, lends itself to interpretation that need not strictly follow the subjective aim of the Organization's founders but rather respects subsequent developments and changing circumstances.[6] Subsequent practice, it is argued, offers many instances in which self-determination has been recognized as offering a concrete legal basis to populations seeking self-government and independence.

This is evident with regard to the Trust Territories of the United Nations, comprising territories that were (a) territories held as mandates of the League of Nations; (b) territories detached from enemy states as a result of the Second World War; and (c) territories voluntarily placed under the Trusteeship System by states responsible for their administration (a purely hypothetical mechanism that was never implemented). Among the basic objectives of the Trusteeship Council (UN Charter, Chapter XII) was the responsibility to promote, "progressive development toward self-government or independence as may be appropriate to the particular circumstances of each territory and its peoples and the freely expressed wishes of the peoples concerned."[7] Over the years the Council worked toward these objectives with respect to the

---

[4] The idea of secession as a right was considered particularly disturbing. In 1921, for example, an International Commission refused to give weight to wishes of a majority of people of the Aaland Islands to secede from Finland and join Sweden, on the grounds that this was incompatible with the very idea of the State as a territorial and political unity. See Frederic L Kirgis, Jr., "The Degrees of Self-Determination in the United Nations Era," *American Journal of International Law*, vol. 88 (1994), p. 304.
[5] Ruth B. Russell and Jeanette E. Muther, *A History of the United Nations Charter: The Role of the United States, 1940–45* (Washington, DC: Brookings, 1958), pp. 810–811.
[6] For an in-depth discussion see, "Self Determination," in Bruno Simma (ed.), *The Charter of the United Nations: A Commentary*, 2nd edn. (Oxford: Oxford University Press, 2002), pp. 48–63. See, also Thomas M. Franck, *Recourse to Force: State Action Against Threats and Armed Attacks* (Cambridge: Cambridge University Press, 2002), pp. 1–19.
[7] Article 76 of the UN Charter.

eleven territories placed under its aegis, and in 1994 its task was effectively completed with the independence of Palau.

In the materials that follow, note the efforts by the Trusteeship Council and the General Assembly, to interpret the meaning of the terms "self-government or independence." Self-government has not been seen to be merely a subsidiary form of independence, but to include such alternatives as joining the administering state in a form of permanent union, or choosing union with another already-independent neighboring state. It will also become apparent in reading these materials that an important question, antecedent to the choice of status, is the means for determining that choice through the inhabitants' "progressive development towards self-government or independence" (UN Charter, Article 76(b)). Consider, too, whether the principles developed in the course of decolonization after World War II are relevant to peoples seeking independence from independent states in the post-colonial era.

Note, also, that decolonization under the Charter occurred in the context of two different systems of UN supervision: those applicable to Trust Territories (Chapter XII of the Charter) and those applicable to Non-Self Governing Territories, for which Chapter XI provide a more limited basis for UN supervision. Even though the term "self-determination" was not mentioned in Chapter XII of the Charter, which deals with the Trusteeship System, the exhortation to prepare peoples for self-government or independence differentiates it from the provisions for mandate territories under the Covenant of the League of Nations, under which territories were classified into groups (A, B, or C), with groups B and C designated as territories having little or no chance of attaining independence. In contrast all Trust territories were given the right to choose independence under the UN Charter and by 1994 they had achieved this.See Table 12-1.

There are still sixteen Non-Self-Governing Territories. See Table 12-2.

This chapter considers the common claim that self-determination is a "right" before considering some specific cases in which that right has been asserted. Particular problems include the relationship between claims of a group to self-determination and claims of a state to territorial integrity. The cases considered are (i) Western Sahara, a former Spanish colony claimed both by Morocco and the indigenous Sahrawi population, still being mediated by the United Nations; (ii) the contested territory of North Borneo, control of which had been variously exercised by the Sultan of Brunei, the Sultan of Sulu, an Austrian businessman, his British employer, and the British Crown, before it voted to join Malaysia, more recently being the subject of a claim by the Philippines before the ICJ; and (iii) the Falkland Islands/Islas Malvinas, which in 1982 was the basis for a brief war between Britain and Argentina.

12.1 Self-Determination as a Right

In the practice of the General Assembly, the right of self-determination came to be extended to colonies, which in the early years of the United Nations

Table 12-1 Trust Territories of the United Nations

Trust Territory	Administering Power	Status
Togoland	Britain	United with the Gold Coast (Colony and Protectorate), a Non-Self-Governing Territory administered by Britain, in 1957 to form Ghana
Somaliland	Italy	United with British Somaliland Protectorate in 1960 to form Somalia
Togoland	France	Became independent as Togo in 1960
Cameroons	France	Became independent as Cameroon in 1960
Cameroons	Britain	Northern territory joined Nigeria and Southern territory joined Cameroon (1961)
Tanganyika	Britain	Became independent in 1961 (in 1964, Tanganyika and the former protectorate of Zanzibar, which had become independent in 1963, united as a single State under the name of the United Republic of Tanzania)
Ruanda-Urundi	Belgian	Voted to divide into the two sovereign States of Rwanda and Burundi in 1962
Western Samoa	New Zealand	Became independent as Samoa in 1962
Nauru	Australia on behalf of Australia, New Zealand, and Britain	Became independent in 1968
New Guinea	Australia	United with the Non-Self-Governing Territory of Papua, also administered by Australia, to become the independent State of Papua New Guinea in 1975
Trust Territory of the Pacific Islands:	United States	(a) Federated States of Micronesia—Became fully self-governing in free Association with the United States in 1990 (b) Republic of the Marshall Islands—Became fully self-governing in free Association with the United States in 1990 (c) Commonwealth of the Northern Mariana Islands—Became fully self-governing as Commonwealth of the United States in 1990 (d) Palau—Became fully self-governing in free Association with the United States in 1994

were far more numerous than the Trust Territories. Self-determination as a "right" of the peoples, is expressly provided for General Assembly resolutions 1514(XV) (1960) and 1541(XV) (1960), excerpted below. These resolutions reiterate the right of self-determination of non-self-governing territories and set out the duties of administering powers to lead them to self-government.

Table 12-2 Non-Self-Governing Territories Listed by the General Assembly

Territory	Administering Power	Population (approximate)
American Samoa	United States	57,291
Anguilla	Britain	11,960
Bermuda	Britain	6,997
British Virgin Islands	Britain	23,000
Cayman Islands	Britain	39,410
Falkland Islands (Malvinas)	Britain	2,391
Gibraltar	Britain	26,703
Guam	United States	154,805
Montserrat	Britain	5,000
New Caledonia	France	215,904
Pitcairn	Britain	46
St. Helena	Britain	6,000
Tokelau	New Zealand	1,518
Turks and Caicos Islands	Britain	24,000
United States Virgin Islands	United States	108,612
Western Sahara	Spain (terminated in 1976); Morocco is recognized as the de facto authority	Disputed

GENERAL ASSEMBLY RESOLUTION 1514(XV) (1960): DECLARATION ON THE GRANTING OF INDEPENDENCE TO COLONIAL COUNTRIES AND PEOPLES

1. The subjection of peoples to alien subjugation, domination and exploitation constitutes a denial of fundamental human rights, is contrary to the Charter of the United Nations and is an impediment to the promotion of world peace and co-operation.

2. All peoples have the right to self-determination; by virtue of that right they freely determine their political status and freely pursue their economic, social and cultural development.

3. Inadequacy of political, economic, social or educational preparedness should never serve as a pretext for delaying independence.

4. All armed action or repressive measures of all kinds directed against dependent peoples shall cease in order to enable them to exercise peacefully and freely their right to complete independence, and the integrity of their national territory shall be respected.

5. Immediate steps shall be taken, in Trust and Non-Self-Governing Territories or all other territories which have not yet attained independence, to

transfer all powers to the peoples of those territories, without any conditions or reservations, in accordance with their freely expressed will and desire, without any distinction as to race, creed or colour, in order to enable them to enjoy complete independence and freedom.

6. Any attempt aimed at the partial or total disruption of the national unity and the territorial integrity of a country is incompatible with the purposes and principles of the Charter of the United Nations.

7. All States shall observe faithfully and strictly the provisions of the Charter of the United Nations, the Universal Declaration of Human Rights and the present Declaration on the basis of equality, non-interference in the internal affairs of all States, and respect for the sovereign rights of all peoples and their territorial integrity.

Under the guise of laying down the extent of the obligation of states to transmit information to the Secretary-General under Article 73(e) of the UN Charter, the second resolution also fleshed out the parameters against which the achievement of effective self-government must be evaluated, perhaps also asserting a right of the General Assembly to supervise this process.

GENERAL ASSEMBLY RESOLUTION 1541(XV) (1960): PRINCIPLES WHICH SHOULD GUIDE MEMBERS IN DETERMINING WHETHER OR NOT AN OBLIGATION EXISTS TO TRANSMIT THE INFORMATION CALLED FOR UNDER ARTICLE 73(E) OF THE CHARTER

Principle I

The authors of the Chapters of the United Nations had in mind that Chapter XI should be applicable to territories which were then known to be of the colonial type. An obligation exists to transmit information under Article 73 e of the Charter in respect of such territories whose peoples have not yet attained a full measure of self-government.

Principle II

Chapter XI of the Charter embodies the concept of Non-Self-Governing Territories in a dynamic state of evolution and progress towards a "full measure of self-government." As soon as a territory and its peoples attain a full measure of self-government, the obligation ceases. Until this comes about, the obligation to transmit information under Article 73 e continues.

Principle III

The obligation to transmit information under Article 73 e of the Charter constitutes an international obligation and should be carried out with due regard to the fulfilment of international law.

Principle IV

Prima facie there is an obligation to transmit information in respect of a territory which is geographically separate and is distinct ethnically and/or culturally from the country administering it.

Principle V

Once it has been established that such a *prima facie* case of geographical and ethnical or cultural distinctness of a territory exists, other elements may then be brought into consideration. These additional elements may be, *inter alia*, of an administrative, political, juridical, economic or historical nature. If they affect the relationship between the metropolitan State and the territory concerned in a manner which arbitrarily places the latter in a position or status of subordination, they support the presumption that there is an obligation to transmit information under Article 73 e of the Charter.

Principle VI

A Non-Self-Governing Territory can be said to have reached a full measure of self-government by:
  (a) Emergence as a sovereign independent State;
  (b) Free association with an independent State; or
  (c) Integration with an independent State.

Principle VII

(a) Free association should be the result of a free and voluntary choice by the peoples of the territory concerned expressed through informed and democratic processes. It should be one which respects the individuality and the cultural characteristics of the territory and its peoples, and retains for the peoples of the territory which is associated with an independent State the freedom to modify the status of that territory through the expression of their will by democratic means and through constitutional processes.

(b) The associated territory should have the right to determine its internal constitution without outside interference, in accordance with due constitutional processes and the freely expressed wishes of the people. This does not preclude consultations as appropriate or necessary under the terms of the free association agreed upon.

Principle VIII

Integration with an independent State should be on the basis of complete equality between the peoples of the erstwhile Non-Self-Governing Territory and those of the independent country with which it is integrated. The peoples of both territories should have equal status and rights of citizenship and equal guarantees of fundamental rights and freedoms without any distinction or discrimination; both should have equal rights and opportunities for representation and effective participation at all levels in the executive, legislative and judicial organs of government.

Principle IX

Integration should have come about in the following circumstances:

(a) The integrating territory should have attained an advanced stage of self government with free political institutions so that its people should have the capacity to make a responsible choice through informed and democratic processes;

(b) The integration should be the result of the freely expressed wishes of the territory's peoples acting with full knowledge of the change in their status, their wishes having been expressed through informed and democratic processes, impartially conducted and based on universal adult suffrage. The United Nations could, when it deems necessary, supervise these processes.

Principle X

The transmission of information in respect of Non-Self-Governing Territories under Article 73 e of the Charter is subject to such limitation as security and constitutional considerations may require. This means that the extent of the information may be limited in certain circumstances, but the limitation in Article 73 e cannot relieve a Member State of the obligations of Chapter XI. The "limitation" can relate only to the quantum of information of economic, social and educational nature to be transmitted.

Principle XI

The only constitutional considerations to which Article 73 e of the Charter refers are those arising from constitutional relations of the territory with the Administering Member. They refer to a situation in which the constitution of the territory gives it self-government in economic, social and educational matters through freely elected institutions. Nevertheless, the responsibility for transmitting information under Article 73 e continues, unless these constitutional relations preclude the Government or parliament of the Administering Member from receiving statistical and other information of a technical nature relating to economic, social and educational conditions in the territory.

Principle XII

Security considerations have not been invoked in the past. Only in very exceptional circumstances can information on economic, social and educational conditions have any security aspect. In other circumstances, therefore, there should be no necessity to limit the transmission of information on security grounds.

The right of self-determination has since been reiterated also in instruments unrelated to decolonization, such as human rights instruments,[8] the Definition of Aggression,[9] and the Helsinki Declaration.[10]

Its invocation in practice, however, even with respect to decolonization, has been contested. This is primarily because there is a fundamental tension between the concept of self-determination—the right of "peoples"—and the right to territorial integrity of states. General Assembly resolution 1514(XV) (1960), for example, specifically provides that "[a]ny attempt aimed at the partial or total disruption of the national unity and the territorial integrity of a country," is incompatible with the UN Charter. In some cases it is possible to interpret the right of self-determination fairly harmoniously with territorial integrity—in case of "blue-water colonialism" or occupation by one state of another it is relatively easy to argue that the occupying state does not have a tenable territorial claim. However, in many other situations, such as where a minority seeks to separate from the state in which it is located or where during decolonization a neighboring state claims "historic title" to the colony, the conflict between self-determination and territorial integrity is apparent. Of course, separation or "independence" is not the only choice available to non-self-governing peoples. Principle VI of resolution 1541(XV) (1960) recognized the attainment of self-government of such groups in cases of their: (a) emergence as a sovereign independent state; (b) free association with an independent state; or (c) integration with an independent state. It may also be argued that in a post-colonial era, the concept of self-determination may be satisfied by a people being allowed freely to participate on the basis of equality with all others who are citizens in the governance of a democratic state, rather than by a right of secession. Such a definition of self-determination, while limited, may be more reconcilable with a nation's right to its "territorial integrity."

---

[8] Article 1, International Covenant on Civil and Political Rights, G.A. res. 2200A (XXI), 21 UN GAOR Supp. (No. 16) at 52, UN Doc. A/6316 (1966), 999 UNTS 171, *entered into force* Mar. 23, 1976; Article 1 International Covenant on Economic, Social and Cultural Rights, G.A. res. 2200A (XXI), 21 UNGAOR Supp. (No. 16) at 49, UN Doc. A/6316 (1966), 993 UNTS 3, *entered into force* Jan. 3, 1976.
[9] G.A. Res. 3314(XXIX) (1974).
[10] Question 1(a) VIII, Final Act of the Conference on Security and Cooperation in Europe, 14 ILM 1292, 1 August 1975.

QUESTIONS ....

1. Does the right of self-determination persist into the post colonial-era? If so, does it necessarily entail a right to independence? If not, what right does it entail? What is the content of the 1960 declarations?
2. Does the right of self-determination exist objectively, as a right of all minorities, or only contextually, as when a minority is actually oppressed or denied equal rights in a state from which it seeks to secede?
3. Has "independence" as an option ceased to be meaningful in a globalized world in which so many of the prerogatives of sovereignty once exercised by independent states have been assumed by regional and international treaty-based "regimes" such as the United Nations, the General Agreement on Tariffs and Trade, etc?

12.2 Western Sahara

The conflict began with a bid for independence by the Sahrawi people, the inhabitants of the Spanish Sahara, in the late 1950s. In 1963 the territory was put on the UN General Assembly's list of countries entitled to self-determination—the so-called 73(e) list (after Article 73(e) of the UN Charter), which set out territories as to which the colonial power was obliged to report to a Committee of the General Assembly. Although Spain initially refused to make the requisite reports, two years later the UN General Assembly re-affirmed the inalienable right of self-determination by the Sahrawi people and requested Spain to end its colonial rule.[11] This was supported by the Spanish Sahara's neighbors, Morocco and Mauritania, as well as by the Organization of African Unity (OAU). In 1966 the United Nations proposed a referendum to allow the Sahrawi people to choose whether they would prefer independence, or Spanish rule.[12] While some steps were taken, the referendum was not realized and the repression of Saharan demonstrations for independence continued. In 1973, the Frente Polisario, the organization that has since played a major role as a representative of the Sahrawi people, was formed.

Following more that a year of attacks by the Polisario, requests by the Jema'a (the Democratic Assembly of the Sahrawi People) for greater autonomy, and calls for fulfilment of the free exercise of the right of self-determination of the Sahrawi people by the United Nations and neighboring countries, Spain finally announced that it would grant greater internal autonomy to the region. However, by this time Morocco and Mauritania had begun to put forward their own claims to parts of the Western Sahara. These claims, based on assertions of historic legal ties with the people of the Western Sahara, were confronted by another neighboring state, Algeria, which

---

[11] GA Res. 2072(XX) (1965).
[12] GA Res. 2229(XXI) (1966).

began to back the Sahrawi demand for self-determination and offered support to the Frente Polisario.

Spain, undergoing its own regime change with the ending of the long regime of dictator Francisco Franco, announced its intention of holding a referendum in the first half of 1975. The General Assembly passed resolution 3292(XXIX) (1974), presenting the following questions to the ICJ for its advisory opinion:

> I. Was Western Sahara (Río de Oro and Sakiet El Hamra) at the time of colonization by Spain a territory belonging to no one (*terra nullius*)?
> If the answer to the first question is in the negative,
> II. What were the legal ties between this territory and the Kingdom of Morocco and the Mauritanian entity?

The resolution also urged Spain to postpone the referendum until the General Assembly had decided on the policy to be followed in order to accelerate the decolonization process in the territory.

Spain considered that the questions were irrelevant, as the United Nations had already decided upon a referendum as the means of decolonization. Morocco and Mauritania took the view that the opinion of the court was relevant. Morocco held that the General Assembly was free to choose from a wide range of solutions in the light of two basic principles enunciated in resolution 1514(XV): self-determination, and national unity and territorial integrity. Mauritania stated that the principle of self-determination could not be dissociated from that of respect for national unity and territorial integrity; and in several instances, the General Assembly had given priority to the latter, particularly in situations where the territory had been created by a colonizing power to the detriment of the state to which the territory had previously belonged. Algeria held that self-determination is the fundamental principle governing decolonization, and that it had been recognized as such by the General Assembly, the administering Power and by regional institutions, international conferences, and the neighboring countries.

WESTERN SAHARA CASE (ADVISORY OPINION), 1975 ICJ REPORTS 12

53. . . . [R]esolution 3292 (XXIX) is the latest of a long series of General Assembly resolutions dealing with Western Sahara . . . [I]n order to appraise the correctness or otherwise of Spain's view . . . it is necessary to recall briefly the basic principles governing the decolonization policy of the General Assembly, the general lines of previous resolutions on the question, and the preparatory work and context of resolution 3292 (XXIX). . . .

81. In the present instance, the information furnished to the Court shows that at the time of colonization Western Sahara was inhabited by peoples which, if nomadic, were socially and politically organized in tribes and under chiefs competent to represent them. It also shows that, in colonizing Western Sahara, Spain did not proceed on the basis that it was establishing its sovereignty over *terrae nullius*. In its Royal Order of 26 December 1884 . . . Spain proclaimed that the King was taking the Rio de Oro under his protection on the basis of agreements which had been entered into with the chiefs of the local tribes: the Order referred expressly to "the documents which the independent tribes of this part of the coast" had "signed with the representative of the Sociedad Espanola de Africanistas," and announced that the King had confirmed "the deeds of adherence" to Spain. Likewise, in negotiating with France concerning the limits of Spanish territory to the north of the Rio de Oro, that is, in the Sakiet El Hamra area, Spain did not rely upon any claim to the acquisition of sovereignty over a *terra nullius*.

82. Before the Court, differing views were expressed concerning the nature and legal value of agreements between a State and local chiefs. But the Court is not asked to pronounce upon the legal character or the legality of the titles which led to Spain becoming the administering Power of Western Sahara. It is asked only to state whether Western Sahara . . . at the time of colonization by Spain was "a territory belonging to no one (*terra nullius*)." As to this question, the Court is satisfied that, for the reasons which it has given, its answer must be in the negative. Accordingly, the Court does not find it necessary first to pronounce upon Morocco's view that the territory was not *terra nullius* at that time because the local tribes, so it maintains, were then subject to the sovereignty of the Sultan of Morocco; nor upon Mauritania's corresponding proposition that the territory was not *terra nullius* because the local tribes, in its view, formed part of the . . . Mauritanian entity. Any conclusions that the Court may reach with respect to either of these points of view cannot change the negative character of the answer which, for other reasons already set out, it has found that it must give to Question I. . . .

84. Question II asks the Court to state "what were the legal ties between [Western Sahara] . . . and the Kingdom of Morocco and the Mauritanian entity." The scope of this question depends upon the meaning to be attached to the expression "legal ties" in the context of the time of the colonization of the territory by Spain. That expression, however, unlike *"terra nullius"* . . . - was not a term having in itself a very precise meaning. Accordingly, in the view of the Court, the meaning . . . has to be found rather in the object and purpose of General Assembly resolution 3292 (XXIX) . . .

85. Analysis of this resolution, as the Court has already pointed out, shows that the two questions have been put to the Court in the context of proceedings in the General Assembly directed to the decolonization of Western Sahara in conformity with resolution 1514 (XV) . . . During the discussion of this item, according to resolution 3292 (XXIX), a legal controversy arose over the status of Western Sahara at the time of its colonization by Spain; and the records of the proceedings make it plain that the "legal controversy" in

question concerned pretensions put forward [by Morocco and Mauritania that the territory had been part of their Kingdom and entity respectively] . . . Accordingly, it appears to the Court that in Question II the words "legal ties between this territory and the Kingdom of Morocco and the Mauritanian entity" must be understood as referring to such "legal ties" as may affect the policy to be followed in the decolonization of Western Sahara. In this connection, the Court cannot accept the view that the legal ties the General Assembly had in mind . . . were limited to ties established directly with the territory and without reference to the people who may be found in it. Such an interpretation would unduly restrict the scope of the question, since legal ties are normally established in relation to people.

86. The Court further observes that, inasmuch as Question II had its origin in the contentions of Morocco and Mauritania, it was for them to satisfy the Court in the present proceedings that legal ties existed between Western Sahara and the Kingdom of Morocco or the Mauritanian entity at the time of the colonization of the territory by Spain. . . .

128. Examination of the various elements adduced by Morocco in the present proceedings does not, therefore, appear to the Court to establish the international recognition by other States of Moroccan territorial sovereignty in Western Sahara at the time of the Spanish colonization. Some elements, however, more especially the material relating to the recovery of shipwrecked sailors, do provide indications of international recognition at the time of colonization of authority or influence of the Sultan . . .

130. . . . [T]he position of the Islamic Republic of Mauritania in relation to Western Sahara at that date differs from that of Morocco for the reason that there was not then any Mauritanian State in existence. In the present proceedings Mauritania has expressly accepted that the "Mauritanian entity" did not then constitute a State; and also that the present statehood of Mauritania "is not retroactive." Consequently, it is clear that it is not legal ties of State sovereignty with which the Court is concerned in the case of the "Mauritanian entity" but other legal ties. . . .

162. The materials and information presented to the Court show the existence, at the time of Spanish colonization, of legal ties of allegiance between the Sultan of Morocco and some of the tribes living in the territory of Western Sahara. They equally show the existence of rights, including some rights relating to the land, which constituted legal ties between the Mauritanian entity, as understood by the Court, and the territory of Western Sahara. On the other hand, the Court's conclusion is that the materials and information presented to it do not establish any tie of territorial sovereignty between the territory of Western Sahara and the Kingdom of Morocco or the Mauritanian entity. Thus the Court has not found legal ties of such a nature as might affect the application of resolution 1514 (XV) in the decolonization of Western Sahara and, in particular, of the principle of self-determination through the free and genuine expression of the will of the peoples of the Territory.

The consequences of this opinion were twofold. First, as the following resolutions indicate, it reinforced the United Nations' resolve to take adequate measures to resolve the situation in the Western Sahara:

SECURITY COUNCIL RESOLUTION 377 (1975)

The Security Council, . . .

1. *Acting* in accordance with Article 34 of the Charter of the United Nations and without prejudice to any action which the General Assembly might take under the terms of its resolution 3292(XXIX) of 13 December 1974 or to negotiations that the parties concerned and interested might undertake under Article 33 of the Charter, *requests* the Secretary-General to enter into immediate consultations with the parties concerned and interested and to report to the Security Council as soon as possible on the results of his consultations in order to enable the Council to adopt the appropriate measures to deal with the present situation concerning Western Sahara;

2. *Appeals* to the parties concerned and interested to exercise restraint and moderation, and to enable the mission of the Secretary-General to be undertaken to satisfactory conditions.

SECURITY COUNCIL RESOLUTION 379 (1975)

The Security Council, . . .

Having noted with concern that the situation in the area remains grave, . . .

1. *Urges* all the parties concerned and interested to avoid any unilateral or other action which might further escalate the tension in the area;

2. *Requests* the Secretary-General to continue and intensify his consultations with the parties concerned and interested, and to report to the Security Council as soon as possible on the results of these consultations in order to enable the Council to adopt any further appropriate measures that may be necessary.

Secondly, it evoked protests from Morocco and Mauritania. On 6 November 1975, on the orders of their King, 350,000 Moroccans crossed "peacefully" into

Western Sahara, occupying the territory. This was condemned by the Security Council in meeting convened on the same day.

SECURITY COUNCIL RESOLUTION 380 (1975)

The Security Council,
Noting with grave concern that the situation concern Western Sahara has seriously deteriorated, . . .
1. *Deplores* the holding of the march;
2. *Calls upon* Morocco immediately to withdraw from the Territory of Western Sahara all the participants in the march.
3. *Calls upon* Morocco and all other parties concerned and interested, without prejudice to any action the General Assembly might take under the terms of its resolution 3292 (XXIX) of 13 December 1974 or any negotiations that the parties concerned and interested might undertake under Article 33 of the Charter, to cooperate fully with the Secretary-General in the fulfilment of the mandate entrusted to him in Security Council resolutions 377 (1975) and 379 (1975).

A Declaration of Principles was agreed in Madrid on 14 November 1975 under which Spain proposed definitively to terminate its presence in the Territory by 28 February 1976 and in the interim to transfer its powers and responsibilities to a temporary administration that would be constituted by Spain's Governor General and two Deputy Governors nominated by Morocco and Mauritania. Algeria, the other neighboring state, was against this tripartite agreement and pushed for the right of the people of the Territory to self-determination and independence. It supported the position of the Frente Polisario.

On 9 December 1975 the Permanent Representative of Algeria to the United Nations transmitted to the Secretary-General a document signed at Guelta Zemmur on 28 November sixty sheikhs and notables of the Saharan tribes. The signatories stated that the only way of consulting the Saharan people was by allowing them to decide their own future and to obtain independence free of any outside interference. As the Jema'a had not been democratically elected, the signatories considered that it could not decide upon self-determination of the Saharan people; and, in order to avoid being used, the Jema'a by unanimous vote of the members present, had decided on its final dissolution. The Document declared the Frente Polisario as the sole and legitimate authority of the people.

The General Assembly debated upon this on the following day and adopted the following resolution:

GENERAL ASSEMBLY RESOLUTION 3458(XXX) (1975): QUESTION OF SPANISH SAHARA

A

The General Assembly, . . .

1. *Reaffirms* the rights of the people of the Spanish Sahara to self-determination in accordance with General Assembly resolution 1514 (XV).

2. *Reaffirms* . . . its concern to see that principle applied to the inhabitants of the territory of Spanish Sahara within a framework that guarantees and permits them the free and genuine expression of their will, in accordance with the relevant resolutions of the United Nations;

3. *Reaffirms* the responsibility of the administering Power and of the United Nations with regard to the decolonization of the Territory and the guaranteeing of the free expression of the people of Spanish Sahara; . . .

7. *Requests* the government of Spain, as the administering Power . . . to take immediately all necessary measures, in consultation with all the parties concerned and interested, so that all Saharans originating in the Territory may exercise fully and freely, under United Nations supervision, their inalienable right to self-determination.

8. *Requests* the Secretary-General, in consultation with the Government of Spain, as the administering Power, and the Special Committee on the situation with regard to the implementation of the Declaration on the Granting of Independence to Colonial Countries and Peoples, to make the necessary arrangements for the supervision of the act of self-determination referred to in paragraph 7 above.

B

The General Assembly, . . .

1. *Takes note* of the tripartite agreement concluded at Madrid on 14 November 1975 by the Governments of Mauritania, Morocco and Spain, the text of which was transmitted to the Secretary-General of the United Nations on 18 November 1975; . . .

3. *Requests* the parties to the Madrid Agreement to ensure respect for the freely expressed aspirations of the Saharan populations;

4. *Requests* the interim administration to take all necessary steps to ensure that all the Saharan populations originating in the Territory will be able to exercise their inalienable right to self-determination through free consultations organized with the assistance of a representative of the United Nations appointed by the Secretary-General.

Spain withdrew its presence from region, as it had committed to do. Moroccan forces moved into the northern and eastern areas of the Territory and Mauritanian forces into parts of the southern area. In some places, these forces met with armed confrontation by forces of the Frente Polisario, which had announced its intention to continue the guerrilla war.

On 27 February 1976, the permanent Mission of Morocco to the United Nations transmitted to the Secretary-General, a message from the President of the Jema'a informing him the Jema'a had unanimously approved the reintegration of the territory of Sahara with Morocco and Mauritania in conformity with historical realities and the links which had always united the Saharan population to those two countries. Western Sahara was thus partitioned into two and Moroccan and Mauritanian civil administration and military forces were established in their respective parts. Algeria continued to oppose these developments as against the wishes of the Saharan people.

Conflict ensued between the Polisario and Morocco and Mauritania for the next two years. On 5 August 1979 the Polisario and Mauritania signed the Algiers Agreement, by which Mauritania renounced its claim to Western Sahara. At this time Morocco moved to annex the southern part of Western Sahara after Mauritania's withdrawal. Hostilities between Morocco and the Frente Polisario continued for almost ten years. During this period, the OAU admitted the Sahrawi Arab Democratic Republic (SADR) as a full member and called for self-determination of the Sahrawi people.

A breakthrough appeared to have been achieved with the adoption of a UN Settlement plan, formulated by the Secretary-General and approved by the Security Council in resolution 658 (1990), which reinforced a cease-fire agreement arrived at between Morocco and the Frente Polisario and provided for a referendum to be conducted in January 1992. To monitor the cease-fire and to assist the Secretary-General in holding of a Referendum for the self-determination of the people of Western Sahara, the Security Council established the United Nations Mission for the Referendum in Western Sahara (MINURSO) by resolution 690 (1991) in April 1991. The other functions that the Minurso was supposed to perform included: verification of the reduction of Moroccan troops in the Territory; monitoring the confinement of Moroccan and Frente Polisario troops to designated locations; taking steps with the parties to ensure the release of all Western Saharan political prisoners or detainees; overseeing the exchange of prisoners of war (with the ICRC); implementation of the repatriation program (with UNHCR); identification and registration of qualified voters; organizing and ensuring a free and fair referendum and proclamation of the results. The referendum was never achieved because of disputes over who could participate.

After years of fruitless negotiations, the Personal Envoy of the Secretary-General asked the parties to come up with their own proposals. Morocco proposed an alternate plan under which it would agree to a substantial devolution of Authority over a ten-year transitory period, during which the implementation of a self-determination referendum would be studied. The Secretary-General proposed abandonment of the original settlement plan and adoption of the Moroccan proposal as a framework agreement. The envoy of the Secretary-General thereafter met with the Frente Polisario, and the governments of Mauritania and Algeria to discuss their reservations to this Framework Agreement. Later however, the Polisario rejected the Agreement. Soon after, Morocco repudiated the original Settlement Plan as obsolete. It stressed that it was willing to provide greater autonomy to the Sahrawi but that the territory must be a part of Morocco.

After many months of efforts to bring the parties to a common understanding, James Baker, the Secretary-General's special envoy, acknowledged there was no easy solution to this issue. He offered the following suggestions, adopted by the Secretary-General in his Report to the Security Council:

REPORT OF THE SECRETARY-GENERAL ON THE SITUATION CONCERNING WESTERN SAHARA (2002)[13]

48. As a first option, the United Nations could, once again, resume trying to implement the settlement plan, but without requiring the concurrence of both parties before action could be taken. This effort would begin with the appeals process but, even under this nonconsensual approach, the United Nations would in the years ahead face most of the problems and obstacles that it has faced during the past 10 years. Morocco has expressed unwillingness to go forward with the settlement plan; the United Nations might not be able to hold a free and fair referendum whose results would be accepted by both sides; and there would still be no mechanism to enforce the results of the referendum. Under this option, the Identification Commission of MINURSO would be reinforced and indeed the overall size of the operation would be increased.

49. As a second option, my Personal Envoy could undertake to revise the draft framework agreement, taking into account the concerns expressed by the parties and others with experience in such documents. However, in this event, my Personal Envoy would not seek the concurrence of the parties as has been done in the past with respect to the settlement plan and the draft framework agreement. The revised framework agreement would be submitted to the Security Council, and the Council would then present it to the parties on a non-negotiable basis. Should the Security Council agree to this option, MINURSO could be downsized further.

50. As a third option, the Security Council could ask my Personal Envoy to explore with the parties one final time whether or not they would now be willing to discuss, under his auspices, directly or through proximity talks, a possible division of the Territory, with the understanding that nothing would

---

[13] UN Doc. S/2002/178 (2002).

be decided until everything was decided. Were the Security Council to choose this option, in the event that the parties would be unwilling or unable to agree upon a division of the Territory by 1 November 2002, my Personal Envoy would also be asked to thereafter show to the parties a proposal for division of the Territory that would also be presented to the Security Council. The Council would present this proposal to the parties on a non-negotiable basis. This approach to a political solution would give each party some, but not all, of what it wants and would follow the precedent, but not necessarily the same territorial arrangements, of the division agreed to in 1976 between Morocco and Mauritania. Were the Security Council to choose this option, MINURSO could be maintained at its present size, or it could be reduced even more.

51. As a fourth option, the Security Council could decide to terminate MINURSO, thereby recognizing and acknowledging that after more than 11 years and the expenditure of sums of money nearing half a billion dollars, the United Nations is not going to solve the problem of Western Sahara without requiring that one or the other or both of the parties do something that they do not wish to voluntarily agree to do.

52. I am aware that none of the above-mentioned options will appear ideal to all the parties and interested countries. In order to give the Security Council time to decide, I recommend that the mandate of MINURSO be extended for two months, until 30 April 2002.

The position of the Security Council and the concerns arising out of the events during this period, as perceived by the Secretary-General are detailed below:

SECURITY COUNCIL RESOLUTION 1394 (2002)

The Security Council, . . .

Taking note of the report of the Secretary-General of 19 February 2002 (S/2002/178),

1. *Decides*, as recommended by the Secretary-General in his report of 19 February 2002, to extend the mandate of the United Nations Mission for the Referendum in Western Sahara (MINURSO) until 30 April 2002 and to consider actively the options described in his report, addressing this issue in its programme of work;

2. *Requests* the Secretary-General to provide a report on the situation before the end of the present mandate . . .

REPORT OF THE SECRETARY-GENERAL ON THE SITUATION CONCERNING WESTERN SAHARA, 19 APRIL 2002[14]

VI. Observations and Recommendations

19. The humanitarian aspects of the overall situation affecting the question of Western Sahara remain a source of great concern. The detention of 1,362 prisoners of war continues to be one of the most pressing humanitarian issues. As the Council is aware, I have already asked my Special Representative to assist ICRC in the discharge of its critical tasks. It is my earnest hope that members of the Council will join me once again in urging the Frente POLISARIO to release all remaining prisoners of war without further delay. I also hope that both parties will continue to cooperate with the efforts of ICRC to solve the problem of the fate of all those unaccounted for since the beginning of the conflict.

20. Given the current low levels of food supply in the refugee camps in the Tindouf area, I am also urging the international community to extend its financial support to enable UNHCR and WFP to meet the humanitarian needs of the refugees. . . . [M]y Special Representative has been in close contact with UNHCR and WFP to support efforts to address this problem. As the same time, I expect Morocco and the Frente POLISARIO to cooperate without further delay with UNHCR in the implementation of the long overdue confidence-building measures, as repeatedly called for by the Security Council since 1999. The plight of the separated refugee families demands no less.

21. It is my hope that the Security Council will decide by the end of the current mandate period how it wishes to proceed with regard to the future of the peace process in Western Sahara and that it will take action, as appropriate on the mandate of MINURSO. I believe that by choosing the option that it considers most likely to help resolve the conflict, the Council will indicate to the parties its determination to continue to look actively for a realistic solution to the conflict that will also contribute to long-term peace, stability and prosperity in the Maghreb region.

22. My Personal Envoy stands ready to undertake the activities that will be required under the option the Security Council chooses, in order to steer the parties towards a resolution of their dispute over Western Sahara, provided that the Council does not support any changes to options one, two or three that would require the concurrence of the parties. Such changes, as my Personal Envoy told the Council on 27 February 2002, would simply encourage a continuation of the conflict and the current stalemate. As always, I intend to lend all my support to my Personal Envoy in his difficult task.

---

[14] UN Doc. S/2002/467 (2002).

In 2003, an attempt was made to revive a modified version of the Framework Agreement, however, even though the Polisario appeared to be willing to support it, the Moroccan government was not and the plan, like its predecessor, was finally shelved. Currently, while some improvements have been seen in the situation on the ground, including release of prisoners, as well as movement across the wall that had been built by Morocco to separate the territory of the Western Sahara occupied by it, from the unoccupied land to the east, where Polisario held sway, no immediate fulfilment of the right of self-determination of the Sahrawi people appears to be in sight. Morocco continues to rule with all the prerogatives of an occupying power and to introduce new settlers into the region with a view to altering its demographics.

QUESTIONS

4. If Morocco had been able to establish historic title to Western Sahara, would the ICJ advisory opinion have been different? See in particular paragraph 162 of the judgment.
5. Compare the situation of Western Sahara with that of East Timor/Timor-Leste, discussed in chapter 9. Should the two situations have been treated similarly?

12.3 North Borneo

The claim of the Philippines to North Borneo is also somewhat similar to the Moroccan and Mauritanian claims over the Western Sahara and the Argentine claim over the Falklands, in that it is another instance of a state attempting to obtain control over a territory on the basis of historical association with it.

North Borneo, renamed "Sabah" is currently a part of Malaysia. The Philippines, however, asserts a claim derived from that of the heirs of the Sultan of Sulu, to whom the Sultan of Brunei had ceded this territory in 1703, in return for military assistance. In the late nineteenth century, control of this territory passed into the hands of the British, via a lease in favour of an Austrian who had a British trading partner. After the First World War, which saw the end of the Austro-Hungarian Empire, the British incorporated Sabah into the British Empire. On attaining its independence from the US, the Philippines kept alive its claim to North Borneo In 1963, when the British retreated from the region, North Borneo was one of the states that after an election fought on the issue of future affiliation, came together to form the Malaysian Federation. At this time, the Philippines, Malaysia, and Indonesia entered into a peace and cooperation treaty termed the Manila Accord. The portion relevant to North Borneo states as follows:

THE MANILA ACCORD, 31 JULY 1963[15]

Malaysia and North Borneo

10. The Ministers reaffirmed their countries' adherence to the principle of self-determination for the peoples of non-self-governing territories. In this context, Indonesia and the Philippines stated that they would welcome the formation of Malaysia provided the support of the people of the Borneo territories is ascertained by an independent and impartial authority, the Secretary-General of the United Nations or his representative.

11. The Federation of Malaya expressed appreciation for this attitude of Indonesia and the Philippines and undertook to consult the British Government and the Governments of the Borneo territories with a view to inviting the Secretary-General of the United Nations or his representative to take the necessary steps in order to ascertain the wishes of the people of those territories,

12. The Philippines made it clear that its position on the inclusion of North Borneo in the Federation of Malaysia is subject to the final outcome of the Philippine claim to North Borneo. The Ministers took note of the Philippine claim and the right of the Philippines to continue to pursue it in accordance with international law and the principle of the pacific settlement of disputes. They agreed that the inclusion of North Borneo in the Federation of Malaysia would not prejudice either the claim or any right thereunder. Moreover, in the context of their close association, the three countries agreed to exert their best endeavours to bring the claim to a just and expeditious solution by peaceful means, such as negotiation, conciliation, arbitration, or judicial settlement as well as other peaceful means of the parties' own choice, in conformity with the Charter of the United Nations and the Bandung Declaration.

13. In particular, considering the close historical ties between the peoples of the Philippines and North Borneo as well as their geographical propinquity, the Ministers agreed that in the event of North Borneo joining the proposed Federation of Malaysia the Government of the latter and the Government of the Philippines should maintain and promote the harmony and the friendly relations subsisting in their region to ensure the security and stability of the area.

On 9 July 1964, representatives of Singapore,[16] Sarawak, Sabah (North Borneo), and the Federation of Malaya signed an agreement in London to unite. A United Nations inquiry was conducted into the willingness of population of North Borneo to join the union was conducted and approved its joining in

---

[15] Available at http://www.fordham.edu/halsall/mod/1963manila1.html.
[16] Singapore later became an independent state on 9 August 1965 and a Member of the United Nations on 21 September 1965.

what became Malaysia. Indonesia refused to recognize the existence of the new state and threatened that if it took a position on the Security Council, to which it had been elected, Indonesia would withdraw from the United Nations. Malaysia was elected and Indonesia followed through on its threat in January 1965. By telegram on 19 September 1966, it announced its decision "to resume full cooperation with the United Nations and to resume participation in its activities." On 28 September 1966, the General Assembly took note of this decision and the President invited representatives of Indonesia to take seats in the Assembly.

Decades later, in a case involving title to disputed islands off the coast of Borneo, the parties, Malaysia and Indonesia (as heirs, respectively, of the British and Dutch East Indies empires) were faced with a request to the ICJ by the Philippines to be allowed to intervene. The intervener did not claim any historic interest in the disputed islands, but argued that the disposition of the case might prejudice its historic title-based claim to North Borneo by deciding ancillary matters relating to that claim.

While Indonesia took no position on this matter, Malaysia strongly resisted the request. It asserted that the Philippine claim over other parts of Sabah had been comprehensively rejected by the people of the region and also because Sabah was recognized by all States as a part of Malaysia.[17] Excerpted below is a separate opinion supporting the Court's rejection of the Philippine application to intervene in the case based on its claim of historic title to part of the territory adjacent to the disputed islands. The Court refused to allow the Philippines to intervene but did so on narrow technical grounds. The Indonesian Judge *ad hoc*, in a separate opinion, addressed the issue of historic title.

. . . .

SOVEREIGNTY OVER PULAU LIGITAN AND PULAU SIPADAN (INDONESIA/MALAYSIA) (APPLICATION BY THE PHILIPPINES FOR PERMISSION TO INTERVENE) INTERNATIONAL COURT OF JUSTICE, JUDGMENT OF 23 OCTOBER 2001, SEPARATE OPINION OF JUDGE AD HOC FRANCK

2. . . . The point of law is quite simple, but ultimately basic to the international rule of law. It is this: historic title, no matter how persuasively claimed

---

[17] Opening Statement by the Agent for Malaysia Tan Sri Abdul Kadir Mohamad Secretary General Ministry of Foreign Affairs (June 26, 2001), Case Concerning Sovereignty over Palau Ligitan and Palau Sipadan (Indonesia/Malaysia): Application by the Philippines for Permission to Intervene, available at http://domino.kln.gov .my/kln/statemen.nsf/de82d75f2a0f57f8c8256b3d0042ab77/3b6ddf83965ef93848256 a770033f78a?OpenDocument.

on the basis of old legal instruments and exercises of authority, cannot except in the most extraordinary circumstances prevail in law over the rights of non-self-governing people to claim independence and establish their sovereignty through the exercise of bona fide self-determination.

1. The Nature of the "Legal Interest" Claimed by the Philippines

3. In the present case, the Application for permission to intervene admits to having no interest in the precise subject-matter of the case . . . which comes before this Court as a territorial dispute over two islands, the ownership of which is contested by Indonesia and Malaysia The basis of the Philippine intervention, in sharp contrast, is its claim to historic sovereignty over much of North Borneo. The Philippines has sometimes characterized this as a territorial claim but, in fact, throughout the pleadings it is clear that what the Philippines seeks to protect by intervention is its claim that the sovereign title of the Sultan of Sulu has become the sovereign title of the Philippines. What the Philippines seeks to preserve is not simply its rights in a territorial dispute with Malaysia about a mutual boundary, but its sovereign title to most of what is now a federated Malaysian state . . .

4. . . . It is in essence a claim to a territory that had been administered as a British dependency, an interest in reversing that territory's decolonization almost 40 years ago.

2. Court's Role in Determining the Philippine Application for Intervention

5. The role of the Court is therefore to determine whether the Philippines claim of title to territories in North Borneo amounts, under international law, to a "legal interest" which justifies its intervention in the main action.

6. What interests does the Philippines advance? It wishes to ensure that this Court is aware of, and duly respects, its interest in sovereignty over most of North Borneo. In exercising its discretion, the Court must consider, and has considered, whether that interest is sufficient and has been demonstrated. But the Court may also consider whether the interest is one which, even if it had been found both weighty and amply demonstrated, is also an interest that is barred by international law.

7. In making that determination, the Court is not confined to the Parties' submissions. Under Article 62, paragraph 2, of the Statute of the Court, it is for the Court itself to decide whether the applicant-intervener possesses a "legal interest" in the main action to be decided by the Court (*Continental Shelf (Tunisia/Libyan Arab Jamahiriya), Application for Permission to Intervene, Judgment, I.C.J. Reports 1981*, p. 12, para. 17). [Judge Franck also cited the *Fisheries Jurisdiction* case: *I.C.J. Reports 1974*, p. 9, para 17].

3. The Impact of Self-determination on Historic Title

9. Under traditional international law, the right to territory was vested exclusively in rulers of States. Lands were the property of a sovereign to be defended or conveyed in accordance with the laws relevant to the recognition, exercise and transfer of sovereign domain. In order to judicially determine a claim to territorial title *erga omnes*, it was necessary to engage with the forms of international conveyancing, tracing historic title through to a critical date or dates to determine which State exercised territorial sovereignty at that point in time. Under modern international law, however, the enquiry must necessarily be broader, particularly in the context of decolonization. In particular, the infusion of the concept of the rights of a "people" into this traditional legal scheme, notably the right of peoples to self-determination, fundamentally alters the significance of historic title to the determination of sovereign title.

10. Previous judgments of this Court [*Legal Consequences for States of the Continued Presence of South Africa in Namibia (Advisory Opinion)*, I.C.J. Reports 1971, pp. 31–32; and *Western Sahara (Advisory Opinion)*, I.C.J. Reports 1975, pp. 31–33] contribute to and recognize the development of the right of non-self-governing peoples to self-determination which "requires a free and genuine expression of the will of the peoples concerned." In the [*East Timor* case], the Court recognized the principle of self-determination to be "one of the essential principles of contemporary international law" [*Case Concerning East Timor (Portugal v. Australia)*, I.C.J. Reports 1995, p. 102, para. 29].

11. The decisions of this Court confirm the prime importance of this principle of self-determination of peoples. The firm basis for the principle is also anchored in universal treaty law, State practice and *opinio juris*. . . . [The opinion cites Articles 1 (2), 55, 73 and 76(b) of the UN Charter; common article 1 of the International Covenant on Civil and Political Rights and the International Covenant on Economic Social and Cultural Rights; General Assembly resolution 637 (VII) of 1952; the unanimously adopted Declaration on the Granting of Independence to Colonial Countries and Peoples, General Assembly resolution 1514(XV) (1960); General Assembly resolution 1541(XV) (1960); the Declaration on the Inadmissibility of Intervention in the Domestic Affairs of States and the Protection of Their Independence and Sovereignty, General Assembly resolution 2131(XX) (1965); the Declaration on Principles of International Law concerning Friendly Relations and Co-operation among States in accordance with the Charter of the United Nations, adopted by consensus as the Annex to General Assembly resolution 2625(XXV) (1970).]

13. The independence of North Borneo was brought about as the result of the expressed wish of the majority of the people of the territory in a 1963 election. The Secretary-General of the United Nations was entrusted under the Manila Accord of 31 July 1963 with the task of ascertaining the wishes of the people of North Borneo, and reported that the majority of the peoples of North Borneo had given serious and thoughtful consideration to their future and: "[had] concluded that they wish to bring their dependent status to an end and to realize their independence through freely chosen association with

other peoples in their region with whom they feel ties of ethnic association, heritage, language, religion, culture, economic relationship, and ideals and objectives." (Quoted by the Representative of Malaysia to the General Assembly, 1219th meeting, 27 September 1963, *Official Records of the General Assembly*, 18th Session, UN Doc. A/PV.1219).

14. In 1963, Britain filed its last report to the United Nations on North Borneo as an Article 73(e) Non-Self-Governing Territory . . . Thereafter, the United Nations removed North Borneo from the list of colonial territories under its decolonization jurisdiction . . . thereby accepting that the process of decolonization had been completed by a valid exercise of self-determination.

15. Accordingly, in light of the clear exercise by the people of North Borneo of their right to self-determination, it cannot matter whether this Court, in any interpretation it might give to any historic instrument or efficacy, sustains or not the Philippines claim to historic title. Modern international law does not recognize the survival of a right of sovereignty based solely on historic title; not, in any event, after an exercise of self-determination conducted in accordance with the requisites of international law, the bona fides of which has received international recognition by the political organs of the United Nations. Against this, historic claims and feudal pre-colonial titles are mere relics of another international legal era, one that ended with the setting of the sun on the age of colonial imperium. . . .

4. Conclusion

18. To allow the Philippines to proceed to intervene in the merits phase of this case, when the legal interest it claims would have no chance of succeeding by operation of law, cannot discharge the Court's duties. Even if the probity of all the Applicant's evidence were to be wholly confirmed, its interest would still be solely political: perhaps susceptible of historic, perhaps of political, but in any event not of judicial, vindication.

When the Court reached the merits of the case, it ultimately decided that Malaysia's claim prevailed over Indonesia. The two territories, Pulau Ligitan and Pulau Sipadan, islands off the coast of Sabah, therefore are under the jurisdiction and sovereignty of Malaysia. It should be noted that the islands, being uninhabited, did not raise any issue of self-determination.

QUESTIONS

6. The majority of the Court, in dismissing the Philippine request to intervene (under Article 62 of the Statute of the ICJ), preferred to make no comment on the claim of historic title on which the applicant had based its claim that it might potentially "be affected by the decision in the case." Was the Court wise to have avoided the issue? Why?

7. Why did Judge *Ad Hoc* Franck seek to close the door on arguments of historic title? What would have been the consequence in this case? In other cases where self-determination is claimed?

12.4 The Falkland Islands/Islas Malvinas and Gibraltar

The Falkland Islands (in Spanish the Islas Malvinas) were at various points the subject of dispute between Britain, France, and Spain; after Argentina's independence from Spain it also asserted a claim to the islands.

In the First and Second World Wars, the Falklands provided a strategic location for the British to conduct operations against the Germans, and two significant naval battles—the Battle of Falkland Islands (December 1914) and the Battle of the River Plate (December 1939) were fought from the Royal Navy Station at Stanley, the capital of the Falklands.

After the Second World War, Argentina pursued its claim to the islands through the United Nations. Negotiations were proposed between the two countries in the 1960s but no settlement followed. A major sticking point was resistance to change on the part of the 2,000 inhabitants of mainly British descent who preferred that the islands remain British territory.

In the 1980s, tension escalated between the two sides with speculation about an invasion of the Falklands being planned by Argentina, which, at the time, was ruled by a military junta. The invasion appeared imminent by the end of March, and on 1 April 1982 the President of the Security Council issued the following appeal to the parties.

STATEMENT BY THE PRESIDENT OF THE SECURITY COUNCIL, 1 APRIL 1982[18]

The Secretary-General, who has already seen the representatives of the United Kingdom and Argentina earlier today, renews his appeal for maximum restraint on both sides. He will, of course, return to Headquarters at any time, if the situation demands it. . . .

The Security Council, mindful of its primary responsibility under the Charter of the United Nations for the maintenance of international peace and security, expresses its concern about the tension in the region of the Falkland Islands (Islas Malvinas). The Security Council accordingly calls on the Governments of Argentina and the United Kingdom to exercise the utmost restraint at this time and in particular to refrain from the use or threat of force in the region and to continue the search for a diplomatic solution.

---

[18] UN Doc. S/14944 (1982).

The invasion took place the next day. In an emergency meeting the British representative on the Security Council proposed a draft resolution[19] that was nearly identical to the resolution finally adopted. There was some debate as to whether Britain could, as an interested party, vote on the matter. The President of the Security Council decided that this resolution was to be issued under Chapter VII and not Chapter VI of the Charter, and therefore the representative of Britain did have a right to vote. (See UN Charter, art. 27(3).) Resolution 502 was adopted the day after the invasion, on 3 April 1982.

SECURITY COUNCIL RESOLUTION 502 (1982)

The Security Council, . . .
Deeply disturbed at reports of an invasion on 2 April 1982 by armed forces of Argentina,
Determining that there exists a breach of the peace in the region of the Falkland Islands (Islas Malvinas),
1. *Demands* an immediate cessation of hostilities;
2. *Demands* an immediate withdrawal of all Argentine forces from the Falkland Islands (Islas Malvinas);
3. *Calls on* the Governments of Argentina and the United Kingdom to seek a diplomatic solution to their differences and to respect fully the purposes and principles of the Charter of the United Nations.

On the same day, a British Task Force was dispatched to the Falklands, landing there on 21 May 1982. Military operations were commenced on air, land, and sea. On 26 May 1982, the Council attempted once more to contain the hostilities.

SECURITY COUNCIL RESOLUTION 505 (1982)

The Security Council, . . .
Noting with the deepest concern that the situation in the region of the Falkland Islands (Islas Malvinas) has seriously deteriorated, . . .
Concerned to achieve as a matter of the greatest urgency a cessation of hostilities and an end to the present conflict between the armed forces of Argentina and of the United Kingdom of Great Britain and Northern Ireland, . . .

---
[19] UN Doc. S/14947 (1982).

2. *Requests* the Secretary-General, on the basis of the present resolution, to undertake a renewed mission of good offices bearing in mind Security Council resolution 502 (1982) and the approach outlined in his statement of 21 May 1982;

3. *Urges* the parties to the conflict to co-operate fully with the Secretary-General in his mission with a view to ending the present hostilities in and around the Falkland Islands (Islas Malvinas);

4. *Requests* the Secretary-General to enter into contact immediately with the parties with a view to negotiating mutually acceptable terms for a cease-fire, including, if necessary, arrangements for the dispatch of United Nations observers to monitor compliance with the terms of the cease-fire;

5. *Requests* the Secretary-General to submit an interim report to the Security Council as soon as possible and, in any case, not later than seven days after the adoption of the present resolution.

A final attempt was made in the Security Council to check the hostilities, via a draft resolution introduced by Panama and Spain on 4 June 1982, which would have given broad powers to the Secretary-General.

DRAFT SECURITY COUNCIL RESOLUTION PROPOSED BY PANAMA AND SPAIN, 4 JUNE 1982[20]

The Security Council, . . .

1. *Requests* the parties to the dispute to cease fire immediately in the region of the Falkland Islands (Islas Malvinas) and to initiate, simultaneously with the cease fire, the implementation of resolutions 502 (1982) and 505 (1982) in their entirety;

2. *Authorizes* the Secretary-General to use such means as he may deem necessary to verify compliance with this resolution;

3. *Requests* the Secretary-General to submit an interim report to the Security Council within 72 hours and to keep the Council informed concerning the implementation of this resolution.

As the British forces had clearly begun to gain an upper hand by this time, the resolution was vetoed by the representatives of Britain and the United States. On 14 June 1982, the Argentine troops in Stanley surrendered to the British.

---

[20] UN Doc. S/15156/Rev. 2 (1982).

Following the war, the Falkland Islanders were granted full British citizenship. Fearing further threats from Argentina, Britain also increased its military presence on the islands, constructing RAF Mount Pleasant, a military base for the Royal Air Force, thirty miles southwest of Stanley and increasing the military garrison. Britain and Argentina resumed diplomatic relations in 1989.

The Falklands issue has not been fully resolved. In June 2003 the issue was brought before the UN Special Committee on Decolonization. The views of the parties are summarized in their comments upon a draft resolution adopted by the Special Committee on Decolonization in 2004:

DECOLONIZATION COMMITTEE SAYS ARGENTINA, UNITED KINGDOM SHOULD RENEW EFFORTS ON FALKLAND ISLANDS (MALVINAS) QUESTION: RESOLUTION SEEKS PEACEFUL SOLUTION TO SOVEREIGNTY DISPUTE, REITERATING COMMITMENT TO HELP PARTIES COMPLY WITH ASSEMBLY REQUEST, 18 JUNE 2004[21]

The Special Committee on Decolonization this morning adopted without a vote a draft resolution on the question of the Falkland Islands (Malvinas) (A/AC.109/2004/L.8), requesting the Governments of Argentina and the United Kingdom to resume as soon as possible a peaceful solution to the sovereignty dispute over the Falkland Islands (Malvinas). . . .

Speaking before the adoption of the draft resolution, Rafael Bielsa, Minister of Foreign Affairs of Argentina, recalled that British forces had expelled the Argentine inhabitants and authorities of the Malvinas Islands on January 3, 1883, thereby establishing their illegal occupation of the Islands. Noting that disruption of the national unity and territorial integrity of any country was incompatible with the purposes and principles of the United Nations Charter, he said the United Kingdom's nineteenth-century violation of the sovereignty and territorial integrity of the independent republic of Argentina meant that the principle of territorial integrity must prevail over that of self-determination. Since continental Argentines had been prevented from settling on the islands since their expulsion in 1883, granting the island's inhabitants the right to self-determination would allow the colonial power to justify its usurpation of territory.

Mr. Bielsa further stressed that the people of Argentina remained fully committed to the peaceful settlement of the dispute and urged the Committee to continue to support the prompt resumption of negotiations on sovereignty.

Petitioners representing the Falkland Islands Government called on the Committee to grant the people of the Falkland Islands the basic right to self-

---

[21] UN Press Release GA/COL/3105 (2004).

determination—the right to pursue their own political ambitions and choice of sovereign status. The draft resolution before the Committee did not take into account the wishes and ambitions of Falkland Islanders and did not respect their right to determine their own future, said Roger Edwards, Legislative Councillor of the Falkland Islands Government. He said Falkland Islanders did not wish to see a change from British sovereign status and he, therefore, urged all delegates not to adopt the resolution.

Mike Summers, Legislative Councillor of the Falkland Islands Government, added that his country was not a colony, that the people neither felt they lived in a colony, nor did the Government of the United Kingdom treat the Falklands as a colony. The Falkland Islands (Malvinas) were geographically, geologically, culturally, linguistically and historically different from Argentina. The international community, he said, must not tolerate those who pursued territorial disputes, while manifestly ignoring the wishes of the people inhabiting, developing and caring for the environment and communities in those territories.

Another petitioner, Alejandro Betts, a former resident of the Falkland Islands (Malvinas), said that although the United Kingdom had been in possession of the Falkland Islands (Malvinas) since their invasion of the islands in the nineteenth century, it was a legal fact that possession alone did not give legitimacy. He said the Committee must work to help the United Kingdom to put aside its opposition to negotiation on the status of the Islands, stressing that Argentina's claim to have her legitimate sovereign rights recognized fell perfectly within international law.

....

Like the Falklands, Gibraltar is another illustration of a territory whose historic link to one nation has been largely eclipsed by its coming under the control of another. As a Spanish possession, Gibraltar was ceded to Britain by Spain under the Treaty of Utrecht in 1713. The treaty allowed British control over the territory in perpetuity, with the caveat that if the British government ever sought to withdraw or transfer control, the territory would be offered back to Spain.[22] Britain thus ruled over Gibraltar for more than two centuries, and the population long favoured its British status. Nevertheless the UK government, in 1946, added Gibraltar to the list of non-self-governing territories in the list maintained by the newly formed UN Special Committee for Decolonization.[23]

---

[22] For the English translation of the text, see http://www.gibnet.com/texts/utrecht.htm.

[23] GA Res. 66(I) 1946. For a complete list see Independence of Colonial Peoples, Encyclopedia of the Nations available at http://www.nations encyclopedia.com/United-Nations/Independence-of-Colonial-Peoples-progress-of-decolonization.html.

In the 1950s, Franco's Spain renewed its old claim upon "the rock" based on the Treaty of Utrecht. Spain argued for the application of the principle of territorial integrity over the principle of self-determination and on this basis demanded that the UK cede the territory to Spain.[24] The UN General Assembly's Decolonization Committee appeared to favor Spain's argument, and the General Assembly passed resolution 2231(XXI) (1966), stating that it

> *Calls upon* the two parties to continue their negotiations, taking into account the interests of the people of the Territory, and asks the administering Power to expedite, without any hindrance and in consultation with the Government of Spain, the decolonization of Gibraltar.

Britain went ahead and conducted a referendum, in which, like in Falklands, the population overwhelmingly voted in favor of continuing under British rule.[25] The General Assembly, still according primacy to "territorial integrity," and regretting the interruption of the negotiations proposed in resolution 2231(XXI), stated its conclusion that:

> the holding of the referendum of 10th September 1967, by the administering Power to be a contravention of the provisions of General Assembly Resolution 2231 (XXI) and of those of the Resolution approved on 1st September 1967 by the Special Committee on the Situation with regard to the Implementation of the Declaration on the Granting of Independence to Colonial Countries and Peoples.[26]

Spain, taking this as support for its position, closed its border with Gibraltar, effectively keeping it under siege, for more than a decade.[27] Politically, Gibraltar stayed aligned with Britain. In 1969 a new constitution for Gibraltar was introduced,[28] under which Gibraltar attained a high degree of internal self-government, with an elected House of Assembly. This Constitution also effectively gave the people of Gibraltar the power to veto any decision regarding the transfer of sovereignty from Britain to any other state.[29] In 1973, it

---

[24] See J.J. Bossano, "The Role of International Law in the Twenty-First Century: The Decolonization of Gibraltar," *Fordham International Law Journal*, vol. 18 (1995), p. 1641. Bossano was the Chief Minister of Gibraltar at the time of writing this article.
[25] Thomas M. Franck and Paul Hoffman, "The Right of Self-Determination in Very Small Places," *New York University Journal of International Law and Politics*, vol. 8 (1976), p. 373.
[26] GA Res. 2353(XXII) (1968).
[27] U.K. Foreign Commonwealth Office, Gibraltar—A General Briefing Note 1–2 (Oct. 1994).
[28] Gibraltar Constitutional Order 1969 (Britain).
[29] The preamble of this Order states in part: "Her Majesty's Government will never enter into arrangements under which the people of Gibraltar would pass under the sovereignty of another state against their freely and democratically expressed wishes."

adhered to the European Economic Community, as a territory for whose external affairs a member state is responsible.[30]

The death of Franco ushered in a more conciliatory phase, and attempts were made by Britain and Spain to resolve their dispute. Border restrictions were lifted in November 1984, when Britain agreed to reopen the question of sovereignty over Gibraltar.[31]

After joining the European Union in 1986, Spain made a more direct bid for control over Gibraltar, emphasizing its claims under the Utrecht Treaty, and proposed that Spain and Britain should enjoy joint sovereignty over the territory. While the British government appeared willing to consider this proposal[32] the people of Gibraltar consistently opposed it, and in a second referendum conducted on 7 November 2002, the proposal was rejected by a vote of 17,900 to 187.[33] Following this, the *British Overseas Territories Act 2002* was passed which changed the status of Gibraltar to an Overseas Territory and reconfirmed the full British citizenship, which had been granted to the population in 1983.

In October 2004, a final bid was made to commence tripartite talks between Spain, Britain and Gibraltar, with Gibraltar representing itself. So far these talks have failed to bring about any change in the position of Gibraltar, which in 2006 adopted a revised constitution, recognizing its right of self-determination. The main features of the Constitution with respect to Gibraltar's status are summarized by British Foreign Secretary Jack Straw as follows:

> The UK will retain its full international responsibility for Gibraltar, including for Gibraltar's external relations and defence, and as the Member State responsible for Gibraltar in the European Union. Gibraltar will remain listed as a British Overseas Territory in the British Nationality Act of 1981, as amended by the British Overseas Territory Act 2002.
>
> The Preamble to the new Constitution will also make clear that the UK stands by its long-standing commitment that Gibraltar will remain part of Her Majesty's dominions unless and until an Act of Parliament otherwise provides, and furthermore that Her Majesty's Government will never enter into arrangements under which the people of Gibraltar would pass under the sovereignty of another state against their freely and democratically expressed wishes.
>
> The new Constitution confirms that the people of Gibraltar have the right of self-determination and that the realisation of this right must be promoted and respected in conformity with the provisions of the UN Charter and any other applicable international treaties. In the Despatch, I will note that, in the view of

[30] This sort of membership is provided for under article 227(4) of the Treaty Establishing the European Community as Amended by Subsequent Treaties Rome, 25 March, 1957, available at http://www.hri.org/docs/Rome57/Rome57.txt.
[31] The Brussels Agreement of 27 November 1984, available at http://www.gibraltarnewsonline.com/reference_documents/brussels_agreement.html.
[32] Spain and Britain agree Gibraltar talks, BBC News, 26 July 2001, at http://news.bbc.co.uk.1/hi/world/europe/1457652.stm.
[33] See http://www.gibnet.com/texts/ref2.htm.

Her Majesty's Government, Gibraltar's right of self-determination is not constrained by the Treaty of Utrecht except in so far as Article X gives Spain the right of refusal should Britain ever renounce Sovereignty. Thus independence would only be an option with Spanish consent.[34]

QUESTIONS

8. The Argentine case for title to the Falkland Islands rests on "territorial integrity" (they are close to Argentina and far from Britain) and "historic title" (they were part of Spanish South America and Argentina inherited the titles pertaining to its part of the Spanish Empire when it won its independence). In addition, Argentina rebuts the self-determination-based claim of Great Britain by alleging that the British inhabitants are "settlers" who were brought to the territory after the expulsion of the Spanish. In such disputes, what weight should be accorded each of these legal claims? Should the preferences of the current inhabitants always trump other considerations? Would your views have been affected had there been the discovery of a gigantic petroleum reserve under the sea eastward of the Falklands?
9. If the population of Gibraltar voted to become independent of Britain, what, if anything, could Britain do to effect or prevent it? What, if anything, could Spain do to effect or prevent it?

12.5 Territorial Integrity or Self-Determination?

The preceding examples all suggest the complications of translating the principle of self-determination into practice. While, as discussed earlier, cases of "blue-water colonialism" are fairly clear cut, in other instances, where the demand comes from groups for independence from territorially contiguous or ethnically similar nations, the enforcement of this principle is more fraught.

Is this a rational basis for deciding whether a territory's population is entitled to self-determination? After the end of colonial empire, existing states have taken a much less enthusiastic view of self-determination. This is evident in the international community's cool response to the bids for autonomy by Chechnya (from Russia) and Abhkhazia (from Georgia), its acceptance of India's annexation of Goa and the assimilation of West Irian by Indonesia.

Chechnya has been engaged in a struggle for independence from Russia since the late eighteenth century, when it was annexed by the Russian ruler Peter the Great. Russian domination continued through the Tsarist and

---

[34] Speech announcing the successful conclusion of the Gibraltar Constitutional negotiations, House of Commons, 27 March 2006, available at http://www.gibnet.com/texts/con061.htm.

Communist periods, and despite initial promises of autonomy in the latter period, Chechnya was not given the status of a full-fledged republic in the USSR. Instead, it was recognized only as an "Autonomous Republic" within the Russian Federation, a factor that would later allow Russia, after the break-up of the Soviet Union, to counter Chechnya's claims of self-determination with its own right to "territorial integrity." It has continued to maintain control over the territory through use of military force, claiming the right to put down illegal armed activity within its own borders. In pursuing this policy, Russia has been able to avoid serious criticism from the international community in its handling of the region, the more readily because the Chechen cause has been linked to extreme Islamic terrorist movements that threaten many states, including Islamic ones.[35] While the United Nations has on occasion condemned the excessive use of force in the region, by Russia,[36] Chechnya's claims for independence continue to be unrecognized.

Abkhazia is also, like Chechnya, part of the Caucasus region. It was absorbed by Russia around the same time as Chechnya, and was then included in the territory of the Georgian Republic of the Soviet Union, being accorded only the status of an autonomous republic within Georgia. Its identification with Georgia continued after Georgia's accession to independence, despite Abkhazia having declared its own independence in the 1990s. In February 1992, the post-Soviet Georgia reverted back to its old Constitution of the 1920s. This took away much of the limited autonomy the Abkhazians had been able to secure during the Soviet phase. Abkhazia and Georgia subsequently went to war, with Russia reportedly supporting the Abkhazians, in the belief that they wanted to integrate with Russia. However, after Abkhazia defeated Georgia, announced its sovereignty in a new Constitution adopted on 4 November 1994, and elected a President, the Commonwealth of Independent States (CIS) imposed sanctions on the territory and both Georgia and Russia formally blockaded it.[37] Peacekeeping forces were deployed and continue to the present.

In 2004 another Presidential election was held in Abkhazia, where the Russian-supported candidate was defeated and a pro-Georgian candidate elected. Rioting followed and Russia openly announced that it would directly intervene in Abkhazian developments in case of threats to its interests in this republic. In response Georgia called upon the international community to

---

[35] NATO Secretary General Lord Robertson, for example, has stated that "Russia has the right to deal with breaches of law and order in its own territory." See "Putin Unleashes his Fury Against Chechen Guerillas," *New York Times*, 12 November 2002.
[36] Russia: UN Human Rights Chief Senses "Climate Of Fear" In Chechnya, 24/02/2006, available at http://www.rferl.org/featuresarticle/2006/02/2a748f8f-513a-4b9a-ae82-99590974ac25.html.
[37] For an in depth discussion see Galina Starovoitova, "Sovereignty after Empire Self-Determination Movements in the Former Soviet Union," available at http://www.usip.org/pubs/peaceworks/pwks19/ pwks19.html; Republic of Abkhazia Review of Events for the Year 1996 available at http://www.abkhazia.org.

reiterate its support to Georgia's full sovereignty and territorial integrity and to warn Russia to abstain from any interference in Georgia's internal affairs. Finally toward the end of 2004, the two rival candidates came to an agreement to jointly contest another election, and following this set up joint administration in the territory.

The Organization for Security and Co-operation in Europe, the European Union, and the United Nations continue to recognize Abkhazia as a part of Georgia.[38] The Georgian government, too, insists on its "territorial integrity" and has offered Abkhazia a high degree of internal autonomy, short of independence. Abkhazia has countered with a peace proposal, the "Key to the Future" which recognizes Abkhazia's sovereignty.[39] The de facto separatist government and the separatist opposition parties resolutely oppose reunification with Georgia, although they are more ambivalent about integration with Russia, which continues to stake a claim.[40]

Goa had a different history. Since the Portuguese invasion in the sixteenth century, for a period of 450 years, right through the British occupation of India, Goa remained a Portuguese colony. After India attained independence, it began to consolidate its territory and asserted its rights over Goa on the basis of territorial contiguity. This continued through the repressive years of the Salazar (Portuguese) dictatorship. After years of fruitless negotiations with Portugal, in which Portugal refused to acknowledge the colonial nature of its control over Goa, India launched Operation Vijay (Victory) to oust the Portuguese from Goa and from Daman-Diu, another colony on the same coast. On 19 December 1961, after two days of fighting, the Portuguese Governor General surrendered and Goa passed into India's hands. This issue remained in debate in the Security Council at the time of the fighting, and India was charged with the violation of Article 2(4). India responded by asserting that its action merely challenged the colonial occupation of Goa; the Indian representative stated that "[The invasion of Goa] is a question of getting rid of the last vestiges of colonialism in India. That is a matter of faith with us. Whatever anyone else may think, Charter or no Charter, Council or no Council, that is our basic faith which we cannot afford to give up at any cost."[41] At the same time, India rejected the suggestion that the Goanese be asked to choose through plebiscite, stating that there was no question that the Goans were Indians, and were furthermore keen to overthrow the Portuguese for that reason.[42] In doing so it ignored the real cultural dissimilarities be-

---

[38] See for instance, Report of the Secretary-General on Abkhazia, Georgia, UN Doc. S/2005/657 (2005).

[39] Tbilisi Unveils Principles of Abkhazia Peace Plan, Civil Georgia, 9 June 2006, available at http://www.civil.ge/eng/detail.php?id=12789.

[40] See Abkhaz Leader Sergei Bagapsh Confirms Goal of Secession from Georgia, 22 August 2005 available at http://www.unpo.org/news_detail.php?arg=03&par=2889.

[41] Speech of SC Jha, UN SCOR, 987th mtg., at 9, para. 40, S/PV. 987 (1961).

[42] Speech of SC Jha, UN SCOR, 988th mtg., at 18, para. 83–84, S/PV. 988 (1961).

tween the Goanese people, who were mostly Roman Catholic and had adopted the Portuguese language and parts of Portuguese culture, and the rest of India. In rebuffing the claim to a right to self-determination, India asserted its right to territorial integrity and its own historic title to the territory. It also claimed to be implementing General Assembly resolutions on self-determination.

India ignored, as Portugal did, the fact that Goa had been placed by the General Assembly on the list of non-self-governing territories drawn up pursuant to resolution 1541. In accordance with that resolution, Goa's integration with India could only have been achieved in compliance with Principle IX of the resolution: "the result of the freely expressed wishes of the territory's people acting with full knowledge of the change in their status, their wishes having been expressed through informed and democratic processes impartially conducted and based on universal adult suffrage." However, because of India's standing within the non-aligned movement and within the United Nations more broadly, its stand was soon accepted. Goa was fully integrated into the Indian union.[43]

Debate in the Security Council over Goa revealed a significant split between developing countries (so many of which had been colonized) and those of the more industrialized North. India also was able to count on its strategic partner of that time, the Soviet Union, to veto on 18 December 1961 a Western resolution calling on India to withdraw. (Ceylon, Liberia, and the United Arab Republic also voted against the draft resolution.) However, the Council at the time also failed to adopt a resolution supported by the four members opposing the Western text to reject the Portuguese complaint. In these circumstances, several authors have contended that the Council's silence suggests implied disapproval of the Indian action and not authorization.[44]

West Irian was similar to Goa in terms of being a former European colony (Dutch) claimed by a newly liberated Asian country (Indonesia). In other ways it was different. First, the transfer of West Irian from the Netherlands to Indonesia was peaceful; for though Indonesia threatened war, the Netherlands were persuaded by the international community to accept a compromise solution, whereby the territory would pass for seven months to a UN Temporary Executive Administration. As a result, the territory was passed to

---

[43] For a discussion see Bonnie Lubega, Goa: An African Writer's Perspective, 6 March 1964, available at http://www.colaco.net/1/goa1964e.htm. For an analysis of Goa's history and political system see Aureliano Fernandes, "Political Transition in Post-Colonial Societies: Goa in Perspective," *Lusotopie* (2000), pp. 341–358, available at www.lusotopie.sciencespobordeaux.fr/fernandes.rtf.

[44] See Quincy Wright, "The Goa Incident," *American Journal of International Law*, vol. 56 (1962), pp. 617–629; Jules Lobel and Michel Ratner, "Bypassing the Security Council: Ambiguous Authorizations to Use Force, Cease-Fires and the Iraqi Inspection Regime," *American Journal of International Law*, vol. 93 (1999), p. 152 n21. For an Indian interpretation of these events, see J. S. Bains, *India's International Disputes: A Legal Study* (Bombay: Asia Publishing House, 1962).

Indonesia, but within the parameters of a very questionable act of self-de-termination. Only after the territory passed under Indonesia's direct control was there an effort to consult the population in 1969. The normal international standard of "one person, one vote" was rejected in favor of a scheme under which the eight regional councils already existing in the territory, would be enlarged and special Assemblies created, which would then each reach a collective decision on whether or not to remain with Indonesia. The addi-tional members would be appointed on the following basis: one group would be chosen by existing approved political, social, and cultural organizations, a second group would consist of "traditional" tribal chiefs selected by the ex-isting council members, and a third group was to be elected by the people themselves (but was never chosen). This method was justified by Indonesia, on the basis of national security and the backwardness of the Irians, and the skeletal UN team sent to monitor the referendum verified the result, despite the fact that it was obviously unrepresentative of the people. Indeed John Saltford, a British academic, posits that neither Indonesia nor the United Nations ever intended to enforce the right of self-determination of the Irian people—it was essentially a token to make the transfer of the territory seem more legitimate.[45]

In sum, most international actors were satisfied that the motions of holding a referendum were gone through; that, in substance, it was not an exercise of free choice did not trouble them unduly, predisposed as they were toward the strength of Indonesia's political and military power, if not the strengths of its legal claims.

QUESTIONS

10. What, if anything, do unorthodox concepts of sovereignty such as "condominium," have to say to complex problems confronting territories such as Northern Ireland, Kashmir, and Gibraltar?
11. Goa is about the same territorial size as Kuwait and has a comparable population. The United Nations went to war to prevent Kuwait from being reunited with Iraq by force, even though the ethnicity of the two populations are similar. How do you distinguish the two cases in terms of applicable legal principles?

Further Reading

Cassese, Antonio. *Self-Determination of Peoples: A Legal Reappraisal*. Cambridge: Cam-bridge University Press, 1995.

---

[45] See John Saltford, *The United Nations and the Indonesian Takeover of West Papua, 1962–1969: The Anatomy of Betrayal* (London: RoutledgeCurzon, 2002).

Franck, Thomas M. "The Stealing of the Sahara." *American Journal of International Law*, vol. 70 (1976), p. 694.

Franck, Thomas M., et al. "The Falklands/Malvinas Crisis." *Proceedings of the American Society of International Law*, vol. 76 (1982), p. 267.

Franck, Thomas M. "Dulce et Decorum Est: The Strategic Role of Legal Principles in the Falklands War." *American Journal of International Law*, vol. 77 (1983), p. 109.

Franck, Thomas M. "Fairness to 'Peoples' and Their Right to Self-Determination." In *Fairness in International Law and Institutions*, edited by Thomas M. Franck. Oxford: Clarendon Press, 1995, pp. 140–172.

Kirgis, Frederic L., Jr. "The Degrees of Self-Determination in the United Nations Era." *American Journal of International Law*, vol. 88 (1994), p. 304.

Knight, David B. "Territory and People or People and Territory? Thoughts on Postcolonial Self-Determination." *International Political Science Review*, vol. 6(2) (1985), p. 248.

Laver, Roberto. "The Falklands/Malvinas: A New Framework for Dealing with the Anglo-Argentine Sovereignty Dispute." *Fletcher Forum of World Affairs*, vol. 25 (2001), p. 147.

Meadows, Martin. "The Philippine Claim to North Borneo." *Political Science Quarterly*, vol. 77(3) (1962), p. 321.

Merrills, J.G. "Sovereignty over Pulau Ligitan and Pulau Sipadan (Indonesia v. Malaysia): The Philippines' Intervention." *International and Comparative Law Quarterly*, vol. 51 (2002), p. 718.

Reisman, W. Michael. "The Struggle for the Falklands." *Yale Law Journal*, vol. 93 (1983), p. 287.

Saltford, John. *The United Nations and the Indonesian Takeover of West Papua, 1962–1969: The Anatomy of Betrayal*. London: RoutledgeCurzon, 2002.

Tomuschat, Christian, ed. *Modern Law of Self-Determination*. Dordrecht: Martinus Nijhoff, 1993.

chapter thirteen
....

Human Rights

The tension between sovereignty and human rights in the international legal order established after the Second World War is clear from the opening words of the UN Charter. War is to be renounced as an instrument of national policy; human rights are to be affirmed. But in its substantive provisions, the Charter appears to privilege peace over dignity: the threat or use of force is prohibited in Article 2(4); protection of human rights is limited to the more or less hortatory provisions of Articles 55 and 56.

Over time, however, human rights have come to be recognized as a core function of the United Nations. By 2005, Secretary-General Kofi Annan could argue that human rights formed one of the three core purposes of the United Nations, along with security and development.[1]

The seeds of this important change were laid elsewhere in the Charter. In the absence of agreement to incorporate a bill of rights in the Charter itself, Article 68 provided that the Economic and Social Council (ECOSOC) "shall set up commissions in economic and social fields and for the promotion of human rights." The UN Commission on Human Rights was established under this provision in 1946.

The Commission—which was abolished in 2006 and replaced by a Human Rights Council—provides a useful lens through which to view the evolution of human rights as understood within the UN system. Early successes in this area were generally attributed to its openness of membership and lack of coercive powers: precisely the faults that later led to sustained criticism into the early twenty-first century.

The first major task of the Commission on Human Rights was submitting reports and proposals on an international bill of rights. Opinion was divided on whether this should take the form of a legally binding instrument that member states might ratify, or a more general declaration in the form of a

---

[1] *In Larger Freedom: Towards Development, Security, and Human Rights for All,* UN Doc. A/59/2005 (2005), available at http://www.un.org/largerfreedom.

recommendation by the General Assembly that would exert moral and political influence on member states. The latter path was chosen and the Commission proposed a draft declaration in 1948, adopted by the General Assembly as the Universal Declaration on Human Rights. Forty-eight states voted in favor; eight abstained (Saudi Arabia, South Africa, and six Soviet bloc states).

The Universal Declaration was intended to form the basis of a more detailed convention with binding force. In the years that followed, however, the ideological divisions of the Cold War were reflected even in debates over human rights. In 1952 the decision was made to divide its provisions between two treaties: one elaborating civil and political rights, the other providing for economic, social, and cultural rights. These are sometimes referred to as first generation and second generation rights respectively, or negative rights (limiting government power) and positive rights (requiring government action). A further fourteen years passed as the documents made their parallel ways through the Commission, the Third Committee of the General Assembly, and the Assembly itself.[2] In 1966 the Assembly approved the two treaties—the International Covenant on Civil and Political Rights (ICCPR) and the International Covenant on Economic, Social, and Cultural Rights (ICESCR). It took another decade to achieve sufficient ratifications for them to enter into force.[3]

These normative developments have been matched by an expanding network of bodies dedicated to the promotion and protection of human rights. Some operate under the UN Charter; others under the two covenants and other treaties. Within the Charter regime, the Commission on Human Rights established mechanisms to address either specific country situations or thematic issues. Known as "special procedures," these typically involve the appointment of a special rapporteur who reports back to the Commission. In 2006 there were thirteen country mandates and twenty-eight thematic mandates. There is also a Sub-Commission on the Promotion and Protection of Human Rights, established as the Commission's main subsidiary body and functioning as a kind of think tank on human rights issues. (Until 1999 its title was the Sub-Commission on Prevention of Discrimination and Protection of Minorities.)

Not created under the UN Charter but part of the broader UN system, a further seven human rights treaty bodies monitor implementation of the core international human rights treaties: the Human Rights Committee (established by the ICCPR); the Committee on Economic, Social and Cultural Rights (established by the ICESCR); the Committee on the Elimination of Racial Discrimination; the Committee on the Elimination of Discrimination Against

---

[2] An important milestone was the International Convention on the Elimination of All Forms of Racial Discrimination, adopted and opened for signature and ratification by GA Res. 2106(XX) (1965).

[3] As of October 2007, the ICCPR had 160 parties; the ICESCR had 156.

Women; the Committee Against Torture; the Committee on the Rights of the Child; and the Committee on Migrant Workers.

This chapter focuses on the UN bodies, emphasizing the tension between sovereignty and human rights pointed out earlier. A central question is whether it is possible for an organization of states to protect human rights when the main violators of human rights are states themselves. This is considered in section 1. A second set of issues concerns the restructuring of the human rights mechanisms that took place in 2006. Will this make the United Nations more effective in promoting and monitoring human rights? A final section considers the surprisingly contentious question of whether the United Nations is bound by its own human rights norms.

13.1 Sovereignty and Human Rights

The Charter provisions on human rights are far more general than those relating to peace and security. Contrast the following provisions with the adoption in 2005 of the Responsibility to Protect, discussed in chapters 1 and 17.

UN CHARTER

Preamble

WE THE PEOPLES OF THE UNITED NATIONS DETERMINED . . .

to reaffirm faith in fundamental human rights, in the dignity and worth of the human person, in the equal rights of men and women and of nations large and small . . .

Article 1

The Purposes of the United Nations are: . . .
3. To achieve international cooperation in solving international problems of an economic, social, cultural, or humanitarian character, and in promoting and encouraging respect for human rights and for fundamental freedoms for all without distinction as to race, sex, language, or religion; . . .

Article 13

1. The General Assembly shall initiate studies and make recommendations for the purpose of: . . .
(b) promoting international cooperation in the economic, social, cultural, educational, and health fields, and assisting in the realization of human rights

and fundamental freedoms for all without distinction as to race, sex, language, or religion. . . .

Article 55

With a view to the creation of conditions of stability and well-being which are necessary for peaceful and friendly relations among nations based on respect for the principle of equal rights and self-determination of peoples, the United Nations shall promote:

(a) higher standards of living, full employment, and conditions of economic and social progress and development;

(b) solutions of international economic, social, health, and related problems; and international cultural and educational cooperation; and

(c) universal respect for, and observance of, human rights and fundamental freedoms for all without distinction as to race, sex, language, or religion.

Article 56

All Members pledge themselves to take joint and separate action in co-operation with the Organization for the achievement of the purposes set forth in Article 55. . . .

Article 62

1. The Economic and Social Council may make or initiate studies and reports with respect to international economic, social, cultural, educational, health, and related matters and may make recommendations with respect to any such matters to the General Assembly, to the Members of the United Nations, and to the specialized agencies concerned.

2. It may make recommendations for the purpose of promoting respect for, and observance of, human rights and fundamental freedoms for all. . . .

Article 68

The Economic and Social Council shall set up commissions in economic and social fields and for the promotion of human rights, and such other commissions as may be required for the performance of its functions.

As indicated earlier, the first major achievement of the United Nations in this area was the Universal Declaration of Human Rights. This was not intended to be a binding instrument, yet is now frequently regarded as reflecting customary international law.

UNIVERSAL DECLARATION OF HUMAN RIGHTS, GENERAL ASSEMBLY RESOLUTION 217A(III) (1948)

Preamble

Whereas recognition of the inherent dignity and of the equal and inalienable rights of all members of the human family is the foundation of freedom, justice and peace in the world,

Whereas disregard and contempt for human rights have resulted in barbarous acts which have outraged the conscience of mankind, and the advent of a world in which human beings shall enjoy freedom of speech and belief and freedom from fear and want has been proclaimed as the highest aspiration of the common people,

Whereas it is essential, if man is not to be compelled to have recourse, as a last resort, to rebellion against tyranny and oppression, that human rights should be protected by the rule of law,

Whereas it is essential to promote the development of friendly relations between nations,

Whereas the peoples of the United Nations have in the Charter reaffirmed their faith in fundamental human rights, in the dignity and worth of the human person and in the equal rights of men and women and have determined to promote social progress and better standards of life in larger freedom,

Whereas Member States have pledged themselves to achieve, in cooperation with the United Nations, the promotion of universal respect for and observance of human rights and fundamental freedoms,

Whereas a common understanding of these rights and freedoms is of the greatest importance for the full realization of this pledge,

Now, therefore,

The General Assembly,

Proclaims this Universal Declaration of Human Rights as a common standard of achievement for all peoples and all nations, to the end that every individual and every organ of society, keeping this Declaration constantly in mind, shall strive by teaching and education to promote respect for these rights and freedoms and by progressive measures, national and international, to secure their universal and effective recognition and observance, both among the peoples of Member States themselves and among the peoples of territories under their jurisdiction.

Article 1

All human beings are born free and equal in dignity and rights. They are endowed with reason and conscience and should act towards one another in a spirit of brotherhood.

Article 2

Everyone is entitled to all the rights and freedoms set forth in this Declaration, without distinction of any kind, such as race, colour, sex, language, religion, political or other opinion, national or social origin, property, birth or other status.

Furthermore, no distinction shall be made on the basis of the political, jurisdictional or international status of the country or territory to which a person belongs, whether it be independent, trust, non-self-governing or under any other limitation of sovereignty.

Article 3

Everyone has the right to life, liberty and security of person.

Article 4

No one shall be held in slavery or servitude; slavery and the slave trade shall be prohibited in all their forms.

Article 5

No one shall be subjected to torture or to cruel, inhuman or degrading treatment or punishment.

Article 6

Everyone has the right to recognition everywhere as a person before the law.

Article 7

All are equal before the law and are entitled without any discrimination to equal protection of the law. All are entitled to equal protection against any discrimination in violation of this Declaration and against any incitement to such discrimination.

Article 8

Everyone has the right to an effective remedy by the competent national tribunals for acts violating the fundamental rights granted him by the constitution or by law.

Article 9

No one shall be subjected to arbitrary arrest, detention or exile.

Article 10

Everyone is entitled in full equality to a fair and public hearing by an independent and impartial tribunal, in the determination of his rights and obligations and of any criminal charge against him.

Article 11

1. Everyone charged with a penal offence has the right to be presumed innocent until proved guilty according to law in a public trial at which he has had all the guarantees necessary for his defence.
2. No one shall be held guilty of any penal offence on account of any act or omission which did not constitute a penal offence, under national or international law, at the time when it was committed. Nor shall a heavier penalty be imposed than the one that was applicable at the time the penal offence was committed.

Article 12

No one shall be subjected to arbitrary interference with his privacy, family, home or correspondence, nor to attacks upon his honour and reputation. Everyone has the right to the protection of the law against such interference or attacks.

Article 13

1. Everyone has the right to freedom of movement and residence within the borders of each State.
2. Everyone has the right to leave any country, including his own, and to return to his country.

Article 14

1. Everyone has the right to seek and to enjoy in other countries asylum from persecution.
2. This right may not be invoked in the case of prosecutions genuinely arising from non-political crimes or from acts contrary to the purposes and principles of the United Nations.

Article 15

1. Everyone has the right to a nationality.
2. No one shall be arbitrarily deprived of his nationality nor denied the right to change his nationality.

Article 16

1. Men and women of full age, without any limitation due to race, nationality or religion, have the right to marry and to found a family. They are entitled to equal rights as to marriage, during marriage and at its dissolution.

2. Marriage shall be entered into only with the free and full consent of the intending spouses.

3. The family is the natural and fundamental group unit of society and is entitled to protection by society and the State.

Article 17

1. Everyone has the right to own property alone as well as in association with others.

2. No one shall be arbitrarily deprived of his property.

Article 18

Everyone has the right to freedom of thought, conscience and religion; this right includes freedom to change his religion or belief, and freedom, either alone or in community with others and in public or private, to manifest his religion or belief in teaching, practice, worship and observance.

Article 19

Everyone has the right to freedom of opinion and expression; this right includes freedom to hold opinions without interference and to seek, receive and impart information and ideas through any media and regardless of frontiers.

Article 20

1. Everyone has the right to freedom of peaceful assembly and association.

2. No one may be compelled to belong to an association.

Article 21

1. Everyone has the right to take part in the government of his country, directly or through freely chosen representatives.

2. Everyone has the right to equal access to public service in his country.

3. The will of the people shall be the basis of the authority of government; this will shall be expressed in periodic and genuine elections which shall be by universal and equal suffrage and shall be held by secret vote or by equivalent free voting procedures.

Article 22

Everyone, as a member of society, has the right to social security and is entitled to realization, through national effort and international co-operation and in accordance with the organization and resources of each State, of the economic, social and cultural rights indispensable for his dignity and the free development of his personality.

Article 23

1. Everyone has the right to work, to free choice of employment, to just and favourable conditions of work and to protection against unemployment.

2. Everyone, without any discrimination, has the right to equal pay for equal work.

3. Everyone who works has the right to just and favourable remuneration ensuring for himself and his family an existence worthy of human dignity, and supplemented, if necessary, by other means of social protection.

4. Everyone has the right to form and to join trade unions for the protection of his interests.

Article 24

Everyone has the right to rest and leisure, including reasonable limitation of working hours and periodic holidays with pay.

Article 25

1. Everyone has the right to a standard of living adequate for the health and well-being of himself and of his family, including food, clothing, housing and medical care and necessary social services, and the right to security in the event of unemployment, sickness, disability, widowhood, old age or other lack of livelihood in circumstances beyond his control.

2. Motherhood and childhood are entitled to special care and assistance. All children, whether born in or out of wedlock, shall enjoy the same social protection.

Article 26

1. Everyone has the right to education. Education shall be free, at least in the elementary and fundamental stages. Elementary education shall be compulsory. Technical and professional education shall be made generally available and higher education shall be equally accessible to all on the basis of merit.

2. Education shall be directed to the full development of the human personality and to the strengthening of respect for human rights and funda-

mental freedoms. It shall promote understanding, tolerance and friendship among all nations, racial or religious groups, and shall further the activities of the United Nations for the maintenance of peace.

3. Parents have a prior right to choose the kind of education that shall be given to their children.

Article 27

1. Everyone has the right freely to participate in the cultural life of the community, to enjoy the arts and to share in scientific advancement and its benefits.

2. Everyone has the right to the protection of the moral and material interests resulting from any scientific, literary or artistic production of which he is the author.

Article 28

Everyone is entitled to a social and international order in which the rights and freedoms set forth in this Declaration can be fully realized.

Article 29

1. Everyone has duties to the community in which alone the free and full development of his personality is possible.

2. In the exercise of his rights and freedoms, everyone shall be subject only to such limitations as are determined by law solely for the purpose of securing due recognition and respect for the rights and freedoms of others and of meeting the just requirements of morality, public order and the general welfare in a democratic society.

3. These rights and freedoms may in no case be exercised contrary to the purposes and principles of the United Nations.

Article 30

Nothing in this Declaration may be interpreted as implying for any State, group or person any right to engage in any activity or to perform any act aimed at the destruction of any of the rights and freedoms set forth herein.

Human rights were initially considered within the United Nations in the context of voluntary regimes of a non-binding character. An important step toward a form of accountability was the creation of the "1235 Procedure," referring to ECOSOC resolution 1235, adopted in 1967, which provided for an annual public debate focusing on "gross violations of human rights and fundamental freedoms."

This development accompanied the adoption of the two international covenants (ICCPR and ICESCR), but reflected a desire to establish a non-treaty-based procedure to examine human rights violations as part of the struggle against racist and colonialist policies. Such a change was possible in part due to the expansion of membership of the United Nations in the course of decolonization. It was driven by Third World countries, with support from Eastern Europe, but was not limited in its application to the regimes identified in the text of the resolution.

ECOSOC RESOLUTION 1235 (XLII) OF 6 JUNE 1967

The Economic and Social Council, . . .

1. *Welcomes* the decision of the Commission on Human Rights to give annual consideration to the item entitled "Question of the violation of human rights and fundamental freedoms, including policies of racial discrimination and segregation and of apartheid, in all countries, with particular reference to colonial and other dependent countries and territories," . . .

2. *Authorizes* the Commission on Human Rights and the Sub-Commission on Prevention of Discrimination and Protection of Minorities, . . . to examine information relevant to gross violations of human rights and fundamental freedoms, as exemplified by the policy of apartheid as practised in the Republic of South Africa and in the Territory of South West Africa . . . , and to racial discrimination as practiced notably in Southern Rhodesia . . . ;

3. *Decides* that the Commission on Human Rights may, in appropriate cases, and after careful consideration of the information thus made available to it, in conformity with the provisions of paragraph 1 above, make a thorough study of situations which reveal a consistent pattern of violations of human rights, as exemplified by the policy of apartheid as practised in the Republic of South Africa and in the Territory of South West Africa . . . , and racial discrimination as practised notably in Southern Rhodesia, and report, with recommendations thereon, to the Economic and Social Council; . . .

Three years later, ECOSOC established a second procedure authorizing the examination of communications concerning "situations which appear to reveal a consistent pattern of gross and reliably attested violations of human rights requiring consideration by the Commission." The "1503 Procedure" developed more quickly than the 1235 Procedure and is frequently used as a precursor to the latter. A key difference is that discussion of 1503 communications (or complaints) are conducted in closed session. By 2000 approximately 50,000 complaints were being received each year.[4]

ECOSOC RESOLUTION 1503 (XLVIII) OF 27 MAY 1970

The Economic and Social Council, . . .

1. *Authorizes* the Sub-Commission on Prevention of Discrimination and Protection of Minorities to appoint a Working Group consisting of not more than five of its members, with due regard to geographical distribution, to meet once a year in private meetings for a period not exceeding ten days immediately before the sessions of the Sub-Commission to consider all communications, including replies of Governments thereon, received by the Secretary-General under Council resolution 728F (XXVIII) of 30 July 1959 with a view to bringing to the attention of the Sub-Commission those communications, together with replies of Governments, if any, which appear to reveal a consistent pattern of gross and reliably attested violations of human rights and fundamental freedoms within the terms of reference of the Sub-Commission; . . .

4. *Further requests* the Secretary-General:

(a) To furnish to the members of the Sub-Commission every month a list of communications prepared by him in accordance with Council resolution 728F (XXVIII) and a brief description of them, together with the text of any replies received from Governments;

(b) To make available to the members of the working group at their meetings the originals of such communications listed as they may request . . .;

5. *Requests* the Sub-Commission on Prevention of Discrimination and Protection of Minorities to consider in private meetings, in accordance with paragraph 1 above, the communications brought before it in accordance with the decision of a majority of the members of the working group and any replies of Governments relating thereto and other relevant information, with a view to determining whether to refer to the Commission on Human Rights particular situations which appear to reveal a consistent pattern of gross and reliably attested violations of human rights requiring consideration by the Commission;

6. *Requests* the Commission on Human Rights after it has examined any situation referred to it by the Sub-Commission to determine:

---

[4] Henry J. Steiner and Philip Alston, *International Human Rights in Context: Law, Politics, Morals*, 2nd edn. (Oxford: Oxford University Press, 2000), p. 615.

(a) Whether it requires a thorough study by the Commission and a report and recommendations thereon to the Council in accordance with paragraph 3 of Council resolution 1235 (XLII); . . .

8. *Decides* that all actions envisaged in the implementation of the present resolution by the Sub-Commission on Prevention of Discrimination and Protection of Minorities or the Commission on Human Rights shall remain confidential until such a time as the Commission may decide to make recommendations to the Economic and Social Council; . . .

10. *Decides* that the procedure set out in the present resolution for dealing with communications relating to violations of human rights and fundamental freedoms should be reviewed if any new organ entitled to deal with such communications should be established within the United Nations or by international agreement.

In addition to the UN procedures outlined here, the ICCPR included an Optional Protocol that enabled states to allow individual complaints to be put forward by individuals directly to the Human Rights Committee. Decisions of the Committee have been influential in persuading some states parties (such as Canada) to adjust their administrative practices and sometimes their laws. By 1980 only twenty-two states had acceded to the Optional Protocol. By 1990 this number increased to forty-eight; by 2000 it was ninety-six. In 2007 there were a total of one hundred and nine states parties.

A related debate on the Right to Development is addressed in chapter 11.

QUESTIONS

1. What obligations are assumed by the members of the United Nations under the Charter provisions on human rights?
2. If the Universal Declaration on Human Rights was a process chosen explicitly to avoid binding commitments, how is it that it is now seen as reflecting customary international law?
3. If the division of the rights in the Universal Declaration on Human Rights into civil and political on the one hand, and economic, social, and cultural rights on the other was a function of Cold War ideology, why do we speak of first and second generation rights? Are the latter enforceable?
4. If one accepts that the main violators of human rights are states, is it possible to protect human rights through an organization of states such as the United Nations? Do the 1235 and 1503 procedures support or undermine your answer?

13.2 The Human Rights Council

By 2005 the Commission on Human Rights was being routinely criticized as lacking impartiality, credibility, and professionalism.[5] Identifying membership as the most difficult and sensitive issue, the High-Level Panel appointed by the Secretary-General in 2003 to propose major reforms in the UN system recommended avoiding the problem through universal membership.[6]

REPORT OF THE HIGH-LEVEL PANEL ON THREATS, CHALLENGES, AND CHANGE: A MORE SECURE WORLD: OUR SHARED RESPONSIBILITY, 1 DECEMBER 2004[7]

282. One of the central missions of the United Nations is to protect human rights, a mission reaffirmed by the Millennium Declaration. The Commission on Human Rights is entrusted with promoting respect for human rights globally, fostering international cooperation in human rights, responding to violations in specific countries and assisting countries in building their human rights capacity.

283. In recent years, the Commission's capacity to perform these tasks has been undermined by eroding credibility and professionalism. Standard-setting to reinforce human rights cannot be performed by States that lack a demonstrated commitment to their promotion and protection. We are concerned that in recent years States have sought membership of the Commission not to strengthen human rights but to protect themselves against criticism or to criticize others. The Commission cannot be credible if it is seen to be maintaining double standards in addressing human rights concerns.

284. Reform of this body is therefore necessary to make the human rights system perform effectively and ensure that it better fulfils its mandate and functions. We support the recent efforts of the Secretary-General and the United Nations High Commissioner for Human Rights to ensure that human rights are integrated throughout the work of the United Nations, and to support the development of strong domestic human rights institutions, especially in countries emerging from conflict and in the fight against terrorism. Member States should provide full support to the Secretary-General and the High Commissioner in these efforts.

[5] A More Secure World: Our Shared Responsibility (Report of the High-Level Panel on Threats, Challenges, and Change), UN Doc. A/59/565 (1 December 2004), available at http://www.un.org/secureworld, para. 283.
[6] The Report of the High-Level Panel is also discussed in chapters 1, 4, 9, and 17.
[7] UN Doc. A/59/565 (2004).

285. In many ways, the most difficult and sensitive issue relating to the Commission on Human Rights is that of membership. In recent years, the issue of which States are elected to the Commission has become a source of heated international tension, with no positive impact on human rights and a negative impact on the work of the Commission. Proposals for membership criteria have little chance of changing these dynamics and indeed risk further politicizing the issue. Rather, we recommend that the membership of the Commission on Human Rights be expanded to universal membership. This would underscore that all members are committed by the Charter to the promotion of human rights, and might help to focus attention back on to substantive issues rather than who is debating and voting on them.

286. In the first half of its history, the Commission was composed of heads of delegation who were key players in the human rights arena and who had the professional qualifications and experience necessary for human rights work. Since then this practice has lapsed. We believe it should be restored, and we propose that all members of the Commission on Human Rights designate prominent and experienced human rights figures as the heads of their delegations.

287. In addition, we propose that the Commission on Human Rights be supported in its work by an advisory council or panel. This council or panel would consist of some 15 individuals, independent experts (say, three per region), appointed for their skills for a period of three years, renewable once. They would be appointed by the Commission on the joint proposal of the Secretary-General and the High Commissioner. In addition to advising on country-specific issues, the council or panel could give advice on the rationalization of some of the thematic mandates and could itself carry out some of the current mandates dealing with research, standard-setting and definitions.

288. We recommend that the High Commissioner be called upon to prepare an annual report on the situation of human rights worldwide. This could then serve as a basis for a comprehensive discussion with the Commission. The report should focus on the implementation of all human rights in all countries, based on information stemming from the work of treaty bodies, special mechanisms and any other sources deemed appropriate by the High Commissioner.

289. The Security Council should also more actively involve the High Commissioner in its deliberations, including on peace operations mandates. We also welcome the fact that the Security Council has, with increasing frequency, invited the High Commissioner to brief it on country-specific situations. We believe that this should become a general rule and that the Security Council and the Peacebuilding Commission should request the High Commissioner to report to them regularly about the implementation of all human rights–related provisions of Security Council resolutions, thus enabling focused, effective monitoring of these provisions.

290. More also needs to be done with respect to the funding situation of the Office of the High Commissioner. We see a clear contradiction between a regular budget allocation of 2 per cent for this Office and the obligation under

the Charter of the United Nations to make the promotion and protection of human rights one of the principal objectives of the Organization. There is also a need to redress the limited funding available for human rights capacity-building. Member States should seriously review the inadequate funding of this Office and its activities.

291. In the longer term, Member States should consider upgrading the Commission to become a "Human Rights Council" that is no longer subsidiary to the Economic and Social Council but a Charter body standing alongside it and the Security Council, and reflecting in the process the weight given to human rights, alongside security and economic issues, in the Preamble of the Charter.

Though it was generally accepted that the Panel's diagnosis of the problems with the Commission on Human Rights was correct, the Secretary-General's response took a different tack by proposing more limited membership for a Human Rights Council, whose members would be elected directly by the General Assembly by a two-thirds majority. The 2005 Summit Outcome Document endorsed the principle of establishing a Council, but left all details to the sixtieth session of the Assembly that was about to begin.

IN LARGER FREEDOM: TOWARDS DEVELOPMENT, SECURITY, AND HUMAN RIGHTS FOR ALL (REPORT OF THE SECRETARY-GENERAL), 21 MARCH 2005[8]

181. The Commission on Human Rights has given the international community a universal human rights framework, comprising the Universal Declaration on Human Rights, the two International Covenants and other core human rights treaties. During its annual session, the Commission draws public attention to human rights issues and debates, provides a forum for the development of United Nations human rights policy and establishes a unique system of independent and expert special procedures to observe and analyse human rights compliance by theme and by country. The Commission's close engagement with hundreds of civil society organizations provides an opportunity for working with civil society that does not exist elsewhere.

182. Yet the Commission's capacity to perform its tasks has been increasingly undermined by its declining credibility and professionalism. In particular, States have sought membership of the Commission not to strengthen

---

[8]UN Doc. A/59/2005 (2005).

human rights but to protect themselves against criticism or to criticize others. As a result, a credibility deficit has developed, which casts a shadow on the reputation of the United Nations system as a whole.

183. If the United Nations is to meet the expectations of men and women everywhere—and indeed, if the Organization is to take the cause of human rights as seriously as those of security and development—then Member States should agree to replace the Commission on Human Rights with a smaller standing Human Rights Council. Member States would need to decide if they want the Human Rights Council to be a principal organ of the United Nations or a subsidiary body of the General Assembly, but in either case its members would be elected directly by the General Assembly by a two-thirds majority of members present and voting. The creation of the Council would accord human rights a more authoritative position, corresponding to the primacy of human rights in the Charter of the United Nations. Member States should determine the composition of the Council and the term of office of its members. Those elected to the Council should undertake to abide by the highest human rights standards.

Membership was the key fault line in subsequent negotiations, with the United States and a number of other countries pushing for the two-thirds requirement recommended by the Secretary-General. The United States also pressed hard for automatic exclusion of states that were the subject of coercive measures imposed by the Security Council related to human rights abuses or terrorism. (Some concerns were expressed within the US State Department that more restrictive criteria could preclude the United States itself from membership.) Failure to include these provisions led the United States to vote against the draft resolution, which was adopted on 15 March 2006 by a recorded vote of one hundred and seventy in favor to four against (Israel, Marshall Islands, and Palau joining the United States) with Belarus, Iran, and Venezuela abstaining. The United States also expressed opposition to the inclusion of term limits, which prevent states from serving more than six years out of every seven, apparently on the basis that this might mean that the United States would, automatically be forced to rotate off the new body every six years for at least a year.

The new Council has forty-seven members that are elected directly and individually by secret ballot by a majority of members of the General Assembly. This ballot is constrained by a requirement to distribute seats among the regional groupings (thirteen from the African Group; thirteen from the Asian Group; six from the Eastern European Group; eight from the Latin American and Caribbean Group; and seven from WEOG). When electing members of the Council, states are asked to "take into account the contribution of candidates to the promotion and protection of human rights and their voluntary pledges and commitments." Once on the Council, members are to uphold the highest standards and cooperate with the new body; a member that commits gross and systematic violations of human rights may be suspended by a two-thirds majority of votes in the General Assembly. The bar to expulsion is extremely high, but the key provision is individual election of members by an absolute majority of the General Assembly, as opposed to a majority of members present and voting. This should prevent regional slates being presented and remove regional solidarity as a rationale for appointing countries with dubious human rights records to the Council—a common problem confronting its predecessor, the Commission on Human Rights.

As in the case of the Security Council, more time and energy was focused on the membership of the Human Rights Council rather than on what it might do once constituted. Key substantive innovations include sitting through the year (rather than for an annual six-week session) and undertaking a "universal periodic review, based on objective and reliable information, of the fulfilment by each State of its human rights obligations and commitments." Diffusing the political contests surrounding election of members and the annual fight over censoring resolutions has created the possibility for the Council to play a more constructive role than the Commission, but it is far from clear that agreement on what the Council should *not* be will ensure agreement on what it should do.

GENERAL ASSEMBLY RESOLUTION 60/251 (2006): THE HUMAN RIGHTS COUNCIL

The General Assembly,

Reaffirming the purposes and principles contained in the Charter of the United Nations, including developing friendly relations among nations based on respect for the principle of equal rights and self-determination of peoples, and achieving international cooperation in solving international problems of an economic, social, cultural or humanitarian character and in promoting and encouraging respect for human rights and fundamental freedoms for all,

Reaffirming also the Universal Declaration of Human Rights[9] and the Vienna Declaration and Programme of Action,[10] and recalling the International Covenant on Civil and Political Rights,[11] the International Covenant on Economic, Social and Cultural Rights[11] and other human rights instruments,

Reaffirming further that all human rights are universal, indivisible, interrelated, interdependent and mutually reinforcing, and that all human rights

---

[9] GA Res. 217A(III) (1948).
[10] UN Doc. A/CONF.157/24 (1993) (Part I), chap. III.
[11] See GA Res. 2200A(XXI) (1966), Annex.

must be treated in a fair and equal manner, on the same footing and with the same emphasis,

Reaffirming that, while the significance of national and regional particularities and various historical, cultural and religious backgrounds must be borne in mind, all States, regardless of their political, economic and cultural systems, have the duty to promote and protect all human rights and fundamental freedoms,

Emphasizing the responsibilities of all States, in conformity with the Charter, to respect human rights and fundamental freedoms for all, without distinction of any kind as to race, colour, sex, language or religion, political or other opinion, national or social origin, property, birth or other status,

Acknowledging that peace and security, development and human rights are the pillars of the United Nations system and the foundations for collective security and well-being, and recognizing that development, peace and security and human rights are interlinked and mutually reinforcing,

Affirming the need for all States to continue international efforts to enhance dialogue and broaden understanding among civilizations, cultures and religions, and emphasizing that States, regional organizations, non-governmental organizations, religious bodies and the media have an important role to play in promoting tolerance, respect for and freedom of religion and belief,

Recognizing the work undertaken by the Commission on Human Rights and the need to preserve and build on its achievements and to redress its shortcomings,

Recognizing also the importance of ensuring universality, objectivity and non-selectivity in the consideration of human rights issues, and the elimination of double standards and politicization,

Recognizing further that the promotion and protection of human rights should be based on the principles of cooperation and genuine dialogue and aimed at strengthening the capacity of Member States to comply with their human rights obligations for the benefit of all human beings,

Acknowledging that non-governmental organizations play an important role at the national, regional and international levels, in the promotion and protection of human rights,

Reaffirming the commitment to strengthen the United Nations human rights machinery, with the aim of ensuring effective enjoyment by all of all human rights, civil, political, economic, social and cultural rights, including the right to development, and to that end, the resolve to create a Human Rights Council,

1. *Decides* to establish the Human Rights Council, based in Geneva, in replacement of the Commission on Human Rights, as a subsidiary organ of the General Assembly; the Assembly shall review the status of the Council within five years;

2. *Decides* that the Council shall be responsible for promoting universal respect for the protection of all human rights and fundamental freedoms for all, without distinction of any kind and in a fair and equal manner;

3. *Decides also* that the Council should address situations of violations of human rights, including gross and systematic violations, and make recommendations thereon. It should also promote the effective coordination and the mainstreaming of human rights within the United Nations system;

4. *Decides further* that the work of the Council shall be guided by the principles of universality, impartiality, objectivity and non-selectivity, constructive international dialogue and cooperation, with a view to enhancing the promotion and protection of all human rights, civil, political, economic, social and cultural rights, including the right to development;

5. *Decides* that the Council shall, inter alia:

(*a*) Promote human rights education and learning as well as advisory services, technical assistance and capacity-building, to be provided in consultation with and with the consent of Member States concerned;

(*b*) Serve as a forum for dialogue on thematic issues on all human rights;

(*c*) Make recommendations to the General Assembly for the further development of international law in the field of human rights;

(*d*) Promote the full implementation of human rights obligations undertaken by States and follow-up to the goals and commitments related to the promotion and protection of human rights emanating from United Nations conferences and summits;

(*e*) Undertake a universal periodic review, based on objective and reliable information, of the fulfilment by each State of its human rights obligations and commitments in a manner which ensures universality of coverage and equal treatment with respect to all States; the review shall be a cooperative mechanism, based on an interactive dialogue, with the full involvement of the country concerned and with consideration given to its capacity-building needs; such a mechanism shall complement and not duplicate the work of treaty bodies; the Council shall develop the modalities and necessary time allocation for the universal periodic review mechanism within one year after the holding of its first session;

(*f*) Contribute, through dialogue and cooperation, towards the prevention of human rights violations and respond promptly to human rights emergencies;

(*g*) Assume the role and responsibilities of the Commission on Human Rights relating to the work of the Office of the United Nations High Commissioner for Human Rights, as decided by the General Assembly in its resolution 48/141 of 20 December 1993;

(*h*) Work in close cooperation in the field of human rights with Governments, regional organizations, national human rights institutions and civil society;

(*i*) Make recommendations with regard to the promotion and protection of human rights;

(*j*) Submit an annual report to the General Assembly;

6. *Decides also* that the Council shall assume, review and, where necessary, improve and rationalize all mandates, mechanisms, functions and responsibilities of the Commission on Human Rights in order to maintain a system of

special procedures, expert advice and a complaint procedure; the Council shall complete this review within one year after the holding of its first session;

7. *Decides further* that the Council shall consist of forty-seven Member States, which shall be elected directly and individually by secret ballot by the majority of the members of the General Assembly; the membership shall be based on equitable geographical distribution, and seats shall be distributed as follows among regional groups: Group of African States, thirteen; Group of Asian States, thirteen; Group of Eastern European States, six; Group of Latin American and Caribbean States, eight; and Group of Western European and other States, seven; the members of the Council shall serve for a period of three years and shall not be eligible for immediate re-election after two consecutive terms;

8. *Decides* that the membership in the Council shall be open to all States Members of the United Nations; when electing members of the Council, Member States shall take into account the contribution of candidates to the promotion and protection of human rights and their voluntary pledges and commitments made thereto; the General Assembly, by a two-thirds majority of the members present and voting, may suspend the rights of membership in the Council of a member of the Council that commits gross and systematic violations of human rights;

9. *Decides also* that members elected to the Council shall uphold the highest standards in the promotion and protection of human rights, shall fully cooperate with the Council and be reviewed under the universal periodic review mechanism during their term of membership;

10. *Decides further* that the Council shall meet regularly throughout the year and schedule no fewer than three sessions per year, including a main session, for a total duration of no less than ten weeks, and shall be able to hold special sessions, when needed, at the request of a member of the Council with the support of one third of the membership of the Council;

11. *Decides* that the Council shall apply the rules of procedure established for committees of the General Assembly, as applicable, unless subsequently otherwise decided by the Assembly or the Council, and also decides that the participation of and consultation with observers, including States that are not members of the Council, the specialized agencies, other intergovernmental organizations and national human rights institutions, as well as non-governmental organizations, shall be based on arrangements, including Economic and Social Council resolution 1996/31 of 25 July 1996 and practices observed by the Commission on Human Rights, while ensuring the most effective contribution of these entities;

12. *Decides also* that the methods of work of the Council shall be transparent, fair and impartial and shall enable genuine dialogue, be results-oriented, allow for subsequent follow-up discussions to recommendations and their implementation and also allow for substantive interaction with special procedures and mechanisms;

13. *Recommends* that the Economic and Social Council request the Commission on Human Rights to conclude its work at its sixty-second session, and that it abolish the Commission on 16 June 2006;

14. *Decides* to elect the new members of the Council; the terms of membership shall be staggered, and such decision shall be taken for the first election by the drawing of lots, taking into consideration equitable geographical distribution;

15. *Decides also* that elections of the first members of the Council shall take place on 9 May 2006, and that the first meeting of the Council shall be convened on 19 June 2006;

16. *Decides further* that the Council shall review its work and functioning five years after its establishment and report to the General Assembly.

Given the focus on the mechanism to select members of the new Council, the first elections were watched closely. Despite efforts to prevent regions fielding slates of candidates, the Africa group proposed thirteen candidates for thirteen seats. Other regions had competitive elections, with the inclusion of Azerbaijan, China, Cuba, Pakistan, and Saudi Arabia being criticized by some human rights organizations and certain states. The failure of Iran and Venezuela to secure a position was seen by some as a success of the new Council. The United States, having voted against the creation of the Council, ultimately decided not to seek a seat in 2006 or 2007, citing a lack of confidence that the institution would be different in more than name from the Commission it was intended to replace.

QUESTIONS

5. Is the Human Rights Council structure and mandate an improvement over the Commission on Human Rights? What problems identified with the Commission remain in the new structure?
6. Were US criticisms of the Human Rights Council fair? With these criticisms in mind, what arguments might be put forward for not seeking a position on the new Council?

13.3 Is the UN Bound by Its Own Human Rights Norms?

The United Nations is not a party to the human rights treaties negotiated under its auspices or monitored through its agencies. In part this reflects the traditional view that only states properly enter into such treaties, a view based on the understanding that it is primarily states that violate or protect human rights. As the United Nations has assumed state-like functions, however—including administrations that ran entire territories, discussed in chapter 9—the question of whether the United Nations is required to abide by basic human rights standards has become more pressing.

In the early 1990s, the end of the Cold War led to increased hopes that the United Nations would become a major vehicle for promoting human rights. In documents such as the Vienna Declaration and Programme of Action, excerpted below, is there any indication of a wariness that the United Nations itself might have trouble living up to the standards it is espousing?

VIENNA DECLARATION AND PROGRAMME OF ACTION, AS ADOPTED BY THE WORLD CONFERENCE ON HUMAN RIGHTS, 25 JUNE 1993[12]

Recognizing and affirming that all human rights derive from the dignity and worth inherent in the human person, and that the human person is the central subject of human rights and fundamental freedoms, and consequently should be the principal beneficiary and should participate actively in the realization of these rights and freedoms,

Reaffirming their commitment to the purposes and principles contained in the Charter of the United Nations and the Universal Declaration of Human Rights,

Reaffirming the commitment contained in Article 56 of the Charter of the United Nations to take joint and separate action, placing proper emphasis on developing effective international cooperation for the realization of the purposes set out in Article 55, including universal respect for, and observance of, human rights and fundamental freedoms for all,

Emphasizing the responsibilities of all States, in conformity with the Charter of the United Nations, to develop and encourage respect for human rights and fundamental freedoms for all, without distinction as to race, sex, language or religion,

Recalling the Preamble to the Charter of the United Nations, in particular the determination to reaffirm faith in fundamental human rights, in the dignity and worth of the human person, and in the equal rights of men and women and of nations large and small, . . .

Emphasizing that the Universal Declaration of Human Rights, which constitutes a common standard of achievement for all peoples and all nations, is the source of inspiration and has been the basis for the United Nations in making advances in standard setting as contained in the existing international human rights instruments, in particular the International Covenant on

---

[12] UN Doc. A/Conf.157/23 (1993).

Civil and Political Rights and the International Covenant on Economic, Social and Cultural Rights. . . .

Recognizing that the activities of the United Nations in the field of human rights should be rationalized and enhanced in order to strengthen the United Nations machinery in this field and to further the objectives of universal respect for observance of international human rights standards, . . .

Invoking the spirit of our age and the realities of our time which call upon the peoples of the world and all States Members of the United Nations to rededicate themselves to the global task of promoting and protecting all human rights and fundamental freedoms so as to secure full and universal enjoyment of these rights, . . .

Solemnly adopts the Vienna Declaration and Programme of Action.

I

1. The World Conference on Human Rights reaffirms the solemn commitment of all States to fulfil their obligations to promote universal respect for, and observance and protection of, all human rights and fundamental freedoms for all in accordance with the Charter of the United Nations, other instruments relating to human rights, and international law. The universal nature of these rights and freedoms is beyond question.

In this framework, enhancement of international cooperation in the field of human rights is essential for the full achievement of the purposes of the United Nations.

Human rights and fundamental freedoms are the birthright of all human beings; their protection and promotion is the first responsibility of Governments. . . .

35. The full and effective implementation of United Nations activities to promote and protect human rights must reflect the high importance accorded to human rights by the Charter of the United Nations and the demands of the United Nations human rights activities, as mandated by Member States. To this end, United Nations human rights activities should be provided with increased resources.

Arguments that the United Nations should be bound sometimes proceed on the basis that such a conclusion is self-evident from the purposes and principles of the UN Charter.

A second approach asserts that the United Nations has sufficient legal personality to be bound by customary international law. Legal personality has been discussed with respect to the *Reparations* case in chapter 3. The Statute of the International Court of Justice is commonly regarded to be an authoritative statement of the sources of international law. (The United Nations cannot be brought before the International Court of Justice; only states may be parties to contentious proceedings.)

STATUTE OF THE INTERNATIONAL COURT OF JUSTICE

Article 38

1. The Court, whose function is to decide in accordance with international law such disputes as are submitted to it, shall apply:

(a) international conventions, whether general or particular, establishing rules expressly recognized by the contesting states;

(b) international custom, as evidence of a general practice accepted as law;

(c) the general principles of law recognized by civilized nations;

(d) . . . judicial decisions and the teachings of the most highly qualified publicists of the various nations, as subsidiary means for the determination of rules of law.

A third approach focuses on the activities of the United Nations and the state-like functions that it is now exercising. Since it is widely held that all states are subject to at least basic human rights law it is questionable whether those states can avoid such obligations by acting through the United Nations. A key problem in this regard is Article 103 of the UN Charter, discussed in the Introduction. This came before the European Court of First Instance when Security Council resolutions freezing the assets of alleged terrorists were claimed to violate European human rights norms.

Security Council resolution 1267 (1999) established a committee (the "1267 Committee") to oversee implementation of a sanctions regime that initially targeted Afghanistan's Taliban government but was later expanded to apply to Osama bin Laden and "individuals and entities associated with him as designated by the Committee, including those in the Al-Qaida organization."[13] In January 2002, following the September 11, 2001, attacks on the United States and the successful military operation in Afghanistan, the regime was further expanded with the removal of a geographic connection to Afghanistan and any time-limit on its application.[14]

The targeted sanctions in question entailed the worldwide freezing of an individual's assets. The process for identifying those individuals whose assets should be frozen, however, was somewhat opaque. Only in January 2004, with the passage of resolution 1526, were member states proposing individuals to be listed called upon to provide information demonstrating an association with al Qaida. The same resolution *encourage[d]* member states to inform such individuals that their assets were being frozen. In July 2005—almost six years after the listing regime was first established—resolution 1617

---

[13] SC Res. 1333 (2000), para. 8(c).
[14] SC Res. 1390 (2002), para. 3.

required that when states proposed additional names for the consolidated list they should henceforth provide to the Committee a "statement of case describing the basis of the proposal." This did not affect the more than four hundred individuals and entities that had been listed without such a formal statement of case. The resolution also *"request[ed]* relevant States to inform, to the extent possible, and in writing where possible, individuals and entities included in the Consolidated List of the measures imposed on them, the Committee's guidelines, and, in particular, the listing and delisting procedures." Meanwhile, the sanctions regime had been challenged in European courts on the basis that assets were being frozen without adequate legal protections.

AHMED ALI YUSUF AND AL BARAKAAT INTERNATIONAL FOUNDATION V. COUNCIL OF THE EUROPEAN UNION AND COMMISSION OF THE EUROPEAN COMMUNITIES (CASE T-306/01) (COURT OF FIRST INSTANCE OF THE EUROPEAN COMMUNITIES, 21 SEPTEMBER 2005)

226. The Court can properly rule on the plea alleging breach of the applicants' fundamental rights only in so far as it falls within the scope of its judicial review and as it is capable, if proved, of leading to annulment of the contested regulation.

227. In this instance, the [Council of the European Union, the Commission of the European Communities] and the United Kingdom maintain, in essence, that neither of those two conditions is satisfied, because the obligations imposed on the Community and its Member States by the Charter of the United Nations prevail over every other obligation of international, Community or domestic law. Consideration of those parties' arguments thus appears to be a precondition to any discussion of the applicants' arguments. . . .

231. From the standpoint of international law, the obligations of the Member States of the United Nations under the Charter of the United Nations clearly prevail over every other obligation of domestic law or of international treaty law including, for those of them that are members of the Council of Europe, their obligations under the [European Convention on Human Rights] and, for those that are also members of the Community, their obligations under the EC Treaty.

232. As regards, first, the relationship between the Charter of the United Nations and the domestic law of the Member States of the United Nations, that rule of primacy is derived from the principles of customary international law. Under Article 27 of the Vienna Convention on the Law of Treaties, which consolidates those principles (and Article 5 of which provides that it is to apply to "any treaty which is the constituent instrument of an international

organization and to any treaty adopted within an international organization"), a party may not invoke the provisions of its internal law as justification for its failure to perform a treaty.

233. As regards, second, the relationship between the Charter of the United Nations and international treaty law, that rule of primacy is expressly laid down in Article 103 of the Charter which provides that, "[i]n the event of a conflict between the obligations of the Members of the United Nations under the present Charter and their obligations under any other international agreement, their obligations under the present Charter shall prevail." In accordance with Article 30 of the Vienna Convention on the Law of Treaties, and contrary to the rules usually applicable to successive treaties, that rule holds good in respect of Treaties made earlier as well as later than the Charter of the United Nations. . . .

234. That primacy extends to decisions contained in a resolution of the Security Council, in accordance with Article 25 of the Charter of the United Nations, under which the Members of the United Nations agree to accept and carry out the decisions of the Security Council. . . .

239. Resolutions adopted by the Security Council under Chapter VII of the Charter of the United Nations are thus binding on all the Member States of the Community which must therefore, in that capacity, take all measures necessary to ensure that those resolutions are put into effect . . .

270. . . . [T]he resolutions of the Security Council at issue were adopted under Chapter VII of the Charter of the United Nations. In these circumstances, determining what constitutes a threat to international peace and security and the measures required to maintain or re-establish them is the responsibility of the Security Council alone and, as such, escapes the jurisdiction of national or Community authorities and courts, subject only to the inherent right of individual or collective self-defence mentioned in Article 51 of the Charter.

271. Where, acting pursuant to Chapter VII of the Charter of the United Nations, the Security Council, through its Sanctions Committee, decides that the funds of certain individuals or entities must be frozen, its decision is binding on the members of the United Nations, in accordance with Article 48 of the Charter.

272. . . . [T]he claim that the Court of First Instance has jurisdiction to review indirectly the lawfulness of such a decision according to the standard of protection of fundamental rights as recognised by the Community legal order, cannot be justified either on the basis of international law or on the basis of Community law . . .

276. It must therefore be considered that the resolutions of the Security Council at issue fall, in principle, outside the ambit of the Court's judicial review and that the Court has no authority to call in question, even indirectly, their lawfulness in the light of Community law. On the contrary, the Court is bound, so far as possible, to interpret and apply that law in a manner compatible with the obligations of the Member States under the Charter of the United Nations.

277. None the less, the Court is empowered to check, indirectly, the lawfulness of the resolutions of the Security Council in question with regard to *jus cogens*, understood as a body of higher rules of public international law binding on all subjects of international law, including the bodies of the United Nations, and from which no derogation is possible.

278. In this connection, it must be noted that the Vienna Convention on the Law of Treaties, which consolidates the customary international law and Article 5 of which provides that it is to apply "to any treaty which is the constituent instrument of an international organization and to any treaty adopted within an international organization," provides in Article 53 for a treaty to be void if it conflicts with a peremptory norm of general international law (*jus cogens*), defined as "a norm accepted and recognised by the international community of States as a whole as a norm from which no derogation is permitted and which can be modified only by a subsequent norm of general international law having the same character." Similarly, Article 64 of the Vienna Convention provides that: "If a new peremptory norm of general international law emerges, any existing treaty which is in conflict with that norm becomes void and terminates."

279. Furthermore, the Charter of the United Nations itself presupposes the existence of mandatory principles of international law, in particular, the protection of the fundamental rights of the human person. In the preamble to the Charter, the peoples of the United Nations declared themselves determined to "reaffirm faith in fundamental human rights, in the dignity and worth of the human person." In addition, it is apparent from Chapter I of the Charter, headed "Purposes and Principles," that one of the purposes of the United Nations is to encourage respect for human rights and for fundamental freedoms.

280. Those principles are binding on the Members of the United Nations as well as on its bodies. Thus, under Article 24(2) of the Charter of the United Nations, the Security Council, in discharging its duties under its primary responsibility for the maintenance of international peace and security, is to act "in accordance with the Purposes and Principles of the United Nations." The Security Council's powers of sanction in the exercise of that responsibility must therefore be wielded in compliance with international law, particularly with the purposes and principles of the United Nations.

281. International law thus permits the inference that there exists one limit to the principle that resolutions of the Security Council have binding effect: namely, that they must observe the fundamental peremptory provisions of *jus cogens*. If they fail to do so, however improbable that may be, they would bind neither the Member States of the United Nations nor, in consequence, the Community.

282. The indirect judicial review carried out by the Court in connection with an action for annulment of a Community act adopted, where no discretion whatsoever may be exercised, with a view to putting into effect a resolution of the Security Council may therefore, in some circumstances, extend to determining whether the superior rules of international law falling

within the ambit of *jus cogens* have been observed, in particular, the mandatory provisions concerning the universal protection of human rights, from which neither the Member States nor the bodies of the United Nations may derogate because they constitute "intransgressible principles of international customary law" . . .

284. The arguments put forward by the applicants in relation to the alleged breach of their fundamental rights may be grouped under three headings: breach of their right to make use of their property, breach of the right to a fair hearing and breach of their right to an effective judicial remedy.

Concerning the alleged breach of the applicants' right to make use of their property . . .

288. It falls therefore to be assessed whether the freezing of funds provided for by the contested regulation . . . and, indirectly, by the resolutions of the Security Council put into effect by those regulations, infringes the applicants' fundamental rights.

289. The Court considers that such is not the case, measured by the standard of universal protection of the fundamental rights of the human person covered by *jus cogens*, and that there is no need here to distinguish the situation of the entity Al Barakaat, as a legal person, from that of Mr. Yusuf, as a natural person.

290. On this point, it is to be emphasised straight away that the contested regulation, in the version amended by Regulation No 561/2003, adopted following Resolution 1452 (2002) of the Security Council, provides, among other derogations and exemptions, that on a request made by an interested person, and unless the Sanctions Committee expressly objects, the competent national authorities may declare the freezing of funds to be inapplicable to the funds necessary to cover basic expenses, including payments for foodstuffs, rent, medicines and medical treatment, taxes or public utility charges . . . In addition, funds necessary for any "extraordinary expense" whatsoever may henceforth be unfrozen, on the express authorisation of the Sanctions Committee.

291. The express provision of possible exemptions and derogations thus attaching to the freezing of the funds of the persons in the Sanctions Committee's list clearly shows that it is neither the purpose nor the effect of that measure to submit those persons to inhuman or degrading treatment.

292. Moreover, it must be noted that while Article 17(1) of the Universal Declaration of Human Rights, adopted by the General Assembly of the United Nations on 10 December 1948, provides that "[e]veryone has the right to own property alone as well as in association with others," Article 17(2) of that Universal Declaration specifies that "[n]o one shall be arbitrarily deprived of his property."

293. Thus, in so far as respect for the right to property must be regarded as forming part of the mandatory rules of general international law, it is only an arbitrary deprivation of that right that might, in any case, be regarded as contrary to *jus cogens*.

294. Here, however, it is clear that the applicants have not been arbitrarily deprived of that right.

299. . . . [F]reezing of funds is a precautionary measure which, unlike confiscation, does not affect the very substance of the right of the persons concerned to property in their financial assets but only the use thereof. . . .

303. It follows from the foregoing that the applicants' arguments alleging breach of their right to make use of their property must be rejected.

The alleged breach of the right to a fair hearing

. . .

319. The fact remains that any opportunity for the applicants effectively to make known their views on the correctness and relevance of the facts in consideration of which their funds have been frozen and on the evidence adduced against them appears to be definitively excluded. Those facts and that evidence, once classified as confidential or secret by the State which made the Sanctions Committee aware of them, are not, obviously, communicated to them, any more than they are to the Member States of the United Nations to which the Security Council's resolutions are addressed.

320. None the less, in circumstances such as those of this case, in which what is at issue is a temporary precautionary measure restricting the availability of the applicants' property, the Court of First Instance considers that observance of the fundamental rights of the persons concerned does not require the facts and evidence adduced against them to be communicated to them, once the Security Council or its Sanctions Committee is of the view that there are grounds concerning the international community's security that militate against it.

321. It follows that the applicants' arguments alleging breach of their right to be heard by the Sanctions Committee in connection with their inclusion in the list of persons whose funds must be frozen pursuant to the resolutions of the Security Council in question must be rejected.

Concerning the alleged breach of the right to an effective judicial remedy . . .

339. Nor does it fall to the Court to verify that there has been no error of assessment of the facts and evidence relied on by the Security Council in support of the measures it has taken or, subject to the limited extent defined in paragraph 337 above, to check indirectly the appropriateness and proportionality of those measures. It would be impossible to carry out such a check without trespassing on the Security Council's prerogatives under Chapter VII of the Charter of the United Nations in relation to determining, first, whether there exists a threat to international peace and security and, second, the appropriate measures for confronting or settling such a threat. Moreover, the question whether an individual or organization poses a threat to international peace and security, like the question of what measures must be adopted vis-à-vis the persons concerned in order to frustrate that threat, entails a political assessment and value judgments which in principle fall within the exclusive competence of the authority to which the international community has entrusted primary responsibility for the maintenance of international peace and security.

340. It must thus be concluded that, to the extent set out in paragraph 339 above, there is no judicial remedy available to the applicant, the Security

Council not having thought it advisable to establish an independent international court responsible for ruling, in law and on the facts, in actions brought against individual decisions taken by the Sanctions Committee.

341. However, it is also to be acknowledged that any such lacuna in the judicial protection available to the applicants is not in itself contrary to *jus cogens*. . . .

343. In this instance, the Court considers that the limitation of the applicants' right of access to a court, as a result of the immunity from jurisdiction enjoyed as a rule, in the domestic legal order of the Member States of the United Nations, by resolutions of the Security Council adopted under Chapter VII of the Charter of the United Nations, in accordance with the relevant principles of international law (in particular Articles 25 and 103 of the Charter), is inherent in that right as it is guaranteed by *jus cogens*.

344. Such a limitation is justified both by the nature of the decisions that the Security Council is led to take under Chapter VII of the Charter of the United Nations and by the legitimate objective pursued. In the circumstances of this case, the applicants' interest in having a court hear their case on its merits is not enough to outweigh the essential public interest in the maintenance of international peace and security in the face of a threat clearly identified by the Security Council in accordance with the Charter of the United Nations. In this regard, special significance must attach to the fact that, far from providing for measures for an unlimited period of application, the resolutions successively adopted by the Security Council have always provided a mechanism for re-examining whether it is appropriate to maintain those measures after 12 or 18 months at most have elapsed (see paragraphs 16, 26, 37 and 313 above).

345. Last, the Court considers that, in the absence of an international court having jurisdiction to ascertain whether acts of the Security Council are lawful, the setting-up of a body such as the Sanctions Committee and the opportunity, provided for by the legislation, of applying at any time to that committee in order to have any individual case re-examined, by means of a procedure involving both the "petitioned government" and the "designating government" (see paragraphs 310 and 311 above), constitute another reasonable method of affording adequate protection of the applicants' fundamental rights as recognised by *jus cogens*.

346. It follows that the applicants' arguments alleging breach of their right to an effective judicial remedy must be rejected.

- -

This and three similar cases were all appealed to the European Court of Justice.

For further discussion of the possibility that the United Nations might have violated its own human rights norms, see the discussion of detention in Kosovo on executive orders in chapter 16.

QUESTIONS ....

7. Does the United Nations need to be bound by human rights norms in order to comply with those norms? How might this be different from states that are "bound" by human rights obligations that may lack any enforcement mechanism?

8. What role for the United Nations is envisaged in the treaties included in this chapter? What role is envisaged in declarations such as that which emerged from the World Conference on Human Rights in 1993?

9. Do you agree with the reasoning in the *Yusuf* case? Would your position change if the assets frozen were held for thirty years? If they were not released upon the death of an alleged terrorist financier?

10. Instead of freezing assets, could the Security Council authorize the detention of an individual? Can the Council authorize torture

Further Reading

Alston, Philip, and Frédéric Mégret, eds. *The United Nations and Human Rights: A Critical Appraisal.* 2nd edn. Oxford: Oxford University Press, 2003.

Chesterman, Simon. "The Spy Who Came In from the Cold War: Intelligence and International Law." *Michigan Journal of International Law*, vol. 27 (2006), p. 1071.

Donnelly, Jack. *International Human Rights.* 3rd edn. Boulder, CO: Westview, 2007.

Forsythe, David. *Human Rights in International Relations.* 2nd edn. Cambridge: Cambridge University Press, 2006.

Hannum, Hurst, ed. *Guide to International Human Rights Practice.* 4th edn. Ardsley, NY: Transnational, 2004.

Mégrét, Fréderic, and Florian Hoffman. "The UN as a Human Rights Violator? Some Reflections on the United Nations Changing Human Rights Responsibilities." *Human Rights Quarterly*, vol. 25(2) (2002), p. 314.

Morsink, Johannes. *The Universal Declaration of Human Rights: Origins, Drafting, and Intent.* Philadelphia: University of Pennsylvania Press, 2000.

Steiner, Henry J., Philip Alston, and Ryan Goodman. *International Human Rights in Context: Law, Politics, Morals.* 3rd edn. Oxford: Oxford University Press, 2007.

chapter fourteen
··················

Humanitarian Assistance

Humanitarian assistance and development assistance (considered in chapter 12) are discrete forms of aid. Humanitarian assistance is, in theory, driven by need and intended to relieve suffering. Development assistance aims more generally at helping an economy to grow and, in theory, become self-sustaining. In reality, humanitarian and development assistance are both supply rather than demand driven, and donors may fail to distinguish between the two. Donor governments commit funds largely on the basis of their domestic priorities and capacity; international agencies must balance the need to treat human suffering fairly against the opportunity that telegenic crises offer to increase available resources. For this reason, the crises in the Balkans typically received far more assistance per capita assistance than comparable or worse crises in Africa.[1]

In addition to determining which crises receive funds, these considerations also determine how those funds are allocated and with what political conditions attached. Here the distinction between humanitarian and development assistance becomes more important, as the attachment of political conditions to humanitarian assistance arguably removes its "humanitarian" character.

The fact that donor countries wish to retain control over how their money is spent is not, in itself, controversial. In most cases, this money comes from taxes paid by citizens who hold their respective governments accountable for how tax revenue is spent. Although donor behavior may be rational from the donor government's perspective, however, the sum total of donor policies rarely presents a rational whole.[2]

---

[1] In 1999, for example, the annual per capita assistance received in the Democratic Republic of the Congo was $8; in Sierra Leone it was $16; in Angola it was $48; for the former Yugoslavia the figure was $207: Oxfam, *An End to Forgotten Emergencies?* (Oxford: Oxfam GB Briefing Paper 5/00, May 2000), available at http://www .oxfam.org.uk.

[2] This subsection draws upon work in progress at the Humanitarianism and War Project at Tufts University. See http://hwproject.tufts.edu.

One of the most important forms of coordination for donors is the pledging conference. In the absence of funds that can be disbursed quickly to a recovery process, significant external resources typically arrive only after such a conference, which brings donor states, UN agencies, and the International Financial Institutions together with local representatives to evaluate proposed reconstruction plans. Within the UN framework, the consolidated inter-agency appeal process (CAP) is nominally the vehicle for coordinating humanitarian assistance.[3] It is far from clear, however, whether a CAP is primarily intended to set priorities, coordinate efforts, or simply to raise funds. Different donors appear to view the process differently, but it cannot function effectively as all three. The variable funding also lends a certain artificiality to the process. In 2001, the CAP realized only 55 percent of its overall requests; provisional figures for 2002 showed 68 percent of total requests being met, varying by country or region from 20 percent to 95 percent.[4] This creates a vicious circle where agencies artificially inflate requests, leading in turn to donor scepticism about the merits of supporting a CAP in its entirety.[5]

Coordination problems also arise at the operational level. There is now a proliferation of inter-governmental and non-governmental organizations dedicated to various forms of humanitarian relief, as well as the many agencies of individual governments. Within the United Nations system, these comprise the Food and Agricultural Organization (FAO), the Office for the Coordination of Humanitarian Affairs (OCHA), the UN Children's Fund (UNICEF), the UN Development Programme (UNDP), the UN High Commissioner for Refugees (UNHCR), the UN Population Fund (UNFPA), the World Food Programme (WFP), and the World Health Organization (WHO). These are all members of the Inter-Agency Standing Committee (IASC), which was established in 1992 to improve preparation for, as well as rapid and coherent response to, natural disasters and other emergencies. In addition to the eight full members, standing invitees to the IASC include two other UN bodies—the Office of the High Commissioner for Human Rights (OHCHR) and the Office of the Special Representative of the Secretary-General on the Human Rights of Internally Displaced Persons (RSG on HR of IDPs)—the International Committee of the Red Cross (ICRC), the International Federation of Red Cross and Red Crescent Societies (IFRC), the International Organization for Migration (IOM), the International Council of Voluntary Agencies (ICVA), the American Council for Voluntary Interna-

---

[3] See GA Res. 46/182 (1991).
[4] UN Office for the Coordination of Humanitarian Assistance, Consolidated Inter-Agency Humanitarian Assistance Appeals: Summary of Requirements and Contributions by Affected Country/Region, available at http://www.reliefweb.int/fts.
[5] Stewart Patrick, "The Donor Community and the Challenge of Postconflict Recovery," in Shepard Forman and Stewart Patrick (eds.), *Good Intentions: Pledges of Aid for Postconflict Recovery* (Boulder, CO: Lynne Rienner, 2000), p. 43.

tional Action (InterAction), the Steering Committee for Humanitarian Response (SCHR), and the World Bank (World Bank).

This chapter first examines the principles of humanitarian assistance with particular reference to the question of political conditions that may be placed on aid. Section two then considers a specific vulnerable population—refugees—and the content of international obligations that are intended to protect them. Section three considers the perverse effects that large scale humanitarian assistance may have on a territory and efforts to minimize such unintended consequences of efforts intended to relieve suffering but which may delay recovery.

14.1 Principles

As the humanitarian operations of the United Nations have become more complex, various attempts have been made to rationalize the institutions and procedures that respond to natural and manmade disasters.

GENERAL ASSEMBLY RESOLUTION 46/182 (1991), ANNEX: STRENGTHENING OF THE COORDINATION OF HUMANITARIAN EMERGENCY ASSISTANCE OF THE UNITED NATIONS

I. Guiding Principles

1. Humanitarian assistance is of cardinal importance for the victims of natural disasters and other emergencies.

2. Humanitarian assistance must be provided in accordance with the principles of humanity, neutrality and impartiality.

3. The sovereignty, territorial integrity and national unity of States must be fully respected in accordance with the Charter of the United Nations. In this context, humanitarian assistance should be provided with the consent of the affected country and in principle on the basis of an appeal by the affected country.

4. Each State has the responsibility first and foremost to take care of the victims of natural disasters and other emergencies occurring on its territory. Hence, the affected State has the primary role in the initiation, organization, coordination, and implementation of humanitarian assistance within its territory.

5. The magnitude and duration of many emergencies may be beyond the response capacity of many affected countries. International cooperation to address emergency situations and to strengthen the response capacity of

affected countries is thus of great importance. Such cooperation should be provided in accordance with international law and national laws. Intergovernmental and nongovernmental organizations working impartially and with strictly humanitarian motives should continue to make a significant contribution in supplementing national efforts.

6. States whose populations are in need of humanitarian assistance are called upon to facilitate the work of these organizations in implementing humanitarian assistance, in particular the supply of food, medicines, shelter and health care, for which access to victims is essential.

7. States in proximity to emergencies are urged to participate closely with the affected countries in international efforts, with a view to facilitating, to the extent possible, the transit of humanitarian assistance.

8. Special attention should be given to disaster prevention and preparedness by the Governments concerned, as well as by the international community.

9. There is a clear relationship between emergency, rehabilitation and development. In order to ensure a smooth transition from relief to rehabilitation and development, emergency assistance should be provided in ways that will be supportive of recovery and long-term development. Thus, emergency measures should be seen as a step towards long-term development.

10. Economic growth and sustainable development are essential for prevention of and preparedness against natural disasters and other emergencies. Many emergencies reflect the underlying crisis in development facing developing countries. Humanitarian assistance should therefore be accompanied by a renewal of commitment to economic growth and sustainable development of developing countries. In this context, adequate resources must be made available to address their development problems.

11. Contributions for humanitarian assistance should be provided in a way which is not to the detriment of resources made available for international cooperation for development.

12. The United Nations has a central and unique role to play in providing leadership and coordinating the efforts of the international community to support the affected countries. . . . The United Nations system needs to be adapted and strengthened to meet present and future challenges in an effective and coherent manner. It should be provided with resources commensurate with future requirements. The inadequacy of such resources has been one of the major constraints in the effective response of the United Nations to emergencies.

II. Prevention

13. The international community should adequately assist developing countries in strengthening their capacity in disaster prevention and mitigation, both at the national and regional levels, for example, in establishing and enhancing integrated programmes in this regard. . . .

VII. Continuum from Relief to Rehabilitation and Development

40. Emergency assistance must be provided in ways that will be supportive of recovery and long-term development. Development assistance organizations of the United Nations system should be involved at an early stage and should collaborate closely with those responsible for emergency relief and recovery, within their existing mandates.

41. International cooperation and support for rehabilitation and reconstruction should continue with sustained intensity after the initial relief stage. The rehabilitation phase should be used as an opportunity to restructure and improve facilities and services destroyed by emergencies in order to enable them to withstand the impact of future emergencies.

42. International cooperation should be accelerated for the development of developing countries, thereby contributing to reducing the occurrence and impact of future disasters and emergencies.

Political conditions are frequently attached to nominally humanitarian assistance, as in the European Union's "Energy for Democracy" program (1999–2000), which allowed the delivery of heating oil to "democratic" Serbian municipalities—meaning those which had voted for opponents of President Slobodan Milosevic.

OFFICE FOR THE COORDINATION OF HUMANITARIAN AFFAIRS, BELGRADE: HUMANITARIAN RISK ANALYSIS NO. 12—HUMANITARIAN PRINCIPLES AND HUMANITARIAN ASSISTANCE, 9 AUGUST 2000[6]

1 Introduction

In a recent publication by OCHA on behalf of the Inter-Agency Standing Committee (IASC), the President of the International Committee of the Red Cross (ICRC) noted that humanitarian action has been used by states over the past decade as a tool for exerting political influence in difficult conflicts:

> When their efforts at prevention or reconciliation had proved unsuccessful, it sometimes seemed the only way to proceed with a clear conscience when all else had failed. Unwilling to endanger human lives (those of their soldiers) and anxious not to alienate public opinion by sustaining losses, States sometimes saw the activities of humanitarian workers—who were there, after all, of their own free will!—as the solution to their problems. At the same time, the States' generosity made it possible to save many lives.

---

[6] Available at www.reliefweb.int. Notes omitted.

One example of this is the controversial link that has been made between assistance to [the Federal Republic of Yugoslavia (FRY)] and political conditions in programmes such as the European Union's "Energy for Democracy" programme.

Major political differences exist between FRY and donor governments. It is the position of the humanitarian community in FRY (excluding Kosovo)—comprising UN Agencies and humanitarian non-governmental organisations (NGOs)—that these political differences must be kept separate from humanitarian assistance. There is a legal basis for this separation, supported by policy considerations that have been affirmed and reaffirmed by the humanitarian community.

A second area of controversy has been the role of local NGOs in FRY. Donor governments have expressed concern over the engagement of such local actors in the provision of aid, citing, among other things, the possible impact of political influence.

This Humanitarian Risk Analysis (HRA) examines the legal and political basis for a principled approach to such issues. . . .

2 Humanitarian Principles

International law does not prescribe clear principles according to which humanitarian assistance can or should be delivered. The majority of treaty law on the subject concerns the right of *access*, and conditions imposed on humanitarian assistance in order to fall within this right. It is possible, however, to draw from this body of treaty law certain normative conclusions about what constitutes humanitarian assistance, and how it should be delivered.

2.1 International Humanitarian Law

The right of access is affirmed explicitly in the Geneva Conventions of 1949 and the two Additional Protocols of 1977 in relation to international armed conflicts. In other cases it is more limited.

In situations of international armed conflict, the most detailed provisions apply to the civilian population of occupied territory. Only Additional Protocol I applies to a state party's own civilian population in need, providing for relief actions subject to the consent of the parties concerned.

In situations of non-international armed conflict, there is a general statement in Article 3 common to the Geneva Conventions that "An impartial humanitarian body, such as the International Committee of the Red Cross, *may offer its services* to the Parties to the conflict" (emphasis added). Additional Protocol II extends this by providing that relief actions of an "exclusively humanitarian and impartial nature and which are conducted without any adverse distinction shall be undertaken," but this is also subject to the consent of the states parties concerned.

For present purposes, these strict principles are not directly applicable because there is not a continuing international or non-international armed conflict; and FRY is not, in general, prohibiting access.

However, as will be discussed below, it is possible to draw more general principles from international humanitarian law and other documents concerning humanitarian assistance. The right of access is premised upon a balance between the needs of the civilian population and the concerns of the state in whose territory they are located. Continuing tensions within FRY and throughout the region emphasise the need for this balance to be struck delicately. In addition, many elements of the complex emergency in South-Eastern Europe are war-related.

As a starting point, then, the definition that must be satisfied to ensure a right of access is adopted here as a minimum standard for humanitarian assistance to FRY more generally.

In brief, humanitarian assistance to the civilian population in FRY should be *humanitarian*, and *impartial*. In addition, *neutrality* and *effectiveness* are sometimes included as additional criteria. There is a further requirement that it be "subject to the *consent*" of the party concerned. These issues will be discussed in turn.

2.2 Humanitarian

The commentary to the Geneva Conventions defines "humanitarian" as "being concerned with the condition of man considered solely as a human being, regardless of his value as a military, political, professional or other unit," and "not affected by any political or military consideration." This focuses on the motivation for offering assistance, rather than the method of carrying it out.

The International Court of Justice considered this question in *Nicaragua v United States*. The ICJ held that an "essential feature of truly humanitarian aid is that it is given 'without discrimination' of any kind." To satisfy this criterion, the ICJ held that such assistance would have to be given "to all in need in Nicaragua, not merely to the *contras* and their dependants."

The interpretation that assistance must be given to *all* parties in order to qualify as humanitarian assistance has been challenged. The *Nicaragua* case was unusual, however, in that the US Congress had passed a resolution providing that assistance was *only* to be given to the *contras*. This would not affect, for example, assistance given where access was physically possible only to one party (eg, for logistical or security reasons). In other words, where equal access is prevented by conditions on the ground rather than by donor policy, provision of assistance to some but not others does not deprive assistance of its humanitarian character.

A second question raised by the requirement that assistance be "humanitarian" concerns the level of assistance granted. Is there a point at which assistance ceases to be "humanitarian"? Programmes such as the Sphere Project have attempted to establish minimum standards for assistance, but it is not clear whether maximum standards are also appropriate. Certainly, items such as sealed roads and internet access (both proposed in relation to FRY) go beyond life-sustaining assistance and are not generally claimed to be "humanitarian" in the strict sense of the word, but where is the line (if any) to be drawn?

The position adopted here is that it is unnecessary to define the precise point at which assistance ceases to be "humanitarian." In general, however, items that are typically considered to be essential to the survival of the civilian population should be delivered in accordance with the principles outlined here. In Additional Protocol I, such items are said to include food, medical supplies, clothing, bedding, means of shelter, and other supplies essential to the survival of the civilian population (such as heating fuel). The Sphere Project defines such assistance as "basic requirements which meet people's needs for adequate water, sanitation, nutrition, food, shelter and health care."

It might be argued that the provision of certain types or certain amounts of such assistance (eg, a wide range of foods, building/reconstruction of houses as opposed to provision of temporary shelters) go beyond that necessary to sustain life and are therefore not strictly "humanitarian." It might be further argued that such assistance may therefore be provided with political conditions. Nevertheless, the difficulty of drawing a clear division between what is humanitarian and what is not would politicise the entire relief effort. If there is doubt about whether a certain type of assistance is "humanitarian," the issue should be resolved by discussion between donors and the humanitarian community.

2.3 Impartial

Whereas the "humanitarian" component refers to the motive and nature of the assistance, the characteristic of "impartiality" refers to the manner in which it is delivered. The commentary on Additional Protocol I identifies three elements of impartiality: non-discrimination—the absence of objective discrimination on the basis of membership of a social "group," including race, colour, religion or faith, sex, birth or wealth or any other similar criteria (the list is drawn from common Article 3); proportionality—in principle, assistance should be delivered on the basis of need; and no subjective decisions— no individual determinations as to whether beneficiary X is innocent or guilty, good or bad.

Note that this is not intended to exclude the possibility of specific actions, for example, for the benefit of children or handicapped people.

It is a notable feature of assistance to FRY that donors have been less insistent on the criterion of proportionality than in other regions. In certain sectors, the level and type of assistance given to FRY has been specifically modulated according to political conditions, rather than need, giving more or less assistance in accordance with political (rather than humanitarian) criteria.

2.4 Neutrality

The question of neutrality is often raised in this context. General Assembly resolution 46/182 (1991) on "Strengthening of the coordination of humanitarian emergency assistance of the United Nations," for example, states that "humanitarian assistance must be provided in accordance with the principles of humanity, neutrality and impartiality."

Neutrality has a particular meaning in international law relating to the position of non-belligerent states that is not directly applicable to the question of humanitarian assistance. Notably, neutrality is not mentioned as a requirement for humanitarian assistance in the Geneva Conventions. Aid given to one side only may well fall foul of other elements, however, as the International Court of Justice held in relation to US aid to the *contras* in Nicaragua, discussed above.

Nevertheless, the reference to neutrality in resolution 46/182 is representative of a general policy that humanitarian assistance should be neutral in its application.

2.5 Effectiveness

A further requirement sometimes discussed is that control over the assistance be effectively supervised. Article 23 of the Fourth Geneva Convention provides that the obligation to allow free passage of essential relief materials is subject to the state being satisfied that there "are no serious reasons for fearing" that the consignments may be diverted from their destination, the control may not be effective, or that a definite advantage may accrue to the military efforts or economy of the enemy through the substitution of the above-mentioned consignments for goods which would otherwise be provided or produced by the enemy or through the release of such material, services or facilities as would otherwise be required for the production of such goods.

These provisions relate to the question of whether a state should allow such materials free passage, and do not establish criteria for the *supply* of such materials. Nevertheless, it is possible to draw from this provision a basic principle that a relief organisation should be expected to exercise due diligence in ensuring that humanitarian assistance is used as such. (Indeed, such criteria have been important to donors in ensuring accountability of humanitarian actors.)

2.6 Consent

There is a further requirement that the right of access is "subject to the *consent*" of the party concerned. This consent is not unfettered, however.

The commentary on Additional Protocol II, Article 18 states that

> The fact that consent is required does not mean that the decision is left to the discretion of the parties. If the survival of the population is threatened and a humanitarian organisation fulfilling the required conditions of impartiality and non-discrimination is able to remedy this situation, relief actions must take place. In fact, they are the only way of combating starvation when local resources have been exhausted. The authorities responsible for safeguarding the population in the whole of the territory of the State cannot refuse such relief without good grounds. Such a refusal would be equivalent to a violation of the rule prohibiting the use of starvation as a method of combat as the population would be left deliberately to die of hunger without any measures being taken. Consequently this would be a violation of Article 14 of the Protocol.

This requirement of consent is clearly inapplicable to situations in which the Security Council has passed a resolution providing for the delivery of assistance. In Somalia, for example, resolution 794 (1992) authorised member states to use "all necessary means to establish as soon as possible a secure environment for humanitarian relief operations in Somalia."

3 Conditionality

From the general principles outlined in Section 2, it is clear that "humanitarian assistance" must be humanitarian in character and impartial. But what if organisations or states impose other, political conditions on the provision of assistance?

An answer to this question may be found in the general principles discussed above. These principles reflect practice in the area of humanitarian assistance. In many cases, they are designed to protect both the beneficiaries and those who provide assistance. Compromising these principles may endanger future access to beneficiaries, and the safety of humanitarian workers.

This HRA will consider only one type of conditionality relevant to FRY: restricting certain forms of assistance to people living in "democratic" municipalities.

As indicated above (Section 2.2), a basic principle of humanitarian assistance is that it is concerned with the "condition of man considered solely as a human being, regardless of his value as a military, political, professional or other unit," and "not affected by any political or military consideration." Imposing conditions that link the provision of essential assistance to political beliefs or activities would clearly contradict this principle (as would a condition that assistance be given only to members of a certain ethnic group, economic class, etc).

Note, however, that these principles are only relevant in determining whether certain acts qualify as humanitarian assistance. It is entirely possible to argue that additional "gifts" that go beyond "humanitarian assistance" in the strict sense of the word can be provided on a conditional basis. Indeed, it might be argued that much of the assistance provided in South-Eastern Europe falls within this category, with the exceptions of essential food and medicine provided to refugees and IDPs, and limited heating facilities provided to vulnerable populations who would otherwise be at mortal risk. (This is entirely separate from the practical question of whether such conditional assistance achieves the desired ends.)

The problem in FRY is that such "gifts" are sometimes represented as if they are in fact humanitarian assistance, when they do not comply with the criteria established here. Notably, the European Union's "Energy for Democracy" programme was represented on various occasions, by both donors and recipients, as "humanitarian" in nature. This is at odds with its formal status as an exemption from EU sanctions that is distinct from the "humanitarian" exemption.

This confusion of the category has been opposed by the humanitarian community, as the provision of conditional assistance (in this case, heating oil to democratic municipalities) politicises the humanitarian relief effort.

The desire of donors to extend dialogue on the transition to democracy beyond selected opposition parties and regions to engage civil society more generally is welcome. However, humanitarian assistance should not be used as a medium or an "instrument" for this clearly political engagement. There are many tools by which donors can engage in support to civil society or promote democratic change (including support to independent media, universities and research institutes, provision of internet access, etc). At the same time, a clear distinction should be maintained between assistance that is humanitarian and assistance that is not.

4 Involvement of Local NGOs

Most of international humanitarian law considers populations *in extremis*. In occupied territory, in areas ravaged by war, there is minimal scope for organised local assistance. Nevertheless, there is an increasing recognition that there is a need to involve local NGOs in relief efforts.

One reason for involving local NGOs in relief efforts is that it assists in the transition from relief efforts to durable solutions. This was recognised in General Assembly resolution 46/182:

> There is a clear relationship between emergency, rehabilitation and development. In order to ensure a smooth transition from relief to rehabilitation and development, emergency assistance should be provided in ways that will be supportive of recovery and long-term development. Thus, emergency measures should be seen as a step towards long-term development.

A second reason is that the involvement of local NGOs helps to ensure that relief efforts are relevant to their target populations. As the Director General of the International Organisation for Migration states:

> Humanitarian action must grow from the ground up. Only by close contact with the people caught up in suffering can we discover their real needs. Only by seeking to address those needs directly can we be sure we are working for them and not for ourselves.

The value of involving local populations in relief efforts is not seriously contested. Rather, in situations such as FRY, these benefits are said to be outweighed by other factors, such as corruption, waste, and political influence. It is important, however, to distinguish between concerns based on the humanitarian nature of the assistance, and concerns based on purely political considerations.

The possibility of corruption and wastage of resources is often raised in relation to dealing with local NGOs. In FRY in particular, concerns have been raised about the susceptibility of local NGOs to political pressure. Such concerns are real, particularly in a situation as political charged as FRY.

Nevertheless, these concerns must be balanced against the strong policy considerations in favour of involving local NGOs. It is also necessary to consider the political pressures that are placed on international NGOs, as well as the increased transaction costs associated with operating through international NGOs.

Moreover, it is necessary to distinguish between concerns about misappropriation of goods and concerns about the political significance attributed to the delivery of relief. The danger that goods may be misappropriated or delivered incorrectly is a reason for increased monitoring of a local NGO. Where such an NGO is shown to be unreliable or prone to corruption, this may justify refusing to work with it in future. The fact that an otherwise reliable NGO has previously worked with a particular government does not.

5 Conclusion

This HRA has examined the legal basis for a principled approach to humanitarian assistance. Drawing on the Geneva Conventions, their Additional Protocols, and relevant UN documents, it is clear that humanitarian assistance should not be made subject to political conditions, and that where possible, it is desirable that such assistance be delivered in conjunction with local NGOs.

On this basis, the present HRA concludes that:

(i) Schemes that use commodities associated with relief to achieve political ends (such as "Energy for Democracy") cannot be considered humanitarian.

(ii) Humanitarian assistance to FRY should be delivered free of political conditions. This applies to supplies that are essential to the survival of the civilian population, but also to items that are generally regarded as "humanitarian" in character, such as food, medical supplies, heating fuel, etc.

(iii) If there is doubt about whether a certain type of assistance is "humanitarian" in character, the issue should be resolved by discussion between donors and the humanitarian community.

(iv) Assistance to FRY that is not humanitarian in character (eg, the EU's "Asphalt for Democracy" scheme) may be linked to conditions. However, such assistance (a) is not guaranteed a right of access under international humanitarian law, and (b) should be clearly distinguished from humanitarian assistance.

(v) It is desirable that, where possible, assistance to FRY (humanitarian and otherwise) be delivered in conjunction with local NGOs.

Whatever conditions are attached to assistance, these may be less disruptive to economic reconstruction than the fact that a significant proportion of pledged resources either does not materialize—or does so very slowly.[7] As the World Bank itself has observed, "pledges are made, but commitment takes longer, and there is a considerable lag before actual disbursement takes

---

[7] Shepard Forman and Stewart Patrick, "Introduction" in Forman and Patrick (eds.), p. 1.

place. Sustainable transitions out of conflict take several years, yet there is a tendency for donors to disengage once the conflict has receded from public attention."[8] For example, $880 million was pledged at the Conference on Rehabilitation and Reconstruction of Cambodia in June 1992. By the time the new government was formed in September 1993, only $200 million had actually been spent, rising to only $460 million by the end of 1995.[9]

The reasons for unfulfilled and delayed pledges are attributable both to donors and recipients. On the "supply" side, ostensibly generous pledges at multilateral conferences may in fact simply repackage previously committed funds. Lengthy bureaucratic formalities, legislative reviews, and inefficient procurement procedures add to these delays. Donors tend to focus on their own political interests—including the interests of their national service providers, who may be tasked with implementing reconstruction contracts. And poor coordination among donors and recipients may result in duplicated or contradictory efforts. On the "demand" side, states recovering from war may lack the capacity to absorb large sums of money and in-kind assistance. Administrative structures may be inadequate to receive funds from diverse sources and for multiple purposes. Inadequate legal structures may encourage inefficiency and corruption.[10]

This has improved slightly. In Afghanistan, for example, three-quarters of the $2 billion pledged for 2002 had been disbursed by the end of the calendar year, though much of it was on emergency relief and revealed that donors had underestimated need in the first years of recovery.[11] This highlights a different bottleneck for international assistance: the lag between disbursement and the financing of effective projects. By May 2003, completed reconstruction projects in Afghanistan had a total expenditure of less than $200 million.[12]

QUESTIONS

1. What does the label "humanitarian" mean? What significance does "humanitarian" have for an actor seeking access to a conflict zone? How

[8] *World Bank, Post-Conflict Reconstruction: The Role of the World Bank* (Washington, DC: World Bank, 1998), 21.
[9] Shepard Forman, Stewart Patrick, and Dirk Salomons, *Recovering from Conflict: Strategy for an International Response* (New York: Center on International Cooperation, 2000), available at http://www.cic.nyu.edu, p. 51.
[10] Forman and Patrick, "Introduction," 9. Cf Graham Hancock, *Lords of Poverty: The Free-Wheeling Lifestyles, Power, Prestige, and Corruption of the International Aid Business* (London: Macmillan, 1989).
[11] Mukesh Kapila and Karin Wermester, "The Afghan Job Is Bigger than Expected," *International Herald Tribune*, 14 January 2003.
[12] Barnett R. Rubin, Humayun Hamidzada, and Abby Stoddard, *Through the Fog of Peacebuilding: Evaluating the Reconstruction of Afghanistan* (New York: Center on International Cooperation, June 2003), available at http://www.cic.nyu.edu.

might a combatant see things differently? How does a "humanitarian" objective differ from the promotion of "human rights"?

2. The provision of humanitarian relief is essentially a voluntary act. Can governments of recipient (or donor) countries place political conditions on such humanitarian assistance? Should they?

14.2 Vulnerable Populations: Refugees

Though the United Nations and other organizations provide assistance to many vulnerable populations, refugees have become the subject of a special regime that outlines obligations of states. The 1951 Convention was remarkable at the time for imposing such obligations, though they were assumed with significant limitations.

· ·

CONVENTION RELATING TO THE STATUS OF REFUGEES, DONE AT GENEVA 28 JULY 1951[13]

The High Contracting Parties,

Considering that the Charter of the United Nations and the Universal Declaration of Human Rights approved on 10 December 1948 by the General Assembly have affirmed the principle that human beings shall enjoy fundamental rights and freedoms without discrimination, . . .

Considering that the grant of asylum may place unduly heavy burdens on certain countries, and that a satisfactory solution of a problem of which the United Nations has recognized the international scope and nature cannot therefore be achieved without international co-operation,

Expressing the wish that all States, recognizing the social and humanitarian nature of the problem of refugees, will do everything within their power to prevent this problem from becoming a cause of tension between States,

Noting that the United Nations High Commissioner for Refugees is charged with the task of supervising international conventions providing for the protection of refugees, and recognizing that the effective co-ordination of measures taken to deal with this problem will depend upon the co-operation of States with the High Commissioner,

Have agreed as follows:

Article 1—Definition of the Term "Refugee"

A. For the purposes of the present Convention, the term "refugee" shall apply to any person who: . . .

---

[13] 189 UNTS 150, entered into force 22 April 1954.

(2) As a result of events occurring before 1 January 1951 and owing to well-founded fear of being persecuted for reasons of race, religion, nationality, membership of a particular social group or political opinion, is outside the country of his nationality and is unable, or owing to such fear, is unwilling to avail himself of the protection of that country; or who, not having a nationality and being outside the country of his former habitual residence as a result of such events, is unable or, owing to such fear, is unwilling to return to it.

In the case of a person who has more than one nationality, the term "the country of his nationality" shall mean each of the countries of which he is a national, and a person shall not be deemed to be lacking the protection of the country of his nationality if, without any valid reason based on well-founded fear, he has not availed himself of the protection of one of the countries of which he is a national.

B. (1) For the purposes of this Convention, the words "events occurring before 1 January 1951" in article 1, section A, shall be understood to mean either (a) "events occurring in Europe before 1 January 1951"; or (b) "events occurring in Europe or elsewhere before 1 January 1951"; and each Contracting State shall make a declaration at the time of signature, ratification or accession, specifying which of these meanings it applies for the purpose of its obligations under this Convention.

(2) Any Contracting State which has adopted alternative (a) may at any time extend its obligations by adopting alternative (b) by means of a notification addressed to the Secretary-General of the United Nations. . . .

D. This Convention shall not apply to persons who are at present receiving from organs or agencies of the United Nations other than the United Nations High Commissioner for Refugees protection or assistance.

When such protection or assistance has ceased for any reason, without the position of such persons being definitively settled in accordance with the relevant resolutions adopted by the General Assembly of the United Nations, these persons shall ipso facto be entitled to the benefits of this Convention.

E. This Convention shall not apply to a person who is recognized by the competent authorities of the country in which he has taken residence as having the rights and obligations which are attached to the possession of the nationality of that country.

F. The provisions of this Convention shall not apply to any person with respect to whom there are serious reasons for considering that:

(a) He has committed a crime against peace, a war crime, or a crime against humanity, as defined in the international instruments drawn up to make provision in respect of such crimes;

(b) He has committed a serious non-political crime outside the country of refuge prior to his admission to that country as a refugee;

(c) He has been guilty of acts contrary to the purposes and principles of the United Nations. . . .

Article 32—Expulsion

1. The Contracting States shall not expel a refugee lawfully in their territory save on grounds of national security or public order.

2. The expulsion of such a refugee shall be only in pursuance of a decision reached in accordance with due process of law. Except where compelling reasons of national security otherwise require, the refugee shall be allowed to submit evidence to clear himself, and to appeal to and be represented for the purpose before competent authority or a person or persons specially designated by the competent authority.

3. The Contracting States shall allow such a refugee a reasonable period within which to seek legal admission into another country. The Contracting States reserve the right to apply during that period such internal measures as they may deem necessary.

Article 33—Prohibition of Expulsion or Return ("refoulement")

1. No Contracting State shall expel or return ("refouler") a refugee in any manner whatsoever to the frontiers of territories where his life or freedom would be threatened on account of his race, religion, nationality, membership of a particular social group or political opinion.

2. The benefit of the present provision may not, however, be claimed by a refugee whom there are reasonable grounds for regarding as a danger to the security of the country in which he is, or who, having been convicted by a final judgement of a particularly serious crime, constitutes a danger to the community of that country.

The limitations of the 1951 Convention were eventually removed in a 1967 Protocol.

PROTOCOL RELATING TO THE STATUS OF REFUGEES, DONE AT NEW YORK ON 31 JANUARY 1967

The States Parties to the present Protocol,

Considering that the Convention relating to the Status of Refugees done at Geneva on 28 July 1951 (hereinafter referred to as the Convention) covers only those persons who have become refugees as a result of events occurring before 1 January 1951,

Considering that new refugee situations have arisen since the Convention was adopted and that the refugees concerned may therefore not fall within the scope of the Convention,

Considering that it is desirable that equal status should be enjoyed by all refugees covered by the definition in the Convention irrespective of the dateline 1 January 1951,

Have agreed as follows:

Article 1. General Provision

1. The States Parties to the present Protocol undertake to apply articles 2 to 34 inclusive of the Convention to refugees as hereinafter defined.

2. For the purpose of the present Protocol, the term "refugee" shall, except as regards the application of paragraph 3 of this article, mean any person within the definition of article 1 of the Convention as if the words "As a result of events occurring before 1 January 1951 and . . . " and the words ". . . as a result of such events," in article 1 A (2) were omitted.

3. The present Protocol shall be applied by the States Parties hereto without any geographic limitation, save that existing declarations made by States already Parties to the Convention in accordance with article 1 B (1) (a) of the Convention, shall, unless extended under article 1 B (2) thereof, apply also under the present Protocol.

A coup in Haiti in 1991 ushered in a period of severe unrest. Among other consequences, significant numbers of people tried to flee Haiti and reach the United States by boat. The United States sought to reduce the number of refugees through an interdiction program that directed the Coast Guard to intercept vessels illegally transporting passengers and to return those passengers to Haiti without first determining whether they qualified as refugees. Such forced repatriation was authorized "to be undertaken only beyond the territorial sea of the United States." Representatives of Haitians turned away by the program sought a restraining order, arguing among other things that the Executive Order violated Article 33 of the UN Convention Relating to the Status of Refugees. An eight to one majority of the US Supreme Court overturned a Court of Appeals decision that the Convention's provisions extended to protect refugees even on the high seas.

SALE V. HAITIAN CENTERS INC, 509 US 155 (1993)
(SUPREME COURT OF THE UNITED STATES)

Under the second paragraph of Article 33 an alien may not claim the benefit of the first paragraph if he poses a danger to the country in which he is located. If the first paragraph did apply on the high seas, no nation could invoke the second paragraph's exception with respect to an alien there: an alien intercepted on the high seas is in no country at all. If Article 33.1 applied extra-territorially, therefore, Article 33.2 would create an absurd anomaly: dangerous aliens on the high seas would be entitled to the benefits of 33.1 while those residing in the country that sought to expel them would not. It is more reasonable to assume that the coverage of 33.2 was limited to those already in the country because it was understood that 33.1 obligated the signatory state only with respect to aliens within its territory.

Article 33.1 uses the words "expel or return ('refouler')" as an obvious parallel to the words "deport or return" in § 243(h)(1). There is no dispute that "expel" has the same meaning as "deport"; it refers to the deportation or expulsion of an alien who is already present in the host country. The dual reference identified and explained in our opinion in *Leng May Ma* v. *Barber*, suggests that the term "return ('refouler')" refers to the exclusion of aliens who are merely "on the threshold of initial entry."

This suggestion—that "return" has a legal meaning narrower than its common meaning—is reinforced by the parenthetical reference to *"refouler,"* a French word that is *not* an exact synonym for the English word "return." Indeed, neither of two respected English–French Dictionaries mentions *"refouler"* as one of many possible French translations of "return." Conversely, the English translations of *"refouler"* do not include the word "return." They do, however, include words like "repulse," "repel," "drive back," and even "expel." To the extent that they are relevant, these translations imply that "return" means a defensive act of resistance or exclusion at a border rather than an act of transporting someone to a particular destination. In the context of the Convention, to "return" means to "repulse" rather than to "reinstate."

The text of Article 33 thus fits with Judge Edwards' understanding "that 'expulsion' would refer to a 'refugee already admitted into a country' and that 'return' would refer to a 'refugee already within the territory but not yet resident there.' Thus, the Protocol was not intended to govern parties' conduct outside of their national borders." From the time of the Convention, commentators have consistently agreed with this view.

The drafters of the Convention and the parties to the Protocol—like the drafters of § 243(h)—may not have contemplated that any nation would gather fleeing refugees and return them to the one country they had desperately sought to escape; such actions may even violate the spirit of Article 33; but a treaty cannot impose uncontemplated extraterritorial obligations on those who ratify it through no more than its general humanitarian intent. Because the text of Article 33 cannot reasonably be read to say anything at all about a nation's actions toward aliens outside its own territory, it does not prohibit such actions.

B. The Negotiating History of the Convention

In early drafts of the Convention, what finally emerged as Article 33 was numbered 28. At a negotiating conference of plenipotentiaries held in Geneva, Switzerland on July 11, 1951, the Swiss delegate explained his understanding that the words "expel" and "return" covered only refugees who had entered the host country. . . .

No one expressed disagreement with the position of the Swiss delegate on that day or at the session two weeks later when Article 28 was again discussed. At that session, the delegate of the Netherlands recalled the Swiss delegate's earlier position:

> Baron van BOETZELAER (Netherlands) recalled that at the first reading the Swiss representative had expressed the opinion that the word "expulsion" related to a refugee already admitted into a country, whereas the word "return" ("*refoulement*") related to a refugee *already within the territory but not yet resident there*. According to that interpretation, article 28 would not have involved any obligations in the possible case of mass migrations across frontiers or of attempted mass migrations.
>
> He wished to revert to that point, because the Netherlands Government attached very great importance to the scope of the provision now contained in article 33. The Netherlands could not accept any legal obligations in respect of large groups of refugees seeking access to its territory.
>
> At the first reading the representatives of Belgium, the Federal Republic of Germany, Italy, the Netherlands and Sweden had supported the Swiss interpretation. From conversations he had since had with other representatives, he had gathered that the general consensus of opinion was in favour of the Swiss interpretation.
>
> In order to dispel any possible ambiguity and to reassure his Government, he wished to have it placed on record that the Conference was in agreement with the interpretation that the possibility of mass migrations across frontiers or of attempted mass migrations was not covered by article 33.
>
> There being no objection, the PRESIDENT *ruled* that the interpretation given by the Netherlands representative should be placed on record.
>
> Mr. HOARE (United Kingdom) remarked that the Style Committee had considered that the word "return" was the nearest equivalent in English to the French term "*refoulement*." He assumed that the word "return" as used in the English text had no wider meaning.
>
> The PRESIDENT suggested that in accordance with the practice followed in previous Conventions, the French word "*refoulement*" ("*refouler*" in verbal uses) should be included in brackets and between inverted commas after the English word "return" wherever the latter occurred in the text. (Emphasis added.)

Although the significance of the President's comment that the remarks should be "placed on record" is not entirely clear, this much cannot be denied: at one time there was a "general consensus," and in July of 1951 several delegates understood the right of *non refoulement* to apply only to aliens physically present in the host country. There is no record of any later disagreement with that position. Moreover, the term "*refouler*" was included in the English version of the text to avoid the expressed concern about an inappropriately broad reading of the English word "return."

Therefore, even if we believed that Executive Order 12807 violated the intent of some signatory states to protect all aliens, wherever they might be found, from being transported to potential oppressors, we must acknowledge that other signatory states carefully—and successfully—sought to avoid just that implication. The negotiating history, which suggests that the Convention's limited reach resulted from a deliberate bargain, is not dispositive, but it solidly supports our reluctance to interpret Article 33 to impose obligations on the contracting parties that are broader than the text commands. We do not read that text to apply to aliens interdicted on the high seas.

Respondents contend that the dangers faced by Haitians who are unwillingly repatriated demonstrate that the judgment of the Court of Appeals fulfilled the central purpose of the Convention and the Refugee Act of 1980. While we must, of course, be guided by the high purpose of both the treaty and the statute, we are not persuaded that either one places any limit on the President's authority to repatriate aliens interdicted beyond the territorial seas of the United States.

It is perfectly clear that 8 USC § 1182(f), . . . grants the President ample power to establish a naval blockade that would simply deny illegal Haitian migrants the ability to disembark on our shores. Whether the President's chosen method of preventing the "attempted mass migration" of thousands of Haitians—to use the Dutch delegate's phrase—poses a greater risk of harm to Haitians who might otherwise face a long and dangerous return voyage, is irrelevant to the scope of his authority to take action that neither the Convention nor the statute clearly prohibits. As we have already noted, Acts of Congress normally do not have extraterritorial application unless such an intent is clearly manifested. That presumption has special force when we are construing treaty and statutory provisions that may involve foreign and military affairs for which the President has unique responsibility. We therefore find ourselves in agreement with the conclusion expressed in Judge Edwards' concurring opinion in *Gracey*:

> This case presents a painfully common situation in which desperate people, convinced that they can no longer remain in their homeland, take desperate measures to escape. Although the human crisis is compelling, there is no solution to be found in a judicial remedy.

The judgment of the Court of Appeals is reversed.

Dissenting Opinion of Justice Blackmun

I believe that the duty of non-return expressed in both the Protocol and the statute is clear. The majority finds it "extraordinary" that Congress would have intended the ban on returning "any alien" to apply to aliens at sea. That Congress would have meant what it said is not remarkable. What is extraordinary in this case is that the Executive, in disregard of the law, would take to the seas to intercept fleeing refugees and force them back to their persecutors—and that the Court would strain to sanction that conduct.

I begin with the Convention, for it is undisputed that the Refugee Act of 1980 was passed to conform our law to Article 33 . . .

The terms are unambiguous. Vulnerable refugees shall not be returned. The language is clear, and the command is straightforward; that should be the end of the inquiry. Indeed, until litigation ensued . . . the Government consistently acknowledged that the Convention applied on the high seas.

The majority, however, has difficulty with the Treaty's use of the term "return ('*refouler*')." "Return," it claims, does not mean return, but instead has a distinctive legal meaning. For this proposition the Court relies almost entirely on the fact that *American* law makes a general distinction between *deportation* and *exclusion*. Without explanation, the majority asserts that in light of this distinction the word "return" as used in the Treaty somehow must refer only to "the exclusion of aliens who are . . . 'on the threshold of initial entry'."

Setting aside for the moment the fact that respondents in this case seem very much "on the threshold of initial entry"—at least in the eyes of the Government that has ordered them seized for "attempting to come to the United States by sea without necessary documentation"—I find this tortured reading unsupported and unnecessary. The text of the Convention does not ban the "exclusion" of aliens who have reached some indeterminate "threshold"; it bans their "return." It is well settled that a treaty must first be construed according to its "ordinary meaning." The ordinary meaning of "return" is "to bring, send, or put (a person or thing) back to or in a former position." That describes precisely what petitioners are doing to the Haitians. By dispensing with ordinary meaning at the outset, and by taking instead as its starting point the assumption that "return," as used in the Treaty, "has a legal meaning narrower than its common meaning," the majority leads itself astray.

The straightforward interpretation of the duty of non-return is strongly reinforced by the Convention's use of the French term "*refouler*." The ordinary meaning of "*refouler*," as the majority concedes, . . . is "[t]o repulse, . . . ; to drive back, to repel." Thus construed, Article 33.1 of the Convention reads: "No contracting state shall expel or [repulse, drive back, or repel] a refugee in any manner whatsoever to the frontiers of territories where his life or freedom would be threatened . . . " That, of course, is exactly what the Government is doing. It thus is no surprise that when the French press has described the very policy challenged here, the term it has used is "*refouler*." . . .

And yet the majority insists that what has occurred is not, in fact, "*refoulement*." It reaches this conclusion in a peculiar fashion. After acknowledging that the ordinary meaning of "*refouler*" is "repulse," "repel," and "drive back," the majority without elaboration declares: "To the extent that they are relevant, these translations imply that 'return' means a defensive act of resistance or exclusion at a border . . . " . . . I am at a loss to find the narrow notion of "exclusion at a border" in broad terms like "repulse," "repel," and "drive back." Gage was repulsed (initially) at Bunker Hill. Lee was repelled at Gettysburg. Rommel was driven back across North Africa. The majority's puzzling progression (*"refouler"* means repel or drive back; therefore "return" means only exclude at a border; therefore the treaty does not apply) hardly justifies a departure from the path of ordinary meaning. The text of Article 33.1 is clear, and whether the operative term is "return" or *"refouler,"* it prohibits the Government's actions.

Article 33.1 is clear not only in what it says, but also in what it does not say: it does not include any geographical limitation. It limits only where a refugee may be sent "to," not where he may be sent from. This is not surprising, given that the aim of the provision is to protect refugees against persecution.

Article 33.2, by contrast, *does* contain a geographical reference, and the majority seizes upon this as evidence that the section as a whole applies only within a signatory's borders. That inference is flawed. Article 33.2 states that the benefit of Article 33.1 "may not . . . be claimed by a refugee whom there are reasonable grounds for regarding as a danger to the security of the country in which he is, or who, having been convicted by a final judgment of a particularly serious crime, constitutes a danger to the community of that country."

The signatories' understandable decision to allow nations to deport criminal aliens who have entered their territory hardly suggests an intent to permit the apprehension and return of noncriminal aliens who have not entered their territory, and who may have no desire ever to enter it. One wonders what the majority would make of an exception that removed from the Article's protection all refugees who "constitute a danger to their families." By the majority's logic, the inclusion of such an exception presumably would render Article 33.1 applicable only to refugees with families.

Far from constituting "an absurd anomaly," the fact that a state is permitted to "expel or return" a small class of refugees found within its territory but may not seize and return refugees who remain outside its frontiers expresses precisely the objectives and concerns of the Convention. Non return is the rule; the sole exception (neither applicable nor invoked here) is that a nation endangered by a refugee's very presence may "expel or return" him to an unsafe country if it chooses. The tautological observation that only a refugee already in a country can pose a danger to the country "in which he is" proves nothing.

The majority further relies on a remark by Baron van Boetzelaer, the Netherlands' delegate at the Convention's negotiating conference, to support its contention that Article 33 does not apply extraterritorially. This reliance, for two reasons, is misplaced. First, the isolated statement of a delegate to the Convention cannot alter the plain meaning of the Treaty itself. Second, placed in its proper context, van Boetzelaer's comment does not support the majority's position.

It is axiomatic that a treaty's plain language must control absent "extraordinarily strong contrary evidence." Reliance on a treaty's negotiating history (*travaux preparatoires*) is a disfavored alternative of last resort, appropriate only where the terms of the document are obscure or lead to "manifestly absurd or unreasonable" results. Moreover, even the general rule of treaty construction allowing limited resort to *travaux preparatoires* "has no application to oral statements made by those engaged in negotiating the treaty which were not embodied in any writing and were not communicated to the government of the negotiator or to its ratifying body." There is no evidence that the comment on which the majority relies was ever communicated to the United States' Government or to the Senate in connection with the ratification of the Convention.

The pitfalls of relying on the negotiating record are underscored by the fact that Baron van Boetzelaer's remarks almost certainly represent, in the words of the United Nations High Commissioner for Refugees, a mere "parliamentary gesture by a delegate whose views did *not* prevail upon the negotiating conference as a whole" (emphasis in original). The Baron, like the Swiss delegate whose sentiments he restated, expressed a desire to reserve the right to *close borders* to *large groups* of refugees. "According to [the Swiss delegate's] interpretation, States were not compelled to allow large groups of persons claiming refugee status to cross [their] frontiers." Article 33, van Boetzelaer maintained, "would not have involved any obligations in the possible case of mass migrations across frontiers or of attempted mass migrations" and this was important because "[t]he Netherlands could not accept any legal obligations in respect of large groups of refugees seeking access to its territory." Yet no one seriously contends that the Treaty's protections depend on the number of refugees who are fleeing persecution. Allowing a state to disavow "any obligations" in the case of mass migrations or attempted mass migrations would eviscerate Article 33, leaving it applicable only to "small" migrations and "small" attempted migrations.

There is strong evidence as well that the Conference rejected the right to close land borders where to do so would trap refugees in the persecutors' territory. Indeed, the majority agrees that the Convention *does* apply to refugees who have reached the border. The majority thus cannot maintain that van Boetzelaer's interpretation prevailed.

That it did not is evidenced by the fact that Baron van Boetzelaer's interpretation was merely "placed on record," unlike formal amendments to the Convention which were "agreed to" or "adopted." It should not be assumed that other delegates agreed with the comment simply because they did not object to their colleague's request to memorialize it, and the majority's statement that "this much cannot be denied: at one time there was a 'general consensus,' " is wrong. All that can be said is that at one time Baron van Boetzelaer remarked that "he had gathered" that there was a general consensus, and that his interpretation was placed on record.

In any event, even if van Boetzelaer's statement *had* been "agreed to" as reflecting the dominant view, this is not a case about the right of a nation to close its borders. This is a case in which a nation has gone forth to *seize* aliens who are *not* at its borders and *return* them to persecution. Nothing in the comments relied on by the majority even hints at an intention on the part of the drafters to countenance a course of conduct so at odds with the Convention's basic purpose.

In sum, the fragments of negotiating history upon which the majority relies are not entitled to deference, were never voted on or adopted, probably represent a minority view, and in any event do not address the issue in this case. It goes without saying, therefore, that they do not provide the "extraordinarily strong contrary evidence," required to overcome the Convention's plain statement: "No Contracting State shall expel or return (*'refouler'*) a refugee in any manner whatsoever to the frontiers of territories where his life or freedom would be threatened . . ."

UN HIGH COMMISSIONER FOR REFUGEES RESPONDS TO US SUPREME COURT DECISION IN *SALE V. HAITIAN CENTERS COUNCIL*, 22 JUNE 1993, 32 ILM 1215

In a statement released June 22, 1993, the UNHCR expressed concern over the Court's decision in Sale v. Haitian Centers Council. The Commissioner called attention to the apparent conflict between the ruling and existing international legislation and norms regarding the treatment and rights of refugees.

According to the statement, in its amicus curiae brief of December 21, 1992, the "UNHCR took the position that blocking the flight of refugees and summarily repatriating them to a place where their lives or freedom would be threatened is contrary to the applicable international refugee treaties and to the international principle of 'non-return' of refugees. These treaties—1951 Convention and the 1967 Protocol relating to the Status of Refugees—prohibit the involuntary return of refugees 'in any manner whatsoever.' "

The UNHCR goes on to conclude on the basis of 40 years of experience that "the obligation not to return refugees to persecution arises irrespective of whether governments are acting within or outside their borders. UNHCR bases its position on the language and structure of the treaties and on the treaties' overriding humanitarian purpose, which is to protect especially vulnerable individuals from persecution. UNHCR's position is also based on the broader human right of refugees to seek asylum from persecution as set out in the Universal Declaration of Human Rights."

The statement continues by saying: "Under the Court's decision, governments are obliged to protect refugees if they already have arrived at the country's territory, but this obligation does not arise if governments intercept the fleeing refugees on the high seas before they arrive. This decision is contrary to the views of UNHCR's Executive Committee that refugees should not be refused entry to a country where they are seeking asylum, and that asylum seekers rescued at sea should always be admitted, at least on a temporary basis. It is UNHCR's position that refugees, wherever they may be, should not be returned to persecution."

"UNHCR considers the Court's decision a setback to modern international refugee law which has been developing for more than forty years, since the end of World War II. It renders the work of the Office of the High Commissioner in its global refugee protection role more difficult and sets a very unfortunate example."

QUESTIONS

3. What rights does a refugee have?
4. Why was the definition of refugee given a time limitation? Why was an optional geographic limitation included also?
5. Article 1(D) of the 1951 Convention Relating to the Status of Refugees was included in order to preserve the special status of a large group that might otherwise have plausibly claimed refugee status. At the time the Refugee Convention was concluded, this group numbered around 900,000; the number of persons registered with the "other" UN agency—the UN Relief and Works Agency (UNRWA)—exceeded 4 million by 2006. What is the group?
6. Are refugees and internally displaced persons (IDPs) treated differently in the UN system? Should they be?
7. Did the United States act lawfully when it drove Haitian refugees away from its coastline? Would it have mattered if the boats had been driven out to the high seas? To Canada?

14.3 Perverse Effects

The road to Hell, as the sixteenth-century proverb has it, is paved with good intentions. One of the least studied aspects of humanitarian and development assistance is the perverse effects that a large international presence can have on an economy. This is particularly acute in post-conflict reconstruction, where an unusually large influx of expatriate personnel dominates the local economy for a period of years—precisely the period in which international assistance should be making its greatest contribution to the establishment of a self-sustaining economy.

Afghanistan's economy before the overthrow of the Taliban in 2001 was based on agriculture and narcotics. By 2003 it was based on agriculture, narcotics, and the international presence. These three sectors sometimes intersected in unusual ways. For example, WFP guidelines prevented it from purchasing grain from the relatively fertile south of the country in order to address food shortages in the north. Meanwhile, efforts to reduce opium production led to Afghan farmers being offered cash if they switched from poppies to crops like grain. Enterprising grain farmers thus switched from grain to poppies in order to be paid to switch back again.

When disputes have arisen over the microeconomic impact of the UN presence, they have tended to focus on the question of salaries. The average monthly salary of an Afghan civil servant working for the government in early 2002 was about $28, a figure that rose to $40 for some ministers, or $80 for a supreme court judge. An Afghan national doing the same work for the United Nations or an international NGO earned between 15 and 400 times that amount, according to salary scales established by the International Civil Services Commission (ICSC). In May 2002, this figure was increased. Such differences foster and deepen the bubble economy, with staff leaving government positions to take the short-term international jobs on offer—even if it means that a judge is working as a driver, or an electrical engineer as a security guard. This causes predictable problems as staff are poached from one place to the next, with organizations losing their institutional memories and such local capacity as actually exists being distorted into servicing the needs of the internationals.

Raising basic pay and increasing the differential on the basis of responsibility might help reduce the incentive for skilled local staff to leave their positions, but a post-conflict government will never be able to compete with the United Nations and international NGOs. Innovative solutions have been mooted, such as a proactive policy to recruit UN staff from diaspora communities, and establishing two-way secondments between UN agencies and the government. In the short-term, basic respect for notice requirements in contracts would help minimize the disruption of sudden staff changes in the various programs. This could be enforced through a code of conduct—if such things were routinely adopted. Ultimately, such problems solve themselves. As the international presence peaks and begins to decline, the job and property balloon bursts.

The Code of Conduct for The International Red Cross and Red Crescent Movement and NGOs in Disaster Relief, was developed and agreed upon by eight of the world's largest disaster response agencies in the summer of 1994 and represents a huge leap forward in setting standards for disaster response. It is used by the International Federation to monitor its own standards of relief delivery and to encourage other agencies to set similar standards.

CODE OF CONDUCT FOR THE INTERNATIONAL RED CROSS AND RED CRESCENT MOVEMENT AND NGOs IN DISASTER RELIEF, 1994[14]

Purpose

This Code of Conduct seeks to guard our standards of behaviour. It is not about operational details, such as how one should calculate food rations or set

---

[14] Available at http://www.ifrc.org/publicat/conduct.

up a refugee camp. Rather, it seeks to maintain the high standards of independence, effectiveness and impact to which disaster response NGOs and the International Red Cross and Red Crescent Movement aspires. It is a voluntary code, enforced by the will of organisation accepting it to maintain the standards laid down in the Code.

In the event of armed conflict, the present Code of Conduct will be interpreted and applied in conformity with international humanitarian law.

The Code of Conduct is presented first. Attached to it are three annexes, describing the working environment that we would like to see created by Host Governments, Donor Governments and Intergovernmental Organisations in order to facilitate the effecti ve delivery of humanitarian assistance.

Definitions

NGOs—NGOs (Non Governmental Organisations) refers here to organisations, both national and international, which are constituted separate from the government of the country in which they are founded.

NGHAs—For the purposes of this text, the term Non Governmental Humanitarian Agencies (NGHAs) has been coined to encompass the components of the International Red Cross and Red Crescent Movement—The International Committee of the Red Cross, The Internatio nal Federation of Red Cross and Red Crescent Societies and its member National Societies— and the NGOs as defined above. This code refers specifically to those NGHAs who are involved in disaster response.

IGOs—IGOs (Inter Governmental Organisations) refers to organisations constituted by two or more governments. It thus includes all United Nations Agencies and regional organisations.

Disasters—A disaster is a calamitous event resulting in loss of life, great human suffering and distress, and large scale material damage.

The Code of Conduct

Principles of Conduct for The International Red Cross and Red Crescent Movement and NGOs in Disaster Response Programmes

1: The Humanitarian imperative comes first: The right to receive humanitarian assistance, and to offer it, is a fundamental humanitarian principle which should be enjoyed by all citizens of all countries. As members of the international community, we recognise our obligation to provide humanitarian assistance wherever it is needed. Hence the need for unimpeded access to affected populations, is of fundamental importance in exercising that responsibility. The prime motivation of our response to disaster is to alleviate human suffering amongst those least able to withstand the stress caused by disaster. When we give humanitarian aid it is not a partisan or political act and should not be viewed as such.

2: Aid is given regardless of the race, creed or nationality of the recipients and without adverse distinction of any kind. Aid priorities are calculated on the basis of need alone: Wherever possible, we will base the provision of relief aid upon a thorough assessment of the needs of the disaster victims and the local capacities already in place to meet those needs. Within the entirety of our programmes, we will reflect consideratio ns of proportionality. Human suffering must be alleviated whenever it is found; life is as precious in one part of a country as another. Thus, our provision of aid will reflect the degree of suffering it seeks to alleviate. In implementing this approach, we recognise the crucial role played by women in disaster prone communities and will ensure that this role is supported, not diminished, by our aid programmes. The implementation of such a universal, impartial and independent policy, can only be effective if we and our partners have access to the necessary resources to provide for such equitable relief, and have equal access to all disaster victims.

3: Aid will not be used to further a particular political or religious standpoint: Humanitarian aid will be given according to the need of individuals, families and communities. Not withstanding the right of NGHAs to espouse particular political or religious opinions, we affirm that assistance will not be dependent on the adherence of t he recipients to those opinions. We will not tie the promise, delivery or distribution of assistance to the embracing or acceptance of a particular political or religious creed.

4: We shall endeavour not to act as instruments of government foreign policy: NGHAs are agencies which act independently from governments. We therefore formulate our own policies and implementation strategies and do not seek to implement the policy of any government, except in so far as it coincides with our own independent policy. We will never knowingly—or through negligence—allow ourselves, or our employees, to be used to gather information of a political, military or economically sensitive nature for governments or other bodies that may serve purposes other than those which are strictly humanitarian, nor will we act as instruments of foreign policy of donor governments. We will use the assistance we receive to respond to needs and this assistance should not be driven by the need to dispose of donor commodity surpluses, nor by the political interest of any particular donor. We value and promote the voluntary giving of labour and finances by concerned individuals to support our work and recognise the independence of action promoted by such voluntary motivation. In order to protect our independence we will seek to avoid dependence upon a single funding source.

5: We shall respect culture and custom: We will endeavour to respect the culture, structures and customs of the communities and countries we are working in.

6: We shall attempt to build disaster response on local capacities: All people and communities—even in disaster—possess capacities as well as vulnerabilities. Where possible, we will strengthen these capacities by employing local staff, purchasing local materials and trading with local companies. Where possible, we will work through local NGHAs as partners in planning and implementation, and co-operate with local government structures where appropriate. We will place a high priority on the proper co-ordination of our emergency responses. This is best done within the countries concerned by those most directly involved in the relief operations, and should include representatives of the relevant UN bodies.

7: Ways shall be found to involve programme beneficiaries in the management of relief aid: Disaster response assistance should never be imposed upon the beneficiaries. Effective relief and lasting rehabilitation can best be achieved where the intended beneficiaries are involved in the design, management and implementation of the assistance programme. We will strive to achieve full community participation in our relief and rehabilitation programmes.

8: Relief aid must strive to reduce future vulnerabilities to disaster as well as meeting basic needs: All relief actions affect the prospects for long term development, either in a positive or a negative fashion. Recognising this, we will strive to implement relief programmes which actively reduce the beneficiaries' vulnerability to future disasters and help create sustainable lifestyles. We will pay particular attention to environmental concerns in the design and management of relief programmes. We will also endeavour to minimise the negative impact of humanitarian assistance, seeking to avoid long term beneficiary dependence upon external aid.

9: We hold ourselves accountable to both those we seek to assist and those from whom we accept resources: We often act as an institutional link in the partnership between those who wish to assist and those who need assistance during disasters. We therefore hold ourselves accountable to both constituencies. All our dealings with donors and beneficiaries shall reflect an attitude of openness and transparency. We recognise the need to report on our activities, both from a financial perspective and the perspective of effectiveness. We recognise the obligation to ensure appropriate monitoring of aid distributions and to carry out regular assessments of the impact of disaster assistance. We will also seek to report, in an open fashion, upon the impact of our work, and the factors limiting or enhancing that impact. Our programmes will be based upon high standards of professionalism and expertise in order to minimise the wasting of valuable resources.

10: In our information, publicity and advertising activities, we shall recognise disaster victims as dignified humans, not hopeless objects: Respect for the disaster victim as an equal partner in action should never be lost. In our public information we shall portray an objective image of the disaster situation where the capacities and aspirations of disaster victims are highlighted, and not just their vulnerabilities and fears. While we will co-operate with the media in order to enhance public response, we will not allow external or internal demands for publicity to take precedence over the principle of maximising overall relief assistance. We will avoid competing with other disaster response agencies for media coverage in situations where such coverage may be to the detriment of the service provided to the beneficiaries or to the security of our staff or the beneficiaries.

QUESTION ....

8. How can the perverse effects of a sudden inflow of foreign money be minimized?

Further Reading

Guiding Principles on Internal Displacement, UN Doc. E/CN.4/1998/53/Add.2 (1998).

Berdal, Mats R., and David M. Malone, eds. *Greed and Grievance: Economic Agendas in Civil Wars.* Boulder, CO: Lynne Rienner, 2000.

Boyce, James K. *Investing in Peace: Aid and Conditionality After Civil Wars*, Adelphi Paper 351. Oxford: Oxford University Press, 2002.

Collier, Paul. *Breaking the Conflict Trap: Civil War and Development Policy.* New York: Oxford University Press, 2003.

Forman, Shepard, and Stewart Patrick, eds. *Good Intentions: Pledges of Aid for Post-conflict Recovery.* Boulder, CO: Lynne Rienner, 2000.

Hancock, Graham. *Lords of Poverty: The Free-Wheeling Lifestyles, Power, Prestige, and Corruption of the International Aid Business.* London: Macmillan, 1989.

Loescher, Gil. *The UNHCR and World Politics: A Perilous Path.* Oxford: Oxford University Press, 2001.

Macrae, Joanna. *Aiding Recovery? The Crisis of Aid in Chronic Political Emergencies.* New York: Zed Books, 2001.

Woodward, Susan L. "Economic Priorities for Successful Peace Implementation." In *Ending Civil Wars: The Implementation of Peace Agreements,* edited by Stephen John Stedman, Donald Rothchild, and Elizabeth M. Cousens. Boulder, CO: Lynne Rienner, 2002, p. 183.

Part Four **Accountability**

chapter fifteen
·················

Immunity and Responsibility

Norms concerning the special privileges of diplomats are among the oldest in international law. Traditionally, these were limited to the representatives of states. From the nineteenth century, however, a gradual extension of traditional privileges and immunities began to include international organizations.

Similarly, responsibility for wrongs in international law was initially limited to those entities capable of acting as full subjects: states. The law of state responsibility determines when and how a state may be held responsible for the breach of an international obligation. Because it separates the consequences of breach from the obligation itself, it is referred to as a set of "secondary" rules as distinct from "primary" or substantive rules. As with immunities and privileges, there has been a gradual—but far more recent—extension of these rules to embrace international organizations.

Both trends indicate the increasing importance of international organizations—especially, but not only, the United Nations—as actors in international affairs. The legal personality of the United Nations was discussed in chapter 3. In this chapter, the focus is on specific issues that have arisen in relation to acts carried out in the name of the Organization.

Section 1 considers immunities and privileges. It was generally accepted when the UN Charter was being drafted that the Organization and its representatives should be granted whatever privileges and immunities were necessary to exercise the functions entrusted to them. The United Nations itself enjoys absolute immunity as a legal person and with respect to UN property. This is protected in the Convention on Privileges and Immunities and has never been a matter of serious dispute. Where no alternative form of legal recourse is available, the immunity may be waived in accordance with the Convention.

The status of officials has been more complicated. The Secretary-General and Assistant Secretaries-General (including Under-Secretaries-General) enjoy diplomatic privileges and immunities. Other officials receive "functional" immunity, meaning that immunity is restricted to official acts and words spoken or written in an official capacity. A key question, in such situations, is who decides whether the relevant words or deeds were indeed performed in an official capacity.

After extracting key provisions from the Charter and the Convention, the chapter looks at two groups of "officials": peacekeepers and special rapporteurs. As we will see in the next chapter on accountability in practice, peacekeepers may present special problems of accountability for the United Nations—both because of the situations in which they operate and the terms according to which their home state sends them on mission. Here we limit ourselves to considering the manner in which the immunities and privileges of the position is presented to them. Special rapporteurs may be employed on a part-time basis and sometimes take on mandates that are not welcomed by the territories in which they operate.

Section 2 turns to the responsibility question. It seems axiomatic that the violation of international law entails responsibility and the obligation to make some form of reparation.[1] States, for example, are normally responsible for internationally wrongful acts that can be attributed to them.[2]

International organizations such as the United Nations raise more complicated issues concerning the attribution of acts by individuals to the Organization; in addition it may sometimes be unclear whether responsibility for a wrong is most appropriately located in an international organization or in the states that created it. (Similar issues may arise in a corporation being punished for the wrongs of its directors.)

This was a marginal issue until the collapse of the International Tin Council in the mid-1980s, which led to much litigation in the English courts and, a decade later, the emergence of a new field of study. The present chapter will briefly consider some of the positions put forward in the Tin Council litigation before examining efforts to codify and develop law in this area.

Establishing the legal rules for accountability is an important foundation. To be meaningful, accountability should not require the creation of new institutions or procedures but should exist as of right. In this way, it is hoped, such institutions and procedures will not merely punish abuse but encourage good behavior. As we shall see in the next chapter, however, deficits in institutions and procedures are sometimes compounded by the political context within which accountability issues arise.

---

[1] See, e.g., *Factory at Chorzów (Jurisdiction)* (1927) PCIJ, Series A, No. 9, p. 21.
[2] See generally James Crawford, *The International Law Commission's Articles on State Responsibility: Introduction, Text and Commentaries* (Cambridge: Cambridge University Press, 2002).

15.1 Immunities and Privileges

UN CHARTER, ART. 105

1. The Organization shall enjoy in the territory of each of its Members such privileges and immunities as are necessary for the fulfilment of its purposes.

2. Representatives of the Members of the United Nations and officials of the Organization shall similarly enjoy such privileges and immunities as are necessary for the independent exercise of their functions in connection with the Organization.

3. The General Assembly may make recommendations with a view to determining the details of the application of paragraphs 1 and 2 of this Article or may propose conventions to the Members of the United Nations for this purpose.

Exercising its powers under Article 105(3) of the Charter, the General Assembly adopted resolution 22(I) (1946), proposing the following resolution for accession by the members of the United Nations.

CONVENTION ON THE PRIVILEGES AND IMMUNITIES OF THE UNITED NATIONS, 13 FEBRUARY 1946, 1 UNTS 15

Whereas Article 104 of the Charter of the United Nations provides that the Organization shall enjoy in the territory of each of its Members such legal capacity as may be necessary for the exercise of its functions and the fulfilment of its purposes and

Whereas Article 105 of the Charter of the United Nations provides that the Organization shall enjoy in the territory of each of its Member such privileges and immunities as are necessary for the fulfilment of its purposes and that representatives of the Members of the United Nations and officials of the Organization shall similarly enjoy such privileges and immunities as are necessary for the independent exercise of their functions in connection with the Organization.

Consequently the General Assembly by a Resolution adopted on the 13 February 1946, approved the following Convention and proposed it for accession by each Member of the United Nations.

Article I—Juridical Personality

Section 1. The United Nations shall possess juridical personality. It shall have the capacity:

(a) to contract;

(b) to acquire and dispose of immovable and movable property;

(c) to institute legal proceedings.

Article II—Property, Funds and Assets

Section 2. The United Nations, its property and assets wherever located and by whomsoever held, shall enjoy immunity from every form of legal process except insofar as in any particular case it has expressly waived its immunity. It is, however, understood that no waiver of immunity shall extend to any measure of execution.

Section 3. The premises of the United Nations shall be inviolable. The property and assets of the United Nations, wherever located and by whomsoever held, shall be immune from search, requisition, confiscation, expropriation and any other form of interference, whether by executive, administrative, judicial or legislative action.

Section 4. The archives of the United Nations, and in general all documents belonging to it or held by it, shall be inviolable wherever located.

Section 5. Without being restricted by financial controls, regulations or moratoria of any kind,

(a) The United Nations may hold funds, gold or currency of any kind and operate accounts in any currency;

(b) The United Nations shall be free to transfer its funds, gold or currency from one country to another or within any country and to convert any currency held by it into any other currency.

Section 6. In exercising its rights under Section 5 above, the United Nations shall pay due regard to any representations made by the Government of any Member insofar as it is considered that effect can be given to such representations without detriment to the interests of the United Nations.

Section 7. The United Nations, its assets, income and other property shall be:

(a) Exempt from all direct taxes; it is understood however, that the United Nations will not claim exemption from taxes which are, in fact, no more than charges for public utility services;

(b) Exempt from customs duties and prohibitions and restrictions on imports and exports in respect of articles imported or exported by the United Nations for its official use. It is understood, however, that articles imported under such exemption will not be sold in the country into which they were imported except under conditions agreed with the Government of that country;

(c) Exempt from customs duties and prohibitions and restrictions on imports and exports in respect of its publications.

Section 8. While the United Nations will not, as a general rule, claim exemption from excise duties and from taxes on the sale of movable and immovable property which form part of the price to be paid, nevertheless when the United Nations is making important purchases for official use of property on which such duties and taxes have been charged or are chargeable, Members will, whenever possible, make appropriate administrative arrangements for the remission or return of the amount of duty or tax.

Article III—Facilities in Respect of Communications

Section 9. The United Nations shall enjoy in the territory of each Member for its official communications treatment not less favourable than that accorded by the Government of that Member to any other Government including its diplomatic mission in the matter of priorities, rates and taxes on mails, cables, telegrams, radiograms, telephotos, telephones and other communications; and press rates for information to the press and radio. No censorship shall be applied to the official correspondence and other official communications of the United Nations.

Section 10. The United Nations shall have the right to use codes and to dispatch and receive its correspondence by courier or in bags, which shall have the same immunities and privileges as diplomatic couriers and bags.

Article IV—The Representatives of Members

Section 11. Representatives of Members to the principal and subsidiary organs of the United Nations and to conferences convened by the United Nations, shall, while exercising their functions and during the journey to and from the place of meeting, enjoy the following privileges and immunities:

(a) Immunity from personal arrest or detention and from seizure of their personal baggage, and, in respect of words spoken or written and all acts done by them in their capacity as representatives, immunity from legal process of every kind;

(b) Inviolability for all papers and documents;

(c) The right to use codes and to receive papers or correspondence by courier or in sealed bags;

(d) Exemption in respect of themselves and their spouses from immigration restrictions, alien registration or national service obligations in the State they are visiting or through which they are passing in the exercise of their functions;

(e) The same facilities in respect of currency or exchange restrictions as are accorded to representatives of foreign governments on temporary official missions;

(f) The immunities and facilities in respect of their personal baggage as are accorded to diplomatic envoys, and also;

(g) Such other privileges, immunities and facilities not inconsistent with the foregoing as diplomatic envoys enjoy, except that they shall have no right to claim exemption from customs duties on goods imported (otherwise than as part of their personal baggage) or from excise duties or sales taxes.

Section 12. In order to secure, for the representatives of Members to the principal and subsidiary organs of the United Nations and to conferences convened by the United Nations, complete freedom of speech and independence in the discharge of their duties, the immunity from legal process in respect of words spoken or written and all acts done by them in discharging their duties shall continue to be accorded, notwithstanding that the persons concerned are no longer the representatives of Members.

Section 13. Where the incidence of any form of taxation depends upon residence, periods during which the representatives of Members to the principal and subsidiary organs of the United Nations and to conferences convened by the United Nations are present in a state for the discharge of their duties shall not be considered as periods of residence.

Section 14. Privileges and immunities are accorded to the representatives of Members not for the personal benefit of the individuals themselves, but in order to safeguard the independent exercise of their functions in connection with the United Nations. Consequently a Member not only has the right but is under a duty to waive the immunity of its representative in any case where in the opinion of the Member the immunity would impede the course of justice, and it can be waived without prejudice to the purpose for which the immunity is accorded.

Section 15. The provisions of Sections 11, 12 and 13 are not applicable as between a representative and the authorities of the state of which he is a national or of which he is or has been the representative.

Section 16. In this article the expression "representatives" shall be deemed to include all delegates, deputy delegates, advisers, technical experts and secretaries of delegations.

Article V—Officials

Section 17. The Secretary-General will specify the categories of officials to which the provisions of this Article and Article VII shall apply. He shall submit these categories to the General Assembly. Thereafter these categories shall be communicated to the Governments of all Members. The names of the officials included in these categories shall from time to time be made known to the Governments of Members.

Section 18. Officials of the United Nations shall:

(a) Be immune from legal process in respect of words spoken or written and all acts performed by them in their official capacity;

(b) Be exempt from taxation on the salaries and emoluments paid to them by the United Nations;

(c) Be immune from national service obligations;

(d) Be immune, together with their spouses and relatives dependent on them, from immigration restrictions and alien registration;

(e) Be accorded the same privileges in respect of exchange facilities as are accorded to the officials of comparable ranks forming part of diplomatic missions to the Government concerned;

(f) Be given, together with their spouses and relatives dependent on them, the same repatriation facilities in time of international crisis as diplomatic envoys;

(g) Have the right to import free of duty their furniture and effects at the time of first taking up their post in the country in question.

Section 19. In addition to the immunities and privileges specified in Section 18, the Secretary-General and all Assistant Secretaries-General shall be accorded in respect of themselves, their spouses and minor children, the privileges and immunities, exemptions and facilities accorded to diplomatic envoys, in accordance with international law.

Section 20. Privileges and immunities are granted to officials in the interests of the United Nations and not for the personal benefit of the individuals themselves. The Secretary-General shall have the right and the duty to waive the immunity of any official in any case where, in his opinion, the immunity would impede the course of justice and can be waived without prejudice to the interests of the United Nations. In the case of the Secretary-General, the Security Council shall have the right to waive immunity.

Section 21. The United Nations shall cooperate at all times with the appropriate authorities of Members to facilitate the proper administration of justice, secure the observance of police regulations and prevent the occurrence of any abuse in connection with the privileges, immunities and facilities mentioned in this Article.

Article VI—Experts on Missions for the United Nations

Section 22. Experts (other than officials coming within the scope of Article V) performing missions for the United Nations shall be accorded such privileges and immunities as are necessary for the independent exercise of their functions during the period of their missions, including the time spent on journeys in connection with their missions. In particular they shall be accorded:

(a) Immunity from personal arrest or detention and from seizure of their personal baggage;

(b) In respect of words spoken or written and acts done by them in the course of the performance of their mission, immunity from legal process of every kind. This immunity from legal process shall continue to be accorded notwithstanding that the persons concerned are no longer employed on missions for the United Nations;

(c) Inviolability for all papers and documents;

(d) For the purpose of their communications with the United Nations, the right to use codes and to receive papers or correspondence by courier or in sealed bags;

(e) The same facilities in respect of currency or exchange restrictions as are accorded to representatives of foreign governments on temporary official missions;

(f) The same immunities and facilities in respect of their personal baggage as are accorded to diplomatic envoys.

Section 23. Privileges and immunities are granted to experts in the interests of the United Nations and not for the personal benefit of the individuals themselves. The Secretary-General shall have the right and the duty to waive the immunity of any expert in any case where, in his opinion, the immunity would impede the course of justice and it can be waived without prejudice to the interests of the United Nations.

Article VII—United Nations Laissez-Passer

Section 24. The United Nations may issue United Nations laissez-passer to its officials. These laissez-passer shall be recognized and accepted as valid travel documents by the authorities of Members, taking into account the provisions of Section 25.

Section 25. Applications for visas (where required) from the holders of United Nations laissez-passer, when accompanied by a certificate that they are traveling on the business of the United Nations, shall be dealt with as speedily as possible. In addition, such persons shall be granted facilities for speedy travel.

Section 26. Similar facilities to those specified in Section 25 shall be accorded to experts and other persons who, though not the holders of United Nations laissez-passer, have a certificate that they are travelling on the business of the United Nations.

Section 27. The Secretary-General, Assistant Secretaries-General and Directors travelling on United Nations laissez-passer on the business of the United Nations shall be granted the same facilities as are accorded to diplomatic envoys.

Section 28. The provisions of this article may be applied to the comparable officials of specialized agencies if the agreements for relationship made under Article 63 of the Charter so provide.

Article VIII—Settlement of Disputes

Section 29. The United Nations shall make provisions for appropriate modes of settlement of:

(a) Disputes arising out of contracts or other disputes of a private law character to which the United Nations is a party;

(b) Disputes involving any official of the United Nations who by reason of his official position enjoys immunity, if immunity has not been waived by the Secretary-General.

Section 30. All differences arising out of the interpretation or application of the present convention shall be referred to the International Court of Justice, unless in any case it is agreed by the parties to have recourse to another mode of settlement. If a difference arises between the United Nations on the one hand and a Member on the other hand, a request shall be made for an advisory opinion on any legal question involved in accordance with Article 96 of the Charter and Article 65 of the Statute of the Court. The opinion given by the Court shall be accepted as decisive by the parties.

Final Article

Section 31. This convention is submitted to every Member of the United Nations for accession.

Section 32. Accession shall be affected by deposit of an instrument with the Secretary-General of the United Nations and the Convention shall come into force as regards each Member on the date of deposit of each instrument of accession.

Section 33. The Secretary-General shall inform all Members of the United Nations of the deposit of each accession.

Section 34. It is understood that, when an instrument of accession is deposited on behalf of any Member, the Member will be in a position under its own law to give effect to the terms of this Convention.

Section 35. This convention shall continue in force as between the United Nations and every Member which has deposited an instrument of accession for so long as that Member remains a Member of the United Nations, or until a revised general convention has been approved by the General Assembly and that Member has become a party to this revised Convention.

Section 36. The Secretary-General may conclude with any Member or Member supplementary agreements adjusting the provisions of this Convention so far as that Member or those Members are concerned. These supplementary agreements shall in each case be subject to the approval of the General Assembly.

Immunity is a very powerful tool that may easily be abused. The following is a pocket card that is given to peacekeepers and explains the behavior that is expected of UN peacekeepers.

WE ARE UNITED NATIONS PEACEKEEPERS (POCKET CARD DISTRIBUTED TO UN PEACEKEEPERS)

The United Nations Organization embodies the aspirations of all the people of the world for peace. In this context the United Nations Charter requires that all personnel must maintain the highest standards of integrity and conduct.

We will comply with the Guidelines on International Humanitarian Law for Forces Undertaking United Nations Peacekeeping Operations and the applicable portions of the Universal Declaration of Human Rights as the fundamental basis of our standards.

We, as peacekeepers, represent the United Nations and are present in the country to help it recover from the trauma of a conflict. As a result we must consciously be prepared to accept special constraints in our public and private lives in order to do the work and to pursue the ideals of the United Nations Organization.

We will be accorded certain privileges and immunities arranged through agreements negotiated between the United Nations and the host country solely for the purpose of discharging our peacekeeping duties. Expectations of the world community and the local population will be high and our actions, behaviour and speech will be closely monitored.

We will always:

- Conduct ourselves in a professional and disciplined manner, at all times;
- Dedicate ourselves to achieving the goals of the United Nations;
- Understand the mandate and mission and comply with their provisions;
- Respect the environment of the host country;
- Respect local customs and practices through awareness and respect for the culture, religion, traditions and gender issues;
- Treat the inhabitants of the host country with respect, courtesy and consideration;
- Act with impartiality, integrity and tact;
- Support and aid the infirm, sick and weak;
- Obey our United Nations superiors and respect the chain of command;
- Respect all other peacekeeping members of the mission regardless of status, rank, ethnic or national origin, race, gender, or creed;
- Support and encourage proper conduct among our fellow peacekeepers;
- Maintain proper dress and personal deportment at all times;
- Properly account for all money and property assigned to us as members of the mission; and
- Care for all United Nations equipment placed in our charge.

We will never:

- Bring discredit upon the United Nations, or our nations through improper personal conduct, failure to perform our duties or abuse of our positions as peacekeepers;
- Take any action that might jeopardize the mission;
- Abuse alcohol, use or traffic in drugs;
- Make unauthorized communications to external agencies, including unauthorized press statements;
- Improperly disclose or use information gained through our employment;
- Use unnecessary violence or threaten anyone in custody;

- Commit any act that could result in physical, sexual or psychological harm or suffering to members of the local population, especially women and children;
- Become involved in sexual liaisons which could affect our impartiality, or the well-being of others;
- Be abusive or uncivil to any member of the public;
- Willfully damage or misuse any United Nations property or equipment;
- Use a vehicle improperly or without authorisation;
- Collect unauthorized souvenirs;
- Participate in any illegal activities, corrupt or improper practices; or
- Attempt to use our positions for personal advantage, to make false claims or accept benefits to which we are not entitled.

We realize that the consequences of failure to act within these guidelines may:

- Erode confidence and trust in the United Nations;
- Jeopardize the achievement of the mission; and
- Jeopardize our status and security as peacekeepers.

Immunity questions have arisen on numerous occasions with respect to human rights monitoring by the United Nations.[3] In 1994 the Commission on Human Rights appointed Dato' Param Cumaraswamy, a Malaysian jurist, as the Commission's Special Rapporteur on the Independence of Judges and Lawyers. In 1995 he gave an interview to *International Commercial Litigation*, a magazine published in London, in which he commented on certain litigation in the Malaysian courts. Two Malaysian companies subsequently claimed that the article that published his remarks contained defamatory words that had "brought them into public scandal, odium and contempt." This was the first of a total of four defamation suits brought against Mr. Cumaraswamy in the Malaysian courts.

The Secretary-General issued a note confirming that "the words which constitute the basis of plaintiffs' complaint in this case were spoken by the Special Rapporteur in the course of his mission" and that the Secretary-General therefore maintained that Mr. Cumaraswamy was immune from legal process with respect to those words. A judge of the Malaysian High Court for Kuala Lumpur concluded that she was "unable to hold that the Defendant is absolutely protected by the immunity he claims," in part because she considered that the Secretary-General's note was merely "an opinion" with scant probative value and no binding force upon the court.

---

[3] See, e.g., *Applicability of Article VI, Section 22, of the Convention on the Privileges and Immunities of the United Nations (Advisory Opinion)* (International Court of Justice, 15 December 1989), available at www.icj-cij.org.

When further discussions did not produce agreement, the Economic and Social Council, at the request of the Secretary-General, sought an advisory opinion on the matter from the International Court of Justice.

ECOSOC DECISION 1998/297 (5 AUGUST 1998)

The Economic and Social Council, . . .
Considering that a difference has arisen between the United Nations and the Government of Malaysia, within the meaning of Section 30 of the Convention on the Privileges and Immunities of the United Nations . . .
1. *Requests* . . . an advisory opinion from the International Court of Justice on the legal question of the applicability of Article VI, Section 22, of the Convention on the Privileges and Immunities of the United Nations in the case of Dato' Param Cumaraswamy as Special Rapporteur of the Commission on Human Rights on the independence of judges and lawyers, . . .
2. *Calls upon* the Government of Malaysia to ensure that all judgements and proceedings in this matter in the Malaysian courts are stayed pending receipt of the advisory opinion of the International Court of Justice, which shall be accepted as decisive by the parties.

The following April the ICJ delivered its advisory opinion.

DIFFERENCE RELATING TO IMMUNITY FROM LEGAL PROCESS OF A SPECIAL RAPPORTEUR OF THE COMMISSION ON HUMAN RIGHTS (ADVISORY OPINION) (INTERNATIONAL COURT OF JUSTICE, 29 APRIL 1999)

38. The Court will initially examine the first part of the question laid before the Court by the Council, which is: "the legal question of the applicability of Article VI, Section 22, of the Convention on the Privileges and Immunities of the United Nations in the case of Dato' Param Cumaraswamy as Special Rapporteur of the Commission on Human Rights on the independence of judges and lawyers, taking into account the circumstances set out in paragraphs 1 to 15 of the note by the Secretary-General . . ."
39. From the deliberations which took place in the Council on the content of the request for an advisory opinion, it is clear that the reference in the request to the note of the Secretary-General was made in order to provide the Court with the basic facts to which to refer in making its decision. The request of the Council therefore does not only pertain to the threshold question whether Mr. Cumaraswamy was and is an expert on mission in the sense of

Article VI, Section 22, of the General Convention but, in the event of an affirmative answer to this question, to the consequences of that finding in the circumstances of the case.

40. . . . Acting in accordance with Article 105 of the Charter, the General Assembly approved the General Convention on 13 February 1946 and proposed it for accession by each Member of the United Nations. Malaysia became a party to the General Convention, without reservation, on 28 October 1957. . . .

42. In its Advisory Opinion of 14 December 1989 on the *Applicability of Article VI, Section 22, of the Convention on the Privileges and Immunities of the United Nations*, the Court examined the applicability of Section 22 *ratione personae, ratione temporis* and *ratione loci.*

In this context the Court stated: "The purpose of Section 22 is . . . evident, namely, to enable the United Nations to entrust missions to persons who do not have the status of an official of the Organization, and to guarantee them 'such privileges and immunities as are necessary for the independent exercise of their functions'. . . . The essence of the matter lies not in their administrative position but in the nature of their mission."

In that same Advisory Opinion, the Court concluded that a Special Rapporteur who is appointed by the Sub-Commission on Prevention of Discrimination and Protection of Minorities and is entrusted with a research mission must be regarded as an expert on mission within the meaning of Article VI, Section 22, of the General Convention.

43. The same conclusion must be drawn with regard to Special Rapporteurs appointed by the Human Rights Commission, of which the Sub-Commission is a subsidiary organ. It may be observed that Special Rapporteurs of the Commission usually are entrusted not only with a research mission but also with the task of monitoring human rights violations and reporting on them. But what is decisive is that they have been entrusted with a mission by the United Nations and are therefore entitled to the privileges and immunities provided for in Article VI, Section 22, that safeguard the independent exercise of their functions.

44. By a letter of 21 April 1994, the Chairman of the Commission informed the Assistant Secretary-General for Human Rights of Mr. Cumaraswamy's appointment as Special Rapporteur. The mandate of the Special Rapporteur is contained in resolution 1994/41 of the Commission entitled "Independence and Impartiality of the Judiciary, Jurors and Assessors and the Independence of Lawyers." This resolution was endorsed by the Council in its decision 1994/251 of 22 July 1994. The Special Rapporteur's mandate consists of the following tasks:

"*(a)* to inquire into any substantial allegations transmitted to him or her and report his or her conclusions thereon;

(b) to identify and record not only attacks on the independence of the judiciary, lawyers and court officials but also progress achieved in protecting and enhancing their independence, and make concrete recommendations, including accommodations for the provision of advisory services or technical assistance when they are requested by the State concerned;

(c) to study, for the purpose of making proposals, important and topical questions of principle with a view to protecting and enhancing the independence of the judiciary and lawyers."

45. The Commission extended by resolution 1997/23 of 11 April 1997 the Special Rapporteur's mandate for a further period of three years.

In the light of these circumstances, the Court finds that Mr. Cumaraswamy must be regarded as an expert on mission within the meaning of Article VI, Section 22, as from 21 April 1994, that by virtue of this capacity the provisions of this Section were applicable to him at the time of his statements at issue, and that they continue to be applicable.

46. The Court observes that Malaysia has acknowledged that Mr. Cumaraswamy, as Special Rapporteur of the Commission, is an expert on mission and that such experts enjoy the privileges and immunities provided for under the General Convention in their relations with States parties, including those of which they are nationals or on the territory of which they reside. Malaysia and the United Nations are in full agreement on these points, as are the other States participating in the proceedings.

47. The Court will now consider whether the immunity provided for in Section 22 (b) applies to Mr. Cumaraswamy in the specific circumstances of the case; namely, whether the words used by him in the interview, as published in the article in *International Commercial Litigation* (November issue 1995), were spoken in the course of the performance of his mission, and whether he was therefore immune from legal process with respect to these words. . . .

50. In the process of determining whether a particular expert on mission is entitled, in the prevailing circumstances, to the immunity provided for in Section 22 (b), the Secretary-General of the United Nations has a pivotal role to play. The Secretary-General, as the chief administrative officer of the Organization, has the authority and the responsibility to exercise the necessary protection where required. This authority has been recognized by the Court when it stated: "Upon examination of the character of the functions entrusted to the Organization and of the nature of the missions of its agents, it becomes clear that the capacity of the Organization to exercise a measure of functional protection of its agents arises by necessary intendment out of the Charter." (*Reparation for Injuries Suffered in the Service of the United Nations, Advisory Opinion, I.C.J. Reports 1949*, p. 184.)[4]

51. Article VI, Section 23, of the General Convention provides that "[p]rivileges and immunities are granted to experts in the interests of the United Nations and not for the personal benefit of the individuals themselves." In exercising protection of United Nations experts, the Secretary-General is therefore protecting the mission with which the expert is entrusted. In that respect, the Secretary-General has the primary responsibility and authority to protect the interests of the Organization and its agents, including experts on mission. As the Court held: "In order that the agent may perform his duties satisfactorily, he must feel that this protection is assured to him by

---

[4] See chapter 3, section 3.1.

the Organization, and that he may count on it. To ensure the independence of the agent, and, consequently, the independent action of the Organization itself, it is essential that in performing his duties he need not have to rely on any other protection than that of the Organization . . . " (*Ibid.*, p. 183.)

52. The determination whether an agent of the Organization has acted in the course of the performance of his mission depends upon the facts of a particular case. In the present case, the Secretary-General, or the Legal Counsel of the United Nations on his behalf, has on numerous occasions informed the Government of Malaysia of his finding that Mr. Cumaraswamy had spoken the words quoted in the article in *International Commercial Litigation* in his capacity as Special Rapporteur of the Commission and that he consequently was entitled to immunity from "every kind" of legal process.

53. As is clear from the written and oral pleadings of the United Nations, the Secretary-General was reinforced in this view by the fact that it has become standard practice of Special Rapporteurs of the Commission to have contact with the media. This practice was confirmed by the High Commissioner for Human Rights who, in a letter dated 2 October 1998, included in the dossier, wrote that: "it is more common than not for Special Rapporteurs to speak to the press about matters pertaining to their investigations, thereby keeping the general public informed of their work."

54. . . . Mr. Cumaraswamy was explicitly referred to several times in the article "Malaysian Justice on Trial" in *International Commercial Litigation* in his capacity as United Nations Special Rapporteur on the Independence of Judges and Lawyers. In his reports to the Commission . . . , Mr. Cumaraswamy had set out his methods of work, expressed concern about the independence of the Malaysian judiciary, and referred to the civil lawsuits initiated against him. His third report noted that the Legal Counsel of the United Nations had informed the Government of Malaysia that he had spoken in the performance of his mission and was therefore entitled to immunity from legal process.

55. . . . [I]n its various resolutions the Commission took note of the Special Rapporteur's reports and of his methods of work. In 1997, it extended his mandate for another three years . . . The Commission presumably would not have so acted if it had been of the opinion that Mr. Cumaraswamy had gone beyond his mandate and had given the interview to *International Commercial Litigation* outside the course of his functions. Thus the Secretary-General was able to find support for his findings in the Commission's position.

56. The Court is not called upon in the present case to pass upon the aptness of the terms used by the Special Rapporteur or his assessment of the situation. In any event, in view of all the circumstances of this case, . . . the Court is of the opinion that the Secretary-General correctly found that Mr. Cumaraswamy, in speaking the words quoted in the article in *International Commercial Litigation*, was acting in the course of the performance of his mission as Special Rapporteur of the Commission. Consequently, Article VI, Section 22 (*b*), of the General Convention is applicable to him in the present case and affords Mr. Cumaraswamy immunity from legal process of every kind.

57. The Court will now deal with the second part of the Council's question, namely, "the legal obligations of Malaysia in this case."

58. Malaysia maintains that it is premature to deal with the question of its obligations. It is of the view that the obligation to ensure that the requirements of Section 22 of the Convention are met is an obligation of result and not of means to be employed in achieving that result. It further states that Malaysia has complied with its obligation under Section 34 of the General Convention, which provides that a party to the Convention must be "in a position under its own law to give effect to [its] terms," by enacting the necessary legislation; finally it contends that the Malaysian courts have not yet reached a final decision as to Mr. Cumaraswamy's entitlement to immunity from legal process.

59. The Court wishes to point out that the request for an advisory opinion refers to "the legal obligations of Malaysia in this case." The difference which has arisen between the United Nations and Malaysia originated in the Government of Malaysia not having informed the competent Malaysian judicial authorities of the Secretary-General's finding that Mr. Cumaraswamy had spoken the words at issue in the course of the performance of his mission and was, therefore, entitled to immunity from legal process . . . It is as from the time of this omission that the question before the Court must be answered.

60. As the Court has observed, the Secretary-General, as the chief administrative officer of the Organization, has the primary responsibility to safeguard the interests of the Organization; to that end, it is up to him to assess whether its agents acted within the scope of their functions and, where he so concludes, to protect these agents, including experts on mission, by asserting their immunity. This means that the Secretary-General has the authority and responsibility to inform the government of a member State of his finding and, where appropriate, to request it to act accordingly and, in particular, to request it to bring his finding to the knowledge of the local courts if acts of an agent have given or may give rise to court proceedings.

61. When national courts are seized of a case in which the immunity of a United Nations agent is in issue, they should immediately be notified of any finding by the Secretary-General concerning that immunity. That finding, and its documentary expression, creates a presumption which can only be set aside for the most compelling reasons and is thus to be given the greatest weight by national courts.

The governmental authorities of a party to the General Convention are therefore under an obligation to convey such information to the national courts concerned, since a proper application of the Convention by them is dependent on such information.

Failure to comply with this obligation, among others, could give rise to the institution of proceedings under Article VIII, Section 30, of the General Convention.

62. The Court concludes that the Government of Malaysia had an obligation, under Article 105 of the Charter and under the General Convention, to inform its courts of the position taken by the Secretary-General. According to a well-established rule of international law, the conduct of any organ of a State must be regarded as an act of that State. This rule, which is of a customary character, is reflected in Article 6 of the Draft Articles on State Re-

sponsibility adopted provisionally by the International Law Commission . . .

Because the Government did not transmit the Secretary-General's finding to the competent courts, and the Minister for Foreign Affairs did not refer to it in his own certificate, Malaysia did not comply with the above-mentioned obligation.

63. Section 22 *(b)* of the General Convention explicitly states that experts on mission shall be accorded immunity from legal process of every kind in respect of words spoken or written and acts done by them in the course of the performance of their mission. By necessary implication, questions of immunity are therefore preliminary issues which must be expeditiously decided *in limine litis* [at the very outset of the proceedings]. This is a generally-recognized principle of procedural law, and Malaysia was under an obligation to respect it. The Malaysian courts did not rule *in limine litis* on the immunity of the Special Rapporteur . . . thereby nullifying the essence of the immunity rule contained in Section 22 *(b)*. Moreover, costs were taxed to Mr. Cumaraswamy while the question of immunity was still unresolved. As indicated above, the conduct of an organ of a State—even an organ independent of the executive power—must be regarded as an act of that State. Consequently, Malaysia did not act in accordance with its obligations under international law.

64. In addition, the immunity from legal process to which the Court finds Mr. Cumaraswamy entitled entails holding Mr. Cumaraswamy financially harmless for any costs imposed upon him by the Malaysian courts, in particular taxed costs.

65. According to Article VIII, Section 30, of the General Convention, the opinion given by the Court shall be accepted as decisive by the parties to the dispute. Malaysia has acknowledged its obligations under Section 30.

Since the Court holds that Mr. Cumaraswamy is an expert on mission who under Section 22 *(b)* is entitled to immunity from legal process, the Government of Malaysia is obligated to communicate this advisory opinion to the competent Malaysian courts, in order that Malaysia's international obligations be given effect and Mr. Cumaraswamy's immunity be respected.

66. Finally, the Court wishes to point out that the question of immunity from legal process is distinct from the issue of compensation for any damages incurred as a result of acts performed by the United Nations or by its agents acting in their official capacity.

The United Nations may be required to bear responsibility for the damage arising from such acts. However, as is clear from Article VIII, Section 29, of the General Convention, any such claims against the United Nations shall not be dealt with by national courts but shall be settled in accordance with the appropriate modes of settlement that "[t]he United Nations shall make provisions for" pursuant to Section 29.

Furthermore, it need hardly be said that all agents of the United Nations, in whatever official capacity they act, must take care not to exceed the scope of their functions, and should so comport themselves as to avoid claims against the United Nations.

In July 2000 the Malaysian High Court ruled that Param was immune from all legal process and dismissed the lawsuits.

QUESTIONS

1. To whom are UN officials accountable for their conduct? What mechanisms are available to challenge the abuse of power by UN staff? Who decides whether conduct is performed in an "official capacity"?
2. Is it appropriate for UN peacekeepers to operate with immunity? Why or why not?
3. Article 19 of the Convention on the Privileges and Immunities, grants the Secretary-General and Assistant Secretaries-General (including Under-Secretaries-General) "the privileges and immunities, exemptions and facilities accorded to diplomatic envoys, in accordance with international law." Such law does not normally protect diplomats from the jurisdiction of their home state. Does the Secretary-General enjoy immunity in his or her home state?
4. In what circumstances may immunity of a UN official be waived? Is it ever required to be waived? Who determines whether the immunity of the Secretary-General should be waived?
5. Are diplomats at the United Nations required to pay parking fines?

15.2 Responsibility of International Organizations

The International Tin Council was an organization of thirty-two members, including the European Economic Community, based on an International Tin Agreement and headquartered in Britain. The Tin Council bought and sold tin on the world market in order to keep prices stable. In 1985 it ran out of money and defaulted on numerous contracts. A key question was whether the members could be held accountable for the sins of the organization.

INTERNATIONAL TIN COUNCIL LITIGATION (HOUSE OF LORDS, 26 OCTOBER 1989)[5]

Lord Templeman

The Sixth International Tin Agreement ("I.T.A.6") was a treaty between the United Kingdom Government, 22 other sovereign states and the European

---

[5] *J.H. Rayner (Mincing Lane) Ltd. v Department of Trade and Industry; Maclaine Watson & Co. Ltd. v Department of Trade and Industry; Maclaine Watson & Co. Ltd. v International Tin Council* [1990] 2 AC 418.

Economic Community ("the member states"). I.T.A.6 continued in existence the International Tin Council ("the I.T.C.") as an international organisation charged with regulating the worldwide production and marketing of tin in the interests of producers and consumers. By article 16 of I.T.A.6, the member states agreed that:

> 1. The council shall have legal personality. It shall in particular have the capacity to contract, to acquire and dispose of moveable and immoveable property and to institute legal proceedings.

Pursuant to the provisions of I.T.A.6, an Headquarters Agreement was entered into between the I.T.C. and the United Kingdom in order to define "the status, privileges and immunities of the council" in the United Kingdom. Article 3 of the Headquarters Agreement provided that:

> The council shall have legal personality. It shall in particular have the capacity to contract and to acquire and dispose of movable and immovable property and to institute legal proceedings.

No part of I.T.A.6 or the Headquarters Agreement was incorporated into the laws of the United Kingdom but the International Tin Council (Immunities and Privileges) Order 1972 (S.I. 1972 No. 120) made under the International Organisations Act 1968 provided in article 5 that: "The council shall have the legal capacities of a body corporate."

The I.T.C. entered into contracts with each of the appellants. The appellants claim, and it is not disputed, that the I.T.C. became liable to pay and in breach of contract has not paid to the appellants sums amounting in the aggregate to millions of pounds. In these proceedings the appellants seek to recover the debts owed to them by the I.T.C. from the member states.

The four alternative arguments adduced by the appellants in favour of the view that the member states are responsible for the debts of the I.T.C. were described throughout these appeals as submissions A, B(1), B(2) and C.

Submission A relies on the fact that the Order of 1972 did not incorporate the I.T.C. but only conferred on the I.T.C. the legal capacities of a body corporate. Therefore, it is said, under the laws of the United Kingdom the I.T.C. has no separate existence as a legal entity apart from its members; the contracts concluded in the name of the I.T.C. were contracts by the member states.

Submission A reduces the Order of 1972 to impotence. The appellants argue that the Order of 1972 was only intended to facilitate the carrying on in the United Kingdom of the activities of 23 sovereign states and the E.E.C. under the collective name of "the International Tin Council." Legislation is not necessary to enable trading to take place under a collective name. The appellants suggested that the Order of 1972 was intended to enable the member states to hold land in the United Kingdom in the name of a nominee. Legislation is not necessary for that purpose either. The appellants then suggested that the Order of 1972 was necessary to relieve the member states from a duty to register the collective name of the I.T.C. and from complying with the other provisions of the Registration of Business Names Act 1916. This trivial suggestion was confounded when, at a late stage in the hearing, the Act of 1916 (now repealed) was examined and found not to apply to an international organisation established by sovereign states. The Order of 1972 did not confer on 23 sovereign states and the E.E.C. the rights to trade under a name and to hold land in the name of the I.T.C. The Order of 1972 conferred on the I.T.C. the legal capacities of a body corporate. The appellants submitted that if Parliament had intended to do more than endow 23 sovereign states and the E.E.C. trading in this country with a collective name, then Parliament would have created the I.T.C. a body corporate. But the Government of the United Kingdom had by treaty concurred in the establishment of the I.T.C. as an international organisation. Consistently with the treaty, the United Kingdom could not convert the I.T.C. into a United Kingdom organisation. In order to clothe the I.T.C. in the United Kingdom with legal personality in accordance with the treaty, Parliament conferred on the I.T.C. the legal capacities of a body corporate. The courts of the United Kingdom became bound by the Order of 1972 to treat the activities of the I.T.C. as if those activities had been carried out by the I.T.C. as a body incorporated under the laws of the United Kingdom. The Order of 1972 is inconsistent with any intention on the part of Parliament to oblige or allow the courts of the United Kingdom to consider the nature of an international organisation. The Order of 1972 is inconsistent with any intention on the part of Parliament that creditors and courts should regard the I.T.C. as a partnership between 23 sovereign states and the E.E.C. trading in the United Kingdom like any private partnership. The Order of 1972 is inconsistent with any intention on the part of Parliament that contracts made by the I.T.C. with metal brokers, bankers, staff, landlords, suppliers of goods and services and others, shall be treated by those creditors or by the courts of the United Kingdom as contracts entered into by 23 sovereign states and the E.E.C. The Order of 1972 conferred on the I.T.C. the legal capacities of a body corporate. Those capacities include the power to contract. The I.T.C. entered into contracts with the appellants.

The appellants submitted that if there had been no Order of 1972, the courts would have been compelled to deal with the I.T.C. as though it were a collective name for an unincorporated association. But the rights of the creditors of the I.T.C. and the powers of the courts of the United Kingdom must depend on the effect of the Order of 1972 and that Order cannot be construed as if it did not exist. An international organisation might have been treated by the courts of the United Kingdom as an unincorporated association if the Order of 1972 had not been passed. But the Order of 1972 was passed. When the I.T.C. exercised the capacities of a body corporate, the effect of that exercise was the same as the effect of the exercise of those capacities by a body corporate. The I.T.C. cannot exercise the capacities of a body corporate and at the same time be treated as if it were an unincorporated association. The Order of 1972 brought into being an entity which must be recognised by the courts of the United Kingdom as a legal personality distinct in law from its membership and capable of entering into contracts as principal. None of the authorities cited by the appellants were of any assistance in construing the effect of the grant by Parliament of the legal capacities of a body corporate to an international organisation pursuant to a treaty obligation to confer legal personality on that organisation. In my opinion the effect is plain; the I.T.C. is a separate legal personality distinct from its members. . . .

The third argument described as submission B(2) is that a rule of international law imposes on sovereign states, members of an international organisation, joint and several liability for the default of the organisation in the payment of its debts unless the treaty which establishes the international organisation clearly disclaims any liability on the part of the members. No plausible evidence was produced of the existence of such a rule of international law before or at the time of I.T.A.6 in 1982 or thereafter. The appellants submitted that this House was bound to accept or reject such a rule of international law and should not shrink from inventing such a law and from publishing a precedent which might persuade other states to accept such law.

My Lords, if there existed a rule of international law which implied in a treaty or imposed on sovereign states which enter into a treaty an obligation (in default of a clear disclaimer in the treaty) to discharge the debts of an international organisation established by that treaty, the rule of international law could only be enforced under international law. Treaty rights and obligations conferred or imposed by agreement or by international law cannot be enforced by the courts of the United Kingdom. The appellants concede that the alleged rule of international law must imply and include a right of contribution whereby if one member state discharged the debts of the I.T.C., the other member states would be bound to share the burden. The appellants acknowledge that such right of contribution could only be enforced under international law and could not be made the subject of an order by the courts of the United Kingdom. This acknowledgement is inconsistent with the appellants' submission B(2). An international law or a domestic law which imposed and enforced joint and several liability on 23 sovereign states without imposing and enforcing contribution between those states would be devoid of logic and justice. If the present appeal succeeded the only effective remedy of the appellants in this country would be against the United Kingdom. This remedy would be fully effective so that in practice every creditor of the I.T.C. would claim to be paid, and would be paid, by the United Kingdom the full amount and any interest payable to the creditor by the I.T.C. The United Kingdom Government would then be embroiled, as a result of a decision of this House, in negotiations and possibly disagreements with other member states in order to obtain contribution. The causes of the failure of the I.T.C. and liability for its debts are disputed. Some states might continue to deny the existence of any obligation, legal or moral, municipal or international, to pay the debts of the I.T.C. or to contribute to such payment. Some states might be willing to contribute rateably with every other state, each bearing one-twenty-third. A state which under I.T.A.6 was only liable to contribute one percent of the capital of the I.T.C. might, on the other hand, only be prepared to contribute one per cent. to the payment of the debts. The producing states which suffered more from the collapse of the I.T.C. than the consuming states might not be willing to contribute as much as the consuming states. Some member states might protest that I.T.A.6 shows an intention that member states should only be liable to contribute to the activities of the I.T.C. a buffer stock of metal and cash intended to be worth £500m. and lost as a result of the fall in tin prices on the metal exchanges which the I.T.C. strove to avoid and which resulted in the collapse of the I.T.C.

The courts of the United Kingdom have no power to enforce at the behest of any sovereign state or at the behest of any individual citizen of any sovereign state rights granted by treaty or obligations imposed in respect of a treaty by international law. It was argued that the courts of the United Kingdom will construe and enforce rights and obligations resulting from an agreement to which a foreign law applies in accordance with the provisions of that foreign law. For example, an English creditor of a Puerto-Rican corporation could sue and recover in the courts of the United Kingdom against the members of the corporation if, by the law of Puerto Rico, the members were liable to pay the debts of the corporation. By analogy, it was submitted, an English creditor of an international organisation should be able to sue in the courts of the United Kingdom the members of the international organisation if by international law the members are liable to pay the debts of the organisation. But there is no analogy between private international law which enables the courts of the United Kingdom to resolve differences between different laws of different states, and a rule of public international law which imposes obligations on treaty states. Public international law cannot alter the meaning and effect of United Kingdom legislation. If the suggested rule of public international law existed and imposed on a state any obligation towards the creditors of the I.T.C., then the Order of 1972 would be in breach of international law because the Order failed to confer rights on creditors against member states. It is impossible to construe the Order of 1972 as imposing any liability on the member states. The courts of the United Kingdom only have power to enforce rights and obligations which are made enforceable by the Order. . . .

Lord Griffiths

My Lords, I have had the advantage of reading the speeches of Lord Templeman and Lord Oliver of Aylmerton. I agree that for the reasons they give the appellants can obtain no redress through English law and that these appeals must be dismissed. I reach this conclusion with regret because in my view the appellants have suffered a grave injustice which Parliament never envisaged at the time legislation was first enacted to enable international organisations to operate under English law.

If during the passage of the Diplomatic Privileges (Extension) Bill through Parliament the Minister of State had been asked by a member what would happen if an international organisation refused to honour a contract on the ground that it had no money I believe that the answer would have been that such a state of affairs would be unthinkable because the governments that had set up the organisation would provide the funds necessary to honour its obligations. . . .

The rules concerning responsibility of International Organizations have been advanced through the work of the International Law Commission, a body of experts who seek to codify and progressively develop international law.

INTERNATIONAL LAW COMMISSION, DRAFT ARTICLES ON RESPONSIBILITY OF INTERNATIONAL ORGANIZATIONS

CHAPTER I—INTRODUCTION

Article 1—Scope of the Present Draft Articles

1. The present draft articles apply to the international responsibility of an international organization for an act that is wrongful under international law.

    2. The present draft articles also apply to the international responsibility of a State for the internationally wrongful act of an international organization.

Article 2—Use of Terms

For the purposes of the present draft articles, the term "international organization" refers to an organization established by a treaty or other instrument governed by international law and possessing its own international legal personality. International organizations may include as members, in addition to States, other entities.

Article 3—General Principles

1. Every internationally wrongful act of an international organization entails the international responsibility of the international organization.

    2. There is an internationally wrongful act of an international organization when conduct consisting of an action or omission:

    (a) Is attributable to the international organization under international law; and

    (b) Constitutes a breach of an international obligation of that international organization.

CHAPTER II—ATTRIBUTION OF CONDUCT TO AN INTERNATIONAL ORGANIZATION

Article 4—General rule on Attribution of Conduct to an International Organization

1. The conduct of an organ or agent of an international organization in the performance of functions of that organ or agent shall be considered as an act of that organization under international law whatever position the organ or agent holds in respect of the organization.

2. For the purposes of paragraph 1, the term "agent" includes officials and other persons or entities through whom the organization acts.

3. Rules of the organization shall apply to the determination of the functions of its organs and agents.

4. For the purpose of the present draft article, "rules of the organization" means, in particular: the constituent instruments; decisions, resolutions and other acts taken by the organization in accordance with those instruments; and established practice of the organization.

Article 5—Conduct of Organs or Agents Placed at the Disposal of an International Organization by a State or Another International Organization

The conduct of an organ of a State or an organ or agent of an international organization that is placed at the disposal of another international organization shall be considered under international law an act of the latter organization if the organization exercises effective control over that conduct.

Article 6—Excess of Authority or Contravention of Instructions

The conduct of an organ or an agent of an international organization shall be considered an act of that organization under international law if the organ or agent acts in that capacity, even though the conduct exceeds the authority of that organ or agent or contravenes instructions.

Article 7—Conduct Acknowledged and Adopted by an International Organization as Its Own

Conduct which is not attributable to an international organization under the preceding draft articles shall nevertheless be considered an act of that international organization under international law if and to the extent that the organization acknowledges and adopts the conduct in question as its own.

CHAPTER III—BREACH OF AN INTERNATIONAL OBLIGATION

Article 8—Existence of a Breach of an International Obligation

1. There is a breach of an international obligation by an international organization when an act of that international organization is not in conformity

with what is required of it by that obligation, regardless of its origin and character.

2. Paragraph 1 also applies to the breach of an obligation under international law established by a rule of the international organization.

Article 9—International Obligation in Force
for an International Organization

An act of an international organization does not constitute a breach of an international obligation unless the international organization is bound by the obligation in question at the time the act occurs.

Article 10—Extension in Time of the Breach
of an International Obligation

1. The breach of an international obligation by an act of an international organization not having a continuing character occurs at the moment when the act is performed, even if its effects continue.

2. The breach of an international obligation by an act of an international organization having a continuing character extends over the entire period during which the act continues and remains not in conformity with the international obligation.

3. The breach of an international obligation requiring an international organization to prevent a given event occurs when the event occurs and extends over the entire period during which the event continues and remains not in conformity with that obligation.

Article 11—Breach Consisting of a Composite Act

1. The breach of an international obligation by an international organization through a series of actions and omissions defined in aggregate as wrongful, occurs when the action or omission occurs which, taken with the other actions or omissions, is sufficient to constitute the wrongful act.

2. In such a case, the breach extends over the entire period starting with the first of the actions or omissions of the series and lasts for as long as these actions or omissions are repeated and remain not in conformity with the international obligation.

CHAPTER IV—RESPONSIBILITY OF AN INTERNATIONAL ORGANIZATION IN CONNECTION WITH THE ACT OF A STATE OR ANOTHER INTERNATIONAL ORGANIZATION

Article 12—Aid or Assistance in the Commission
of an Internationally Wrongful Act

An international organization which aids or assists a State or another international organization in the commission of an internationally wrongful act by the State or the latter organization is internationally responsible for doing so if:

(a) That organization does so with knowledge of the circumstances of the internationally wrongful act; and

(b) The act would be internationally wrongful if committed by that organization.

Article 13—Direction and Control Exercised over the Commission of an Internationally Wrongful Act

An international organization which directs and controls a State or another international organization in the commission of an internationally wrongful act by the State or the latter organization is internationally responsible for that act if:

(a) That organization does so with knowledge of the circumstances of the internationally wrongful act; and

(b) The act would be internationally wrongful if committed by that organization.

Article 14—Coercion of a State or Another International Organization

An international organization which coerces a State or another international organization to commit an act is internationally responsible for that act if:

(a) The act would, but for the coercion, be an internationally wrongful act of the coerced State or international organization; and

(b) The coercing international organization does so with knowledge of the circumstances of the act.

Article 15—Decisions, Recommendations and Authorizations Addressed to Member States and International Organizations

1. An international organization incurs international responsibility if it adopts a decision binding a member State or international organization to commit an act that would be internationally wrongful if committed by the former organization and would circumvent an international obligation of the former organization.

2. An international organization incurs international responsibility if:

(a) It authorizes a member State or international organization to commit an act that would be internationally wrongful if committed by the former organization and would circumvent an international obligation of the former organization, or recommends that a member State or international organization commit such an act; and

(b) That State or international organization commits the act in question in reliance on that authorization or recommendation.

3. Paragraphs 1 and 2 apply whether or not the act in question is internationally wrongful for the member State or international organization to which the decision, authorization or recommendation is directed.

Article 16-Effect of this Chapter

This chapter is without prejudice to the international responsibility of the State or international organization which commits the act in question, or of any other State or international organization.

QUESTIONS

6. If an international organization is composed by and acts through member states, should responsibility for a wrong committed by the Organization be attributed to the Organization or its members?
7. Can the United Nations be held internationally responsible for wrongful acts by a state acting pursuant to an authorization, such as an enforcement action authorized by the Security Council?

Further Reading

Bekker, Pieter H. F. *The Legal Position of Intergovernmental Organizations—A Functional Necessity Analysis of Their Legal Status and Immunities*. The Hague: Martinus Nijhoff, 1994.

Amerasinghe, C. F., *Principles of the Institutional Law of International Organizations*. Cambridge: Cambridge University Press, 1996.

Reinisch, August. *International Organizations Before National Courts*. Cambridge: Cambridge University Press, 2000.

Schermers, Henry G., and Niels M. Blokker. *International Institutional Law: Unity Within Diversity*. 4th edn. Leiden: Brill, 2004.

Klabbers, Jan. *An Introduction to International Institutional Law*. Cambridge: Cambridge University Press, 2002.

Crawford, James. *The International Law Commission's Articles on State Responsibility: Introduction, Text and Commentaries*. Cambridge: Cambridge University Press, 2002.

Denza, Eileen. *Diplomatic Law: A Commentary on the Vienna Convention on Diplomatic Relations*. 2nd edn. Oxford: Clarendon Press, 1998.

Sands, Philippe, and Pierre Klein. *Bowett's Law of International Institutions*. London: Sweet & Maxwell, 2001.

Wellens, Karel. *Remedies Against International Organisations*. Cambridge: Cambridge University Press, 2002.

chapter sixteen

....

Accountability in Practice

Several UN bodies possess sweeping jurisdiction under the UN Charter, notably the power to determine the limits of their own jurisdiction—*kompetenz-kompetenz* as the German say. None of these bodies (the Security Council, the General Assembly, the International Court of Justice) is directly accountable to any other. This facilitates decision making, but also creates an apparent accountability deficit. To whom are these bodies accountable?

In theory, the answer may appear to be no one. This chapter tests that theory by examining some high-profile UN failures and abuses that happened in the course of UN operations. The chapter focuses on five situations. The first two are the inability of the UN to prevent widespread killing in Rwanda in 1994 and Srebrenica (Bosnia and Herzegovina) in 1995. The third is the questionable use of authority in the UN Interim Administration in Kosovo, where individuals were detained at length without trial. The fourth concerns allegations of sexual exploitation against UN peacekeepers. The fifth is the management (or mismanagement) of the Oil-for-Food Programme, which allowed a humanitarian exemption from embargoes on the sale of Iraqi oil from 1995–2003 but was the subject of great criticism.

As indicated in the previous chapter, there are various ways of holding power to account, some more or less effective than others. The tendency through each of these incidents has been to rely primarily on a public airing of the facts, though the terms of reference of such an airing is typically selective. The United Nations, for example, opened itself to significant criticism over its action and inaction in Rwanda and Srebrenica. Without diminishing the justified nature of that criticism, it is clear that a number of member states also bore responsibility for what happened—or didn't happen—in Rwanda in particular. Unusually, Kosovo had an institutionalized reporting capacity in the person of the Ombudsperson Institution, established by the OSCE as part of the UN mission. This is typically more effective than after-the-fact reporting, but the Ombudsperson lacked any power to do more than publicize his findings. Sexual abuse in the Congo operation (MONUC) was merely the most prominent and widespread example of a problem that affects many peace operations, particularly those with large military deployments. It also highlights some of the problems with immunity regimes discussed in the previous chapter. Finally, the Oil-for-Food scandal demonstrates the problem with narrowly construing the terms of reference of an inquiry—poor performance by the Secretariat should not be excused, but nor should it be used to excuse poor oversight by member states.

There are occasional exceptions. US President Bill Clinton is alone among the leaders of the permanent five members of the Security Council in having made a serious effort to apologize for the disastrous inaction during Rwanda's genocide. On Srebrenica, member states engaged in a degree of finger pointing, but only the Netherlands, which issued a scathing report on the performance of its peacekeeping contingent in Srebrenica, took a serious stab at self-analysis on events in which poor decision making in the Security Council, in the UN Secretariat, by the headquarters of the UN peacekeeping operation in Bosnia, within NATO, and by several UN member states actively contributed to the loss of thousands of lives. No state has a particular interest in having its own peacekeepers investigated for allegations of sexual abuse—leading to the suppression of even the names of the countries involved in the incident described here, with the result that the abuse was attributed to "the United Nations" generally. And, as we shall see, the Oil-for-Food Programme was a deeply politicized institution from its very creation.

16.1 Rwanda

The failure of prevention in Rwanda was considered in chapter 7. Here we consider the role of the UN peacekeeping operation, UNAMIR. The report by the UN Panel established by Secretary-General Annan to inquire into these events is a long and still quite controversial document.[1] In order to provide a flavor of some of the panel's further findings, the following summary is from UN Yearbook.[2]

SUMMARY OF THE INDEPENDENT INQUIRY INTO THE ACTIONS OF THE UNITED NATIONS DURING THE 1994 GENOCIDE IN RWANDA, UN YEAR BOOK 1999[3]

The Secretary-General . . . informed the Security Council of his intention to set up an independent inquiry into the actions taken by the United Nations at

---

[1] UN Doc. S/1999/12571 (1999).
[2] See also *Rwanda: The Preventable Genocide* (Addis Ababa: Organization of African Unity, International Panel of Eminent Personalities, 2000).
[3] See also excerpts from the report in chapter 7 of this volume.

the time of the 1994 genocide in Rwanda. In view of the enormity of the genocide, he stated, questions continued to surround the actions of the United Nations immediately before and during the period of the crisis. The primary purpose of the inquiry would be to establish the facts and to draw conclusions as to the UN response to the tragedy. The President of the Council stated . . . that the members supported the Secretary-General's proposed course of action.

The Independent Inquiry, which was chaired by Ingvar Carlsson, former Prime Minister of Sweden, and included Han Sung-Joo, former Foreign Minister of the Republic of Korea, and Lieutenant-General Rufus M. Kupolati of Nigeria, submitted its report to the Secretary-General on 15 December. On the same date, the Secretary-General forwarded the report to the Council. The Inquiry's terms of reference were to establish a chronology of key events pertaining to UN involvement in Rwanda from October 1993 to July 1994; to evaluate the mandate and resources of the United Nations Assistance Mission for Rwanda (UNAMIR) and how they affected the UN response to the events relating to the massacres; and to draw conclusions and identify the lessons to be learned from the tragedy. The Inquiry had unrestricted access to all UN documentation and persons involved.

The report stated that approximately 800,000 people were killed during the 1994 genocide in Rwanda. The systematic slaughter of men, women and children took place over the course of about 100 days between April and July 1994, during which atrocities were committed by militia and the armed forces, but also by civilians against other civilians. The international community did not prevent the genocide, nor did it stop the killing once the genocide had begun. The failure by the United Nations to prevent and subsequently to stop the genocide was a failure by the UN system as a whole. The fundamental failure was the lack of resources and political commitment devoted to the situation in Rwanda and to the UN presence there. There was a persistent lack of political will by Member States to act, or to act with enough assertiveness, thus affecting the response by the Secretariat and decision-making by the Security Council; it was also evident in the difficulties in obtaining sufficient troops for UNAMIR. Despite the Mission's chronic lack of resources and political priority, serious mistakes were made with the resources that were at the disposal of the United Nations.

The Inquiry noted that the 1948 Convention on the Prevention and Punishment of the Crime of Genocide established the criteria for determining genocide and the Security Council had used the same criteria in outlining the mandate of the International Criminal Tribunal for Rwanda, which had determined that the mass killings of Tutsi in Rwanda in 1994 constituted genocide. The Inquiry concluded that the genocide was planned and incited by Hutu extremists against the Tutsi.

The Inquiry found that the UN response before and during the genocide failed in a number of respects. The responsibility for the failure to prevent and stop the genocide lay with a number of different actors, in particular the Secretary-General, the Secretariat, the Security Council, UNAMIR and the broader membership of the United Nations. The Organization and Member States concerned owed a clear apology to the Rwandan people. In addition, efforts should be made to bring to justice those Rwandans who planned, incited and carried out the genocide against their countrymen. The overriding failure in the UN response before and during the genocide was summarized by the Inquiry as a lack of resources and a lack of will.

UNAMIR, the main component of the UN presence in Rwanda, was not planned, dimensioned, deployed or instructed in a way that provided for a proactive and assertive role in dealing with a peace process in serious trouble. The Mission's mandate was based on an analysis of the peace process that proved erroneous and that was never corrected, despite significant warning signs that the original mandate had become inadequate. In the time of deepest crisis, the Mission experienced a lack of political leadership, lack of military capacity, severe problems of command and control and lack of coordination and discipline. Despite facing a deteriorating security situation that should have motivated a more assertive and preventive UN role, no steps were taken to adjust the mandate to the reality of the needs in Rwanda.

The Inquiry addressed the matter of the 11 January 1994 cable[4] sent by UNAMIR Force Commander Brigadier-General Romeo A. Dallaire to the Secretary-General's Military Adviser, Major-General Maurice Baril, stating that Dallaire had received information regarding a strategy to provoke the killing of Belgian soldiers and the Belgian battalion's withdrawal from Rwanda. He had also been informed that trained men were scattered throughout Kigali, that all Tutsi in Kigali were to be registered, probably for their extermination, and that there was a major arms cache for that purpose. In response to Dallaire's request to take military action, senior Secretariat officials responded that such an operation went beyond UNAMIR's mandate. The Inquiry believed that serious mistakes were made in dealing with the cable, both in UNAMIR and in the Secretariat. The leadership of the Department of Peacekeeping Operations did not brief the Secretary-General and the Security Council was not informed. The Inquiry also found it incomprehensible that more was not done to follow up on the information received. However, it saw no reason to criticize the Secretariat's decision on the mandate issue but felt that the matter should have been raised with the Council. Further, the threat against the Belgian contingent should have been followed up more clearly.

Regarding failure to respond to the genocide, the Inquiry noted that UNAMIR was in disarray. It was also under rules of engagement not to use force except in self-defence. The operation was prevented from performing its political mandate, incapable of protecting the civilian population or civilian UN staff and at risk itself. Further, UNAMIR was sidelined in relation to the national evacuation operations conducted by Belgium, France, Italy and the United States. The responsibility for that situation, said the Inquiry, had to be

---

[4] See chapter 7 of this volume.

shared between the leadership of UNAMIR, the Secretariat and troop-contributing countries.

As to the withdrawal of the Belgian contingent following the killing of 10 of its members, the Inquiry believed it was essential to preserve the unity of UN command and control and that troop-contributing countries, despite domestic political pressures, should refrain from unilateral withdrawal to the detriment and even risk of ongoing peacekeeping operations. The subsequent Council decision to reduce UNAMIR to a minimal force rather than make every effort to muster the political will to stop the killing led to widespread bitterness in Rwanda; it was a decision that the Inquiry found difficult to justify and it felt that the Council bore a responsibility for its lack of political will to do more.

Rwanda was to prove a turning point in UN peacekeeping, and came to symbolize a lack of will to commit to peacekeeping and, above all, to take risks in the field, said the Inquiry. From its inception, UNAMIR suffered from a lack of resources and logistics. During the massacres, the Mission and the Secretariat continued to focus on achieving a ceasefire and too little attention was given to the massacres. Furthermore, there was a weakness in the capacity for political analysis, in particular within UNAMIR but also at Headquarters. The Mission also failed to protect civilians, political leaders and Rwandan UN staff members who expected or sought protection.

The Inquiry believed that there were institutional lessons to be learned from the Rwandan crisis with regard to the capacity and willingness of the United Nations to conduct peacekeeping operations, and there were lessons to be learned relating to the relationship between the United Nations and Rwanda. The aftermath of the genocide was still a reality—in the suffering, in the efforts to build reconciliation, in bringing those responsible to justice, and in the continued problems of those displaced and the needs of the survivors. It was also a reality in the continued existence of the Interahamwe as an armed force in the Great Lakes region, and in the continued instability in that region.

The Inquiry made a number of recommendations for future peacekeeping efforts:

(1) the Secretary-General should initiate an action plan to prevent genocide involving the whole UN system;

(2) efforts should be made to improve UN peacekeeping capacity, including the availability of resources and clarity as to which rules of engagement should apply;

(3) the United Nations—and in particular the Security Council and troop-contributing countries—should be prepared to prevent acts of genocide or gross violations of human rights;

(4) the UN early warning capacity should be improved, both with outside actors and within the Secretariat;

(5) protection of civilians in conflict situations should be improved;

(6) the security of UN and associated personnel, including local staff, needed to be improved;

(7) cooperation between officials responsible for the security of different categories of staff in the field needed to be ensured;

(8) an effective flow of information needed to be ensured;

(9) improvements should be made in the flow of information to the Council;

(10) the flow of information on human rights issues should be improved;

(11) national evacuation operations should be coordinated with UN missions on the ground;

(12) further study should be given to suspending participation of a Member State on the Security Council in exceptional circumstances, such as the Rwandan crisis;

(13) the international community should support efforts in Rwanda to rebuild the society; and

(14) the United Nations should acknowledge its part of the responsibility for not having done enough to prevent or stop the genocide in Rwanda.

These very significant failings at the United Nations occurred at a time when parallel problems in other UN peacekeeping operations were inspiring a degree of reticence on the part of potential troop contributors. The UN operation in the former Yugoslavia, UNPROFOR, was bogged down between belligerents engaged in a war of attrition and saddled with mandates not much clearer or more useful than that of UNAMIR. Similarly, the UN's setbacks in Somalia, along with crucial US military losses there, had created a fear in Washington of African "quagmires." Without US leadership, any international response was always likely to be meek. French involvement in Rwanda had produced—to say the least—complex and not always helpful policy responses from Paris. Belgium, the former colonial power in Rwanda, was effectively intimidated by the slaughter of ten of its UNAMIR peacekeepers and withdrew. In this context, the lack of political will in the Council is more readily understandable, however deplorable.

Several Council members, notably its President in April 1994, New Zealand, and Nigeria argued for more forceful action to counter the genocide, but they were over-ridden by those with the means to make a difference on the ground. That Rwanda happened at the time also to hold one of the elected seats on the Council is one of the ironies of this sad chapter in Council history. The recommendations of the Panel outlined above were all sensible. But it is not clear their either Security Council or Secretariat took them entirely to heart.

QUESTION

1. While "the United Nations" is widely blamed for the failure to forestall genocide in Rwanda in 1994, how would you assess and assign legal and

political responsibility to different actors within the United Nations (Security Council members, UN Secretariat officials, UN staff—including UNAMIR peacekeepers—on the ground)? Have any of these actors paid a price for their mistakes?

16.2 Srebrenica

The disaster at Srebrenica remains a terrible stain on the record of UN peacekeeping and an indictment of strategies in the UN Security Council premised as much on wishful thinking and the "art of the possible" as on realistic planning for harsh realities on the ground. Around 7,000 men and boys were killed after the "safe area" fell to Serb forces despite the presence of a Dutch battalion of peacekeepers intended to deter attack. NATO was also involved due to the "air cover" (through air strikes) it was providing for the UN mission. The NATO strikes requested by the local UN commander failed to materialize after squabbling among UN, NATO, and national officials. The UN report on these sorry events—also commissioned by Secretary-General Kofi Annan—was widely praised as the frankest document of its sort to have been published by the United Nations.[5] Again, a sense of the report is provided by the summary from the UN Year Book.

SUMMARY OF THE REPORT OF THE SECRETARY-GENERAL PURSUANT TO GENERAL ASSEMBLY RESOLUTION 53/35: THE FALL OF SREBRENICA, UN YEAR BOOK 1999

In response to General Assembly resolution 53/35, the Secretary-General submitted a comprehensive report [A/54/549] on the events dating from the establishment of the safe area of Srebrenica on 16 April 1993 until the endorsement of the Peace Agreement by the Security Council in resolution 1031 (1995).

The Secretary-General said the tragedy that occurred after the fall of Srebrenica was shocking for the magnitude of the crimes committed and because the enclave's inhabitants believed that the Council's authority, the presence of the United Nations Protection Force (UNPROFOR) peacekeepers and the might of NATO's air power would ensure their safety. Instead, the Bosnian Serb forces ignored the Council, pushed aside UNPROFOR troops and overran the safe area of Srebrenica, assessing correctly that air power would not be used against them. They proceeded to depopulate the territory

[5] UN Doc. A/54/549 (1999).

within 48 hours and executed and buried thousands of men and boys within a matter of days, while their leaders negotiated with the international community.

The Secretary-General said that many of the errors the United Nations made flowed from its well-intentioned effort to keep the peace and apply the rules of peacekeeping when there was no peace to keep. Knowing that any other course of action would jeopardize the lives of the troops, the Council and Member States tried to create or imagine an environment in which the tenets of peacekeeping could be upheld, to stabilize the situation on the ground through ceasefire agreements and to eschew the use of force, except in self-defence. The international community's response to the war in Bosnia and Herzegovina, comprising an arms embargo, humanitarian aid and the deployment of a peacekeeping force, was a poor substitute for more decisive and forceful action to prevent the unfolding horror, the Secretary-General stated.

None of the conditions for the deployment of peacekeepers had been met: there was no peace agreement, not even a functioning ceasefire, and there was no clear will to peace and no clear consent by the belligerents. It had become clear that the ability to adapt mandates to the reality on the ground was of critical importance to ensuring that the appropriate force under the appropriate structure was deployed. None of that flexibility was present in the management of UNPROFOR.

There was neither the will to use decisive air power against Serb attacks on the safe areas, nor the means on the ground to repulse them.

Two of the safe areas, Srebrenica and Zepa, were demilitarized to a far greater extent than any of the others. However, instead of enhancing their security, it only made them easier targets for the Serbs. The failure to fully comprehend the extent of the Serb war aims might explain in part why the Secretariat and the peacekeeping mission did not react more quickly and decisively when the Serbs initiated their attack on Srebrenica. In fact, the Council was given the impression that the situation was under control and many believed that to be the case. Some instances of incomplete and inaccurate information being given to the Council could be attributed to problems with reporting from the field, but in other instances the reporting might have been illustrative of a more general tendency to assume that the parties were equally responsible for the transgressions that occurred. It was not clear, in any event, that the provision of more fully accurate information to the Council would have led to appreciably different results.

In the end, the Bosnian Serb war aims were repulsed on the battlefield and not at the negotiating table, yet the Secretariat had convinced itself that the broader use of force by the international community was beyond its mandate and undesirable.

The fall of Srebrenica was replete with lessons for the Organization and its Member States: when peacekeeping operations were used as a substitute for political consensus they were likely to fail; and peacekeepers should never be deployed where there was no ceasefire or peace agreement, or told to use their peacekeeping tools—lightly armed soldiers in scattered positions—to impose the ill-defined wishes of the international community by military means. If the necessary resources were not provided, and the political, military and moral judgements were not made, the job simply could not be done. Protected zones and safe areas should be demilitarized and established by the agreement of the belligerents, as in the case of the "protected zones" and "safe havens" recognized by international humanitarian law, or they should be truly safe areas, fully defended by a credible military deterrent.

The responsibility for allowing that tragic course of events by its prolonged refusal to use force in the early stages of the war was shared by the Council, the Contact Group and other Governments, which contributed to that delay, as well as by the Secretariat and the mission in the field. Clearly, however, the primary and most direct responsibility lay with the architects and implementers of the attempted genocide in Bosnia. The cardinal lesson of Srebrenica was that a deliberate and systematic attempt to terrorize, expel or murder an entire people should be met decisively with all necessary means, and with the political will to carry the policy through to its logical conclusion.

The Secretary-General concluded that through error, misjudgement and an inability to recognize the scope of the evil, the United Nations failed to help save the people of Srebrenica from the Serb campaign of mass murder, crystallizing a truth understood only too late by the United Nations and the world at large: that Bosnia was as much a moral cause as a military conflict.

Importantly, the report identifies a mismatch between Security Council strategies (peacekeeping) and the situation on the ground (no peace to keep). The summary above rather underplays the Secretariat's attempts in 1993 and 1994 to secure the larger numbers of peacekeepers for UNPROFOR that might have deterred the Serb attack on Srebrenica, but it rightly points to the determination of the Serb military leadership and strategies largely discouraging the use of force by the United Nations and NATO. There was either reprehensible confusion or doubly reprehensible finessing of what UN "safe areas" were meant to represent. They certainly did not have the deterrent military capacity that would have made them truly safe.

Were any lessons learned from this episode? Importantly, did the United Nations subsequently insist on peace agreements before deploying peacekeepers? Did peacekeepers subsequently deploy in sufficient numbers and so equipped as to be able to defend their mandates? Too often they did not. The case of Sierra Leone, discussed in chapter 8, is one of several in which UN peacekeepers were easily overrun by local combatants. By 2005, the UN Secretariat (eventually supported by the Security Council), clearly fed up with the UN's own frequent military incapacity and ineffectiveness, adopted tougher strategies on the ground in the Congo after a French-led EU "coalition of the willing," Operation Artemis, had restored order. Perhaps as a consequence, MONUC also absorbed larger casualties there in 2005 and 2006 than had earlier been the case. It remains the case that UN peacekeeping operations are frequently caught between demanding situations on the ground and the expediency with which members of the Security Council are all too often driven to adopt mandates seriously under-resourced relative to their objectives.

QUESTION

2. How would you contrast the responsibility of the United Nations for action or inaction in Srebrenica, in comparison with the responsibility of the United Nations for events in Rwanda?

16.3 Kosovo

We have seen in chapter 2 and again in chapter 9 how extensive were the powers conferred on the UN Special Representative of the Secretary-General (SRSG) in Kosovo by Security Council resolution 1244 (1999). Considerable unease grew not only over these powers, but also over the virtually unlimited nature of such powers available to the international community's High Representative in Bosnia under the Dayton agreements and to the SRSG in East Timor during the United Nations' period of transitional administration there. While the ability to "check and balance" local political actors engaged in irresponsible pandering to their own communities was seen by many as a positive feature of robust mandates for the leading international actor in challenging theaters of operation, the local effects of prolonged undemocratic rule by international fiat has been less discussed. In a case in point, the international ombudsperson in Kosovo (an office created by the Organization for Security and Cooperation in Europe, OSCE, one of several organizations charged with implementing resolution 1244) sought to rein in the SRSG, on legal and human rights grounds.

One of the consequences of the diminished credibility of UNMIK and its own lack of faith in the local judiciary was recourse to detention on executive orders. On 28 May 2000, Afram Zeqiri, a Kosovar Albanian and former Kosovo Liberation Army (KLA) fighter, was arrested on suspicion of murdering three Serbs in the village of Cernica, including the shooting of a four-year-old boy. An Albanian prosecutor ordered him released for lack of evidence, raising suspicions of judicial bias. The decision was upheld by an international judge, but SRSG Bernard Kouchner nevertheless ordered that Zeqiri continue to be detained under an "executive hold," claiming that the authority to issue such orders derived from "security reasons" and Security Council resolution 1244 (1999).

Similar orders were made by Kouchner's successor, Hans Haekkerup. In February 2001, a bus carrying Serbs from Nis into Kosovo was bombed, killing eleven. British KFOR troops arrested Florim Ejupi, Avdi Behluli, Çelë Gashi, and Jusuf Veliu in mid-March on suspicion of being involved, but on 27 March a panel of international judges of the District Court of Pristina ordered that Behluli, Gashi, and Veliu be released. The following day, Haekkerup issued an executive order extending their detention for thirty days, later extended by six more such orders. (Ejupi was subsequently reported to have "escaped" from the high-security detention facility at Camp Bondsteel.)[6]

SPECIAL REPORT NO. 3, ON THE CONFORMITY OF DEPRIVATIONS OF LIBERTY UNDER "EXECUTIVE ORDERS" WITH RECOGNISED INTERNATIONAL STANDARDS, 29 JUNE 2001

[Addressed to Mr. Hans Haekkerup, Special Representative of the Secretary-General of the United Nations]

Pursuant to his authority under Sections 1.1 and 4.1 of UNMIK Regulation No. 2000/38 on the Establishment of the Ombudsperson Institution in Kosovo and Rule 22, paras. 3 and 4 of the Rules of Procedure of the Ombudsperson Institution, the Ombudsperson has issued the above Special Report.

The Ombudsperson found that deprivations of liberty imposed under "Executive Orders" or any other form of executive instruction, decree or decision issued by the Special Representative of the Secretary-General of the United Nations (SRSG) do not conform with recognised international standards. He found that any such deprivation of liberty cannot be considered to be lawful in the sense of para. 1 of Article 5 of the European Convention on Human Rights, that the absence of judicial control over deprivations of liberty imposed under Executive Orders constitutes a violation of paras. 3 and 4 of Article 5 of the Convention and that the lack of an enforceable right to compensation for unlawful deprivations of liberty constitutes a violation of para. 5 of Article 5.

The Ombudsperson recommended that the SRSG immediately cease the practice of issuing Executive Orders imposing on any individual in Kosovo a deprivation of liberty. The Ombudsperson further recommended that the SRSG, no later than 20 July 2001, convene one or more panels composed of international judges to review, on an urgent basis, the lawfulness of detentions of individuals currently deprived of their liberty under Executive Orders, such review to conform with the requirements of Article 5 of the European Convention on Human Rights. The Ombudsperson also re-

---

[6] Simon Chesterman, *You, the People: The United Nations, Transitional Administration and State-Building* (Oxford: Oxford University Press, 2004), pp. 167-168.

commended that the SRSG should undertake to comply with decisions on deprivations of liberty taken by the judicial panels convened in accordance with the recommendations.

The Ombudsperson also recommended that the SRSG, no later than 31 August 2001, promulgate a Regulation setting forth the legal bases for compensation claims for unlawful deprivations of liberty and proper judicial proceedings in this respect and, on the date of its entry into force, disseminate it through all appropriate channels in all languages widely used in Kosovo. The Ombudsperson further recommended that the new Regulation should be distributed to all persons who have been deprived of their liberty under Executive Orders issued by the SRSG and to all judges, judicial officers or others exercising judicial authority in Kosovo.

Following criticism by the OSCE Ombudsperson, as well as international human rights organizations such as Human Rights Watch and Amnesty International, a Detention Review Commission of international experts was established by UNMIK in August 2001 to make final decisions on the legality of administrative detentions. The Commission approved extension of the detentions of the alleged Nis bombers until 19 December 2001—a few weeks after Kosovo's first provincial elections—ruling that "there are reasonable grounds to suspect that each of the detained persons has committed a criminal act." At the end of that period, the three-month mandate of the Commission had not been renewed; in its absence, the Kosovo Supreme Court ordered the release of the three detainees. The last person held under an Executive Order, Afrim Zeqiri, was released by a judge on bail in early February 2002 after approximately twenty months in detention.

QUESTION

3. The Kosovo case outlined above relates to the special (and potentially unlimited) powers of UN representatives in territories under UN rule. Are there judicial or other international processes that should be set in place to serve as checks on such powers whenever they are established? How could this be done practically, without creating cumbersome and expensive bureaucracies?

16.4 Sexual Exploitation by UN Peacekeepers

The issue of sexual exploitation across borders grew in prominence during the 1990s, and early in the 2000s attention started to focus on the conduct of UN and other international personnel, in light of complaints that the UN peacekeepers in the Balkans and in Africa had engaged in sexual exploitation of those they were meant to protect. Concern crystallized in 2004 over reports of widespread sexual exploitation by troops and civilian staff of MONUC, the UN's large peacekeeping operation in the Democratic Republic of the Congo. The Secretary-General, acknowledging the gravity of the allegations, commissioned a report from a panel led by the Jordanian Ambassador to the United Nations, Prince Zeid Ra'ad Zeid Al-Hussein, himself a former civilian peacekeeper in Bosnia.

A COMPREHENSIVE STRATEGY TO ELIMINATE FUTURE SEXUAL EXPLOITATION AND ABUSE IN UNITED NATIONS PEACEKEEPING OPERATIONS, 24 MARCH 2005[7]

3. United Nations peacekeeping has a distinguished history of helping many States and peoples to emerge from conflict with the hope of a better future. Many peacekeeping personnel have given their lives to realize that goal, and their achievements and sacrifices must not be forgotten. But despite the distinguished role that United Nations peacekeeping personnel have played over the last half-century, there regrettably will always be those who violate codes of conduct and thereby dishonour the many who have given their lives in the cause of peace. Sexual exploitation and abuse by military, civilian police and civilian peacekeeping personnel is not a new phenomenon. Such acts cover a wide spectrum of behaviour, from breaches of the Organization's standards of conduct, such as solicitation of adult prostitutes, which may be legal in some countries, to acts that would be considered a criminal offence in any national jurisdiction, for example rape and paedophilia. . . .

6. The reality of prostitution and other sexual exploitation in a peace-keeping context is profoundly disturbing to many because the United Nations has been mandated to enter into a broken society to help it, not to breach the trust placed in it by the local population. Moreover, the Organization should not in any way increase the suffering of vulnerable sectors of the population, which has often been devastated by war or civil conflict. For example, in the Democratic Republic of the Congo, it would appear that sexual exploitation and abuse mostly involves the exchange of sex for money (on average $1–$3 per encounter), for food (for immediate consumption or to barter later) or for jobs (especially affecting daily workers). Some young girls whom I spoke with in the Democratic Republic of the Congo talked of "rape disguised as prostitution," in which they said they were raped and given money or food afterwards to give the rape the appearance of a consensual transaction. Once young girls are in this situation, a situation of dependency

---

[7] UN Doc. A/59/710 (2005).

is created which tends to result in a continued downward spiral of further prostitution, with its attendant violence, desperation, disease and further dependency. A consequence of sexual exploitation and abuse is the presence of abandoned "peacekeeper babies," children fathered and abandoned by peacekeeping personnel. The absence of a functioning legal system means that the protections afforded to citizens of most countries against this type of abuse are absent. . . .

II. The Rules

. . .

15. United Nations staff have the status and the privileges and immunities of officials under the Convention on the Privileges and Immunities of the United Nations (the General Convention), which also sets out the conditions under which their immunity may be waived by the Secretary-General. . . .

16. United Nations Volunteers are also employed in peacekeeping missions. Recent status-of-forces agreements extend to them the privileges and immunities of officials granted under the General Convention. . . .

17. Individual contractors and consultants are also employed by peacekeeping missions. They are subject to local law and are bound by the standards set out in the Organization's standard conditions of contract for individual contractors and consultants.

18. Civilian police and military observers have the status and the privileges and immunities of experts on mission granted under the General Convention (military liaison officers and military staff officers are also considered experts on mission). . . .

19. Military members of national contingents have the privileges and immunities specified in the status-of-forces agreement or, if none has been concluded, in the model status-of-forces agreement, which the Security Council makes applicable to peacekeeping operations pending the conclusion of a status-of-forces agreement with the host State. The model status-of-forces agreement provides that the troop-contributing country has criminal and disciplinary jurisdiction over military members of the contingents (A/45/594, annex, para. 47 (b)). However, as an administrative measure, the Secretary-General may order the repatriation of any military member of a contingent who has been found culpable of serious misconduct in a mission investigation. Troop-contributing countries have over the years universally accepted the general standards of conduct set out in the publications entitled "Ten Rules: Code of Personal Conduct for Blue Helmets" and "We Are United Nations Peacekeepers." . . .

21. The basic standards of conduct and integrity required of the various categories of peacekeeping personnel—set out in the Staff Regulations and Rules, the Ten Rules and We Are United Nations Peacekeepers—are similar because they are all derived from principles established in Article 101, paragraph 3, of the Charter, which requires the highest standards of integrity of United Nations officials. But those documents are general in nature; they do

not give specific instructions on precisely what acts of sexual exploitation and abuse are prohibited. The 2003 bulletin fills that gap by setting out such detailed prohibitions. The bulletin was welcomed by the Special Committee on Peacekeeping Operations (Special Committee) and by the General Assembly in its resolution 58/315 of 1 July 2004, but it must be noted that the bulletin applies of its own force only to United Nations staff.

22. There is thus an extensive mosaic of provisions drafted at varying points in time and with varying degrees of legal force dealing with sexual exploitation and abuse that apply to the various categories of peacekeeping personnel. As noted above, only United Nations staff members are unquestionably bound by the prohibitions set out in the 2003 Secretary-General's bulletin. Civilian police and military observers agree to be bound by directives, which, since approximately mid-2004, have included a summary of those prohibitions. The situation of military members of contingents is unclear. Rules can be made binding on military members of contingents only with the agreement of and action by the troop-contributing country concerned. . . .

27. The General Assembly should reiterate its approval of the standards set out in the 2003 bulletin and make them applicable to all categories of peacekeeping personnel, without exception. It should also request the Secretary-General to ensure that all civilian personnel are bound by them. Furthermore, the Assembly should decide that those standards and the standards contained in Ten Rules and We Are United Nations Peacekeepers be included in the model memorandums of understanding, and the troop-contributing countries should undertake to issue the standards in a form binding on their personnel. The Secretary-General and troop-contributing countries should cooperate to issue the standards set out in the 2003 bulletin, as well as those contained in Ten Rules and We are United Nations Peacekeepers, to troop-contributing country personnel in convenient card form in the languages of those personnel, with the troop-contributing country providing the translation and the mission arranging for publication of the cards at its cost. . . .

V. Individual Disciplinary, Financial and Criminal Accountability

67. Some of the difficulties faced by troop-contributing countries in acting on what they perceived to be flawed preliminary investigations and board of inquiry reports were explained earlier in the present report. Also examined were the difficulties faced by the Department of Peacekeeping Operations in investigating allegations of sexual exploitation and abuse where traditional methods of identification through witnesses proved difficult if not impossible. Underlying such problems of investigative technique are two more fundamental problems that are more difficult to resolve:

(a) In respect of military members of national contingents, troop-contributing countries are often reluctant to admit publicly to acts of wrong doing and consequently lack the will to court-martial alleged offenders;

(b) In respect of staff and experts on mission, the lack of a legal system in some peacekeeping areas that meets minimum international human rights standards makes it difficult for the Secretary-General to waive the immunity of staff accused of serious crimes in the mission area. . . .

68. Personnel who violate the standards established in the 2003 Secretary-General's bulletin ought to be subjected to disciplinary action unless, in the case of staff or experts on mission, the Secretary-General, in lieu of such action, accepts an immediate resignation and a designation that the individual is never to be re-employed by the United Nations is placed in his or her file. . . .

71. It is recommended that the model memorandum of understanding be amended to provide that troop-contributing countries undertake to institute disciplinary action against military members of their contingents found to have violated the standards set out in the 2003 bulletin by means of an investigation conducted in accordance with the recommendations set out in section II above.

Individual Criminal Accountability

Military Members of Contingents   78. Under the model status-of-forces agreement, military members are subject to the criminal authority of the troop-contributing country concerned. Because military members of national contingents are not subject to the criminal jurisdiction of the host State, the model status-of-forces agreement, which has been repeatedly endorsed by the Security Council, specifically envisaged that the Secretary-General would obtain formal assurances from the troop-contributing country concerned that it would exercise jurisdiction with respect to crimes that might be committed by their forces in the mission area (see A/45/594, annex, para. 48). In a footnote to that provision, it was noted that such formal assurances would be inserted into the country-specific memorandum of understanding. The practice of the Organization no longer follows that understanding, but it should. . . .

79. . . . The model memorandum of understanding should also provide that if those authorities conclude that prosecution is not appropriate, the troop-contributing country will submit a report to the Secretary-General explaining why prosecution was not appropriate. The model memorandum of understanding also ought to require the troop-contributing country to agree to inform the Secretary-General within 120 days after a case has been referred to it of measures it has taken under its national law and to inform him of progress achieved every 120 days thereafter until the case is finalized.

80. It must be emphasized that the provisions outlined above do not obligate a troop-contributing country to prosecute. A decision whether or not to prosecute is an act of sovereignty. However, these provisions will require a troop-contributing country to submit the case to the appropriate authorities, who must decide whether or not to prosecute in the same way as they would for an offence of a similar grave nature under their laws in their own jurisdiction. The suggested provisions would also obligate the troop-contributing country to report the outcome of the case in its jurisdiction. . . .

82. The Secretary-General, in his annual report to the Special Committee, should describe in general terms the actions taken by troop-contributing countries in response to cases referred to them. The Secretary-General should, in a separate section of the report, set out the details of cases in which a troop-contributing country failed to inform him of the action taken as a result of the mission's investigation. In such cases the report shall name the troop-contributing country and provide details of the alleged conduct, of course without revealing the identity of the member of the contingent alleged to have committed those acts. . . .

United Nations Staff and Experts on Mission   84. The 1945 United Nations Conference on International Organization decided that personnel of the Organization would be immune from national jurisdiction only with respect to acts performed by them in their official capacity unless that immunity were waived by the United Nations. . . .

85. . . . It further provides that the Secretary-General shall have the right and the duty to waive the immunity of any official in any case where, in his opinion, the immunity would impede the course of justice and can be waived without prejudice to the interests of the United Nations . . ..

86. The practice of the Secretary-General in implementing this provision is clear. If staff or experts on mission commit criminal acts in their duty station and the host State seeks to prosecute, the Secretary-General will first make a determination as to whether the acts in question were performed in the course of official duties. If the acts were not performed in the course of official duties, the Secretary-General will inform the local authorities that no functional immunity exists. . . . If the acts in question have some connection to official duties, such as driving of a United Nations vehicle, while drunk, or if the official enjoys the immunity of a diplomatic envoy and the host State seeks to prosecute, the Secretary-General must waive that immunity if . . . continued immunity would impede the course of justice and where immunity can be waived without prejudice to the interests of the United Nations. This policy, of course, must be rigorously applied in peacekeeping operations to acts of sexual exploitation and abuse that constitute crimes under the laws of the host State. But it must be remembered that not all the acts of sexual exploitation and abuse specified in the 2003 Secretary-General's bulletin constitute crimes under national law; for example, in many jurisdictions purchasing sex from prostitutes over the age of 18 is not a crime.

87. In the great majority of cases the application of the tests in the Convention is clear. What was not anticipated at the time the General Convention was drafted was that the United Nations would, on occasion, be operating in areas where there was no functioning legal system or where the legal system was so devastated by conflict that it no longer satisfied minimum international human rights standards. In such cases it would not be in the interests of the United Nations to waive immunity because its Charter requires it to uphold, promote and respect human rights. In other words, it would not be in the interest of the Organization for the Secretary-General to permit a staff

member to be subjected to a criminal process that did not respect basic international human rights standards.

88. In such cases, making United Nations personnel criminally accountable depends upon whether another State has jurisdiction under its laws to prosecute. A number of States assert criminal jurisdiction over their nationals, but whether an effective prosecution can be launched depends on whether the offence is a crime under the law of the prosecuting State, whether sufficient evidence for prosecution under the applicable substantive and procedural law can be obtained and whether the prosecuting State can obtain custody of the accused. Whether those factors combine to enable prosecution is fortuitous. This is unsatisfactory. The intention of the Organization's founders to make United Nations personnel criminally accountable for their misdeeds may be thwarted.

89. It is not easy to devise a solution. It may be possible to develop an international convention that would subject United Nations personnel to the jurisdiction of States parties for specified crimes committed *by* such personnel (the Convention on the Safety of United Nations and Associated Personnel does this for specified crimes *against* United Nations personnel). The difficulty with this alternative is that it would apply only to the parties to the convention. Another possibility, at least for peacekeeping operations with a rule-of-law mandate from the Security Council, might be to try to get agreement with the host State when negotiating the status-of-forces agreement for the United Nations to provide assistance to the host State to ensure that criminal proceedings against United Nations personnel satisfied international human rights standards. The difficulty with this alternative is that it would be seen as instituting two standards of justice: one for local inhabitants and one for international officials. This is not an attractive proposition. But at least there would be criminal accountability for acts of sexual exploitation and abuse committed by officials and experts on mission that constituted crimes under local law.

As often happens at the United Nations, these recommendations point to the diffusion of responsibility when failure to meet minimal standards of behavior involves "UN" staff. In this instance, peacekeeping troops supplied by member states were primarily involved. Ultimately, poor behavior of such staff needs to be corrected (and prosecuted) by the troop-contributing nations rather than the United Nations itself.

QUESTION

4. In cases where sexual abuse is perpetrated by UN peacekeeping personnel provided by member states, what measures can the United Nations take

to ensure punishment of guilty parties? What policy should be adopted with respect to UN civilian officials?

16.5 The Iraq Oil-for-Food Programme Inquiry

The Oil-for-Food Programme (OFFP) was created as a humanitarian exemption to the comprehensive sanctions imposed on Iraq from 1990. The program was authorized by Security Council resolution 986 (1995), but only became operational in December 1996, seven months after a long-delayed Memorandum of Understanding was concluded between the United Nations and the Government of Iraq. During the seven years of the program, $64 billion of Iraqi oil was exported, of which $37 billion was spent in Iraq on humanitarian relief. ($18 billion was allocated for Iraqi compensation of claims arising from Iraq's invasion of Kuwait; a further 2.2 percent—about $1.4 billion—was reserved for funding UN administration of the program.)

While a degree of leakage and sanctions-busting was anticipated, wholesale flouting of the program's parameters was not. In late 2003 and early 2004, media reports increasingly drew attention not only to possible mismanagement of the OFFP, but also to alleged corruption of UN officials. In response, Kofi Annan in April 2004 created an Independent Inquiry Committee into the OFFP, a decision endorsed by the Security Council in resolution 1534 (2004). The Committee comprised Paul Volcker (former Chair of the US Federal Reserve), Richard Goldstone (a former South African justice and International Criminal Tribunal Prosecutor), and Mark Pieth (an international expert on money-laundering).

The Committee released a series of reports, the most important of which was the third, published in September 2005. This extensive report was covered by a press release, the contents of which were shaped by discussions among the Committee's member themselves and by them with UN Secretary-General Kofi Annan and his deputy Louise Fréchette.

PRESS RELEASE—INDEPENDENT INQUIRY COMMITTEE FINDS MISMANAGEMENT AND FAILURE OF OVERSIGHT: UN MEMBER STATES AND SECRETARIAT SHARE RESPONSIBILITY[8]

The Independent Inquiry Committee today issues its definitive Report on the overall management and oversight of the "temporary" Oil-for-Food Programme, a programme which stretched to seven years with more than $100

[8] For the full report, date 7 September 2005, see www.iic-offp.org.

billion in transactions (over $64 billion in oil sales and approximately $37 billion for food). In preceding interim reports and briefing papers, the Committee has reported the results of its investigations on specific aspects of the Oil-for-Food Programme.

This very large and very complex Programme accomplished many vital goals in Iraq. It reversed a serious and deteriorating food crisis, preventing widespread hunger and probably reducing deaths due to malnutrition. While there were problems with the sporadic delivery of equipment and medical supplies, undoubtedly many lives were saved. At the same time, things went wrong, damaging the reputation and credibility of the United Nations.

With respect to the Programme as a whole, the Committee's central conclusion is that the United Nations requires stronger executive leadership, thoroughgoing administrative reform, and more reliable controls and auditing.

However, responsibility for what went wrong with the Programme cannot be laid exclusively at the door of the Secretariat. Members of the Security Council and its 661 Committee must shoulder their share of the blame in providing uneven and wavering direction in the implementation of the Programme.

What Went Wrong

However well-conceived the Programme was, in principle, the Security Council failed to clearly define the broad parameters, policies and administrative responsibilities for the Programme. This lack of clarity was exacerbated by permitting the Iraqi regime to exercise too much initiative in the Programme design and its subsequent implementation. Compounding that difficulty, the Security Council, in contrast to most past practice, retained through its 661 Committee, substantial elements of administrative control. As a result, neither the Security Council nor the Secretariat leadership was in overall control.

For all that uncertainty, the Secretariat had significant responsibilities in implementing and administering the Programme. As the Chief Administrative Officer of the United Nations, the Secretary-General, in turn, carried oversight and management responsibilities for the entire Secretariat. That included auditing and controls functions that had demonstrable problems with respect to the Programme.

Within the Programme itself, problems arose almost from the start. This report records the reluctance of both the Secretary-General and the Deputy Secretary-General to recognize their own responsibility for the Programme's shortcomings, their failure to ensure that critical evidence was brought to the attention of the Security Council and the 661 Committee, and their minimal efforts to address sanctions violations with Iraqi officials; altogether there was a lack of oversight concerning OIP's administration of the $100 billion Oil-for-Food Programme, and, above all a failure shared by them both to provide oversight of the Programme's Executive Director, Benon Sevan.

In sum, in light of these circumstances, the cumulative management performance of the Secretary-General and the Deputy Secretary-General fell short of the standards that the United Nations Organization should strive to maintain. In making these findings, the Committee has recognized the difficult administrative demands imposed upon the Secretariat and the Secretary-General, both by the design of the Programme and the overlapping Security Council responsibilities.

The Committee's investigation clearly makes the point that, as the Programme expanded and continued, Saddam Hussein found ways and means of turning it to his own advantage, primarily through demands for surcharges and kickbacks from companies doing business with the Programme. For UN agencies, the work went beyond their core competencies of overseeing the distribution of humanitarian goods—from monitoring, planning, and consulting—to infrastructure rebuilding, thus multiplying problems. Nor was there much success in coordinating so large a programme among UN Agencies accustomed to zealously defending their institutional autonomy.

Illicit Income

To put the Programme's flaws and the manipulation by the Saddam Hussein regime into perspective, it is important to note that the regime derived far more revenues from smuggling oil *outside* the Programme than from its demands for surcharges and kickbacks from companies that contracted *within* the Programme. Thousands of vehicles and trucks carried smuggled goods—in both directions across the Iraqi border—with limited, if any, kind of inspection or oversight by the United Nations or, for that matter, member states involved. By the Programme's design, these inspectors were charged only with the inspection of oil and goods that were financed under the Programme. The value of oil smuggled outside of the Programme is estimated by the Committee to be USD 10.99 billion as opposed to an estimated USD 1.8 billion of illicit revenue from Saddam Hussein's manipulation of the Programme.

Kofi and Kojo Annan

In the light of new information relating to *Kojo* Annan's activities to assist Cotecna win the humanitarian goods inspection contract, and a document suggesting that the Secretary-General may have been informed of Cotecna's bid, the Committee reviewed its findings concerning the Secretary-General in its Second Interim Report. After a careful examination of the new information, the Committee has affirmed its prior finding that, weighing all of the information and the credibility of witnesses, the evidence is not reasonably sufficient to conclude that the Secretary-General knew that Cotecna had submitted a bid on the humanitarian inspection contract in 1998.

The Committee also affirms its prior finding that no evidence exists that the Secretary-General influenced, or attempted to influence, the procurement process in 1998 leading to the selection of Cotecna.

As to the adequacy of the Secretary-General's response to press reports in January 1999 of a possible conflict of interest, the Committee re-emphasizes its earlier conclusion that the Secretary-General was not diligent and effective in pursuing an investigation of the procurement of Cotecna. What is now known about Kojo Annan's efforts to intervene in the procurement process, underscores the Committee's prior finding that a thorough and independent investigation of the allegations regarding Kojo Annan's relationship with Cotecna was required in 1999. A resolution of the questions much earlier would likely have resolved the issues arising from the Cotecna bid process and the consequent conflict of interest concerns.

The "Backchannel" and the MOU Negotiations

This Report deals with the negotiations that resulted in the Memorandum of Understanding between the UN and Saddam Hussein. It also records Iraqi attempts to pass money to former Secretary-General Boutros Boutros-Ghali, principally through an Iraqi-American businessman, Samir Vincent, and a Korean lobbyist, Tongsun Park. The Iraqi leadership hoped that Secretary-General Boutros-Ghali would be "more flexible" and would take steps to "ease the conclusion" in the oil-for-food negotiations. The Committee has determined that well over $1 million was paid to Mr. Vincent and Mr. Park. However, the Committee has not found evidence that Secretary-General Boutros-Ghali received or agreed to receive monies from Mr. Park and Mr. Vincent.

Also reported are Iraq's efforts to secure another high-level contact at the United Nations in 1997 when Mr. Park introduced his Iraqi contacts to a Canadian, Maurice Strong—Secretary-General Annan's newly-appointed Executive Coordinator for United Nations Reform. In the course of Mr. Park's relationship with Mr. Strong, he obtained $1 million in cash from his Iraqi contacts which he used to consummate a stock purchase in a company controlled by Strong's family. While there is an indication that Iraqi officials tried to establish a relationship with Mr. Strong, the Committee has found no evidence that Mr. Strong was involved in Iraqi affairs or matters relating to the Programme.

Reform Proposals

On the central matter of United Nations reform, the Committee's investigation leads it to make six major recommendations:

• Create the position of Chief Operating Officer ("COO"). The COO would have authority over all aspects of administration and would be appointed by the General Assembly on the recommendation of the Security Council.

The position would report to the Secretary-General and the United Nations Charter should be amended as appropriate.

- Establish an Independent Oversight Board (IOB) with a majority of independent members. In discharging its mandate, the IOB should have functional responsibility for all independent audit, investigation and evaluation activities, both internal and external, across the United Nations Secretariat and those agencies receiving funds from the United Nations and for which the Secretary-General appoints the executive heads.
- Improve the coordination and the oversight framework for cross-Agency programs.
- Strengthen the quality of the United Nations management and management practices.
- Extend the financial disclosure requirement well below the current assistant secretary-general level within the organization and specifically include the Secretary-General and the Deputy Secretary-General as well as all UN staff who have any decision-making role in the disbursement or award of UN funds (eg. Procurement Department, Office of the Controller).
- Expand and better define the United Nations conflict of interest rules so that they encompass actual, potential and apparent conflicts of interest.
- Agencies involved in a United Nations programme are entitled to reasonable support for "overhead" as well as direct expenses. In the context of the Oil-for-Food Programme, those charges were excessive and the Agencies involved should return up to $ 50 million in excess compensation secured as a result of work performed under Security Council Resolution 1483.

Emphasizing points expressed in the Report's Preface, the Committee's Chairman, Paul A Volcker, stated, "The inescapable conclusion from the Committee's work is that the United Nations Organization needs thoroughgoing reform—and it needs it urgently. What is important—*what has been recognized by one investigation after another*—is that real change must take place, and change over a wide area. Clear benchmarks for measuring progress must be set. The General Assembly should insist, in its forthcoming meeting, that key reforms be put in place no later than the time of its regular meeting in 2006. To settle for less, to permit delay and dilution, would be to invite failure. It would, in reality, further erode public support, undercut effectiveness, and dishonor the ideals upon which the United Nations is built."

He added, "Before concluding its work, the Committee also intends a more comprehensive listing of firms participating in the Programme, either in the purchase of oil or the sale of humanitarian goods, as well as a more detailed analysis of the manner in which Iraq and its vendors and oil purchasers unlawfully manipulated the Programme."

The Committee members were not intimately involved in the drafting of the report but did, as noted above, influence the terms of this press release and some of the report's prefatory paragraphs, placing the responsibility of the Secretary-General and Deputy Secretary-General in a degree of context, and, in particular, weighing it against that of the Security Council. The Committee's staff, adopting a more prosecutorial tone and mode, had largely elided the issue of Security Council oversight of its own Iraq Sanctions Committee (the so-called 661 Committee), in which the widely known sanctions-busting by Turkey and Jordan was supported by the avowed policy of several Council members. Further, the 661 Committee had approved many contracts widely thought to be of dubious compliance with OFFP terms. Sticking narrowly to the mandate set for the IIC, the staff avoided issues of political responsibility and focused instead of bureaucratic responsibility, financial accountability, and corruption, which led to, apparently, some corrective drafting at the request of Committee members. Nevertheless, the media focused overwhelmingly on the sins of omission and commission by UN Secretariat members, including Annan and Fréchette, mostly providing the Security Council with a "free pass."

The Report, in its preface, did point to a particular challenge faced by the Secretary-General:

> The reality is that the Secretary-General has come to be viewed as chief diplomatic and political agent of the United Nations. The present Secretary-General is widely respected for precisely those qualities. In these turbulent times, those responsibilities tend to be all consuming. The record amply reflects consequent administrative failings.

While the appointment of a Chief Operating Officer, leaving the Secretary-General free to devote himself full-time to his diplomatic responsibilities, could serve to improve accountability at the top, the Charter and most member states do not appear to regard the Secretary-General's diplomatic and administrative responsibilities as quite so severable.

QUESTION

5. The IIC convincingly held Secretary-General Annan, his deputy, and several other officials to account for their failures of oversight of the Iraq OFFP. How might member states, particularly those in the Security Council, also be held accountable for their parallel failures of oversight or in some cases for their active collusion with sanctions-busting?

Further Reading

Byers, Michael, and Simon Chesterman, "Changing the Rules About Rules? Unilateral Humanitarian Intervention and the Future of International Law." In *Humanitarian*

Intervention: Ethical, Legal and Political Dilemmas," edited by J. L. Holzgrefe and Robert O. Keohane. Cambridge: Cambridge University Press, 2003, pp. 177–203.

Chesterman, Simon. *You, the People: The United Nations, Transitional Administration, and State-Building.* Oxford: Oxford University Press, 2004, pp. 126–153.

Franck, Thomas M. *Recourse to Force: State Action Against Threats and Armed Attacks.* Cambridge: Cambridge University Press, 2002, pp. 1–19.

Malone, David M. *The International Struggle for Iraq: Politics in the UN Security Council, 1980–2005.* Oxford: Oxford University Press, 2006, pp. 114–151.

Meyer, Jeffrey A., and Mark G. Califano. *Good Intentions Corrupted: The Oil-for-Food Scandal and the Threat to the UN.* New York: Public Affairs, 2006.

Power, Samantha. *A Problem from Hell: America and the Age of Genocide.* New York: Basic Books, 2002, pp.247–327.

Roberts, Adam, and Richard Guelff. *Documents on the Laws of War.* 3rd edn. Oxford: Oxford University Press, 2000, pp. 1–46.

Wheeler, Nicholas J. *Saving Strangers: Humanitarian Intervention in International Society.* Oxford: Oxford University Press, 2000, pp. 208–241.

Zwanenburg, Marten. *Accountability of Peace Support Operations: International Humanitarian Law.* Heidelberg: Springer Books, 2005.

chapter seventeen

....

Reform

In addition to the perennial problems of dysfunctional institutions, inadequate resources, and ephemeral political will, the United Nations has always faced crises of expectations. At the beginning of the 1990s the United States, while proclaiming itself the victor of the Cold War, magnanimously asserted that this provided an opportunity for the United Nations to fulfill its long-promised role as the guardian of international peace and security. The Security Council saw new possibilities for action without the paralyzing veto; Secretary-General Boutros Boutros-Ghali laid out grand plans with *An Agenda for Peace*. In the words of US President George H. W. Bush the rule of law would supplant "the rule of the jungle."[1]

The rhetoric was euphoric, utopian, and short-lived. International security issues continued to be resolved by reference to Great Power interests; economic development attracted more speeches than resources. (Indeed, global development assistance levels dropped sharply in the 1990s.) Rhetoric has its own significance, however, and the language of human rights and the rule of law became more accepted through this period, as was the principle of greater international engagement in areas previously considered to lie solely within the domestic jurisdiction of member states. Whether such principles should be supported by action remained a bone of some contention.

In this context, discussion of reform has always begged the question of whether that reform must take place primarily in the structures, procedures, and personnel that make up the United Nations, or in the willingness of member states to use them. Past efforts at creating and reshaping the international institutions to promote peace and security have tended to be driven by political will, which is most plentiful in a time of crisis. The First World War was the backdrop for establishment of the League of Nations; the League's failure to prevent the Second World War led to its replacement by the

---

[1] George H. W. Bush, "Address Before a Joint Session of the Congress on the Persian Gulf Crisis and the Federal Budget Deficit," 11 September 1990.

United Nations. Importantly, US President Franklin Roosevelt pushed for the negotiation of the UN Charter to be held in San Francisco while the bombs of the Second World War were still falling. Unlike the Covenant of the League of Nations, which was negotiated as one agreement among many at Versailles in 1919, the UN Charter was the main event in San Francisco and its references to "the scourge of war" were reinforced by daily reports of final battles in the worldwide conflict.

For some, the US-led invasion of Iraq in March 2003 represented a similar challenge not merely to the institutions but to the very idea of international order. The war split the Security Council, divided NATO and the European Union, and prompted the creation of a high-level panel to rethink the very idea of collective security in a world dominated by US military power.[2] In the wake of the Iraq war, anxiety concerning the role and relevance of the United Nations was widespread. But leadership on the reform agenda came, unusually, from the Secretary-General. It was Kofi Annan who appointed the High-Level Panel on Threats, Challenges, and Change, which attempted to grapple with legitimate US security concerns while broadening discussion of international threats beyond its counter-terrorism and non-proliferation agenda. He had already commissioned Jeffrey Sachs's UN Millennium Project to propose strategies for achieving the Millennium Development Goals.[3] And in March 2005 these security and development agendas were joined by a third, human rights, in a Secretary-General's report unusual for its ambition.

That report, *In Larger Freedom*, was intended to set both the tone and the substantive agenda for the sixtieth General Assembly, which included a Summit of Heads of State on 14–16 September 2005. The report was broad in scope, seeking to define a new security consensus based on the interdependence of threats and responses, and narrow in detail, setting specific targets for official development assistance, calling for the creation of a Peacebuilding Commission, and outlining a long-awaited definition of terrorism. On the most contested political question of Security Council expansion, however, the report endorsed the fence-sitting position of the High-Level Panel, laying out options but not choosing between them, while urging member states to take a decision on Council expansion even if consensus was not possible.[4] Such discretion did not detract from larger anomalies in this approach: that the Secretary-General was trying to use reform to generate political will rather than reflect it, and that he was taking a lead role just when his political and moral credibility was being called into question by allegations of corruption and mismanagement in the Oil-for-Food Programme.

---

[2] The Report of the High-Level Panel is also discussed in chapters 1, 4, 9, and 13.

[3] Investing in Development: A Practical Plan to Achieve the Millennium Development Goals (Report of the UN Millennium Project to the Secretary-General) (17 January 2005), available at http://www.unmillenniumproject.org/reports.

[4] In Larger Freedom: Towards Development, Security, and Human Rights for All, UN Doc. A/59/2005 (21 March 2005), available at http://www.un.org/largerfreedom.

This chapter examines the context within which reform of the United Nations takes place, examining first the Charter and two commonly bemoaned constraints: the membership of the Security Council and the veto power of its permanent members. The chapter then turns to larger questions of political will, looking at efforts to articulate new visions of international cooperation by experts, UN officials, and the representatives of member states.

17.1 The Charter

As suggested in the Introduction, the Charter bears many similarities to a constitution. And, like most constitutions, it is designed to be difficult to amend.[5]

UN CHARTER

Article 108

Amendments to the present Charter shall come into force for all Members of the United Nations when they have been adopted by a vote of two thirds of the members of the General Assembly and ratified in accordance with their respective constitutional processes by two thirds of the Members of the United Nations, including all the permanent members of the Security Council.

Article 109

1. A General Conference of the Members of the United Nations for the purpose of reviewing the present Charter may be held at a date and place to be fixed by a two-thirds vote of the members of the General Assembly and by a vote of any seven members of the Security Council. Each Member of the United Nations shall have one vote in the conference.

2. Any alteration of the present Charter recommended by a two-thirds vote of the conference shall take effect when ratified in accordance with their respective constitutional processes by two thirds of the Members of the United Nations including all the permanent members of the Security Council.

3. If such a conference has not been held before the tenth annual session of the General Assembly following the coming into force of the present Charter,

---

[5] See the discussion of whether the Charter might be considered a constitution in the Introduction to this volume.

the proposal to call such a conference shall be placed on the agenda of that session of the General Assembly, and the conference shall be held if so decided by a majority vote of the members of the General Assembly and by a vote of any seven members of the Security Council.

The three Charter amendments to date all took place between 1963 and 1973. The first expanded Security Council membership from eleven to fifteen and increased the number of votes necessary to pass a resolution from seven to nine; it also expanded the membership of the Economic and Social Council (ECOSOC) from eighteen to twenty-seven. The second corrected the amendment procedures themselves, in line with the increased size of the Security Council, requiring that nine (rather than seven) members be required to support a call for a General Conference of member states for the purposes of reviewing the Charter. The third further increased the membership of ECOSOC from twenty-seven to fifty-four.

QUESTIONS

1. Do the permanent members of the Security Council have a veto over amending the Charter?
2. It is sometimes said that debate over UN reform is intractable because, like academic politics, the stakes are so small. Does UN reform matter?

17.2 Institutions: The Security Council

Since the Security Council is widely seen as the most influential part of the UN system, much discussion of reform focuses on its membership. In 1993, the General Assembly established an open-ended working group (that is, open to all members of the United Nations) to consider, among other things, the question of increasing Council membership.[6] More than a decade into its deliberations there is still no agreement on an appropriate formula for Security Council representation and the body is jokingly referred to as the "never-ending working group." Issues of general consensus are that the Council should be expanded and probably include new permanent members—but perhaps without granting newcomers the coveted veto, currently held by only the P-5.

In March 1997, Razali Ismail, chairman of the working group, presented a paper synthesizing the majority view on expansion of the Security Council.

---

[6] GA Res. 48/26 (1993).

Now known as the "Razali Plan," it proposed increasing Council membership from fifteen to twenty-four by adding five permanent members (one each from the developing states of Africa, Asia, and Latin America and the Caribbean, and two from the industrialized states—generally recognized as Germany and Japan) and four non-permanent members (one each from Africa, Asia, Eastern Europe, and Latin America and the Caribbean). Though unable to generate much enthusiasm, the Razali Plan became the benchmark for other reform proposals.[7]

REPORT OF THE HIGH-LEVEL PANEL ON THREATS, CHALLENGES, AND CHANGE: A MORE SECURE WORLD: OUR SHARED RESPONSIBILITY, 1 DECEMBER 2004[8]

244. The founders of the United Nations conferred primary responsibility on the Security Council for the maintenance of international peace and security. The Security Council was designed to enable the world body to act decisively to prevent and remove threats. It was created to be not just a representative but a responsible body, one that had the capacity for decisive action. The five permanent members were given veto rights but were also expected to shoulder an extra burden in promoting global security. Article 23 of the Charter of the United Nations established that membership in the Council as a whole was explicitly linked not just to geographical balance but also to contributions to maintaining peace and security.

245. Since the Council was formed the threats and challenges to international peace and security have changed, as has the distribution of power among members. But the Security Council has been slow to change. Decisions cannot be implemented just by members of the Security Council but require extensive military, financial and political involvement by other States. Decisions taken and mandates given have often lacked the essential components of realism, adequate resources and the political determination to see them through. The Secretary-General is frequently holding out a begging bowl to implement Security Council decisions. Moreover, the paucity of representation from the broad membership diminishes support for Security Council decisions.

246. Since the end of the cold war, the effectiveness of the Council has improved, as has its willingness to act; but it has not always been equitable in

---

[7] Paper by the Chairman of the Open-Ended Working Group on the Question of Equitable Representation on and Increase in the Membership of the Security Council and Other Matters Related to the Security Council, 20 March 1997.
[8] UN Doc. A/59/565 (2004).

its actions, nor has it acted consistently or effectively in the face of genocide or other atrocities. This has gravely damaged its credibility. The financial and military contributions to the United Nations of some of the five permanent members are modest compared to their special status, and often the Council's non-permanent members have been unable to make the necessary contribution to the work of the Organization envisaged by the Charter. Even outside the use of a formal veto, the ability of the five permanent members to keep critical issues of peace and security off the Security Council's agenda has further undermined confidence in the body's work.

247. Yet recent experience has also shown that the Security Council is the body in the United Nations most capable of organizing action and responding rapidly to new threats.

248. Thus, the challenge for any reform is to increase both the effectiveness and the credibility of the Security Council and, most importantly, to enhance its capacity and willingness to act in the face of threats. This requires greater involvement in Security Council decision-making by those who contribute most; greater contributions from those with special decision-making authority; and greater consultation with those who must implement its decisions. It also requires a firm consensus on the nature of today's threats, on the obligations of broadened collective security, on the necessity of prevention, and on when and why the Council should authorize the use of force.

249. We believe that reforms of the Security Council should meet the following principles:

(a) They should, in honouring Article 23 of the Charter of the United Nations, increase the involvement in decision-making of those who contribute most to the United Nations financially, militarily and diplomatically—specifically in terms of contributions to United Nations assessed budgets, participation in mandated peace operations, contributions to voluntary activities of the United Nations in the areas of security and development, and diplomatic activities in support of United Nations objectives and mandates. Among developed countries, achieving or making substantial progress towards the internationally agreed level of 0.7 per cent of GNP for ODA should be considered an important criterion of contribution;

(b) They should bring into the decision-making process countries more representative of the broader membership, especially of the developing world;

(c) They should not impair the effectiveness of the Security Council;

(d) They should increase the democratic and accountable nature of the body.

250. The Panel believes that a decision on the enlargement of the Council, satisfying these criteria, is now a necessity. The presentation of two clearly defined alternatives, of the kind described below as models A and B, should help to clarify—and perhaps bring to resolution—a debate which has made little progress in the last 12 years.

251. Models A and B both involve a distribution of seats as between four major regional areas, which we identify respectively as "Africa," "Asia and Pacific," "Europe" and "Americas." We see these descriptions as helpful in making and implementing judgements about the composition of the Security Council, but make no recommendation about changing the composition of the current regional groups for general electoral and other United Nations purposes. Some members of the Panel, in particular our Latin American colleagues, expressed a preference for basing any distribution of seats on the current regional groups.

252. Model A provides for six new permanent seats, with no veto being created, and three new two-year term non-permanent seats, divided among the major regional areas as follows:

Model A

Regional area	No. of States	Permanent seats (continuing)	Proposed new permanent seats	Proposed two-year seats (non-renewable)	Total
Africa	53	0	2	4	6
Asia and Pacific	56	1	2	3	6
Europe	47	3	1	2	6
Americas	35	1	1	4	6
Totals model A	191	5	6	13	24

253. Model B provides for no new permanent seats but creates a new category of eight four-year renewable-term seats and one new two-year non-permanent (and non-renewable) seat, divided among the major regional areas as follows:

Model A

Regional area	No. of States	Permanent seats (continuing)	Proposed four-year renewable seats	Proposed two-year seats (non-renewable)	Total
Africa	53	0	2	4	6
Asia and Pacific	56	1	2	3	6
Europe	47	3	2	1	6
Americas	35	1	2	3	6
Totals model B	191	5	8	11	24

254. In both models, having regard to Article 23 of the Charter of the United Nations, a method of encouraging Member States to contribute more

to international peace and security would be for the General Assembly, taking into account established practices of regional consultation, to elect Security Council members by giving preference for permanent or longer-term seats to those States that are among the top three financial contributors in their relevant regional area to the regular budget, or the top three voluntary contributors from their regional area, or the top three troop contributors from their regional area to United Nations peacekeeping missions.

255. The Panel was strongly of the view that no change to the composition of the Security Council should itself be regarded as permanent or unchallengeable in the future. Therefore, there should be a review of the composition of the Security Council in 2020, including, in this context, a review of the contribution (as defined in para. 249 above) of permanent and non-permanent members from the point of view of the Council's effectiveness in taking collective action to prevent and remove new and old threats to international peace and security.

Germany, Japan, India, and Brazil swiftly constituted themselves as a candidate group for permanent seats but there was some division over which African states should be selected, in particular as between South Africa, Nigeria, and Egypt. This combined with resistance from other members—both permanent members wary of diluting their powers, and other members suspicious of the value to them of neighbors receiving permanent seats on a body to which they might only occasionally aspire—meant that agreement was impossible.

QUESTIONS

3. Should the Council be more representative of the membership of the United Nations? Why, or why not—and what reform might best achieve this goal?
4. Would making the Council more representative make it more effective? Should a trade-off be considered? Can it be avoided?

17.3 Procedures: The Veto

The veto power of the five permanent members of the Security Council is sometimes cited as a barrier to the effectiveness of the United Nations. As Article 108 makes clear, however, any proposal to abolish or modify it would require endorsement by those five permanent members. Various efforts have been made to circumvent this requirement or at least limit the impact of the veto.

INTERNATIONAL COMMISSION ON INTERVENTION AND STATE SOVEREIGNTY, THE RESPONSIBILITY TO PROTECT, DECEMBER 2001

6.19 A common theme in a great many of the Commission's consultations was the democratic legitimacy of the fifteen-member Security Council, which can hardly claim to be representative of the realities of the modern era so long as it excludes from permanent membership countries of major size and influence, in particular from Africa, Asia and Latin America. The Security Council was also variously claimed to be neither answerable to the peoples of the world, nor accountable to the plenary General Assembly nor subject to juridical supervision and scrutiny. There is no doubt that reform of the Security Council, in particular to broaden and make more genuinely representative its composition, would help in building its credibility and authority—though not necessarily making the decision making process any easier. But this is not a debate into which this Commission need enter for the purposes of this report.

6.20 An issue which we cannot avoid addressing, however, is that of the veto power enjoyed by the present Permanent Five. Many of our interlocutors regarded capricious use of the veto, or threat of its use, as likely to be the principal obstacle to effective international action in cases where quick and decisive action is needed to stop or avert a significant humanitarian crisis. As has been said, it is unconscionable that one veto can override the rest of humanity on matters of grave humanitarian concern. Of particular concern is the possibility that needed action will be held hostage to unrelated concerns of one or more of the permanent members—a situation that has too frequently occurred in the past. There is another political problem. Those states who insist on the right to retaining permanent membership of the UN Security Council and the resulting veto power, are in a difficult position when they claim to be entitled to act outside the UN framework as a result of the Council being paralyzed by a veto cast by another permanent member. That is, those who insist on keeping the existing rules of the game unchanged have a correspondingly less compelling claim to rejecting any specific outcome when the game is played by those very rules.

6.21 For all these reasons, the Commission supports the proposal put to us in an exploratory way by a senior representative of one of the Permanent Five countries, that there be agreed by the Permanent Five a "code of conduct" for the use of the veto with respect to actions that are needed to stop or avert a significant humanitarian crisis. The idea essentially is that a permanent member, in matters where its vital national interests were not claimed to be involved, would not use its veto to obstruct the passage of what would otherwise be a majority resolution. The expression "constructive abstention" has been used in this context in the past. It is unrealistic to imagine any amendment of the Charter happening any time soon so far as the veto power and its distribution are concerned. But the adoption by the permanent members of a more formal, mutually agreed practice to govern these situations in the future would be a very healthy development.

REPORT OF THE HIGH-LEVEL PANEL ON THREATS, CHALLENGES, AND CHANGE: A MORE SECURE WORLD: OUR SHARED RESPONSIBILITY, 1 DECEMBER 2004[9]

256. . . . We recognize that the veto had an important function in reassuring the United Nations most powerful members that their interests would be safeguarded. We see no practical way of changing the existing members' veto powers. Yet, as a whole the institution of the veto has an anachronistic character that is unsuitable for the institution in an increasingly democratic age and we would urge that its use be limited to matters where vital interests are genuinely at stake. We also ask the permanent members, in their individual capacities, to pledge themselves to refrain from the use of the veto in cases of genocide and large-scale human rights abuses. We recommend that under any reform proposal, there should be no expansion of the veto.

257. We propose the introduction of a system of "indicative voting," whereby members of the Security Council could call for a public indication of positions on a proposed action. Under this indicative vote, "no" votes would not have a veto effect, nor would the final tally of the vote have any legal force. The second formal vote on any resolution would take place under the current procedures of the Council. This would, we believe, increase the accountability of the veto function.

258. In recent years, many informal improvements have been made to the transparency and accountability of the Security Council's deliberative and decision-making procedures. We also remind the Security Council that troop contributors have rights under Article 44 of the Charter to be fully consulted concerning the deployment of troops to Council-mandated operations. We recommend that processes to improve transparency and accountability be incorporated and formalized in the Council's rules of procedure.

259. Many delegations on the Security Council lack access to professional military advice. Yet they are frequently called upon to take decisions with far-ranging military implications. We recommend therefore that the Secretary-

---

[9] UN Doc. A/59/565 (2004).

General's Military Adviser and the members of his staff be available on demand by the Security Council to offer technical and professional advice on military options.

260. We welcome greater civil society engagement in the work of the Security Council.

None of these reforms was adopted, and the Council continues to operate under "provisional" rules of procedure.

QUESTIONS

5. Is it possible to abolish the veto? What other mechanisms might limit its impact on Council decision making? What lessons, if any, may be drawn from the acceptance that abstention by a permanent member is not regarded as a failure to "concur" within the meaning of Article 27(3) of the UN Charter?
6. Is reform most needed in the institutions and procedures of the United Nations, or in the willingness of states to use them? Which type of change is more difficult?

17.4 Political Will: Interdependence of Threats

Underlying questions of reform of the United Nations are different visions of its role in addressing distinct species of threat. In 2004 the High-Level Panel explored the possibility that the United Nations could bridge these distinct threats.

REPORT OF THE HIGH-LEVEL PANEL ON THREATS, CHALLENGES, AND CHANGE: A MORE SECURE WORLD: OUR SHARED RESPONSIBILITY, 1 DECEMBER 2004[10]

1. The United Nations was created in a spirit of optimism fuelled by the end of the Second World War and the will to avoid a repeat of its horrors and those of its predecessor. For many of the States most traumatized by two world wars, the experiment has been successful. Over the subsequent 60

---

[10] UN Doc. A/59/565 (2004).

years, many parts of the world have enjoyed unparalleled peace and prosperity. The dynamics and tensions that led to the Second World War were laid to rest, war between the great Powers was avoided and a stable peace emerged in Europe. Japan, Germany and Italy were successfully integrated into the family of nations and are currently the second, third and sixth largest financial contributors to the United Nations.

2. In the first 30 years of the United Nations, dozens of new States emerged from colonial systems that, until recent times, tied half of mankind to a handful of capitals. Assisting new States into being was a seminal contribution of the United Nations during this period. Decolonization in turn transformed the United Nations. At the creation of the United Nations in 1945, there were 51 members; today there are 191. The General Assembly was transformed from a body composed of States that largely resembled one another to one whose membership varied dramatically. By the mid-1960s, developing countries formed a majority in the General Assembly and through it gained a voice in international politics largely denied to them outside the institution.

3. The second half of the twentieth century was a struggle for the viability of these new States and the well-being of their citizens. They inherited arbitrary colonial boundaries and colonial economies designed to serve the needs of the metropole. Independence was the start of a race to educate and develop the professional, scientific and technological expertise to run modern States and economies. All of this took place in an era of huge expectations about what States could and should deliver, when most models of economic growth relied on heavy State control.

4. In the last 40 years, life expectancy in developing countries has increased by 20 years, and per capita income has doubled in such countries as Botswana, Brazil, China, the Republic of Korea and Turkey in less than a third of the time it took to do so in the United Kingdom or the United States a century or more earlier. Despite such progress, however, large parts of the world remained mired in life-threatening poverty. Between 1975 and 1999, sub-Saharan Africa saw no overall increase in its per capita income.

5. By the 1980s, many of these new States faced crises of State capacity and legitimacy, reflected in the rise of internal wars as the dominant form of warfare in the second half of the twentieth century.

6. As we enter the twenty-first century, these struggles are far from over. More than a billion people lack access to clean water, more than two billion have no access to adequate sanitation and more than three million die every year from water-related diseases. Fourteen million people, including six million children, die every year from hunger. There were 842 million undernourished people in 2000; 95 per cent lived in poor countries.

7. Almost 30 million people in Africa now have HIV/AIDS. In the worst-affected States, middle-aged urban elites are heavily afflicted, eroding State capacity and decimating the economic activity of what should be a State's most productive group. The increasing number of infected women and girls is threatening food and agricultural production. If trends are not reversed,

some of these States face collapse under the combined weight of poverty a.
HIV/AIDS.

8. Decolonization was only one of the forces that shaped the United Nations. The United Nations founders did not anticipate that the United States and the former Soviet Union would soon embark on a global rivalry, developing and deploying tens of thousands of nuclear weapons capable of destroying the world many times over.

9. Controlling the destructive capability of nuclear technology and harnessing its promise became central to the work of the United Nations. The very first resolution adopted by the General Assembly in 1946 called for the disarmament of "weapons adaptable to mass destruction."

10. The cold war shaped much of global politics for the next 45 years. The rivalry between the United States and the former Soviet Union blocked the Security Council from playing a dominant role in maintaining international peace and security. Nearly all armed conflicts and struggles for liberation were viewed through the prism of East-West rivalry until the historic collapse of the former Soviet Union and the end of communist rule in Eastern Europe.

11. Nonetheless, without the United Nations the post-1945 world would very probably have been a bloodier place. There were fewer inter-State wars in the last half of the twentieth century than in the first half. Given that during the same period the number of States grew almost fourfold, one might have expected to see a marked rise in inter-State wars. Yet that did not occur and the United Nations contributed to that result. The United Nations diminished the threat of inter-State war in several ways. Peace was furthered by the invention of peacekeeping; diplomacy was carried out by the Secretary-General; disputes were remedied under the International Court of Justice; and a strong norm was upheld against aggressive war.

12. The dramatic but peaceful end of the cold war opened an opportunity for collective security to flourish. The first years after the end of the cold war seemed to point towards a new role for the United Nations. In 1990, the Security Council authorized the use of force against Iraq to liberate Kuwait. The Security Council broadened the interpretation of threats to international peace and security to authorize an intervention for humanitarian purposes in Somalia. The United Nations helped bring to an end several protracted wars in Central America and Southern Africa.

13. The moment was short-lived. It quickly became apparent that the United Nations had exchanged the shackles of the cold war for the straitjacket of Member State complacency and great Power indifference. Although the United Nations gave birth to the notion of human security, it proved poorly equipped to provide it. Long-standing regional conflicts, such as those involving Israel/Palestine and Kashmir, remained unresolved. Failures to act in the face of ethnic cleansing and genocide in Rwanda and Bosnia eroded international support. Optimism yielded to renewed cynicism about the willingness of Member States to support the Organization.

14. The terrorist attacks of 11 September 2001 on New York and Washington, D.C., brought with them a glimpse of the potential for renewed

collective security. On 12 September 2001, France introduced and the Security Council unanimously passed resolution 1368 (2001), which condemned the attacks and opened the way for United States-led military action against the Taliban regime in self-defence. On the same day, the General Assembly condemned terrorism and the attacks. On 28 September 2001, the Security Council adopted resolution 1373 (2001), which obligates all Member States, under Chapter VII of the Charter of the United Nations, to take specific actions to combat terrorism. Three months later, the United Nations presided over the Bonn Agreement, which created an interim government to replace the deposed Taliban regime. The United Nations stood behind the interim government in Afghanistan as custodian of the peace process and helped to draft the country's new constitution.

15. This spirit of international purpose lasted only months and was eroded by divisions over the United States-led war in Iraq in 2003.

16. The attacks of 11 September 2001 revealed that States, as well as collective security institutions, have failed to keep pace with changes in the nature of threats. The technological revolution that has radically changed the worlds of communication, information-processing, health and transportation has eroded borders, altered migration and allowed individuals the world over to share information at a speed inconceivable two decades ago. Such changes have brought many benefits but also great potential for harm. Smaller and smaller numbers of people are able to inflict greater and greater amounts of damage, without the support of any State. A new threat, transnational organized crime, undermines the rule of law within and across borders. Technologies designed to improve daily life can be transformed into instruments of aggression. We have yet to fully understand the impact of these changes, but they herald a fundamentally different security climate—one whose unique opportunities for cooperation are matched by an unprecedented scope for destruction.

II. The Case for Comprehensive Collective Security

A. Threats Without Boundaries

17. Today, more than ever before, threats are interrelated and a threat to one is a threat to all. The mutual vulnerability of weak and strong has never been clearer.

18. Global economic integration means that a major terrorist attack anywhere in the developed world would have devastating consequences for the well-being of millions of people in the developing world. The World Bank estimates that the attacks of 11 September 2001 alone increased the number of people living in poverty by 10 million; the total cost to the world economy probably exceeded 80 billion dollars. These numbers would be far surpassed by an incident involving nuclear terrorism.

19. Similarly, the security of the most affluent State can be held hostage to the ability of the poorest State to contain an emerging disease. Because in-

ternational flight times are shorter than the incubation periods for many infectious diseases, any one of 700 million international airline passengers every year can be an unwitting global disease-carrier. Severe acute respiratory syndrome (SARS) spread to more than 8,000 people in 30 countries in three months, killing almost 700. The influenza pandemic of 1919 killed as many as 100 million people, far more than the First World War, over a period of a little more than a year. Today, a similar virus could kill tens of millions in a fraction of the time.

20. Every threat to international security today enlarges the risk of other threats. Nuclear proliferation by States increases the availability of the materiel and technology necessary for a terrorist to acquire a nuclear weapon. The ability of non-State actors to traffic in nuclear materiel and technology is aided by ineffective State control of borders and transit through weak States.

21. International terrorist groups prey on weak States for sanctuary. Their recruitment is aided by grievances nurtured by poverty, foreign occupation and the absence of human rights and democracy; by religious and other intolerance; and by civil violence—a witch's brew common to those areas where civil war and regional conflict intersect. In recent years, terrorists have helped to finance their activities and moved large sums of money by gaining access to such valuable commodities as drugs in countries beset by civil war.

22. Poverty, infectious disease, environmental degradation and war feed one another in a deadly cycle. Poverty (as measured by per capita gross domestic product (GDP)) is strongly associated with the outbreak of civil war. Such diseases as malaria and HIV/AIDS continue to cause large numbers of deaths and reinforce poverty. Disease and poverty, in turn, are connected to environmental degradation; climate change exacerbates the occurrence of such infectious disease as malaria and dengue fever. Environmental stress, caused by large populations and shortages of land and other natural resources, can contribute to civil violence.

23. Transnational organized crime facilitates many of the most serious threats to international peace and security. Corruption, illicit trade and money-laundering contribute to State weakness, impede economic growth and undermine democracy. These activities thus create a permissive environment for civil conflict. The prospect of organized criminal groups providing nuclear, radiological, chemical or biological weapons to terrorists is particularly worrying. Increasing drug trade partly accounts for rapidly increasing levels of HIV/AIDS infections, especially in Eastern Europe and parts of Asia. And organized criminal activities undermine peacebuilding efforts and fuel many civil wars through illicit trade in conflict commodities and small arms.

B. The Limits of Self-Protection

24. No State, no matter how powerful, can by its own efforts alone make itself invulnerable to today's threats. Every State requires the cooperation of other States to make itself secure. It is in every State's interest, accordingly, to cooperate with other States to address their most pressing threats, because

doing so will maximize the chances of reciprocal cooperation to address its own threat priorities.

25. Take, as one example, the threat of nuclear terrorism. Experts estimate that terrorists with 50 kilograms of highly enriched uranium (HEU), an amount that would fit into six one-litre milk cartons, need only smuggle it across borders in order to create an improvised nuclear device that could level a medium-sized city. Border controls will not provide adequate defence against this threat. To overcome the threat of nuclear terrorism requires the cooperation of States, strong and weak, to clean up stockpiles of HEU, better protect shipping containers at ports and agree on new rules regulating the enrichment of uranium. Cooperation in the sharing of intelligence by States is essential for stopping terrorism.

26. Similarly, in order to stop organized crime States must cooperate to fight money-laundering, trafficking in drugs and persons, and corruption. International efforts to stem the problem are only as strong as the weakest link. Ineffective collective security institutions diminish the security of every region and State.

27. The most robust defence against the possible terrorist use of nuclear, chemical or biological weapons would seek to control dangerous materials, deter and capture terrorists, and address the broader threats that increase the risk of terrorist action. Civil war, disease and poverty increase the likelihood of State collapse and facilitate the spread of organized crime, thus also increasing the risk of terrorism and proliferation due to weak States and weak collective capacity to exercise the rule of law. Preventing mass-casualty terrorism requires a deep engagement to strengthen collective security systems, ameliorate poverty, combat extremism, end the grievances that flow from war, tackle the spread of infectious disease and fight organized crime.

28. Thus all States have an interest in forging a new comprehensive collective security system that will commit all of them to act cooperatively in the face of a broad array of threats.

C. Sovereignty and Responsibility

29. In signing the Charter of the United Nations, States not only benefit from the privileges of sovereignty but also accept its responsibilities. Whatever perceptions may have prevailed when the Westphalian system first gave rise to the notion of State sovereignty, today it clearly carries with it the obligation of a State to protect the welfare of its own peoples and meet its obligations to the wider international community. But history teaches us all too clearly that it cannot be assumed that every State will always be able, or willing, to meet its responsibilities to protect its own people and avoid harming its neighbours. And in those circumstances, the principles of collective security mean that some portion of those responsibilities should be taken up by the international community, acting in accordance with the Charter of the United Nations and the Universal Declaration of Human Rights, to help build the necessary capacity or supply the necessary protection, as the case may be.

30. What we seek to protect reflects what we value. The Charter of the United Nations seeks to protect all States, not because they are intrinsically good but because they are necessary to achieve the dignity, justice, worth and safety of their citizens. These are the values that should be at the heart of any collective security system for the twenty-first century, but too often States have failed to respect and promote them. The collective security we seek to build today asserts a shared responsibility on the part of all States and international institutions, and those who lead them, to do just that.

D. Elements of a Credible Collective Security System

31. To be credible and sustainable a collective security system must be effective, efficient and equitable. In all these respects, the multilateral system as we now know it, in responding to the major security threats which the world has confronted in recent decades, has shown that it can perform. But it must be strengthened to perform better—in all the ways we spell out in the present report.

1. Effectiveness   32. Whether by reducing the demand for nuclear weapons, mediating inter-State conflict or ending civil wars, collective security institutions have made critical contributions to the maintenance of international peace and security, although those contributions are often denigrated, both by those who would have the institutions do more and by those who would have them do less.

33. Collective security institutions are rarely effective in isolation. Multilateral institutions normally operate alongside national, regional and sometimes civil society actors, and are most effective when these efforts are aligned to common goals. This is as true of mediation as it is of post-conflict reconstruction, poverty-reduction strategies and non-proliferation measures.

34. States are still the front-line responders to today's threats. Successful international actions to battle poverty, fight infectious disease, stop transnational crime, rebuild after civil war, reduce terrorism and halt the spread of dangerous materials all require capable, responsible States as partners. It follows that greater effort must be made to enhance the capacity of States to exercise their sovereignty responsibly. For all those in a position to help others build that capacity, it should be part of *their* responsibility to do so.

35. Collective action often fails, sometimes dramatically so. Collective instruments are often hampered by a lack of compliance, erratic monitoring and verification, and weak enforcement. Early warning is only effective when it leads to early action for prevention. Monitoring and verification work best when they are treated as complements to, not substitutes for, enforcement.

36. Collective security institutions have proved particularly poor at meeting the challenge posed by large-scale, gross human rights abuses and genocide. This is a normative challenge to the United Nations: the concept of State and international responsibility to protect civilians from the effects of war and human rights abuses has yet to truly overcome the tension between the competing claims of sovereign inviolability and the right to intervene. It is

also an operational challenge: the challenge of stopping a Government from killing its own civilians requires considerable military deployment capacity.

2. Efficiency 37. Some collective security instruments have been efficient. As the institutional embodiment of the Treaty on the Non-Proliferation of Nuclear Weapons and of considerable long-term success in preventing widespread proliferation of nuclear weapons, the International Atomic Energy Agency (IAEA)—with its regular budget of less than $275 million—stands out as an extraordinary bargain. Similarly, the Secretary-General's mediation efforts, though grossly underresourced, have helped reduce international tensions.

38. But more collective security instruments have been inefficient. Post-conflict operations, for example, have too often been characterized by countless ill-coordinated and overlapping bilateral and United Nations programmes, with inter-agency competition preventing the best use of scarce resources.

39. The biggest source of inefficiency in our collective security institutions has simply been an unwillingness to get serious about preventing deadly violence. The failure to invest time and resources early in order to prevent the outbreak and escalation of conflicts leads to much larger and deadlier conflagrations that are much costlier to handle later.

3. Equity 40. The credibility of any system of collective security also depends on how well it promotes security for all its members, without regard to the nature of would-be beneficiaries, their location, resources or relationship to great Powers.

41. Too often, the United Nations and its Member States have discriminated in responding to threats to international security. Contrast the swiftness with which the United Nations responded to the attacks on 11 September 2001 with its actions when confronted with a far more deadly event: from April to mid-July 1994, Rwanda experienced the equivalent of three 11 September 2001 attacks every day for 100 days, all in a country whose population was one thirty-sixth that of the United States. Two weeks into the genocide, the Security Council withdrew most of its peacekeepers from the country. It took almost a month for United Nations officials to call it a genocide and even longer for some Security Council members. When a new mission was finally authorized for Rwanda, six weeks into the genocide, few States offered soldiers. The mission deployed as the genocide ended.

42. Similarly, throughout the deliberation of the High-level Panel on Threats, Challenges and Change, we have been struck once again by the glacial speed at which our institutions have responded to massive human rights violations in Darfur, Sudan.

43. When the institutions of collective security respond in an ineffective and inequitable manner, they reveal a much deeper truth about which threats matter. Our institutions of collective security must not just assert that a threat to one is truly a threat to all, but perform accordingly.

QUESTIONS ....

7. Member states of the United Nations perceive threats differently. Should a state concerned with, say, terrorism, be prepared to compromise on action in response to threats perceived as more pressing by another state, such as under-development?

8. If a "grand bargain" that recognized and addressed the different threats facing different countries were possible, who would be the most likely broker of such an agreement?

17.5 Visions of Order

The United States is the most powerful of the member states of the United Nations. In September 2002 US President George W. Bush used his address to the General Assembly to call on the United Nations to help confront what he described as the threat posed by Iraq.

US PRESIDENT GEORGE W. BUSH'S ADDRESS TO THE UNITED NATIONS GENERAL ASSEMBLY, 12 SEPTEMBER 2002

Mr. Secretary General, Mr. President, distinguished delegates, and ladies and gentlemen: We meet one year and one day after a terrorist attack brought grief to my country, and brought grief to many citizens of our world. Yesterday, we remembered the innocent lives taken that terrible morning. Today, we turn to the urgent duty of protecting other lives, without illusion and without fear. . . .

The United Nations was born in the hope that survived a world war—the hope of a world moving toward justice, escaping old patterns of conflict and fear. The founding members resolved that the peace of the world must never again be destroyed by the will and wickedness of any man. We created the United Nations Security Council, so that, unlike the League of Nations, our deliberations would be more than talk, our resolutions would be more than wishes. After generations of deceitful dictators and broken treaties and squandered lives, we dedicated ourselves to standards of human dignity shared by all, and to a system of security defended by all.

Today, these standards, and this security, are challenged. Our commitment to human dignity is challenged by persistent poverty and raging disease. The suffering is great, and our responsibilities are clear. The United States is joining with the world to supply aid where it reaches people and lifts up lives, to extend trade and the prosperity it brings, and to bring medical care where it is desperately needed. . . .

Above all, our principles and our security are challenged today by outlaw groups and regimes that accept no law of morality and have no limit to their violent ambitions. In the attacks on America a year ago, we saw the destructive intentions of our enemies. This threat hides within many nations, including my own. In cells and camps, terrorists are plotting further destruction, and building new bases for their war against civilization. And our greatest fear is that terrorists will find a shortcut to their mad ambitions when an outlaw regime supplies them with the technologies to kill on a massive scale.

In one place—in one regime—we find all these dangers, in their most lethal and aggressive forms, exactly the kind of aggressive threat the United Nations was born to confront.

Twelve years ago, Iraq invaded Kuwait without provocation. And the regime's forces were poised to continue their march to seize other countries and their resources. Had Saddam Hussein been appeased instead of stopped, he would have endangered the peace and stability of the world. Yet this aggression was stopped—by the might of coalition forces and the will of the United Nations.

To suspend hostilities, to spare himself, Iraq's dictator accepted a series of commitments. The terms were clear, to him and to all. And he agreed to prove he is complying with every one of those obligations. . . .

Delegates to the General Assembly, we have been more than patient. We've tried sanctions. We've tried the carrot of oil for food, and the stick of coalition military strikes. But Saddam Hussein has defied all these efforts and continues to develop weapons of mass destruction. The first time we may be completely certain he has nuclear weapons is when, God forbid, he uses one. We owe it to all our citizens to do everything in our power to prevent that day from coming.

The conduct of the Iraqi regime is a threat to the authority of the United Nations, and a threat to peace. Iraq has answered a decade of UN demands with a decade of defiance. All the world now faces a test, and the United Nations a difficult and defining moment. Are Security Council resolutions to be honored and enforced, or cast aside without consequence? Will the United Nations serve the purpose of its founding, or will it be irrelevant?

The United States helped found the United Nations. We want the United Nations to be effective, and respectful, and successful. We want the resolutions of the world's most important multilateral body to be enforced. And right now those resolutions are being unilaterally subverted by the Iraqi regime. Our partnership of nations can meet the test before us, by making clear what we now expect of the Iraqi regime. . . .

My nation will work with the UN Security Council to meet our common challenge. If Iraq's regime defies us again, the world must move deliberately, decisively to hold Iraq to account. We will work with the UN Security Council for the necessary resolutions. But the purposes of the United States should not be doubted. The Security Council resolutions will be enforced—the just demands of peace and security will be met—or action will be unavoidable. And a regime that has lost its legitimacy will also lose its power.

The failure to agree on a strategy with respect to Iraq has been discussed in chapter 2. The High-level Panel on Threats, Challenges, and Change was set up in response to the political crisis that followed the March 2003 invasion of Iraq. Speaking to the General Assembly a year after President Bush's address quoted above, Secretary-General Annan was blunt about the challenges confronting the United Nations.

SECRETARY-GENERAL'S ADDRESS TO THE UNITED NATIONS GENERAL ASSEMBLY, 23 SEPTEMBER 2003[11]

Excellencies, we have come to a fork in the road. This may be a moment no less decisive than 1945 itself, when the United Nations was founded. At that time, a group of far-sighted leaders, led and inspired by President Franklin D. Roosevelt, were determined to make the second half of the 20th century different from the first half. They saw that the human race had only one world to live in, and that unless it managed its affairs prudently, all human beings may perish. So they drew up rules to govern international behaviour, and founded a network of institutions, with the United Nations at its centre, in which the peoples of the world could work together for the common good.

Now we must decide whether it is possible to continue on the basis agreed then, or whether radical changes are needed. And we must not shy away from questions about the adequacy, and effectiveness, of the rules and instruments at our disposal.

British Prime Minister Tony Blair was sometimes accused of using British diplomacy to make US foreign policy more palatable. Three years after the Iraq war, he gave a speech that sought to map out a new agenda for foreign policy.

BRITISH PRIME MINISTER TONY BLAIR, FOREIGN POLICY SPEECH AT GEORGETOWN UNIVERSITY, 26 MAY 2006[12]

We all agree that the characteristic of the modern world is interdependence. We haven't yet thought through its consequences.

[11] Reprinted with permission of the United Nations.
[12] Available at http://www.number-10.gov.uk/output/Page9549.asp

In Government, I realised this first at the time of the Asian financial crisis shortly after taking office. Within weeks, all of us who had been initially holding back, waiting for the market to correct itself, wondering how a market meltdown in Thailand could possibly destabilise our own economies, were coming together, agreeing packages to prevent contagion, supporting Brazil and others who looked like they might be the next to go. In the process every conventional doctrine about markets was amended to prevent catastrophe.

A year later, Kosovo happened and the spectre of ethnic cleansing returned to Europe. We put pressure on Milosevic. We threatened diplomatic action. We eventually took military action by air strikes. But it was only when, with considerable courage President Clinton indicated—and it was only an indication—he might be prepared to use ground force, that suddenly Milosevic collapsed and the crisis was resolved.

What these two events taught me was that the rule book of international politics has been torn up. Interdependence—the fact of a crisis somewhere becoming a crisis everywhere—makes a mockery of traditional views of national interest. You can't have a coherent view of national interest today without a coherent view of the international community. Nations, even ones as large and powerful as the USA, are affected profoundly by world events; and not affected, in time or at the margins but at breakneck speed and fundamentally. Why is immigration the No.1 domestic policy issue in much of Europe and in the US today? What are the solutions? The answer is that globalisation is making mass migration a reality; and only global development will make it a manageable reality. . . .

The point is that in respect of any of these challenges, certain things stand out. They affect us all. They can only be effectively tackled together. And they require a pre-emptive and not simply reactive response.

Here is where it becomes very difficult. In the old days—I mean a few decades back—countries could wait, assess over time, even opt out—at least until everything was clear. We could act when we knew. Now we have to act on the basis of precaution.

What is more, such action will often require intervention, far beyond our own boundaries. The terrorism we are fighting in Britain, wasn't born in Britain, though on 7th July last year it was British born terrorists that committed murder. The roots are in schools and training camps and indoctrination thousands of miles away, as well as in the towns and cities of modern Britain. The migration we experience is from Eastern Europe, and the poverty-stricken states of Africa and the solution to it lies there at its source not in the nation feeling its consequence.

What this means is that we have to act, not react; we have to do so on the basis of prediction not certainty; and such action will often, usually indeed, be outside of our own territory. And what all that means is: that this can't be done easily unless it is done on an agreed basis of principle, of values that are shared and fair. Common action only works when founded on common values.

Therefore, to meet effectively the challenge that faces us, we must fashion an international community that both embodies, and acts in pursuit of global values: liberty, democracy, tolerance, justice. These are the values we believe in. These are the values universally accepted across all nations, faiths and races, though not by all elements within them. These are values that can inspire and unify. So, how, at this moment in time, in an international community that has been riven, do we achieve such unity around such values? . . .

The scale of this agenda is enormous. It means that today's leaders of nations must analyse, cope with, deal with, a vast array of international problems as well as the myriad of challenges thrown up by each of our systems of healthcare, pensions, welfare, law and order. Except that, these problems are no longer simply international. They intrude into domestic politics. There is globalisation in politics, too.

All of the issues raised today, require immense focus, commitment and drive to get things done. Increasingly, there is a hopeless mismatch between the global challenges we face and the global institutions to confront them. After the Second World War, people realised that there needed to be a new international institutional architecture. In this new era, in the early 21st century, we need to renew it.

I want to make some tentative suggestions for change.

First, the UN Secretary General, Kofi Annan, has done an extraordinary job in often near impossible circumstances. He has also proposed reforms of the UN that should certainly be done.

But a Security Council which has France as a permanent member but not Germany, Britain but not Japan, China but not India to say nothing of the absence of proper representation from Latin America or Africa, cannot be legitimate in the modern world. I used to think this problem was intractable. The competing interests are so strong. But I am now sure we need reform. If necessary let us agree some form of interim change that can be a bridge to a future settlement. But we need to get it done.

We should give the UNSG new powers: over the appointments in the Secretariat—it is absurd they have to be voted on, one by one, in the General Assembly; and over how the resources of the UN are spent. We should streamline radically the humanitarian and development operations so that the UN can act effectively as one agency in country: single UN offices, with one leader, one country plan and one budget. There is even a case for establishing one humanitarian agency that allows for better prediction of an impending crisis; for swifter action to remedy it; and sees the different aspects, from short-term relief to longer term development as linked not distinct.

We should also strengthen the UNSG's powers to propose action to the Security Council for the resolution of long-standing disputes; and encourage him in doing so.

Second, the World Bank and IMF. These institutions together play an important role in global stability and prosperity. There is a case, as has been argued before, for merger. But in any event, there is certainly a powerful case for reform. . . .

Third, there is a strong argument for establishing a multilateral system for "safe enrichment" for nuclear energy. . . .

Fourth, the G8 now regularly meets as the G8 +5. That should be the norm.

Finally, we need a UN Environment Organisation, commensurate with the importance the issue now has on the international agenda. . . .

Leaders should do more. But it's the system itself that is at fault, not because of indolence but because of time. Occasionally I look at our international institutions and think as I do about our welfare state: the structures of 1946 trying to meet the challenges of 2006.

What's the obstacle? It is that in creating more effective multilateral institutions, individual nations yield up some of their own independence. This is a hard thing to swallow. Let me be blunt. Powerful nations want more effective multilateral institutions—when they think those institutions will do their will. What they fear is effective multilateral institutions that do their own will.

But the danger of leaving things as they are, is ad hoc coalitions for action that stir massive controversy about legitimacy; or paralysis in the face of crisis.

No amount of institutional change will ever work unless the most powerful make it work. The EU doesn't move forward unless its leading countries agree. That is the reality of power; size; economic, military, political weight.

But if there is a common basis for working—agreed aims and purposes— then no matter how powerful, countries gain from being able to sub-contract problems that on their own they cannot solve. Their national self-interest becomes delivered through effective communal action.

Today, after all the turmoil and disagreement of the past few years, there is a real opportunity to bring us together. We all of us face the common security threat of global terrorism; we all of us depend on a healthy global financial system; all of us, at least in time, will feel the consequences of the poverty of millions living in a world of plenty; we all of us know that secure and clean energy is a common priority. All of us have an interest in stability and a fear of chaos. That's the impact of interdependence.

Above all, though in too many countries and in too many ways, global values are not followed, there is no dissent about their desirability. From the moment the Afgans came out and voted in their first ever election, the myth that democracy was a Western concept, was exploded. The Governments of the world do not all believe in freedom. But the people of the world do.

In my nine years as Prime Minister I have not become more cynical about idealism. I have simply become more persuaded that the distinction between a foreign policy driven by values and one driven by interests, is obviously wrong. Globalisation begets interdependence. Interdependence begets the necessity of a common value system to make it work. In other words, the idealism becomes the real politik. None of that will eliminate the setbacks, fallings short, inconsistencies and hypocrisies that come with practical decision-making in a harsh world. But it does mean that the best of the human spirit, that which, throughout the ages, has pushed the progress of humanity along, is also the best hope for the world's future. Our values are our guide.

To make it so, however, we have to be prepared to think sooner and act quicker in defence of those values—progressive pre-emption, if you will. There is an agenda for it, waiting to be gathered and capable of uniting a world once divided. There wouldn't be a better moment for it.

Two weeks later, Kofi Annan's deputy, Mark Malloch Brown, gave a speech that he later said had been intended to encourage greater involvement by the United States in the United Nations.

SPEECH BY DEPUTY SECRETARY-GENERAL MARK MALLOCH BROWN AT THE CENTURY FOUNDATION, 6 JUNE 2006

Thank you for allowing me to speak to you today on Power and Global Leadership. I often get asked to talk about leadership, but rarely about power. I wonder why.

With that thought as my starting point, I am going to give what might be regarded as a rather un-UN speech. Some of the themes—that the United Nations is misunderstood and does much more than its critics allow—are probably not surprising. But my underlying message, which is a warning about the serious consequences of a decades-long tendency by US Administrations of both parties to engage only fitfully with the UN, is not one a sitting United Nations official would normally make to an audience like this.

But I feel it is a message that urgently needs to be aired. And as someone who has spent most of his adult life in this country, only a part of it at the UN, I hope you will take it in the spirit in which it is meant: as a sincere and constructive critique of US policy towards the UN by a friend and admirer. Because the fact is that the prevailing practice of seeking to use the UN almost by stealth as a diplomatic tool while failing to stand up for it against its domestic critics is simply not sustainable. You will lose the UN one way or another.

Founders' Vision

Multilateral compromise has always been difficult to justify in the American political debate: too many speeches, too many constraints, too few results. Yet it was not meant to be so.

The all-moral-idealism-no-power institution was the League of Nations. The UN was explicitly designed through US leadership and the ultimate coalition of the willing, its World War II allies, as a very different creature, an antidote to the League's failure. At the UN's core was to be an enforceable concept of collective security protected by the victors of that war, combined with much more practical efforts to promote global values such as human rights and democracy.

Underpinning this new approach was a judgement that no President since Truman has felt able to repeat: that for the world's one super-Power— arguably more super in 1946 than 2006—managing global security and development issues through the network of a United Nations was worth the effort. Yes it meant the give and take of multilateral bargaining, but any dilution of American positions was more than made up for by the added clout of action that enjoyed global support.

Today, we are coming to the end of the 10-year term of arguably the UN's best-ever Secretary-General, Kofi Annan. But some of his very successes— promoting human rights and a responsibility to protect people from abuse by their own Governments; creating a new status for civil society and business at the UN—are either not recognized or have come under steady attacks from anti-UN groups.

To take just one example, 10 years ago UN peacekeeping seemed almost moribund in the aftermath of tragic mistakes in Rwanda, Somalia and Yugoslavia. Today, the UN fields 18 peacekeeping operations around the world, from the Congo to Haiti, Sudan to Sierra Leone, Southern Lebanon to Liberia, with an annual cost that is at a bargain bin price compared to other US-led operations. And the US pays roughly one quarter of those UN peacekeeping costs—just over $1 billion this year.

That figure should be seen in the context of estimates by both the GAO and RAND Corporation that UN peacekeeping, while lacking heavy armament enforcement capacity, helps to maintain peace—when there is a peace to keep—more effectively for a lot less than comparable US operations. Multilateral peacekeeping is effective cost-sharing on a much lower cost business model and it works.

That is as it should be and is true for many other areas the UN system works in, too, from humanitarian relief to health to education. Yet for many policymakers and opinion leaders in Washington, let alone the general public, the roles I have described are hardly believed or, where they are, remain discreetly underplayed. To acknowledge an America reliant on international institutions is not perceived to be good politics at home.

However, inevitably a moment of truth is coming. Because even as the world's challenges are growing, the UN's ability to respond is being weakened without US leadership.

Take the issue of human rights.

When Eleanor Roosevelt took the podium at the UN to argue passionately for the elaboration of a Universal Declaration of Human Rights, the world responded. Today, when the human rights machinery was renewed with the formation of a Human Rights Council to replace the discredited Commission on Human Rights, and the US chose to stay on the sidelines, the loss was everybody's.

I hope and believe the new Council will prove itself to be a stronger and more effective body than its predecessor. But there is no question that the US decision to call for a vote in order to oppose it in the General Assembly, and then to not run for a seat after it was approved by 170 votes to 4, makes the challenge more difficult.

More broadly, Americans complain about the UN's bureaucracy, weak decision-making, the lack of accountable modern management structures and the political divisions of the General Assembly here in New York. And my response is, "guilty on all counts."

But why?

In significant part because the US has not stuck with its project—its professed wish to have a strong, effective United Nations—in a systematic way. Secretary Albright and others here today have played extraordinary leadership roles in US-UN relations, for which I salute them. But in the eyes of the rest of the world, US commitment tends to ebb much more than it flows. And in recent years, the enormously divisive issue of Iraq and the big stick of financial withholding have come to define an unhappy marriage.

As someone who deals with Washington almost daily, I know this is unfair to the very real effort all three Secretaries of State I have worked with— Secretary Albright, Secretary Powell and Secretary Rice—put into UN issues. And today, on a very wide number of areas, from Lebanon and Afghanistan to Syria, Iran and the Palestinian issue, the US is constructively engaged with the UN. But that is not well known or understood, in part because much of the public discourse that reaches the US heartland has been largely abandoned to its loudest detractors such as Rush Limbaugh and Fox News. That is what I mean by "stealth" diplomacy: the UN's role is in effect a secret in Middle America even as it is highlighted in the Middle East and other parts of the world.

Exacerbating matters is the widely held perception, even among many US allies, that the US tends to hold on to maximalist positions when it could be finding middle ground.

We can see this even on apparently non-controversial issues such as renovating the dilapidated UN Headquarters in New York. While an architectural landmark, the building falls dangerously short of city codes, lacks sprinklers, is filled with asbestos and is in most respects the most hazardous workplace in town. But the only Government not fully supporting the project is the US. Too much unchecked UN-bashing and stereotyping over too many years—manifest in a fear by politicians to be seen to be supporting better premises for overpaid, corrupt UN bureaucrats—makes even refurbishing a building a political hot potato.

Making Reform Work

One consequence is that, like the building itself, the vital renewal of the Organization, the updating of its mission, its governance and its management tools, is addressed only intermittently. And when the US does champion the right issues like management reform, as it is currently doing, it provokes more suspicion than support.

Last December, for example, largely at US insistence, instead of a normal two-year budget, Member States approved only six months' worth of expenditure—a period which ends on June 30. Developing and developed countries, the latter with the US at the fore, are now at loggerheads over whether sufficient reform has taken place to lift that cap, or indeed whether there should be any links between reform and the budget. Without agreement, we could face a fiscal crisis very soon.

There has been a significant amount of reform over the last 18 months, from the creation of a new Ethics Office and whistle-blower policy, to the establishment of a new Peacebuilding Commission and Human Rights Council. But not enough.

The unfinished management reform agenda, which the US sensibly supports, is in many ways a statement of the obvious. It argues that systems and processes designed 60 years ago for an organization largely devoted to running conferences and writing reports simply don't work for today's operational UN, which conducts multibillion-dollar peacekeeping missions, humanitarian relief operations and other complex operations all over the world. The report sets out concrete proposals for how this can be fixed while also seeking to address the broader management, oversight and accountability weaknesses highlighted by the "oil-for-food" programme.

One day soon we must address the massive gap between the scale of world issues and the limits of the institutions we have built to address them. However, today even relatively modest proposals that in any other organization would be seen as uncontroversial, such as providing more authority and flexibility for the Secretary-General to shift posts and resources to organizational priorities without having to get direct approval from Member States, have been fiercely resisted by the G-77, the main group of developing countries, on the grounds that this weakens accountability. Hence the current deadlock.

What lies behind this?

It is not because most developing countries don't want reform. To be sure, a few spoilers do seem to be opposed to reform for its own sake, and there is no question that some countries are seeking to manipulate the process for their own ends with very damaging consequences. But in practice, the vast majority is fully supportive of the principle of a better run, more effective UN; indeed they know they would be the primary beneficiaries, through more peace, and more development.

So why has it not so far been possible to isolate the radicals and build a strong alliance of reform-minded nations to push through this agenda?

I would argue that the answer lies in questions about motives and power.

Motives, in that, very unfortunately, there is currently a perception among many otherwise quite moderate countries that anything the US supports must have a secret agenda aimed at either subordinating multilateral processes to Washington's ends or weakening the institutions, and therefore, put crudely, should be opposed without any real discussion of whether they make sense or not.

And power, that in two different ways revolves around perceptions of the role and representativeness of the Security Council.

First, in that there has been a real, understandable hostility by the wider membership to the perception that the Security Council, in particular the five permanent members, is seeking a role in areas not formally within its remit, such as management issues or human rights.

Second, an equally understandable conviction that those five, veto-wielding permanent members who happen to be the victors in a war fought 60 years ago, cannot be seen as representative of today's world—even when looking through the lens of financial contributions. Indeed, the so-called G-4 of Security Council aspirants—Japan, India, Brazil and Germany—contribute twice as much as the P-4, the four permanent members excluding the US

Prime Minister Tony Blair acknowledged exactly this point on his trip to Washington last month, and it is something which does need to be addressed. More broadly, the very reasonable concerns of the full UN membership that the fundamental multilateral principle that each Member State's vote counts equally in the wider work of the UN needs to be acknowledged and accommodated within a broader framework of reform. If the multilateral system is to work effectively, all States need to feel they have a real stake.

New Global Challenges

But a stake in what system?

The US—like every nation, strong and weak alike—is today beset by problems that defy national, inside-the-border solutions: climate change, terrorism, nuclear proliferation, migration, the management of the global economy, the internationalization of drugs and crime, the spread of diseases such as HIV and avian flu. Today's new national security challenges basically thumb their noses at old notions of national sovereignty. Security has gone global, and no country can afford to neglect the global institutions needed to manage it.

Kofi Annan has proposed a restructuring of the UN to respond to these new challenges with three legs: development, security and human rights supported, like any good chair, by a fourth leg, reformed management. That is the UN we want to place our bet on. But for it to work, we need the US to support this agenda—and support it not just in a whisper but in a coast to coast shout that pushes back the critics domestically and wins over the sceptics internationally. America's leaders must again say the UN matters.

When you talk better national education scores, you don't start with "I support the Department of Education." Similarly for the UN it starts with politicians who will assert the US is going to engage with the world to tackle climate change, poverty, immigration and terrorism. Stand up for that agenda consistently and allow the UN to ride on its coat-tails as a vital means of getting it done. It also means a sustained inside-the-tent diplomacy at the UN. No more "take it or leave it," red-line demands thrown in without debate and engagement.

Let me close with a few words on Darfur to make my point.

A few weeks ago, my kids were on the Mall in Washington, demanding President Bush to do more to end the genocide in Darfur and President Bush wants to do more. I'd bet some of your kids were there as well. Perhaps you were, too. And yet what can the US do alone in the heart of Africa, in a region the size of France? A place where the Government in Khartoum is convinced the US wants to extend the hegemony it is thought to have asserted in Iraq and Afghanistan.

In essence, the US is stymied before it even passes "Go." It needs the UN as a multilateral means to address Sudan's concerns. It needs the UN to secure a wide multicultural array of troop and humanitarian partners. It needs the UN to provide the international legitimacy that Iraq has again proved is an indispensable component to success on the ground. Yet, the UN needs its first parent, the US, every bit as much if it is to deploy credibly in one of the world's nastiest neighbourhoods.

Back in Franklin and Eleanor Roosevelt's day, building a strong, effective UN that could play this kind of role was a bipartisan enterprise, with the likes of Arthur Vandenberg and John Foster Dulles joining Democrats to support the new body. Who are their successors in American politics? Who will campaign in 2008 for a new multilateral national security?

For many developing countries, however, reform of the United Nations is less about whether the United States participates or not, than it is about how decisions are made and resources allocated.

STATEMENT BY DUMISANI KUMALO, PERMANENT REPRESENTATIVE OF SOUTH AFRICA TO THE UNITED NATIONS, ON BEHALF OF THE GROUP OF 77 AND CHINA, TO GENERAL ASSEMBLY, 8 MAY 2006

The Group of 77 and China has been supportive of a number of major reforms. We supported the approval of the resources needed for the Human Rights Council. It was the Group of 77 and China that fought to have a peacebuilding support office be funded from predictable new resources and not from within existing budget levels or through establishing temporary posts. It is the Group of 77 and China that wants to ensure that we deal with development challenges in more concrete and tangible ways. As it is, we are still awaiting our negotiating partners to join in a consensus that will build on the global partnership that was confirmed by the September Summit.

We were instrumental in the approval of an amount of $100 million that the Secretary-General urgently needed to proceed with the Capital Master Plan. It was the developing countries that have always insisted that the Secretary-General should receive adequate and predictable resources to undertake effectively the numerous tasks of this Organization. It was also the Group of 77 and China that supported the budget level requested by the Secretary-General in 2005 and opposed the spending cap.

Since the adoption of the Outcome Document last September, the Group of 77 and China has supported the creation of an ethics office, the finalization of the whistle-blower policy and increasing the investigation and auditing capacity of the Office of Internal Oversight Services.

Clearly, the suggestion that the Group of 77 and China is somehow blocking or delaying reform is at best misleading or at worst absolutely untrue.

We want to reassure all Member States that the resolution we have just adopted does not in any way delay or prevent the reform of the United Nations. In fact, a careful reading of this resolution will show that many of the proposals in it are meant to make this a better Organization. A large part of this resolution captures areas in which there is general agreement among Member States about their importance and necessity. The exceptions are those proposals that would have amended the oversight role of Member States, through the General Assembly.

In addition to the governance issues, the elements in the resolution that we differed on with our negotiating partners were on the enforcement of gender targets in the Secretariat, ensuring equitable geographical representation in the recruitment of the Secretariat, in particular at senior levels, and increasing procurement opportunities for developing countries. These elements are important to developing countries and to suggest that fighting for them would detract from the reform initiatives of the Secretary-General is misleading.

Everyone in this Assembly knows that this Organization does not reflect the international character of its Membership, in particular at senior levels that seem to be monopolized by nationals from a few countries. This is despite repeated calls on this matter by the General Assembly. The suggestion that nationals from developing countries are somehow less qualified and not able to meet the standards that we have set for our international civil servants in the Charter of the United Nations is untrue.

The Secretariat must stop paying more than just lip service to the calls to ensure a greater gender balance and equitable geographical representation in the recruitment and promotion of its staff. Our resolution is merely asking for proposals on gender targets and geographical distribution to be included in the September 2006 report. To suggest that these requests will delay the proposals of the Secretary-General or halt the reform exercise is false.

The June report on procurement inter alia will elaborate on the Secretary-General's proposal to move towards a lead agency concept where provisions of the General Assembly resolutions may not apply. Our resolution simply requests that an assessment of the internal controls of these organizations be undertaken to ensure effective oversight. The Group of 77 and China is therefore not delaying reform by asking that Member States receive assurances that the provisions of General Assembly resolutions will be respected and effective internal controls will be in place.

The Group of 77 and China supports the Secretary-General as chief administrative officer of the United Nations. The Secretary-General is elected by the Member States and therefore we believe that he is accountable to the General Assembly. For this reason, we did not understand, or even accept, that in order for the Secretary-General to carry out his duties, this should be accompanied by denying the majority of Member States the right to pronounce on the administration of the United Nations. The Group of 77 and China has continued to maintain that for a "small but representative group of Members States" to replace the role of all Member States in carrying out the oversight responsibilities of the General Assembly, is an attempt to deny every Member of the United Nations the role due to them.

QUESTIONS

9. US President Bush said the response of the United Nations to Iraq would determine whether the organization would be relevant or not. What might this mean? Did the UN pass the test? Did it pass some other form of "test"?

10. The June 2006 speech by the Deputy Secretary-General was greeted with apoplexy by various US officials. Was giving such a speech wise? Was it helpful?

11. How should concerns relating to legitimacy, such as those expressed by the Permanent Representative of South Africa, be balanced against the desire for an effective and efficient United Nations?

Further Reading

www.reformtheun.org

Chesterman, Simon, "Reforming the United Nations: Legitimacy, Effectiveness, and Power After Iraq." *Singapore Year Book of International Law*, vol. 10 (2006), pp. 1–28.

Chesterman, Simon, ed. *Secretary or General? The UN Secretary-General in World Politics.* Cambridge: Cambridge University Press, 2007.

Heinbecker, Paul, and Patricia Goff, eds. *Irrelevant or Indispensable? The United Nations in the 21st Century.* Waterloo, ON: Wilfrid Laurier University Press, 2005.

Luck, Edward C. *UN Security Council: Practice and Promise.* London and New York: Routledge, 2006, pp. 111–126.

Malone, David M. "The High Level Panel and the Security Council." *Security Dialogue*, vol. 36(3) (September 2005), pp. 370–372.

Thakur, Ramesh. *The United Nations, Peace and Security: From Collective Security to the Responsibility to Protect*. Cambridge: Cambridge University Press, 2006.

Weiss, Thomas G., David P. Forsythe, Roger A. Coate, and Kelly Kate Pease. *The United Nations and Changing World Politics*. 5th edn. Boulder, CO: Westview, 2007.

Charter of the United Nations[1]

WE THE PEOPLES OF THE UNITED NATIONS DETERMINED

to save succeeding generations from the scourge of war, which twice in our lifetime has brought untold sorrow to mankind, and

to reaffirm faith in fundamental human rights, in the dignity and worth of the human person, in the equal rights of men and women and of nations large and small, and

to establish conditions under which justice and respect for the obligations arising from treaties and other sources of international law can be maintained, and

to promote social progress and better standards of life in larger freedom,

AND FOR THESE ENDS

to practice tolerance and live together in peace with one another as good neighbours, and

to unite our strength to maintain international peace and security, and

to ensure by the acceptance of principles and the institution of methods, that armed force shall not be used, save in the common interest, and

to employ international machinery for the promotion of the economic and social advancement of all peoples,

HAVE RESOLVED TO COMBINE OUR EFFORTS TO ACCOMPLISH THESE AIMS

Accordingly, our respective Governments, through representatives assembled in the city of San Francisco, who have exhibited their full powers found to be in good and due form, have agreed to the present Charter of the United Nations and do hereby establish an international organization to be known as the United Nations.

CHAPTER I—PURPOSES AND PRINCIPLES

Article 1

The Purposes of the United Nations are:

1. To maintain international peace and security, and to that end: to take effective collective measures for the prevention and removal of threats to the peace, and for the suppression of acts of aggression or other breaches of the peace, and to bring about by peaceful means, and in conformity with the principles of justice and international law, adjustment or settlement of international disputes or situations which might lead to a breach of the peace;

---

[1]Signed at San Francisco, 26 June 1945 and entered into force on 24 October 1945.

2. To develop friendly relations among nations based on respect for the principle of equal rights and self-determination of peoples, and to take other appropriate measures to strengthen universal peace;

3. To achieve international cooperation in solving international problems of an economic, social, cultural, or humanitarian character, and in promoting and encouraging respect for human rights and for fundamental freedoms for all without distinction as to race, sex, language, or religion; and

4. To be a centre for harmonizing the actions of nations in the attainment of these common ends.

Article 2

The Organization and its Members, in pursuit of the Purposes stated in Article 1, shall act in accordance with the following Principles.

1. The Organization is based on the principle of the sovereign equality of all its Members.

2. All Members, in order to ensure to all of them the rights and benefits resulting from membership, shall fulfil in good faith the obligations assumed by them in accordance with the present Charter.

3. All Members shall settle their international disputes by peaceful means in such a manner that international peace and security, and justice, are not endangered.

4. All Members shall refrain in their international relations from the threat or use of force against the territorial integrity or political independence of any state, or in any other manner inconsistent with the Purposes of the United Nations.

5. All Members shall give the United Nations every assistance in any action it takes in accordance with the present Charter, and shall refrain from giving assistance to any state against which the United Nations is taking preventive or enforcement action.

6. The Organization shall ensure that states which are not Members of the United Nations act in accordance with these Principles so far as may be necessary for the maintenance of international peace and security.

7. Nothing contained in the present Charter shall authorize the United Nations to intervene in matters which are essentially within the domestic jurisdiction of any state or shall require the Members to submit such matters to settlement under the present Charter; but this principle shall not prejudice the application of enforcement measures under Chapter VII.

CHAPTER II—MEMBERSHIP

Article 3

The original Members of the United Nations shall be the states which, having participated in the United Nations Conference on International Organization at San Francisco, or having previously signed the Declaration by United Nations of January 1, 1942, sign the present Charter and ratify it in accordance with Article 110.

Article 4

1. Membership in the United Nations is open to all other peace-loving states which accept the obligations contained in the present Charter and, in the judgment of the Organization, are able and willing to carry out these obligations.

2. The admission of any such state to membership in the United Nations will be effected by a decision of the General Assembly upon the recommendation of the Security Council.

Article 5

A member of the United Nations against which preventive or enforcement action has been taken by the Security Council may be suspended from the exercise of the rights and privileges of membership by the General Assembly upon the recommendation of the Security Council. The exercise of these rights and privileges may be restored by the Security Council.

Article 6

A Member of the United Nations which has persistently violated the Principles contained in the present Charter may be expelled from the Organization by the General Assembly upon the recommendation of the Security Council.

CHAPTER III—ORGANS

Article 7

1. There are established as the principal organs of the United Nations: a General Assembly, a Security Council, an Economic and Social Council, a Trusteeship Council, an International Court of Justice, and a Secretariat.

2. Such subsidiary organs as may be found necessary may be established in accordance with the present Charter.

Article 8

The United Nations shall place no restrictions on the eligibility of men and women to participate in any capacity and under conditions of equality in its principal and subsidiary organs.

CHAPTER IV—THE GENERAL ASSEMBLY

Composition

Article 9

1. The General Assembly shall consist of all the Members of the United Nations.
2. Each member shall have not more than five representatives in the General Assembly.

Functions and Powers

Article 10

The General Assembly may discuss any questions or any matters within the scope of the present Charter or relating to the powers and functions of any organs provided for in the present Charter, and, except as provided in Article 12, may make recommendations to the Members of the United Nations or to the Security Council or to both on any such questions or matters.

Article 11

1. The General Assembly may consider the general principles of cooperation in the maintenance of international peace and security, including the principles governing disarmament and the regulation of armaments, and may make recommendations with regard to such principles to the Members or to the Security Council or to both.

2. The General Assembly may discuss any questions relating to the maintenance of international peace and security brought before it by any Member of the United Nations, or by the Security Council, or by a state which is not a Member of the United Nations in accordance with Article 35, paragraph 2, and, except as provided in Article 12, may make recommendations with regard to any such questions to the state or states concerned or to the Security Council or to both. Any such question on which action is necessary shall be referred to the Security Council by the General Assembly either before or after discussion.

3. The General Assembly may call the attention of the Security Council to situations which are likely to endanger international peace and security.

4. The powers of the General Assembly set forth in this Article shall not limit the general scope of Article 10.

Article 12

1. While the Security Council is exercising in respect of any dispute or situation the functions assigned to it in the present Charter, the General Assembly shall not make any recommendation with regard to that dispute or situation unless the Security Council so requests.

2. The Secretary-General, with the consent of the Security Council, shall notify the General Assembly at each session of any matters relative to the maintenance of international peace and security which are being dealt with by the Security Council and shall similarly notify the General Assembly, or the Members of the United Nations if the General Assembly is not in session, immediately the Security Council ceases to deal with such matters.

Article 13

1. The General Assembly shall initiate studies and make recommendations for the purpose of:

a. promoting international cooperation in the political field and encouraging the progressive development of international law and its codification;

b. promoting international cooperation in the economic, social, cultural, educational, and health fields, and assisting in the realization of human rights and fundamental freedoms for all without distinction as to race, sex, language, or religion.

2. The further responsibilities, functions and powers of the General Assembly with respect to matters mentioned in paragraph 1(b) above are set forth in Chapters IX and X.

Article 14

Subject to the provisions of Article 12, the General Assembly may recommend measures for the peaceful adjustment of any situation, regardless of origin, which it deems likely to impair the general welfare or friendly relations among nations, including situations resulting from a violation of the provisions of the present Charter setting forth the Purposes and Principles of the United Nations.

Article 15

1. The General Assembly shall receive and consider annual and special reports from the Security Council; these reports shall include an account of the measures that the Security Council has decided upon or taken to maintain international peace and security.

2. The General Assembly shall receive and consider reports from the other organs of the United Nations.

Article 16

The General Assembly shall perform such functions with respect to the international trusteeship system as are assigned to it under Chapters XII and XIII, including the approval of the trusteeship agreements for areas not designated as strategic.

Article 17

1. The General Assembly shall consider and approve the budget of the Organization.

2. The expenses of the Organization shall be borne by the Members as apportioned by the General Assembly.

3. The General Assembly shall consider and approve any financial and budgetary arrangements with specialized agencies referred to in Article 57 and shall examine the administrative budgets of such specialized agencies with a view to making recommendations to the agencies concerned.

Voting

Article 18

1. Each member of the General Assembly shall have one vote.

2. Decisions of the General Assembly on important questions shall be made by a two-thirds majority of the members present and voting. These questions shall include: recommendations

with respect to the maintenance of international peace and security, the election of the non-permanent members of the Security Council, the election of the members of the Economic and Social Council, the election of members of the Trusteeship Council in accordance with paragraph 1(c) of Article 86, the admission of new Members to the United Nations, the suspension of the rights and privileges of membership, the expulsion of Members, questions relating to the operation of the trusteeship system, and budgetary questions.

3. Decisions on other questions, including the determination of additional categories of questions to be decided by a two-thirds majority, shall be made by a majority of the members present and voting.

Article 19

A Member of the United Nations which is in arrears in the payment of its financial contributions to the Organization shall have no vote in the General Assembly if the amount of its arrears equals or exceeds the amount of the contributions due from it for the preceding two full years. The General Assembly may, nevertheless, permit such a Member to vote if it is satisfied that the failure to pay is due to conditions beyond the control of the Member.

Procedure

Article 20

The General Assembly shall meet in regular annual sessions and in such special sessions as occasion may require. Special sessions shall be convoked by the Secretary-General at the request of the Security Council or of a majority of the Members of the United Nations.

Article 21

The General Assembly shall adopt its own rules of procedure. It shall elect its President for each session.

Article 22

The General Assembly may establish such subsidiary organs as it deems necessary for the performance of its functions.

CHAPTER V—THE SECURITY COUNCIL

Article 23

[1945 text]

1. The Security Council shall consist of eleven Members of the United Nations. The Republic of China, France, the Union of Soviet Socialist Republics, the United Kingdom of Great Britain and Northern Ireland, and the United States of America shall be permanent members of the Security Council.

[1963 text][2]

1. The Security Council shall consist of fifteen Members of the United Nations. The Republic of China, France, the Union of Soviet Socialist Republics, the United Kingdom of Great Britain and Northern Ireland, and the United States of America shall be permanent members of the Security Council.

---

[2] Amendment adopted by the General Assembly on 17 December 1963, and entered into force on 31 August 1965.

The General Assembly shall elect six other Members of the United Nations to be non-permanent members of the Security Council, due regard being specially paid, in the first instance to the contribution of Members of the United Nations to the maintenance of international peace and security and to the other purposes of the Organization, and also to equitable geographical distribution.

2. The non-permanent members of the Security Council shall be elected for a term of two years. In the first election of the non-permanent members, however, three shall be chosen for a term of one year. A retiring member shall not be eligible for immediate re-election.

The General Assembly shall elect ten other Members of the United Nations to be non-permanent members of the Security Council, due regard being specially paid, in the first instance to the contribution of Members of the United Nations to the maintenance of international peace and security and to the other purposes of the Organization, and also to equitable geographical distribution.

2. The non-permanent members of the Security Council shall be elected for a term of two years. In the first election of the non-permanent members after the increase of the membership of the Security Council from eleven to fifteen, two of the four additional members shall be chosen for a term of one year. A retiring member shall not be eligible for immediate re-election.

3. Each member of the Security Council shall have one representative.

Functions and Powers

Article 24

1. In order to ensure prompt and effective action by the United Nations, its Members confer on the Security Council primary responsibility for the maintenance of international peace and security, and agree that in carrying out its duties under this responsibility the Security Council acts on their behalf.

2. In discharging these duties the Security Council shall act in accordance with the Purposes and Principles of the United Nations. The specific powers granted to the Security Council for the discharge of these duties are laid down in Chapters VI, VII, VIII, and XII.

3. The Security Council shall submit annual and, when necessary, special reports to the General Assembly for its consideration.

Article 25

The Members of the United Nations agree to accept and carry out the decisions of the Security Council in accordance with the present Charter.

Article 26

In order to promote the establishment and maintenance of international peace and security with the least diversion for armaments of the world's human and economic resources, the Security Council shall be responsible for formulating, with the assistance of the Military Staff Committee referred to in Article 47, plans to be submitted to the Members of the United Nations for the establishment of a system for the regulation of armaments.

Voting

Article 27

1. Each member of the Security Council shall have one vote.

[1945 text]

2. Decisions of the Security Council on procedural matters shall be made by an affirmative vote of seven members.
3. Decisions of the Security Council on all other matters shall be made by an affirmative vote of seven members including the concurring votes of the permanent members; provided that, in decisions under Chapter VI, and under paragraph 3 of Article 52, a party to a dispute shall abstain from voting.

[1963 text][3]

2. Decisions of the Security Council on procedural matters shall be made by an affirmative vote of nine members.
3. Decisions of the Security Council on all other matters shall be made by an affirmative vote of nine members including the concurring votes of the permanent members; provided that, in decisions under Chapter VI, and under paragraph 3 of Article 52, a party to a dispute shall abstain from voting.

Procedure

Article 28

1. The Security Council shall be so organized as to be able to function continuously. Each member of the Security Council shall for this purpose be represented at all times at the seat of the Organization.

2. The Security Council shall hold periodic meetings at which each of its members may, if it so desires, be represented by a member of the government or by some other specially designated representative.

3. The Security Council may hold meetings at such places other than the seat of the Organization as in its judgment will best facilitate its work.

Article 29

The Security Council may establish such subsidiary organs as it deems necessary for the performance of its functions.

Article 30

The Security Council shall adopt its own rules of procedure, including the method of selecting its President.

Article 31

Any Member of the United Nations which is not a member of the Security Council may participate, without vote, in the discussion of any question brought before the Security Council whenever the latter considers that the interests of that Member are specially affected.

Article 32

Any Member of the United Nations which is not a member of the Security Council or any state which is not a Member of the United Nations, if it is a party to a dispute under consideration by

---

[3] Amendment adopted by the General Assembly on 17 December 1963 and entered into force on 31 August 1965.

the Security Council, shall be invited to participate, without vote, in the discussion relating to the dispute. The Security Council shall lay down such conditions as it deems just for the participation of a state which is not a Member of the United Nations.

CHAPTER VI—PACIFIC SETTLEMENT OF DISPUTES

Article 33

1. The parties to any dispute, the continuance of which is likely to endanger the maintenance of international peace and security, shall, first of all, seek a solution by negotiation, enquiry, mediation, conciliation, arbitration, judicial settlement, resort to regional agencies or arrangements, or other peaceful means of their own choice.

2. The Security Council shall, when it deems necessary, call upon the parties to settle their dispute by such means.

Article 34

The Security Council may investigate any dispute, or any situation which might lead to international friction or give rise to a dispute, in order to determine whether the continuance of the dispute or situation is likely to endanger the maintenance of international peace and security.

Article 35

1. Any Member of the United Nations may bring any dispute, or any situation of the nature referred to in Article 34, to the attention of the Security Council or of the General Assembly.

2. A state which is not a Member of the United Nations may bring to the attention of the Security Council or of the General Assembly any dispute to which it is a party if it accepts in advance, for the purposes of the dispute, the obligations of pacific settlement provided in the present Charter.

3. The proceedings of the General Assembly in respect of matters brought to its attention under this Article will be subject to the provisions of Articles 11 and 12.

Article 36

1. The Security Council may, at any stage of a dispute of the nature referred to in Article 33 or of a situation of like nature, recommend appropriate procedures or methods of adjustment.

2. The Security Council should take into consideration any procedures for the settlement of the dispute which have already been adopted by the parties.

3. In making recommendations under this Article the Security Council should also take into consideration that legal disputes should as a general rule be referred by the parties to the International Court of Justice in accordance with the provisions of the Statute of the Court.

Article 37

1. Should the parties to a dispute of the nature referred to in Article 33 fail to settle it by the means indicated in that Article, they shall refer it to the Security Council.

2. If the Security Council deems that the continuance of the dispute is in fact likely to endanger the maintenance of international peace and security, it shall decide whether to take action under Article 36 or to recommend such terms of settlement as it may consider appropriate.

Article 38

Without prejudice to the provisions of Articles 33 to 37, the Security Council may, if all the parties to any dispute so request, make recommendations to the parties with a view to a pacific settlement of the dispute.

CHAPTER VII—ACTION WITH RESPECT TO THREATS TO THE PEACE, BREACHES OF THE PEACE, AND ACTS OF AGGRESSION

Article 39

The Security Council shall determine the existence of any threat to the peace, breach of the peace, or act of aggression and shall make recommendations, or decide what measures shall be taken in accordance with Articles 41 and 42, to maintain or restore international peace and security.

Article 40

In order to prevent an aggravation of the situation, the Security Council may, before making the recommendations or deciding upon the measures provided for in Article 39, call upon the parties concerned to comply with such provisional measures as it deems necessary or desirable. Such provisional measures shall be without prejudice to the rights, claims, or position of the parties concerned. The Security Council shall duly take account of failure to comply with such provisional measures.

Article 41

The Security Council may decide what measures not involving the use of armed force are to be employed to give effect to its decisions, and it may call upon the Members of the United Nations to apply such measures. These may include complete or partial interruption of economic relations and of rail, sea, air, postal, telegraphic, radio, and other means of communication, and the severance of diplomatic relations.

Article 42

Should the Security Council consider that measures provided for in Article 41 would be inadequate or have proved to be inadequate, it may take such action by air, sea, or land forces as may be necessary to maintain or restore international peace and security. Such action may include demonstrations, blockade, and other operations by air, sea, or land forces of Members of the United Nations.

Article 43

1. All Members of the United Nations, in order to contribute to the maintenance of international peace and security, undertake to make available to the Security Council, on its call and in accordance with a special agreement or agreements, armed forces, assistance, and facilities, including rights of passage, necessary for the purpose of maintaining international peace and security.

2. Such agreement or agreements shall govern the numbers and types of forces, their degree of readiness and general location, and the nature of the facilities and assistance to be provided.

3. The agreement or agreements shall be negotiated as soon as possible on the initiative of the Security Council. They shall be concluded between the Security Council and Members or between the Security Council and groups of Members and shall be subject to ratification by the signatory states in accordance with their respective constitutional processes.

Article 44

When the Security Council has decided to use force it shall, before calling upon a Member not represented on it to provide armed forces in fulfilment of the obligations assumed under Article 43, invite that Member, if the Member so desires, to participate in the decisions of the Security Council concerning the employment of contingents of that Member's armed forces.

Article 45

In order to enable the United Nations to take urgent military measures, Members shall hold immediately available national air-force contingents for combined international enforcement action. The strength and degree of readiness of these contingents and plans for their combined action shall be determined within the limits laid down in the special agreement or agreements referred to in Article 43, by the Security Council with the assistance of the Military Staff Committee.

Article 46

Plans for the application of armed force shall be made by the Security Council with the assistance of the Military Staff Committee.

Article 47

1. There shall be established a Military Staff Committee to advise and assist the Security Council on all questions relating to the Security Council's military requirements for the maintenance of international peace and security, the employment and command of forces placed at its disposal, the regulation of armaments, and possible disarmament.

2. The Military Staff Committee shall consist of the Chiefs of Staff of the permanent members of the Security Council or their representatives. Any Member of the United Nations not permanently represented on the Committee shall be invited by the Committee to be associated with it when the efficient discharge of the Committee's responsibilities requires the participation of that Member in its work.

3. The Military Staff Committee shall be responsible under the Security Council for the strategic direction of any armed forces placed at the disposal of the Security Council. Questions relating to the command of such forces shall be worked out subsequently.

4. The Military Staff Committee, with the authorization of the Security Council and after consultation with appropriate regional agencies, may establish regional sub-committees.

Article 48

1. The action required to carry out the decisions of the Security Council for the maintenance of international peace and security shall be taken by all the Members of the United Nations or by some of them, as the Security Council may determine.

2. Such decisions shall be carried out by the Members of the United Nations directly and through their action in the appropriate international agencies of which they are members.

Article 49

The Members of the United Nations shall join in affording mutual assistance in carrying out the measures decided upon by the Security Council.

Article 50

If preventive or enforcement measures against any state are taken by the Security Council, any other state, whether a Member of the United Nations or not, which finds itself confronted with special economic problems arising from the carrying out of those measures shall have the right to consult the Security Council with regard to a solution of those problems.

Article 51

Nothing in the present Charter shall impair the inherent right of individual or collective self-defence if an armed attack occurs against a Member of the United Nations, until the Security Council has taken measures necessary to maintain international peace and security. Measures taken by Members in the exercise of this right of self-defence shall be immediately reported to the Security Council and shall not in any way affect the authority and responsibility of the Security Council under the present Charter to take at any time such action as it deems necessary in order to maintain or restore international peace and security.

CHAPTER VIII—REGIONAL ARRANGEMENTS

Article 52

1. Nothing in the present Charter precludes the existence of regional arrangements or agencies for dealing with such matters relating to the maintenance of international peace and security as are appropriate for regional action, provided that such arrangements or agencies and their activities are consistent with the Purposes and Principles of the United Nations.

2. The Members of the United Nations entering into such arrangements or constituting such agencies shall make every effort to achieve pacific settlement of local disputes through such regional arrangements or by such regional agencies before referring them to the Security Council.

3. The Security Council shall encourage the development of pacific settlement of local disputes through such regional arrangements or by such regional agencies either on the initiative of the states concerned or by reference from the Security Council.

4. This Article in no way impairs the application of Articles 34 and 35.

Article 53

1. The Security Council shall, where appropriate, utilize such regional arrangements or agencies for enforcement action under its authority. But no enforcement action shall be taken under regional arrangements or by regional agencies without the authorization of the Security Council, with the exception of measures against any enemy state, as defined in paragraph 2 of this Article, provided for pursuant to Article 107 or in regional arrangements directed against renewal of aggressive policy on the part of any such state, until such time as the Organization may, on request of the Governments concerned, be charged with the responsibility for preventing further aggression by such a state.

2. The term enemy state as used in paragraph 1 of this Article applies to any state which during the Second World War has been an enemy of any signatory of the present Charter.

Article 54

The Security Council shall at all times be kept fully informed of activities undertaken or in contemplation under regional arrangements or by regional agencies for the maintenance of international peace and security.

CHAPTER IX—INTERNATIONAL ECONOMIC AND SOCIAL CO-OPERATION

Article 55

With a view to the creation of conditions of stability and well-being which are necessary for peaceful and friendly relations among nations based on respect for the principle of equal rights and self-determination of peoples, the United Nations shall promote:

a. higher standards of living, full employment, and conditions of economic and social progress and development;

b. solutions of international economic, social, health, and related problems; and international cultural and educational co-operation; and

c. universal respect for, and observance of, human rights and fundamental freedoms for all without distinction as to race, sex, language, or religion.

Article 56

All Members pledge themselves to take joint and separate action in co-operation with the Organization for the achievement of the purposes set forth in Article 55.

Article 57

1. The various specialized agencies, established by intergovernmental agreement and having wide international responsibilities, as defined in their basic instruments, in economic, social, cultural, educational, health, and related fields, shall be brought into relationship with the United Nations in accordance with the provisions of Article 63.

2. Such agencies thus brought into relationship with the United Nations are hereinafter referred to as specialized agencies.

Article 58

The Organization shall make recommendations for the coordination of the policies and activities of the specialized agencies.

Article 59

The Organization shall, where appropriate, initiate negotiations among the states concerned for the creation of any new specialized agencies required for the accomplishment of the purposes set forth in Article 55.

Article 60

Responsibility for the discharge of the functions of the Organization set forth in this Chapter shall be vested in the General Assembly and, under the authority of the General Assembly, in the Economic and Social Council, which shall have for this purpose the powers set forth in Chapter X.

CHAPTER X—THE ECONOMIC AND SOCIAL COUNCIL

Composition

Article 61

[1945 text]

1. The Economic and Social Council shall consist of eighteen Members of the United Nations elected by the General Assembly.
2. Subject to the provisions of paragraph 3, six members of the Economic and Social Council shall be elected each year for a term of three years. A retiring member shall be eligible for immediate re-election.
3. At the first election, eighteen members of the Economic and Social Council shall be chosen. The term of office of six members so chosen shall expire at the end of one

[1971 text][4]

1. The Economic and Social Council shall consist of fifty-four Members of the United Nations elected by the General Assembly.
2. Subject to the provisions of paragraph 3, eighteen members of the Economic and Social Council shall be elected each year for a term of three years. A retiring member shall be eligible for immediate re-election.
3. At the first election after the increase in the membership of the Economic and Social Council from twenty-seven[5] to fifty-four members, in addition to the members

---

[4] Amendment adopted by the General Assembly on 17 December 1963 and entered into force on 31 August 1965. A further amendment was adopted by the General Assembly on 20 December 1971, and entered into force on 24 September 1973.

[5] Text reflects the earlier amendment, which expanded membership of the Economic and Social Council from eighteen to twenty-seven.

year, and of six other members at the end of two years, in accordance with arrangements made by the General Assembly.

elected in place of the nine members whose term of office expires at the end of that year, twenty-seven additional members shall be elected. Of these twenty-seven additional members, the term of office of nine members so elected shall expire at the end of one year, and of nine other members at the end of two years, in accordance with arrangements made by the General Assembly.

4. Each member of the Economic and Social Council shall have one representative.

Functions and Powers

Article 62

1. The Economic and Social Council may make or initiate studies and reports with respect to international economic, social, cultural, educational, health, and related matters and may make recommendations with respect to any such matters to the General Assembly, to the Members of the United Nations, and to the specialized agencies concerned.

2. It may make recommendations for the purpose of promoting respect for, and observance of, human rights and fundamental freedoms for all.

3. It may prepare draft conventions for submission to the General Assembly, with respect to matters falling within its competence.

4. It may call, in accordance with the rules prescribed by the United Nations, international conferences on matters falling within its competence.

Article 63

1. The Economic and Social Council may enter into agreements with any of the agencies referred to in Article 57, defining the terms on which the agency concerned shall be brought into relationship with the United Nations. Such agreements shall be subject to approval by the General Assembly.

2. It may coordinate the activities of the specialized agencies through consultation with and recommendations to such agencies and through recommendations to the General Assembly and to the Members of the United Nations.

Article 64

1. The Economic and Social Council may take appropriate steps to obtain regular reports from the specialized agencies. It may make arrangements with the Members of the United Nations and with the specialized agencies to obtain reports on the steps taken to give effect to its own recommendations and to recommendations on matters falling within its competence made by the General Assembly.

2. It may communicate its observations on these reports to the General Assembly.

Article 65

The Economic and Social Council may furnish information to the Security Council and shall assist the Security Council upon its request.

Article 66

1. The Economic and Social Council shall perform such functions as fall within its competence in connection with the carrying out of the recommendations of the General Assembly.

2. It may, with the approval of the General Assembly, perform services at the request of Members of the United Nations and at the request of specialized agencies.

3. It shall perform such other functions as are specified elsewhere in the present Charter or as may be assigned to it by the General Assembly.

Article 67

1. Each member of the Economic and Social Council shall have one vote.

2. Decisions of the Economic and Social Council shall be made by a majority of the members present and voting.

Procedure

Article 68

The Economic and Social Council shall set up commissions in economic and social fields and for the promotion of human rights, and such other commissions as may be required for the performance of its functions.

Article 69

The Economic and Social Council shall invite any Member of the United Nations to participate, without vote, in its deliberations on any matter of particular concern to that Member.

Article 70

The Economic and Social Council may make arrangements for representatives of the specialized agencies to participate, without vote, in its deliberations and in those of the commissions established by it, and for its representatives to participate in the deliberations of the specialized agencies.

Article 71

The Economic and Social Council may make suitable arrangements for consultation with non-governmental organizations which are concerned with matters within its competence. Such arrangements may be made with international organizations and, where appropriate, with national organizations after consultation with the Member of the United Nations concerned.

Article 72

1. The Economic and Social Council shall adopt its own rules of procedure, including the method of selecting its President.

2. The Economic and Social Council shall meet as required in accordance with its rules, which shall include provision for the convening of meetings on the request of a majority of its members.

CHAPTER XI—DECLARATION REGARDING NON-SELF-GOVERNING TERRITORIES

Article 73

Members of the United Nations which have or assume responsibilities for the administration of territories whose peoples have not yet attained a full measure of self-government recognize the principle that the interests of the inhabitants of these territories are paramount, and accept as a sacred trust the obligation to promote to the utmost, within the system of international peace and security established by the present Charter, the well-being of the inhabitants of these territories, and, to this end:

a. to ensure, with due respect for the culture of the peoples concerned, their political, economic, social, and educational advancement, their just treatment, and their protection against abuses;

b. to develop self-government, to take due account of the political aspirations of the peoples, and to assist them in the progressive development of their free political institutions, according to the particular circumstances of each territory and its peoples and their varying stages of advancement;

c. to further international peace and security;

d. to promote constructive measures of development, to encourage research, and to co-operate with one another and, when and where appropriate, with specialized international bodies with a view to the practical achievement of the social, economic, and scientific purposes set forth in this Article; and

e. to transmit regularly to the Secretary-General for information purposes, subject to such limitation as security and constitutional considerations may require, statistical and other information of a technical nature relating to economic, social, and educational conditions in the territories for which they are respectively responsible other than those territories to which Chapter XII and XIII apply.

Article 74

Members of the United Nations also agree that their policy in respect of the territories to which this Chapter applies, no less than in respect of their metropolitan areas, must be based on the general principle of good-neighborliness, due account being taken of the interests and well-being of the rest of the world, in social, economic, and commercial matters.

CHAPTER XII—INTERNATIONAL TRUSTEESHIP SYSTEM

Article 75

The United Nations shall establish under its authority an international trusteeship system for the administration and supervision of such territories as may be placed thereunder by subsequent individual agreements. These territories are hereinafter referred to as trust territories.

Article 76

The basic objectives of the trusteeship system, in accordance with the Purposes of the United Nations laid down in Article 1 of the present Charter, shall be:

a. to further international peace and security;

b. to promote the political, economic, social, and educational advancement of the inhabitants of the trust territories, and their progressive development towards self-government or independence as may be appropriate to the particular circumstances of each territory and its peoples and the freely expressed wishes of the peoples concerned, and as may be provided by the terms of each trusteeship agreement;

c. to encourage respect for human rights and for fundamental freedoms for all without distinction as to race, sex, language, or religion, and to encourage recognition of the interdependence of the peoples of the world; and

d. to ensure equal treatment in social, economic, and commercial matters for all Members of the United Nations and their nationals and also equal treatment for the latter in the administration of justice without prejudice to the attainment of the foregoing objectives and subject to the provisions of Article 80.

Article 77

1. The trusteeship system shall apply to such territories in the following categories as may be placed thereunder by means of trusteeship agreements:

a. territories now held under mandate;

b. territories which may be detached from enemy states as a result of the Second World War; and

c. territories voluntarily placed under the system by states responsible for their administration.

2. It will be a matter for subsequent agreement as to which territories in the foregoing categories will be brought under the trusteeship system and upon what terms.

Article 78

The trusteeship system shall not apply to territories which have become Members of the United Nations, relationship among which shall be based on respect for the principle of sovereign equality.

Article 79

The terms of trusteeship for each territory to be placed under the trusteeship system, including any alteration or amendment, shall be agreed upon by the states directly concerned, including the mandatory power in the case of territories held under mandate by a Member of the United Nations, and shall be approved as provided for in Articles 83 and 85.

Article 80

1. Except as may be agreed upon in individual trusteeship agreements, made under Articles 77, 79, and 81, placing each territory under the trusteeship system, and until such agreements have been concluded, nothing in this Chapter shall be construed in or of itself to alter in any manner the rights whatsoever of any states or any peoples or the terms of existing international instruments to which Members of the United Nations may respectively be parties.

2. Paragraph 1 of this Article shall not be interpreted as giving grounds for delay or postponement of the negotiation and conclusion of agreements for placing mandated and other territories under the trusteeship system as provided for in Article 77.

Article 81

The trusteeship agreement shall in each case include the terms under which the trust territory will be administered and designate the authority which will exercise the administration of the trust territory. Such authority, hereinafter called the administering authority, may be one or more states or the Organization itself.

Article 82

There may be designated, in any trusteeship agreement, a strategic area or areas which may include part or all of the trust territory to which the agreement applies, without prejudice to any special agreement or agreements made under Article 43.

Article 83

1. All functions of the United Nations relating to strategic areas, including the approval of the terms of the trusteeship agreements and of their alteration or amendment, shall be exercised by the Security Council.

2. The basic objectives set forth in Article 76 shall be applicable to the people of each strategic area.

3. The Security Council shall, subject to the provisions of the trusteeship agreements and without prejudice to security considerations, avail itself of the assistance of the Trusteeship Council to perform those functions of the United Nations under the trusteeship system relating to political. economic, social, and educational matters in the strategic areas.

Article 84

It shall be the duty of the administering authority to ensure that the trust territory shall play its part in the maintenance of international peace and security. To this end the administering authority may make use of volunteer forces, facilities, and assistance from the trust territory in carrying out the obligations towards the Security Council undertaken in this regard by the administering authority, as well as for local defense and the maintenance of law and order within the trust territory.

Article 85

1. The functions of the United Nations with regard to trusteeship agreements for all areas not designated as strategic, including the approval of the terms of the trusteeship agreements and of their alteration or amendment, shall be exercised by the General Assembly.

2. The Trusteeship Council, operating under the authority of the General Assembly, shall assist the General Assembly in carrying out these functions.

CHAPTER XIII—THE TRUSTEESHIP COUNCIL

Composition

Article 86

1. The Trusteeship Council shall consist of the following Members of the United Nations:

a. those Members administering trust territories;

b. such of those Members mentioned by name in Article 23 as are not administering trust territories; and

c. as many other Members elected for three-year terms by the General Assembly as may be necessary to ensure that the total number of members of the Trusteeship Council is equally divided between those Members of the United Nations which administer trust territories and those which do not.

2. Each member of the Trusteeship Council shall designate one specially qualified person to represent it therein.

Functions and Powers

Article 87

The General Assembly and, under its authority, the Trusteeship Council, in carrying out their functions, may:

a. consider reports submitted by the administering authority;

b. accept petitions and examine them in consultation with the administering authority;

c. provide for periodic visits to the respective trust territories at times agreed upon with the administering authority; and

d. take these and other actions in conformity with the terms of the trusteeship agreements.

Article 88

The Trusteeship Council shall formulate a questionnaire on the political, economic, social, and educational advancement of the inhabitants of each trust territory, and the administering authority for each trust territory within the competence of the General Assembly shall make an annual report to the General Assembly upon the basis of such questionnaire.

Voting

Article 89

1. Each member of the Trusteeship Council shall have one vote.
2. Decisions of the Trusteeship Council shall be made by a majority of the members present and voting.

Procedure

Article 90

1. The Trusteeship Council shall adopt its own rules of procedure, including the method of selecting its President.
2. The Trusteeship Council shall meet as required in accordance with its rules, which shall include provision for the convening of meetings on the request of a majority of its members.

Article 91

The Trusteeship Council shall, when appropriate, avail itself of the assistance of the Economic and Social Council and of the specialized agencies in regard to matters with which they are respectively concerned.

CHAPTER XIV—THE INTERNATIONAL COURT OF JUSTICE

Article 92

The International Court of Justice shall be the principal judicial organ of the United Nations. It shall function in accordance with the annexed Statute which is based upon the Statute of the Permanent Court of International Justice and forms an integral part of the present Charter.

Article 93

1. All Members of the United Nations are ipso facto parties to the Statute of the International Court of Justice.
2. A state which is not a Member of the United Nations may become a party to the Statute of the International Court of Justice on conditions to be determined in each case by the General Assembly upon the recommendation of the Security Council.

Article 94

1. Each Member of the United Nations undertakes to comply with the decision of the International Court of Justice in any case to which it is a party.
2. If any party to a case fails to perform the obligations incumbent upon it under a judgment rendered by the Court, the other party may have recourse to the Security Council, which may, if it deems necessary, make recommendations or decide upon measures to be taken to give effect to the judgment.

Article 95

Nothing in the present Charter shall prevent Members of the United Nations from entrusting the solution of their differences to other tribunals by virtue of agreements already in existence or which may be concluded in the future.

Article 96

1. The General Assembly or the Security Council may request the International Court of Justice to give an advisory opinion on any legal question.

2. Other organs of the United Nations and specialized agencies, which may at any time be so authorized by the General Assembly, may also request advisory opinions of the Court on legal questions arising within the scope of their activities.

CHAPTER XV—THE SECRETARIAT

Article 97

The Secretariat shall comprise a Secretary-General and such staff as the Organization may require. The Secretary-General shall be appointed by the General Assembly upon the recommendation of the Security Council. He shall be the chief administrative officer of the Organization.

Article 98

The Secretary-General shall act in that capacity in all meetings of the General Assembly, of the Security Council, of the Economic and Social Council, and of the Trusteeship Council, and shall perform such other functions as are entrusted to him by these organs. The Secretary-General shall make an annual report to the General Assembly on the work of the Organization.

Article 99

The Secretary-General may bring to the attention of the Security Council any matter which in his opinion may threaten the maintenance of international peace and security.

Article 100

1. In the performance of their duties the Secretary-General and the staff shall not seek or receive instructions from any government or from any other authority external to the Organization. They shall refrain from any action which might reflect on their position as international officials responsible only to the Organization.
2. Each Member of the United Nations undertakes to respect the exclusively international character of the responsibilities of the Secretary-General and the staff and not to seek to influence them in the discharge of their responsibilities.

Article 101

1. The staff shall be appointed by the Secretary-General under regulations established by the General Assembly.
2. Appropriate staffs shall be permanently assigned to the Economic and Social Council, the Trusteeship Council, and, as required, to other organs of the United Nations. These staffs shall form a part of the Secretariat.
3. The paramount consideration in the employment of the staff and in the determination of the conditions of service shall be the necessity of securing the highest standards of efficiency, competence, and integrity. Due regard shall be paid to the importance of recruiting the staff on as wide a geographical basis as possible.

CHAPTER XVI—MISCELLANEOUS PROVISIONS

Article 102

1. Every treaty and every international agreement entered into by any Member of the United Nations after the present Charter comes into force shall as soon as possible be registered with the Secretariat and published by it.

2. No party to any such treaty or international agreement which has not been registered in accordance with the provisions of paragraph I of this Article may invoke that treaty or agreement before any organ of the United Nations.

Article 103

In the event of a conflict between the obligations of the Members of the United Nations under the present Charter and their obligations under any other international agreement, their obligations under the present Charter shall prevail.

Article 104

The Organization shall enjoy in the territory of each of its Members such legal capacity as may be necessary for the exercise of its functions and the fulfillment of its purposes.

Article 105

1. The Organization shall enjoy in the territory of each of its Members such privileges and immunities as are necessary for the fulfillment of its purposes.

2. Representatives of the Members of the United Nations and officials of the Organization shall similarly enjoy such privileges and immunities as are necessary for the independent exercise of their functions in connection with the Organization.

3. The General Assembly may make recommendations with a view to determining the details of the application of paragraphs 1 and 2 of this Article or may propose conventions to the Members of the United Nations for this purpose.

CHAPTER XVII—TRANSITIONAL SECURITY ARRANGEMENTS

Article 106

Pending the coming into force of such special agreements referred to in Article 43 as in the opinion of the Security Council enable it to begin the exercise of its responsibilities under Article 42, the parties to the Four-Nation Declaration, signed at Moscow October 30, 1943, and France, shall, in accordance with the provisions of paragraph 5 of that Declaration, consult with one another and as occasion requires with other Members of the United Nations with a view to such joint action on behalf of the Organization as may be necessary for the purpose of maintaining international peace and security.

Article 107

Nothing in the present Charter shall invalidate or preclude action, in relation to any state which during the Second World War has been an enemy of any signatory to the present Charter, taken or authorized as a result of that war by the Governments having responsibility for such action.

CHAPTER XVIII—AMENDMENTS

Article 108

Amendments to the present Charter shall come into force for all Members of the United Nations when they have been adopted by a vote of two thirds of the members of the General Assembly and ratified in accordance with their respective constitutional processes by two thirds of the Members of the United Nations, including all the permanent members of the Security Council.

Article 109

[1945 text]

1. A General Conference of the Members of the United Nations for the purpose of reviewing the present Charter may be held at a date and place to be fixed by a two-thirds vote of the members of the General Assembly and by a vote of any seven members of the Security Council. Each Member of the United Nations shall have one vote in the conference.

[1965 text][6]

1. A General Conference of the Members of the United Nations for the purpose of reviewing the present Charter may be held at a date and place to be fixed by a two-thirds vote of the members of the General Assembly and by a vote of any nine members of the Security Council. Each Member of the United Nations shall have one vote in the conference.

2. Any alteration of the present Charter recommended by a two-thirds vote of the conference shall take effect when ratified in accordance with their respective constitutional processes by two thirds of the Members of the United Nations including all the permanent members of the Security Council.

3. If such a conference has not been held before the tenth annual session of the General Assembly following the coming into force of the present Charter, the proposal to call such a conference shall be placed on the agenda of that session of the General Assembly, and the conference shall be held if so decided by a majority vote of the members of the General Assembly and by a vote of any seven members of the Security Council.

CHAPTER XIX—RATIFICATION AND SIGNATURE

Article 110

1. The present Charter shall be ratified by the signatory states in accordance with their respective constitutional processes.

2. The ratifications shall be deposited with the Government of the United States of America, which shall notify all the signatory states of each deposit as well as the Secretary-General of the Organization when he has been appointed.

3. The present Charter shall come into force upon the deposit of ratifications by the Republic of China, France, the Union of Soviet Socialist Republics, the United Kingdom of Great Britain and Northern Ireland, and the United States of America, and by a majority of the other signatory states. A protocol of the ratifications deposited shall thereupon be drawn up by the Government of the United States of America which shall communicate copies thereof to all the signatory states.

4. The states signatory to the present Charter which ratify it after it has come into force will become original Members of the United Nations on the date of the deposit of their respective ratifications.

Article 111

The present Charter, of which the Chinese, French, Russian, English, and Spanish texts are equally authentic, shall remain deposited in the archives of the Government of the United States of America. Duly certified copies thereof shall be transmitted by that Government to the Governments of the other signatory states.

IN FAITH WHEREOF the representatives of the Governments of the United Nations have signed the present Charter.

DONE at the city of San Francisco the twenty-sixth day of June, one thousand nine hundred and forty-five.

---

[6] Amendment adopted by the General Assembly on 20 December 1965 and entered into force on 12 June 1968.

Statute of the International Court of Justice

Article 1

The International Court of Justice established by the Charter of the United Nations as the principal judicial organ of the United Nations shall be constituted and shall function in accordance with the provisions of the present Statute.

CHAPTER I — ORGANIZATION OF THE COURT

Article 2

The Court shall be composed of a body of independent judges, elected regardless of their nationality from among persons of high moral character, who possess the qualifications required in their respective countries for appointment to the highest judicial offices, or are jurisconsults of recognized competence in international law.

Article 3

1. The Court shall consist of fifteen members, no two of whom may be nationals of the same state.

2. A person who for the purposes of membership in the Court could be regarded as a national of more than one state shall be deemed to be a national of the one in which he ordinarily exercises civil and political rights.

Article 4

1. The members of the Court shall be elected by the General Assembly and by the Security Council from a list of persons nominated by the national groups in the Permanent Court of Arbitration, in accordance with the following provisions.

2. In the case of Members of the United Nations not represented in the Permanent Court of Arbitration, candidates shall be nominated by national groups appointed for this purpose by their governments under the same conditions as those prescribed for members of the Permanent Court of Arbitration by Article 44 of the Convention of The Hague of 1907 for the pacific settlement of international disputes.

3. The conditions under which a state which is a party to the present Statute but is not a Member of the United Nations may participate in electing the members of the Court shall, in the absence of a special agreement, be laid down by the General Assembly upon recommendation of the Security Council.

Article 5

1. At least three months before the date of the election, the Secretary-General of the United Nations shall address a written request to the members of the Permanent Court of Arbitration belonging to the states which are parties to the present Statute, and to the members of the national groups appointed under Article 4, paragraph 2, inviting them to undertake, within a given time, by national groups, the nomination of persons in a position to accept the duties of a member of the Court.

2. No group may nominate more than four persons, not more than two of whom shall be of their own nationality. In no case may the number of candidates nominated by a group be more than double the number of seats to be filled.

Article 6

Before making these nominations, each national group is recommended to consult its highest court of justice, its legal faculties and schools of law, and its national academies and national sections of international academies devoted to the study of law.

Article 7

1. The Secretary-General shall prepare a list in alphabetical order of all the persons thus nominated. Save as provided in Article 12, paragraph 2, these shall be the only persons eligible.

2. The Secretary-General shall submit this list to the General Assembly and to the Security Council.

Article 8

The General Assembly and the Security Council shall proceed independently of one another to elect the members of the Court.

Article 9

At every election, the electors shall bear in mind not only that the persons to be elected should individually possess the qualifications required, but also that in the body as a whole the representation of the main forms of civilization and of the principal legal systems of the world should be assured.

Article 10

1. Those candidates who obtain an absolute majority of votes in the General Assembly and in the Security Council shall be considered as elected.

2. Any vote of the Security Council, whether for the election of judges or for the appointment of members of the conference envisaged in Article 12, shall be taken without any distinction between permanent and non-permanent members of the Security Council.

3. In the event of more than one national of the same state obtaining an absolute majority of the votes both of the General Assembly and of the Security Council, the eldest of these only shall be considered as elected.

Article 11

If, after the first meeting held for the purpose of the election, one or more seats remain to be filled, a second and, if necessary, a third meeting shall take place.

Article 12

1. If, after the third meeting, one or more seats still remain unfilled, a joint conference consisting of six members, three appointed by the General Assembly and three by the Security Council, may be formed at any time at the request of either the General Assembly or the Security Council, for the purpose of choosing by the vote of an absolute majority one name for each seat

still vacant, to submit to the General Assembly and the Security Council for their respective acceptance.

2. If the joint conference is unanimously agreed upon any person who fulfills the required conditions, he may be included in its list, even though he was not included in the list of nominations referred to in Article 7.

3. If the joint conference is satisfied that it will not be successful in procuring an election, those members of the Court who have already been elected shall, within a period to be fixed by the Security Council, proceed to fill the vacant seats by selection from among those candidates who have obtained votes either in the General Assembly or in the Security Council.

4. In the event of an equality of votes among the judges, the eldest judge shall have a casting vote.

Article 13

1. The members of the Court shall be elected for nine years and may be re-elected; provided, however, that of the judges elected at the first election, the terms of five judges shall expire at the end of three years and the terms of five more judges shall expire at the end of six years.

2. The judges whose terms are to expire at the end of the above-mentioned initial periods of three and six years shall be chosen by lot to be drawn by the Secretary-General immediately after the first election has been completed.

3. The members of the Court shall continue to discharge their duties until their places have been filled. Though replaced, they shall finish any cases which they may have begun.

4. In the case of the resignation of a member of the Court, the resignation shall be addressed to the President of the Court for transmission to the Secretary-General. This last notification makes the place vacant.

Article 14

Vacancies shall be filled by the same method as that laid down for the first election subject to the following provision: the Secretary-General shall, within one month of the occurrence of the vacancy, proceed to issue the invitations provided for in Article 5, and the date of the election shall be fixed by the Security Council.

Article 15

A member of the Court elected to replace a member whose term of office has not expired shall hold office for the remainder of his predecessor's term.

Article 16

1. No member of the Court may exercise any political or administrative function, or engage in any other occupation of a professional nature.

2. Any doubt on this point shall be settled by the decision of the Court.

Article 17

1. No member of the Court may act as agent, counsel, or advocate in any case.

2. No member may participate in the decision of any case in which he has previously taken part as agent, counsel, or advocate for one of the parties, or as a member of a national or international court, or of a commission of enquiry, or in any other capacity.

3. Any doubt on this point shall be settled by the decision of the Court.

Article 18

1. No member of the Court can be dismissed unless, in the unanimous opinion of the other members, he has ceased to fulfill the required conditions.

2. Formal notification thereof shall be made to the Secretary-General by the Registrar.

3. This notification makes the place vacant.

Article 19

The members of the Court, when engaged on the business of the Court, shall enjoy diplomatic privileges and immunities.

Article 20

Every member of the Court shall, before taking up his duties, make a solemn declaration in open court that he will exercise his powers impartially and conscientiously.

Article 21

1. The Court shall elect its President and Vice-President for three years; they may be re-elected.

2. The Court shall appoint its Registrar and may provide for the appointment of such other officers as may be necessary.

Article 22

1. The seat of the Court shall be established at The Hague. This, however, shall not prevent the Court from sitting and exercising its functions elsewhere whenever the Court considers it desirable.

2. The President and the Registrar shall reside at the seat of the Court.

Article 23

1. The Court shall remain permanently in session, except during the judicial vacations, the dates and duration of which shall be fixed by the Court.

2. Members of the Court are entitled to periodic leave, the dates and duration of which shall be fixed by the Court, having in mind the distance between The Hague and the home of each judge.

3. Members of the Court shall be bound, unless they are on leave or prevented from attending by illness or other serious reasons duly explained to the President, to hold themselves permanently at the disposal of the Court.

Article 24

1. If, for some special reason, a member of the Court considers that he should not take part in the decision of a particular case, he shall so inform the President.

2. If the President considers that for some special reason one of the members of the Court should not sit in a particular case, he shall give him notice accordingly.

3. If in any such case the member Court and the President disagree, the matter shall be settled by the decision of the Court.

Article 25

1. The full Court shall sit except when it is expressly provided otherwise in the present Statute.

2. Subject to the condition that the number of judges available to constitute the Court is not thereby reduced below eleven, the Rules of the Court may provide for allowing one or more judges, according to circumstances and in rotation, to be dispensed from sitting.

3. A quorum of nine judges shall suffice to constitute the Court.

Article 26

1. The Court may from time to time form one or more chambers, composed of three or more judges as the Court may determine, for dealing with particular categories of cases; for example, labour cases and cases relating to transit and communications.

2. The Court may at any time form a chamber for dealing with a particular case. The number of judges to constitute such a chamber shall be determined by the Court with the approval of the parties.

3. Cases shall be heard and determined by the chambers provided for in this article if the parties so request.

Article 27

A judgment given by any of the chambers provided for in Articles 26 and 29 shall be considered as rendered by the Court.

Article 28

The chambers provided for in Articles 26 and 29 may, with the consent of the parties, sit and exercise their functions elsewhere than at The Hague.

Article 29

With a view to the speedy dispatch of business, the Court shall form annually a chamber composed of five judges which, at the request of the parties, may hear and determine cases by summary procedure. In addition, two judges shall be selected for the purpose of replacing judges who find it impossible to sit.

Article 30

1. The Court shall frame rules for carrying out its functions. In particular, it shall lay down rules of procedure.
2. The Rules of the Court may provide for assessors to sit with the Court or with any of its chambers, without the right to vote.

Article 31

1. Judges of the nationality of each of the parties shall retain their right to sit in the case before the Court.
2. If the Court includes upon the Bench a judge of the nationality of one of the parties, any other party may choose a person to sit as judge. Such person shall be chosen preferably from among those persons who have been nominated as candidates as provided in Articles 4 and 5.
3. If the Court includes upon the Bench no judge of the nationality of the parties, each of these parties may proceed to choose a judge as provided in paragraph 2 of this Article.
4. The provisions of this Article shall apply to the case of Articles 26 and 29. In such cases, the President shall request one or, if necessary, two of the members of the Court forming the chamber to give place to the members of the Court of the nationality of the parties concerned, and, failing such, or if they are unable to be present, to the judges specially chosen by the parties.
5. Should there be several parties in the same interest, they shall, for the purpose of the preceding provisions, be reckoned as one party only. Any doubt upon this point shall be settled by the decision of the Court.
6. Judges chosen as laid down in paragraphs 2, 3, and 4 of this Article shall fulfill the conditions required by Articles 2, 17 (paragraph 2), 20, and 24 of the present Statute. They shall take part in the decision on terms of complete equality with their colleagues.

Article 32

1. Each member of the Court shall receive an annual salary.
2. The President shall receive a special annual allowance.
3. The Vice-President shall receive a special allowance for every day on which he acts as President.
4. The judges chosen under Article 31, other than members of the Court, shall receive compensation for each day on which they exercise their functions.
5. These salaries, allowances, and compensation shall be fixed by the General Assembly. They may not be decreased during the term of office.
6. The salary of the Registrar shall be fixed by the General Assembly on the proposal of the Court.

7. Regulations made by the General Assembly shall fix the conditions under which retirement pensions may be given to members of the Court and to the Registrar, and the conditions under which members of the Court and the Registrar shall have their travelling expenses refunded.

8. The above salaries, allowances, and compensation shall be free of all taxation.

Article 33

The expenses of the Court shall be borne by the United Nations in such a manner as shall be decided by the General Assembly.

CHAPTER II — COMPETENCE OF THE COURT

Article 34

1. Only states may be parties in cases before the Court.

2. The Court, subject to and in conformity with its Rules, may request of public international organizations information relevant to cases before it, and shall receive such information presented by such organizations on their own initiative.

3. Whenever the construction of the constituent instrument of a public international organization or of an international convention adopted thereunder is in question in a case before the Court, the Registrar shall so notify the public international organization concerned and shall communicate to it copies of all the written proceedings.

Article 35

1. The Court shall be open to the states parties to the present Statute.

2. The conditions under which the Court shall be open to other states shall, subject to the special provisions contained in treaties in force, be laid down by the Security Council, but in no case shall such conditions place the parties in a position of inequality before the Court.

3. When a state which is not a Member of the United Nations is a party to a case, the Court shall fix the amount which that party is to contribute towards the expenses of the Court. This provision shall not apply if such state is bearing a share of the expenses of the Court

Article 36

1. The jurisdiction of the Court comprises all cases which the parties refer to it and all matters specially provided for in the Charter of the United Nations or in treaties and conventions in force.

2. The states parties to the present Statute may at any time declare that they recognize as compulsory ipso facto and without special agreement, in relation to any other state accepting the same obligation, the jurisdiction of the Court in all legal disputes concerning:

a. the interpretation of a treaty;

b. any question of international law;

c. the existence of any fact which, if established, would constitute a breach of an international obligation;

d. the nature or extent of the reparation to be made for the breach of an international obligation.

3. The declarations referred to above may be made unconditionally or on condition of reciprocity on the part of several or certain states, or for a certain time.

4. Such declarations shall be deposited with the Secretary-General of the United Nations, who shall transmit copies thereof to the parties to the Statute and to the Registrar of the Court.

5. Declarations made under Article 36 of the Statute of the Permanent Court of International Justice and which are still in force shall be deemed, as between the parties to the present Statute, to be acceptances of the compulsory jurisdiction of the International Court of Justice for the period which they still have to run and in accordance with their terms.

6. In the event of a dispute as to whether the Court has jurisdiction, the matter shall be settled by the decision of the Court.

Article 37

Whenever a treaty or convention in force provides for reference of a matter to a tribunal to have been instituted by the League of Nations, or to the Permanent Court of International Justice, the matter shall, as between the parties to the present Statute, be referred to the International Court of Justice.

Article 38

1. The Court, whose function is to decide in accordance with international law such disputes as are submitted to it, shall apply:

a. international conventions, whether general or particular, establishing rules expressly recognized by the contesting states;

b. international custom, as evidence of a general practice accepted as law;

c. the general principles of law recognized by civilized nations;

d. subject to the provisions of Article 59, judicial decisions and the teachings of the most highly qualified publicists of the various nations, as subsidiary means for the determination of rules of law.

2. This provision shall not prejudice the power of the Court to decide a case *ex aequo et bono*, if the parties agree thereto.

CHAPTER III — PROCEDURE

Article 39

1. The official languages of the Court shall be French and English. If the parties agree that the case shall be conducted in French, the judgment shall be delivered in French. If the parties agree that the case shall be conducted in English, the judgment shall be delivered in English.

2. In the absence of an agreement as to which language shall be employed, each party may, in the pleadings, use the language which it prefers; the decision of the Court shall be given in French and English. In this case the Court shall at the same time determine which of the two texts shall be considered as authoritative.

3. The Court shall, at the request of any party, authorize a language other than French or English to be used by that party.

Article 40

1. Cases are brought before the Court, as the case may be, either by the notification of the special agreement or by a written application addressed to the Registrar. In either case the subject of the dispute and the parties shall be indicated.

2. The Registrar shall forthwith communicate the application to all concerned.

3. He shall also notify the Members of the United Nations through the Secretary-General, and also any other states entitled to appear before the Court.

Article 41

1. The Court shall have the power to indicate, if it considers that circumstances so require, any provisional measures which ought to be taken to preserve the respective rights of either party.

2. Pending the final decision, notice of the measures suggested shall forthwith be given to the parties and to the Security Council

Article 42

1. The parties shall be represented by agents.

2. They may have the assistance of counsel or advocates before the Court.

3. The agents, counsel, and advocates of parties before the Court shall enjoy the privileges and immunities necessary to the independent exercise of their duties.

Article 43

1. The procedure shall consist of two parts: written and oral.

2. The written proceedings shall consist of the communication to the Court and to the parties of memorials, counter-memorials and, if necessary, replies; also all papers and documents in support.

3. These communications shall be made through the Registrar, in the order and within the time fixed by the Court.

4. A certified copy of every document produced by one party shall be communicated to the other party.

5. The oral proceedings shall consist of the hearing by the Court of witnesses, experts, agents, counsel, and advocates.

Article 44

1. For the service of all notices upon persons other than the agents, counsel, and advocates, the Court shall apply direct to the government of the state upon whose territory the notice has to be served.

2. The same provision shall apply whenever steps are to be taken to procure evidence on the spot.

Article 45

The hearing shall be under the control of the President or, if he is unable to preside, of the Vice-President; if neither is able to preside, the senior judge present shall preside.

Article 46

The hearing in Court shall be public, unless the Court shall decide otherwise, or unless the parties demand that the public be not admitted.

Article 47

1. Minutes shall be made at each hearing and signed by the Registrar and the President.

2. These minutes alone shall be authentic.

Article 48

The Court shall make orders for the conduct of the case, shall decide the form and time in which each party must conclude its arguments, and make all arrangements connected with the taking of evidence.

Article 49

The Court may, even before the hearing begins, call upon the agents to produce any document or to supply any explanations. Formal note shall be taken of any refusal.

Article 50

The Court may, at any time, entrust any individual, body, bureau, commission, or other organization that it may select, with the task of carrying out an enquiry or giving an expert opinion.

Article 51

During the hearing any relevant questions are to be put to the witnesses and experts under the conditions laid down by the Court in the rules of procedure referred to in Article 30.

Article 52

After the Court has received the proofs and evidence within the time specified for the purpose, it may refuse to accept any further oral or written evidence that one party may desire to present unless the other side consents.

Article 53

1. Whenever one of the parties does not appear before the Court, or fails to defend its case, the other party may call upon the Court to decide in favour of its claim.

2. The Court must, before doing so, satisfy itself, not only that it has jurisdiction in accordance with Articles 36 and 37, but also that the claim is well founded in fact and law.

Article 54

1. When, subject to the control of the Court, the agents, counsel, and advocates have completed their presentation of the case, the President shall declare the hearing closed.

2. The Court shall withdraw to consider the judgment.

3. The deliberations of the Court shall take place in private and remain secret.

Article 55

1. All questions shall be decided by a majority of the judges present.

2. In the event of an equality of votes, the President or the judge who acts in his place shall have a casting vote.

Article 56

1. The judgment shall state the reasons on which it is based.

2. It shall contain the names of the judges who have taken part in the decision.

Article 57

If the judgment does not represent in whole or in part the unanimous opinion of the judges, any judge shall be entitled to deliver a separate opinion.

Article 58

The judgment shall be signed by the President and by the Registrar. It shall be read in open court, due notice having been given to the agents.

Article 59

The decision of the Court has no binding force except between the parties and in respect of that particular case.

Article 60

The judgment is final and without appeal. In the event of dispute as to the meaning or scope of the judgment, the Court shall construe it upon the request of any party.

Article 61

1. An application for revision of a judgment may be made only when it is based upon the discovery of some fact of such a nature as to be a decisive factor, which fact was, when the judgment was given, unknown to the Court and also to the party claiming revision, always provided that such ignorance was not due to negligence.

2. The proceedings for revision shall be opened by a judgment of the Court expressly recording the existence of the new fact, recognizing that it has such a character as to lay the case open to revision, and declaring the application admissible on this ground.

3. The Court may require previous compliance with the terms of the judgment before it admits proceedings in revision.

4. The application for revision must be made at latest within six months of the discovery of the new fact.

5. No application for revision may be made after the lapse of ten years from the date of the judgment.

Article 62

1. Should a state consider that it has an interest of a legal nature which may be affected by the decision in the case, it may submit a request to the Court to be permitted to intervene.

2. It shall be for the Court to decide upon this request.

Article 63

1. Whenever the construction of a convention to which states other than those concerned in the case are parties is in question, the Registrar shall notify all such states forthwith.

2. Every state so notified has the right to intervene in the proceedings; but if it uses this right, the construction given by the judgment will be equally binding upon it.

Article 64

Unless otherwise decided by the Court, each party shall bear its own costs.

CHAPTER IV — ADVISORY OPINIONS

Article 65

1. The Court may give an advisory opinion on any legal question at the request of whatever body may be authorized by or in accordance with the Charter of the United Nations to make such a request.

2. Questions upon which the advisory opinion of the Court is asked shall be laid before the Court by means of a written request containing an exact statement of the question upon which an opinion is required, and accompanied by all documents likely to throw light upon the question.

Article 66

1. The Registrar shall forthwith give notice of the request for an advisory opinion to all states entitled to appear before the Court.

2. The Registrar shall also, by means of a special and direct communication, notify any state entitled to appear before the Court or international organization considered by the Court, or, should it not be sitting, by the President, as likely to be able to furnish information on the question, that the Court will be prepared to receive, within a time limit to be fixed by the President, written statements, or to hear, at a public sitting to be held for the purpose, oral statements relating to the question.

3. Should any such state entitled to appear before the Court have failed to receive the special communication referred to in paragraph 2 of this Article, such state may express a desire to submit a written statement or to be heard; and the Court will decide.

4. States and organizations having presented written or oral statements or both shall be permitted to comment on the statements made by other states or organizations in the form, to the extent, and within the time limits which the Court, or, should it not be sitting, the President, shall decide in each particular case. Accordingly, the Registrar shall in due time communicate any such written statements to states and organizations having submitted similar statements.

Article 67

The Court shall deliver its advisory opinions in open court, notice having been given to the Secretary-General and to the representatives of Members of the United Nations, of other states and of international organizations immediately concerned.

Article 68

In the exercise of its advisory functions the Court shall further be guided by the provisions of the present Statute which apply in contentious cases to the extent to which it recognizes them to be applicable.

CHAPTER V — AMENDMENT

Article 69

Amendments to the present Statute shall be effected by the same procedure as is provided by the Charter of the United Nations for amendments to that Charter, subject however to any provisions which the General Assembly upon recommendation of the Security Council may adopt concerning the participation of states which are parties to the present Statute but are not Members of the United Nations.

Article 70

The Court shall have power to propose such amendments to the present Statute as it may deem necessary, through written communications to the Secretary-General, for consideration in conformity with the provisions of Article 69.

Index

Page references followed by *f, t,* and *n* refer to figures, tables, and notes respectively; page references in bold refer to document excerpts.

CPSIA information can be obtained at www.ICGtesting.com
Printed in the USA
BVOW021207030113

309594BV00003B/11/P